The Sociology of American Drug Use

Second Edition

Charles E. Faupel
AUBURN UNIVERSITY

Alan M. Horowitz
UNIVERSITY OF DELAWARE

Greg S. Weaver
AUBURN UNIVERSITY

New York   Oxford
OXFORD UNIVERSITY PRESS
2010

Oxford University Press, Inc., publishes works that further Oxford University's
objective of excellence in research, scholarship, and education.

Oxford   New York
Auckland   Cape Town   Dar es Salaam   Hong Kong   Karachi
Kuala Lumpur   Madrid   Melbourne   Mexico City   Nairobi
New Delhi   Shanghai   Taipei   Toronto

With offices in
Argentina   Austria   Brazil   Chile   Czech Republic   France   Greece
Guatemala   Hungary   Italy   Japan   Poland   Portugal   Singapore
South Korea   Switzerland   Thailand   Turkey   Ukraine   Vietnam

Published by Oxford University Press, Inc.
198 Madison Avenue, New York, New York, 10016
http://www.oup.com

Oxford is a registered trademark of Oxford University Press

Library of Congress Cataloging-in-Publication Data

Faupel, Charles E.
    The sociology of American drug use / Charles Faupel, Alan Horowitz,
Greg Weaver. — 2nd ed.
        p. cm.
    Includes bibliographical references and index.
    ISBN 978-0-19-537528-2 (alk. paper)
    1. Substance abuse—Social aspects.   2. Drug abuse—Social aspects.
    I. Horowitz, Alan M. (Alan Mark), 1952–   II. Weaver, Gregory.   III. Title.
    HV4998.F385   2010
    362.29—dc22   2009021442

Printing number: 9 8 7 6 5 4 3 2 1

Printed in the United States of America
on acid-free paper

To Our Students

CONTENTS

The Sociology of American Drug Use is written especially for undergraduates in sociology or criminology and criminal justice programs with a strong sociological focus. All of the authors are sociologically trained criminologists, and we all have taught courses in the sociology of drug use. The first edition of this text was conceived out of the frustration that we have had in finding a text that is appropriate for the courses that we teach. We had to make do with texts that, although solid in content, did not fit with how we were accustomed to approaching the substantive material as sociologically trained criminologists. This situation has not changed much since the first edition appeared. Other criminology courses that we have taught focus on issues such as measurement and problems in measuring crime, theoretical perspectives on crime, social correlates of crime, and societal reaction to crime. These courses have a long list of textbooks that facilitate this focus. This is not the case with textbooks on the sociology of drug use, however. We seek to mainstream the study of the sociology of drug use within the broader study of crime and delinquency by bringing such a focus to *The Sociology of American Drug Use*, both in content and in organization.

The first section, "A Sociological Approach to Drug Use" provides an overview of some of the basic concepts and issues involved in the study of drug use from a sociological perspective. Chapter 1, "The Sociological Study of Drug Use," lays out the foundation for a sociology of drug use by identifying and defining some of the basic concepts that any student in the field must know. This chapter focuses especially on the social construction of drug use as a social problem. We give special attention to the concepts of drug set and drug setting in understanding the social construction of drug use as a social issue in our society.

Chapter 2, "A Brief History of Drug Use and Drug Control in America," provides a valuable historical context for understanding drug use in this country, from prior to our founding as a nation to the present day. This chapter addresses both the history of drug use and of societal reaction to drug use.

Chapter 3, "Classifying Psychoactive Drugs," presents a pharmacological typology of drugs. The emphasis of this book is the social context of drug use and drug experience, but drugs differ in how they affect the central nervous system. This typology, which is commonly used in the field today, provides students with an important grounding in the pharmacology of drugs and drug use. Because of their importance in recent years, we have added a sixth category to this typology, Other Mood- and Performance-Enhancing Drugs. Two specific types of drugs are included in this category: *antidepressants*, which seek to moderate extremes of mood, and performance-enhancing *anabolics*.

Chapter 4, "Official and Unofficial Data Sources," provides students with an extensive discussion of the major sources of information that researchers utilize in coming to an empirical understanding of drug use. This chapter underscores the importance of empirical observation as a basis for theorizing as well as policy making. Chapter 5, "Theoretical Explanations for Drug Use and Addiction," summarizes the theories that have been used to explain initiation into drug use and/or addiction. This chapter focuses heavily on sociological theories, though it also summarizes other important theories from the fields of philosophy, biology, and psychology as well.

The second section, "Social Correlates of Drug Use," focuses on some of the predominant social features that tend to be associated with drug use in America. Chapter 6, "Demographic Correlates of Drug Use," highlights specifically gender, race, age, and social class as correlates of substance use and misuse. Chapter 7, "Institutional Correlates of Drug Use," discusses the use of drugs in the military, in the medical profession, among athletes, and in the criminal justice system, as well as the use of drugs in religious contexts such as Rastafarian use of marijuana and the use of hallucinogenic drugs in the Native American Church. Both Chapters 6 and 7 are expanded from the first edition.

Chapter 8, "Health Correlates of Drug Use," focuses first on the negative consequences of drug use, recognizing that not only might pharmacological factors of the drugs themselves negatively affect health, but also synergistic and lifestyle factors among drug users are not always recognized for their contribution to negative health consequences of drug use. Additionally, Chapter 8 addresses some of the ways in which drugs can positively affect our health. Three specific issues are discussed, namely medical marijuana, the unrestricted use of narcotics in terminally ill patients, and the use of alcohol in moderation.

Chapter 9, "Economic Correlates of Drug Use," takes both a macroeconomic look at the drug industry, highlighting the impact of the drug trade on the larger economy both in the United States and other countries, and a microeconomic look at the underground economy of drug use. The chapter also examines the problems of drugs in the workplace and the response of business and industry to this use.

Chapter 10, "Cultural and Subcultural Correlates of Drug Use," underscores the importance of social and cultural context in understanding drug use. After a general discussion of the nature of drug cultures and subcultures, we examine three specific drug subcultures: the rave subculture, the street-heroin subculture, and the subculture of blunts smokers. The chapter concludes with a discussion of drug use as a career.

Chapter 11, "Violent and Criminal Correlates of Drug Use," addresses the relationship between drug use and both violent and nonviolent crime. This relationship is examined both theoretically and empirically. The common-sense notion that drug use causes crime through either direct pharmacological action or through economic compulsion is critically analyzed, and alternative ways of understanding the drugs-crime nexus are also explored.

The final section of the text, "Societal Response to Drug Use" explores important areas of drug policy. Chapter 12, "Legal Responses to Drug Problems," examines the broad policy options of prohibition, legalization, and decriminalization in terms of both the benefits and the limitations of each. A fourth broad policy option, harm reduction, is introduced as an alternative to minimize the negative impacts of drug use in American society.

Chapter 13, "Therapeutic Responses to Drug Problems," focuses on drug treatment. A variety of philosophies governing the treatment of substance abuse are addressed in this chapter, including the effectiveness of the various modalities. Chapter 14, "Preventive Responses to Drug Use," examines two broad preventive initiatives, drug education and drug testing.

Finally, Chapter 15, "Drug Policy for the Twenty-First Century," is admittedly somewhat speculative as we attempt to offer creative suggestions for a workable drug policy for the century ahead. Our suggestions are based upon a commitment to harm reduction. There are certainly differences of opinion about what harm reduction means and how it should be implemented, but this is a philosophical ideal to which we are committed. The details of what such a policy might look like are beyond the scope of this chapter and this text, yet we do try to provide some specific ideas about some of the elements that might comprise such a policy.

We are excited about the approach we are taking in this text. We have updated this second edition in several ways that we hope will represent an improvement over the first edition. In addition to updating statistical material, we have examined new issues and concerns in the world of drug use, such as our discussion of the blunts subculture. Additionally, we have added new boxed material under the theme "Drugs: Myths and Reality" in which we address issues often viewed through a stereotyped lens and reveal something of the reality behind the stereotypes. We have also reorganized the text slightly, even better to parallel the organization of typical texts in criminology and juvenile delinquency courses. In the process of making these changes, we have also expanded one of the chapters on correlates of drug use to two separate chapters, one on demographic correlates and a second on what we are terming *institutional correlates* comprising both occupational correlates religion as a context for drug use.

In all of this, we have attempted to maintain the flavor and approach of the first edition of this text. We hope that the frustration that generated the writing of this book will not be in vain, but that others, who may have experienced similar frustrations, will find this text responsive to their needs. We recognize that not everyone who teaches a course on drug use will find our approach useful; for those who do, however, we welcome any feedback that you may have for how we might communicate the sociological perspective on drug use more effectively.

Acknowledgments

We recognize that any major writing project that is successful is a team effort. As authors, we are keenly aware of the importance of teamwork in the division of labor on this book. We are especially appreciative of the contributions made by the substantive reviewers of this manuscript:

Peter Adler, University of Denver
Andrew Golub, University of Vermont
Greg Haase, Western State College
Angel Hoekstra, University of Colorado, Boulder
Robert Keel, University of Missouri, St. Louis
David N. Khey, University of Florida

Each of these individuals provided valuable suggestions for improvement over the first edition, and we are extremely grateful for their act of service to us and to the profession. There responses were not only insightful, but also framed in a most encouraging way. We are especially thankful to Andrew Golub, not only for his robust and stimulating comments on the reviews, but also for the wealth of information he has contributed on the blunts subculture through his various publications. I (Faupel) want to add a personal note of thanks to Peter Adler, who has been a source of great personal encouragement in his response to the first edition of this text in phone conversations and at those long, long, l o n g meetings of the executive council of Alpha Kappa Delta. They were always a little shorter when you were there, Peter.

We also want to recognize our colleagues at Auburn University. Although they did not directly contribute to the content of the book, their words of encouragement and their willingness to act as sounding boards is deeply appreciated. We are also very appreciative of the support provided to Alan Horowitz by the Parallel Program of the University of Delaware and to his students for their valuable contribution to the pedagogical material in this text. Finally, we want to acknowledge the editorial staff at Oxford University Press who so patiently worked with us throughout this process. We are especially grateful to the untiring work of Sherith Pankratz and Whitney Laemmli. You guys have been nothing short of awesome in your responsiveness to our questions and concerns.

A SOCIOLOGICAL APPROACH TO DRUG USE

CHAPTER **1**

The Sociological Study of Drug Use

Five suburban Philadelphia high school girls, four of them honor students, die in an accident after their car leaves the road and hits a tree; all five had been "huffing" the fumes of a well-known cleaning product shortly before their death. An elderly woman in rural West Virginia takes OxyContin, a potent synthetic narcotic for pain caused by bone cancer; she sells some of her prescription to a young addict for forty dollars per pill, a stash which he promptly pulverizes and inhales. Two members of the Native American Church of North America ingest peyote, a naturally occurring hallucinogenic drug, in a church-sponsored religious ritual in Oregon; because they violated state law in doing so, they are fired from their jobs as drug abuse counselors. A Delaware teenager commits suicide at a time when he was smoking the herb salvia several times a week; his journal entries suggest that the drug influenced him to view his life as pointless. An Olympic track and field star is disqualified from competition for using anabolic steroids, which are on the banned substances list; his wife, a multiple gold medal winner, is tainted by the scandal. These scenarios all happened to real people and are indicative of the range of drug-related issues this textbook investigates.

Ours is a country of drug users. This statement is not a pejorative one; we are not saying that being a drug user is a bad thing; nor, certainly, are we saying that it is a good thing. Rather, we are simply stating a social fact. The overwhelming majority of Americans, adolescents and older, use substances that have a psychoactive effect and can, from a biochemical perspective, be considered "drugs." **Psychoactive drugs** affect the functioning of the central nervous system in some way, and hence influence our thought processes, our emotional responses, how we perceive the world around us, the mood we are in, and more. We, the authors, are not claiming that most of us are drug abusers, or that most of us are taking great risks, or even that most of us are using illegal drugs or legal drugs in an illegal way. But we do routinely use substances that are legal and may even be widely promoted—substances such as caffeine, nicotine, alcohol, and some prescription drugs—in our daily lives. Consider the number of college students who start their days with a strong cup of coffee (or Red Bull, Mountain Dew, Monster, Amp, and the like), who don't feel "right" until they've done so. Of course, a sizeable minority of the American people also use drugs that are currently illegal, many of whose psychoactive effects are harmful to the user and possibly to others. This is also a social fact, albeit one with profound consequences to American society. The American hunger for illegal drugs will be given the greatest scrutiny in this textbook, though our patterns of alcohol and tobacco use and abuse also are of considerable interest to us. It is safe to say that all facets of American life are touched by psychoactive drug use or abuse.

This opening chapter introduces you to the basics of a sociological perspective on drugs and drug use. We begin this chapter by comparing the sociological perspective with the perspectives provided by other scientific disciplines. This discussion is followed by an explanation of some of the basic terminology that is essential to understanding the nature of drug use in society. We examine terms such as *drug effects*, *dependence*, *addiction*, *drug use*, *drug abuse*, the *drug problem*, and yes, even the term *drug*, all through the lens of the sociological framework.

A Sociological Approach to Studying Drug Use

This textbook is a *sociological* investigation of drug use in America. It is likely that many, if not most, of the students reading *The Sociology of American Drug Use* have had previous courses in sociology and have a working knowledge of the sociological perspective and of sociological concepts such as *culture*, *social structure*, and *society*. Regardless, a brief explanation of a sociological approach to the phenomenon of drug use is in order. To the sociologist, drugs are more than just chemical substances whose effects can be studied in laboratory experiments. They are also social and cultural phenomena. How we define what is and is not a drug, the meanings we attach to drugs and their use, the sorts of drugs we use and the manner in which we use them, and the overall societal impact of drug use are all influenced by social and cultural factors.

Drugs may be researched and theorized about from any number of academic perspectives; each has specific theoretical questions of interest and specific methods of conducting research. One of the tenets of scientific inquiry is that the answers you seek are predicated on the questions you ask. Different research questions will yield different answers. Clinical **pharmacology** is the study of how the biochemical substances we know as drugs affect the structure and function of the human body. Pharmacologists are interested in how drugs work as pharmacological entities, testable by experiments; they pay somewhat less attention to the role of social or environmental influences on drug effects. Pharmacologists interested in the absorption and distribution patterns of cocaine by the human body, for example, have an important research agenda. They might ask: What are the factors that promote or block absorption of cocaine into the bloodstream? Courses in pharmacology, or more specifically **psychopharmacology**, which focus on the action of psychoactive drugs, would be of great benefit to nursing, premedical, or medical students, to those studying for a career in clinical pharmacology, or perhaps to those wishing to be drug and alcohol counselors. They might be of somewhat less importance to the college student who is looking to be a police officer or who is seeking other employment in the criminal justice system. The student who is interested in the social science dimensions of deviant or disapproved of behavior wouldn't find her answers there. Drug and alcohol counselors would certainly need additional grounding in research on drug abuse that looks at extra-pharmacological factors. And individuals who want to understand the consequences of the drug abuse of a family member or friend might also wish to look elsewhere. Social scientific perspectives on drugs would be of great value to them.

Drugs are much more than biochemical substances to sociologists and other social scientists. "In addition to their inherent pharmacological properties, drugs are also taken *in certain ways, by certain people, for certain reasons*; moreover, they are also social, cultural, political, and symbolic phenomena…" (Goode 1999, 27; emphasis in original). Pharmacologists simply aren't interested, professionally, in studying these dimensions of drugs. Nor should they be.

Inciardi and Rothman (1990, 12–13) acknowledge that cocaine use is sufficiently widespread to stimulate considerable research from the perspectives of each of the social sciences. *Anthropologists*, whose focus is often on traditional, nonindustrial societies, have examined the practice of coca leaf chewing by the indigenous peoples of the Andes mountains of South America where coca has been grown and chewed for centuries. (Cocaine is derived from the coca plant). In studying the coca rituals and beliefs of these people, they may note that coca chewing is a mildly stimulating pastime considered comparable to our well-established practice of taking a coffee break. Coca leaves contain relatively small amounts of active stimulant, and chewing them releases the substance into the system quite slowly. The role of coca use as an aspect of peasant folk medicine, in brewed coca tea for example, might also considered; as could be the religious properties of coca, which was associated with the divine by the Incan people (see Weil 1972 on natural drug use). Anthropologists have also studied drug use in American society, using ethnographic methods including direct observation and a variety of open-ended interviewing techniques. Drug ethnography in American cities was, in fact, pioneered by an anthropologist named Edward Preble.

Political scientists, with their emphasis on political and governmental processes, and the means by which power is acquired and used, might be concerned with issues like the destabilizing or corrupting effects of cocaine trafficking on a government's functioning, such as in Colombia in the 1980s and 1990s, or of opium trafficking more recently in Afghanistan, or on the relationships between the governments of multiple countries such as tension between Peru and the United States over coca eradication policies. The considerable amount of money and influence wielded by drug-trafficking cartels, who have a vested interest in reducing governmental control of their operations, may be profoundly corrupting of democratic process. Other interests of political scientists might include the political debates at the origin of many of our drug laws and of drug legislation in general (a topic we look at in Chapter 2). A number of scholars (among them Brecher 1972; Grinspoon and Bakalar 1976; Musto 1999) have argued that the anticocaine legislation of the early 1900s was racist in its implementation and enforcement, being based on mythologies that black Americans would be especially likely to use cocaine and especially violent when they did. The use of political power to control an "undesirable" segment of society for its alleged or expected drug abuse is of interest to sociologists as well, whose scope of study overlaps that of the political scientist.

The economics of the crack cocaine trade, the effect of windfall drug-dealing profits on a country's economy, or the impact of drug abuse on economic productivity might be of interest to *economists*. Colombia, home of the famous Medellin and Cali cocaine cartels, was affected throughout the 1980s by the billions of dollars a year that cocaine brought to the country's economy (Inciardi 2002), Flooded with money, specifically U.S. dollars, the Colombian currency was devalued and hyperinflation ensued. A black market in American dollars thrived; for example, American automobiles sold for several times their asking price in the United States. Conversely, Americans were estimated to be spending upward of $100 billion a year on illegal drugs in the 1980s (estimates for today are far lower, as both drug prices and consumption rates have dropped compared with twenty to thirty years ago). This is money that largely was unavailable to aid the bottom line of legitimate industries (Mills 1987; Nadelmann 1989).

Historians, who study drug use throughout American history, help to remind us that drug use often was practiced many years ago. The recreational use of psychoactive drugs was not invented yesterday or by the hippies of the 1960s, despite what the popular belief might be. David F. Musto (2001), a professor of child psychiatry and the history of medicine at Yale University, and a recognized expert on drug use in the United States in the nineteenth and early twentieth centuries, writes that the recreational use of inhalants dates back to the early nineteenth century. At his own Ivy League university in the 1820s, students staged "ether frolics" and used nitrous oxide (known then and now as laughing gas) at parties. So college students and others today who do "whip-its" are continuing a centuries-old practice. Inhalation-based drug experiences are more covert today because, although nitrous oxide is legally available, using it for intoxication is currently illegal. We know a great deal more about the damage done by inhalant abuse today than we did many years ago. Just because a substance that alters one's consciousness can be purchased legally (because it has other, more common uses) should never lead one to conclude that it is therefore safe to use. As historians remind us, the legal status of chemical substances changes not only when harm is recognized, but for many other social and political reasons as well (Goode 1975).

Each of the social sciences mentioned so far differs from sociology in that they are disciplines focused on a relatively narrow slice of human behavior (political behavior, economic behavior, etc.). *Psychologists* engaged in drug studies differ from sociologists not in the scope of the discipline, as both study the full range of human behavior, but in its focus on the individual as the unit of analysis, whereas sociologists study human behavior within social groups ranging from the very small to the quite large. Psychologists might be interested in studying what personality characteristics are found in those who are more likely to choose one drug, such as cocaine, over another. They are also interested in the effects of cocaine use on one's personality, on thinking, on emotions, on motivation. Psychic dependence on the drug's mood elevation or induced feelings of well-being, which fosters compulsive cocaine use known as "binging," may be studied by psychologists who wish to understand the brain-behavior link. And psychologists would be interested in the link between drug abuse and psychosis: Does abusing drugs lead to psychotic episodes? Or are those with serious underlying mental illnesses more likely to abuse drugs? Or are both possible?

Inciardi and Rothman (1990, 13) claim that sociologists have been especially concerned with studying patterns of cocaine use and abuse in the United States. Sociologists collect and analyze data on the **incidence** and **prevalence** of cocaine use. That is, they are concerned with how frequently someone takes a dose of a given drug (incidence) and what segment of the population has used a given drug, or drugs in general, in a specified period of time (prevalence), ranging from their lifetime ("Have they ever used, even once?") to daily ("Have they used in the last 24 hours?"). Unlike psychologists, who attempt to predict an individual's behavior, including drug-using behavior, by researching factors *endogenous* to an individual, sociologists look at the linkage between the behavioral patterns of subgroups in the society and the *exogenous* factors to which they are exposed.

What are the combination of theoretical points of view and approaches to conducting research that are characteristic of sociological approaches to the study of drug use in America? Note that we say *approaches*, not approach. We do so because, although there are common elements comprising their discipline about which all sociologists agree, there are many research- and theory-based issues about which sociologists might legitimately differ, such as what methods to use when conducting social research or what general theories of society inform their professional work. *Sociology is a general behavioral science* that studies all forms of human behavior, including those studied by more narrowly focused disciplines like political science. You would have a difficult time coming up with a type of social behavior that has not been studied by sociologists. *The focus of sociologists is on social groups and their structure, organization, and cultural elements.* When studying social behavior—including drug use and abuse, drug trafficking, and drug control—the sociologist is ever mindful of the social forces shaping that behavior and the group response to that behavior. To that end, sociology reminds us that human behavior exists within a social and cultural context that cannot be ignored. Ignoring the social dimensions of drug-oriented behavior leads to incomplete or distorted research and theory.

A sociological view of the world affects the academic understanding of drugs in American society in four important ways. Most of what is written in this textbook directly or indirectly touches on one or more of these dimensions.

- To define what a drug is, or is not, we must look beyond the biochemical substances studied by pharmacologists and include the social contexts within which social definitions take place. What the concept "drug" means is affected by a variety of social influences.
- To understand psychoactive drug effects, we must have an awareness of social factors that influence how drugs affect those who take them and how those users experience their drug taking independent of any pharmacological processes that are occurring.
- Drug use, drug abuse, and drug addiction and/or dependence are all social constructions; that is, the meaning attached to each of these ideas is a matter of social negotiation. We will be defining these concepts for you, but we ask you to recognize that other professionals in this field, with other interests, may disagree with our interpretations.
- To comprehend our society's concern over the social problem of drug abuse, we must investigate not only the objective harm done by and to drug abusers but also the subjective dimensions of concern. Social problems are both conditions that cause observable harm and subjectively constructed campaigns led by those who claim that something is harmful.

The impact of drug abuse in this society profoundly affects our social institutions and our social relationships. Drug abuse affects all aspects of social life: family dynamics are strained, economic productivity decreases, the health care system must meet increased demands, and the landscape of crime and justice shifts. In short, drug abuse raises the costs of running a society, it is associated with a host of social pathologies, and it is destructive of interpersonal trust.

The Sociological Definition of "Drug"
This may seem like an unnecessary section of this book. After all, we all know what a drug is, don't we? Were you to do a survey of people in your community, you might find that they agree about whether substance A or B should count as a drug. But what would be the bases for that decision? Would your respondents be considering the psychopharmacological actions of the substance in question? That is, would they

be thinking of drugs as chemical substances that alter the way we feel or think, or the ways in which our bodies function? Without question, drugs are such chemical entities. It is likely, however, that those examples considered drugs by the subjects of your survey weren't selected on this basis alone. An additional dimension would be whether your survey respondents would classify Drug A or Drug B as "good drugs" or "bad drugs." This distinction is particularly influenced by extrapharmacological factors of a social, cultural, or political nature. Many Americans consider marijuana to be a drug but do not consider alcohol to be a drug, yet both substances have a psychoactive effect when used in sufficient doses. Psychoactive drugs—those that exert an influence on our central nervous system and have the capacity to alter our mood or emotion, our sensation or perception, or our cognition (thinking)—are the central subject of this textbook. Psychoactivity alone, though, doesn't explain why marijuana is more frequently thought of as a drug than is alcohol, a substance that in many ways is more powerful and has a wider range of psychoactive effects and societal consequences than does marijuana. Alcohol's effect on motor skills performance, such as driving a car, is more profound. Alcohol abuse precipitates violent behavior, from fighting to rape to homicide, in ways marijuana does not (Parker 1995). Where there is interpersonal violence in America, alcohol is likely to be a contributing factor. It isn't the level of actual *social harm* done by abusing a particular substance that leads to it being considered a drug, or a dangerous drug, or a bad drug. Purported social harm is used to indict certain practices that are deemed unacceptable, however. What leads the public—at a given point in time, since public attitudes change—to label a substance as a drug is a complex process of **social construction**.

Sociologists are particularly interested in understanding the social and cultural factors that influence common perceptions of what drugs are and are not. For sociologists, the political climate matters, the prevailing culture matters, a society's awareness of a threat in its midst matters. Drugs are multidimensional phenomena. They are pharmacological substances that affect human anatomy and physiology, the structure and functioning of the human body, to be sure. But they are also political and economic phenomena; they are grounded in our history and our folklore and our popular culture; they are an integral part of our national psyche. We must take these varied contexts into consideration when naming, classifying, evaluating, and judging drugs. Sociologist Erich Goode offers this consideration of **drug**: "…any accurate and valid definition of drugs must include the social, cultural, and contextual dimension. The concept drug is in part a cultural artifact, a social fabrication, applied to certain types of substances in specific contexts or settings. *A drug is something that has been defined by certain segments of the society as a drug"* (1999, 58; emphasis in original).

According to this perspective, what is most important is how social elements get defined by a society at a specific point in time. It recognizes the variability of social concern and societal responses about things we might call drugs. Currently, marijuana is viewed as a drug; its recreational use is illegal in all states (though not necessarily a criminal offense, as it has been decriminalized in eleven states as of 2008).[1]

With the exception of some "dry" counties or municipalities and, of course, for those who are under the age of 21, alcohol is legal, available, and widely promoted. It wasn't always so. Eighty-plus years ago, during Prohibition, alcohol consumption was illegal by federal law as a result of the Eighteenth Amendment to the Constitution of the United States. Marijuana use, in contrast, was a legal, though somewhat disreputable, pursuit in every state. Sociologists stress that one's status as a criminal or as a societal outsider (Becker 1963, 1–18) is always the result of being associated with behaviors whose prevailing social definitions deem them unacceptable. In the public mind, being a user of drugs (meaning "bad" drugs) conveys such disrepute based upon images of drug use as dirty, destructive, dangerous, and the like.

The point being made by sociologists is that, although the chemical properties of a substance certainly matter, what gets defined as a drug, and hence which practices get defined as drug use or abuse, hinges on the prevailing social and political perspectives. The "reality" of drug use is a social and political phenomenon (Goode 1975). It shifts with the times and with changes in the groups who wield political power and moral influence (see Gusfield 1963 on shifting perceptions of drinkers of alcohol). A commonly used phrase in sociology is, "Reality is socially constructed." We distinguish "drugs" from "drink," though both act pharmacologically on our bodies. We distinguish "drugs" from "medicine," because they are purported to be used for different purposes. Yet sometimes a substance shifts in the collective wisdom from medicine to drug, as was the case with OxyContin around 2000. Throughout this book, but particularly in Chapter 2, we will see that the drugs with which we are most concerned, the "most dangerous drugs," go through cycles of public recognition.

Psychoactive Drug Effects

One of the most commonly asked questions by students in a course on the Sociology of Drug Use, or by the population in general, is "What effect does taking a drug have on the user?" As we shall soon see, this is an imprecise question, because the questioner may have several different goals in mind. She might be asking, "If I take this drug, how will it make me feel?" Alternately, the intention might be to discover whether any deleterious effects of using this substance might be likely: "If I take this drug, might it lead me to go crazy?" (There's a popular myth that anyone who "trips" on LSD seven times—or is it 11?—is legally insane.) Or perhaps the intention is to ferret out long-term consequences of using a particular drug on one's health and well-being. We really are talking about several different kinds of effects associated with psychoactive drug use—*objective drug effects*, *subjective drug effects*, and *chronic drug effects*. Each will be discussed now.

Objective drug effects result from being under the influence of a substance and can be measured reliably. Although they are less likely to be the reasons motivating drug use in the first place, they are quite valuable to researchers and scientists. For example, users of marijuana may experience a *tachycardial effect*; that is, smoking marijuana produces a measurable increase in one's heart rate. This effect doesn't

Drugs: Myths and Reality

The Battle Over Salvia: A Twenty-First Century Controversy

The social and legal status of *Salvia divinorum* is a hotly debated issue, reminiscent of earlier battles over the meaning of LSD, peyote, and ecstasy. The trajectory of public discourse about salvia during the first decade of the twenty-first century—Is it a relatively harmless psychedelic? Is it a dangerous hallucinogen? Does it have profound religious and spiritual dimensions? Is it a medically useful substance?—with interest groups lined up on all sides of the issue, demonstrates once again how what is real and true is never simplistic or black-and-white when it comes to subjective drug effects. The meanings attached to chewing or smoking salvia is an excellent example of what sociologists call the *social construction of reality*.

First, the facts. Salvia is an herb, botanically a member of the mint family, whose psychoactive compound is salvinorin A. It is native to Oaxaca, Mexico, where it was used originally by Mazatec shamans as an aid to experiencing spiritual revelations. It is relatively new on the American drug scene; its presence in society and popular culture dates to perhaps the year 2000. So far, it is legally sold online and in specialty shops. It has various street names (*Sally D*, the *magic mint*) as all substances that garner subcultural support acquire. It is increasingly popular with college students, with males 18 to 25 the most common salvia-using demographic. According to a National Survey on Drug Use and Health report (SAMHSA 2008), it is estimated that 1.8 million people aged 12 or older used *Salvia divinorum* in their lifetime, and approximately 750,000 did so in the past year. And thousands of those college students have made "under the influence of salvia" videos a staple of YouTube. Herein lies a central concern for drug control agencies and interest groups.

As we emphasize in this textbook, the same substance can be used by different groups in different ways for different purposes with radically different effects. Consequently, it is difficult to argue that there is one and only one undeniable "salvia experience." Those seeking intoxicated thrills—and posting their antics and incoherence online—have one relationship with salvia. Even if this is the most common way salvia is used in this country, should this be used as a reason to preclude other salvia experiences of a spiritual or medically useful nature? The federal government (through the Drug Enforcement Administration) has answered this question Yes with substances like ecstasy and LSD, which are prohibited for all purposes, "legitimate" or not. A Yes answer has consequences: "Pharmacologists who believe salvia could open new frontiers for the treatment of addiction, depression and pain fear that its criminalization would make it burdensome to obtain and store the plant, and difficult to gain permission for tests on human subjects" (Sack and McDonald 2008). Hence, the interests of scientific inquiry and medical advancement get intertwined with the drive to regulate salvia by law enforcement interests in some of our largest states (a number of smaller states, like Delaware, have banned it for several years) and at the federal level.

This battle over the status of salvia within societal institutions and in the culture at large exists these days for several reasons. First, herbs whose subjective effects alternatively may be classified as psychedelic or hallucinogenic, the first designation more favorable than the second, are inherently controversial. The debate over LSD, ecstasy, and peyote has frequently been highly emotional precisely because these substances produce intense experiences and elicit such angry passions on both sides of the issue. Salvia's subjective effects are similarly intense, but are much

Drugs: Myths and Reality *(continued)*

shorter lived than any of the aforementioned drugs. Second, research on salvia is relatively recent, so issues like chronic (long-term) effects have not been studied. When little data are available, enforcers like the Drug Enforcement Administration do not know whether to subsume it under the Controlled Substances Act. Third, our society has had a relatively prohibitionist stance toward drugs in recent years, frustrating those who believe that, despite abuse by some, many substances have great potential to be rewarding or beneficial to others, and prohibition thwarts the discovery or awareness of these benefits. Inevitably, then, interest groups have clashed (and will continue to do so) over whether salvia is benign or threatening, whether it holds promise therapeutically and pharmaceutically or lacks medical utility, whether it is a pipe dream or a genuine tool for spiritual enhancement, and whether it should be left alone or prohibited or regulated (perhaps like tobacco or alcohol). The reality of salvia has yet to be determined.

generally motivate people to use the drug; in fact, the elevated heart rate may be experienced by the user as an uncomfortably anxious feeling. Yet this knowledge is valuable, since it would seem to indicate that individuals with underlying heart conditions should be especially cautious about smoking marijuana, because for them the risks of doing so might be greater than for other individuals. Drugs affect different users in different ways; the health history of the user, among many other factors, is relevant to the consequences he or she might experience from using drugs. Remember, risk associated with drug use is not an either-or proposition; degree of risk varies along a continuum from slight to quite serious, based on many factors.

Another objective drug effect, one with far greater consequences, can be seen in the discoordinating effects of alcohol intoxication. Nearly ever reader of this text is aware of the effect of alcohol in sufficient doses on speech and motor coordination. One's performance in driving a car, a measurable skill, is adversely affected by alcohol consumption, and the degree of diminished performance, correlated with blood-alcohol concentration, is reliably shown in study after study. Researchers can then pinpoint how much alcohol one would need to consume, on average, to yield a particular level of increased risk. And public policy makers could employ such data in setting laws, as in the recent movement to have states lower the threshold for DUI offenses from the once standard 0.10% BAC to the more restrictive 0.08% BAC.

To sum up, objective drug effects are measurable effects resulting from the direct ingestion of a drug or drugs by a user. They are observable, independent of whatever the user believes that he or she is experiencing. Marijuana intoxication is associated with decreased driving performance, though not as clearly so as alcohol intoxication. Yet a significant number of marijuana smokers mistakenly believe themselves to be better drivers when high. They confuse the subjective experience of their greater awareness of the need to be careful with their objective driving performance. Objective drug effects matter to the study of drug use in America and are of some interest to sociologists, yet in many ways subjective effects are the more valuable to look at. And they are certainly more controversial.

Subjective drug effects cannot be measured on a consistent scale and are grounded in the experiential reality of the user. Note that just because an outside observer may not be able to measure such effects, that doesn't make them any less real. Perhaps an example of subjective reality in an allied field will be helpful here. Recently, hospitals have been required to ask their patients about the level of pain they are experiencing and to make pain management a higher therapeutic priority. Patients are asked to rate their current pain on a scale of 1 to 10, something which they are generally able to do. We are aware that one person's pain experience may differ from another's, based on factors such as tolerance for pain, and that the reporting of pain may be mediated through factors such as gender ("tough men don't show they are hurting"). So two patients undergoing similar treatment may report subjectively experienced levels of pain that are quite different.

So it is with subjective drug effects—the use of a particular drug may yield different experiences for different users. These differences may be heightened further because of the difficulty in precisely articulating subjective effects. We know about subjective effects primarily through user-reported experiences, as opposed to external observation, and such reportage is often imprecise because drug experiences may be so personal and profound that an agreed upon vocabulary of effects is not possible. Obviously, this makes them somewhat tougher to study by sociologists and other drug researchers. They are also more controversial, since it is easier to make claims about subjective drug effects that are wildly divergent and that support different agendas. There is great difficulty evaluating the "rightness" of perspectives based on subjective experience, just as there is with many other social issues today, such as abortion or capital punishment.

What is the experience of being "high" like? Is being high on marijuana like being drunk on alcohol? How are the similarities and differences articulated? Here you see how hard it is to explain to others—to sociologists who are studying drug use, or to those who might wish to experiment with a drug themselves—the subjective nature of drug experience. These experiences may or may not be related to objective, observable changes in the user's vital signs, blood chemistry, or appearance. In other words, subjective drug effects may be more than the user's psychic experience of changes in objective conditions. They may be wholly unique phenomena sui generis—in and of themselves.

LSD (lysergic acid diethylamide-25), commonly known as acid, is a potent drug that provides a wide range of profound subjective experiences for its users, experiences that they may have difficulty articulating to others who might wish to know what their drug "trip" was like. Imagine an experience where one's senses cross heretofore unheard of boundaries—attributing colors to different musical sounds, for example, or reporting that one could "taste" musical notes. Or consider the "eureka experience" (Goode 1999, 247) where one makes connections between things that appear to the user to represent some important truth, but will seem silly or incomprehensible if explained to an observer. A female college student told one of the authors of the following experience: "I had come to the great 'aha.' And that was that Herman Munster [of the TV show *The Munsters*] and Prince [the musical artist] were one and the same person, because you never saw them in the same place and the shoes they wore were identical." Needless to say, she had great difficulty persuading others at the time that the green and physically imposing Munster was one and the same with the diminutive Prince. Given that LSD renders its users extremely emotionally labile, she was distraught when no one else could see her point of view, since conveying this important truth to others had become a mission for her. Days later, sober, she could understand why her fellows had not bought into the Munster-Prince unified theory of pop culture.

For the most part, subjective effects are the ones that users seek, that motivate them to use psychoactive drugs initially, regularly, or even habitually. Experiencing a "high," "tripping," and having a sense of drug-induced well-being are all subjective effects. It must be noted that whereas a pleasurable subjective drug experience may be sought by users, not all such effects are pleasurable and may, in fact, result in profoundly uncomfortable sensations or experiences. Powerful drugs may yield powerfully negative subjective experiences, such as sensations of paranoia or of being suffocated or of experiencing nightmares from which one may not easily awaken. Traumatic drug experiences, although relatively rare occurrences, can indelibly implant themselves on unfortunate users.

Subjective drug effects are influenced by many factors that are of particular interest to sociologists and other behavioral scientists. One's expectations prior to a drug-using experience or one's emotional state or mood, known as the user's **set**, can influence whether one gets intoxicated and whether or not that intoxication is defined as pleasurable. It can also influence the behavior one considers appropriate while intoxicated. Experimental psychologist Kim Fromme and her associates did research on "alcohol outcome expectancies," using student subjects (of legal age) in a simulated tavern. Some of her research subjects would be served mix drinks containing a measured amount of alcohol, others would drink nonalcoholic counterparts of similar appearance, and still others would be given some of each. Subjects often would report feeling intoxicated and they "acted drunk," even when no or little alcohol had been consumed, because they were around others who had imbibed alcohol, and their behavioral expectations were adjusted accordingly. Behaviors that might seem purely alcohol induced, Fromme argues, including risk-taking sexual behaviors, may be products more of one's expectations of the alcohol experience than of pharmacological disinhibition, including the expectation held by many college men that the consequences of coercing sex are reduced when alcohol is a factor (Fromme and Wendel 1995). This is important, because it leads us away from the simplistic assessment that the pharmacological action of drugs alone causes a host of unwanted and risky behaviors, and leads us toward looking at psychological and sociocultural influences on our comportment while under the influence.

These emotional states and expectations, the drug user's **set**, is a concept frequently paired with the **setting** within which drug use takes place. Setting has a number of dimensions: physical surroundings, the presence or absence of others and one's relationship to those present, and the prevailing legal and political climate. All of these affect the comfort level of the user, and being comfortable or uncomfortable in a drug-using episode can alter the nature of the experience. This isn't difficult to see. If one wishes to use a substance—say marijuana—in an environment where there are well-known social or legal consequences for doing so, the behavior will be more surreptitious due to fear of being discovered, and this can result in feeling suspicious or paranoid of others. It is not the pharmacological action of the marijuana that is causing such feelings (though the tachycardial effect mentioned previously might play a modest role), it is the unsafe environment. The experience of drugs like marijuana, and especially hallucinogens like LSD, whose impact on cognition and mood are pronounced, may be altered profoundly by how one perceives the immediate and social environments. Set and setting are important, nonpharmacological influences on the nature of subjective drug experience.

Pharmacological influences on objective and subjective drug effects are also worthy of mention. **Route of administration**, the method by which drugs are introduced into one's physiological systems, can greatly alter the effects of using the drug. There are many such routes of administration, including: "mainlining," intravenous injection directly into the bloodstream; "skin-popping," or subcutaneous injection; "snorting" or intranasal administration; smoking or inhaling vapors; oral ingestion, swallowing a solid or liquid containing the active ingredient; and transdermal absorption through the skin, as with a nicotine or fentanyl patch. They vary in the speed and efficiency of the onset of effects. Intravenous injection and smoking are extremely rapid, effects being felt within a matter of seconds. (There is some disagreement in the drug research literature about which of these is faster, though the effects of IV injection are more profound.) Drugs that are swallowed take effect or "kick in" much more slowly, taking perhaps 30 to 60 minutes in many cases. That time lag may make it harder for the user to connect the effects experienced with the substance ingested, especially in **polydrug use** situations, those where an individual is using multiple substances in the same time period. Coca products, for example, may be injected in solution form, smoked in rock form ("crack"), snorted in powdered form, or even orally ingested, as with chewing coca leaves or drinking brewed coca tea (or in Coca-Cola in its earliest formulations more than a century ago). The intensity and duration of the drug-using episode will vary with different routes of administration. The route of administration one chooses to employ may be affected by drug-using peers or by financial considerations, so we can see that social processes remain important factors on drug effects and experiences.

Other pharmacological factors influencing psychoactive drug effects are *dose*, *potency*, *purity*, *tolerance*, and *drug interaction*. Most drugs have effects that are **dose** related, with a known **effective dose** and **lethal dose**. Pharmaceuticals have a recommended **therapeutic dose**. What is the dose that is most often appropriate for the

DRUGS AND EVERYDAY LIFE

Vietnam, Drug Setting, and Heroin Addiction

Sociologists who study drug use emphasize the importance of setting, the social context in which drugs are used, in understanding the effects that drugs can have on the user. The importance of setting was brought home to policy makers with the publication of a book commissioned by the federal government itself, entitled *The Vietnam Drug User Returns.* The study was prompted when two United States congressmen visited the war zone in Vietnam and came back with claims that some 10 to 15 percent of our military personnel in Vietnam were addicted to heroin. When they reported this, there was, understandably, great concern that when these soldiers returned stateside, they would continue in their addiction, and trained in the use of firearms as they were, American citizens would be placed in great risk of being victimized by violent crime. Psychiatrist Lee Robins was asked to lead the study of drug use among soldiers returning from Vietnam.

Robins (1974) found that only about one percent of American servicemen had used narcotic drugs more than a few times prior to going to Vietnam, though most were very experienced with alcohol and tobacco. After their arrival in Vietnam, however, some 45 percent of these servicemen tried heroin or opium, and about 20 percent of those who tried became addicted. What greatly concerned government officials was that just about half of these narcotics users continued to use after arriving back on American soil. Robins' research revealed, however, that only about 6 percent became readdicted to heroin

after returning from Vietnam. Typically, previous research revealed that about two-thirds of patients treated in hospitals would relapse in about a year. This finding challenged the common knowledge of the day that heroin was an inherently addicting drug. It is assumed that even occasional use of the drug will inevitably lead to addiction, and that once addicted, it is almost impossible for the user to quit. So how was it that American servicemen experienced such a high rate of use and addiction while in Vietnam, but so few continued that use after returning?

The answer to this question is clearly found in a setting that was relatively conducive to narcotics use in Vietnam. It has been suggested, first, that American GIs encountered a highly threatening environment in Vietnam. Circumstances such as what they were facing are highly conducive to the use of drugs, particularly narcotics, as a way of coping with the intensive stress of an unpredictable battle zone. Second, these soldiers were away from family and friends, and living with others who were also using. The normative constraints against the use of such drugs were not there. These two factors, combined with the ready availability of narcotics, provided a setting that encouraged the use of and even addiction to narcotics. These social conditions were not present when they returned to the United States, however. Narcotics were not freely available, and when they were available, the came in a much more diluted form than available in Vietnam. There were, moreover, strong normative proscriptions against the use of narcotics in the United States, even the threat of arrest. The result? Only a handful of Vietnam addicts returned to continue their addiction in the United States.

effect one wishes to achieve? Anabolic steroids have a therapeutically recommended dose appropriate for tissue repair. Yet someone who is interested in increasing muscle and strength rapidly will seek a much higher effective dose, many times the therapeutic dose, which yields the desired benefits but does so with greatly enhanced risks. Or consider drinkers of alcohol, who might seek the gentle relaxation that one mixed drink and a slightly elevated blood alcohol level provides, or may desire, as binge-drinking college students do, a greater level of intoxication in which one would feel drunk. The latter effect might be found at a blood-alcohol level of 0.15 percent (though many drink beyond that

1.1 The effect that drugs have on the individual user depends greatly on the setting or social context in which drugs are used. (Photo: Véronique Burger/ Photo Researchers)

point)—not all that far from the median lethal dose for alcohol, which is right around 0.40%. The ratio between effective and lethal dose for alcohol, being relatively narrow, makes lethal levels of alcohol intoxication a possibility, particularly for the naive drinker who might be talked into drinking games. In contrast, marijuana, a less toxic drug, has a lethal dose that is virtually unreachable.

Potency and **purity** are allied terms. Potency refers to the strength of the drug in question, specifically to how much of that drug is necessary for an effective dose. The more potent the drug, the smaller is the effective dose. LSD is an extremely potent drug, with an effective dose of perhaps 100 micrograms (µg), about one ten-thousandth of a gram. An aspirin-sized tablet, 325 milligrams (mg), of pure LSD would yield around 3,250 doses! Drugs like marijuana or psilocybin mushrooms, grown as opposed to synthesized in a laboratory, have variable potency, though they are far less potent than LSD. Marijuana cultivators can breed strains of the cannabis plant with higher levels of THC (delta-9-tetrahydrocannabinol), its active ingredient, that are more in demand and fetch a higher price because of the increased potency. In contrast, purity refers to the percentage of the drug sample that is actually the drug itself. Marijuana, whatever its potency, is generally 100% pure (though it may be occasionally mixed with other drugs). Powdered street drugs, like heroin and cocaine, may vary widely in purity; some samples contain little drug and much inactive ingredient or adulterant, other samples have higher rates of purity. In recent years, the purity of street drug samples has increased because of the glut of drugs on the market. A user not accustomed to higher levels of purity might be at greater risk of overdose, perhaps fatally so.

Drug tolerance is a cumulative resistance to the pharmacological effects of a drug that develops in some users of some drugs. In drugs where tolerance may develop—among them LSD, alcohol, and the narcotics—regular, chronic, or habitual use may raise the effective dose for such users. Consider the case of the individual who can "drink others under the table"; he or she may have developed a tolerance to alcohol, which may serve as a warning sign that alcohol dependence or alcoholism has begun to set in. Drug tolerance and **drug dependence** are believed to be related phenomena. At the very least, behaviorally and pharmacologically, experienced drinkers have subjective drug effects different from the inexperienced drinker. Interestingly, though the effective dose of such drinkers is higher, moving closer to the known lethal dose, such users are less likely to die of acute alcohol intoxication because of their drinking experience. The chronic or cumulative effects of alcohol abuse are another story, as we shall see shortly.

Finally, we must consider **drug interaction** effects. These are vitally important for two reasons: polydrug use, the mixing of substances, is an extremely common practice; and when drugs are mixed together, their cumulative effect may be synergistic, antagonistic, or idiosyncratic, and hence dangerous. This is true for both recreational drug use and the use of pharmaceutical drugs for medical purposes. For this reason, physicians ask their patients for lists of all current medications (especially elderly patients who take pills for more ailments and whose livers metabolize drugs more slowly), and pharmacies have computerized records which flag potentially dangerous combinations.[2] One form of danger is known as **synergism effects**. Synergism is the condition where two or more drugs taken in combination have an effect that is greater than a simple additive effect. Many drugs, particularly central nervous depressants like tranquilizers or narcotic pain relievers, when combined with alcohol (itself a CNS, central nervous system, depressant), exhibit synergism, often dangerously so. Some drugs are **antagonistic** to one another, and cancel out each other's effects. Some drugs in combination have **idiosyncratic effects**: the effect of one of the drugs may be greatly heightened by the presence of the other drug, whose effect is muted, or the effects of both drugs may be heightened, as with the injectable heroin-cocaine mix known as a "speedball." An awareness of the ways in which drugs—legal and illegal, recreational and therapeutic—interact, is critical for users and health practitioners alike.

Chronic effects are those that accumulate over time as one continues to use or abuse a particular substance. For the most part, they are objective health-related consequences of a history of drug abuse. Perhaps this is most easily understood by looking at tobacco smoking. Tobacco does little harm to the vast majority of users in any given episode of use. We have been warned by the Surgeon General about the deleterious effects of smoking since the 1960s, but such warnings are not of the "one puff could lead to insanity or to lung cancer" variety. Rather, we are confronted with powerful evidence that many years of smoking tobacco products, most notably cigarettes, is associated with some of America's leading causes of death, among them heart disease and chronic lung disorders such as lung cancer and emphysema. Recent estimates of smoking-related deaths range from 400,000 to 450,000 people every year, even though the number of active smokers in society has dropped.

Clearly, the chronic effects of tobacco consumption contribute mightily to mortality (death) and morbidity (sickness) statistics.

Another chronic effect of drug abuse is addiction, a concept we deal with elsewhere in this chapter. Despite alarmist claims to the contrary, no drug is "instantly addictive," regardless of its potential for producing dependency in its user. Addiction results from regular and repeated use of a drug by an individual. It must be noted that, although there is no magic timetable for when addiction occurs—as drugs vary in their addictive potential from low to quite high, and users vary somewhat in terms of their susceptibility to addiction—the biochemical alterations occurring within the addict are the result of an accumulative process and hence must be considered chronic effects.

Drug Use, Drug Abuse, and Drug Addiction

So far in this chapter, the concepts of drug use and drug abuse have appeared repeatedly. They are often conflated by casual observers of the drug scene, by the mass media, and by those who may have an ideological axe to grind. It is time for us to differentiate these terms because they are not interchangeable and should not be used interchangeably by anyone who takes the study of psychoactive drugs in America seriously. **Drug use** is an extremely broad concept, for it refers to the use of any chemical substance that acts like a drug or that is believed to act like a drug. This includes a wide range of both legal and illegal substances. It includes every level of involvement with psychoactive substances, from the most occasional user to the frequent social user to the person who uses habitually (perhaps due to drug dependence). When we wrote earlier that ours is a nation of psychoactive drug users, and that this is a social fact and not a pejorative view of the American people, we were acknowledging the universality of drug using in this country. And the majority of this drug use is socially acceptable and even promoted. We joke about needing our caffeine "fix" in the mornings, but rarely must going into a coffee shop be done secretly. The majority of American adults drink alcoholic beverages in any given month; lifetime prevalence approaches 6 out of every 7 of us (SAMHSA 2000b). After work or college classes, drinking establishments attract the thirsty, the overworked, and the stressed-out with Happy Hours or Attitude Adjustment Sessions; societal protest is minimal. The point is, the *use* of substances that alter emotion and mood is ingrained in American society. That is why we can say that drug use is an American way of life. The broadness and ubiquity of psychoactive drug use makes *drug use* a less useful concept than *drug abuse*.

There are those who argue—usually on religious, moral, or ethical grounds—that using anything psychoactive constitutes **drug abuse**. Although this is not a mainstream cultural position, it should be acknowledged. Students at Brigham Young University, which is run according to Latter Day Saints' principles (the Mormon Church), sign a pledge that they will abstain from all drugs, even soft drinks containing caffeine. Violation of this pledge is considered drug abuse in the eyes of school administrators. Other colleges and universities, and other religious organizations have similar bans. As noted, this is not a widely held position. Much more widely believed by the public at large, and some drug abuse professionals, is that the recreational use of any illegal drug constitutes drug abuse. After all, the word *abuse* connotes a negative evaluation of a practice, and the *abuser* is a wrongdoer, a violator of acceptable standards of behavior. And it is wrong to do things that are against the law. So why not combine the two, allowing the criminal law to be the arbiter of whether or not a practice qualifies as drug abuse?

We believe that the "any use of an illegal drug constitutes drug abuse" argument is overly simplistic and falls short in two important areas. First, it fails in any way to distinguish the degree of involvement one has with drugs; the one-time-only user of an illegal drug and the habitual user are lumped together and are tarred with the same damning brush. Drug abuse should not be considered an all-or-nothing phenomenon, where, for example, smoking marijuana once or a few times is equated with hard core, intractable, consequential behavior. The second shortcoming, and the more critical, is that it legalistically assumes that the law assesses with impartiality and scientific precision those drugs whose use represents a threat and hence should be designated as abusive.

Drug legislation is not created in a social and political vacuum, and is affected by more than the best drug research available. Nor are drugs politically neutral entities about which we can be dispassionate. The legislative process is always swayed by the prevailing political winds; drug legislation is especially political. The distinction between legal drugs and illegal drugs is a political one, not a scientific one. This doesn't mean that the distinction is worthless or unimportant. It matters vitally which substances can lead to legal consequences for those who use them. But it is a great mistake to assume that illegal drugs are inevitably harmful and that the use of their legal counterparts is essentially a risk-free endeavor. Yet we make this mistake all of the time, dichotomizing "good" drugs from "bad" on the basis of legal status alone, and in doing so attribute far greater wisdom and scientific basis to the legislative process than it deserves.

As sociologists, we believe that it makes much more sense to assess whether drug involvement should be considered drug abuse by looking at the individual, interpersonal, and social consequences of drug-involved behavior. This restores the concept of social harm, allows us to ground our understanding of drug abuse in measurable adversity, and permits us to see abuse on a sliding scale from slight to great, since the consequences of actions are not of uniform severity. Let us therefore define drug abuse as "the use of a substance or substances in such a way that it leads to measurable personal, interpersonal, or social consequences" (adapted from Fuqua 1978, 8–9). Many of these consequences will come from over-involvement with a substance, some will come from misusing a substance, and still others will be the result of bad luck. We mention the last of these because, although most episodes of drug use result in no harm whatsoever, one should never assume that using a drug, even a relatively benign one, is entirely without risk. And although we can calculate the probability of risk to some extent by attending to the many factors that affect the pharmacological action of a drug, there are no guarantees of safety.

What are some of the consequences that might stem from drug involvement? Impaired physical and mental health functioning is one. Every human physiological system is potentially affected: the cardiovascular system by drugs that accelerate the development of heart disease or by stimulant drugs such as cocaine that may overstimulate the heart; the respiratory system by drugs that are smoked or inhaled, contributing to chronic obstructive lung diseases or lung cancer; the central nervous system, which may experience irreversible damage to brain functioning. The damage may be done by legal drugs like tobacco products and alcohol as well as illegal drugs such as heroin, cocaine, and marijuana. That is why judging abuse by legal status alone is an inappropriate strategy.

Or consider the following interpersonal and social consequences of the overuse or misuse of drugs, which potentially affect every social role that we might be called on to play, within every social institution.

- Fathers and mothers who abdicate parenting roles because they are debilitated by a drug's effects, or because they are wrapped up in the pursuit of the drugs or the money with which to purchase drugs.
- Significant others who withdraw from intimacy and commitment because of drug involvement. When drug abuse enters a relationship, it becomes an unhealthy love triangle that tends to squeeze out the nonabusing partner.
- Religious or spiritual individuals whose relationship with God withers as drug abusing becomes more central to their lives. Drug abusers may be pursuing "false gods," seeking comfort and meaning in chemicals.
- Committed students whose love of learning and outstanding academic records get thrust aside by overinvolvement with drugs. A history of drug abuse can often be intuited by looking at student transcripts that follow all too predictable patterns.
- Once-productive employees whose absences become more frequent, whose post-lunch break performance declines, and whose interaction with coworkers suffers are often abusing drugs.
- Law-abiding people who find that their moral objections to committing crimes dissolve when drug hunger requires money that they cannot earn legitimately. The sharp increase in prison populations in the last generation is primarily fueled by increased penalties for drug-related crimes.

Perhaps this paints an overly pessimistic view of drug abuse; however, it is important for students to recognize that drug abuse has the potential to destroy lives utterly, and not only the lives of the abusers themselves but often those who are tied to them in a variety of social relationships. Remember that drug use is not the same as drug abuse; it is a rhetorical overreach, a convenient myth that those who wage war on drugs would like us to believe. Any drug may be used safely by some, even the drugs about which we are most frequently warned. Not all drug abusers are irreparably harmed. Drug abuse, although it has serious consequences and is one of our nation's social problems, may not be the scourge that some have painted it to be. But it is surely a fact of life in American society that has consequences, now and in the future.

No concept in the study of drugs has been as variably used and as misused as **drug addiction**. Addiction is a disease where a misconfigured brain chemistry produces drug cravings. No, it's not; it is a product of moral breakdown or moral inferiority that comes from associating oneself with undesirable drugs. Really? Drugs have negative associations in our society, therefore addiction likely must be viewed pejoratively as well. The concept of addiction has been broadened beyond the realm of chemical abuse. Public discourse—talk shows, self-help advocates—now refers to gambling as an addiction, to sex and love addiction, to refined sugar and simple carbohydrate addiction, to Internet addiction, and more. In science—and sociology adheres to principles of scientific inquiry and method—concepts need precise definition, as precise as language allows. In the realm of drug studies, we have been extremely imprecise when we talk about drug abuse, "the dangerous drug problem," and especially about drug addiction. We need to clear up this conceptual confusion.

Addiction originally was used to connote an enslavement of a person to a substance, which became the master (see Brecher 1972). When drugs began to be studied scientifically in the 1800s, what became known as a "classical" model of addiction emerged, one which focused on physical addiction, on craving and on drug withdrawal, as in the following definition from a recent drugs text: "Addiction is a drug craving accompanied by physical dependence, which motivates continued usage, resulting in a tolerance to a drug's effects and a syndrome of identifiable symptoms when the drug is abruptly withdrawn" (Inciardi and McElrath 1998, xiii).

To become addicted in the classical sense, one must use a potentially addictive drug, in adequate doses and for a sufficiently long time, that one undergoes biochemical alterations that produce such a physical dependence. All narcotic drugs are physically addicting, as are most other central nervous system depressants including alcohol. Nicotine, a stimulant, is also an addicting drug. Not all drugs, however, regardless of how frequently they are used, produce such a physical dependence in their users. Cannabis products like marijuana and hashish do not. Hallucinogenic drugs like LSD, peyote, and ecstasy do not. Most stimulants, including cocaine and the amphetamines, are not physically addicting. This may sound like semantic hairsplitting, but a drug may not be physically addicting, yet be powerfully habit forming. Cocaine clearly is such a drug, as it is used habitually and harmfully by many. In other words, physical addiction is just one type of **drug dependence**. Dependence can also exist at the psychological level and at the behavioral level as well.

Why don't we simply speak of drug dependence then, rather than of both drug addiction and nonaddictive drug dependence? What is the value of maintaining separate researching and theorizing on drug addiction? We will understand physical withdrawal symptoms better—some are dangerous, even life threatening, whereas others are merely uncomfortable—which allows us to make detoxification a safer process. Drug treatment programs will have higher success rates as the phenomenon of addiction is understood more fully. Alfred Lindesmith (1938), a giant in the field of understanding drug addiction, constructed a theory of addiction that focused on how the pain associated with opiate withdrawal made it more difficult to perform a variety of social roles and often led the addict to continue using to keep those painful symptoms at bay. An awareness of this might reduce relapse, which at one time was seen as an inevitable part of the addiction process. Alan Leshner, the former Director of the National Institute on Drug Abuse, claims that drug addiction treatment is as successful as treatment for other chronic diseases as diabetes, high blood pressure, and asthma (1999, 1321). The profound changes in brain functioning wrought by addiction make addiction a brain disease, according to Leshner, but one that is eminently treatable.

Increasingly, researchers have focused their attention on the role of psychological (or psychic) dependence, both with drugs that have a potential to be physically addicting and those without. The reason for the increasing attention to the concept of psychological dependence starting in the 1970s—a period of rising rates of drug usage—seemed clear. Users of drugs that were not physically addicting, particularly cocaine, were exhibiting patterns of drug dependence very similar to those using physically addicting substances. If the dependence was not physical, which meant that there weren't physical cravings or withdrawal symptoms when the drug was removed, then what could explain continued abuse of these drugs, even in the face of accumulating negative consequences? Lindesmith (1938) emphasized avoidance of withdrawal symptoms as the primary motivator for continued opiate use by the addict, downplaying the role of the pursuit of euphoria, which he believed wasn't experienced once true addiction set in. He argued that his theory of addiction was truly sociological, because one could only interpret the distress of drug withdrawal within a cultural pattern of knowledge and beliefs about drugs.

More modern drug theorists take issue with Lindesmith's contention that pursuing euphoria does not drive addicts to continue using. Addicts who have undergone detoxification and remained clean for periods of time relapse into opiate use. And as mentioned before, nonaddicting drugs were being abused in patterns similar to the opiates. Why? McAuliffe and Gordon (1974) challenged Lindesmith and theorized that pursuit of euphoria, of feeling good through using chemicals, might be the answer. Psychologists argue that substance use (among a wide range of pleasurable practices), can be highly reinforcing, and such reinforcement might be at the core of psychological dependence. We've heard of the laboratory rats who will push a lever many hundreds of times if there is a possibility of receiving a small dose of cocaine. Positive pharmacological reinforcement would seem to explain this. Could such findings be transferred to human subjects as well? Could this be the key to compulsive drug abuse, even among drugs that are physically addicting? Are drugs so pleasurable for some abusers that they will risk the serious consequences of continued use to their health and to their social relationships?

The answer seems to be yes, though the existence of psychological dependence is somewhat harder to establish than is the existence of physical addiction. Drug users may be physically addicted, psychologically dependent, or both. Physically addicting drugs, heroin for example, may also produce profound psychological dependence. Psychological dependence would seem to be especially useful in explaining patterns of cocaine dependence, since cocaine seems to be the most reinforcing of all drugs. Research subjects who are given cocaine, but are unaware that is what they have taken, report higher levels of pleasure than with any other drug (Grinspoon and Bakalar 1976). With a million or more hardcore cocaine users—those who use the drug more frequently than ten times in a week in this country—we must be interested in explaining compulsive drug abuse. Although psychological dependence is a concept still in formation, it seems to be a useful tool for understanding and possibly controlling compulsive and consequential drug-abusing behavior.

Sociology and the Classification of Drugs

Chapter 3 of this book presents a taxonomy of drugs, a classification schema by which we can understand similarities and differences among substances we consider to be drugs. It is worth mentioning here, albeit briefly, the role that sociology plays in understanding drug classification when it asks the question, How do social and political influences affect the way our society classifies drugs? Some drug classifications are made on the basis of pharmacological or biochemical factors, largely outside the scope of sociology. Whether a drug is deemed psychoactive or not is based on whether the chemical substance acts on the central nervous system (CNS). The type of influence on the central nervous system is likewise largely pharmacological; a CNS stimulant like cocaine and a CNS depressant like heroin have widely divergent effects. A user who desires to use one when she is actually using the other will experience unwanted drug effects, regardless of how powerful her expectations, as was vividly demonstrated when Uma Thurman's character in the film *Pulp Fiction* had a seizure after snorting high-grade heroin she mistook for cocaine.

A number of drug classification dimensions are very much influenced by social and political forces, including: whether or not drugs are considered medically useful; whether or not drugs should be legalized; and whether or not a drug is seen as having a high potential for addiction or abuse. As we will see in Chapter 2, these factors are at the root of how the federal government classifies psychoactive drugs. Consider the current debate over whether marijuana has legitimate medicinal properties that might benefit those with glaucoma or AIDS or certain forms of cancer. Is marijuana medicine or is it merely a drug? Physicians find themselves at odds with most politicians who are upset with pro-marijuana activists. The debate has pitted different levels of government against one another (State of California: pro; Federal Government: con). This clearly indicates that something other than scientific reliance on empirical evidence is going on here. Political ideologies, vested social interests, images of morality, and public opinion affect how marijuana will be classified.

The sociological perspective recognizes and assesses the roles these factors play in the debate.

Understanding Social Concern about the "Drug Problem"

We have discussed how, from a sociological point of view, the concepts of drug, drug abuse, drug addiction, and drug classification are all socially constructed concepts, acquiring diverse meanings in different social contexts. To these social constructions we wish to add one other, the drug problem: how the American drug problem—or more accurately, drug problems—are understood as a product of our time and place, and the social and political forces that predominate. This does not mean that drug problems are social fabrications, woven out of thin air. We are arguing that the presence of objectively harmful conditions is relevant but not sufficient for us to understand why some forms of drug use are labeled as problematic and others are not. In other words, the way our society considers drugs to be a threat, which we certainly do, is not a purely scientific decision. Many interests—moral, political, economic—weigh in on what our drug problem is and what we ought to be doing about it. This is an important point: the drug policies that emerge in any era are based on the way we socially construct, and hence come to understand, the drug problem.

Our collective governments—federal, state, and local—control the use or distribution of a great many psychoactive substances. They also permit, but regulate, many drugs, including prescribed pharmaceuticals, tobacco products, and alcohol. Still others are essentially unregulated, like over-the-counter medications and caffeine. How substances are classified are based as much on perceived threat as anything else. How harmful/dangerous/threatening is substance X perceived to be? And by whom? Obviously, some people or groups in our society have more power to influence our perceptions than others. There is political advantage to be gained from declaring certain drugs to be harmful and conducting campaigns against them. Drug controls in this society are influenced by political lobbyists representing interests supporting or fighting the criminalization of the use of a particular drug. The history of drug controls in America, which we will cover in Chapter 2, makes this clear.

Sociologist Howard Becker (1963) calls individuals or groups who argue that they are the ones who should define "the reality" of drugs and their users **moral entrepreneurs** (sometimes this concept appears as "politico-moral entrepreneurs"). Moral entrepreneurs take it upon themselves to tell us what we should be threatened by and what we should, as a society, do about that threat. Accordingly, defining the drug problem and implementing drug controls is a moral and political enterprise. Think of the range of societal actors who might benefit professionally from placing drugs in a negative light and having us be "at war" with drugs: politicians who are trying to build political capital by declaring themselves tough on drugs (in today's climate, few politicians get reelected by pushing for drug legalization or for less restrictions); religious leaders who preach that drug use is a sign of moral breakdown or turning away from God; and law enforcement personnel who argue that drug users commit more crimes and make their jobs much harder. To the extent that these groups have power or access to the powerful, and access to the media to get their message out, they shape the perception that drugs are a serious problem in America and something must be done now. Troy Duster (1970) is among the critics who say that this leads to the dangerous practice of legislating morality, using the law to uphold the primacy of one among several competing moral ideologies.

Moral entrepreneurs, at their most successful, generate a subjective concern over drugs that is out of proportion with the objective threat. Such a situation is called a "moral panic" (Goode 1990), a "drug scare" (Reinarman 2000), or a "drug panic" (Jenkins 2001). Sociologist Craig Reinarman writes: "Drug 'wars,' anti-drug crusades, and other periods of marked public concern about drugs are never merely reactions to the various troubles people can have with drugs. These drug scares are recurring cultural and political phenomena *in their own right* and must, therefore, be understood sociologically on their own terms...especially so for U.S. society, which has had *recurring* anti-drug crusades and a *history* of repressive anti-drug laws" (2000, 147; emphases in original). There have been many such drug scares scattered over the last hundred years, ranging from concern over "demon alcohol" by temperance movement leaders in the early 1900s, which led to the Volstead Act of 1919 and Prohibition (Gusfield 1963), to the "reefer madness" scare of the 1930s fostered by the then head of the Federal Bureau of Narcotics (today called the Drug Enforcement Administration), Harry Anslinger, which led to the Marihuana Tax Act of 1937, to the overheated rhetoric and exploding social concern of the crack cocaine scare of the late 1980s. Drug scares create a crisis mentality in the minds of Americans, who believe that the drug scourge threatens to overwhelm our society. This may be seen most astonishingly in a September 1989 *New York Times*/CBS News poll, which found that 64 percent of the respondents, five out of every eight people, answered that drugs were the most important concern of our country (Goode 1999, 71)! As we have stated before, drug abuse produces consequences about which we should be justly concerned. But they are not now, nor have they ever been, the greatest threat to American society, at least not in objective terms.

Reinarman (2000, 151–153) and Goode (1999, 73–75) discuss the ingredients, the objective and especially the subjective factors, that can serve as a "recipe" for drug hysteria and the repressive drug laws that often ensue. Drug scares are built upon kernels of truth—people do abuse drugs—and drug scares often follow an increase in drug abuse or deaths from drug abuse. This is an objective factor. The mass media magnify the problem by engaging in what Reinarman calls "the routinization of caricature" in which worst-case scenarios are portrayed as more typical than they actually are to sell the news. Moral entrepreneurs and prominent spokespersons make claims about the social evil of drugs, and create and enforce rules prohibiting them, often furthering their own vested interests. Professional interest groups—churches, law enforcement agencies, the drug treatment industry, and others—compete for definitional "ownership" of the problem by claiming that their special knowledge makes them the legitimate authority. Clearly, the media, moral entrepreneurs, and interest groups "pop" the kernel of truth, making it both larger and somehow less substantial than it was. This inflation of the problem occurs against a historical context of conflict between groups in the society, which creates a "level of cultural anxiety that provides fertile ideological soil" (Reinarman 2000, 152) for drug prohibition. Drug scares have often included a conception of a "dangerous class" of folk-devil drug abusers about whom we should be wary. The combination of a disreputable and immoral group (often based on thinly veiled racist or ethnic assumptions) and a substance said to increase the threat to us who are "innocent" is a powerful ideological weapon. Finally, "drugs are richly functional scapegoats. They provide elites with fig leaves to place over unsightly social ills that are endemic to the social system over which they preside. And they provide the public with a restricted aperture of attribution in which only a chemical bogeyman or the lone deviants who ingest it are seen as the cause of a cornucopia of complex problems" (Reinarman 2000, 153). This is part of the American tendency to embrace simplistic and individualistic explanations for problems that really demand nuanced and complex social investigation. Sociologists must reject such simplicity in their research projects and in their theorizing.

Summary: Sociologists on American Drug Use

Among the many intellectual approaches to studying and understanding drug use, we will be focusing our attention on only one of them, the sociological approach. Sociology, because it is a social science, looks at empirical evidence about drugs. It also points out when others are being patently unscientific. Much of what we "know" about drugs is untrue or partially true because our society permits the debate over drugs to be distorted by ideology, morality, and partisan politics. Sociologists stress that the social context of drug use is vital to understanding its meaning. Whether or not a psychoactive substance is considered a drug involves contextual interpretation. So does the divide between "good" and "bad" drugs, between safe and unsafe, between medically useful and not. Harmfulness gets determined not by objective standards but by political persuasiveness. The "drug problem" and solutions to said problem are grounded in prevailing cultural beliefs, however unscientifically generated they may be. With great zeal, drugs are presented to us as being "dangerous" or "highly addicting" or "an epidemic" or "a plague" or "a crisis" (see Jenkins 2001) to whip up subjective concern. Sociologists help us make sense of the divide between such concern and the empirical reality or actual social harm done by drugs.

As you read this textbook, we ask you to examine critically your own beliefs, favorable or unfavorable, about drugs. Are you willing to set aside some of what you know, if you are shown that it is built on faulty assumptions? We hope so. Sociology is about learning truths and coming up with more valid beliefs about social phenomena, including drugs. As we are instructed by the eminent sociologist Peter

Berger, "there is a debunking motif inherent in sociological consciousness.... The sociological frame of reference... carries with it a logical imperative to unmask the pretensions and the propaganda by which men cloak their actions with each other" (Berger 1963, 38). Drugs are complex social phenomena, and we hope that students reading this book are willing to understand the difference between facts and value judgments, and between science and ideology.

Key Terms

antagonistic effect
chronic effect
dose
drug
drug abuse
drug addiction
drug dependence
drug interaction
drug tolerance
drug use
effective dose
idiosyncratic effect
incidence
lethal dose
moral entrepreneur
objective drug effect
pharmacology
polydrug use
potency
prevalence
psychoactive drug
psychopharmacology
purity
route of administration
set
setting
social construction
subjective drug effect
synergism effect
therapeutic dose

Thinking Critically...

1. Studying sociology can be uncomfortable for some students because the discipline challenges many of their strongly held beliefs. How does the sociological

perspective, as discussed in this chapter, challenge beliefs that you hold regarding drugs, drug use, and drug users in American society?

2. Explain the sociological argument that the concept of drug is a cultural artifact, a social fabrication. With this understanding, what sorts of substances might be considered drugs? How does this challenge common-sense beliefs?

3. What is the difference between drug *set* and drug *setting*? Why do sociologists regard these features as important as the chemistry of the drug itself?

4. The text defines drug abuse as drug involvement that "leads to measurable personal, interpersonal, or social consequences." How is this definition different from how most people define drug abuse? Using this definition of abuse, what are some ways in which substances might be abused that might not normally be considered abuse?

5. What is "the drug problem?" Why is it defined in the way that it is? For example, why don't we consider the restriction of people's freedom to use drugs in ways that do not harm other people to be a "drug problem"?

Learning from the Internet

1. Go to the website www.youtube.com. In the search window, type in "salvia trips." Most of the videos available are amateur videos of individuals filming friends on the hallucinogenic drug salvia. Watch three or four of these short videos. Describe how the *drug set* of the user and/or the *drug setting* in which the drug was used might have affected the experience of the user.

2. Using the Internet search engine of your choice, type in "the drug problem" (using the quotation marks). Go to a sampling of the sites that the search engine brings up. (Note: Normally it is best to use the sites on the first two or three pages for the most directly pertinent results.) Identify how each of the sites you visited define "the drug problem." Make a note about who administered the site: for example, was it a drug treatment program? the United States government? a law enforcement agency? an organization seeking the reform of drug laws? How is the definition of "the drug problem" shaped by the political or ideological perspective of the organization hosting the site?

Notes

1. This statement is true as of the fall of 2008.
2. The concern here is over drug misuse, where prescription medications or over-the-counter drugs are used in inappropriate ways. The more our population ages, the greater the likelihood that drug misuse and its consequences will rise.

CHAPTER **2**

A Brief History of Drug Use and Drug Control in America

We established in the last chapter that drug use and abuse are socially constructed problems. By that we mean that whether or not drug use is seen as a problem is determined by the social context of that behavior. It is difficult, however, to understand that the problem of drug abuse is socially constructed when we observe people dying from drug overdoses, becoming addicted to the point of neglecting their families and other social roles, and suffering from physical ailments such as hepatitis-B, AIDS, and cardiac disease—to name just a few—that result from drug abuse. Are these not direct, objective consequences of the use of the drug? History helps us understand how such problems, some of which seem to be intrinsic to the drugs themselves, are often the result of much larger social and political processes. That is why sociologist Peter Berger (1963) describes the sociologist and the historian as fellow travelers with a close intellectual bond. History is also important because it provides valuable lessons for future public policy and practice. Failure to consider the lessons of history when it comes to drug use and drug policy stifles our ability to move beyond emotionally laden rhetoric and to avoid knee-jerk reactions to this rhetoric. As philosopher George Santayana wrote, "those who cannot remember the past are condemned to repeat it" (1905, 284). Indeed, we shall see how relevant Santayana's observation is to the study of drugs in American history, since we have often repeated our mistakes. Before examining the American experience with drug use and drug policy, however, we begin by looking back further into global history as a context for the American drug experience. We will then focus our attention on drug use in nineteenth- and twentieth-century America.

Drugs through the Ages

Drug use and abuse are not unique to American society, nor to contemporary global experience. Drug taking has been found in most societies that have existed over the last ten thousand years or so, and it is not at all a stretch to suggest that drug use is virtually a cultural universal.

The oldest known mind-altering substance consumed by humans was mead, an alcoholic drink made from fermented honey, which was first produced around 8,000 B.C. Other forms of fermented alcohol such as beer and berry wines appeared over the next two millennia. Because yeast is neutralized by alcohol, the highest level of alcoholic content that can be produced through natural fermentation is about 15 percent. Higher-concentration beverages can only be produced through an elaborate process of distillation, which has a much more recent history, dating to about 800 A.D. Today, distilled liquors are usually measured in proof—the highest concentration possible being 200 proof, or pure, 100 percent alcohol.[1]

Opium and its derivatives also have a long history of use and abuse. The earliest known reference to opium is about 4,000 B.C. when mention is made of a "joy plant" on a Sumerian tablet (Ray 1978). Recent evidence also suggests a very early use of opium in Switzerland in the Neolithic period in the fourth millennium B.C. (Booth 1998; Merlin 1984). Ancient Greek culture was particularly fond of the poppy plant, and its legends contain several references to opium, which is derived from the poppy. Here, opium was used medicinally, recreationally, and ritualistically. Hippocrates was also fond of opium as a medicine and believed that the white poppy juice mixed with nettle seeds would cure a host of ailments (Booth 1998).

The use of opium as a ritualistic and pleasure drug in Greek culture is also apparent. Its presence is evident in Greek literature, including Homer's *Odyssey*. Homer makes reference to "nepenthe," the "drug of forgetfulness":

> Helen, daughter of Zeus, poured a drug, nepenthe, into the wine they were
> drinking which made them forget all evil. Those who drank of the mixture did not

shed a tear all day long, even if their mother or father had died, even if a brother or beloved son was killed before their own eyes by the weapons of the enemy. (Booth 1998, 18)

Opiates also found favor with numerous nineteenth-century Romantic literary figures in Europe, including Samuel Taylor Coleridge, William Wordsworth, Percy Shelley, John Keats, and perhaps most notably Thomas De Quincy, who in 1821 published *Confessions of an English Opium-Eater*. The drug of choice for many of these writers as well as artists of the time was laudanum, an alcohol-morphine combination. It is generally acknowledged that Coleridge's *The Rime of the Ancient Mariner* and *Kubla Kahn* were both written under the influence of opiates (Booth 1998).

Other drugs have been targeted at various points in history as both "problems" and "cures." One such drug is caffeine, usually consumed in the form of coffee. Legend has it that coffee was first discovered when an ancient Arabian goatherd named Kaldi could not understand why his goats were bouncing about so energetically all over the hillside. When he investigated, he discovered that the goats were eating wild red berries. He tried them himself, and as the story goes, he experienced the first coffee buzz! As we have seen with so many drugs, as caffeine became more widely known, it was believed to have special curative powers. An Arabian medical text from around 900 A.D. suggested that coffee was a panacea for everything from curing measles to lust (Ray 1978).

Coffee, and caffeine generally, is arguably the most widely used drug today, though we do not usually think of it as a drug. It is indeed a drug, however, and it was not always so widely tolerated. A certain group of women in England published a pamphlet in 1674 entitled *The Women's Petition Against Coffee*. It read, in part:

> Our countrymen's palates are become as fanatical as their Brains; how else is't possible they should *Apostatize* from the good old primitive way of ale-drinking, to run a *Whoreing* after such variety of destructive Foreign Liquors, to trifle away their time, scald their *Chops*, and spend their *Money*, all for a little *base, black, thick, nasty bitter stinking, nauseous* Puddle water. (Meyer 1954; cited in Ray 1978, 187)

Concern with caffeine consumption was expressed in the United States as well. One medical professional categorized coffee addiction with addictions to narcotics and alcohol when he claimed that it induced delusional states. He went on to describe a prominent general in a noted battle in the Civil War: "...after drinking several cups of coffee, he appeared on the front line, exposing himself with great recklessness, shouting and waving his hat as if in a delirium, giving orders and swearing in the most extraordinary manner. He was supposed to be intoxicated. Afterward it was found that he had used nothing but coffee" (Crothers 1902, 303–304; cited in Brecher 1972, 197).

Dr. Crothers went on to claim that coffee drinkers will often become less than satisfied with coffee and go on to more destructive drugs such as narcotics. This is a very familiar claim, and one that we often hear regarding marijuana today. Coffee was then, as marijuana is today, considered a "gateway drug." (See Chapter 3 for further discussion of this argument.)

Tobacco has also had an uneven social history, with periods of tolerance followed by periods of intolerance. During one such intolerant period in the early seventeenth century in England, King James I was especially anxious to rid his country of tobacco. His strategy was to identify tobacco with evil foreigners who represented a threat to a civilized way of life—a strategy not unlike what would be used centuries later in this country with early drug laws having racist origins. Yet while it has been villified, tobacco has also enjoyed strong support from the medical community throughout much of its pharmacological history, having been touted as a cure for headaches, abscesses, and even the common cold. Not until the 1890s was tobacco removed from the *United States Pharmacopeia*, a document analogous to today's *Physician's Desk Reference*, which contains information on drugs used for treating various maladies. To be part of a society's pharmacopeia is to have a recognized medical utility, an important part of the way psychoactive drugs get classified. Such was our 400-year dance with the medical marvel tobacco.

The recreational use of tobacco did not, of course, end in the 1890s, nor did it begin there. Almost certainly before they even arrived home from their explorations, Columbus and his crew were enjoying the pleasures of this drug. These sailors discovered early that drinking the smoke of tobacco provides energy when that is needed, but also eases tension during times of anxiety. From the late 1700s to the turn of the twentieth century, however, tobacco smoking gave way to other forms of tobacco use, primarily chewing and snuff dipping. During this time ordinances were passed that actually forbade the use of smoking tobacco in some cities. Indeed, by 1921, 14 states had laws prohibiting the use of cigarettes with another 28 states considering such legislation (Brecher 1972). This did not deter tobacco smoking; in fact, by the 1920s, the use of smoking tobacco once again surpassed other forms of tobacco use.

Marijuana has a long history dating to 4000 B.C. in China (Grinspoon and Bakalar 1997). The earliest known medical reference to cannabis came in 2737 B.C. in a pharmacy book written by the Chinese emperor Shen Nung. Here it is referred to as "Liberator of Sin," suggesting doubt and uncertainty about the euphoric effects of the drug. The emperor did, however, recognize certain medicinal benefits to marijuana, including treatment for malaria, constipation, female problems, and even absentmindedness (Grinspoon and Bakalar 1997, 3). Marijuana did not make its way into the New World until about 1545 when the Spaniards introduced it into Chile. It was also introduced into North America in Jamestown in 1611, where it was cultivated for its fiber. It came to be a fairly important part of the agricultural economy in the colonies. One writer has pointed out that "Virginia awarded bounties for hemp culture and manufacture, and imposed penalties upon those who did not produce it" (Boyce 1900, 35; cited in Brecher 1972, 403). Even George Washington grew hemp on his Mount Vernon estate, and while he was almost certainly growing it for its fibrous content, evidence from his diary suggests that he was also interested in its pharmacological properties:

> *May 12–13, 1765:* Sowed Hemp at Muddy hole by Swamp
>
> *August 7, 1765:* –began to separate the Male from the Female Hemp…rather too late (Andrews and Vinkenoog 1967, 34; cited in Brecher 1972, 403)

The assertion that Washington was concerned about the pharmacology of hemp rests on the recognition even at that time that the potency of the marijuana resin was enhanced if the male and female plants were separated before they had the opportunity to pollinate. Marijuana had clearly found a place in early American pharmacology.

We highlight this early history not to provide an exhaustive account of drug use throughout history, but simply to document the fact that drugs have been part of recorded human history virtually from the beginning. Moreover, societal reaction to drug use can also be observed across time, though the drugs being praised or vilified have varied greatly throughout this history. We shall discover in the sections that follow that the American drug experience is also varied as is American reaction to drug use.

Nineteenth-Century America: A "Dope-Fiend's Paradise"

Nineteenth-century America can be characterized as, among other things, a century of widespread medicinal and recreational drug use. Rufus King (1972) has referred to this period as "the sensible century." Edward Brecher (1972) has noted that the use of drugs, particularly narcotics, was so prevalent in the 1800s that this century could appropriately be described as a "dope fiend's paradise."

Narcotic Use in the Nineteenth Century

The use of narcotics by literary figures of the nineteenth century is well known largely through their own writings, such as Thomas De Quincy's *Confessions of an English Opium-Eater* first published in book form in 1823. Other nineteenth-century literary figures whose use of opium and morphine was well known include Samuel Taylor Coleridge and Edgar Allen Poe (King 1972). Narcotics were not restricted to the elite of the literary world at this time, however. Opium and its derivatives were readily available through prescriptions given to patients for a variety of complaints. They were available in over-the-counter preparations under a variety of brand name **patent medicines** that were popularized early in the nineteenth century. Young (1961) has noted that, whereas in 1771 no American brands of patent medicines were being marketed commercially, by 1804 some 80 to 90 brands were being advertised in a New York catalog of medicines. Some of the brands appearing in the nineteenth century included Dr. James' Cordial, McMunn's Elixir of Opium, and Mrs. Winslow's Soothing Syrup (a mixture marketed as a teething syrup for infants that contained

Drugs: Myths and Reality

Mrs. Winslow's Soothing Syrup for Children Teething

Letter from a Mother in Lowell, Massachusetts

Dear Sir: I am happy to be able to certify to the efficiency of MRS. WINSLOW'S SOOTHING SYRUP, and to the truth of what it is represented to accomplish. Having a little boy suffering greatly from teething, who could not rest, and at night by his cries would not permit any of the family to do so, I purchased a bottle of the SOOTHING SYRUP, in order to test the remedy, and, when given to the boy according to directions, its effect upon him was like magic; he soon went to sleep, and all pain and nervousness disappeared. We have had no trouble with him since, and the little fellow will pass through with comfort the excruciating process of teething, by the sole aid of MRS. WINSLOW'S SOOTHING SYRUP. Every mother who regards the health and life of her children should possess it.

Mrs. H.A. Alger
Lowell, Mass.

Source: *New York Times*, December 4, 1860.

morphine sulfate). Other preparations contained cannabis indica, chloral hydrate, and cocaine. A popular method of marketing these medicines, especially during the last two decades of the nineteenth century, was the medicine show. These were rather elaborate performances, complete with magic or other forms of entertainment, culminating in a "pitch man" who, when the crowd was sufficiently worked up, convinced them of the need for the tonics available for sale (Young 1961). These products were essentially unregulated, and prior to the Pure Food and Drug Act of 1906, patent medicines and soothing syrups were not even required to have their ingredients listed on the bottle.

Nineteenth-century physicians became so enamored of morphine's pharmacology that it was commonly referred to in this profession as G.O.M., God's Own Medicine, a reference introduced by the eminent Canadian physician Sir William Osler, who was an expert in treating addiction and himself a narcotics addict (Booth 1998). Most of the consumers of these drugs were middle-class women, many of whom became addicted as a result of using narcotics to treat physical symptoms. Brecher (1972) notes that one late-nineteenth-century textbook listed no less than 54 symptoms that were treatable by morphine including angina, diabetes, insanity, menstrual cramps, and even nymphomania! Morphine is a pain reliever with wonderful therapeutic properties, but as was often the case in the nineteenth century for a variety of substances, advocates overstated the benefits. Morphine use became especially prevalent during the Civil War to treat wounded soldiers. So widespread was morphine abuse during the war that dependence on it would eventually come to be called "soldier's disease" or "the army disease" (King 1972, 16). This drug

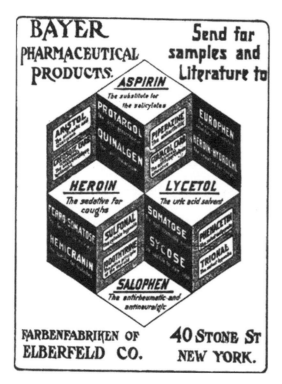

BAYER
PHARMACEUTICAL
PRODUCTS.

Send for samples and Literature to

ASPIRIN
The substitute for the salicylates

ARISTOL
PROTARGOL
QUINALGEN

PIPERAZINE

EUROPHEN

HEROIN HYDROCHL

HEROIN
The sedative for coughs

LYCETOL
The uric acid solvent

FERRO-SOMATOSE
SOMATOSE
SULFONAL
PHENACETIN
HEMICRANIN
SYCOSE
TRIONAL

SALOPHEN
The antirheumatic and antineuralgic

FARBENFABRIKEN OF
ELBERFELD CO.

40 STONE ST
NEW YORK.

2.1 Heroin and other narcotics were used as principle active ingredients in many patent medicines in the nineteenth and early twentieth centuries. (Image: Wikipedia Commons)

was so well received that many confederate states grew the poppy plant for its morphine production during the war, and the federal government did not make its cultivation illegal until 1942.

Morphine also came to be viewed as an alternative to recreational drinking and as a form of treatment for opium addiction. Dr. J. R. Black, in a scientific paper read to colleagues, noted that morphine "is less inimical to healthy life than alcohol.... [It] calms in place of exciting the baser passions, and hence is less productive of acts of violence and crime; in short...the use of morphine in place of alcohol is but a choice of evils, and by far the lesser" (1889; quoted in Brecher 1972, 8). Lord Lister was even more pointed: "Opium soothes; alcohol maddens" (King 1972, 18), Many physicians attempted to convert alcoholics to morphine, a practice continued into the 1930s and even early 1940s by many older doctors (Brecher 1972).

The use of morphine was further spread when, by the late nineteenth century, the medical profession recognized the addictive potential of opium and came to believe that the use of morphine in place of opium might be a cure for opium addiction. More particularly, with the invention of the hypodermic syringe in 1853, many in the field believed that injection of morphine was less addictive than the orally ingested opium. We now know that this is not the case, and indeed, mainline injection is a particularly addictive method of administration.

The waning years of the nineteenth century witnessed the introduction of a new, semisynthetic narcotic that would later become the scourge of the twentieth century. This new wonder drug was heroin, so named because of the "heroic" powers it was alleged to possess (derived from the German *heroisch*, which means heroic or powerful). Heroin was developed in 1874 but not marketed commercially until 1898 by the German pharmaceutical company Bayerische AG, more commonly known as Bayer Laboratories, makers of Bayer aspirin. It was initially marketed as a powerful analgesic and a cough suppressant, but soon became touted as an effective cure for morphine and opium addiction, continuing the fruitless pursuit of finding a nonaddictive narcotic. The nation's honeymoon with heroin was short lived, however, and by 1910, Bayer had removed heroin from its pharmacopeia. Heroin was discovered to be powerfully addictive and would be the object of intensive law enforcement for the remainder of the twentieth century.

The historical circumstances that gave rise to America's concern with opiates in the late nineteenth century are important to note. Throughout the latter half of the nineteenth century, tens of thousands of Chinese men and boys immigrated into the United States, working on the railroads during the great Western expansion. Along with other customs, they brought with them their opium-smoking habits. In time, these Chinese immigrants moved into cities that were mushrooming in the West, working for low wages and incurring the hostility of residents of these cities. Of such concern were the Chinese that in 1862 California enacted legislation that levied a "Chinese Police Tax" of $2.50 per month on all Chinese 18 years of age and older. The purpose of this act was stated clearly in its subtitle: "An Act to Protect Free White Labor Against Competition with Chinese Coolie Labor and to Discourage the Immigration of the Chinese Into the State of California." It is no surprise, then, that opium was suddenly defined as a major problem. Many women—the principle users of narcotics besides the Chinese—were frequenting opium dens, incurring the wrath and fear of their husbands and the city fathers.

All of this culminated in a series of antinarcotics laws in the late nineteenth century. The first of these was an 1872 law that held that "the administration of laudanum, an opium preparation, or any other narcotic to any person with the intent thereby to facilitate the commission of a felony" was itself a felony (Levine 1973, 96). The law was ineffective in curtailing opium use, and cities began developing local ordinances, the first in San Francisco in 1875, "forbidding the practice under penalty of a heavy fine or imprisonment or both" (Terry and Pellens 1928, 73). Opium smoking had been practiced by San Franciscans for years, but only when the use of this drug came to be identified with the Chinese, a despised and feared minority group, was this practice denounced. This is a pattern that we will observe with other drugs as well: a tendency to villify minorities and minority drug use when that minority is perceived as a threat to the dominant community. Other western cities followed San Francisco's lead, and in 1877, Nevada became the first state to criminalize the sale of opiate products (without a physician's prescription) on a state-wide basis (Levine 1973).

Alcohol Use in the Nineteenth Century

Alcohol had been widely tolerated in America prior to the nineteenth century, though drunkenness was not generally accepted. Most of the early colonists drank beer and hard cider, though by the 1700s distilled liquors were becoming increasingly available. They drank heavily by contemporary standards, seemingly at odds with the Puritan reputation of the colonists. There were voices of concern over the overuse of alcohol during this time, most notably by Philadelphia psychiatrist Benjamin Rush, one of the signers of the Declaration of Independence. He went so far as to label it a destructive disease (Lender and Martin 1987). These voices were not given a great deal of credence, however, and the practice and the legal status of drinking remained relatively unchanged. In short, it was not perceived to be a social problem.

Social drinking continued to be commonplace throughout much of the nineteenth century, and in amounts greater than the previous century. As the western frontier expanded, many of the original settlers and explorers were single men, isolated from their families and other human contact. Drinking was often quite unrestrained and frequently coincided with gambling, fighting, and womanizing. It was during this time that Native American tribes were also introduced to alcohol by western frontiersmen. The belief was, generally, that as long as one's drinking was not harmful to others, it was not a social concern (Lender and Martin 1987).

The mid-nineteenth century witnessed a massive immigration of Europeans, initially from Ireland, who brought robust drinking habits with them. Americans had little love for the Irish. Most were very poor and no doubt willing to work for wages much lower than domestic labor. They were also overwhelmingly Roman Catholic with a strong allegiance to the Church and to the hierarchical order it represented. The Irish were indeed an alien culture in American society, both feared and despised. Irish drinking habits became a symbol of moral inferiority, and America's tolerance of alcohol diminished substantially (Lender and Martin 1987).

Organized opposition to alcohol also began to emerge in the nineteenth century. The first evidence of any real organized effort to oppose alcohol came in 1811 at the General Assembly of the Presbyterian Church held that year in Philadelphia. Benjamin Rush, now up in years, implored those in attendance to deliver strong temperance messages from their pulpits, which they did. The Presbyterian effort was mirrored by other denominations including the Methodists and Baptists. These efforts eventually resulted in the formation of the American Society for the Promotion of Temperance (later shortened to the American Temperance Society, then the American Temperance Union) in 1826. The goals of this organization were truly **temperance**—moderation, not abstinence—except for distilled liquors, which were seen to be intrinsically evil. There were, to be sure, numerous voices for **prohibition** (abstinence), but it would be until the late nineteenth century that prohibition emerged as a strong political force in America, the culmination of which would not be seen until the early twentieth century (Lender and Martin 1987). A strong prohibition sentiment can be seen in collections of stories that tell of the horrible evils of alcohol and the consequences it wreaks on families. One such collection edited by Elton R. Shaw is entitled *The Curse of Drink; or Stories of Hell's Commerce* (1909). Stories such as "A Bottle of Tears," "Married to a Drunkard," and "The Saloon Keeper's Daughter," all ostensibly true, describe the horrors of alcohol on individual and family life. Some have direct reference to the Irish as in "Timmy Flannigan and His Promotion" and "Tom M'Hardy's Battlements." Songs and poems were also written, often to popular tunes of the time, to galvanize the increasing prohibitionist fervor in the waning years of the nineteenth century.

DRUGS AND EVERYDAY LIFE

When Rum Shall Cease to Reign

Written to the tune of "When Johnny Comes Marching Home"

Get ready for the jubilee,
    Hurrah! Hurrah!
When this our country shall be free,
    Hurrah! Hurrah!
The girls will sing, the boys will shout,
    When alcohol is driven out:
And we'll all feel gay when whiskey is no
    more.
And we'll all feel gay when whiskey is no
    more.

We're only children now, you know,
    Hurrah! Hurrah!
But temp'rance children always grow,
    Hurrah! Hurrah!
The girls will all be women then,
    The boys, of course, will all be men,
And we'll all fight rum 'till rum shall be no
    more.
And we'll all fight rum 'till rum shall be
    no more.

From Maine to California,
    Hurrah! Hurrah!
From Delaware to Canada,
    Hurrah! Hurrah!
The struggle now is going on,
    And when the mighty victory's
    won,
We'll all feel gay that whiskey reigns no
    more.
We'll all feel gay that whiskey reigns no
    more.

It will not do to simply say,
    Hurrah! Hurrah!
But do your duty, then you may
    Hurrah! Hurrah!
Assist the weak, yourself deny,
    Stand by the right, and bye and
    bye,
We'll all feel gay that whiskey reigns no
    more.
We'll all feel gay that whiskey reigns no
    more.

Edward Carswell

Reprinted in Elton Shaw (ed.), *The Curse of Drink* (1909)

Cocaine Use in the Nineteenth Century

The chewing of coca leaves has been practiced for centuries by Native American tribes, particularly the Incas. The earliest record that we have of such activity is found in a grave in Peru that is dated to about 500 A.D. By 1000 A.D., the coca leaf was used as part of religious ritual in the Inca civilization and was even used as a form of monetary exchange.

The coca leaf was introduced into the European world when the Spanish *conquistadors* invaded Peru and established a European presence there. The coca leaf was not immediately popular in Europe, and when it did finally catch the imagination of the European people, it was used in prepared drinks rather than chewed as it had been in the New World. A particularly popular drink in Europe was Mariani's Wine, a red wine containing coca and named after its manufacturer Signor Angelo Mariani.

Cocaine, the alkaloid base and active ingredient in the coca leaf, was not isolated until 1844. The drug enjoyed about a half-century honeymoon period, being touted as a cure for both depression and morphine addiction (Brecher 1972; Ray 1978). Perhaps the most notable cocaine user was Sigmund Freud, the father of psychoanalysis. Freud found that the drug was almost instantaneously helpful in overcoming his own depression. He almost immediately recommended it to his fiancée Martha Bernays and to his close friend Ernst von Fleischl, who was suffering from morphine addiction. Freud was so elated with the drug that he referred to it as "the magical drug" and promptly wrote a medical treatise on its benefits, *The Cocaine Papers*, that was published within two months of his own initial experimentation in 1884. We get a glimpse into Freud's early high regard for the drug in a letter to Martha Bernays:

> If it goes well, I will write an essay on it and I expect it will win its place in therapeutics, by the side of morphium and superior to it. I have other hopes and intentions about it. I take very small doses of it regularly against depression and against indigestion, and with the most brilliant success. I hope it will be able to abolish the most intractable vomiting, even when this is due to severe pain; in short it is only now that I feel I am a doctor, since I have helped one patient and hope to help more. (Jones 1953, 81)

His enthusiasm was short-lived however, when a year later his friend von Fleischl developed a full-fledged cocaine psychosis, complete with hallucinations of snakes crawling over his skin (Brecher 1972). Freud would later denounce the use of cocaine, and by 1890, the dependency potential of cocaine was fully appreciated by medical practitioners.

Cocaine, like opium and its derivatives, was also an ingredient in many of the popular patent medicines of the time, which were marketed under various names such as Coca Cordial. Pharmaceutical companies, Parke-Davis among them, openly advertised cocaine in their products, which included coca-leaf cigarettes, tablets, hypodermic injections, sprays, and ointments (Musto 1973). In addition to patent medicines, the beverage industry discovered cocaine. About the time that Freud was experimenting with cocaine, Atlanta druggist Dr. John Stythe Pemberton was developing a beverage that included extracts from the coca plant. Initially, he combined it with alcohol, naming it French Wine Coca—Ideal Nerve and Tonic Stimulant, which he marketed in 1885. The following year he developed yet another product that replaced the alcohol with an extract of the kola nut, which contains about 2 percent caffeine. This product was named Coca Cola, a beverage that in modified form (minus the coca extract) is the biggest-selling soft drink today (Brecher 1972).

By the end of the nineteenth century, cocaine was generally regarded as a public menace. Musto (1973) notes the widely held belief that cocaine spurred violence against whites by African Americans in the South. Stories also abounded of black men on cocaine with superhuman strength and that cocaine use by blacks improved their pistol marksmanship. One of the more incredible myths was that cocaine rendered black users impenetrable to .32-caliber bullets, which supposedly resulted in many southern police departments issuing .38-caliber handguns to their officers. These beliefs almost certainly contributed to the eventual vilification of cocaine. There is, of course, no evidence that cocaine had this effect on African Americans of that day (or any other day), but the troublesome aspect of this belief is the reaction that it spurred: this fear coincided with a peak period in the lynching of blacks in the South. Once again, we see the consequences of racist thought and action, and of how a drug scare can be fomented based on little or no evidence.

Marijuana Use in the Nineteenth Century

As we have seen, marijuana has been part of the American experience practically since the founding of the colonies in New England. Its use in medical practice spanned the nineteenth century and part of the twentieth. The drug was accepted into the *United States Pharmacopeia* in 1850 and remained there until 1942. It was recommended for a variety of ailments including neuralgia, gout, rheumatism, hysteria, insanity, uterine hemorrhage tetanus, among many others. It was also believed to act as an aphrodisiac and an appetite accelerant, a generally recognized effect today (Brecher 1972; Grinspoon and Bakalar 1997). Pharmaceutical companies, such as Parke-Davis, Squibb, and Lilly, marketed fluid extracts of the drug to meet growing medical demands, and one company, Grimault and Sons, marketed marijuana cigarettes for use by asthma patients. By the early twentieth century, as other drugs became more available, medical dependency on marijuana declined, though the medical community continued to accept the medical legitimacy of marijuana until the passing of the Marihuana Tax Act of 1937 (Brecher 1972).

Marijuana was also widely used recreationally in the nineteenth century. Several accounts have been written of the experiences of marijuana users, some of these in highly regarded magazines of the time, including *Putnams* and *Harper's New Monthly Magazine*. Recreational use at this time was typically referred to as "hashish eating," suggesting that the hashish resin was used, often baked into other foods but also taken directly in liquid form (Brecher 1972).

Recreational use of marijuana did not become widely popular until the early twentieth century, however. The efforts of the Women's Christian Temperance Union and other groups seeking to outlaw alcohol were rewarded when the Eighteenth Amendment, ratified in 1919 and implemented one year later, and the subsequent Volstead Act made the manufacture and sale of alcohol illegal on a national basis. The impact of this legislation on marijuana consumption was almost immediate: marijuana use and possession was not illegal at this time, and "tea pads"—marijuana smoking establishments—were established throughout the major cities of the United States. It is estimated that by 1930 there were 500 such establishments in New York City alone (Brecher 1972). Brecher further reports that it was smoked in exclusive gentlemen's clubs. Cultivation of the cannabis plant became commonplace throughout the United States; it can be grown pretty much anywhere.

There was, to be sure, heightened concern over the use of this drug during the 1920s because of its easy availability. Of particular concern was access to marijuana by children. The concern over marijuana was fueled by reports in the Southwest that Mexican immigrants were bringing the drug into the country. Fears were heightened when a series of articles linking marijuana use and crime was published in a New Orleans newspaper about the same time (Ray 1978). Once again, public reaction intensified as drugs become identified with ethnic minorities. This concern would ultimately result in the passage of the Marihuana Tax Act in 1937, which had the effect of outlawing marijuana distribution at the federal level.

The Beginnings of the Prescription Drug Industry in the Nineteenth Century

Finally, the nineteenth century witnessed the emergence of a prescription drug industry that has left an indelible mark on the pharmacological history of America and most other countries of the world. This industry has its roots in the early patent medicines containing narcotics, cocaine, and alcohol that had been marketed throughout the nineteenth century. As the century progressed, however, pharmaceutical laboratories were turning out new synthetic drugs that would be marketed through medical practitioners as safe and effective for treatment of a variety of maladies, including emotional disorders. This would be an extremely lucrative industry that continues to this day, with billions of dollars in annual profits to commercial pharmaceutical companies. Many of the drugs developed and manufactured by these companies eventually become diverted into underground markets and used for recreational purposes as well.

The story of the modern prescription drug industry might well be traced to the discovery of the barbiturates, which itself is a fascinating story. As the story goes, Adolf von Baeyer, Nobel prize–winning chemist and founder of Bayer Pharmaceuticals, discovered barbituric acid—a combination of urea and malonic acid—on December 4, 1862. There are two accounts of the naming of this new compound. According to one, Bayer was in love with a barmaid named Barbara who donated the urea (urine) that was used to make the compound. He originally named the compound "Barbara's urates," later shortened to "barbituric" acid in honor of her. According to the second account, Bayer celebrated the discovery by stopping for a drink at a tavern popular among artillery officers. That particular day happened to be the Day of Saint Barbara, patron saint of artillary officers, and the new compound was named "Barbara's Urates," in honor of Saint Barbara.

Since this fateful December day in 1862, some 2,500 barbiturates, as well as new families of drugs such as meprobamate (Miltown) and the benzodiazepines (Librium and Valium), have been synthesized. Similarly, prescription stimulants in the form of the amphetamines would make their way to commercial markets by the 1930s. Where cocaine was once prescribed for fatigue and depression, the amphetamines became the new drug of choice. These new synthesized prescription drugs would emerge as popular alternatives to cocaine and the narcotics. Indeed, the prohibition of cocaine and narcotics played an important role in the rise of the prescription drug industry, as the demand for a pharmaceutical solution to physical and emotional maladies did not diminish just because cocaine, heroin, and other nineteenth-century favorites were no longer legally available. We discuss the prohibition of the nineteenth-century pharmacopeia and the subsequent rise of alternative drug strategies in the following section.

The Twentieth Century: Age of Legal Repression and Experimentation

The nation's fascination with drug use in the early 1900s gave way to a sober awareness of the abuse potential of these substances by the end of the century. Moreover, we have seen that these drugs lost their innocence as their use became associated with ethnic minorities who were perceived as a threat by those in dominant racial groups who held political power. As a consequence, the twentieth century witnessed a rather strong social and legal reaction against the use of drugs, particularly the drugs that we have discussed above. The prohibitionist reaction generally took the form of one or more of the following themes that can be observed in the prohibitionist literature (White 1979):

1. A despised or feared subgroup, typically an ethnic minority, is identified with use of the drug.
2. Many of the problems in the society are depicted as resulting from drug use.
3. A culture's survival is depicted as dependent on successful prohibition of the drug.
4. Drug "use" and drug "addiction" are essentially equated.
5. Corruption of children is linked to drug use.
6. The drug user and seller are regarded as "fiends" seeking to create more addicts.
7. Policy options are presented as either/or: total prohibition or total access.
8. Anyone questioning the above characterizations is attacked and characterized as being part of the problem.

The mood of the nation was both reflected in and, to some extent at least, shaped by men such as Richmond Pearson Hobson, a celebrated Navy captain. After unsuccessfully attempting to mobilize public opinion against a growing "yellow peril" (the Japanese), he turned his attention to alcohol as the "great destroyer." Hobson eloquently portrayed the battle against alcohol as the battle between good and evil, positing that "95 percent of all acts and crimes of violence are committed by drunkards" (Epstein 1977, 24). He theorized that alcohol attacked "the top of the brain...since the upper brain is the physical basis of thought, feeling, judgment, self-control, and it is the physical organ of the will, of the consciousness of God, of the sense of right and wrong, of ideas of justice, duty, love, mercy, self-sacrifice and all that makes character" (24). Furthermore, he maintained that the effect of alcohol on "negroes" was a degeneration "to the level of the cannibal." Similarly, alcohol caused "peacable redmen" to become "savages" (25).

Ironically, Hobson's very success as a moral entrepreneur (see Chapter 1) left him once again in search of a cause. The Prohibition movement succeeded in making alcohol illegal across the country, but unfortunately for Hobson's theorizing, the crime rate did not go down significantly as a result. In the meantime, the Harrison Narcotics Act of 1914 was drawing the nation's attention to the evils associated with cocaine, opium, morphine, and heroin. Hobson saw another opportunity for a moral crusade. In 1928, he claimed over national radio, "Most of the daylight robberies, daring holdups, cruel murders, and similar crimes of violence are now known to be committed chiefly by drug addicts who constitute the primary cause of our alarming crime wave" (Epstein 1977, 28). Hobson's explanation for how these drugs caused crime was remarkably similar to what he said a decade earlier about alcohol:

> The entire brain is immediately affected when narcotics are taken into the system. The upper cerebral regions, whose more delicate tissues, apparently the most recently developed and containing the shrine of the spirit, all those attributes of the man which raise him above the level of the beast, are at first tremendously stimulated and then—quite soon—destroyed.... At the same time the tissues of the lower brain, where reside all the selfish instincts and impulses, receive the same powerful stimulation. With the restraining forces of the higher nature gone, the addict feels no compunction whatever in committing any act that will contribute to a perverted supposition of his own comfort or welfare. (27)

Already by 1875, as we have seen, city governments were enacting ordinances against opiate use. This wave of lawmaking was followed by national legislation beginning very early in the twentieth century. The course was being set for a repressive legal response to cultural problems in this country, an approach that would distinguish the United States from many other western countries. The use and misuse of psychoactive substances is one such problem that came to be especially defined as a legal problem with a legal solution. In this section, we examine the following pieces of national anti-drug legislation: the Pure Food and Drug Act of 1906; the Harrison Narcotics Act of 1914; the Eighteenth Amendment and the National Prohibition (Volstead) Act of 1919; the Marihuana Tax Act of 1937; the Controlled Substances Act of 1970; and the Anti-Drug Abuse Act of 1988. In addition, we will briefly examine antismoking efforts in the latter part of the century, commonly known as the Great American Smokeout, and the recent litigation against tobacco companies.

Pure Food and Drug Act of 1906
The **Pure Food and Drug Act** was a sweeping policy change that had as its goal making food and drugs safer for American consumers. The drugs primarily targeted by this act were the unregulated patent medicines, concoctions that contained alcohol,

narcotics, cocaine, cannabis extracts, and other psychoactive drugs. The Pure Food and Drug Act was the culmination of more than a quarter-century of advocacy that was met with strong opposition from the business sector, which was making a good profit from patent medicines affected by this legislation. A series of events took place that resulted in the successful passage of the Pure Food and Drug Act. The American Medical Association (AMA) began to take a more active interest in regulating the patent medicine industry, as did the American Pharmaceutical Association (APhA). There were also exposés written on the patent medicine industry and published in widely circulated magazines. Samuel Hopkins Adams wrote an impassioned series in *Colliers* under the title "The Great American Fraud," in which he severely attacked the patent medicine industry (Brecher 1972). Perhaps the triggering event for the Pure Food and Drug Act, however, was Upton Sinclair's disturbing exposé of the meat packing industry in Chicago, a thinly veiled novel titled *The Jungle*, published in 1906. Sinclair's portrayal was so disturbing that President Theodore Roosevelt sent investigators to Chicago to verify Sinclair's charges. Their report confirmed Sinclair's claims and identified further problems as well (Ihde 1982). Later that year the Pure Food and Drug Act became law.

Among other things, the act required that manufacturers of patent medicines indicate on their labeling whether certain specified drugs, including alcohol and narcotics, were contained therein. Later amendments to the Act would also require a listing of quantities and concentrations of these drugs. The Act was, essentially, a truth-in-advertising act that had the effect of protecting both addicts and innocent consumers from undue concentrations that could result in health problems (Brecher 1972; Young 1961). Whatever safeguarding effect that this act would have on the lives of addicts, however, was temporary. Merely eight years later, in 1914, Congress would pass the Harrison Narcotics Act, which, in effect, made distribution of narcotics a federal offense and shifted the federal focus from health concerns to sociolegal ones.

Harrison Narcotics Act of 1914

The origins of the Harrison Narcotics Act can be traced back to mid-nineteenth century concern over Chinese opium use and the early anti-opium ordinances passed, first in San Francisco and then in other western cities. America's concern and sensitivity over narcotics rose considerably throughout the last 30 years of the nineteenth century.

Following the Spanish-American War in 1898, the United States gained control over a number of Spanish colonies, including Puerto Rico, Guam, and the Philippines. American occupation of the Philippines revealed that the Spanish had operated an opium distribution monopoly. Episcopal Bishop Charles Henry Brent, perhaps the first American missionary to the Philippines, quickly learned of the opium monopoly and determined to address the opium problem there. Bishop Brent was assigned to head a commission, known as the Brent Commission, to study alternatives to dealing with the narcotics distribution problem in the Philippines.

The Brent Commission urged international intervention and control of narcotics, realizing that this was indeed not merely a national problem. This resonated well with the State Department. Two opium wars had already been fought in 1839 and 1858 over the British bringing underpriced opium from India into China, undercutting trade for Chinese opium. Moreover, American businessmen in China had been complaining that much of the Chinese trade was being diverted for British opium, making American trade more difficult. American missionaries to China were also raising concerns about what high levels of opium consumption were doing to the Chinese people (Brecher 1972; Musto 1973).

An international group representing 13 nations, known as the Shanghai Opium Commission and chaired by Bishop Brent, met in Shanghai in 1909 to discuss and make recommendations for international narcotics control. Several recommendations came out of this conference; however, failing to get the representative nations to agree to a second meeting, the United States began to organize international narcotics control. Two years following the meeting of the Shanghai Commission, representatives from 12 nations met at The Hague in the Netherlands to discuss international control of narcotics. In this conference, participating representatives hammered out the first international narcotics agreement in what was known as The Hague Convention of 1912. The Convention was not immediately enforced, however, because only 12 of the 46 world world were at the table. Moreover, Germany—not one of the original 12 nations at the table—questioned the resolve of the United States to enact their own legislation to implement the provisions of the Convention. If the United States was to avoid international embarrassment, it would be necessary to enact comprehensive federal legislation (Musto 1973).

The United States thus began to consider domestic legislation, which eventually became known as the Harrison Act of 1914, named after Representative Francis Burton Harrison who promoted the bill in the House of Representatives. Very little was mentioned about the evils of narcotics during the congressional debates, which lasted several days. Rather, the issue was debated on the basis of international obligation that the United States had incurred at The Hague (Brecher 1972). Neither the morality of narcotics use or addiction nor crime and other antisocial behavior that we now associate with narcotics use were part of the debates. Indeed, crime and antisocial behavior were not major problems stemming from narcotics use until after the criminalization of these drugs.

Because the federal government has only very limited powers to criminalize behavior, the Harrison Narcotics Act of 1914 was written in language that ostensibly imposed a tax on importers and distributors of narcotics. Indeed, the official title of the Harrison Act was "An Act to provide for the registration of, with collectors of internal revenue, and to impose a special tax upon all persons who produce, import, manufacture, compound, deal in, dispense, sell, distribute, or give away opium or coca leaves, their salts, derivatives, or preparations, and for other purposes" (U.S. Congress 1914; cited in Brecher 1972).

The Harrison Act was, prima facie, a revenue measure. It required that medical practitioners, doctors and pharmacists, as well as manufacturers and importers of narcotics (which in the language of this Act also included cocaine, a non-narcotic stimulant) register with the U.S. government, obtain a license, pay a modest fee for this privilege and a small excise tax (one cent per ounce), and maintain paperwork on all drug transactions (Brecher 1972; Lindesmith 1965). Patent medicines, incidentally, were exempt from the licensing, taxation, and reporting provisions provided that they maintained specified minimum concentrations of narcotics in their remedies. The Pure Food and Drug Act had earlier required labeling of these concentrations and made provision for testing them.

Although on its face merely a revenue act, the Harrison Act made it unlawful to sell, barter, or give away narcotics except in pursuance of a written order of the person to whom the drug is to be sold, an order that must be on a special form issued by the Internal Revenue Service (Terry and Pellens 1928). The exception to this provision was the "distribution...to a patient by a physician, dentist, or veterinary surgeon registered under this Act in the course of his professional practice only" (985). The last phrase, "in the course of his professional practice only," was something of a hook. This phrase would later be interpreted by law enforcement agencies and by the courts to mean that prescribing narcotics to addicts for maintenance purposes was *not* within the course of professional practice. Law enforcement agencies reasoned that addiction was not a disease, and hence opiates prescribed to addicts were not administered in the course of professional practice. The effect of the Harrison Act, therefore, was to criminalize narcotics for all but narrowly circumscribed medical purposes. Indeed, many physicians were arrested, convicted, and imprisoned for distributing drugs to addicts following the Harrison Act.

That physicians would interpret prescribing heroin and morphine to addicts for maintenance purposes as an acceptable professional practice is not difficult to understand. Narcotics addiction is tenacious, and efforts to cure addicts had not often been successful. Hence, physicians, having taken the Hippocratic Oath, felt bound to alleviate the suffering of their patients. The Oath reads, in part, "I will follow that method of treatment which according to my ability and judgment, I consider for the benefit of my patient." Relief of withdrawal symptoms was clearly in keeping with the spirit of this tradition.

The Legislature and the Supreme Court, however, generally sided with the interpretation of the Harrison Act held by law enforcement. Congress enacted several laws in the years following the Harrison Act that clarified its intent to prohibit the recreational use of narcotics, and particularly heroin. The Narcotic Drug Import and Export Act was enacted in 1922, which made importation of narcotic drugs illegal for all but strictly medical purposes. This was followed by the Heroin Act in 1924 which specifically made the manufacture and possession of heroin illegal. The Supreme Court also acted decisively on the side of a law enforcement interpretation of the Harrison Act. Five cases were particularly significant. The first, *United States v.*

Jin Fuey Moy (1916), concluded that the possession of drugs by addicts was illegal under the provisions of the Harrison Act. The defense for this case argued that the section of the act that stated that unregistered persons possessing narcotics were presumed guilty of violation applied only to *those who were required to register*, namely doctors and pharmacists. The Court ruled otherwise, which essentially made criminals of all addicts who were in possession of narcotics that were not prescribed by a registered physician (Lindesmith 1965).

A second case, *Webb et al. v. United States* (1919) directly addressed the legality of physicians prescribing maintenance dosages to addicts. In this case, Dr. Webb, a practicing physician in Memphis, Tennessee, had been prescribing narcotics to addicted patients. Dr. Webb was indicted under provisions of the Harrison Act. The Supreme Court issued a very short opinion in which they concluded that "to call such an order for the use of morphine a physician's prescription would be so plain a perversion of meaning that no discussion of the subject is required" (U.S. Supreme Court 1919). The Webb case was upheld one year later in *Jin Fuey Moy v. United States* (1920). A closely related case in 1922 upheld the findings of the latter *Jin Fuey Moy* decision in that the physician in question, Dr. Behrman, was prescribing such large doses of narcotics and cocaine that the court found no reasonable interpretation could conclude that they were being prescribed for medical purposes (*United States v. Behrman* 1922). With the Behrman case, the criminal status of the addict seemed sealed.

One final case, *Lindner v. United States* (1925), softened the impact of these prior cases, however. In this case, Seattle physician Charles Lindner prescribed only four tablets to a patient who later reported him to authorities. Lindner was convicted on the basis of the prior interpretations of the Harrison Act; however, his conviction was reversed by the high court, which argued that the small amount of drug prescribed must be considered when considering the legality of prescribing narcotics, even to addicts. With this decision, the court modified its previous stance and left open the door to prescription for maintenance purposes, at least in smaller dosages. Addiction was not a crime, in and of itself, nor was the addict to be considered a criminal. Rather, *Lindner* held that those addicted to narcotics are "diseased and proper subjects for medical treatment." This position was bolstered further in the 1962 case of *Robinson v. California*, which struck down a California statute that made it a misdemeanor to "be addicted to the use of narcotics." The status of being an addict could not be construed as a criminal status, as it would violate the Eighth and Fourteenth Amendments' ban on cruel and unusual punishment. An individual cannot be criminalized, therefore, for looking sickly or for having needle marks on the arm. *Being an addict is an illness and is hence different from using an addictive drug, which may be declared illegal*, though the two may obviously be related (U.S. Supreme Court 1962). The Supreme Court seemed to be arguing for a public health response to the problem of addiction, rather than a criminal justice response. Our century-long policy of criminalization speaks otherwise.

Consequences of the Harrison Act

The Rise of the Prescription Drug Industry. The Harrison Act and the subsequent Supreme Court decisions that interpreted it have been the cornerstone of American drug policy throughout most of the twentieth century. Two decades later, another influential act, the Marihuana Tax Act, would use the basic architecture of the Harrison Act to criminalize marijuana. More importantly, the Harrison Act established a prohibitionist policy and a repressive mindset toward recreational drug use that has characterized twentieth-century America. Indeed, it was the defining drug legislation until 1970, when Congress passed the Controlled Substances Act.

One result of the Harrison Act as well as earlier narcotics legislation was a substitution of these drugs with other legal **functional alternatives**. An early alternative to narcotics that was especially popular among women (who, along with the Chinese, were the primary users of narcotics) were barbiturates. The barbiturates enjoyed widespread popularity during the early part of the twentieth century, even though potential problems were recognized as early as 1905 when the first barbiturate intoxication and withdrawal symptoms were noted. They continued to be used, however, and it was not until 1942 that concern among the medical community was heightened by an article appearing in *Hygiea* (since renamed *Today's Health*) that warned of the potential dangers of nonmedical use of barbiturates. Other articles would soon follow, including an article with the provocative title "Thrill Pills Can Kill You" in the popular and prestigious *Collier's* in 1949 (Brecher 1972). This was followed by a 1950s study demonstrating the addictive potential and withdrawal hazards of barbiturates. As a result of these and other reports, doctors became more hesitant to prescribe barbiturates, though they continued to be quite widely prescribed well into the 1970s.

When the addictive potential of barbiturates came to be realized, alternatives were sought, resulting in the development of sedatives and minor tranquilizers as whole new classes of drugs. Among the sedatives, methaqualone was most popular. It was synthesized in the 1950s in India and was initially believed to be an effective antimalarial agent (Inciardi 1992). When its sedative qualities were discovered, it was introduced as a safer alternative to barbiturates. Known on the street as "ludes" and "Vitamin Q" among other names, this drug became very popular in the 1960s. Unfortunately, a darker side of the drug soon emerged, as violence and other antisocial behaviors became linked with it. Nausea, dizziness, and even overdose became increasingly common. The result of this was a reclassification of the drug from Schedule II to Schedule I, which denotes that the drug has no medical utility and carries with it stronger law enforcement response (see Table 2.1).

Side effects from the sedatives set the pharmaceutical companies in search of still another alternative, the minor tranquilizers. The most popular and most widely prescribed of these was the wonder drug Valium. At the peak of its popularity in

1975, 61.3 million prescriptions (including refills) had been written. Millions of Americans, especially women who were the primary consumers of Valium, became addicted. This tendency to replace one form of addiction with another did not go unnoticed. In her widely read critique of the prescription drug industry entitled *The Female Fix*, Muriel Nellis observes:

> Just as heroin was perceived as a treatment for morphine addiction, now methadone is the addictive substitute for heroin.... In the same continuum of reduced risk, barbiturates and other heavy sedatives were replaced by the so-called minor tranquilizers. But this breakthrough foisted more of these drugs on larger populations—for a wider variety of milder nondisease conditions. (1980, 8–9)

Prescriptions for Valium declined after 1975 because of the concern over addiction and other adverse effects. There would never again be such a surge of popularity for Valium. This does not mean, however, that minor tranquilizers have been removed from the mood disorder pharmacopeia. Just as the patent for Valium was approaching expiration, a new drug, Xanax, was introduced in 1981. Halcion, another benzodiazepine, followed shortly.

Doctors have learned to be cautious in prescribing Valium, and now Xanax and Halcion. The popularity of these drugs, however, has created a huge underground market, a "gray market," for these prescription drugs. Unlike heroin, cocaine, and methamphetamines, which are illegally manufactured, illegal Valium and other prescription tranquilizers are usually diverted from pharmacies, hospitals, and doctor's offices. Sometimes patients will "physician hop"—visit several doctors complaining of the same symptoms and get several prescriptions filled at different drug stores. Another way in which prescription drugs are diverted to the streets is by burglarizing pharmacies and doctor's offices. In some cases, clever criminals surreptitiously obtain prescription pads from doctor's offices and forge their own prescriptions. However obtained, these drugs are then resold through illegitimate channels for prices much higher than the prescription cost.

In addition to the search for functional alternatives for narcotics, the Harrison Narcotics Act effectively criminalized cocaine as well, necessitating new forms of stimulants. Although amphetamines were initially marketed for treating asthma and other bronchial problems (see Chapter 3), World War II Army physicians were prescribing amphetamines to soldiers suffering from fatigue and to elevate mood. The amphetamines would also find increasing popularity following the war for patients suffering from depression (Brecher 1972). In many ways, twentieth-century use of amphetamines was a functional alternative for the widespread cocaine use of the nineteenth century.

The Emergence of the Drug-Crime Subculture. In addition to the search for functional alternatives, the Harrison Narcotics Act encouraged the development of a drug-using criminal subculture. This topic is explored more thoroughly in Chapters 10,

11, and 12, but we would point out here that when drugs are made illegal, those who continue to use these drugs are faced with a number of problems—including locating dependable supplies of the drug, raising the funds to purchase illegal drugs (which are always more expensive than legal substances), and avoiding detection by the police, among others—for which they inevitably turn to each other for assistance and mutual support. Because illegal users must typically rely on criminal means of income, they cultivate relationships with other criminals as mentors, business associates, and friends. The criminalization of narcotics thus provided a legal milieu that encouraged the emergence of an underground subculture centered around the acquisition and use of illegal substances.

Eighteenth Amendment

Prior to the late nineteenth century, opposition to alcohol was framed primarily in terms of temperance rather than prohibition, reflected in the name of the leading alcohol opposition group of the time, the American Temperance Society. Among other things, this call for temperance resulted in the establishment of many breweries throughout the United States, which would replace the distilleries and encourage the consumption of beer rather than the more potent distilled spirits. Many of these breweries were owned by Germans, a factor that would later figure in the movement to a Constitutional prohibition. The breweries were very effective in marketing the beers that they produced, alcohol consumption (albeit of beer) rose, and the temperance voices soon took on more strident prohibitionist tones (Ray 1978).

The movement to prohibit alcohol began in the mid-nineteenth century when several states, led by Maine in 1851, enacted statewide prohibition statutes. Until the twentieth century, however, the movement to prohibit alcohol proceeded in fits and starts: states would enact prohibition legislation only to repeal those statutes a few years later. The National Prohibition Party, was organized in 1874 specifically to promote a prohibition agenda. More significant, however, was the establishment of the Anti-Saloon League in 1895. This was a nonpartisan organization that lobbied with all political parties, promising to bring votes to whomever would support national prohibition. The Anti-Saloon League also worked with ministers and church groups to gain political support by preaching a prohibitionist message in the pulpits of America. By 1903, more than one-third of the nation lived in states that had enacted prohibition legislation, a figure that would increase to about 50 percent of the population by 1913. This same year also saw the passage of the Webb-Kenyon Act that banned shipment of intoxicating liquors from wet to dry states (Lender and Martin 1987).

The momentum for national prohibition was clearly gaining. The elections of 1916 placed into office so many "dry" candidates that congressional action authorizing a national vote on a constitutional amendment was a near-certainty. Such a resolution was authored by Andrew Volstead, Representative from Minnesota, and passed both houses of congress by December of 1917. Within a month, Mississippi became the first state to ratify the constitutional amendment. The thirty-sixth state to ratify (the minimum needed for the three-fourths of states required) was

Nebraska, on January 16, 1919. (All but two states, Connecticut and Rhode Island, eventually ratified.) Later that year, Congress passed the **National Prohibition Act** (also known as the Volstead Act), a piece of enabling legislation that cleared the way for the practical implementation of Prohibition. As stipulated by the constitution, the Eighteenth Amendment went into effect one year following Nebraska's ratification, on January 16, 1920 (Lender and Martin 1987; Ray 1978). The Amendment was short, consisting of three small sections:

Section 1. After one year from the ratification of this article the manufacture, sale, or transportation of intoxicating liquors within, the importation thereof into, or the exportation thereof from the United States and all territories subject to the jurisdiction thereof for beverage purposes is hereby prohibited.

Section 2. The Congress and the several States shall have concurrent power to enforce this article by appropriate legislation.

Section 3. This article shall be inoperative unless it shall have been ratified as an amendment to the Constitution by the legislatures of the several States, as provided in the Constitution, within seven years from the date of the submission hereof to the States by the Congress.

The Eighteenth Amendment remained in effect for 13 years, from 1920 to 1933. But the political landscape had shifted, and those supporting the reintroduction of legal alcohol had the numbers in their favor. On February 20, 1933, Congress passed legislation proposing a repeal of Prohibition and sent it to the states for ratification. By December of that year, the 36th state ratified the Twenty-First Amendment repealing prohibition. This Amendment, too, was direct and to the point:

Section 1. The eighteenth article of amendment to the Constitution of the United States is hereby repealed.

Section 2. The transportation or importation into any State, Territory, or possession of the United States for delivery or use therein of intoxicating liquors, in violation of the laws thereof, is hereby prohibited.

Section 3. This article shall be inoperative unless it shall have been ratified as an amendment to the Constitution by conventions in the several States, as provided in the Constitution, within seven years from the date of the submission hereof to the States by the Congress.

Individual states also began repealing statewide legislation during this time. Predictably, Mississippi, which had been the first state to ratify the Eighteenth Amendment, was the last state to lift statewide prohibition, not doing so until 1966 (Brecher 1972; Ray 1978).

It is somewhat difficult to assess the impact of alcohol prohibition on American society. Early assessments of prohibition dismissed it as a total failure, insisting that the country, and especially women, were drinking more than ever. Clarence Darrow and coauthor Victor Yarros promoted such a popular view in *Prohibition Mania* (1927). More careful analysis, however, has failed to confirm this popular view. Numerous studies have suggested that the overall amount of alcohol consumption did indeed decline during Prohibition. Moreover, indicators of alcoholism and other alcohol problems, such as hospital admissions, arrests for drunkenness, and drinking-related diseases suggest an overall decline in alcohol consumption during these years (Lender and Martin 1987). Still other research presents a more complex picture. Economist Mark Thornton (1991) suggests that, although drinking levels showed a sharp decline initially after the Eighteenth Amendment went into effect, they then gradually increased, reaching pre-Prohibition levels by the end of the 1920s. Furthermore, economist Clark Warburton (1932) presents data suggesting that distilled liquor consumption comprised a much larger percentage of the overall alcohol consumption in the United States during the years of Prohibition. Moreover, the illegal alcohol most available during this period was distilled in nature—moonshine—and often very toxic. Hence, the risks for toxic reactions and other health problems associated with Prohibition-era alcohol use increased dramatically (Lender and Martin 1987). Such observations lend support to the "Iron Law of Prohibition," which states that the more repressive the law enforcement efforts, the more potent a prohibited substance becomes (Cowan 1986). Although Cowan was referring to narcotics, the same general principle can be applied to alcohol and other substances as well.

Of course, other costs have been borne in American society because of Prohibition. Perhaps most significantly, it was during this era that organized crime first gained a substantial foothold in American economic life (Lender and Martin 1987). These costs must also be considered when considering the success or failure of Prohibition. Most historians and social scientists agree that Prohibition was, on balance, a failed experiment.

Marihuana Tax Act of 1937

Cannabis products were quite widely used as recreational drugs in the early twentieth century, particularly in the 1920s when alcohol was prohibited. Both narcotics and alcohol were illegal during this time, and even if one were willing to break the law, the price of alcohol became prohibitively expensive. Consequently, many people began smoking marijuana as a functional alternative to alcohol and opium.

America's courtship with recreational marijuana in the 1920s was an uneasy one, however. The 1920s was a period of considerable Mexican immigration to southern states from Louisiana to California, and extending north to Colorado and Utah (Musto 1973). Mexicans coming into America, some legally and others illegally, brought marijuana with them, much as the Chinese brought opium with them a half-century earlier. Cheap Mexican labor was welcomed by farmers, but these neighbors from south of the border were also feared and were believed to be responsible for crimes and other forms of deviant behavior. Because marijuana smoking was part of their cultural experience, we find once again a pattern of vilification of both Mexicans as an ethnic minority and marijuana as their drug of choice. Marijuana quickly came to be seen as a cause of violence and crime among Mexican immigrants. It should not be surprising that many of the border states and surrounding states were early advocates of criminalization and became the first to pass state-wide laws prohibiting marijuana.

Despite these concerns, only sixteen states had passed marijuana legislation by 1930. That year, the Federal Bureau of Narcotics was formed in the Treasury Department with Harry J. Anslinger as its Commissioner. Anslinger was an extremely ambitious politician-bureaucrat who presented himself as the nation's drug czar of the time. He gained the respect of leading politicians and community leaders of his day and was described in one article as the man who "has more dope on dope than any other man in the world" (Marsh 1937, 11; cited in Carroll 1991, 23). Initially, however, Anslinger and the Bureau were not especially concerned with marijuana use, as is evidenced in the following from a 1932 report:

> A great deal of public interest has been aroused by newspaper articles appearing from time to time on the evils of the abuse of marihuana.... This publicity tends to magnify the extent of the evil and lends color to an inference that there is an alarming spread of the improper use of the drug, whereas the actual increase in such use may not have been inordinately large. (Bureau of Narcotics 1932, 51; cited in Becker 1963, 138)

Commissioner Anslinger, however, became personally interested in combating marijuana use and began a three-fold strategy of moral entrepreneurship for doing so. First, he began lobbying in state legislatures for adoption of antimarijuana laws. In his report for 1935, Anslinger stressed the importance of state legislation:

> In the absence of Federal legislation on the subject, the States and cities should rightfully assume the responsibility for providing vigorous measures for the extinction of this lethal weed. (Bureau of Narcotics 1936, 30; cited in Brecher 1972, 413)

Largely as a result of Anslinger's sustained lobbying effort at the state level, 46 of the then 48 states adopted antimarijuana laws by 1937. This, despite the fact that marijuana was almost certainly declining in use anyway because of the lifting of prohibition on alcohol.

Anslinger's second strategy was to launch a massive public opinion campaign. The Bureau did this by feeding information from its files to newspapers, magazines, and tabloids. These accounts were often filled with half-truths and had the effect of mobilizing public support for national prohibition as well as compliance with state laws prohibiting marijuana use. One such story printed in *American Magazine* captures the tenor of information being conveyed to the public:

> An entire family was murdered by a youthful addict in Florida. When officers arrived at the home they found the youth staggering about in a human

slaughterhouse. With an ax he had killed his father, mother, two brothers, and a sister. He seemed to be in a daze.... He had no recollection of having committed the multiple crime. The officers knew him ordinarily as a sane, rather quiet young man; now he was pitifully crazed. They sought the reason. They boy said he had been in the habit of smoking something which youthful friends called "muggles," a childish name for marihuana. (Anslinger and Cooper 1937, 19, 50)

The final strategy employed by the Bureau of Narcotics was to seek federal legislation that would prohibit the distribution of marijuana. Again, Commissioner Anslinger was adamant regarding the need for federal legislation. In his report for 1936, Anslinger states:

In the absence of additional Federal legislation, the Bureau of Narcotics can therefore carry on no war of its own against this traffic...the drug has come into wide and increasing abuse in many states, and the Bureau of Narcotics has therefore been endeavoring to impress upon the various States the urgent need for vigorous enforcement of local cannabis laws. (Bureau of Narcotics 1937, 59; cited in Becker 1963, 140)

As with the Harrison Narcotic Act, the **Marihuana Tax Act** was framed as a revenue measure to avoid constitutional problems. Marijuana was used for certain medical purposes at that time. Hence, as with the Harrison Act some 20 years earlier, physicians, dentists, veterinarians, and other established medical professionals were required to register with the federal government and pay a nominal tax. The language of this act also stipulated that these medical professionals must administer marijuana "in the course of their professional practice." Hence, individuals possessing or distributing marijuana without registering and obtaining a tax stamp, or administering the drug in a manner not in keeping with the course of their professional practice, would be subject to sanction.

The public's concern over marijuana, which had been agitated by Anslinger's entrepreneurial campaign, faded once the Tax Act passed. The 1940s and 1950s were periods of minimal marijuana concern and marijuana usage. Yet the legacy of the Marihuana Tax Act, as with the Harrison Act, was enormous: it would be the defining legislation for marijuana control until the introduction of the Controlled Substances Act of 1970 superceded it.

Renewed Drug Experimentation and the Controlled Substances Act of 1970

Following the heightened level of concern over marijuana in the 1930s were a couple of decades of relative calm as our national attention was focused on World War II, returning GIs, establishing families, building the economy, and so forth. It would be inaccurate to say that there was no governmental or public concern about drug use during the 1940s, 1950s, and early 1960s, however. Moral crusader Harry Anslinger and the Bureau of Narcotics were vigilant during this time, even trying to tie the

Bureau's activities with the war effort (Carroll 1991). Moreover, Anslinger waged what seemed to be a personal vendetta against sociologist Alfred Lindesmith, who challenged Anslinger's ideas about narcotics addiction in his provocative 1940 publication "Dope-Fiend Mythology." Anslinger succeeded in creating a general spirit of fear and intimidation directed at anyone who might challenge his agenda (Galliher et al. 1998). This milieu contributed to the enactment of the Boggs Act in 1951 and the Narcotics Control Act in 1956. The Boggs Act placed mandatory minimum sentences for drug law violators, and in the process made penalties much higher. Perhaps more significantly, marijuana and narcotics were lumped together for the first time at the federal level as the act provided for uniform penalties for violations of *either* the Narcotics Drug Import and Export Act *or* the Marihuana Tax Act (Bonnie and Whitebread 1970). The Narcotics Control Act placed even stiffer penalties for drug law violations, even allowing the death penalty for those involved in sale or distribution of heroin when recommended by a jury (King 1972). As significant as these activities were, however, not until the 1960s was the nation's attention fixated once again on recreational drugs.

The first "scare" that would herald a new age of drug experimentation was almost accidental. The drug was toluene, an organic solvent found in model airplane glue. The first recorded event of glue-sniffing seems to have occurred in 1959, though children were certainly breathing the fumes from tubes of cement much earlier than that. On August 2, 1959, *Empire*, the Sunday supplement to the *Denver Post*, featured an article with the headline, "Some Glues are Dangerous: Heavy Inhalation Can Cause Anemia or Brain Damage." The article went on to report how young children were getting high from toluene and even provided quite explicit information about their techniques for sniffing (Fluke and Donato 1959). This and other stories only increased the fascination with the drug, and experts were soon warning that the drug could be fatal. Many juvenile arrests were made, even though this drug was not yet prohibited by law. Laws would soon be passed in several states that would make glue sniffing illegal.

It was not long before the media across the country were filled with reports of deaths from glue sniffing. When these claims were carefully investigated, it turns out that there were a total of nine alleged deaths, each one reported several times as reporters would use secondary sources, which have a tendency to multiply a single case many times over. When these nine deaths were carefully investigated, six of them were found to have been caused by asphyxiation resulting from the victim's head being covered by an air-tight plastic bag—not due to glue fumes at all! It was suspected that the seventh death was an asphyxiation case as well. An eighth case involved a juvenile who had been ill and had sniffed gasoline fumes but was not known to have sniffed glue. The final case was also questioned, as the victim had not been seen sniffing glue before his death, and moreover, no evidence of toluene was found in his body during autopsy (Brecher 1972).

The glue sniffing scare is instructive. As is so frequently the case with juvenile drug use, the publicity surrounding drugs—even when it is negative—only serves to pique the fascination of young people. It is interesting to note that at the beginning of the 1960s, the most popular form of inhalant among young people was gasoline fumes. By the end of that decade, the incidence of gasoline fume inhalation was about the same as it was in the beginning of the decade. Glue sniffing, however, had skyrocketed (Brecher 1972). It seems that sometimes the best-intentioned publicity campaigns can have the most adverse effects. We will address some of these issues in Chapter 14.

The 1960s also witnessed a renewed interest in marijuana among middle-class American youth, who used it in part as a symbol of protest against establishment morality, and a widespread subculture of marijuana use developed. The drug became variously known as pot, herb, weed, and reefer among this generation of users. Studies revealed that by 1979 more than 50 percent of teenagers had at least experimented with marijuana over the 12 months prior to their being questioned.

As the decade of the 1960s progressed, establishment norms were increasingly being challenged by the nation's youth—and especially the middle-class youth. Variously called the Woodstock Generation, Hippies, and the Boomer Generation, this was the large adolescent and college-aged cohort who was challenging many accepted cultural mores and the established hierarchy. Consider these last two verses from the seminal 1964 rallying cry, "The Times They Are A-Changin'" by poet–folk singer Bob Dylan:

> Come mothers and fathers throughout the land
> And don't criticize what you can't understand
> Your sons and your daughters are beyond your command
> Your old road is rapidly agin'....
> The line it is drawn, the curse it is cast
> The slow one now will later be fast
> As the present now will later be past
> The order is rapidly fadin'.
> And the first one now will later be last
> For the times they are a changin'.

Establishment norms were also challenged by the use of hallucinogenic drugs, or as they were known by the users of that day, psychedelics. By far the most notorious of these was d-lysergic acid diethylamide (LSD). This synthetic hallucinogenic was discovered almost accidentally by Swiss chemist Albert Hoffman. Hoffman first synthesized the drug in the laboratories of Sandoz Pharmaceutical Company and promptly set it on the shelf where it stayed for five years. Then, on the afternoon of April 16, 1943, Hoffman would make a "mind-bending" discovery: he accidentally took the world's first LSD "trip." Hoffman recounted his experience a short time later:

> Last Friday, the 16th of April, I was forced to interrupt my work in the laboratory
> in the middle of the afternoon, and go home to seek care, since I was overcome

by a remarkable uneasiness combined with a slight dizziness. At home I lay down and fell into a not unpleasant, intoxicated-like state which was characterized by an extremely exciting fantasy. In a twilight condition with closed eyes (I found the daylight to be annoyingly bright), there crowded before me without interruption, fantastic pictures of extraordinary plasticity, with an intensive, kaleidoscopic play of colors. After about two hours this condition disappeared. (Stoll 1947, 60; cited in Liska 1990, 284)

The recreational use of LSD was promoted by a young Harvard University professor, Timothy Leary. Leary was a highly respected clinical psychology professor at Harvard who had taught classes, collaborated on several text books, and until his encounter with LSD, was a most uncontroversial figure. He experimented with psilocybin while in Mexico, and later experimented with LSD. He began holding sessions with students off campus, touting the marvels of these drugs, and in many cases introducing his students to them. Leary was sincere in his belief that LSD was truly a mind-expanding (psychedelic rather than hallucinogenic) drug that could change the human nervous system in positive ways. Because these young, educated, affluent drug users were not so easily dismissed as criminal or otherwise disposable, there was perceived a need for legislation that would discourage such rampant drug use among the cream of our nation's youth, while not impose sanctions that would destroy their futures. One such piece of legislation was the Narcotic Addict Rehabilitation Act (NARA) in 1966, which authorized the courts to order civil commitment for purposes of drug treatment as an alternative to prison sentences (a policy that is being received favorably today in some states such as California). It was, not coincidentally, about this time when methadone maintenance became widely available as a treatment option for heroin addiction.

The most significant legislation, however, was passed by Congress in1970. This was the Comprehensive Drug Abuse Prevention and Control Act. Title II of that act, known as the **Controlled Substances Act** (CSA), essentially incorporates all changes in drug laws that occurred since the passage of the Harrison Act in 1914 (Shulgin 1992; Winger et al. 1992; McDowell and Spitz 1999). Hence, the CSA supersedes prior legislation and remains the defining legislation for current drug law policy. Furthermore, this legislation contains provisions that place strict requirements on recordkeeping, inventory control, and security (DEA 1999). Finally, and most importantly for purposes of this discussion, the Controlled Substances Act classifies or "schedules" drugs for purposes of legal sanction (see Table 2.1). The CSA does not much focus on specific substances, but rather establishes a set of common standards that are associated with the dangerousness of a drug (Bureau of Justice Statistics 1992). The primary criteria ostensibly used in scheduling a drug are (1) identifying its medical uses, (2) determining its abuse potential, and (3) assessing its threats to human safety (Shulgin 1992; DEA (2005). These criteria are used both to determine whether a drug should be controlled and, if so, to place the

Table 2.1. A summary of drug scheduling of the Controlled Substances Act of 1970.				
Schedule	Examples	Abuse Potential	Medical Use	Available by Prescription
I	Heroin, LSD, methaqualone, marijuana	High	None	No
II	Morphine, cocaine, methamphetamine, PCP, methadone	High	Limited	Yes No refills Written Rx signed by doctor
III	Barbiturates, anabolic steroids, codeine	Moderate	Yes	Yes Refill 5 times in 6 months Refill anytime in 6 months Written or oral Rx
IV	Valium, Darvon, Talwin, Equanil, Xanax	Low	Yes	Yes Refill 5x in 6 months Refill anytime in 6 months Written or oral Rx
V	Over-the-counter cough medications with codeine	Low	Yes	Not required, but available only by licensed pharmacist to persons 18 and older; sale must be recorded.

Source: DEA 2005.

substance in the appropriate schedule (McDowell and Spitz 1999). The Controlled Substances Act contains five different **drug schedules**, Schedule I through Schedule V, with drugs having the highest potential for abuse at Schedule I. The determination of where on the schedule a specific drug should be placed lies with the administrator of the DEA and is a highly political process. Examples of drugs in each of the schedules, as well as definitions of abuse potential, medical utility, and legal availability of these drugs are provided in Table 2.1.

The Process of Scheduling

The process through which a drug is added to one of the five schedules is understandably complex and sometimes controversial. The Drug Enforcement Administration plays an important role in this process. Newly developed drugs automatically undergo a medical and scientific evaluation by the Department of Health and Human Services to identify if CSA scheduling is warranted. This evaluation, which includes a partially binding recommendation, is forwarded to the Drug Enforcement Administration for review (Bureau of Justice Statistics 1992). As noted by Shulgin (1992), the scheduling or enforcement status of a drug may change if a previously unidentified health hazard or abuse potential becomes apparent.

Proceedings to schedule a drug may be initiated by the administrator of the Drug Enforcement Administration, the Department of Health and Human Services, or by petition of any interested party (DEA 2005). At this time, the DEA administrator requests that a scientific and medical evaluation of the drug by the Department of Health and Human Services be conducted to explore the previously mentioned criteria of medical use, abuse potential, and associated safety concerns (DEA 1999). This evaluation also includes a partially binding recommendation on whether the drug should be placed onto a particular schedule (Bureau of Justice Statistics 1992). However, the DEA administrator has the ultimate authority in this regard (Shulgin 1992; DEA 1999).

Concerns in Drug Scheduling

There is some concern that the DEA, particularly the administrator, has excessive influence over the scheduling process and may be unduly influenced by political rather than scientific considerations (Shulgin 1992; Kleber 1994). Not only does the DEA administrator often initiate scheduling proceedings, but this person also plays a significant role in scheduling itself. For example, any evaluation conducted on a drug by the Department of Health and Human Services for scheduling purposes is binding only when the recommendation is *not* to schedule a substance (DEA 1999). Placement onto a specific schedule is determined ultimately by the DEA administrator.

A second issue of importance concerns how scheduling decisions affect the availability and use of drugs for medical purposes. McDowell and Spitz (1999) specifically note the controversy that surrounds the medical use of marijuana, a Schedule I drug. Recall that Schedule I substances are considered to have no accepted medical use and therefore cannot be obtained by prescription. Cocaine, on the other hand, is located in Schedule II because it does have limited medical uses—even though it is generally considered to be the more dangerous of the two. Kleber (1994), on the other hand, suggests that a measure of the support for medical use of marijuana is political because the negative consequences of use outweigh benefits that have yet to be proven. As a result, he contends that the Department of Health and Human Services, not the DEA, should define medical use for the Controlled Substances Act so that decisions are based upon scientific grounds.

The Controlled Substances Act established a new threshold in drug policy. Politically, the issue of drug control was muted in the 1970s as the nation addressed other pressing problems, such as a dignified retreat from the Vietnam War and a searing energy crisis. The drug issue would once again emerge, however, under the presidency of Ronald Reagan in the 1980s.

Anti-Drug Abuse Act of 1988

Several events occurred in the 1980s that resulted in a renewed federal interest in drug control. A conservative president, Ronald Reagan, was elected. Reagan made federal drug control, particularly supply-side (law enforcement, in this context) initiatives a high priority. First Lady Nancy Reagan complemented her husband's drug priorities by making drugs her focus with her "Just Say No" campaign against drug use. Additionally, two high-profile athletes—Len Bias, a basketball player at the University of Maryland, and Don Rogers, a defensive back for the Cleveland Browns—died within a month of each other in 1987 from alleged cocaine overdose. The 1980s also witnessed the introduction and widespread popularity of crack cocaine, a cheaper, ready-to-use, and highly dependence-producing form of cocaine. This was also the decade that a new fatal disease was introduced, acquired immunodeficiency syndrome, AIDS. The connection between AIDS and IV drug use was quickly recognized. As a result of all of these events, the nation was again, by the end of the decade, focused on drug use.

A series of laws enacted in the 1980s represented a return to more repressive drug policies. In 1984, Congress passed the Sentencing Reform Act, which once again placed mandatory minimum sentences for those convicted of drug offenses reflecting a policy instituted in 1951 by the Boggs Act, which had been lifted by the Controlled Substances Act in 1970. Two years later, Congress passed the Anti-Drug Abuse Act of 1986, which, among other things, placed differential mandatory minimum sentences on powder and crack cocaine. Essentially, the penalty for selling 5 grams of crack cocaine (5 years) was equivalent to the penalty for possession of *500 grams* of powder cocaine (Musto 1999). This was, needless to say, a controversial piece of legislation, with many suggesting that the new law was blatantly classist and racist, as crack is a drug used primarily by lower-class and minority individuals. It is not surprising, therefore, that drugs and drug policy were major issues in the 1988 presidential campaign that placed George H. W. Bush in the White House.

This was the social and political context for the **Anti-Drug Abuse Act of 1988.** This multifaceted act addressed a broad range of concerns. First, it addressed alcohol and especially the problem of drunk driving by requiring warning labels on all alcoholic beverages and by providing federal dollars to states that vigorously addressed the problem of drunk driving. This act reinstituted the federal death penalty for major drug traffickers. Also included were provisions to combat money laundering and asset forfeiture of those arrested for drug violations (Musto 1999). This latter provision has also proved controversial because it allowed assets to be seized even prior to a guilty verdict. Finally, the 1988 legislation addressed the fears of drugs in schools and in the workplace by establishing the Drug Free Workplace (see Chapters 9 and 14) and enacting the Drug-Free Schools and Communities Act Amendments of 1989. These amendments required schools to establish a system for maintaining drug-free environments, to inform students and teachers of the penalties for drug use and sale, and to provide information on available treatment (Musto 1999). These provisions established the basis for drug testing in the workplace and in the schools discussed in Chapter 14. Almost a decade later, the Drug-Free Communities Act of 1997 would make federal grants available to coalitions made up of a broad spectrum of communities (youth, businesses, the media, schools, law enforcement, religious organizations, and so forth) in an effort to increase citizen participation in combating drug use in communities across the United States.

The Anti-Drug Abuse Act of 1988, along with the 1984 and 1986 legislation, profoundly affected our criminal justice system, though not always in a positive way. These laws have largely been responsible for serious jail and prison overcrowding. Between 1985 and 1996, the number of prisoners in federal, state, and county facilities rose by about 100 percent. Those sentenced for drug offenses accounted for about half of this increase (Musto 1999). Perhaps the positive side of this is that, as we have incarcerated more and more of our drug offenders, both crime rates and overall drug use have stayed level or declined since the late 1980s (with blips upward for specific drugs in the early 1990s). It is not clear, of course, how much of this results from our nation's tough drug laws and how much from a graying of the population or other demographic or cultural factors.

The Great American Smokeout and the Onset of Tobacco Litigation

The 1960s witnessed a renewed concern over the health hazards associated with smoking. Low tar and nicotine cigarettes were introduced for the first time, and in 1964 the Surgeon General of the United States issued the famous report on smoking and health that ultimately resulted in cigarette manufacturers being required to put a warning label on every package of cigarettes: "Cigarette smoking may be hazardous to your health" (U.S. Surgeon General 1964). The 1970s witnessed the enactment of several state laws that restricted smoking, and by 1978, 33 states and Washington D.C. had passed restrictive measures defining where one could and could not smoke in public places.

The American Cancer Society has also been quite successful in its campaigns to get people to quit smoking, organizing its first Great American Smokeout in 1977 (American Cancer Society n.d.). The event has been held annually for over 30 years on the third Thursday of November, and more people quit smoking on that day than any other day of the year, including New Year's Day. Unfortunately, more than 90 percent of those who try to quit without seeking treatment fail, most within a week (NIDA 2006b).

Other groups have also participated in promoting a smoke-free environment. Groups such as ASH (Action on Smoking and Health) and GASP (Group Against Smokers' Pollution) have been striving to designate public areas as smoke-free out of their concern for passive or secondary smoke. These and other groups that make up what has come to be called the "non-smokers liberation movement" (Matchan 1977) have successfully banned smoking from most public areas. In 1997, two small-town lawyers from Mississippi brought suit against the tobacco companies. Tobacco industries had been sued before, but these suits were almost always unsuccessful because the tobacco companies managed to convince juries with the argument that victims themselves brought on their own demise by voluntarily smoking in the face of evidence of tobacco's ill health effects. However, in 1997, the Mississippi Attorney General Mike Moore and his law school classmate Dick Scruggs took on the companies on behalf of state taxpayers to recoup money spent on health care. They were able to show that the tobacco companies themselves knew about the potential dangers of smoking and suppressed that information. Their efforts were eventually joined by 43 other states in the lawsuit that some would say has finally brought the tobacco industry to its knees. The industry agreed to pay some $368 billion in health-related damages, to discontinue billboard advertising, and to withdraw ads using the "smooth character" Joe Camel because of their appeal to children. In 2000, a jury in Florida found tobacco producers and distributors liable for lying about the dangers of nicotine and for suppressing evidence that they had conspired to boost amounts of nicotine to hasten addiction. This decision, in essence, declared cigarettes to be nicotine-delivery devices.

There is some evidence that the efforts of antismoking groups have been effective. According to the Economic Research Service of the Department of Agriculture, consumption of cigarettes in the United States declined from an all time high of 640 billion cigarettes in 1981 to to 371 billion in 2006 (U.S. Department of Agriculture 2006). It is also worthy of note that cigarette smoking by young people has also been declining throughout the 1990s and into the twenty-first century (Johnston et al., 2003).

Summary

We have examined all too briefly the history of drug use in America. Most of this history has focused on the nineteenth and twentieth centuries. This is so for one primary reason: these consecutive centuries contrast sharply with regard to attitudes and societal responses to drug use. The nineteenth century had wide-open availability of most types of drugs. Virtually no controls were placed on the manufacture, distribution, possession, or use of psychoactive drugs. The twentieth century represented a complete swing of the pendulum to a repressive control strategy on most forms of recreational drug use. There is perhaps no other area of public policy that has experienced such a sea-change.

What might we learn from this history? Hopefully, this question will be answered, in part at least, with discussions in the chapters to follow. There are, however, several points that we might want to consider before proceeding further:

- Characteristics of drugs—such as addictiveness, health consequences, and criminogenic potential—are clearly *not* merely a matter of pharmacology as many presume. These characteristics are socially defined as we have seen by examining the shift in our understanding and policies toward drug use and addiction between the nineteenth and twentieth centuries.

- Drug policy is fickle and subject to factors totally unrelated to the harmfulness (or lack thereof) of drugs; such factors include racial prejudice, economic interests, and political entrepreneurship.
- We have seen in this contrast the extremes of drug policy, from laissez-faire nonintervention to considerable repression; and neither policy has seemed satisfactory. We must search out solutions that can realistically reduce the damage that drug use, and societal reaction to drug use, can cause.

As you explore the remaining chapters of this text, we urge you to keep these first two chapters in mind. They establish an important conceptual, theoretical, and historical context for interpreting contemporary issues and knowledge on the landscape today.

Key Terms

Anti-Drug Abuse Act of 1988
Controlled Substances Act of 1970
drug schedules
functional alternative
Harrison Narcotics Act of 1914
Marihuana Tax Act of 1937
National Prohibition Act of 1919 (Volstead Act)
patent medicine
prohibition
Prohibition
Pure Food and Drug Act of 1906
temperance

Thinking Critically...

1. The authors quote Peter Berger that "the sociologist and the historian are fellow travelers with a close intellectual bond." How does understanding the history of American drug use and drug control help us understand contemporary drug issues?

2. The philosopher George Santayana wrote, "Those who cannot remember the past are condemned to repeat it." After reading this chapter summarizing the history of drug use and drug use policy, what are some lessons that you think we should have learned as a society regarding drug use? How might we do things differently as a result of this understanding?

3. This brief summary of drugs through history has revealed that chemical substances that were once touted as "miraculous" later came to be condemned as a "scourge." (And occasionally, the process goes in the other direction.) This is true of heroin, cocaine, and many other drugs. From what you have read, does this result from an advancement in scientific knowledge, from a change in the prevailing social and political climate, or possibly from something else?

4. You have read how many antidrug laws originated to control groups of purported users who were from undesirable ethnic minority groups. Is this use of law unique to drug legislation, or do you think the law is used as a way of controlling and repressing marginal groups in other areas as well?

5. How were the social conditions and concerns about drug use in the 1960s, which led to the Controlled Substances Act, different from the situations that led to anti-drug legislation earlier in the twentieth century?

Learning from the Internet

1. A valuable website for information about the history of drug use is the Schaffer Drug Library. Go to its history section, http://www.druglibrary.org/schaffer/ History/HISTORY.HTM, and read at least three of the articles listed. Go beyond the brief history written in this chapter and write a more detailed history of one of the drugs or drug laws described in this chapter.

2. One of the advantages of the Internet is that it provides access to many original materials that would not easily be obtained elsewhere. Once again, the Schaffer Drug Library is very helpful as it has collected many such documents. A full text version of the Harrison Narcotics Act can be found at http://www.erowid.org/ psychoactives/law/law_fed_harrison_narcotics_act.shtml. Similarly, the full text of the Marihuana Tax Act can be found at http://www.druglibrary.org/schaffer/ hemp/taxact/mjtaxact.htm. Go to one or both of these websites and read the legislation carefully. By citing the specific portions of the legislation, describe how these federal laws are able to, in effect, criminalize the possession of these drugs.

Note

1. The term "proof" came from early colonial days when alcohol was used to ignite gunpowder. Gunpowder would ignite at about a 50 percent concentration of alcohol, which was then considered "100 proof." This was, as it were, full proof that the alcohol was strong enough to ignite the gunpowder. Pure alcohol is therefore 200 proof.

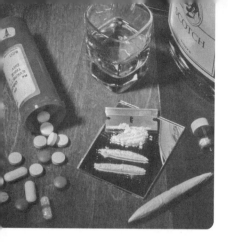

CHAPTER **3**

Classifying Psychoactive Drugs

You may ask, Why classify drugs? What purpose does it serve? Scientists classify information for much the same reason that everybody else does. Confronted with a multitude of data, this information must be placed into categories for it to be meaningful. Hence, plants and animals are classified first into a family, then a genus, then a species, and so forth. These categories are based on particular qualities that the scientists are looking for, and individual plants and animals that possess those qualities are placed into a particular category. Only by classifying the world in this way can the scientist comprehend the world in a meaningful way. Scientists call these classification schemes **taxonomies**.

The classification of psychoactive drugs serves the same sort of purpose. In the first place, classification allows drug researchers and practitioners to make sense of the many substances that are collectively referred to as drugs. But, although these substances share some things in common (e.g., they are all ingested into a living organism), they are also different in many ways. These differences can then provide a basis for classification. One classification scheme was introduced in Chapter 2. This classification system, the Schedule of Drugs, is essentially a legal taxonomy. It purports to arrange drugs according to their addictive potential and medical utility, but it is used primarily as a mechanism for determining criminal sanctions.

Still another classification scheme, introduced by Erich Goode (2008), categorizes drugs on the basis of their intended function, distinguishing drugs recognized for their medical utility, psychoactivity, or illegality as a drug. Among these broad functions, the one we use to define "drug" for this text is psychoactivity: *This text is concerned with substances that in some way affect the operation of the central nervous system.* This narrows the range of substances substantially. We are not, for example, interested in penicillin or birth control pills in this text. But among psychoactive substances, there remains a broad range of drugs that, although sharing the characteristic of affecting the central nervous system in some fashion, nevertheless differ from each other in some important respects.

The remainder of this chapter identifies and discusses a classification scheme that focuses only on psychoactive drugs, a classification scheme which we call a *psychopharmacological taxonomy*. This taxonomy, which is commonly used among drug researchers and practitioners, classifies drugs on the basis of their psychopharmacological effect. Classifying psychoactive drugs according to their pharmacological effect requires consideration of *how these drugs affect the central nervous system.* We now know that most drugs affect the central nervous system through one or more **neurotransmitters**. Many neurotransmitters have been discovered; those which are most closely connected with psychoactive drugs are acetycholine, norepinephrine,

Table 3.1. A pharmacological taxonomy of psychoactive drugs.

Type	Effect on CNS	Examples
Narcotics	Generally depressant; also analgesic and soporific effects	Drugs that derive from the poppy plant or are chemically very similar: opium, morphine, codeine, heroin, methadone, dilaudid
Depressants	Slow down the activity of the central nervous system	alcohol, barbiturates, tranquilizers, sedatives, inhalants such as gasoline fumes and toluene in glue, ether
Stimulants	Speed up the activity of the central nervous system	cocaine, crack, amphetamines, caffeine, nicotine
Hallucinogens	Cause extreme sensory distortion, and cross-sensory stimulation	LSD, psilocybin, mescaline, PCP, nutmeg
Marijuana	Slight depressant effect; mildly euphoric	marijuana, hashish
Other Mood and Performance Enhancing Drugs	Leveling of moods; reduce extremes of emotional states; enhance physical performance	antidepressants, lithium, anabolic steroids, human growth hormones

dopamine, serotonin, gamma-aminobutyric acid (GABA), N-methyl-D-aspartate (NMDA), endorphins, and the cannabinoids (Moak and Anton 1999). These neurotransmitters are chemicals released by neurons into a small space between two neurons called a **synapse**. The neurotransmitters are targeted to a single cell and are very specific in the message that they provide (Ksir et al. 2008).

Most of the psychoactive drugs that we discuss in this text affect in some way one or more of the neurotransmitters identified above. We could classify drugs according to the type of neurotransmitter activated, but some drugs involve more than one neurotransmitter. Furthermore, although such a taxonomy might be meaningful to pharmacologists, it is less useful to social scientists, counselors, policy makers, and lay people who are much more interested in the actual effects of the drugs on the central nervous system and, in turn, on behavior and mood. The classification system in Table 3.1 is the one most widely used by researchers and practitioners in the field today. We include in this table one additional miscellaneous category that we have titled simply "Mood- and Performance-Enhancing Drugs." Drugs in this category include antidepressants and performance-enhancing drugs such as anabolic steroids, which do not clearly possess characteristics of any of the other five categories.

Narcotics

Our English word **narcotic** comes from the Greek word *narkotikos*, "to benumb." Indeed, as we shall see below, this is one of the principle effects of the narcotic drugs. When we think of drug abuse, an image that commonly comes to mind is the narcotics addict, emaciated, unkempt, and willing to do anything for his or her next "fix." This is, furthermore, an image that often drives public policy and plays on people's fears of drugs. There are, however, many misunderstandings about narcotic drugs ranging from what qualifies as a narcotic to the powers that narcotic drugs have over individuals. We begin this section by examining the various drugs that make up this taxonomic category. This discussion will be followed by a brief discussion of the pharmacological effects that these drugs have on the human organism.

What are Narcotics?

There is probably no category of drugs that has been more misidentified than the narcotics. Popular culture has identified everything from marijuana to cocaine to heroin as a narcotic at some time or another. Furthermore, the legal culture defines narcotics as those drugs potentially dangerous and with high addictive potential. Our use of the term in this text, however, is driven by the pharmacological definition. At the risk of oversimplification, narcotic drugs are those that derive from *Papaver somniferum*, the opium poppy plant, or synthesized drugs with a similar chemical structure. For this reason, the narcotics are also sometimes generally referred to as *opioids*, or if derived from the opium alkaloid itself, these natural or semisynthetic narcotics are referred to more specifically as *opiates* (Stine and Kosten 1999). The poppy plant is grown in various parts of the world, but most successfully in areas of the middle and far east, known as the Golden Crescent and Golden Triangle, respectively. We examine some of the more commonly used narcotics below.

The Natural Narcotics

The natural narcotics are those derived directly from the poppy plant, and do not involve the use or mixture of any other chemical compounds. We will look at three of the most commonly used natural narcotics below: opium, morphine, and codeine.

Opium

Our word opium comes from the Greek *opion*, "poppy juice." That is exactly what opium is—the milky extract of the seeds of the poppy plant. Before they completely ripen, the poppy seeds are slit open, and the liquid that drains out, when dried, forms a sticky brown substance called opium. Through the years, opium has been used both medically and recreationally (see Chapter 2). Recreationally, it is typically smoked in an opium pipe, which entails filtering the vapor of the burning residual through water and inhaling deeply into the lungs.

Morphine

The discovery of morphine and codeine in the early nineteenth century represents a major threshold in the medical use of narcotics. Morphine was first isolated as the primary active ingredient in opium by a young German scientist, Frederich Sertürner. Sertürner named his discovery morphium after Morpheus, the Greek god of dreams. Ironically, his wife would later die of an overdose (Lingeman 1974). Morphine is a particularly strong narcotic, some ten times stronger than opium. It was at one time widely used as a recreational drug, with names such as *M, morph, morpho, dreamer, monkey, stuff* and *Miss Emma*. Heroin has largely displaced morphine as the drug of choice among recreational users.

Codeine

The discovery of morphine opened the field of chemistry to pursue other derivatives, resulting in some 30 different alkaloids over the next few decades (Ksir et al. 2008). Perhaps the most important of these came in 1832 in the form of codeine, a narcotic used largely for its analgesic effect. Literally translated from the Greek, "poppy head," codeine quickly caught on as both an analgesic, and an antitussin, a cough suppressant. Many cough formulas using codeine as the active ingredient were patented and sold over the counter as recently as 1970. Codeine was also commonly used recreationally in this form by youthful users and known as *schoolboy* on the street. Codeine is not nearly as potent as morphine and requires at least 12 times the dose to achieve the same analgesic effect (Liska 2004). For this reason, it has been much more popular among physicians as an analgesic when the more powerful morphine is not required.

The Semisynthetic Narcotics

Semisynthetics are the product of a synthesis of naturally occurring narcotics with other chemical substances. The following discussion highlights three of the most commonly used semi-synthetics: heroin, dilaudid, and oxycodone.

Heroin

The story of heroin begins in 1874 when two acetyl groups—which essentially share the chemical properties of vinegar—were attached to morphine to form diacetylmorphine, or more commonly, heroin. Named for its "heroic" powers, this new drug was substantially (some three times) more powerful than morphine (Ksir et al. 2008). Moreover, it was initially believed that heroin was not an addictive drug, and that it was effective in eliminating morphine withdrawal symptoms (Lipton and Maranda 1983). Within about a decade, the addictive potential of heroin became clearly evident. Because of its phenomenally addictive power, there is no accepted medical use of heroin in the United States today. It is legally available in Canada after being banned for 30 years, and it is still available in England and a handful of other countries for certain medical purposes including the legal maintenance of narcotics addicts, though it is no longer widely distributed (Liska 2004). Heroin is, however, a drug of choice among recreational narcotics users. Some of the more common street names for heroin are *smack, horse, H, shit,* and *dope* among many other "brand" names given by dealers of heroin to identify their own supplies (Goldstein et al. 1984).

Dilaudid

Dilaudid (dihydromorphine) is a very powerful narcotic, from two to eight times the potency of morphine (Carroll 1989). Dilaudid is a prescribed medication for the most extreme forms of pain and in some cases for cough suppression. Because of its potency, however, physicians do not readily prescribe it, though it is a drug of choice among addicted medical professionals. In addition, it seems to be the narcotic of choice among heroin addicts when supplies of heroin are temporarily low or cut off (Inciardi 2002). The 1988 film *Drug Store Cowboy*, based on an unpublished novel by James Fogle, depicts the use of Dilaudid by a veteran narcotics addict, who describes it as "the best pharmaceutical dope money can buy."

Oxycodone

Oxycodone is synthesized from a minor constituent of opium known as thebaine. It is similar chemically to codeine but more potent and potentially more addictive. Medically, oxycodone is usually administered as Percodan, a combination of oxycodone and aspirin, or Percocet, a combination of oxycodone and acetaminophen. Both of these combinations have made their way into the underground economy and are taken orally or dissolved in water and mainlined. A new and stronger form of oxycodone was developed and patented in 1996 under the trade name OxyContin. This new drug was originally produced in 10-, 20-, 40-, and 80-milligram tablets, and in July 2000, a 160 milligram tablet was introduced. Percodan and Percocet, by contrast, contain 5 and 2.25 milligrams of oxycodone, respectively. OxyContin is not only a more powerful form of oxycodone, but it is a controlled release drug that acts for up to 12 hours, making it especially effective as a pain treatment. Used recreationally, the drug has been chewed, crushed and snorted, and dissolved in water and injected. When used in these ways, the controlled release function is no longer effective, leading to rapid release and absorption of the drug (NDIC 2001a).

The Synthetic Narcotics

Synthetic narcotics are those with no origin in the poppy plant—that is, they are synthesized, manufactured from beginning to end in a laboratory—but which nevertheless have a chemical structure and pharmacological effect that mimics the natural narcotics. Many synthetics are available today. We will briefly examine five of the more commonly used: methadone; the synthetic analgesics, Demerol, Darvon and Talwin; and Fentanyl.

Methadone

Methadone was first synthesized by chemists in Germany in the 1940s in response to a shortage of morphine. It was not until the 1960s, however, that this drug came to be used as a treatment for heroin addiction, which is its primary use today. Methadone is usually taken orally in liquid form, most often mixed with orange juice or some other pleasant-tasting medium. Because it is usually swallowed, it takes much longer to take effect than heroin, which is usually mainlined. More importantly, methadone has an effective action of 24 to 36 hours, compared with heroin's 4- to 5-hour effect, therefore requiring only a single dosage daily. This quality has made methadone a particularly appealing drug in some treatment circles; methadone maintenance as a treatment program will be discussed more fully in Chapter 13. More recently, the FDA approved an alternative to methadone, buprenorphine, as a Schedule III drug, and it has subsequently found its way into the treatment pharmacopeia. Distributed under the trade names Suboxone and Subutex, this drug is very similar to methadone, but has an effective duration of two to three days. Beyond its use as a treatment for heroin addiction, methadone is sometimes used as a drug of preference by recreational drug users who get it from other users who have diverted it from methadone maintenance clinics. Methadone is often referred to on the street as *Dollies* or *Dolls*.

The Synthetic Analgesics: Demerol, Darvon, and Talwin

Discovered in 1939, Demerol (meperidine) is primarily used as an analgesic. It is stronger than codeine, though only about 15 percent as potent as morphine (Liska 2004). It is commonly used in childbirth to relieve labor and delivery pain, and is frequently prescribed for postoperative discomfort (DEA 2005). Demerol does produce euphoria, particularly when injected, and for that reason is a popular substitute for heroin by addicts who are temporarily cut off from their supply. Contrary to early belief, Demerol is an addictive drug as many physicians discovered when they began to prescribe and use it for minor pain (Liska 2004).

Darvon (propoxyphene) is almost always administered orally and is the least potent of all of the narcotics we have discussed. It is usually taken as an analgesic for mild to moderate pain. Darvon is often manufactured in combination with other analgesics such as acetaminophen (Darvocet-N) and aspirin. Darvon is not a popular drug for recreational use because of potentially severe side effects such as depression and psychosis. The FDA strongly warns physicians not to prescribe this drug to suicidal or extremely depressed patients (Liska 2004).

Another popular narcotic analgesic is Talwin (pentazocine). Talwin has greater analgesic effect than Darvon and is used for moderate to severe pain. It is capable of producing physical dependence, though it is generally considered to have low abuse potential. Although Talwin is considered a synthetic narcotic, it does have some antagonistic effect (Liska 2004). As we shall see in Chapter 13, narcotic antagonists are drugs that block the effects of other narcotic drugs by keeping them from binding to the brain receptors that will in turn cause euphoria. In addition to its antagonistic effect, Talwin seems to have a narcotic effect of its own.

Fentanyl

Fentanyl was first synthesized in the late 1950s in Belgium and was medically introduced as an anaesthetic under the trade name of Sublimaze. It is used during and following surgery for pain relief. Analogues of the original drug were produced shortly thereafter, and by the mid-1970s, the drug was being used illicitly, first in medical circles and eventually in the street culture. Today over a dozen analogues are manufactured in clandestine laboratories. Known by street users as *china white* or sometimes *P dope* (Stine and Kosten 1999), this is an extremely potent narcotic, many times more potent than most heroin available on the street and some 100 times more potent than morphine (Liska 2004).

Pharmacological Features of Narcotics

The narcotics have several pharmacological features in common that, taken together, distinguish them from the other categories of drugs we discuss in this text. These features are addictive potential, analgesic effect, and euphoria.

Addictive Potential

The narcotics are perhaps the most addictive of all drugs, at least from a strictly physiological point of view. Those addicted to heroin and other narcotics describe having a "monkey on their back," which drives them to go back again and again for more drugs. Research by Inciardi (1979), for example, suggests a very rapid transition from experimental to addictive heroin use: among males, only about six months; among females, less than two months.[1] Clearly, with a few notable exceptions such as crack cocaine (discussed below), narcotics have a seduction almost unparalleled among recreational drugs.

Early efforts to explain this attraction relied on theories of weak moral character or personality attributes that were prone to addiction, commonly known as the addictive personality (Chein et al. 1964; Platt 1975). These early attempts at explaining the physiological basis for addiction notwithstanding, it would not be until the 1970s that medical science began to understand the complex chemical and physiological basis for addiction. The key to this understanding is in the chemistry of the brain itself. Scientists have discovered that the brain and the pituitary gland produce morphine-like chemical neurotransmitters, the first of which were named *enkephalins*, and later chemical discoveries that were named **endorphins** (a contraction of the phrase *endogenous morphine*). Addiction to the natural and synthetic opiates results when the brain and pituitary gland cease or diminish production of the body's own chemical narcotics because the heroin or other ingested narcotics attach to the receptor sites and fool the brain into thinking it does not need to produce enkephalins or endorphins. When an individual ceases taking narcotics for whatever reason, the organism experiences acute withdrawal because brain chemical production has been curtailed (Carroll 1989; Liska 2004; Stine and Kosten 1999). Chapter 5 further explores the biochemical basis for narcotics addiction, as well as addiction to other types of drugs.

It is important to point out the psychological and social factors of addiction to narcotics. The late Norman Zinberg (1984) brought to the attention of the scientific community the fact that many individuals who use narcotics *never* become addicted. Zinberg emphasized the importance of drug set (the psychological predisposition of drug users) and setting (the social context of drug use) as important factors in drug addiction. These social dynamics contributing to drug addiction and the experience of drug use generally, are discussed more fully in Chapter 1.

Analgesic Effects

Pain blocking is the most important of the intended effects of the narcotics. As we noted earlier in this section, morphine, dilaudid, codeine, Darvon, and Demerol are all prescribed primarily for their analgesic properties, and indeed, most if not all of the narcotics have been used for this purpose at one time or another. The narcotics are arguably the most effective analgesics available to modern medicine. The mechanism of analgesic action is also found in the endorphins and their receptors found throughout the human body. When the human organism experiences pain, endorphins are sent to those receptors to alleviate the discomfort. Narcotics, having a similar molecular structure and the ability to attach to the same receptors, accomplish the same result (Liska 2004).

Euphoria

All of the drugs that we examine in this chapter are psychoactive, meaning that they affect the functioning of the central nervous system. The narcotics, however, have a rather unique euphoric effect. This effect has been variously described as a "warm feeling," "floating," and simply "at peace with the world." Lingeman describes the euphoric effects of narcotics in a medical setting as "a subjective state of well-being produced by the patient's dramatic release from pain and the anxieties and tensions accompanying it" (1974, 104). The euphoria produced by narcotics is a strong motivator for continued use. Most experienced heroin addicts seldom experience the desired state of euphoria after they become fully addicted because of the large quantity of the drug it would take to achieve this state, and they often report that they are "chasing that first high." Although the euphoria is an important psychological motivation for continued use, most addicts are content to merely ease or forestall the "jones"—withdrawal symptoms resulting from a lack of the drug.

Other Effects

In addition to their addictive potential, analgesic effect, and euphoria, the narcotics produce numerous other physiological reactions. One such effect is suppression of the cough reflex, called an antitussive effect. The narcotic that has been used for this purpose historically is codeine, though other narcotics could accomplish this as well. The narcotics also produce an antidiarrheal effect. Indeed, long-term opiate users sometimes experience constipation because of this narcotic effect. Another symptom associated with opiate use is constriction of the pupils of the eye. A rather harmless effect, such constriction is often used as an indicator that an individual has been using opiates (Stine and Kosten 1999). Narcotics also have a soporific effect, inducing drowsiness in the user. This effect is manifest, for example, when heroin users go "on the nod," which is a sleep-like state with alternating periods of wakefulness.

A final physiological symptom associated with narcotics use that has potential health ramifications is a decrease in central nervous system activity, especially the rate of respiration. This symptom is one shared with other depressants such as alcohol and barbiturates. This feature of narcotics is the basis for **overdose** and death resulting from overdose. Theoretically, if one consumes a large enough amount of narcotics in high enough concentrations, the respiratory system can slow down to such an extent that the brain literally suffocates because of a lack of sufficient oxygen (Liska 2004). There is a great debate in the field about how dangerous heroin and other narcotics are in this regard. Clearly, other factors contribute to most so-called overdose deaths. We will discuss these health consequences of narcotics use in more detail in Chapter 8.

Depressants

The **depressants** share one feature in common with the narcotics: they both act to slow down central nervous system processes. Depressants do not produce many of the other effects of narcotics, however. Five broad categories of depressants are generally distinguished: alcohol, barbiturates, tranquilizers, sedatives, and inhalants.

Alcohol

Alcohol[2] comes in three forms: beer, wine, and distilled spirits. Beer, which is normally the least concentrated of all forms of alcoholic beverages, is produced by the fermentation of grains, usually barley. Most commercial beers in the United States today contain only about 4 percent alcohol; these are called lager beers. More concentrated are malt liquors with up to 5 percent alcohol. Ales contain the most with up to 7 percent alcohol (Carroll 1989).

Wine is also produced through fermentation and can be made from just about any fruit available. Most fruits include sugar that, when combined with yeast and water, will produce the necessary fermentation. Most wines contain a maximum of 15 percent alcohol, or two to three times the concentration in commercially made beers (Carroll 1989). Some wines are "fortified" with distilled spirits and may contain as much as 20 percent alcohol (Ksir et al. 2008).

Distilled spirits are produced by heating a fermented solution until the alcohol boils. This solution is usually a grain mash, but wine is also distilled to produce brandies and liqueurs. The vapors are then captured and allowed to condense. Because alcohol has a lower boiling point than water, it is possible to capture the more pure alcohol vapors before the water boils, and thus when condensed, a much more concentrated alcohol residue remains. Distilled beverages generally range in concentration from 80 to 100 proof, or 40 to 50 percent alcohol content (Carroll 1989).

Although beers, wines, and distilled spirits contain varying concentrations of alcohol, the typical serving sizes are more uniform. This is referred to as the principle of equivalent amounts. As illustrated in the diagram that follows, three individuals— one drinking a 12-ounce can of beer, a second drinking a 4-ounce glass of wine, and a third consuming a 1.25-ounce shot of whiskey—are all consuming about the same amount of alcohol, approximately one-half ounce (Carroll 1989).

Product	Gross Weight	Percent Alcohol	Net Alcohol Consumed
Beer	12 oz.	4%	12 x .04 = 0.48 oz.
Wine	4 oz.	12%	4 x .12 - 0.48 oz.
Distilled Spirits	1.25	40%	1.25 x .40 = 0.50 oz.

Alcohol **intoxication** is usually measured in terms of **blood-alcohol content (BAC)**. BAC refers to the proportion of the content of one's blood supply that is made up of alcohol, measured in grams per 100 milliliters. A blood alcohol content of 0.08, for example (the legal threshold of intoxication in all 50 states), means that alcohol comprises .08 milligram per 100 milligrams of blood (otherwise stated as 8/100 of one percent alcohol). Table 3.2 highlights the behavioral effects of varying levels of blood-alcohol content in the typical individual. It should be pointed out that at least two factors seem to affect the relationship between BAC and behavioral performance, the rate of increase of BAC and the level of tolerance one has developed to alcohol. The faster the rate of increase (resulting from hard and fast drinking), the *greater* the effect on motor performance; and the greater the tolerance one has developed to alcohol, the *lower* the impact on performance (Ksir et al. 2008).

Barbiturates

Barbiturates is the family of central nervous system depressants that were developed and widely prescribed from the late nineteenth century until the 1950s, when doctors became more wary of their addiction potential. More than 2,500 barbiturates have been synthesized, though only about 50 were ever marketed for human consumption. Today, only about a dozen are in medical use (DEA 2005). The barbiturates are

Table 3.2. Performance indicators at select blood alcohol concentrations.	
Percent BAC	**Performance Indicators**
0.05	Lowered level of alertness; lowered inhibitions; impaired judgement
0.10	Increased reaction time; impaired motor function and coordination
0.15	Significantly increased reaction time
0.20	Lowered sensory awareness; substantially impaired motor function
0.25	Staggering and other signs of seriously impaired motor function
0.30	Stuporous but probably conscious; totally unaware of surroundings
0.35	Coma. LD1, the minimal level causing death, meaning that about 1 percent of people with 0.35 concentration will die.
0.40	LD50—about half of people with BAC of 0.40 will die.

Source: Adapted from Ksir, Hart, and Ray, 2008. Reproduced with permission of The McGraw-Hill Companies.

typically categorized as short-acting, intermediate-acting, and long-acting according to how long before the drug takes effect and the duration of the effective time. Short-acting barbiturates are generally used as anesthesia for short-term surgical procedures. They typically take effect within one minute when intravenously injected and have a duration of action of no more than three hours. Because of their extremely short duration, these barbiturates are not commonly used for recreational purposes. Intermediate-acting barbiturates generally take effect in about 15 to 45 minutes and may work for up to six hours. They are most commonly used to induce sleep and quickly replaced alcohol, chloral hydrate, bromides, and the opiates, which had been commonly used for this purpose. Commonly used intermediate-acting barbiturates are Seconal, Amytal, Tuinal, and Nembutal, which, along with others in this category, bear some resemblance to alcohol in their effects. They produce the euphoria and disinhibition characteristic of an alcohol high, and often a similar hangover effect as well. Long-acting barbiturates, such as Luminal, are used primarily for daytime sedation where a longer action period is required. These barbiturates take up to an hour to take effect, but their duration may be as long as 16 hours. The relatively slow onset of these barbiturates discourage their recreational use (Carroll 1989).

The intermediate-acting barbiturates were popular as recreational drugs, especially during the 1960s. According to Brecher (1972), much of this popularity can be attributed to the negative publicity that surrounded them in earlier years. They became a source of fascination for thrill seekers. The barbiturates were marketed on the streets under such names as *reds, blues, yellows, barbs, yellow jackets, goofballs, Christmas trees,* and *red devils* among many others. Used nonmedically, barbiturates can have very serious consequences, including fatalities from overdose and sudden withdrawal.

Nonbarbiturate Sedatives

The oldest nonbarbiturate sedative is chloral hydrate, first synthesized in 1862. It is still in use today, but has not been prescribed with any frequency since the introduction of barbiturates about the turn of the century. Chloral hydrate is perhaps best known today as Mickey Finn or knock-out drops. When mixed with alcohol, chloral hydrate is especially potent and quick acting, and is used intentionally to cause deep sedation for purposes of robbery, kidnaping, rape, or otherwise victimizing a subject. Because of the synergistic effect that chloral hydrate has when mixed with alcohol, the Mickey Finn is a potentially toxic and fatal concoction (Inciardi 1977).

What we more commonly know today as sedatives were developed in response to the concerns over the potentially addictive affects of the barbiturates. One of the early sedatives was glutethimide, synthesized in 1954 and marketed as Doriden and Dormtabs. Glutethemide was a treatment for insomnia and was supposedly less toxic and less addictive than the barbiturates. Unfortunately, it was found to be both addictive and more toxic than the barbiburates it was designed to replace. Glutethimide was succeeded in 1965 by yet another sedative, methaqualone, most commonly known by its trade name Quaalude in the United States. In England and Europe, it was more commonly marketed under the names Sopor or Mandrax. Street users generally refer to the drug simply as *ludes* or *sopers* (Lingeman 1974; Ksir et al. 2008). This drug was considered much safer than the earlier glutethimide, but—in part because of its reputation for being safer—it was much more widely abused. Ironically, when Controlled Substances Act rescheduling of many drugs occurred in 1991, methaqualone was transferred to Schedule I and gluethimide was moved only to Schedule II (DEA 2005).

Tranquilizers

The tranquilizers are generally divided into two broad categories, major tranquilizers and minor tranquilizers.

Major Tranquilizers

The major tranquilizers are almost exclusively limited to medical contexts, with only occasional recreational use. The major tranquilizers are grouped into four broad families: phenothiazines, thioxanthines, butyrophenones, and Rauwolfia alkaloids. The most commonly used are the phenothiazines, which are marketed under trade names such as Thorazine, Mellaril, and Compazine. Contrary to popular opinion, the term "major tranquilizer" does not refer to the extent of their use or abuse. Rather, it has to do with the nature of their impact on the human body and the types of symptoms they address. Also called antipsychotics, the major tranquilizers are used almost exclusively to treat the symptoms of schizophrenia and other psychotic states—if you will, "major" mental illnesses. They have been found effective in reducing hallucinations, delusions, and the anxieties associated with them (Liska 2004).

Minor Tranquilizers

The minor tranquilizers are used to treat a variety of disorders generally termed anxiety disorders, or "minor" forms of mental illness. Because of this, some prefer the term antianxiety agents or ataractics when referring to these drugs. The two most commonly prescribed families of minor tranquilizers are meprobamate and the benzodiazepines. Meprobamate was the first of the minor tranquilizers to be synthesized under the trade name of Miltown, but when the addictive potential of Miltown became apparent, the benzodiazepines were introduced, initially Librium, followed by Valium. Valium quickly became the most widely prescribed drug in America. At the peak of its popularity, in 1975, 61.3 million prescriptions (including refills) had been written (Goode 1999). Millions of Americans, especially women, who were the primary consumers of Valium, became addicted. Valium use declined significantly by the early 1980s, partly because doctors became more hesitant to prescribe Valium, but perhaps mostly because the patent on Valium was running out,[3] and the manufacturer, Hoffman-Laroche, ceased marketing the drug so heavily (*Consumer Reports* 1993).

This did not signal the end of minor tranquilizer use, however. Generic diazepam is now more widely prescribed than trade name Valium by a margin of about ten to one (Goode 2008). New benzodiazepines, most notably Xanax and Halcion, were introduced in the 1980s. It was believed that these drugs would not have the addictive potential of Valium because they are processed and eliminated from the body in less than half a day, and they are typically prescribed to be taken three times a day rather than the one-a-day dosage for Valium. Clinical studies soon found that these rapidly eliminating drugs have an even stronger rebound effect and addictive potential than Valium. These findings were too late for many Americans, who were already dependent. By 1987, Xanax had become the fourth leading drug on the prescription drug list (*Consumer Reports* 1993). On the street, the tranquilizers are called *blues, heavenly blues, valley girls, vals, valums, tranqs,* and *valo,* among other slang terms.

A very recent benzodiazepine with a very troublesome record is flunitrazepam, marketed under the trade name of Rohypnol. Better known as *roofies, rophies, roach, rope, Mexican Valium,* or simply the *date rape drug,* this drug has never been approved in the United States, although about 80 countries have approved it for insomnia. Rohypnol usually begins to take effect within 20 minutes and reaches peak effectiveness within a couple of hours. Rohypnol use in the United States has been especially popular as a club drug. It is also used to facilitate untoward and unwanted sexual advances. This drug is nearly 10 times stronger than Valium and not only sedates an individual, making her powerless to resist, but also causes temporary anterograde amnesia[4] so that victims often do not recall any details of an assault or sexual misadventure. At a cost of only about $5 per tablet, many high school and college males find this to be a cheap form of sexual thrill. A number of actions by the federal government as well as efforts by the manufacturer have resulted in limiting its availability in recent years (DEA 2005).

Inhalants

The inhalants are CNS depressants dispensed in vapor form and breathed. They come in a variety of commercial products, most of which are not intended for medical use. These volatile substances can be found in more than 1,000 common household products, so they are readily available to children. The mind-altering effect of these substances has a very long history, dating to ancient times. Preble and Laury (1967) note, for example, that in the ancient Greek, Judaic, Egyptian, and Babylonian worlds, there is strong evidence that the aroma of burnt spices and other natural vapors were enjoyed and even used as part of worship rituals. These religious practices continue today in the Jewish Havdalah service, which connotes the end of the Sabbath. As our knowledge of chemistry developed, many synthetic solvents were developed that produced even stronger psychoactive effects. We can categorize most inhalants as either organic solvents or anasthetics.

Organic Solvents

Almost universally, organic solvents are commercial products that have been legally manufactured for uses other than human consumption. Most of the organic solvents are petroleum distillates and include such products as gasoline, lighter fluids, paint thinners, varnishes and lacquers, dry cleaning products, and model glue (toluene) among others. All of these products, when inhaled intensely, are capable of producing extreme physiological reactions, sometimes resembling the hallucinogenic drugs (discussed below). These are all depressants in their pharmacological impact on the CNS, however, and in most cases their effects resemble extreme alcohol inebriation. The organic inhalants can be taken in several ways. They can be sniffed directly from the container they are in, squeezed into paper bags, as was toluene during the 1960s experimentation with that drug, or they may be "huffed" from a rag that is soaked with the substance and often placed in a bag so that the vapors are not dispersed into the atmosphere. This practice seems to be most common among 10- to 12-year-olds (DEA 2005).

Anaesthetics

Many of the anaesthetic inhalants are used for medical purposes but have been discovered by recreational drug users for the high that they can experience. Perhaps the oldest of the anaesthetics is nitrous oxide (N_2O), discovered in 1776 by Sir Joseph Priestly and almost simultaneously by Sir Humphrey Davy. Davy discovered that when inhaled, the drug produced a rush of excitement and a compulsion to laugh loudly, which resulted in it being referred to as laughing gas. Medical uses for nitrous oxide were not discovered until later, when dentist Horace Wells quite accidentally discovered its ability to stop pain. By the mid-1840s, this drug was recognized as a medical breakthrough (Brecher 1972). Today the drug continues to be used recreationally, though not on a large scale. Its users, who suck the drug out of gas-filled balloons, call the practice "doing whippits." The high is extremely shortlived (Ksir et al. 2008).

Two other inhalants that have been used both medically and recreationally are ether and chloroform. Ether is produced when distilled alcohol is combined with sulfuric acid. The drug has been used in medicine as an anaesthetic since the early 1700s but became a popular drug of choice during prohibition. Chloroform is a nineteenth-century discovery that was used both recreationally because of its intoxicating effect and, by the mid-nineteenth century, medically as an analgesic during childbirth. Its medical use was discontinued as the potential for overdose was soon discovered, and for the same reason, it is no longer commonly used as a recreational drug (Brecher 1972).

Pharmacological Features of the Depressants

The pharmacological feature common to all depressants is their tendency to depress the actions of the central nervous system and to slow down physiological processes dependant on the CNS. The respiratory system slows down, the heart rate decreases, thought processes slow down, and reaction time increases. This feature of the depressants poses several health threats that are discussed more fully in Chapter 8.

Another effect shared by most of the depressants is that they interact with one another and with certain other drugs, particularly the narcotics, in a synergistic fashion, which can result in overdose-like symptoms (Brady et al. 1999). Finally, studies have demonstrated that most of the depressants produce both tolerance and dependence over time, which means that the user requires higher levels of the drug to achieve the same effect (tolerance) and potentially dangerous withdrawal symptoms are experienced when use of the drug is discontinued (Brady et al. 1999; Moak and Anton 1999; Ksir et al. 2008).

Beyond the general pharmacological effects of the depressants, alcohol affects the human organism in numerous and unique ways. Most of the CNS depressants act primarily through the gamma-aminobutyric acid (GABA) neurotransmitter system (Brady et al. 1999). Alcohol, however, affects multiple neurotransmitter systems including serotonin, dopamine, endorphin, GABA, and NMBA (Kranzler and Anton 1994). Other properties of alcohol pose unique risks to the human organism; these and other health correlates of the depressants will be discussed much more fully in Chapter 8.

Stimulants

The **stimulants** share one important pharmacological characteristic: they stimulate the central nervous system. This feature leads to some common physiological effects that are discussed at the end of this section and in Chapter 8. Some of the stimulants, such as cocaine and its derivatives, are well-known for their abuse potential. Others are not even considered drugs by many people. These non-drug drugs include nicotine and caffeine, drugs that are used by millions of Americans today.

Cocaine

Cocaine is derived from the leaves of the coca plant (*Erythroxylon coca*), which is grown primarily in the high-altitude regions of South America, principally in Colombia, Peru, Ecuador, and Bolivia. A coca paste is formed by pulverizing the coca leaf and soaking it in alcohol and benzol (a petroleum distillate), draining the solution, and adding sulfuric acid. Cocaine crystals containing about a concentration of about 90 percent (compared to about 1 percent concentration in the coca leaf) are left as a residue. These crystals are known as coca paste (Inciardi 2002). The paste is then usually transformed into a powder, cocaine hydrochloride, by diluting it with other substances such as milk sugar or lactose. Powdered cocaine is typically sniffed or "snorted" nasally, but it may also be smoked or injected directly into the bloodstream. When injected in combination with heroin use, it is called speedballing. When used recreationally, cocaine has been referred to variously as *coke, C, big C, lady snow, toot, blow,* and *girl,* among many others. The term *girl* is used to differentiate cocaine from heroin, *boy,* when used in a speedball. Cocaine has always been attractive as a recreational drug and was particularly popular in the disco culture of the 1970s among upwardly mobile young people. Its use peaked during the 1980s and has generally declined since (Johnston et al. 2007). The potentially dangerous consequences of cocaine, at one time denied by users and professionals alike, were highlighted by the closely timed deaths of University of Maryland basketball star Len Bias and Cleveland Browns defensive back Don Rogers.

Freebase

Freebase cocaine, popular during the 1970s, is a form that is smoked. Freebase is formed by treating powder cocaine with a liquid base such as ammonia to remove the hydrochloric acid. The free-standing cocaine base (hence, freebase) is then dissolved, typically in ether, that forms crystals with much lower melting points. It is then melted in a glass pipe and the vapors inhaled. The more concentrated form of cocaine, combined with the form in which it is inhaled, makes freebasing a particularly quick and potent form of high. Because the solution that the freebase is combined with is usually ether or some other volatile substance, freebasing has proven a potentially dangerous pastime (Inciardi 2002). One of the more well-known cases of injury caused by freebasing was when comedian Richard Pryor was severely burned. Freebasing declined with the emergence of the more stable crack cocaine.

Crack

Crack cocaine first emerged in the mid-1980s and has been considered by many to be the scourge of the 1990s. Chitwood, Rivers, and Inciardi document that the first major media mention of crack was "[b]uried within the pages of the Monday edition of the prestigious New York Times" (1996, 1). It was a most casual mention and inappropriately confused crack with freebase. But it caught the attention of other media, and in less than a year over a thousand stories in major media outlets focused on crack cocaine. By 1986, the DEA felt compelled to respond to the hysteria generated by the media. In actuality, crack was, at this time, restricted to inner city neighborhoods in a small number of major cities. It was not the epidemic the media took it to be (Inciardi 2002).

Crack is manufactured by mixing the powdered cocaine hydrochloride with ammonia or, more typically, with sodium bicarbonate (baking soda) and water, and then heated to remove the hydrochloride. What remains is a cocaine-sodium or cocaine-ammonia mixture, which is typically about 30 to 40 percent pure. It is then heated, and the vapors inhaled. The name "crack" derives from the crackling sound when the baking soda is heated. Because crack is so cheap—typically about $3 to $5 for a "rock"—it is highly attractive to young users who have very limited resources to purchase more expensive drugs. Crack is, as Reinarman and Levine (1997) point out, primarily a marketing innovation. It takes substances already available and repackages them in a new and less expensive form, allowing distributors to reach a new clientele—young, minority, inner-city youth. It is seductive, however, in that the high from crack is very immediate (crossing the blood-brain barrier within about six seconds), intense, and very short-lasting, leaving the user with a craving for more. Crack users quickly find themselves craving more of the drug than they can afford, resulting in many spontaneous, poorly planned crimes that frequently turn violent. During the late 1980s and early 1990s, we witnessed the emergence of a crack subculture, complete with argot, crack houses, crack dealers, and crack paraphernalia. Crack goes by many names in the subculture, some of which are *caps, caviar, cookies, hard rock, jelly beans, kryptonite, rooster,* and *white tornado*. Of great concern to public health officials is the spread of HIV among regular crack users, as many will readily prostitute themselves, often within the crack houses, for rocks of crack cocaine (Chitwood et al. 1996; Inciardi et al. 1993). We will take up this issue in greater detail in Chapter 8. There is some evidence for a downturn in the use of crack during the 1990s (ONDCP 1998), though surveys of high school students suggest a level or perhaps even slight increase in crack use as measured in 30-day and annual prevalence (Johnston et al. 2007).

Prescription Stimulants

Normally referred to as amphetamines,[5] these powerful CNS stimulants have some similarities to cocaine, but usually last longer and more pervasively impact the body. There are three broad families of amphetamines: levoamphetamine (Benzedrine), dextroamphetamine (Dexedrine), and methamphetamine (Methedrine). The amphetamines are rather recent additions to the medical and recreational pharmacopeia. Their discovery followed on the heels of discovering the chemical structure of epinephrine (adrenalin). Epinephrine is also found naturally in certain herbs, and was used by the Chinese for some 5,000 years, as well as in Russia and among the Native Americans and Spaniards in the southwestern United States (Grinspoon and Hedblom 1975). Seeking to develop a drug that could, in effect, imitate the effect of adrenalin, chemists first isolated ephedrine, the active ingredient in epinephrine, in 1887, though this drug did not make its way into routine medical practice until 1932. The drug was marketed as Benzedrine, and it was used to clear bronchial passages by shrinking the enlarged nasal mucosa. Other discoveries soon followed. Only three years after it was first marketed, scientists learned that Benzedrine was very effective in treating narcolepsy, a disorder that causes victims to fall asleep suddenly and for no apparent reason. The drug would later be used by truck drivers, students, and others who needed to maintain alertness for long hours without sleep.

Then in 1939, a discovery was made that would eventually place amphetamines in hundreds of thousands of American households. Studies of patients being treated for narcolepsy revealed that they had a significant reduction in appetite. Our cultural preoccupation with thinness created a demand for this new wonder drug, and by mid-century, a generation of women had discovered the marvels of "black beauties" (biphetamines) (Liska 2004). Despite some question about how effective they are as anorectics (inducing weight loss) compared to maintaining careful diets, in the short run at least, patients are able to lose weight. The FDA strongly cautions against the use of amphetamines for weight control, though it does not ban their prescription outright; however, other amphetamine-like drugs have been developed for this purpose (Liska 2004; Ksir et al. 2008).

The methamphetamines are the most recently developed form of amphetamine. This family is much more powerful than either Benzedrine or Dexadrine and has a more rapid onset. Perhaps most significantly, however, methamphetamine is produced in powder form, which makes it easier to snort, smoke, or inject. Consequently, this drug has come into wide recreational use and abuse under such street names as *meth, crank, speed, go, chalk, fire, glass, crystal, crystal meth*, and, *ice*. "Smoking" methamphetamines actually involves heating the substance in a container over a flame and inhaling the fumes through a straw or glass pipe. Intravenous use of the drug has been documented among U.S. servicemen since the 1950s (Brecher 1972); however, this method of use did not spread among civilians until the 1960s. It was particularly popular among heroin addicts, who used the powder methampetamine in place of cocaine in the preparation of speedballs. (In fact, this is probably where it took on the nickname "speed.")

The introduction of methamphetamine was also significant because this is a drug that can be manufactured quite easily in home kitchen or basement laboratories, often called "speed labs." Brecher (1972) notes that, when the government began to restrict legal distribution of methamphetamine, these homemade speed labs sprang up all across the United States, making it virtually impossible for the government to control its spread. In 2005, the Drug Enforcement Administration seized nearly 12,500 clandestine lab operations, virtually all of which were methamphetamine labs. This represents a dramatic increase from just six years earlier, at less than

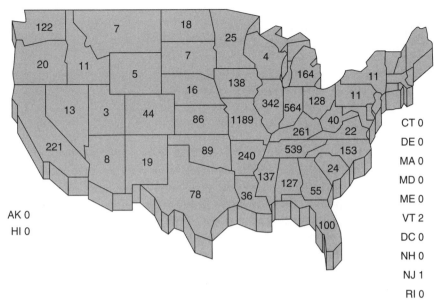

Map last updated January 2008

3.1 Total of all clandestine meth lab incidents, including labs, dumpsites, and chemicals, glass, and equipment, in 2007–5,080.

Source: Drug Enforcement Administration. 2008. "Maps of Methamphetamine Lab Incidents." Available Online: http://www.usdoj.gov/dea/concern/map_lab_seizures.html [Accessed June 20, 2008].

7,500 seizures in 1999. However, as seen in Figure 3.1, the number of lab seizures declined even more dramatically to just over 5,000 seizures in 2008 (DEA 2008).

Speed was a particularly attractive drug because it provided a powerful rush that has been compared to an intense sexual orgasm. Unlike cocaine, however, the high that is afforded by speed lasts much longer, and the user does not feel the need to re-inject nearly so often. The late 1990s witnessed a dramatic increase in the abuse of methamphetamines (or crank) among the young, particularly in the West, but also in the Southeast and Midwest (Albertson et al. 1999).

Ritalin: A Stimulant Paradox

The year 1937 marked a most remarkable and paradoxical discovery in medical science: amphetamines were effective in controlling hyperactivity in children, a condition that would later be linked with attention deficit–hyperactivity disorder (ADHD) (formally referred to as minimal brain dysfunction), affecting an estimated 5 to 10 percent of the general population (Volkow et al. 1998). This is a paradox, because common sense would dictate that to treat such a condition with a stimulant would only increase the level of activity and/or distraction. The primary drug of choice used today to control hyperactivity is methylphenidate, commonly known as Ritalin. Less commonly, Cylert (pemoline), Dexedrine, and other stimulants are also used. All of these drugs are CNS stimulants, though not all (including Ritalin) are amphetamines. Among individuals with ADHD, however, these act upon the central nervous system in unique ways to *lower* the level of hyperactivity and attention deficit. The mechanism by which this takes place is believed to be the ability of these drugs to block the dopamine transporters, thereby increasing the synaptic concentration of dopamine (Volkow et al. 1998). Moreover, research has found that the use of these drugs promotes self-esteem, cognition, and social and family functioning, and greatly lowers the risk of substance abuse among those diagnosed with ADHD (Biederman et al. 1999; Spencer et al. 1996).

The use of Ritalin has increased dramatically. Miller and Leger (2003) estimate that more than 11 million prescriptions are written each year, and that through the mid-1990s the production of Ritalin increased by some 700 percent. Volkow (2006) asserts a four-fold increase in stimulant (mostly Ritalin) prescriptions to youth between 1987 and 1996, with level or slight increases in prescriptions since. Many medical experts believe that Ritalin is being greatly overprescribed. Also of concern, Ritalin has been used by people for whom it has not been prescribed for a variety of reasons, including appetite suppression, staving off sleep, increased cognitive focus, and euphoria. Although certainly of concern, Monitoring the Future, which measures drug use among youth (discussed further in Chapter 4), notes a slight decline in the illicit use of Ritalin since 2001 (Johnston et al. 2007). Ritalin is not widely abused, but the DEA has defined it as a Schedule II drug, indicating a high level of abuse potential (DEA 2005).

Nicotine

The only medium in which nicotine is conveyed is tobacco, so our discussion of nicotine is really the story of tobacco. Today, there is no recognized medical use for tobacco, though this was not always the case, as we have seen in Chapter 2. It is estimated that there are over 45 million adults in the United States who smoke cigarettes, in addition to millions of others who use other tobacco products. Nearly half of regular cigarette smokers will eventually die or experience one or more severe disabilities as a result of their smoking. Approximately 438,000 deaths each year—or 1 death in 5—can be attributed to tobacco (CDC 2008a). The physiological dangers associated with tobacco smoking are immense. Arguably, no other drug poses as many physiological risks to the human organism as does tobacco. Yet, this is a drug that has historically been treated rather lightly by policy makers, treatment specialists, and educators.

The addictive potential of nicotine has been a source of controversy recently, with tobacco companies making strong denials of this claim. Clearly, there is evidence of withdrawal symptoms, including irritability, anxiety, headaches, drowsiness, and gastrointestinal problems among heavy smokers. Moreover, if we measure addiction by compulsive reinforcement, there is perhaps no other drug that produces quite the dependence and need for reinforcement as tobacco. Studies conducted prior to the Great American Smokeout in the 1980s revealed that 85 percent of adolescents who smoked more than one cigarette went on to become regular users. Moreover, of those who became regular users, some 85 percent continued regular smoking patterns at least until age 60. If these statistics are accurate, more than 70 percent of adolescents who smoked more than one cigarette—that is, went beyond experimenting—would become regular smokers for the rest of their lives (Russell 1971; cited in Brecher 1972). Another study found that nearly 70 percent of American smokers smoke more than 15 cigarettes per day (National Clearinghouse for Smoking and Health 1969; cited in Brecher 1972). This is an average of one cigarette (read, one "hit") per waking hour. No other drug commands this level of reinforcement. If we use the frequency of reinforcement as a measure, tobacco is clearly the most addicting drug in existence, a reality underscored by C. Everett Koop, Surgeon General during the Reagan administration.

It is estimated that more than 80 percent of current adult smokers started smoking before the age of 18 (CDC 1994a). This is of particular concern as we witnessed increasing rates of tobacco use among high school and even middle school students through the 1990s. Some of the increased attractiveness of tobacco to younger users came in the form of "bidi" and "kretek," two forms of tobacco which are imported from India and Indonesia, respectively, and are flavored with cloves, fruit, and other things. A study by the Centers for Disease Control and Prevention (2000), revealed that 13 percent of middle school students and 35 percent of high school students use some form of tobacco product. These findings are confirmed by University of Michigan studies that show an increase in cigarette use among high school seniors through 1997, when 36.5 percent of seniors reported using cigarettes within the last 30 days. The good news is that this percentage has declined substantially since 1997, with only 21.6 percent of seniors smoking in the past month in 2006 (Johnston et al. 2007).

Caffeine

The story of caffeine as a psychoactive drug is, for the most part, the story of coffee. We would point out, however, that caffeine itself is part of a larger family of drugs known as the xanthines. The word *xanthine* is a Greek term meaning "yellow," which is the color of the residue of xanthines when heated with nitric acid until dry. In addition to caffeine, the xanthines also include theophylline and theobromine. The last two categories of xanthines are not commonly consumed for their psychoactive effect, though theobromine is a substantial ingredient in cocoa and chocolate, as well as in cola soft drinks. Caffeine is the primary psychoactive ingredient in coffee, as well as some teas and cola drinks.

Some of the psychoactive effects of caffeine consumption are positive and intended. Caffeine is included in many over-the-counter pain remedies such as Anacin, which are used primarily in the treatment of headaches. College students and truck drivers use this drug both in tablet and liquid (coffee) form to stay awake. While commonly used, and not even considered by most people to be a drug, the stimulant potential of caffeine is greatly underestimated by most users. Certainly, while caffeine overdoses are highly unlikely (it would take the equivalent of about 100 cups of coffee within a two- or three-hour-period to die from an overdose), caffeine has produced some bizarre reactions. Panic attacks have been reported, with symptoms of heart palpitations, choking, and general feelings of doom. There is also potential for at least mild physiological addiction with withdrawal symptoms, particularly headaches. Like other stimulants, caffeine increases heart rate, blood pressure, and metabolism rates, as well as gastrointestinal activity (Ksir et al. 2008). These and other physiological symptoms of the stimulants are discussed below.

Pharmacological Features of the Stimulants

The stimulants affect primarily the dopamine and serotonin neurotransmitter systems as well as the hormonal norepinephrine system (Weaver and Schnoll 1999). The stimulants accelerate CNS activity, which results in symptoms such as increases heart rate, blood pressure, metabolism, and generally in the electrical activity of the cerebral cortex. In low to moderate dosages, these symptoms do not pose health risks for most people, though in higher dosages there is certainly the risk for cardiovascular problems. There is also evidence that the stimulants produce both tolerance and dependance. This is particularly true of cocaine (as we discuss below), but all of the stimulants show these symptoms. Some classic withdrawal symptoms include depression, anxiety, problems with memory, and suicide ideation (Weaver and Schnoll, 1999). These drugs also produce some positive effects, including a reduction in appetite and inhibition of one's ability to sleep. When used in normal dosages, studies have found a heightened level of mental acuteness and motor coordination, along with increased levels of energy. Because these drugs are taken in different media, the stimulants also have their own unique effects on the human organism.

Methamphetamine poses potentially severe consequences for the regular and heavy user. Because it induces such a high level of energy over a long period of time, users experience sleeplessness, often for many days in a row. Prolonged heavy use of methamphetamine is also believed to induce psychotic-like episodes, involving hallucinations of insects crawling just under the skin, a phenomenon experts call formication (Liska 2004).

Cocaine is somewhat unique in how rapidly and intensely it produces euphoria, whether taken in powder or rock (crack) form. Crack is particularly intense, but compared with other stimulants, powder cocaine is very intense as well. Not surprisingly, there has been a great deal of debate over the years regarding the addictive quality of cocaine. It was long believed that dependence on cocaine was a purely psychological phenomenon, that the pleasurable experience of cocaine was highly reinforcing psychologically. Researchers have recently discovered regions deep within the brain that produce pleasurable feelings. One area that appears to be particularly responsive to cocaine is an area called the ventral tagmental area (VTA), which releases large amounts of dopamine that is transmitted to the synapses between neurons and binds to specialized proteins called dopamine receptors. Scientists have found that cocaine blocks the removal of dopamine from the synapse, resulting in the accumulation of dopamine, thereby resulting in more continuous stimulation of the receiving neurons and, hence, the euphoria that users experience (NIDA 1999). There is even some suggestion that a tolerance for cocaine may develop, requiring ever larger amounts of cocaine to achieve a similar effect. This would explain, for example, why lab rats and other animals will forego food for cocaine or will push a lever thousands of times for a dose of cocaine. This continues to be debated as more research on the physiology of cocaine use is conducted. Clearly, cocaine in all of its forms is highly reinforcing, producing an intense desire for more of the drug. This seems to be a feature of other stimulants as well, but recent research on cocaine addiction has been especially enlightening in this area (NIDA 1999; Weaver and Schnoll 1999).

Hallucinogens

When most people think about the **hallucinogens**, they think of LSD, a powerful hallucinogen that rose to prominence during the 1960s. The hallucinogens have a long history, however, that precedes LSD by centuries, even millennia. The remainder of this section will examine two broad categories of hallucinogens, the natural hallucinogens and synthetic hallucinogens.

The Natural Hallucinogens

Grinspoon and Bakalar (1979) suggest that of the approximately 5,000 known alkaloid plants throughout the world, probably about one hundred or so would be considered hallucinogenic. The natural hallucinogens have been used for thousands of years as intoxicants, healing remedies, and as part of religious rites. Throughout most of this history, these drugs were not used recreationally, but under the watchful eye of medical or religious specialists (Grinspoon and Bakalar 1979). It is impossible to examine all of the naturally occurring hallucinogens here, but we will be looking at some of the more common ones in use today.

Peyote and Mescaline

Peyote has an interesting history, as this drug has been in continuous use as part of religious rituals from before written history to the present day. Part of the cactus *Lophophora williamsii*, this drug was used by native peoples in America as a component in their religious rituals long before Europeans discovered this land. Spanish explorers who moved into Mexico discovered the use of this plant and noted that it had extreme effects on its users. Early missionaries into Mexico and the southwest United States attempted to stop its use, but this only forced it underground and led to the establishment of a peyote-based religion among Native American peoples. It was used largely underground in Native American religious practice until the establishment in 1918 of the Native American Church of the United States. Despite attempts to make the use of this drug illegal in religious practice, with the official establishment of the Native American church, these attempts failed on grounds of interfering with free religious expression (Grinspoon and Bakalar 1979).

The entire *Lophophora williamsii* cactus has hallucinogenic qualities, though only the portion above the ground can easily be consumed. The upper portion of the cactus, or crown, is typically sliced into "mescal buttons" and eaten. The primary active ingredient in the mescal buttons is mescaline, which is usually taken in a powder or capsule form. Mescaline became quite popular among recreational drug users in the 1960s, along with LSD and other hallucinogenic drugs. It was preferred over LSD by many because it does not produce as intense an effect and often less nausea and other unwanted effects. The psychedelic effect of mescaline is primarily visual distortion, though it does also produce some **synesthesia** (Ksir et al. 2008). Recreational users refer to mescaline as *Big Chief, mescal, mesc, buttons,* and *cactus.*

Psilocybin

A derivative of the *Psilocybe mexicana* mushroom, psilocybin has become a popular drug among recreational hallucinogenic drug users. This drug is also used by some Native Americans in religious rituals, and was used as early as 1,000 B.C. in Guatemala among the Aztecs. Psilocybin was first isolated in the *Psilocybe mexicana* mushroom in 1958 by Albert Hoffman, who twenty years earlier had discovered LSD (Ksir et al. 2008). Psilocybin has many of the same effects as peyote and mescaline. Time and space perception are affected, and subjects are reported to be more suggestible and distracted. Emotions become more labile and extreme, swinging from extreme euphoria and hilarity to deep depression. The effect, however, is more mild than with either peyote or LSD (Grinspoon and Bakalar 1979). Slang terms for psilocybin include *shrooms, magic mushrooms, sacred mushrooms, caps, liberty caps,* and *purple passion.*

Synthetic and Semisynthetic Hallucinogens

The synthetic and semisynthetic hallucinogens are those that are substantially synthesized in a laboratory setting. These range from dextromethorphan (DXM)—which is nothing more than a cough syrup, but when taken in dosages far beyond what is recommended as an antitussin, produces hallucinogenic effects (see the "Drugs and Everyday Life" section in this chapter for a description of one user's experience)—to the widely recognized hallucinogenic, LSD. We will be looking at some of the more commonly used synthetics here.

LSD

Laboratory-synthesized hallucinogens begin with the discovery of LSD[6] (d-lysergic acid diethylamide), known on the street as *microdot, blotter acid, window panes, Bart Simpson, Bartman, blue heaven, tabs,* and most commonly, *acid.* LSD is arguably the most potent drug known to humankind. Normal doses are measured in *micrograms* (μg), 1/1,000 of a milligram. The effective dose of 50 micrograms is but one-twentieth of a milligram. LSD is considered to be about 4,000 times more potent than mescaline (Ksir et al. 2008). A single ounce of the drug would provide enough

DRUGS AND EVERYDAY LIFE

I Felt my Soul Being Ripped from my Body

The following account is provided by an individual who had taken about 720 milligrams of cough syrup containing dextromethorphan (DXM). This is equivalent to two 4-ounce bottles of cough syrup.

Well, I had an experience with some extremely dangerous drugs a few days ago. I used to drink a bottle of Robitussin for fun. Well, I found some concentrated DXM in pill form. My friend, 'O' and I decided to have some fun. A bottle like I used to drink had about 220 milligrams of dextromethorphan. We each took 720 milligrams. About two hours later, back at our house it hit us. I started getting some weird visuals on the wall. 'O' was zonked out and freaked out lying on the couch. We both started hearing crazy sounds. We had total loss of any motor skills. My friend 'R' paged me and asked me to come over to the tavern. I was in no shape to drive and explained this to him and he said okay.

I finally convinced O to unfold the couchbed so that we could both lie down. He did so and I climbed aboard. The entire room was spinning and we could not keep focus on anything. 'Just sleep it off, we thought....'

I got caught in a nasty time-loop. I experienced Hell. I thought that my basement was the only existent Universe and Jason and I were doomed to live it out in this horrible state for all eternity. God was finally punishing us for our foolish sins. I experienced the same events over and over again. Seeing my legs, leaving the bed, looking at my pager, returning to my bed, leaving my body, and then seeing my legs again. Each time I left my body, it seemed days, years, eons passed, but each time I looked at my pager only one minute had passed.

We both thought that we were dying or very close to it. I felt my soul being ripped from my body. I tried to contain it, but my body began to strech and pull and my head started to get yanked from my neck. I could only console myself by assuring myself that we did not do enough to overdose. Intense visuals of torment. I could hear people screaming and dying. I knew my life was about to end.

I woke up about six hours later and we were back to the ground. I was wearing a robe and the entire basement was trashed. We were still heavily high, and we spent the next hour talking about the trip. We then cleaned everything up, got some breakfast and headed to work. I am still high as write this now.

That stuff makes pure LSD seem like ginger beer. There is no comparison. DXM is by far the most intense shit I have ever done.

Raoul

Source: Erowid Experience Vaults 2000.

for about 300,000 doses! Because of its extreme potency, LSD is taken via another medium of transmission, such as in a small sugar cube or on blotter paper.

LSD is the combination of lysergic acid—which is not itself an hallucinogen and is found in ergot, a fungus that grows on various grains—with diethylamide, a synthetic compound. Hence, LSD is technically a semisynthetic hallucinogen. LSD produces all of the effects of hallucinogens cited earlier. Because these experiences are often very intense, users may experience anxiety or panic (though see Chapter 1 for a discussion of the importance of set and setting for how these drugs are experienced). The so-called bad trip results from these intense experiences where the user is at a loss to make sense of what is happening, and typically, other users are not around to help "normalize" or explain that these experiences are to be expected (Grinspoon and Bakalar 1979).

Despite the potency of the drug and its potential for bizarre hallucinogenic reactions, LSD is almost surely not the evil menace merited by the hysteria during the height of our concern in the 1960s and 1970s. Perhaps the most common allegation regarding LSD use is the occurrence of flashbacks, even years after discontinuing use. There seems to be no question about whether these occur; they certainly do. There is, however, some disagreement about *why* they occur. Some see these flashbacks as a result of the pharmacological effect of LSD on the brain and nervous system. A more commonly accepted explanation, however, is that the human mind captures extreme experiences and replays them at later times. War veterans frequently experience this phenomenon. A study by William McGlothlin and David Arnold (1971) revealed that among 247 LSD users, 8 reported symptoms that might be serious enough to call a flashback.

A related concern regarding LSD use is the belief that it induces psychotic reactions that might result in great panic or even suicide. Again, severe reactions do occur. Sociologist Howard Becker (1967) has suggested, however, that the likelihood of such an experience is socially derived. In his research, Becker found that those users who were given LSD in clinical settings, where abnormal reactions were expected, generally experienced the severe symptoms. All of their actions while under the influence of the drug were met with reactions of shock and horror. The situation was defined as one of abnormality. This was a far different response than those users who first used in the context of an experienced subculture of use, which defined these actions and subjective experiences as normal. Becker found far fewer incidents of so-called psychotic episodes in this context. Becker's findings only emphasize the importance that setting plays in the nature of one's experience using LSD. A related concern is the potential for LSD to induce suicide attempts. There have been a small number of suicide attempts among LSD users, but several qualifying factors must be noted. One of these is the set or psychological disposition of the user while using the drug. Those users who are already highly depressed will very possibly be at higher risk for suicide, given the tendency of LSD to make one more emotionally labile. It must also be remembered that because LSD greatly affects spatial perception, many apparent attempts at suicide may be nothing more than an inability to perceive one's environment accurately (which may account for people walking out of multistory windows, for example).

A major charge against LSD that sent shockwaves through communities was that it causes genetic (chromosomal) damage. The concern was first raised in a March 1967 article appearing in *Science*, a popular and highly respected journal (Cohen et al. 1967). It was reported that subjects exposed to repeated dosages of LSD were many more times likely to have white blood cell chromosomal damage than were non-exposed subjects. News of this study spread quickly across the country, and soon the popular media was speculating about the risks of giving birth to deformed or retarded infants. Unfortunately, because the popular press is not constrained to the same level of scientific rigor as scientific report- ing, the fine details are often missed. The reports fail to mention that white blood cell damage bears no necessary relation- ship to germ cells, which are the cells involved in reproduction. The media further failed to report that white blood cell chro- mosomal damage can be caused in many ways—by X-rays, viral infections, and even heavy use of caf- feine (Brecher 1972)!

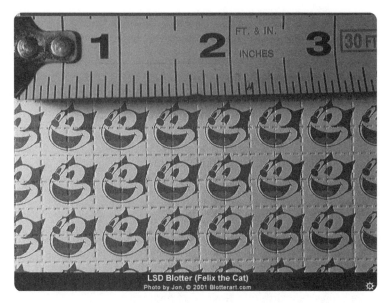

LSD Blotter (Felix the Cat)
Photo by Jon, © 2001 Blotterart.com

3.2 Dealers would often stamp their logo on the blotter paper, which served as a trademark. This practice has evolved into what is now known as blotter art. The typical hit was a 1/4-inch square. (Photo © Jon Blackburn/ blotterart.com)

Ecstasy

A relatively recent addition to the pharmacopeia of drugs is the powerful drug ecstasy. Scientifically, this drug is referred to as MDMA (for its chemical struc- ture, 3-4 methylenedioxymethamphetamine). It was first synthesized in 1912 by a German pharmaceutical company for possible use as an appetite suppressant. Ecstasy has both hallucinogenic and amphetamine-like qualities and today is used almost exclusively as a recreational drug (DEA 2005). It is marketed on the street as *Ecstasy, XTC, Adam, clarity, lover's speed,* or most commonly, simply *X*. Ecstasy is a particularly powerful stimulant and has been linked to brain damage by dam- aging the nerve endings that release serotonin. This is believed to result in memory loss among ecstasy users (Mathias 1999). Warnings of harm notwithstanding, and in spite of its high cost ($25 a hit in 2000), it remains a very popular club drug. This likely results from its association with "rave culture" or rave parties, which are often quite psychedelic themselves, complete with trance-like music and wild color schemes. Raves also generally last until after dawn, so the stimulant component of the drug is attractive as well.

PCP (Phencyclidine)

PCP was originally developed as an anaesthetic and was tested for human use in the 1950s. It was discontinued, however, because of the side effects of confusion and delirium, though it was marketed and used as an animal anesthetic under the trade

Drugs: Myths and Reality

A Brief History of MDMA

MDMA was developed in Germany in the early 1900s as a parent compound to be used to synthesize other pharmaceuticals. During the 1970s in the United States, some psychiatrists began using MDMA as a psychotherapeutic tool, despite the fact that the drug had never undergone formal clinical trials nor received approval from the U.S. Food and Drug Administration (FDA) for use in humans. In fact, it was only in late 2000 that the FDA approved the first small clinical trial for MDMA to determine if the drug can be used safely with two sessions of ongoing psychotherapy under carefully monitored conditions to treat post-traumatic stress disorder. Nevertheless, the drug gained a small following among psychiatrists in the late 1970s and early 1980s, with some even calling it "penicillin for the soul" because it was perceived to enhance communication in patient sessions and reportedly allowed users to achieve insights about their problems. It was also during this time that MDMA first started becoming available on the street. In 1985, the U.S. Drug Enforcement Administration (DEA) banned the drug, placing it on its list of Schedule I drugs, corresponding to those substances with no proven therapeutic value.

Source: NIDA 2006d.

name Sernalyn (Ksir et al. 2008). The drug did, however, become popular among recreational drug users. It is commonly known on the street as angel dust, rocket fuel, embalming fluid, and wack, among other names. PCP, which comes in powder form, is often sprinkled on marijuana leaves to "spike" the smoke. When used in this form, it may be called *killer weed, killer joint,* or *crystal supergrass*. It is easily manufactured in make-shift labs and requires very little knowledge of chemistry.

Ketamine

Ketamine hydrochloride was also developed as a general anaesthetic for human and animal use. This drug produces effects very similar to PCP, though users claim that it is superior to PCP or LSD because its effects are more short lived—typically about an hour, though some of its effects can last up to a day. Ketamine is a relatively recent drug to be used recreationally and is known on the street as *k, ket, vitamin k, special k,* and *psychedelic heroin*. It is used by a relatively small number, primarily teenagers, though that number is increasing as this is also a drug associated with rave culture (DEA 2005; Stephens 1999).

Pharmacological Features of Hallucinogens

The hallucinogens have a very unique psychoactive effect on the user, the exact nature of which has been controversial. Those who see these drugs as dangerous tend to describe these effects as hallucinogenic, suggesting psychotic episodes, hallucinations, and the like. During the 1960s and 1970s when LSD was more prominently defended, this image was contested. Users defined their experience as mind expanding rather than hallucinogenic, and preferred the term **psychedelic**. Both terms, *hallucinogenic* and *psychedelic*, are politically loaded. It is not surprising that today, in the midst of a strong antidrug culture, hallucinogenic is the preferred term. The truth of the matter is that both terms are less than adequate in describing what transpires when one uses these drugs. Although some effects are unique to each of the hallucinogens, all share some characteristics in common. Building on the pioneering work of Harvard psychiatrist Lester Grinspoon and his colleague James Bakalar (1979), Goode identifies nine subjective effects that the hallucinogens tend to share, most of which involve distortion of sensory perceptions:

1. *Synesthesia*—where the user tends to smell colors, or see sounds as bright colors. Indeed, the psychedelic motifs and lighting designs that can still be seen in many nightclubs derive directly from this experience.
2. *Eidetic imagery*—sometimes called eyeball movies, where the user, with eyes closed, sees visual images as though watching a motion picture.
3. *Multilevel reality*—an experience that involves seeing the same object or event from a variety of levels or perspectives.
4. *Fluidity*—objects are in continual flux, much like an amoeba.
5. *Subjective exaggeration*—involves multiplying either the number or the size of objects or events. An LSD user described an incident to one of the authors of this text of being on LSD and having to go to the bathroom to urinate. He described how he felt like a giant 12 feet tall standing over a commode with an opening the size of the dime. He went on to describe how challenging it was to "hit the target" when he urinated. What he was experiencing was a substantial spatial distortion.
6. *Emotional lability*—great swings in mood and temperament.
7. *Timelessness*—time ceases to be relevant, even ceases to exist in the mind of the user.
8. *Ambivalence*—the experience of both good and bad emotions during the same episode, perhaps during the same moment in time.
9. *Sensory overload*—a sense of being bombarded with stimuli and not being able to process it adequately. (1999, 245–248)

In addition to these subjective effects, Jacobs (1987) has identified certain "psychic" effects, which include sudden changes of affect, isolation, and other-worldly sensations. He also suggests a "somatic" effect, which might include nausea, tingling of skin, dizziness, tremors and sudden reflexes. These experiences, which are certainly shaped by social and psychological factors, are also a function of the unique chemistry of the hallucinogens. Although not all users of hallucinogens experience all of these symptoms, these experiences have been reported by users of various drugs in this category.

PCP is somewhat unique among the hallucinogens in that it is primarily an anesthetic that shares some properties with other hallucinogenic drugs such as LSD

(Goode 1999). It can produce very strong and severe reactions in users. A moderate dose causes feelings of estrangement and detachment, numbness, slurred speech, and loss of coordination. In large doses, the user also experiences auditory hallucinations and image distortion and in some cases amnesia (DEA 2005).

The risk of overdosing on hallucinogenic drugs is quite low. Most of the drugs in this category have a high effective dose/lethal dose ratio. The lethal dose for LSD is about 400 times what it takes for an effective dose, so not surprisingly, there has not been a single verified case of LSD overdose. Mescaline has a much lower ratio, the lethal dose being about 10 to 30 times the effective dose (Ksir et al. 2008).

Finally, the hallucinogens produce a high level of tolerance, and quite quickly. It is difficult to produce the desired effect after several days of use, a pattern characteristic of LSD, psilocybin, and mescaline. Moreover, there is a cross-tolerance between these drugs: use of one increases tolerance of others. Tolerance for these drugs abates rather rapidly, however, usually after only a few days. Because of this pattern of tolerance, users of hallucinogens typically "trip" on only a sporadic basis (Stephens 1999). Dependance, characterized by **withdrawal symptoms**, is extremely rare among hallucinogenic users; indeed, these drugs have the lowest rate of dependency development (Gable 1993, Stephens 1999). The one exception to this is PCP, which generates a moderate to high rate of dependency.

Marijuana

Marijuana consists of the leaves and flowering tops of the *Cannabis* plant. There are actually three species of the cannabis plant, all of which can be used for recreational or medicinal use, though not all are equally effective. The most widely used species in this country is *Cannabis sativa*, which originated in Asia but is now grown worldwide and commonly in the United States and Canada. It is also used for hemp fiber in rope and other materials. *Cannabis indica* is a second species of the plant, which is substantially more potent than *Cannabis sativa* but not as widely grown. Still a third species is *Cannabis ruderalis*, which is grown primarily in Russia and has little psychoactive substance in it. There is also nonpsychoactive variant of *Cannabis sativa*, used for its fiber for clothing and other purposes.

Marijuana is known on the street as *pot, grass, reefer, mary jane*, and *apupulco gold*, among other names. Marijuana and marijuana products are consumed in many ways. Most commonly, it is smoked as a hand-rolled cigarette, commonly called a *joint*. Sometimes, however, it is smoked in a pipe (a *bowl*) or a bong, where the smoke is typically filtered through water before being taken into the lungs. Other methods of consumption are also used. Many users prefer the more potent resin from the flowering tops of the female marijuana plant, which is known as *hashish* or simply *hash*. Hashish can be smoked, but it is often eaten in cookies, brownies, and other baked goods. Hashish is more often found in Europe or Asia than in the United States. An even more concentrated form of marijuana is hash oil, which is prepared by boiling the hash resin in a solvent, typically alcohol, and filtering out the remaining solids (Ksir et al. 2008).

The active ingredient in marijuana is delta-9 tetrahydrocannabinol, normally known simply as THC. THC is but one of 61 cannabinoids—chemicals unique to the *Cannabis* plant—and more than 400 total chemicals found in the marijuana plant. The THC content of marijuana varies widely across the species and forms discussed above, and indeed, varies widely even within species. *Cannabis sativa*, for example, typically contains about 2 to 5 percent THC, though it can range from less than 1 percent to about 8 percent. *Cannabis indica*, which is not grown in North America at all, is more potent than *Cannabis sativa*. Hashish generally ranges between 2 and 8 percent, but can be as high as 14 percent, and hash oil may contain more than 50 percent THC content (Ksir et al. 2008).

Some Misconceptions about Marijuana Use

Because of its widespread popularity, and because of antimarijuana campaigns since the 1930s, marijuana has been an alleged culprit in many types of mental, behavioral, and physical disorders. We now know several of these allegations to be false, and there are serious doubts about others. Any sociological assessment of such charges must account for social factors that may come into play in users' experiences of this or any other drug. That is to say, we must be cognizant of the setting in which marijuana is used. Only by accounting for the impact of these contextual factors can we appropriately assess the impact of the drug itself, that is, its pharmacological effect.

One of the primary charges brought against marijuana in the 1970s and still widely believed today is that marijuana destroys ambition, induces laziness, and generally decreases the motivation of the user to engage in constructive activity. Psychologists have referred to this as the **amotivational syndrome**. This is an interesting charge because it is almost diametrically opposed to an earlier charge launched by Harry Anslinger, first Director of the Bureau of Narcotics, that marijuana use incited violence, sexual aggression, and other aggressive forms of behavior (Anslinger and Tompkins 1953). What has changed are the social conditions under which marijuana is used. Marijuana was largely confined to inner-city, lower-class neighborhoods in the late 1930s and 1940s. Users were individuals who were largely segregated from middle-class America, and they were widely feared. It was easy to play on these fears, and the Bureau of Narcotics did precisely this in a number of ways. The 1960s and 1970s users were, by contrast, favored sons and daughters of professional middle-class families. The earlier imagery was not credible. What was credible, however, was the allegation that these young people had lost their drive and ambition. Many were flunking out of college and opting for alternative lifestyles. We can hardly blame this on the marijuana, however! There is simply no convincing data that marijuana has a direct causal relationship on motivation (Joy et al. 1999). Many of these teens were (and are) predisposed to rejecting the values of hard work and getting ahead even before they ever start using marijuana.

There have, indeed, been studies that have shown lower academic achievement on the part of chronic marijuana users. In most cases, however, this pattern was also observed prior to the onset of marijuana use (e.g., see Johnston 1973). There is, furthermore, the fact that when an individual begins to use marijuana, he or she begins to associate with other users who do not reinforce the "Protestant ethic" of hard work and material success. There is a normative component to marijuana use that puts pressure on the user to conform to subcultural expectations. All of these factors make a direct causal linkage between marijuana use and the amotivational syndrome extremely doubtful. Finally, there is the demographic reality that adolescence is a time of rebellion, a time of rejecting parental values for a season to explore the world for one's self. For many young people, this involves experimentation generally with alternative lifestyles, which may involve marijuana. Marijuana may, in fact, be a component of an amotivational syndrome that we observe among many young people in college. It is but one of many factors that converge during this time in life, however, and we must be careful not to single it out as a lone "cause." We must recognize that the amotivational syndrome is a lifestyle feature that is much broader than simply using marijuana.

Another characterization of marijuana that is promoted by our nation's drug enforcement officials is that this drug inevitably leads to the use of other, more serious, dangerous, and expensive drugs. The current labeling of this allegation is that marijuana is a **gateway drug**. Past researchers and practitioners have also referred to it as the *stepping-stone hypothesis* and the *slippery slope hypothesis*. All of these terms refer to essentially the same thing—that once started down a path of drug use, beginning with marijuana, it is difficult to turn back, and users find it necessary to go on to more potent drugs to achieve a satisfactory high. There is a measure of truth to this hypothesis. There is by now almost irrefutable evidence that marijuana users are more likely to use other drugs than those who do not use marijuana. Further, the evidence is strong that they used marijuana at an earlier age than they used the other drugs (Fergusson and Horwood 2000; Kandel et al. 1992; Lessem et al. 2006). Indeed, there are strong relationships among *all* forms of psychoactive drug use (including alcohol and tobacco) and the use of other more expensive psychoactive drugs.

Once again, we must be careful in how we interpret these data. There are, specifically, two fallacies that we must be careful to avoid as we interpret such empirical evidence. One fallacy we would call the *inevitability fallacy*. This fallacy, which is very much a part of a common cultural understanding, is that those individuals who use marijuana, at least beyond a brief experimental level, will almost inevitably go on to use other more potent drugs. The evidence simply does not support such a proposition. Examining the Monitoring the Future study (1999), for example, we can observe that in 2004, 27.5 percent of 10th graders smoked marijuana within the past year; however, two years later (which we would assume to be a reasonable time span to be going on to other drugs), only 1.7 percent of the same cohort (now seniors) used LSD, 0.7 percent used PCP, 5.7 percent used cocaine, 2.1 percent used

crack, and 0.8 percent used heroin (Johnston et al. 2007). Clearly, the overwhelming majority of individuals who smoke marijuana never go on to use more potent
drugs. Part of the problem with the logic of the inevitability fallacy is the tendency
to examine the issue backwards: we tend to look at heroin addicts or crack addicts
and find that most of them used marijuana before they went on to using other drugs.
This is certainly true. It is also true that most of them first used tobacco, alcohol, caffeine, and soda pop!

The second fallacy we call the *causal fallacy*. This fallacy states that those marijuana users who do go on to use more potent drugs are compelled to do so because
of the intrinsic nature of the drug or drug experience. Generally, the argument goes,
marijuana users are not satisfied with the high that marijuana can give and feel the
need to go on and experiment with other drugs. Goode (2008) refers to this as the
pharmacological school or *intrinsic school*, which uses the metaphor of the conveyor
belt: users get on the belt by using marijuana, and then are carried on down the
line of increasingly dangerous drug use. Joy, Watson, and Benson (1999) reserve the
term *stepping stone hypothesis* to refer to this pharmacologically driven movement
to other drugs. Social scientists who have studied this issue carefully have generally
rejected such an explanation. Rather, they suggest that marijuana use is a socially significant step in the process of drug involvement. Indeed, research by Kandel and her
associates suggests that the real gateway drugs are either alcohol or tobacco (Kandel
1975; Kandel and Yamaguchi 1993; Kandel et al. 1992).

Joy, Watson, and Benson (1999) suggest that what is significant about marijuana
in the progression to other types of drugs, such as heroin and cocaine, is that marijuana is the first illicit drug most people use. Marijuana is a threshold of sorts in that
it represents a willingness to engage in behavior beyond what is generally accepted in
society. Goode (2008) advances this idea further in what he calls the "sociocultural"
model: those who use marijuana are more likely to get involved in peer groups that
promote anticonventional activity. After initial contact with close friends who turn
them on to marijuana, they are introduced to others in a subculture of drug use, who
may also be using cocaine or other drugs, and perhaps even committing criminal
acts. If the developing marijuana user continues this association, there is, of course,
a greater likelihood that his or her behavior will increasingly reflect these subcultural values and ideals. This is a process of socialization that is no different from the
socialization that takes place in the military, in churches, and indeed, in drug treatment programs! This understanding of the cause of progression, however, suggests a
much different intervention strategy than the intrinsic school. We will be addressing
these issues of intervention in Chapters 12 to 15 where we examine societal reaction
to drug use.

Pharmacological Features of Marijuana Use

As reported by users, marijuana produces a sense of well-being and euphoria, a
distorted sense of time, which is associated with short-term memory loss, and
heightened physical and emotional sensitivity. Other effects include reduction in

anxiety and alternating periods of talkativeness and laughter, followed by intro-spection and lethargy (Joy et al. 1999). As we have already pointed out, these experiences cannot be fully understood apart from an understanding of the set and especially the setting of the marijuana user. In recent years, scientists have also identified neurochemical factors that seem to be related. About 1990, investiga-tors discovered a specific neuroreceptor for cannabinoids in various regions of the brain. These areas of the brain correspond to long-established effects of marijuana use on fragmented thought patterns, short-term memory, and motor coordination (Stephens 1999).

There is very little evidence that marijuana produces tolerance, and to the extent that it does, the tolerance is very short-lived (Joy et al. 1999). For years it was believed by many users that marijuana use results in a "reverse tolerance"—that the more one uses the drug, the *less* one needs to achieve the desired effect. This phenomenon has never been produced under controlled experimental conditions, however, and it is believed that this effect may be due to the users' learning to inhale more deeply and efficiently (Stephens 1999). Studies have, however, found evi-dence of withdrawal symptoms, especially among heavy users and when withdrawal is sudden. Irritability, insomnia, sweating, restlessness, nausea, cramping, and loss of appetite are commonly reported (Joy et al. 1999; Stephens 1999). Most users, how-ever, do not experience these symptoms or experience them only mildly.

Other Mood- and Performance-Enhancing Drugs

We include in this category two types of drugs that do not fit readily into any of the previous five categories. These drugs, the *antidepressants* and *anabolics*, are neither depressant nor stimulant in their effect, though they may produce symptoms resem-bling some of the effects of depressant or stimulant drugs. These drugs are finding increasing use and are coming under scrutiny by policy makers and practioners alike. Hence, they merit consideration here.

Antidepressants

Perhaps no area of psychoactive pharmacology has advanced more in recent years than the development and refinement of antidepressant medication. Within a few years of its discovery in 1937, the standard treatment for depression was electric shock, or electroconvulsive therapy (ECT). Although still used today, the popular-ity of ECT has waned considerably since the 1970s. This treatment is regarded by many as primitive and inhumane, a reaction prompted in part by media depictions such as that found in the highly successful 1975 film *One Flew Over the Cuckoo's Nest*. Antianxiety medications of various sorts—tranquilizers and other depressants—had been available for years, but they were not effective for treating depression or manic depression (now called bipolar disorder) (Goode 1999).

Drugs introduced specifically for the treatment of depression first appeared in 1955 in the form of monoamine oxidase (MAO) inhibitors. Initially introduced to treat tuberculosis, MAO inhibitors were found to have a substantial mood-elevating effect. Because of severe side effects when taken with certain foods, including severe headaches, heart palpitations, nausea, and severe hypertension, these early antide-pressants have been all but discontinued (Pletscher 1991; Ksir et al. 2008).

A second family of antidepressants, known as the tricyclics, was developed in the late 1950s. These drugs were also discovered quite by accident in the process of searching for a more effective antihistamine. Although not effective for everyone, these drugs are quite effective in lessening the severity of depressive mood disorders (Ksiret al. 2008). Indeed, some evidence suggests that for severe depression, the tricyclics may be more effective than the newer serotonin reuptake inhibitors, which are most widely prescribed for depression today (Boyce and Judd 1999). Tricyclics are still in use today for treating depression, but untoward side effects, including the possibility of lethal dosages, has resulted in physicians and psychiatrists preferring a newer, more stable family of antidepressants known as *selective serotonin reuptake inhibitors (SSRIs)*.

The SSRIs work to increase the level of serotonin in the synapse between neurons. **Serotonin** is a neurotransmitter, which is the key to conducting electri-cal activity across the **synapse**, the microscopic space (only a few millionths of a millimeter) between neurons (Liska 2004). Normally, serotonin released into the synapse that does not immediately bind with receptors will be eliminated (a process called *reuptake*), sometimes too quickly, resulting in less than adequate transmis-sion of neurological impulses. By inhibiting the reuptake process, more serotonin remains in the synapse for a longer period of time, thereby maximizing the neuro-transmission process (Williams College Neuroscience 1998).

A number of SSRIs that have been developed since fluoxetine (Prozac) was first introduced in 1987, though Prozac remains the most popular. Others include ser-traline (Zoloft), paroxetine (Paxil), and venlafaxine (Effexor). All work on the same basic principle of inhibiting serotonin reuptake. The SSRIs do not have the serious side effects of the earlier tricyclics, but there are some, including nausea, vomiting, drowsiness, and tremors (Barbey and Roose 1998). A widely circulated clinical study by Martin Teicher and his colleagues (1990) raised considerable fear among med-ical professionals regarding suicide ideation among patients using the drug to treat depression. This warning, based on six clinically depressed patients, was followed up by several other similar reports alleging the same thing, as well as other symptoms of *akathisia*, or heightened agitation, which could possibly lead to violent behav-ior (Healy 2000). A controversy flared when David Healy, psychiatrist and eminent scholar at the University of Wales College of Medicine, had a job offer revoked from the Centre for Addiction and Mental Health at the University of Toronto because he claimed harmful effects of Prozac and other drugs that were manufactured by Eli Lilly Pharmaceuticals, a major financial supporter of the Centre (Birmingham 2001; Canadian Association of University Teachers 2001). A media frenzy also ensued, as both print and electronic media, including the tabloids, ran feature stories on the Prozac scare (Hegarty 1995). Law suits were also filed against Eli Lilly on behalf of patients who had injured themselves while on the drug as well as victims of Prozac patients, including the children of a man who killed himself and his wife while taking the drug (Zuckoff 2000).

In point of fact, although clinical studies have demonstrated suicide ideation and even instances of bizarre and violent behavior among Prozac patients, there is little evidence to support the inferences drawn from these studies, nor the allegations mounted in the media and the courtrooms. Research by Jick, Dean, and Jick (1995) examining suicides among patients taking various antidepressants reveals that Prozac was less implicated in the suicides than the earlier tricyclics. Hegarty's summary of studies (1995) confirms the findings of Jick, Dean, and Jick that the risk for suicide ideation or aggression under Prozac is no more, and probably considerably less, than under other antidepressants. Indeed, it has been suggested that any increase in suicide ideation may be the result of heightened expectations of such thoughts as a result of the media hype (Ioannou 1992).

A final drug that has been used to treat depression is lithium. Lithium was initially proposed in the 1940s as a salt substitute in heart patients until it was discovered that high levels of lithium could be toxic and even fatal. Research in the late 1940s in Australia revealed that lithium was quite effective in sedating manic patients, though it was not until 1970 that the FDA approved its use as a treatment for depression (Ksir et al. 2008). Lithium has been most effective in the treatment of bipolar disorder (manic depression), with only modest effectiveness with unipolar disorder (simple depression).

Some serious risks are associated with the use of lithium. Excessive concentrations of the drug can lead to a state of confusion, loss of coordination, convulsions, and ultimately death. Fortunately, it is quite easy to monitor blood levels so that dosage adjustments can be made. Clinical evidence continues to show that the benefits of lithium for bipolar patients are favorable enough to outweigh the risks. Research has suggested that is has been especially effective in reducing suicide among bipolar patients (Baldessarini et al. 1999; Tondo et al. 2001). While there has been a trend away from lithium as a treatment, some in the medical research community continue to urge its use (Baldessarini and Tondo 2000, 2001; Baldessarini et al. 2002).

Anabolics

Anabolic literally means "building up," so the drugs that are included in this category are those substances that build up muscle and body mass. The anabolic drugs fall into three broad categories: proteins, steroids, and human growth hormones. These drugs are prescribed medically but have found even more widespread use among athletes. For that reason, we will be discussing these drugs more fully in Chapter 7.

Anabolic proteins are found naturally in the human body, manufactured in the kidneys in the form of erythropoietin (EPO). This protein is also available artificially, and its medical use is to combat anemia associated with kidney failure. Because it greatly increases the oxygen supply in the blood, it is a favorite of athletes as a mechanism to increase their endurance. Unfortunately, when used by individuals such as athletes who already have high levels of oxygen in their blood, there is high risk for blood thickening and clotting (Liska 2004).

Anabolic steroids are also chemicals manufactured naturally in the human body, but available synthetically for performance enhancement as well. Steroids are synthetic derivatives of testosterone, the male sex hormone, and like testosterone, they promote muscle growth as well as other performance-enhancing effects. These drugs have been used experimentally to treat patients with osteoporosis, male impotency, low sexual desire in both men and women, and as a male contraceptive. Its principle use, however, is among athletes to build muscle mass and quickly repair muscle damage. The federal government recognizes the potential medical use of steroids, but the Anabolic Steroids Act of 1990 categorizes steroids and human growth hormones as Schedule III drugs, effectively placing these drugs under the control of the Drug Enforcement Administration, a criminal justice agency, rather than with the Food and Drug Administration, the agency responsible for the oversight of prescription drugs (Mosher and Akins 2007).

Numerous medical and behavioral effects have been associated with synthetic steroid use. There is, first, a strong androgenic effect produced by steroids, which is the development of secondary male sexual characteristics such as facial hair, hardening of muscles, and lowering of voice, in women as well as men. Steroid use has also been associated with a greater likelihood of testicular atrophy in men, decreased sperm production, male pattern baldness, and difficulty in urination (Liska 2004). Steroids also have a psychoactive effect on the user, including euphoria and elevated mood, enhanced sexual desire, and increased alertness, energy, and memory (Mosher and Akins 2007). On the negative side, steroid users have experienced major mood disorders, including severe mania and/or major depression (Pope and Katz 1994). More notably, chronic users experience increased levels of irritability and aggression, a behavioral feature of steroid use that has found popular expression in the term **roid rage**.

Human growth hormone (HGH) is also an anabolic produced naturally by the pituitary gland that regulates human growth. The hormone produced artificially is used in medicine primarily to treat dwarfism. It is widely believed that HGH also improves athletic performance by building muscle mass, a belief for which there is no solid scientific support. Moreover, serious health risks are associated with its use, including carpal tunnel compression (numbness in fingers), giantism (jaw and joint enlargement), and elevated blood sugar potentially leading to diabetes (Liska 2004).

Summary

Classification is an intrinsic and essential part of science and of social life in general. We classify people according to their sex, their weight and height, their hair color, and even the region of the country they are from. We classify objects into animate and inanimate, the living world into plant and animal. Classification allows us to organize our world. The term that scientists use for the classification schemes they develop is *taxonomy*.

This is also why we classify drugs. Among the multitude of dimensions that might be used as the basis for classifying drugs, the most common, and we believe most helpful, is the impact of the drug on the central nervous system. We have termed this classification system a psycho*pharmacological taxonomy* because it classifies drugs based on their psychopharmacology, which is to say, how those drugs affect the central nervous system. The six broad categories included in this taxonomy are: narcotics, other depressants, stimulants, hallucinogens, marijuana, and the general category, mood and performance enhancers. Each of these drugs affects the user in different ways. Moreover, it is important to remember that the effects these drugs have on the user depends not only on the pharmacology of the drugs but also on the set (frame of mind) and setting (immediate environment of drug use) of the use of these drugs. Mode of ingestion also affects how a drug acts upon the central nervous system. Pharmacology is, in short, only one component of a complex set of factors that together account for both subjective and behavioral responses to drug use but it is an important component. Regardless of set or setting, stimulants affect the user in a different way than depressants. Moreover, when a user consumes more than a single drug, the pharmacology of those drugs will determine, to a large extent, whether the user enhances his or her experience or whether he or she suffers an overdose or other negative consequences. Pharmacology is thus an important piece of a larger puzzle that must be in place to understand the impact of drug use on human and social experience.

Key Terms

amotivational syndrome
anabolics
blood-alcohol content (BAC)
CNS stabilizers
depressants
endorphin
gateway drug
hallucinogens
intoxication
narcotics
neurotransmitter
overdose
psychedelic
roid rage
serotonin
stimulants
synapse

synesthesia
taxonomy
withdrawal symptoms

Thinking Critically...

1. Compile a list of the drugs discussed in this chapter, and based on the information presented, rank them in order of most to least harmful. Conduct an informal survey among your friends, family, classmates not taking this class, and others you know: Provide them with the same list, and ask them to rank these drugs from most to least harmful. Are there discrepancies between the lists, especially between your list and those who provided you feed back? How might you account for these differences?

2. Why are alcohol and tobacco (nicotene) so widely used and accepted today despite the fact that they are more harmful pharmacologically than many other drugs that are not found acceptable. An obvious answer is that they are legal whereas other drugs are not, but that begs the question: Why do we find these dangerous drugs acceptable enough to keep them legal, while we make illegal other drugs that are less potentially damaging?

3. Marijuana is misunderstood both by those who stress its harmfulness and those who tout its benefits. What are some of the most prominent marijuana myths and fallacies?

4. Why do you think that all (or many) illegal drugs get classified as narcotics?

5. This chapter has used a taxonomy that categorizes drugs according to their pharmacological properties. Is there another basis for classifying drugs that might be better? If so, why? Identify an alternative basis for classifying drugs, develop a taxonomy complete with category names, and place the drugs into each category.

Learning from the Internet

1. One excellent source of internet information on various drugs is the Lycaeum, located at http://www.lycaeum.org/. Go to this website and research as many drugs or drug types as you can. Describe what you learn here that goes beyond what was discussed in Chapter 3.

2. Another source of information about specific drugs is the United States Government. This information can be found on various websites. Two websites that provide a great deal of descriptive information are provided by the National Institute on Drug Abuse (NIDA) http://www.nida.nih.gov/drugpages.html and the Drug Enforcement Agency (DEA) http://www.usdoj.gov/dea/concern/concern.htm. Read about the same drugs that you investigated at the Lycaeum

website. Is the information on the government websites different from that found at the Lycaeum? In what ways? How might you account for this difference?

Notes

1. Inciardi found that males, on average, first used heroin at 18.7 years of age; their "continued" use of heroin began, on average, at age 19.2. The average age for first heroin use among females was 18.2; first "continued" use was age 18.4 (1979).
2. More precisely, we are referring to ethyl alcohol. This is one of three families of alcohol compounds and the only one safe for human consumption. Neither methyl and isopropyl can be metabolized by the body, and hence are toxic.
3. The patent for prescription drugs in the United States is good for only 28 years.
4. *Anterograde* amnesia is distinguished from *retrograde* amnesia in that individuals suffering from the former remember events from their past except for the period of their intoxication. Retrograde amnesia involves the losing of memory of all or significant portions of past events in one's life.
5. Not all of the prescription stimulants are in the amphetamine family. Ritalin, for example, is not technically an amphetamine. Its structure and effect is very similar, however, so we are considering it and other prescription stimulants in the same category for purposes of this discussion.
6. Sometimes the drug is referred to as "LSD-25." The "25" refers to the fact that LSD was the 25th derivative of lysergic acid to be synthesized.

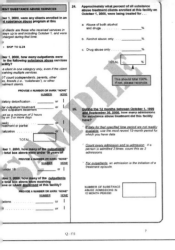

C H A P T E R **4**

Official and Unofficial Data Sources

Wnited States, or that the prevalence of drug use of a certain type is increasing
or declining. You may wonder how such estimates are determined. The task is, in
fact, not an easy one. This is in part because recreational drug use is largely an illegal
activity. People who are involved in illegal behavior risk arrest and are not typically
willing to talk about these activities with strangers. Moreover, people are not always
willing to admit to their use of drugs that are not illegal but nevertheless might be
seen as deviant, such as alcohol or tobacco. Furthermore, unlike other kinds of criminal behavior, we cannot ask the general citizenry if they have ever been a "victim"
of drug use, because drug use is a victimless crime.[1] We can estimate the number of
burglaries or robberies by asking citizens if they have ever been a victim of such a
crime, but we cannot estimate the number of drug users, the number of drug pur-
chases, or the number of times a drug is used by asking citizens about victimization.
When we say that drug use has no victim, we mean simply that the acts of purchasing
and using drugs is not forced upon one adult by another. These acts require voluntary cooperation between drug dealer and drug user. Hence, it is not reasonable to
expect a drug user to say, "Yes, I have been victimized by my drug dealer because he
sold me drugs."

This leaves us with two general methods to obtain information about the level
of drug use. The first way is through **official statistics**, which we define as statistics on drug use which are gathered as a function of day-to-day organizational
procedures conducted by the government or other agencies cooperating with the
government. We will introduce five broad official sources of drug use statistics in
this chapter: criminal justice agencies, including the police and correctional institutions, and noncriminal justice agencies including hospital emergency departments,
medical examiners, and treatment programs. The other sources that are frequently
used in estimating drug use and trends in drug use are **unofficial statistics**. These
are statistics gathered by researchers for the express purpose of identifying drug
users, learning relevant information about them, and estimating incidence and
prevalence. We will introduce three major unofficial sources of drug use statistics:
the Monitoring the Future study, the Youth Risk Behavior Survey, and the National
Survey on Drug Use and Health. Other unofficial sources of drug use data are available, though less widely used; these will be discussed very briefly at the end of the
chapter.

Some Important Terms

If we are to understand and interpret drug statistics appropriately, we must learn to
distinguish two sets of terms that are often confused. These terms are drawn from
the field of medicine but have been borrowed by the social sciences, particularly the
field of criminology. These terms are found frequently throughout the drug literature, and it is appropriate that we look carefully at them before going on to examine
official and unofficial sources of data on drug use.

Epidemiology and Etiology

Epidemiology is derived from three Greek terms *epi*, "over"; *demos*, "people," a "population," or "district"; and *logos*, "discourse" or "study." Translated, it means the *study* of the distribution of a phenomenon *over* a *population*. As far as we know, the term was first used by the Greek physician Hippocrates in a book by the same name, and as the term is commonly used in the medical sciences today, it refers to the study of the spread and distribution of diseases. When medical scientists are examining the epidemiology of diseases such as AIDS, they look for how it is distributed across population groups and regions. For example, epidemiologists learned early in the epidemic that the incidence of AIDS was much higher among intravenous drug-using populations and among male homosexuals. This picture may change over time, but it was a "snapshot in time" of the pattern of this disease.

The social sciences have used this term as well. Although most social scientists no longer see crime and deviance as pathologies, as they did in the early twentieth century, much of the language from that era, which borrowed heavily from the field of medicine, is still used. Social scientists still talk about the epidemiology of crime, for example, which refers to how crime is patterned. This is, in fact, one of the central questions that criminologists ask: Where is the rate of crime, or of specific crimes, the highest? Specifically, the epidemiological profile of crime takes into consideration class, race, gender, occupation, and age, among other factors. These same factors are examined with regard to the epidemiology of drug use. Later chapters in this text examine various dimensions of the epidemiology of drug use including social class, gender, race, and age, as well as various occupations.

Etiology is often confused with epidemiology by lay people. It is quite different, however. Also derived from the Greek—*aitia* meaning "causes" and *logos* meaning "discourse" or "study"—it refers to the study of causes. Hence, rather than examining how a disease is distributed, etiology concerns itself with what causes the disease in the first place. Returning to the AIDS example, etiologists learned that the disease could be traced to the green monkey in Africa. They then began to study the disease at this early point to learn more about its cause. Etiological studies also looked at how it caused human degradation and death by destroying the immune system. This knowledge is often helpful, as it is in the case of the AIDS virus, in searching for cures. This term *etiology* has been borrowed by the social sciences to refer to the process of identifying the causes of crime and other undesirable social phenomena. The central etiological question addressed by criminologists is, *Why do people of a particular social class or age group commit more crimes than individuals in other age categories or social classes?* Generally, these etiological factors are addressed by theories of crime and drug use. Indeed, because the social sciences are not as exacting as medical science, most of our etiological explanations for these phenomena remain in the realm of theory, subject to further verification. We examine some of the major theories for the etiology of drug use (and related behaviors) in the next chapter.

Prevalence and Incidence

These terms are relevant to both the fields of epidemiology and etiology, but are especially important concepts in the field of epidemiology. They, too, are borrowed from the field of medicine, but are used slightly differently there than in the social sciences. When medical researchers talk about the **prevalence** of a disease, they are referring to the total number of individuals in a population who have a disease at any given point in time. **Incidence** refers to the number of new individuals who acquire a disease within a given time period, typically a year. For example, in 2005 it was estimated that there were just under one million cases of AIDS in the United States; there was a *prevalence* of approximately one million people with AIDS in the United States at that time.[2] Let us say that in 2015, there are 1.2 million people with AIDS in the United States; however, 100,000 of the individuals who had AIDS in 2005 died during that 10-year period, leaving a total of 300,000 *new cases* of AIDS reported between 2005 and 2015. This number, 300,000, refers to the *incidence* of AIDS from 2005 to 2015.[3]

The social sciences use *prevalence* and *incidence* in a slightly different way. Normally, when social scientists talk about *prevalence*, they are referring to the total number of *individuals* who have ever engaged in a particular activity such as crime or drug use.[4] *Incidence*, in the social sciences, refers to the number of *cases* or *events* of a particular phenomenon. Survey researchers, for example, will typically ask how frequently a respondent has committed a particular crime or used a particular drug. That figure becomes the basis for the *incidence* of crime or drug use. Police statistics present incidence as the number of arrests for a particular crime or the number of crimes that come to the attention of the police in a particular year. As we shall see when we look at some of the official statistics for drug use, incidence may also be represented by the number of hospital emergency department visits that are reported. In sum, prevalence refers to the number of *individuals* who have ever (or within a specified period of time) used a drug. Incidence, on the other hand, refers to *frequency* or *number of times* a drug was used over a specified period of time.

Rates

One further concept, **rate**, must be introduced for us to be able to interpret and understand drug use statistics. Very often drug use statistics are reported as simply total numbers of users, or **Ns**, which is a straightforward count. Sometimes they will be reported in terms of percentages, which is also straightforward. For example, if among a sample of 10,000 people, 3,000 admit to having used some sort of illicit substance in the past year, we would say that 30 percent of the sample has used some sort of illicit drug in the last 12 months. A percentage is the number of respondents or cases that fit a category per one hundred overall cases.

Rates are similar to percentages, but are not necessarily calculated on a per-100 basis. *Rate* refers to the number of drug users per unit of population. The unit of population may vary, and it is important to know what the unit is to interpret the data accurately. For example, the Uniform Crime Reports, published by the Federal Bureau of Investigation, uses a population unit base of 100,000 for its rates; other sources use a unit base of 1,000. If one is not aware of what the unit of population is, they will draw very inaccurate interpretations about the prevalence of drug use!

Rates are important for two reasons. First, simply providing an N does not really give us a clue as to how pervasive drug use, or a particular type of drug use, may be. That there are an estimated 500,000 to 1,000,000 heroin addicts in the United States sounds like a great deal. However, when we consider that the entire population of the United States is over 300,000,000 people, the rate of heroin use is only 1.7 to 3.3 people per 1,000 people. We can see that reporting in rates rather than Ns provides a much less dramatic but more realistic picture of the level of drug use.

The rate is even more important, however, when looking at trends in drug use over time. Let us use actual FBI statistics from the Uniform Crime Reports to illustrate our point. The estimated number of nonalcohol, drug-related arrests in 1995 was 1,476,100 and 1,846,351 in 2005. That represents a 25.1 percent increase in the number of drug-related arrests. However, the population has also increased during that time, from 262,803,276 in 1995 to 295,560,549 in 2005. The rate of drug-related arrests in 1995 was 561.7 arrests per 100,000 population, compared with 624.7 arrests per 100,000 in 2005. The increase in the *rate* of drug-related arrests was therefore not 25.1 percent, but rather 11.2 percent (FBI 1995, 2005; U.S. Census Bureau n.d., 2000). Rates, in effect, take into account shifts in the population base. In so doing, they provide a much better idea of whether involvement in drugs (or any other behavior for that matter) is increasing or decreasing, or whether increased numbers of drug users or arrests is simply a function of more people. We should also note that, although the figures employed for this example were for the United States as a whole, we could determine rates for any demographic group, say young people aged 10–19 or for men vs. women. By identifying the target population of interest, whether it be the population as a whole or some subpopulation, we can calculate rates of drug use among that population.

Official Drug Use Statistics

We have suggested earlier that official statistics are defined as statistics which are gathered as a function of day to day organizational procedures conducted by the government or other agencies cooperating with the government. Numerous government agencies, such as the National Institute on Drug Abuse, fund special studies on drug use and behaviors related to drug use. The statistics generated by these studies are not what we mean by official statistics, however. Rather, official statistics refer to data that are generated by government and cooperating agencies in the normal course of their work. For example, when police departments make arrests, these arrests are recorded, and then get compiled by the FBI. Similarly, we will look at hospital emergency department and medical examiner data compiled from the charts of emergency departments and medical examiner reports. These are the five types of data we use:

1. **Uniform Crime Reports (UCR)**, reported by local police departments and compiled by the FBI
2. **Arrestee Drug Abuse Monitoring (ADAM)** Program, formerly the Drug Use Forecasting (DUF) system
3. **Correctional data** from a myriad of sources, at federal and local levels, including statistics on probationers
4. **Drug Abuse Warning Network (DAWN)**, comprising data reported by hospital emergency departments and by medical examiners
5. **Treatment data** compiled by the Drug and Alcohol Services Information System (DASIS), the National Survey of Substance Abuse Treatment Services (N-SSATS), and the Treatment Episode Data Set (TEDS).

Uniform Crime Reports (UCR)

Those of you who have had a course in Criminology or Juvenile Delinquency should be familiar with the Uniform Crime Reports. This is a general source of crime statistics gathered from some 17,000 police departments and published by the FBI. The FBI began gathering crime statistics in 1931 in Massachusetts, in response to a legal mandate given the Bureau a year earlier. Reporting by police departments has always been voluntary, and until the 1950s, reporting was not at all systematic, and many police departments failed to report at all. Over the years, with the professionalization of police departments, these statistics have improved substantially in their completeness and usefulness as descriptive tools.

The crimes reported in the Uniform Crime Reports fall into two categories, simply called "Part I Offenses" and "Part II Offenses." Part I Offenses, also known as index crimes, consist of eight categories of crime: homicide, aggravated assault, rape, robbery, burglary, grand larceny, motor vehicle theft, and arson. These are considered the most serious crimes and form the basis for the general crime rate released by the FBI and published and broadcast by the media. Certainly, other crimes could be considered as part of the crime rate and for specific purposes may be used instead of the index crimes. Because the index crimes are considered the most serious, however, they form the basis of a general crime rate.

Part II Offenses consist of 21 additional offenses considered less serious than the index crimes, from forgery and counterfeiting to juveniles running away from home. The categories that interest us are four crime categories tucked away in the Part II Offenses: drug abuse violations, driving under the influence, liquor law violations, and drunkenness. Drug abuse violations are further divided into two categories, sale/manufacture and possession. When reporting both sale/manufacture and possession offenses, the FBI further distinguishes four categories: heroin/cocaine

Table 4.1. Estimated drug and alcohol arrests, 2007.

Offense	Total N	Rate (per 100,000)	Percent change in N, 1998–2007	Percent change in rate, 1998–2007
Drug abuse violations	1,386,394	614.8	17.6	5.4
DUI offenses	1,055,981	468.2	−1.8	−12.0
Liquor law violations	478,671	212.3	−11.4	−20.6
Drunkenness	451,055	200.0	−12.4	−21.5
Total Alcohol	**1,985,707**	**880.5**	**−7.0**	**−16.7**
Total Drugs and Alcohol	**3,372,101**	**1,495.3**	**1.6**	**−9.0**

Source: Constructed from FBI 2007, Tables 31 and 32.

and derivatives, marijuana, synthetic or manufactured drugs, and other dangerous non-narcotic drugs. These categories and subcategories of drug abuse violations are reported only for arrests, and as percentages of all drug abuse violations. No information is provided on rates or on the total number of each subcategory, though both of these statistics could be derived quite readily if one were interested in doing so.

Incidence of Drug Abuse Violations Reported by the UCR

Table 4.1 provides a snapshot of the number and rate of drug and alcohol arrests in 2007. The FBI reports nearly 1.4 million drug arrests for 2007. Possession-related offenses accounted for most of the total (not shown). There were estimated to be nearly 2 million alcohol arrests, most of which were DUI offenses. Between 1998 and 2007, there was an 17.6 percent increase in the number of drug arrests, and a 7 percent decrease in alcohol arrests. Accounting for the change in population, the rate of increase for drug abuse violations over these 10 years was only 5.4 percent, whereas the rate of alcohol-related offenses decreased by 16.7 percent.

Evaluation of UCR Data

We must take great care in our interpretation of these statistics. First, we know that the **dark figure** of crime—that portion of the total crimes committed that are not brought to the attention of the police—is very high, and it is particularly high for crimes of this nature. Hence, these data are going to underestimate overall drug use. Moreover, note that these are *arrest* statistics.[5] Typically, for drug sales offenses, undercover police officers have made several "buys" before making a single arrest so law enforcement may gain access to higher-level dealers. Alcohol statistics do not suffer from these problems, but we know that the dark figure for alcohol violations is also very high. Because of the extremely high dark figure for both drug abuse and alcohol offenses, we must also be wary when interpreting trend data in the Uniform Crime Reports. These statistics suggest a substantial increase in drug arrests, with a slight decrease in alcohol arrests. However, this may be merely an artifact of shifting priorities in law enforcement. With a dark figure for these types of crime in excess of 90 percent—more than 90 percent of these crimes do not come to the attention of the police—a simple change in law enforcement priority or procedure could easily result in these changes, and they may not represent a fundamental shift in the level of drug use or sales at all.

Arrestee Drug Abuse Monitoring (ADAM) Program

The Arrestee Drug Abuse Monitoring Program was instituted in 1997. ADAM replaced an earlier data collection initiative called the Drug Use Forecasting (DUF) system, established in 1987. Some changes were made, including an expansion of the number of metropolitan areas included, but the basic methodology remained the same. Recent arrestees in selected cities throughout the country were randomly selected and interviewed about their drug use within 48 hours of when they were booked. These interviews were then corroborated with urine specimens. Both interviews and urine specimens were voluntary, but in most cities more than 80 percent of the arrestees agreed to the interviews, and of those more than 80 percent agree to the urine samples (ADAM 2003). Due to funding concerns, the ADAM program was terminated on January 29, 2004. Officials stated that their intention was to relaunch the program the following year, but ADAM has not been reintroduced as of this writing. We include a brief discussion of the program here because of its unique methodology.

Interviews were conducted and drug specimens collected over a two-week period, four times per year. Quarterly collection has an important advantage over annual surveys in that seasonal variations in drug use can be measured. Arrestees were questioned about a variety of areas, including education, living arrangement, criminal behavior, and income sources, but the interviews focused most intensively on past and current drug use patterns. Urine specimens were taken to corroborate self-report statements of recent drug use and to provide a valuable validity check. Drug-use data were collected for 10 categories of drugs: amphetamines, barbiturates, benzodiazepines (Valium), cocaine, opiates, PCP, methadone, marijuana, propoxyphene (Darvon), and methaqualone (Quaaludes and other sedatives).

When the original DUF program was launched, data were collected from 21 cities throughout the country. By 2003, 17 additional cities were added to the program, though four of the original 21 cities were no longer included, for a total of 34 cities.

Prevalence of Drug Use Revealed by ADAM

Table 4.2 presents the percentage of arrestees with any drugs in their urine according to the offense for which the were arrested. What is most noteworthy, perhaps, is the high proportion of arrestees testing positive for drug use at the time of their

Table 4.2. Percent of arrestees positive for drugs by offense category, 1999.		
Offense	**Male**	**Female**
Violent offenses	**48.6**	**34.2**
Robbery	65.3	62.5
Assault	44.2	33.1
Weapons	74.1	57.1
Other Violent Offenses	32.7	15.4
Property offenses	**63.3**	**50**
Larceny, theft	57.8	41.7
Burglary	62.9	35.7
Stolen vehicle	68.7	66.7
Other property	63.6	57.1
Drug offenses	**83.9**	**86.9**
Drug sales	82.4	84.6
Drug possession	84.5	86.8
Prostitution	**41.2**	**82.3**
Other offenses	**54.5**	**69.3**

Source: ADAM 2000.

arrest. Depending on the offense, this percentage varies from about 15 percent (for females committing nonspecified violent offenses) to more than 86 percent (for females arrested for drug possession). Although high levels of drug use among those arrested for drug possession is understandable, levels of drug use are extremely high among all arrestees, regardless of the offenses for which they are arrested.

The pattern of drug positives by offense types is itself interesting. We might hypothesize, for example, that people committing violent crimes are more likely to be on drugs than those who commit property crimes or public order offenses such as prostitution. We might reason that drugs make individuals less rational or less in control of their behavior and hence more likely to engage in violent behavior. Property crimes, on the other hand, require more precision and presence of mind. Property offenders, we might thus reason, are less likely to have drugs in their system when arrested. Table 4.2 presents only very limited support for this idea, however. With the exception of robbery, a *lower* percentage of arrestees for violent crimes than for property crimes tested positive for drugs. The reason for this may be, once again, that we are dealing with arrestees. It may well be that our hypothesis is correct, that most property offenders do, in fact, commit their crimes while "clean," and indeed, the reason these arrestees were arrested in the first place is because they were not clear-headed enough to pull off their crime and hence were caught. Such a possibility raises again the limitation of ADAM data in making generalizations to the broader criminal population.

The other interesting observation worthy of note in Table 4.2 is the fact that females are more likely to test positive for drugs for every single crime category except drug sales. We might interpret from these findings that females are more dependent on drugs in the commission of crimes. Insofar as these data are representative of the general criminal population in Los Angeles, such a proposition would be reasonable. Again, however, because only arrestees are represented here, we must be careful in drawing such conclusions.

Evaluation of ADAM

Because data were collected quarterly, ADAM allowed us to track drug use over time. Unfortunately, as it was essentially limited to the 1990s, this program did not have sufficient longevity to be of much value in assessing trends among arrestees. ADAM presented other advantages over most official statistics in two important ways. First, data were collected by trained interviewers for purposes of obtaining drug use information. Because most official statistics are merely by-products of official processing of drug users, the information collected on drug use may not be as valid or reliable. Moreover, ADAM had a built-in verification mechanism, urine samples. No other national data base used such a dependable system of validation.

ADAM data also presented some shortcomings. Perhaps most significantly, data were collected only on arrestees. Years of street drug research have demonstrated that arrestees may not represent the larger population of drug users (e.g., see Faupel 1986; 1991), so the findings are generalizable only to those drug users who have been arrested. A second area of weakness, which was addressed to some extent by the ADAM program, was the fact that data were not truly national but were gathered in a small number of large cities. Although geographically distributed throughout the country, they are not necessarily reflective of smaller cities, towns, and rural communities. Over the years, ADAM established sites in more moderate-sized cities, which strengthened the data considerably. Moreover, the program launched an initiative to supplement the urban data collection with rotating "outreach" collections that included satellite communities and rural areas.

An additional feature of the ADAM program, added in 1998, was the inclusion of international data from eight foreign countries: Australia, Chile, England, the Netherlands, Panama, Scotland, South Africa, and Uruguay. This international effort, known as I-ADAM, was the first international drug abuse prevalence program to generate standardized data on drug abuse.

Correctional Statistics[6]

A small amount of data is available on drug use characteristics of state, federal, and local prisoners. Like the Uniform Crime Reports, the reporting of these data by individual states and local jurisdictions is voluntary, though now all states participate to some degree. Data are collected from state and federal prison facilities in each of the 50 states and the District of Columbia by the U.S. Census Bureau. Reports are submitted twice a year, at mid-year and at year end, and include not only the total count of inmates, but also several demographic and other categories, including race and ethnicity, sex, and offense type. The Census of Jails (COJ), which involves county and municipal facilities, is conducted only about once every five years. In the intervening years, the less comprehensive Annual Survey of Jails (ASJ) has been conducted since 1982. The ASJ is normally conducted on a smaller sample of the full Census of Jails.

Additionally, every five or six years, the U.S. Census Bureau conducts special surveys in federal, state, and local facilities based on scientifically selected samples of the facilities and of the inmates housed in them. These special surveys contain detailed information about prisoners not contained in any other source, including their current offenses, criminal histories, family and personal backgrounds, and prior drug and alcohol use and treatment. Although this information is technically not official data, we are considering it here because it so closely parallels the National Prison Survey (NPS) data in methodology and therefore augments it very well.

Drug Abuse Warning Network (DAWN)

Sponsored by the Substance Abuse and Mental Health Services Administration (SAMHSA), the Drug Abuse Warning Network (DAWN) represents the first of the non–criminal justice sources for official statistics. DAWN has been collecting information from two sources, hospital emergency departments and medical examiners,since 1975. DAWN is a valuable data source because it provides information not available through other official sources on the health consequences of drug use and abuse. Moreover, DAWN taps individuals who do not come to the official attention of the police or other criminal justice agencies.

More recently, DAWN has undergone some rather significant changes in its data collection and recording procedures. In response to concerns that DAWN was not fulfilling its original mandate as completely as it should, an initiative to redesign the methodology was begun in 1997 and was finally implemented in 2003. Design changes affected both emergency department and medical examiner data; these changes are highlighted below as we discuss each of these data sources. Because of these changes, it is not recommended that comparisons be made between data collected after 2002 and that of earlier years.

Emergency Department (ED) Data

The ED data come from a national probability sample of hospitals in all 50 states and are based upon the 2000 census.[7] These national data are augmented by a probability sample of hospitals in 21 metropolitan areas, with plans to add metropolitan areas in the future. Additionally, supplementary samples of hospitals outside the designated metropolitan areas are used to determine national estimates. The hospitals eligible to be included in DAWN are nonfederal, short-stay general hospitals that have a 24-hour emergency department. Because probability samples are used, the data are quite representative of cases coming into emergency departments. The data are collected by nurses and other medically trained personnel after reviewing medical charts for indications that the emergency department visit was related to drug use or abuse. Information in the charts themselves, of course, originates from the attending physicians or other emergency department personnel who have treated the patient.

The criteria are quite broad and less complex than the earlier DAWN data.[8] Data are reported for individuals of all ages and for all types of drug-related ED visits, regardless of whether presenting symptoms are directly related to drug use or abuse. Unlike the earlier methodology, however, only the current drug use history of those drugs related to the ED visit is reported (DAWN 2002, 2005a).

The information contained in the emergency department data is the number of "drug mentions" involved in emergency department episodes. Drug mentions are categorized according to type of drug, including all illicit drugs as well as prescription and over-the-counter medications. Moreover, unlike the earlier DAWN, information is included on alcohol-only cases (when not in combination with other drugs) for those under the age of 21, adverse reactions to drugs, and malicious or accidental poisonings. The earlier DAWN required only that the use of a drug be intentional with the purpose of achieving a psychoactive reaction.

Medical Examiner (ME) Data

The ME data comprises information on deaths attributable to drug abuse. Unlike the emergency department data, the medical examiner portion of DAWN is not drawn from a probability sample, and hence care must be taken when examining these data. Participation in DAWN is voluntary, and not all deaths are investigated by a medical examiner, so these data should not be extended to draw conclusions beyond the locations themselves. In 2003, 122 medical examiner facilities in 35 U.S. metropolitan areas and to 126 county-wide medical examiner offices in six states submitted reports to DAWN (DAWN 2005b). As with the ED data, design changes in the ME reports preclude meaningful comparisons across the two time periods. Perhaps the most important design change is that the only drugs reported to DAWN by medical examiners are those drugs directly implicated in the death, regardless of the reason the decedent used the drug.[9] Other design changes include reporting all ages and

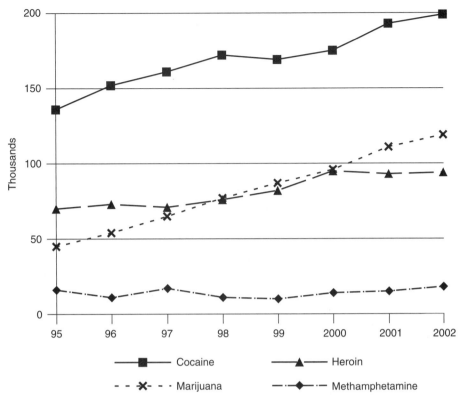

4.1 Emergency Room Episodes, 1995–2002.

Source: Substance Abuse and Mental Health Services Administration. 2003., *Emergency Department Trends from the Drug Abuse Warning Network, Final Estimates, 1995–2002.* DAWN Series D-24, DHHS Publication No. (SMA) 03-3780, Rockville, MD:; Office of Applied Statistics.

reporting alcohol-only cases for decedents under the age of 21, criteria changes also incorporated into the ED data.

Any given case may involve multiple mentions. Forms allow for the recording of up to six different types of drugs in addition to alcohol. Many drug users are polydrug users, so it is not always possible to determine which drug or drug combination was primarily responsible for the death. In addition to the drug-related data surrounding the death, ME reports include demographic information about the decedent as well as information about the circumstances of the death.

Drug Use Patterns Revealed by DAWN

Figure 4.1 reveals that during the latter half of the 1990s and into the new millennium, the number of emergency department episodes related to drug use and abuse increased slightly. It should be noted however, that, except for marijuana, these years reflect a leveling of a significant increase that began during the latter 1980s and into early 1990s (not shown). For example, cocaine episodes increased at an almost alarming rate of more than 70 percent from 100,000 in 1988 (about 80,000 in 1990) to nearly 200,000 in 2002. This dramatic increase almost certainly results from an increased prevalence in crack use (and an increased purity of cocaine) during the early 1990s. Nearly 450,000 emergency department visits for cocaine were reported in 2005, but because of differences in recording practices, this does not necessarily represent an increased trend in problem cocaine use. There were far fewer episodes involving marijuana, heroin, and methamphetamines, but the same trend of increasing rates is evident, particularly among certain age categories, depending on the drug in question. As with cocaine, and largely resulting from systemic recording changes in DAWN data, these drugs were responsible for a vastly increased number of emergency department visits in 2005. Marijuana-related episodes accounted for more than 240,000 visits, heroin for over 160,000, and methamphetamines for nearly 110,000 emergency department visits.

The data on marijuana provide an empirical example of what DAWN data can and cannot tell us. Episodes involving marijuana are lower than cocaine episodes, yet we know from self-report studies that the prevalence of marijuana use is much higher than cocaine. We need to be cautious, therefore, as we interpret the other data as well. *These are cases that involve emergency department treatment.* The reason for the rise might be an increase in the use of a drug or an increase in the potency of the drug. Or it may result from factors that have nothing to do with drug use patterns at all, but rather to patterns of treatment for drug use.

Evaluation of DAWN

A major strength of DAWN data is that they provide information not available in any other official source nor, for that matter, in any unofficial source. Morbidity and mortality statistics seem to offer a vital contribution to our understanding of the potential consequences of drug abuse. Additionally, these data are collected annually so that epidemiological trends in emergency department episodes or drug-related deaths can be tracked. Unfortunately, because DAWN significantly altered their criteria for inclusion and made other substantial methodological changes, it is not possible to compare data collected after 2002 with earlier trends.

There are additional problems associated with the DAWN data. First, these data cannot be used as a reliable estimate of *drug use prevalence*, although they are sometimes interpreted in this way. They are, instead, an indicator of *drug-related health problems*. For example, an increase in the number of emergency department or medical examiner incidents may simply mean that a new drug or drug combination has hit the streets, one that is more potent than that to which local users are accustomed, or it may mean simply that more users are going to emergency departments because of successful public relations campaigns in the area. Changing patterns may also reflect changes in procedure at a hospital. For example, if a municipality has instituted a drug-detoxification unit, hospitals may routinely refer incoming drug-related cases there. It has also been suggested that changes to more sophisticated computer equipment may affect (usually increase) drug-related judgements because they are better able to detect and more effectively record drug involvement.

A second related area of limitation is that emergency department data almost certainly underestimate the drug-related problems in a community. Many users experiencing drug overdoses, synergism, or other complications of drug use may choose to not go to the emergency department. Instead, they may consult their pharmacist, local doctor, or a medically experienced friend. Moreover, until the redesign of DAWN in 2003, alcohol, a major drug of abuse, was not included at all except when in combination with other drugs. The inclusion of alcohol-only incidents since 2003, unfortunately, includes only minors, those under that age of 21. Yet we know that alcohol consumption by adults as well as juveniles is the primary drug implicated in many drunk driving accidents and violent exchanges resulting in emergency department visits or medical examiner reports. Reporting alcohol incidents only for juveniles or reporting such incidents only in conjunction with other drugs minimizes alcohol's harm as a drug of abuse.

Third, the medical examiner data suffer the additional limitation in that reports are often delayed for six months or more because of the extended time required for the completion of autopsy reports. Medical examiner data are only about 80 percent complete after six months, and are not usually fully complete for a year. Moreover, since 1997, DAWN has not aggregated its medical examiner data, making examination of broad trends difficult at best. Trends can be examined for individual cities, however.

Drug and Alcohol Services Information System (DASIS)

Data collection on drug treatment admissions was first mandated on a national level by the Drug Abuse Office and Treatment Act (PL 92-255) in 1972. This act provided federal funding for treatment programs and required reporting on clients entering those programs. The first reporting efforts were initiated as the Client-Oriented Data Acquisition Process (CODAP) in 1973. This program continued for nine years until 1981, and gathered data from nearly 2,000 federally funded programs that admitted some 200,000 patients over that time.

Mandatory CODAP reporting was terminated in 1981 because of the transfer of funding from the federal to state governments under the Alcohol and Drug Abuse and Mental Health Services Block Grant. The block grant program included no reporting requirements, though some states continued to report voluntarily.

In 1988, amendments to the original block grant program mandated federal data collection on clients receiving substance abuse treatment through programs receiving block grant monies. The Treatment Episode Data Set (TEDS) was established in 1989 in response to this mandate under the auspices of the Substance Abuse and Mental Health Services Administration (SAMHSA). SAMHSA had other treatment services data sets as well. The Drug and Alcohol Services Information System (DASIS) was thus created as a mechanism for integrating these sources of information and to avoid redundancy. In addition to TEDS, this need for integration resulted in the creation of the National Master Facility Inventory (NMFI), after 2000 known as the Inventory of Substance Abuse Treatment Services (I-SATS). I-SATS is a continuously updated and comprehensive listing of all known substance abuse treatment facilities, as well as prevention and education facilities identified by the states. I-SATS is the core of DASIS. The third component of DASIS is the Uniform Facility Data Set (UFDS), which also underwent a name change in 2000 and is now called the National Survey of Substance Abuse Treatment Services (N-SSATS). N-SSATS is an annual survey of the characteristics and utilization of alcohol and drug abuse treatment facilities. Below, we briefly describe first the N-SSATS, which is facility-level data, then TEDS, which contains individual client-level data.

National Survey of Substance Abuse Treatment Services (N-SSATS)

N-SSATS collects data from state-recognized treatment facilities on facility and client characteristics. Surveys are sent by mail, with a follow-up phone interview for those facilities that did not respond to the mail survey. Numerous questions are asked regarding the facility and the services it provides as well as client characteristics. Unlike TEDS, which tracks admissions over an entire year, N-SSATS asks for information of one specified day. Since 2002, the reference date for collection is the last weekday in March (SAMHSA 2003b). This methodology does not allow for as many detailed questions about client characteristics, though N-SSATS does contain information not available in TEDS. For example, information is requested on the number of pregnant women in the facility and for individuals being treated for certain diseases such as tuberculosis.

Treatment Episode Data Set (TEDS)

TEDS compiles data on admissions to treatment programs collected by states as mandated under the revised Substance Abuse Prevention and Treatment Block Grant. TEDS data are comprised of two major components, the admissions data set and the discharge data set. The discharge data were established in 2000. The admissions data have been collected for more than 12 years, and consist of a variety of information including: type of drug an individual is being admitted for, method of ingestion (for some drugs), type of service requested, source of referral, frequency of drug use, age at first use, and various demographic information on clients.

Prevalence of Drug Use According to TEDS. Figure 4.2 reveals that alcohol is far and away the most frequently treated substance, with some 725,000 admissions in 2005. It is noteworthy, however, that the number of admissions has declined over the years that TEDS data are available, from nearly 860,000 admissions in 1995. The remaining types of drug admissions are much lower, with admissions ranging from about 100,000 to 322,000. Treatment facility admissions for these drugs has remained quite steady over time with the exception of the stimulants, which have nearly tripled over the 11-year period.

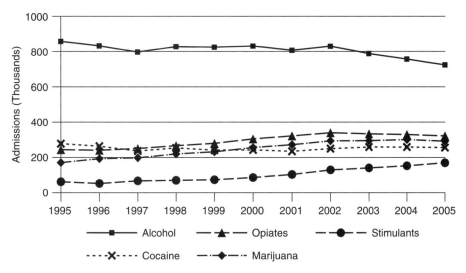

4.2 Treatment Facility Admissions, 1995–2005.

Sources: Substance Abuse and Mental Health Services Administration. 2007a. *Treatment Episode Data Set (TEDS): 1995–2005. National Admissions to Substance Abuse Treatment Services.* DASIS Series S-37, DHHS Publication No. (SMA) 07-4234. Rockville, MD: Office of Applied Studies.

The treatment data seem to contradict the DAWN emergency department data, which show a substantial increase in emergency department episodes over the eight-year period from 1995 to 2002. Cocaine witnessed an especially dramatic increase, yet treatment facilities witnessed a slight decline in admissions for cocaine abuse. It may be that cocaine users, especially crack users, are not willing to go to treatment facilities and end up in the emergency department instead. Similarly, courts may be less likely to send cocaine and crack users to treatment as part of their sentence, being more inclined to send them directly to prison. These inconsistencies can best be addressed with studies especially designed to identify drug users and drug use patterns. Studies of a more ethnographic nature or specially focused on active drug users can intentionally include items that address such anomalies. This is the advantage of unofficial statistics, which we examine in the next section.

Evaluation of TEDS. Because TEDS is based on treatment admissions, certain limitations are inherent to the data. First, not all individuals seek or are referred to treatment, so like any official data source, generalizations to the general population cannot be made. Indeed, because TEDS is only obtained from treatment programs receiving block grant money, the information contained here may not even be representative of all treatment patients. TEDS patients are more likely to be hardcore users, poorer, and probably court-ordered attendees. It must also be recognized that the unit of analysis is the admission and not the individual, so that an individual admitted twice in the same year would count twice in the data. Finally, variation may exist from state to state in the reporting of drug treatment episodes that have nothing to do with actual differences in treatment admissions. States vary in their licensure, certification, and accreditation requirements, as well as in their policies for disbursing public funds. In some states, for example, state substance abuse agencies also regulate private agencies and individual practitioners, whereas in other states private facilities are not so regulated. Those states that do regulate private facilities will be more likely to report admissions to private as well as public agencies, whereas those states that do not so regulate will be reporting only public treatment admissions. Similarly, some states collect data from treatment facilities in prisons, and others do not (SAMHSA 2007a).

Unofficial Drug Use Statistics

Unofficial drug use statistics are those gathered for the express purpose of identifying drug users, learning relevant information about them, and estimating incidence and prevalence. Government agencies may fund or cooperate with these studies, but these data are not part of official censuses or other data routinely gathered by government agencies. Three unofficial sources of drug use data will be explored at length in this chapter:

1. **Monitoring the Future (MTF)**, an annual survey of high school students conducted by the Institute for Social Research at the University of Michigan
2. **Youth Risk Behavior Survey (YRBS)**, a biennial survey of high school students (grades 9–12) conducted by the Centers for Disease Control since 1991, with more than 14,000 students responding in 2007
3. **National Survey on Drug Use and Health (NSDUH)**, sponsored by the Substance Abuse and Mental Health Services Administration and interviewing some 70,000 individuals in households across the country.

In addition to these on-going nationally representative initiatives, we will examine more briefly several other sources of data, including Pulse Check, developed by the Office of National Drug Control Policy, and the Community Epidemiology Work Group (CEWG), which consists of a group of experts from 21 metropolitan areas who report on local indicators of drug use every six months.

Monitoring the Future (MTF)

The Monitoring the Future project began in 1975 at the Survey Research Center of the Institute for Social Research at the University of Michigan. The stated purpose of MTF is "to study changes in the beliefs, attitudes, and behavior of young people in the United States" (1999). When the project began, it was known as the National High School Senior Survey and began with senior classes only. The survey was further expanded in 1991 to include nationally representative samples of 8th and 10th graders.

The survey began in 1975 with approximately 16,000 senior students in about 133 schools nationwide. When 8th and 10th graders were added in 1991, a sample of similar size was drawn for each of these cohorts. Today, approximately 50,000 students in about 420 public and private schools are surveyed annually. Additionally, beginning in 1976, a random sample of the senior class has been tracked on a biennial basis to measure changes in use and attitudes for up to 14 additional years.

Data are collected during the spring of each year. A three-stage sampling process is used to ensure a nationally representative sample:

Stage 1: Select specific geographical areas.
Stage 2: Select one or more schools within each of those areas.
Stage 3: Select classes within each school.

Students are alerted in advance about the upcoming survey through letters and flyers, and participation is voluntary. The questionnaires are group administered in classrooms and in some cases larger group formats such as school assemblies. Follow-up questionnaires are mailed to respondents with a small monetary gift of $10 to help ensure higher response rates.

Prevalence of Drug Use as Measured by MTF

Monitoring the Future reports lifetime, annual, and 30-day prevalence data as the percentage of individuals who report ever using drugs or using a particular type of drug. Figure 4.3 provides trend data from 1975 through 2007 on the number of high school seniors who report having used any of five different types of drugs, including alcohol, during the previous month. The trend is unmistakable. Self-reported drug use seems to have reached a peak in the late 1970s to early 1980s, then steadily declined over the next decade to a low in 1992. The 1990s witnessed an increase in both drug and alcohol use,[10] though self-reported use by high school students has once again levelled off or declined during the late 1990s and into the first decade of the 21st century.

Alcohol use has always been high among high school students, with use during the previous month at or about 70 percent throughout the first half of the 1980s, but declining in the late 1980s. The pattern for illicit drug use is slightly different than alcohol. The early 1980s were a peak period in illicit drug use, as revealed by the combined percentages both for "any illicit drug" and for the individual drugs used, except for narcotics use. Furthermore, the illicit drugs witnessed a fairly sharp downward trend throughout the 1980s and into the early 1990s, though cocaine and narcotics use has always been low, with less than 7 and 4 percent (respectively) of seniors reporting use of these drugs during the previous month. (Most narcotics use involves drugs other than heroin. Annually from 1975 to 2007, less than 1 percent of the sampled high school seniors reported using heroin during the previous month.)

Evaluating MTF

Monitoring the Future is one of the most powerful and reliable measures of drug use in the general population of young people. The care given to obtaining random samples provides a strong base for generalizing to the larger population of high school

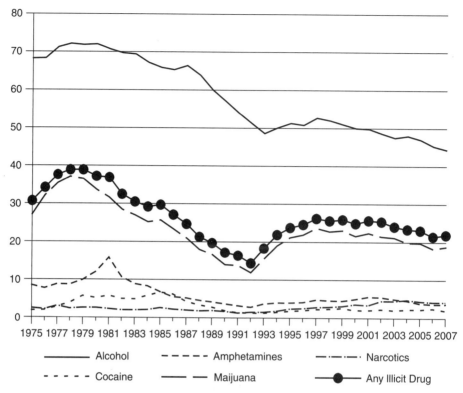

4.3 Monitoring the Future 30-day Prevalence of Drug Use for 12th Graders, 1975–2007.

Sources: Johnston L. D., O'Malley, P. M., Bachman, J. G., & Schulenberg, J. E. 2007a. *Monitoring the Future national survey results on drug use, 1975–2006. Volume I: Secondary school students* (NIH Publication No. 07-6205). Bethesda, MD: National Institute on Drug Abuse. Table 5-2.
Jonston, L. D., O'Malley, P. M., Bachman, J. G., & Schulenberg, J. E. 2008. *Monitoring the Future national results on adolescent drug use: Overview of key findings, 2007* (NIH Publication No. 08-6418). Bethesda, MD: National Institute on Drug Abuse, Table 3.

students and young adults. Moreover, because it is conducted annually and uses more than a single cohort, this project can measure four kinds of change:

1. Changes over time within a single age cohort (sometimes called *period effects*)
2. Developmental changes within a cohort over time
3. Differences among class cohorts over the life cycle
4. Changes associated with changing environments (e.g., from high school to college).

One primary limitation to the MTF is that it is restricted to young people, which, of course, is its purpose. A second limitation is that the questionnaire is administered in large group formats, typically in the classroom. Students do not have the same level of privacy in these settings, which could possibly affect responses.

Youth Risk Behavior Survey (YRBS)

The Youth Risk Behavior Survey (YRBS) has been conducted on a biennial basis since 1991. The CDC developed the survey to respond to a need for state and local data, as well as national data in six specific areas:

1. Behaviors that contribute to unintentional injuries and violence
2. Tobacco use
3. Alcohol and other drug use
4. Sexual behaviors that contribute to unintended pregnancy and STDs (including HIV infection)
5. Unhealthy dietary behavior
6. Physical inactivity.

The "alcohol and other drug use" area contains questions addressing lifetime and current (past 30 days) alcohol, marijuana, and cocaine use, which data we present in the pages that follow. Additionally, the survey includes information on periodic heavy episodic (binge) drinking and lifetime use of illegal injection drugs, inhalants, steroids, hallucinogenics, heroin, methamphetamines, and ecstasy. Other questions regarding alcohol and drug use are also included, such as whether these drugs were used prior to age 13 and whether they were used or sold on school property.

The survey consists of nationally representative samples of public and private school students in grades 9–12 using a three-stage cluster sampling procedure. The first stage, primary sampling units, consisting of counties, subareas of large counties, or grouped adjacent smaller counties. These units are stratified according to their metropolitan statistical area (MSA) status and to the percentage of black and Hispanic students. The second stage involves sampling the schools within the primary sampling units. The third and final stage consists of sampling individual classes—either a required class such as English or social studies, or a required period such as home room—within the selected schools. This process resulted in a total of 14,041 students with usable responses in the 2007 survey (Eaton et al. 2008).

Prevalence of Drug Use as Measured by YRBS

Figure 4.4 presents, in graph form, the biennial data on alcohol, marijuana, and cocaine use by 9th through 12th graders from 1991, when the survey was first administered, through 2007. The YRBS data very closely parallel the trends revealed by the 12th graders responding in the Monitoring the Future survey. Alcohol use remained fairly constant, with about 50 percent of high school students reporting at least one incident of alcohol use in the last 30 days, over the period from 1991 to 2007. This was also found by Monitoring the Future, which reflected a substantially lower involvement with alcohol compared to previous decades. Cocaine use also remained remarkably consistent over the 15 years of the YRBS survey, though the percentage of high school students using cocaine in the last 30 days increased from about 2 percent in 1991 to more than 4 percent in the years from 1997 to 2003, then dropped to just over 3 percent in 2007. These figures are still lower than pre-1990

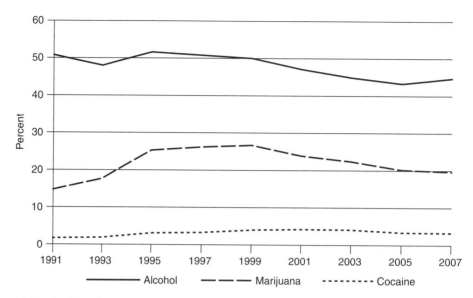

4.4 Youth Risk Behavior Surveillance System Percent High School Students Reporting Use in Past Month, 1991–2007.

Source: Centers for Disease Control. 2008b. *Healthy Youth! YRBSS: Youth Risk Behavior Surveillance System.* Available Online: http://www.cdc.gov/HealthyYouth/yrbs/index.htm [Accessed June 4, 2008.]

levels, some years of which exceeded 6 percent as revealed by Monitoring the Future. Finally, the 1990s witnessed a rise in marijuana use from about 15 percent in the previous month in the early 1990s to nearly 27 percent by the end of that decade. Marijuana use did decline somewhat to under 20 percent by 2007, though not to early 1990 levels. This trend was also noted by Monitoring the Future.

Evaluating YRBS

There are significant similarities between the YRBS and MTF. Both surveys target young people, though MTF has a broader age range, including 8th graders. Also, both surveys utilize a similar three-stage sampling process that ensures a nationally representative sample of young people, resulting in highly credible estimates. They also share the limitation of being administered in large group settings, most often in the classroom.

Unlike the yearly MTF, the YRBS is administered every two years. This should not be a major drawback in measuring long-term trends, though unusual dynamics may be operative in a given year that a biennial survey might miss. Perhaps the greatest disadvantage of the YRBS over the MTF is that the YRBS does not generally report by single age cohorts. Whereas the MTF reports 8th, 10th, and 12th graders separately as unique cohorts, the YRBS reports their combined sample of 9th through 12th graders.[11] This is a critical age period when young people undergo many challenges, identity crises, and lifestyle experimentation, including drug and alcohol use. It is likely that 9th graders will have a very different experience with drugs than will 12th graders. For example, the MTF survey reveals that in 2007, 21.9 percent of 12th graders used an illicit drug in the past 30 days, compared with only 7.4 percent of 8th graders (Johnston et al. 2008). Combining grades 9 through 12 clearly masks significant differences between the age cohorts.

Another limitation of the YRBS is that the number of drugs examined is fairly limited. Recent drug use data (past 30 days) is available only for cocaine, marijuana, and alcohol. Lifetime use is available for a number of other drugs, including inhalants, heroin, ecstasy, methamphetamines, ecstasy, illegal steroids, and illegal injection drug use. MTF, by contrast, includes detailed information on more than 20 illegal drugs in addition to tobacco and alcohol (though it does not include information on illegal steroid use). No information is reported on the percentage of students who engage in *any* illegal drug use, which is a commonly used indicator in other sources of data on drug use, including the MTF.

Perhaps the greatest value of the YRBS is the fact that it confirms the general trends revealed by the MTF, and hence lends even more credibility to an already strongly reliable source of information on drug use among high school youth.

National Survey of Drug Use and Health (NSDUH)

The National Survey on Drug Use and Health has been conducted by the federal government since 1971, in response to the same legislation in 1970 that created the Commission on Marijuana and Drug Abuse. The Commission was charged with the responsibility of reporting to the Congress and the President on the extent of drug use in the United States. The first survey was conducted in 1971 under the name of the Nationwide Study of Beliefs, Information, and Experiences. The project changed names to the National Household Survey on Drug Abuse (NHSDA), and later, in 2002, renamed itself once again to the National Survey on Drug Use and Health (NSDUH) (Kennet and Gfroerer 2005). Between 1971 and 1992, it was conducted on only a periodical basis; since 1992, the survey has been conducted annually under the auspices of the Substance Abuse and Mental Health Services Administration (SAMHSA). Like Monitoring the Future and the Youth Risk Behavior Survey, the NSDUH is a self-report measure of drug use among a representative sample of the United States population. Unlike the MTF and YRBS data, however, the National Survey on Drug Use and Health attempts to represent all age groups. The survey canvasses residents of households, noninstitutional group living quarters (such as shelters and dormitories), and civilians living on military bases. It does not include military personnel, homeless people who are not living in shelters, and institutionalized populations such as jails, prisons, and hospitals.

Face-to-face interviews are conducted with a probability sample of household members aged 12 and older. The annual survey includes interviews with approximately 25,000 people, and in 1999, this number was increased to approximately 70,000 people. The expanded number allows for more accurate estimates of drug-use prevalence at the state level. The survey includes questions on the recency and

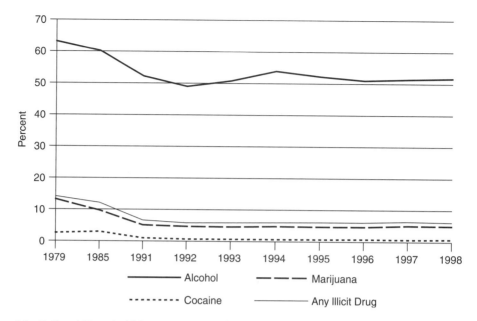

4.5a National Household Survey on Drug Abuse Percent Age 12 and Older Reporting Drug Use, 1979–1998.

Source: Substance Abuse and Mental Health Services Administration. *1999c. Summary of Findings from the 1998 National Household Survey on Drug Abuse.* Washington, DC: Substance Abuse and Mental Health Services Administration.

frequency of drug use, attitudes toward drug use, problems encountered as a result of drug use, and treatment needs and experiences. Also included in the survey is information on demographic characteristics of respondents, employment and education information, income, health status, and access to health care and health insurance, among others.

The methodology employed in this survey was substantially changed on two occasions. First, in 1999, the survey ceased using a paper-and-pencil interviewing technique, implementing instead a computer-assisted interviewing program, which uses audio computer-assisted self-interviewing for more sensitive questions. This is believed to reduce the likelihood of non-, evasive, or false responses to sensitive questions and thereby increase the accuracy of responses. Further design changes were instituted in 2002, most notably the offer of a monetary incentive to participate, which is also believed to improve the response rate substantially. Because of these changes, it is not recommended that post-2002 results be compared with pre-1999 results, thereby limiting the current ability of the survey to measure long-term trends.

Prevalence of Drug Use as Measured by NSDUH

Figure 4.5a presents annual data on use during the previous month for the years 1991–1998. For the most part, overall use changed little during this period. Not

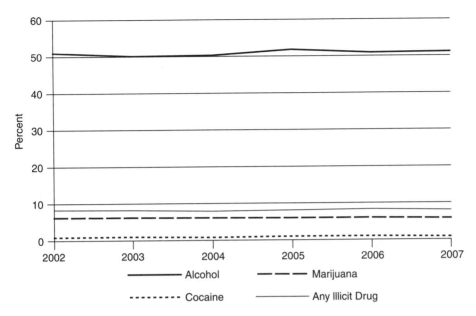

4.5b National Survey of Drug Use and Health Percent Age 12 and Older Reporting Use in Past Month, 2002–2007.

Note: Because of a survey redesign in 1999, and again in 2002, NHSDA data for 1991–1998 are not directly comparable with figures for 2002–2005. Hence, these data are presented separately in Figure 4.5b. Also note the name change.

Sources: Substance Abuse and Mental Health Services Administration. 2004. *Results from the 2003 National Survey on Drug Use and Health: National Findings.* Office of Applied Studies, NSDUH Series H-25, DHHS Publication No. SMA 04-3964 Rockville, MD: Substance Abuse and Mental Health Services Administration. Substance Abuse and Mental Health Services Administration. 2006a. *Results from the 2005 National Survey on Drug Use and Health: National Findings.* Office of Applied Studies, NSDUH Series H-30, DHHS Publication No. SMA 06-4194 Rockville, MD: Substance Abuse and Mental Health Services Administration. Substance Abuse and Mental Health Services Administration. 2008. *Results from the 2007 National Survey on Drug Use and Health: National Findings.* Office of Applied Studies, NSDUH Series H-34, DHHS Publication No. SMA 08-4343. Rockville, MD: Substance Abuse and Mental Health Services Administration.

surprisingly, alcohol is by far the most frequently used drug. In some ways the figures presented in this table are similar to the Monitoring the Future data on high school students during the 1990s. However, when the NSDUH data in Figure 4.5a are compared to MTF data presented in Figure 4.3, an interesting and significant pattern appears. Even though overall use of alcohol and drugs remained stable during this period, use among teenagers appears to have increased during the early 1990s.

It is important not to forget that the National Survey is a sample of all respondents ages 12 and older. It is not examining the same age group over time. Hence, as time passes, and as we move through the period when cohorts of drug users beginning their drug use in the 1960s and then 1970s, more and more people in the population will have used drugs. When reading tables and figures drawn from different populations and using different methodologies, we must examine closely the differences in the populations represented and the methodologies used. Since 2002, drug use remains low, at pre-1999 levels, and alcohol use remains at about 50 percent of the population having used within the past month.

Evaluating NSDUH

The NSDUH, like MTF and YRBS, is a powerful tool in the measurement of drug use prevalence. Its advantage over the high school surveys is that it includes a much broader age range in its sampling procedure. This survey is clearly the most representative survey of the entire United States population, though it does not include institutionalized, military, or homeless samples. One criticism that has been leveled against the National Survey is that it tends to underreport the use of heroin and cocaine (Reuter 1999). This almost certainly results from the lack of representation of institutionalized (including prison) and homeless individuals in the sample. Another limitation of the survey, for current trend analysis at least, is the fact that it has undergone such significant methodological changes in 1999 and 2002. Ultimately, of course, these changes improve the accuracy of the survey, but they do make the interpretation of long-term trends difficult.

Other Unofficial Sources of Drug Use

In addition to the national representative studies discussed above, numerous other research initiatives are available to illuminate the nature and extent of drug use in the United States. We highlight these below.

Pulse Check

The *Pulse Check* report has been published by the Office of National Drug Control Policy (ONDCP) since 1992. Between 1992 and 1996, the ONDCP reported findings on a quarterly basis; since 1996, these data are reported semiannually. The January 2004 *Pulse Check* included information from 25 cities.[12] The data in *Pulse Check* are based on conversations and interviews with representatives in each of the cities with expertise in the following areas:

- **Ethnographic and Epidemiological Sources.** *Pulse Check* identifies some of the most well-known ethnographers and epidemiologists as well as sociologists and psychologists working in the drug use area.
- **Law Enforcement Sources.** Key informants from law enforcement agencies at city, county, and/or federal levels in each of the 25 cities are interviewed.
- **Treatment Provider Sources.** Both methadone and nonmethadone treatment providers are represented.

The specific cities and the number of locations from which this information is obtained varies from report to report, but attempts are made to include an ethnographer, an epidemiologist, a law enforcement official, and a treatment provider from each of the cities.

The January 2004 *Pulse Check* reports on some 10 drug use categories: marijuana, crack, powder cocaine, methamphetamines, heroin, diverted methadone, other diverted opioids, ecstasy, PCP, and other drugs including club drugs. Information that is obtained from the various sources includes the level of use, ease of purchase, who is using, market prices, and purity. Most of the data are provided in narrative form and include information on the level of drug use and drug marketing as perceived by the experts who are interviewed for this reporting program. Table 4.3 provides, in summary form, some of the typical information provided in *Pulse Check* by ethnographers and epidemiologists for several of the drugs reported.

Pulse Check data are not as systematic as other sources of data presented earlier; nor are they as precise. Rather, they provide a narrative overview of drug use and drug-using behavior at various points in time that can be quickly assimilated and understood by policy makers and community groups to gain a sense of the nature of drug use in their communities and regions as compared with others. It is just what it says, a "pulse check." It is not to be used as a full-blown "drug physical." Other data sources are necessary for such information.

The *Pulse Check* reports do, however, draw from data sources not otherwise readily available. The ethnographic data are particularly valuable. **Ethnography** is a research methodology in which researchers spend time in the regular environments of the drug user. Rather than relying on captive samples of prisoners or treatment clients, these data are obtained from drug users in their natural settings. Researchers sometimes interview drug users at length about their drug use and other related behaviors, as well as observe their activity when they are given entree to do so. Valuable information that cannot be obtained even on national self-report surveys such as the National Household Survey or Monitoring the Future can be obtained through this means. Ethnographers studying drug use are some of the best-trained sociologists, psychologists, and other social scientists, seeking to understand drug use *from the perspective of the drug user himself or herself.* Hence, whereas these data are not as systematic and do not lend themselves to generalizations to national level drug use, they do provide valuable information about drug use not readily available elsewhere. The Drugs and Everyday Life feature provides a first-hand account by Richard Curtis, an experienced ethnographer, of the way ethnographers go about doing their work.

Community Epidemiology Work Group (CEWG)
The Community Epidemiology Work Group is a network of epidemiologists and other researchers who have been meeting every other year for some 30 years to review and discuss trends in drug use and abuse. This group is sponsored by the National Institute on Drug Abuse (NIDA). CEWG monitors drug use indicators from 21 cities.[13] These researchers base their reports on numerous epidemiological sources, including many of those we have already discussed (TEDS, DAWN, ADAM, and the UCR), as well as data provided by the Drug Enforcement Agency (DEA), ethnographic sources, focus groups, and other community-based resources.

Table 4.3. *Pulse Check* ethnographers and epidemiologists report on drug use.

Drug	Level of use	Ease of purchase	Changes in who is using	Market prices	Purity
Marijuana	High, stable	Most easily purchased of all drugs; availability stable	Age remains stable	$100/ounce	Range from 1 to 30% THC content
Crack	Less serious use and consequences in some cities	Stable in most cities	Using population continues to age	Range from $2 to $40 per rock; average $10 per rock	From 30 to 85%
Powder cocaine	Stable or declining in most cities	More difficult in some cities; less in others; stable in most cities	Using population remains demographically stable	Varies; average about $100/gram	From 30 to 95%
Heroin	Generally stable; slight increase in some cities	Stable in most cities	New and younger users in many cities	$4 to $30 per bag depending on city; declined in many cities	Varies depending on city; remaining stable in most cities
Methamphetamine	Emerging or increasing as problem in most cities, especially in the West	Quite easy to purchase in most cities, especially in the West	Increase among younger people and possibly females	Price remaining stable	Variable; declining in some cities, increasing in others; stable in most
Other diverted opioids	Diverted Oxycontin increasing problem in most cities	Moderately difficult	New users in some cities; younger siblings and older users	Typically about $1 per milligram	N/A
Ecstasy	Emerging or intensifying as major problem in most cities	More difficult in some cities; less in others; sable in most cities	Using population remains demographically stable	$7.50 to $40 per tablet depending on city; prices remaining stable	N/A

Note: *Pulse Check* provides a broad range of information on various drugs as reported by ethnographers, epidemiologists, and other professionals in the field. It is a quick, snapshot report on such things as market prices, purity, ease of purchase, and the prevalence of drugs of particular interest.

Source: Summarized from ONDCP2004.

DRUGS AND EVERYDAY LIFE

An Ethnographer's Self-Portrait

I am an ethnographer specializing in the study of illegal drugs, primarily in New York City neighborhoods.... Those who might think I could talk with more authority about crime from the victim's rather than the offender's perspective could not be more wrong. In fact, after more than 20 years of intensive and extensive street-level research in New York city's most dangerous neighborhoods, I have never been harmed or have even really feared for my physical safety—except occasionally because of nervous police officers who are surprised to find me in what they consider to be hostile territory, like crack houses or shooting galleries. For the past 10 years I've lived in Brownsville, Brooklyn—Mike Tyson's boyhood neighborhood and the one-time homicide capital of New York City—where my two daughters attend public school and where I've become quite involved in community affairs. My reasons for living in Brownsville are complex. They include my commitment to improving the inner city and my belief that if I want to "talk the talk," I need to "walk the walk." I have never regretted my decision.

What Does an Ethnographer Do?

Ethnographers do many different things. For example, a recent *New York Times* article described how corporations are increasingly turning to ethnographers to better understand how people use their products so that they can devise improvements. The work of an ethnographer—data collection—involves observing individuals over prolonged periods of time and interviewing them about topics of interest. Ethnographers typically study relatively small groups of people,

and although we hope that such intensive scrutiny might lead to generalizations that can be applied to other groups across time and space, that is not always the case. What an ethnographer learns about drug dealing in Harlem or Brooklyn may or may not have relevance to policymakers and public officials outside New York City, except that trends beginning in New York sometimes spread elsewhere.

One might simply say that ethnographers study people's everyday lives. While I do study people's everyday lives, the people I study are involved in illegal activities—typically selling or using drugs. Individuals unfamiliar with the streets or the populations I study often want to know how I actually do the work. First, I am always straightforward about what I am doing with the people I would like to know better. I try never to deceive anyone or misrepresent myself....

Second, I carry no protection while doing research; I rely on the relationships that I develop to ensure my safety. I do not own a gun or carry a knife or any other kind of protection device, and people are generally aware of this. This actually works to my advantage because research subjects are often so concerned about my well-being while I am working in "neighborhood minefields" that they feel obliged to accompany me to ensure my safe passage. On more than one occasion, local "tough guys" who felt it necessary to play bodyguard because they thought I was a walking target for stickup artists were shocked and appalled at how readily I entered crack houses and shooting galleries that even they had been afraid to enter. When they discovered that everyone inside knew me, they were even more surprised. While I do not mean to minimize the dangers involved in this line of work—and there are some if you do not know what you are doing—I have always felt extraordinarily protected by those around me.

The information available through CEWG is not new in the sense of a separate and unique data collection effort; however, researchers in the CEWG do their own unique statistical analyses and interpretations, which provide valuable information and perspectives on drug use in the United States.

Behavioral Risk Factor Surveillance System (BRFSS)

The Behavioral Risk Factor Surveillance System is sponsored by the Centers for Disease Control. This survey is conducted annually by telephone and targets the adult (18 and older) noninstitutionalized population, with a sample size of more than 350,000 individuals each year. Since 2002, it has been conducted in all 50 states plus Washington, D.C., Puerto Rico, the U.S. Virgin Islands, and Guam. This survey collects information on various aspects related to health and health care, including cigarette and alcohol use.

College Alcohol Study (CAS)

Conducted by the Harvard School of Public Health, this survey collects data on alcohol use from students at four-year colleges and universities in 40 states. It is not an annual survey, having been conducted in 1993, 1997, 1999, and 2001. A representative sample of schools was selected in 1993, and subsequent surveys have utilized the same sample (though some of the schools dropped out over the years). Data are based on student responses to mail-out questionnaires.

National Health Interview Survey (NHIS)

This nation-wide survey, conducted since 1957, is sponsored by the National Center for Health Statistics and administered through personal household interviews. The survey is designed to gather information on a variety of health-related measures including cigarette smoking and alcohol use among people 18 and older.

Department of Defense Survey of Health-Related Behaviors among Military Personnel

The Department of Defense have been gathering health-related information on its personnel since 1980 and conducted its ninth survey in 2005. The 2005 sample

Drugs: Myths and Reality

What Do the Statistics Really Say?

We have presented a multitude of data and sources of data in this chapter. Some of these statistics seem to conflict with each other. Some studies, utilizing the same sources of data, seem to suggest that very different things are going on. Sometimes it is difficult to make sense of it all. The task of interpreting statistics is no easier in the field of drug use than in other areas of social life. The following short excerpt by Lana Harrison highlights the importance of carefully understanding the methodology employed in studies.

The problem of misinterpretation of data [is] not new. There are...examples of inap-propriate comparisons and uses of data, such as reports designed to grab headlines with bylines such as "100% increase in cocaine use among youth," when in fact the prevalence rate doubled from 1% to 2%. This is more of an example of over-interpreting results. It is accurate, but the presentation is misleading. There have been a variety of efforts over the years to address internal inconsistencies in a single data source, inconsistencies in information across two or more studies, or to combine information from several sources to create more comprehensive epidemiological data. It's important to examine the methodology of studies to ensure that data comparisons are valid. Good studies discuss their limitations carefully.

Source: Harrison 2001.

consisted of more than 16,000 active-duty military personnel throughout the world who responded to anonymous self-administered questionnaires regarding health-related behaviors, including drug and alcohol use. This is the only systematic source of data on drug use among military personnel. We will discuss this survey further, including highlights from the 2005 survey, in Chapter 7.

Individual Research Efforts

In addition to the research efforts described throughout this chapter, countless researchers from many scientific disciplines are conducting their own research on drug use. Some of this research is funded by federal agencies such as NIDA and SAMHSA, and some of it is being carried out with the assistance of state, local, and private funds. Findings from these research efforts are reported in various drug-related journals[14] as well as books on the subject.

Summary

This chapter has summarized the major sources of information on drug use and on behavior related to drug use. Similar to more general crime statistics, these data sources can generally be divided into official drug use statistics and unofficial drug use statistics. Official statistics are defined as statistics gathered as a function of day-to-day organizational procedures conducted by the government or other agencies cooperating with the government. These agencies include the police, correctional facilities, treatment facilities, hospital emergency departments, and medical examiners. Unofficial statistics are those gathered for the express purpose of identifying drug users, learning relevant information about them, and making estimates of incidence and prevalence. Three major sources of unofficial statistics are: Monitoring the Future, a national survey of 8th, 10th, 12th graders, and young adults is conducted on an annual basis; the Youth Risk Behavior Survey, which is a nationally representative biennial survey of high school students in grades 9 through 12; and the National Survey on Drug Use and Health, which is also a national survey, but of all individuals 12 and older living in a randomly drawn sample of households in the United States. Other sources of information include Pulse Check, which includes information from interviews with ethnographers, epidemiologists, police, and treatment personnel; and the Community Epidemiologists Work Group, a biannual meeting of epidemiologists who report their analyses of statistics gathered through several sources, including many of those studied here.

These sources of data provide varying and even contradictory information. There are several reasons for this. First and most importantly, they are using different sample populations with widely varying drug use experiences. A national random sample will provide very different results than emergency department or treatment samples, for example. Second, the methodologies employed also vary widely. Again, a national random sample will provide a very different profile than will a purposive sample of hard-core street addicts, which is targetted by many ethnographers. When examining any drug use data, it is very important to consider carefully both the target population and the methodology employed. Far too often, inappropriate conclusions are drawn by policy makers, practitioners, community groups, and yes, even researchers themselves because they have not carefully considered the implications of these methodological issues.

Key Terms

dark figure
epidemiology
ethnography
etiology
incidence
N, n
official statistics
prevalence
rate
unofficial statistics

Thinking Critically...

1. Why is it important to determine *rates* of drug use rather than simply reporting the number of drug users? Give some examples of how simply reporting numbers might distort or provide an inaccurate assessment of levels of drug use.

2. Examine carefully each of the four types of official drug use statistic discussed at length in this chapter. (Correctional statistics were not discussed at length.) Why do you think there are such differences in the statistics presented? Identify where these statistics are coming from. Describe specifically what they tell us about drug use. How does this understanding explain these differences?

3. The authors of your text contend that, when it comes to estimating the prevalence of drug use nation wide, unofficial statistics are far more accurate and reliable than official statistics. Based on the discussion in this chapter, why is this so?

4. During the 1990s and into the next decade, emergency room data showed cocaine, heroin, and marijuana abuse to be on the rise, whereas other data, notably treatment data, did not indicate such an increase, and perhaps even a modest decline. Based on what you know about these data sources, speculate why this might be the case.

5. Looking at unofficial data, can you speculate why the National Survey on Drug Use and Health reports that less than 10 percent of their respondents report current (past 30 day) marijuana use, while the Monitoring the Future and Youth Risk Behavior Survey both report percentages in excess of 20 percent? Response to this question requires a consideration of the methodology employed in each survey.

Learning from the Internet

1. Go to the SAMHSA website: http://www.oas.samhsa.gov/. This page contains statistics as from various sources on drug use. Research everything that you can about the nature of the statistics described there. (You can click on the specific statistics in the column on the right.) Describe, as best you can from these pages, how these statistics are collected, the populations that they are drawn from, and any other pertinent information about these statistics.

2. Now go to the Monitoring the Future website (http://www.monitoringthefuture.org/). Maneuver through the site to find the most recent data on drug use among high school students. Look for the following drugs: Any illicit drug use, Marijuana, and Cocaine. If you study the table of contents page you will see that "lifetime," "annual," and "past 30 days" statistics are provided. Report what you find for the most recent years. If you can find the "trend tables," report what you find over the past 10 years. Specifically take note of (a) the differences between

each of these drugs, and (b) the differences between the types of statistics reported (lifetime, annual, and 30-day). Explain why there are differences in both cases.

Notes

1. This is not to say that there are no victims of drug use. Families of alcoholics and drug users are victims in the sense that a spouse, parent, or child may be abusive or may drain the family's physical and emotional resources. Similarly, the person held up at gunpoint for money to buy drugs is, indeed, a victim of drug use. But this is not the sort of information that we are seeking; rather we are seeking to estimate the number of *drug users*.
2. Prevalence statistics are typically presented as percentages or as rates of the affected population. The *prevalence rate* for the United States is approximately 0.60 percent of adults.
3. Incidence figures are often reported as percentages or as rates of the total prevalence from the prior reporting year. Hence, in the example here, of 300,000 new cases from 2005 to 2015, the *incidence* of AIDS from 2005 to 2015 is 300,000, or alternatively an *incidence rate* of 30 percent from 2005 to 2015.
4. Typically, individuals are asked if they have committed any crimes within the last six months (or three months, or one year), or whether they have ever used drugs within the last three months (or six months or one year). The term *prevalence* is used to refer either to "lifetime" prevalence or to prevalence during a particular time period.
5. The FBI does not report these categories in its "Crimes Known to the Police" section for understandable reasons. These are so-called victimless crimes and are not usually reported to the police except tantamount to an arrest.
6. Correctional statistics are comprised mainly of the following: National Prisoner Statistics (NPS), Survey of Inmates in State Correctional Facilities (SISCF), Survey of Inmates in Local Jails (SILJ), Census of Jails (COJ), and Annual Survey of Jails (ASJ).
7. Prior to 2003, data were collected only from the contiguous 48 states, with sampling based on 1980 census.
8. The earlier DAWN procedures established complex criteria for inclusion as a reportable case, including age requirements (between 6 and 97), that the presenting problem must have been induced by or directly related to drug use, that the motive for taking the drug must have been for illicit psychoactive purposes, and so forth.
9. Previously, DAWN included any drugs found in the system of the deceased, but if there was no inferred intent to use any of these drugs to either to cause death, or for illegal psychoactive purposes, the case was not reported to DAWN at all.
10. The exception to this reverse trend is alcohol; however, the wording of the question changed in 1993 to clarify that a drink meant "more than a few sips." Hence, the drop in alcohol use after 1993 probably reflects the more stringent wording.
11. The 2007 surveillance survey reported prevalence statistics by cohort (Eaton et al. 2008), but their data is most frequently presented with the combined cohorts.
12. The cities in *Pulse Check* were: Atlanta, Baltimore, Boston, Chicago, Cincinnati, Cleveland, Dallas, Denver, Detroit, Houston, Los Angeles, Miami, Minneapolis/St. Paul, New York, Philadelphia, Phoenix, Pittsburgh, Portland, Sacramento, St. Louis, San Diego, San Francisco, Seattle, Tampa/St. Petersburg, and Washington, D.C.
13. The cities are: Atlanta, Baltimore, Boston, Chicago, Denver, Detroit, Honolulu, Los Angeles, Miami, Minneapolis/St. Paul, Newark, New Orleans, New York, Philadelphia,

Phoenix, St. Louis, San Diego, San Francisco, Seattle, San Antonio, Texas, and Washington, D.C.

14. Some of the leading journals in the drug and alcohol field are: *The International Journal of the Addictions*; *Journal of Drug Issues*; *Contemporary Drug Problems*; *Quarterly Journal of Studies on Alcohol*; *Drug Abuse and Alcoholism Review*; *Journal of Drug Education*; *Drugs and Society*; *Alcoholism*; *Journal of Health and Social Behavior*; *Drug and Alcohol Dependence*; *American Journal of Drug and Alcohol Abuse*; *Journal of Addictions and Offender Counseling*; and *Chemical Dependencies*.

CHAPTER **5**

Theoretical Explanations for Drug Use and Addiction

This chapter examines various scientific theories that have been offered for drug use and addiction. Simply stated, a **scientific theory** is an explanation for the relationship between two or more phenomena written in such a way that it can be falsified with empirical evidence. Empirical evidence is that which is observed: either through one of the five natural senses—touch, smell, sight, hearing, or taste—or with the use of special instruments such as microscopes, telescopes, seismographs, or survey questionnaires. When sociologists and other social scientists attempt to explain drug use and addiction, they desire to construct theories that are scientific in nature. Some theories ultimately prove to be better than others in that empirical testing tends to support the explanation contained in these theories. A theory that is not supported by the evidence is no less scientific because its hypotheses are not supported. Indeed, that such a theory is not supported by research is evidence that it is scientific! Failure to find support may be because it does not, in fact, explain the evidence, or it may derive from problems with the data, such as with its measurement. None of these problems alone renders a theory unscientific. The theories that are discussed in this chapter ostensibly meet the test for being scientific in nature.

One may wonder why it is important to develop theories in the first place. The answer is quite simple, really: without theory, we would have nothing more than a series of descriptions of things observed. We would not know *why* these things exist as they do, and explaining "Why?" or "How?" is the essence of theory. If it is not known why or how events occur as they do, we would not be able to predict their occurring in the future. Moreover, understanding why something occurs as it does provides a basis for taking preventive action. If we know why a group of people abuse drugs, social and governmental policy can be appropriately designed to reduce the occurrence of abuse.

Usually, we are not interested in developing theories merely for the sake of explaining, though fundamental explanation is the essential role of the basic sciences. Those of us who are basic or "pure" scientists are pleased to let our work end there. We know, however, that there are greater rewards of good theory. When we theorize well, and when those theoretical explanations are supported repeatedly by empirical data, we offer a solid foundation for both prediction and intervention efforts. Without theory, such efforts would be random and likely not particularly effective.

Earlier, the importance of the "Why?" and "How?" aspects were discussed. Before talking about specific theories, it is necessary to clarify the "What?" as well. The phenomena of drug use, abuse, and addiction are complex and involve different behaviors and dynamics, as discussed in Chapter 1. Factors related to first-time use, for example, are likely quite different than the reasons that one goes on to become addicted to these substances. Moreover, factors involved in initial experimentation with drugs are likely to be very different than factors leading to relapse. There is an extensive literature on each of these aspects of drug use. Table 5.1 presents a framework for organizing theories of drug use. You will also notice that there are various levels of explanation for drug use and addiction: nature theories, biological theories, psychological theories, and sociological theories. The discussion in this chapter is organized around this typology. Some of these approaches tend to be more focused on initiation into drug use, while other levels of explanation tend to focus on addiction. Some biological and sociological theories also tackle the question of why rates of drug use vary for different segments of the population, or how drug use is distributed in our society, a pursuit known as drug epidemiology (discussed in Chapter 6). Theoretical understanding of the phenomena of drug use and addiction requires an awareness of the concepts, strengths, and weaknesses of multiple paradigms because at the present, no one theory is sufficient.

Table 5.1. A taxonomy of theories of drug use.

Theoretical level	Behavior to be explained	
	Onset of use	Addiction
Nature	Weil	—
Biological	—	Neurochemical explanations Biogenetic explanations
Psychological	Psychoanalytic theories Personality theories	Psychoanalytic theories Personality theories Behavioral theories
Sociological	Differential association theory Differential reinforcement theory Becker's learning rheory Social control theory Self control theory Strain theory	Differential reinforcement theory Becker's learning theory Winick's integrated theory Cultural deviance theory Labeliing theory

Source: Adapted from Ritz and Kuhar, 1993, p. 52.

Nature Theories

Nature theories suggest that initial drug use and drug addiction result from an intrinsic character of human nature itself. Discussions grounded in human nature are often controversial and unpopular in academic circles. They are argued by many to be less scientific than biological, psychological, or sociological theories because *human nature* is seen as slippery to conceptualize and hence difficult to put to empirical test. Nature theories should be distinguished from biological theories, which focus on how the biological features of individuals who become addicted are different than those of individuals who do not become addicted. Nature theories, by contrast, posit that drug use and addiction are universal human characteristics (Mosher and Atkins 2007).

The earliest nature theories had strong moral overtones. The addict was seen as weak-willed and unable to control his or her impulses, implying a sense of moral inferiority on the part of the addict. These early ideas of drug addiction blended moral judgments of drugs, drug use, and drug users with biology and disease, providing a vivid depiction of the perils of addiction. More recent nature theories do not impose a moral evaluation on drug use or human nature, or at least not a *negative* moral evaluation.

DRUGS AND EVERYDAY LIFE

Hunting Mushrooms

The following excerpt from an article published in the *Journal of Psychedelic Drugs* by Andrew Weil illustrates an important theme of nature theories in explaining drug use: *drugs are a means of altering our consciousness*, a drive which, according to Weil and others, is part of our very nature. It matters little what type of drug that it is; indeed, there are many ways in which people alter their consciousness without the use of drugs at all—through sex, gambling, acts of risk and daring, among others. According to nature theorists, all of these activities, including the use of psychoactive drugs, is a response to this basic human drive to alter our consciousness.

Gradually I became aware of a strange sensation in my stomach, a sort of buzzing vibration that grew slowly in intensity. It was not at all unpleasant, and I knew at once it was the mushrooms. Over the next ten minutes this unusual feeling became stronger, filling my abdomen. Then it began to invade the rest of my body, pushing outward through the muscles to the extremities. I was distinctly aware of a subtle but powerful energy vibrating through the musculature of my whole body. It made me feel warm and strong. As it reached my head, my senses sharpened, and I found myself admiring qualities of the wet pasture I had ignored until then. The green of the grass was of glowing intensity, highlighted by tones of brown and red. The smell of the earth and rain was overpowering. I had no desire to move. If the ground had been dry, I would have stretched out and rolled on the grass.

Our little group slowly drew together. Obviously, we were all feeling the effects of the mushrooms. We moved slowly and gracefully, swinging our arms and laughing at each other. The laughter seemed to bubble up from inside, and the sound of it echoed inside my chest. I was also very conscious of the taste of mushrooms. It was as strong as if fresh in my mouth but was diffused through my whole body. I felt the taste in my muscles.

The rain picked up in intensity. Clearly we could not stay out in the field much longer. It was late afternoon and turning colder. Slowly we wended our way out of the pasture, across the fence, and up a steep bank to the car. I curled up in a corner of the back seat as we started to move. It was an hours drive south along the coast to Greg and Susan's house.

The mushroom energy continued to course around my body. And now it began to pull me away from ordinary awareness into a realm that bordered on sleep but was not sleep. It was an effort to maintain awareness of the car and my fellow passengers, let alone the scenery outside. Instead, I closed my eyes and began to see visions that were somewhere between images in the mind's eye and actual movies projected on the inside of my eyelids. At first there were shadowy patterns that tended to multiply themselves in infinite regressions, but these soon resolved themselves into very clear images of mushrooms. The mushrooms that appeared to me were of one type, not Liberty Caps. They grew in clustered bunches, the stipes arising from a common point, and lacked the Liberty Cap's distinct peak. They also seemed fleshier and bigger. I had never seen them before. Bunches of these visionary mushrooms appeared out of nowhere, springing up at odd angles, swirling and receding. They occupied my attention completely.

"Are you all right?" someone in the front seat asked.

"Yes, I'm seeing mushrooms." I opened my eyes for a moment, surprised by the brightness of the outside light. I closed them

DRUGS AND EVERYDAY LIFE (continued)

quickly and was instantly back in the comfortable night world of visions. I felt sorry for the driver and other front-seat riders who were attending to the road and could not watch the interior show.

We arrived at the house without difficulty just as it was growing dark.

"Are you still seeing mushrooms?" Greg asked me.

I closed my eyes to make sure. "Yes, they're still there."

"A number of people who eat these things see mushrooms," Greg said.

"The ones I'm seeing aren't the ones we ate. I wonder if I'll ever meet up with them."

I told Greg and Susan that Liberty Caps more than lived up to my expectations and thanked them for introducing me to them. Hallowe'en seemed an especially fitting day on which to meet them.

Source: Andrew Weil, "Letters from Andrew Weil: Mushroom Hunting in Oregon 1: One Hundred Pounds of Chanterelles" *Journal of Psychedelic Drugs* 7, 1 (1975), pp. 97–98. Copyright Haight Ashbury Publications, San Francisco, CA. www.hajp.com. Used with Permission.

Andrew Weil, a physician and proponent of alternative medicine, suggests that the desire to alter consciousness is universal: "It is my belief that the desire to alter consciousness periodically is an innate, normal drive analogous to hunger or the sexual drive" (1986, 19). Chemical agents are, of course only one route to altered consciousness; young children, for example, experience such a state when they spin themselves into dizziness. Altered states are also reported by athletes (e.g., seeking a "runner's high") and adventure seekers as a motivation to engage in otherwise painful or risky behavior (Mosher and Atkins 2007). The use of chemical substances is, however, a very common and popular route to altered consciousness. Weil points out that in every known culture (with the exception of Eskimo culture), there are indigenously grown intoxicants and established rituals for using them.

Drug use is, according to Weil, an expression of the universal drive to achieve altered states of consciousness. The goodness or badness of this drive might be questioned, but it is universal. The question that remains is, Why does this drive lead to different forms of consciousness-altering behavior? For some individuals it involves drugs. Others may engage sexual activities or other behaviors that are viewed as adventuresome. Weil's argument about altered states of consciousness cannot explain why this drive is expressed in different ways. Weil's theory is grounded in the idea that, because the desire for an altered state of consciousness is universal, we must not presume that it is bad, though certain means to attain it involve excessive risk to the individual and to others and therefore may be considered behaviorally undesirable. For Weil, human nature does not excuse the choosing of harmful or threatening variations of consciousness alteration.

Biological Theories

Biological theories suggest that people become addicted to chemical substances because of particular biological predispositions. Nineteenth-century theories of addiction used biological disease metaphors in attempts to explain drug addiction. These theories were a product of their time. Germ theory had ascended to a position of dominance in American medicine. Like other maladies, addiction was seen as a disease that was communicable. An underlying belief was that drugs are toxins that accumulate in the body and damage or destroy bodily organs and functions, thereby resulting in addiction and a loss of behavioral control. Detoxification strategies emerged in response to this understanding, for addiction to alcohol and other drugs. Early biological theorizing vaguely defined the biological character of addiction, preferring the power of rhetoric to systematic observation.

Since then, medical researchers and others have attempted to refine our understanding of the biological bases of addiction. Contemporary explanations focusing on biological characteristics can be broadly classified as either neurochemical or genetic in nature.

Neurochemical Explanations

The specific nature of neurochemical explanations varies with the type of drug in question. Each one identifies neurotransmission—particularly in the mesolimbic dopamine system—as the biological source of addiction (Erickson 2007). Sunderwirth defines neurotransmission as "the mechanism by which signals or impulses are sent from one nerve cell (neuron) to the other" (1985, 12). The manner in which various drugs affect the neurotransmission process will be discussed throughout this section.

The work of Dole and Nyswander provided a major breakthrough in understanding biological aspects of opiate addiction. In 1963, they began treating heroin addicts with methadone, a synthetic narcotic. Within two years' time, they noted a considerable drop in the level of heroin use and in the criminality of addicts under their care. This treatment was predicated on the observation that heroin addicts develop a tolerance for heroin, and that if given methadone, an oral medication much longer lasting than heroin, the felt need for heroin would not be present (Dole et al. 1968). In the decades since Dole and Nyswander's groundbreaking work, other researchers have provided additional insight to the instrumental role that neurotransmitters play in addictions to various types of drugs.

In the case of narcotics, protein peptides were discovered in the brain that serve as transmission agents for electrical messages regarding pain, stress, and mood from one brain cell to another (Fishbein and Pease 1990; Terenius 1993). The remarkable discovery that provided clues to the neurological basis of addiction is that these peptides are similar in chemical structure to opiate drugs. These peptides have thus earned the name *endorphins*, short for "endogenous morphine." Because of the affinity between endorphin and opiate drugs, the receptor sites in the brain treat these chemicals as though they are the endogenous peptide endorphin. For this reason, after a period of time, the narcotics addict feels merely normal after using heroin unless he or she takes an unusually large dose. Also, it is for this reason that addicts experience physiological withdrawal symptoms. There is a period of time after the cessation of heroin use before the brain can produce endorphins to send to receptor cells. The addict experiences muscle cramps, diarrhea, profuse sweating, and other unpleasant symptoms during this interim period when there is a lack of either external or internal chemical neurotransmitters; it may last from several hours to several days, depending on the level of tolerance that one has developed.

Neurochemical explanations for addictions to other drugs are similar, though the specific mechanisms vary. Stimulants, particularly cocaine and the amphetamines, are believed to affect the neurotransmitter dopamine as well as norepinephrine and serotonin. These drugs do not imitate dopamine, as narcotics imitate endorphin, but rather block the reabsorption of dopamine by the sender cell. Since dopamine triggers reward mechanisms in the brain, the user experiences an intense high when cocaine blocks its reabsorption. Furthermore, researchers have also discovered that when a chronic cocaine user ceases using the drug, withdrawal symptoms occur because the brain has been getting the message that there is too much dopamine being released in the first place. The result is depression and under-arousal during periods of withdrawal. Only recently has this phenomenon come to be understood. Prior to the 1980s, it was believed that cocaine did not produce physical dependence, and that addiction to cocaine was purely psychological. The discovery of these mechanisms has added a new dimension to our understanding of cocaine addiction (Fishbein and Pease 1990; Gawin 1991). However, it is important to note that this research does not answer why some people are more prone to addiction than are others. Koob and Le Moal (2008) correctly point out that the interactions among biological, psychological, and social factors is complex. Our search for the answer to this question begins by looking at biogenetic explanations for addiction.

Biogenetic Explanations

Most research focusing on genetic predisposition to drug abuse and addiction has focused on alcohol, though some research shows a link between genetics and tobacco use (de Fiebre and Collins 2002). Unlike neurochemical theories, which have isolated specific biological mechanisms that cause dependency symptoms, the genetic linkage is based largely on epidemiological studies. Four broad types of epidemiological studies assess the genetic linkage to alcoholism: studies of animals, family patterns, twins, and adoptees.

Animal Studies. Studies conducted on animals (mostly rats) have shown that it is possible to breed strains that have a decided preference for alcohol over water when given a choice (Erickson 2007). In most of these studies, rats are given free access to food, alcohol, and water. Typically, rats preferring alcohol over water are then bred together, as are rats preferring water over alcohol. Results show that after several generations, the preference for alcohol is even greater in the alcohol-preference breed and even lower in the water-preference breed (Logue 1986). Schuckit (1983) has further noted that some strains of rats consume as much as 80 percent of their fluid intake in the form of alcohol, whereas other strains preferred water almost exclusively.

Family Pattern Studies. Schuckit (1985) noted that a familial linkage to alcoholism has been documented for more than a century. There appears to be a direct and positive relationship between the risk for becoming alcoholic and the number of alcoholic family members, as well as for the genetic closeness of these family members. Cotton (1979) has observed that direct offspring of alcoholics tend to be three to five times more likely to become alcoholic than offspring of nonalcoholics. Schuckit's research (1985) suggests that individuals in families with a history of alcoholism tend to react less intensely to moderate doses of ethanol than do individuals in the lower-risk, nonalcoholic family group. Schuckit proposes that this response may render individuals in high-risk families less capable of discerning appropriate boundaries to drinking behavior.

Twin Studies. Because of the difficulty in separating genetic from environmental influences in family studies, researchers have examined alcoholism patterns among twins, comparing monozygote (MZ) twins with dizygote (DZ) twins. MZ twins, more commonly known as identical twins, are those who share 100 percent of their genetic material, as they split after an egg has been fertilized. DZ twins, or fraternal twins, are the result of separate eggs, and hence are as different genetically as non-twin siblings. Theoretically, if there is a genetic basis for alcoholism, similarity of symptoms should be much more evident in MZ twins than in DZ twins. Studies of twins yield somewhat mixed results, but a genetic factor is suggested. Rates of alcoholism are much more similar among MZ twins than among DZ twins, a finding that is particularly consistent for men (Sher 1991). Sher also reports that other selected aspects of alcoholic behavior, such as willingness to drive drunk, general attitudes about alcohol, and binge drinking may also have a genetic link.

Adoption Studies. Perhaps the strongest evidence for a genetic link to alcoholism comes from research among adoptees that has been conducted most comprehensively in Scandinavia. These studies examine individuals with alcoholic biological parents who have been adopted by nonalcoholic parents at or shortly after birth. Alcoholism rates for these individuals are compared with those adoptees born to and living with nonalcoholic parents. The results are remarkably consistent, showing a much higher likelihood of alcoholism among those children born to alcoholic parents, even though they are raised by nonalcoholic parents. Again, the genetic influence seems to be more consistently present among males (Schuckit 1983; Sher 1991).

In Search of a Cause. Epidemiological studies provide convincing evidence for a genetic influence on alcoholism. In fact, Erickson (2007, 83) contends that

60 percent of the variance in the risk for alcoholism is attributed to genetic factors. There are, however, three questions that remain to be answered by these studies. First, Can we generalize from these studies of alcoholics to other types of drug addicts? Presently, this question remains unanswered in part because research findings are contradictory; see Hesselbrock, Hesselbrock, and Epstein (1999) and Uhl and colleagues (2008) for differing accounts. Second, These studies do not explain all of the variation, so what other factors contribute to alcoholism? These environmental factors will be taken up in our discussion of psychological and sociological theories of addiction.

The third question not answered by these epidemiological studies is, What is the biogenetic mechanism that causes a predisposition to alcoholism? Research suggests several possible mechanisms, though conclusive linkages have yet to be established (Erickson 2007; Schukit 1983). Uhl et al. (2008) suggest that up to 95 genes play a role. Some studies suggest that the rate of absorption and metabolism of ethanol (alcohol) may be under genetic control. One study by Vesell (1975) suggests that the rate of metabolism for ethanol is more similar between MZ twins than between DZ twins. Other studies suggest a genetically influenced difference in central nervous system sensitivity to alcohol. If so, susceptibility to the neurotransmitter factors discussed above may itself have a genetic basis. Still other research points to the possibility of an inherited vulnerability to the consequences of chronic alcohol use, such as cirrhosis of the liver. Finally, there may be a link between certain inherited personality traits and/or psychiatric disorders and the risk for alcoholism (Schuckit 1983). These factors are generally identified and examined by psychologists.

Psychological Theories

Psychological theories of drug use and addiction, like biological theories, focus on the individual user and the characteristics of that individual that somehow differentiate him or her from nonusers. Unlike biological theories, however, which identify the neurochemical and genetic features of drug addicts that predispose them to substance abuse, psychological theories look at the nature and quality of individual experiences that might make one susceptible to drug use, abuse, or addiction, including how these experiences interact with biological and socio-environmental variables. There are three broad types of psychological explanations: psychoanalytic explanations, personality theories, and behavioral theories.

Psychoanalytic Explanations
Psychoanalytic theories comprise a range of explanations that identify the cause of abuse and addiction to be abnormal personality development or adjustment. Addiction is seen as a sickness or pathology, the result of an unhealthy development process often traced to early childhood experiences. Many of these explanations draw upon Sigmund Freud's general theory of human development. Each stage of development poses its own challenges and needs to the developing youngster,

theorizes Freud. Failure to meet the challenges or the needs of the individual may result in an emotional "fixation," meaning that the individual does not adequately develop emotionally beyond that point. In the search for "compensatory gratification" to fill the emotional void left by unfilled needs and unmet challenges, the individual may engage in certain forms of drug use or other deviant behavior. The high or relief sought through the drug is a surrogate ideal, a substitute value, a chemical mythology, that normally would be supplied by the internal sense of meaning, goal directedness, and value orientation (Wurmser 1981, 147–148). Raskin, Petty, and Warren (1957) suggest that the user is one who is not able to make the necessary adjustments required in normal daily living. Drug abuse is a mechanism for alleviating the frustrations and stress resulting from the inability to adjust to these conflicting demands. Psychoanalytic explanations are not especially influential in contemporary theorizing about drugs (Hesselbrock et al. 1999). In a recent review of current psychoanalytic perspectives, Morgenstern and Leeds (1993) suggest that its utility has been limited because substance use is viewed as secondary in relation to psychoanalytic concepts and processes, and because both physiological and social forces are often ignored.

Personality Theories

Some have suggested that those who use or abuse drugs have personalities that are somehow different from those of nonabusers. Jessor defines personality as "that set of relatively enduring psychological attributes that characterize a person and constitute the dimensions of individual differences, including values, attitudes, needs, beliefs, expectations, moral orientations, and other such essentially sociocognitive variables" (1979, 343). These personality traits are usually phrased in evaluative and negative terms. Some of the earliest studies suggested that addicts tended to have psychopathic or sociopathic personalities (Kolb 1925), now usually referred to as *antisocial personality disorders*. Other psychologists suggested that those who abused drugs or who became dependent on them suffered from an **addictive personality** or addiction-prone personality. This idea is rooted largely in a disease model, which sees addiction as a pathology caused by some inadequacy in the individual. Isidor Chein and his colleagues (1964) identified the inadequate personality as a causative factor. They suggest that a lack of goals, interests, and emotional expression predisposes one to drug use and addiction.

Although the idea of an addictive personality remains popular among the general public and among some sectors of the treatment community (Nakken 1988), it is for the most part unsupported (de Wit 2005). Part of the reason that it has fallen from favor as an explanation for addiction is that the early empirical research supporting this concept was quite seriously flawed (Gendreau and Gendreau 1970; Platt and Labate 1976). Moreover, it has become increasingly apparent that the search for a single personality type to explain addiction has not been productive. Psychologists have, rather, identified several personality characteristics that appear to predispose an individual to addiction. These variables include low self-esteem, an inability to trust, and a higher than normal need for stimulation and sensation seeking (Platt and Labate 1976; Cox 1985). Similarly, in a recent review, de Wit suggests that traits related to substance abuse include factors related to sociability, reward, and well-being; of particular importance is recognition of how neurobiological and genetic factors influence personality, particularly the dopamine function (2005, 258–260).

A review of the literature regarding personality characteristics of marijuana users led Jerome Jaffe (1979) to three generalizations that are consistent with a multicharacteristic understanding of personality variables. First, Jaffe suggests that marijuana users tend to score high on scales of nonconventionality. Factors related to nonconventionality include a sense of alienation, critical beliefs about the larger society, and lower rates of religiosity. Second, Jaffe concludes that marijuana users are open to new experiences. They are more spontaneous in nature and receptive to uncertainty and change. Third, marijuana users manifest lower rates of conventional achievement value and achievement satisfaction. Jaffe is careful to point out that these personality characteristics may be history or culture bound.

Personality correlates continue to be examined as predisposing factors in substance abuse, but it is often difficult to distinguish the personality attributes from the behaviors they are attempting to explain. For example, to suggest that sensation-seeking individuals are more likely to abuse drugs seems hardly explanatory. Drug-using behavior *is* sensation seeking, in that one of the reasons people use alcohol and drugs is to experience pleasure or to alleviate discomfort. Similarly, the fact that marijuana users score higher in nonconventionality should hardly be surprising since the use of marijuana, though common, is itself an unconventional behavior. These explanations of addiction frequently identify causes that are attributed to personality features, but perilously close to the very behavior they purport to explain. We call such explanations *tautologies*,[1] a methodological dilemma that sociologists work hard to avoid when theorizing. However, the role of personality attributes should not be discounted. In some ways, personality serves as a bridge of sorts in the complex interaction between biological and social factors associated with alcohol and drug use.

Behavioral Theories

The foundation for behavioral theory was established with the work of the Russian physiologist Ivan Pavlov, who discovered that dogs could be conditioned to salivate at the sound of a bell because the animal made an association between the bell and food when both were presented simultaneously. The pairing of a conditioned stimulus such as a bell, a location, or some contextual factor with an unconditioned stimulus such as alcohol or drugs is referred to as **classical conditioning**. Furthermore, individuals are likely to engage in behaviors that are positively rewarded and avoid those that are produce negative consequences, an idea known as **operant conditioning** (Hesselbrock et al. 1999). Albert Bandura (1969) further extended the notion of operant conditioning by suggesting that individuals model their behavior after significant other people whose opinion and relationship they value. As will be discussed later, this concept is key to understanding influence of social factors upon individuals.

Psychologists have applied principles of behavioral theory to drug use and addiction. For example, McAuliffe (1975) identifies three reinforcing effects of opiates: euphoria, cessation of withdrawal effects, and related analgesic effects. Furthermore, Crowley (1981) distinguishes between primary reinforcers and secondary reinforcers. Primary reinforcers are those objects or situations that are directly pleasurable, such as food or sexual activity. Certain kinds of drug use, Crowley states, are primary reinforcers in that these drugs produce an intrinsically pleasurable experience. Correia (2005) is correct in suggesting that drug use is a very efficient way to experience pleasure. Secondary reinforcers, on the other hand, are those objects or situations that are pleasurable because of the associations that people make with them—a classical and/or operant conditioning response. Just as eating a fine meal or having sex can be pleasurable in and of itself, the context in which these activities occur also plays a role (Correia 2005). For example, Crowley (1981) describes how smoking dried banana peel became a fad in some circles for its presumed hallucinogenic effect. Banana peel has no such primary effect, but the association made between smoking the peel and the psychedelic music, peer group enjoyment, and other aspects of the "banana grass" subculture reinforced the behavior.

Cognitive behavioral theories also recognize the role of operant conditioning in producing a behavioral response when certain stimuli are present. However, these theories explicitly recognize that response to stimuli is not automatic. Rather, when stimuli are presented, a cognitive (thought) process begins to unfold that, in turn, results in behavior. Key to this process is the recognition and evaluation of the potential costs and benefits associated with a particular behavior (Hesselbrock et al. 1999).

The classic cognitive theory of addiction was developed by sociologist Alfred Lindesmith and presented in an article entitled "A Sociological Theory of Addiction" (1938), and in fact this was and remains perhaps the best articulation of a cognitive behavioral framework for understanding addiction. He suggested that addiction to narcotics cannot be accounted for by positive reinforcements of euphoria, for there are many individuals who have used narcotics and experienced the euphoric effects, but have not become addicted. Moreover, addiction cannot be accounted for merely by the absence of withdrawal distress that results from self-medication of narcotics during times of withdrawal. According to Lindesmith, only when a cognitive connection is made between the use of narcotics and the alleviation of withdrawal symptoms does the felt need for the drug arise. That is, only when the would-be addict comes to recognize the effect of narcotics in relieving withdrawal does that individual come to feel a need for the drug. This cognitive recognition is the necessary condition for addiction to develop, according to Lindesmith.

The behavioral theories are similar in many ways to some of the sociological theories discussed in the following section. As we shall see, some of the sociological theories, particularly those commonly known as *social learning theories*, draw many of their ideas from the work of the behaviorists.

Sociological Theories

General sociological theories of drug use and abuse are most often derived from categories of theory originally created to explain crime and delinquency. These theories include: social process theories, social structural theories, and societal reaction theories. Each of these theoretical approaches attempts to answer different theoretical questions. All of them, however, focus explicitly on the social environment of the user, the hallmark of sociological theory. Keep in mind our Chapter 1 discussion on how sociologists approach the study of drugs.

Social Process Theories

Social process theories tend to be social-psychological or microsociological in nature. That is, these theories seek to explain the processes by which social norms, expectations, values, and other social and cultural forces influence an individual's behavior. Social process theories are an important link between psychological theories (particularly behavioral theories) and social structural theories, which are addressed in the next section. There are two primary types of social process theories, social learning theories and social control theories, both of which are relevant to the understanding of drug use and addiction.

Social Learning Theories

Social learning theories begin with the assumption that individuals are not born to be drug users but rather acquire the penchants, values, and skills to do so through a process of socialization. The first major theoretical statement from a social learning perspective was Edwin Sutherland's differential association theory (1939). In some respects, Sutherland's theory is quite simple. It proposes that criminal behavior is learned in association with others who positively value such behavior. Adapted for the study of drug users, his argument is that individuals become involved in a drug culture by associating with others who characterize drug behavior in positive terms. Sutherland further recognizes that our relationships with people vary in *frequency* of interaction, *duration* of those interactions, the *priority* or importance of those relationships, and the *intensity* with which we interact. Hence, those people whom we highly admire and with whom we interact frequently, over a long period of time, and/or intensely will have a much greater impact on our proclivity to become drug involved than less significant relationships involving less frequent and less intense involvement.

Sutherland's theory has been extended by the work of Ronald Akers (1969). Akers, in developing the most widely utilized sociological-criminological perspective of social learning, extended Sutherland's work by elaborating the specific mechanism through which learning occurs, **differential reinforcement**. Akers suggests that behavior is reinforced through reward and punishment. The individuals and groups with whom we interact control the reinforcement we receive. Hence, if we associate primarily with law-abiding or non-drug-using people, law-abiding behavior will be reinforced.

In his 1992 theoretical work on the sociology of drug use, Akers suggests that initially, there is a social reinforcement for drug use by one's peers: "In the initiation of drug use, exposure to definitions favorable to drugs and differential association with other users who provide models and social reinforcement for use are critical" (1992, 97). Akers goes on to say that "[m]any who are exposed to deviant subcultures define drugs in positive terms from the beginning or are exposed to drug-tolerant attitudes" (99). However, reinforcement comes not only from social peers; the drugs themselves often provide an intrinsic reinforcement to the users. Akers suggests that if the initial drug effects are pleasant, drug use is positively reinforced, and it is more likely that use will continue than if the results are unpleasant. Akers also recognizes that once a person becomes addicted, particularly to opiates and other physiologically addicting substances, the motive for continued use may be a negative reinforcement, a way of avoiding the pain of not having the drug. Although the inherent reinforcing effects of the drugs are recognized, Akers' general theory is profoundly social in nature. The key to understanding why some people begin to and continue to use drugs lies in the nature of the reinforcements provided by their social groups and significant others.

Another social learning explanation that has been developed especially for understanding drug-using behavior has been offered by Howard Becker (1963, 1967). Becker (1963) argues that the user who experiments with marijuana does not automatically experience the effects of the drug. Rather, the user must engage in a learning process to experience the positive effects of the drug. There are several components to this learning. First, the novice user must learn the technique of using the drug. The marijuana user must learn to inhale deeply, and to hold the smoke in the lungs for a period of time. The correct technique for smoking is usually learned in the context of marijuana-smoking peers. A similar learning process is reported by narcotics users. They must learn how to "cook" (prepare) the heroin, to "tie up" (prepare their veins), and to insert the needle through the wall of the vein without going all the way through the other wall (Faupel 1991).

It is not enough to learn the technique for smoking (or shooting) if one is going to have a "successful" drug experience, one must also learn to perceive the effects of these drugs. Drugs may produce certain physiological symptoms, but if these symptoms are not recognized as being caused by the drug, the user will not experience it as a high. That is, the subjective effects of the drugs may be perceived as sleepiness or dizziness or a host of other experiences, but not as a high. One of the functions of the drug-using subculture is to normalize these experiences: the user is told that this is a normal experience to be expected when using this drug. These associates thus define the experience as a normal result of using the drug. Moreover, others define these subjective states as pleasurable. Lacking such an interpretation, the novice user

Drugs: Myths and Reality

Becoming a Heroin User

Charles Faupel, in his book *Shooting Dope*, identifies drug availability as a critical determinant of one's level of involvement as a heroin addict. The following excerpt from that book highlights the importance of learning how to self-inject as a factor in drug availability and the process that this learning entails:

There is one final avenue to increased availability that was essential to the transition to the stable-addict phase among the participants in this study, namely, learning the skills and techniques required for self-injection. Almost without exception participants reported dramatic increases in their heroin consumption once they had learned to "spike" themselves. As Gloria recalled, "It wasn't hard for me to learn to spike my own arm—so he [a friend] didn't have to do it anymore. I did it myself....I went on and on, and it got to be so big that it got to the point I wasn't selling, I was just using."

While Gloria mastered self-injection with relative ease, this was not the case for many of the respondents. Some of them had an aversion to needles that had to be overcome. Moreover, it was necessary to learn to "tie up" to expose a vein. Many addicts initially found it difficult to control *rolling* (moving) veins; and having done that, to know at what depth to insert the syringe to avoid extending the needle through both walls of the vein. These addicts also had to learn what mixtures of water to add to the powdered heroin, how long to cook the heroin, and how to draw the mixture into the syringe, avoiding air bubbles and straining impurities. All of this is a complex process, and most users do not become adept at it without considerable practice.

Learning to self-inject is an important milestone in an addict's career because it signifies an independence from older, more experienced addicts and gives users increased stature and respect in the subculture. Little Italy summarized how this rite of passage affected his relationships: "They came back, fixed me up with a shot. I hit. I was hitting myself, man. And they were smiling, 'Oh Man, you know how to hit yourself too now, huh?' So I done graduated. I'm one of the big boys now."

Source: Charles E. Faupel, *Shooting Dope: Career Patterns of Hard-Core Heroin Users*. Gainesville, FL: University of Florida Press, 1991, pp. 69–70. Reprinted with permission of the University Press of Florida.

may well decide that this is not a pleasant experience, and he or she will not care to repeat it. Many initial experiences with drugs, ranging from alcohol and marijuana to heroin, are often unpleasant and uncomfortable.

Faupel (1991) reports that veteran heroin users, reflecting upon their initiation into heroin use, would recall gut-wrenching nausea that would be met with smiles of understanding from their friends. Yet in the words of one female addict, "the more I puked, the higher I got." While intrinsically a negative experience by almost any standard, these experiences were redefined for the beginning user as something to be appreciated and enjoyed. Becker's learning theory, in sum, suggests that if one is to continue substance use of any type beyond an initial experimental level, he or she must literally learn to get high. This learning occurs in a social context, typically among more experienced users who are mentors of sorts in this educational process.

Social Control Theories

Social control theories begin with a fundamentally different premise than do learning theories. According to the social control perspective, human beings are inherently hedonistic and do not need to learn the motives and predispositions to engage in drug use and criminal behavior. In contrast to many theories that seek to answer the general question of "Why?" in regard to behaviors, control theory turns this question on its head, instead asking "Why not?" That is, Why is it that persons choose *not* to become involved in delinquent and criminal activities? Generally speaking, this perspective suggests the answer lies in the development of a social bond to conventional society.

The most concise statement representing control theory comes from Travis Hirschi (1969). He identifies four elements to this social bond:

- *Attachment*, the emotional bonds developed with others who represent conventional values and authority
- *Commitment*, the investment of time, effort, and other resources into conventional lines of activity
- *Involvement*, filling up one's time with conventional activities such as sports or other after-school activities, so that there is little time for illegal activities
- *Belief*, the cognitive affirmation of conventional values and morality.

Hirschi suggests that these elements of the social bond provide certain stakes or interests in conformity. Nonconforming behavior jeopardizes the attachments that one has developed with caring adults or the payoff for the investments involved in commitment. Similarly, behavior that violates one's belief in the integrity of the moral order produces dissonance. However, when one or more of these bonds are lacking or weak, the individual has less at stake and is therefore at higher risk for delinquency, drug use, or other forms of antisocial behavior.

Ironically, whereas control theory has found considerable support for other types of delinquent behavior (Vold et al. 2002), the theory is not particularly effective in explaining drug use. One study by Burkett and Warren (1987) does find indirect support for the theory. Examining both religiosity (a measure of religious commitment) and peer associations together, Burkett and Warren found that religiosity does not have a direct impact on marijuana use, but it did have an impact on the types of peers with whom one associated. Peer associations (a social learning variable) then have a direct impact on the level of marijuana use.[2] When it is operative, it appears that social control variables have their greatest impact in the choice of friends with whom one associates. This is, of course, an important contribution and should not be minimized, for as these studies and others in the tradition of learning theory make convincingly clear, friendship patterns have a powerful effect on the likelihood of drug use.

Hirschi later elaborated social control theory in a revision known as *self-control theory* (Gottfredson and Hirschi 1990). Vold and his colleagues (2002) contend that self-control theory is an abandonment of social control theory. However, a careful examination of the theory, suggests this contention may be an overstatement. Self-control has been described as a "process through which an individual becomes the principal agent in guiding, directing, and regulating those features of behavior that might lead to desired positive consequences) (Goldfried and Merbaum 1973, 11). Hirschi is even more specific: self control is simply the ability to exercise restraint when long-term costs are greater than short term benefits. In fact, "social control and self-control are the same thing" (Hirschi 2004, 543). To understand this apparent contradiction, one must remember that, according to Gottfredson and Hirschi, self-control is developed through the process of socialization, particularly via the ability of parents to monitor the child's behavior and to recognize and punish misbehavior consistently when it occurs. This point is clarified (ironically) by Vold and his colleagues (2002), who suggest that self-control results when external controls are internalized during socialization.

Grasmick, Tittle, Bursik, and Arneklev (1993) provide a widely used measure of self-control that consists of the following elements: *impulsivity*, a here-and-now attitude; a tendency to engage in *risk-seeking* or exciting behavior; a tendency to *prefer simple tasks*, which allows for easier gratification; a *preference for physical tasks*; a *low tolerance for frustration*; and a tendency to be *self-centered*, insensitive to the feelings and needs of others. This index has been widely used in empirical studies that test the theory. However, Marcus (2004) points out that if self-control is a unidimensional characteristic or construct, as claimed by Gottfredson and Hirschi (1990), then the apparent incongruence between the theory and its conceptualization is a serious issue. Beginning with *A General Theory of Crime* and beyond, these authors have viewed self-control as a unidimensional characteristic, but at the same time, they suggest that its components are keys to understanding the weighing of costs versus benefits of particular acts. Hirschi suggests that perhaps the best conceptualization of self-control is as "a count of the number of different acts with long-term negative consequences committed by the individual in a specified period of time—the fewer the better" (2004, 542). Despite much research examining the utility of this perspective, little work has focused specifically on alcohol or drug use per se. This development is somewhat surprising, since in the original text, Gottfredson and Hirschi (1990) suggest that tobacco, alcohol, and drug use are excellent examples of acts (legal and illegal) where short-term benefits take precedence over long-term consequences.

Subcultural Recruitment and Socialization: An Integrated Perspective

Erich Goode (1970, 1999) and Bruce Johnson (1973) find that young people who smoke marijuana tend to share a number of common characteristics. They tend to be less religious than nonsmokers, more sexually permissive, and more likely to hold left-leaning political views. These common characteristics, according to Goode, provide a basis for interaction and mutual attraction. Among potential drug users is a selective recruitment process that draws these individuals together into a common network and subculture. Would-be marijuana users are not recruited randomly into this subculture but are drawn to it because of the common world view and lifestyle characteristics. By contrast, nonusers tend to become involved in friendship networks that are more compatible with conventional values.

Once recruited into such a drug-using peer network, socialization into it begins. Among parents, schools, and other conventional socialization agents such as religion that exert influence in the life of an adolescent, peer groups are particularly powerful agents of socialization when it comes to making immediate lifestyle choices. Denise Kandel (1973), who has studied adolescent drug use patterns perhaps more than any other scholar, suggests that while parents may exert preliminary influence by example in the use of alcohol, the use of drugs is primarily the result of socialization among peers. Later research by Kandel and Davies (1991) further revealed that drug users tended to have even greater intimacy with peers than did nonusers. And they found that as one progresses in the sequence of drug use, there is a greater likelihood that the closest friends are also users. This recent research suggests that, whereas parental and general peer group influence may play a greater role in entry-level drug use such as alcohol, as the adolescent progresses to illegal drug use such as marijuana and especially other more expensive drugs, he or she will more deliberately seek out like-minded peers.

This body of research, which supports what Goode (1999) has called the *selective interaction/socialization model*, suggests that both social control and social learning influences the process of becoming a drug user. Social control factors are primarily at work in the selection of peer associations—people seek out friends who are most closely aligned with their lifestyle and world view. However, once this peer-selection process has taken place, social learning principles become dominant in one's choices to initiate and continue involvement in drug-using sequences.

Social Structural Theories

When we talk about social structural theories, we are referring to explanations that attempt to explain why certain categories of people tend to be more involved in drug use and/or crime than other categories. These epidemiological theories attempt to explain differential levels of crime and drug use rates among various segments of the population. This focus separates social structural theories from earlier theories, which look for links between individual drug users and the social environment of which they are a part. Over the years, two distinct approaches to structural explanations have developed, strain theories and cultural deviance theories.

Strain Theory

Robert Merton, in expanding earlier work of Durkheim, provided the basis by which strain theory (sometimes called *anomie theory*) could be applied to drug use and other deviant behaviors. Merton's theory views social structure primarily in economic or social class terms. In "Social Structure and Anomie" (1938), Merton identifies two interacting elements of society that produce varying levels of strain. The

Table 5.2. Merton's strain theory.

Response	Orientation to socially defined goals	Orientation to culturally approved means	Behavioral examples
Conformity	Positive	Positive	Law-abiding behavior motivated by desire to get ahead
Innovation	Positive	Negative	Property crimes; other crimes driven by profit motive
Ritualism	Negative	Positive	Law-abiding behavior motivated by need to follow the rules
Retreatism	Negative	Negative	Drug and alcohol abuse; generally withdrawal from society
Rebellion	Negative/Positive	Negative/Positive	Counterculture involvement; activity that represents a rejection of conventional values and pursuit of alternative lifestyles

Source: Adapted from Merton, 1938, p. 676.

first is structurally defined goals, which are viewed as desirable by all. In American society, these goals are typically material in nature, and thus we tend to define success in materialistic terms. The second element is the culturally approved means for obtaining these goals. Young people go to college to get higher-paying jobs, thus pursuing the socially defined goal of material success through a socially approved means.

The problem is that the acceptance of culturally defined goals of material success in a particular sector of society does not necessarily mean that socially approved means are acknowledged with the same level of commitment, or that commitment to socially approved means is accompanied by a commitment to the goals. The disjunction between culturally approved goals and socially accepted means for obtaining them produces strain. Strain, in turn, may result in deviance such as drug use. Table 5.2 describes the various possible responses to the goals-means disconnect. According to Merton, the drug addict is likely to be someone who rejects both the goals and the accepted means to achieve them. He called such a person a **retreatist**, in effect a societal dropout. Heroin and alcohol have been cited as especially prominent in the world of the retreatist because they provide an escape from the demanding realities of life.

Many of Merton's ideas were further elaborated by Richard Cloward and Lloyd Ohlin (1960). Their differential opportunity theory posits that retreatism occurs only after attempts to achieve success have proven unsuccessful. Cloward and Ohlin claim that most individuals first attempt to achieve the goals of material success through legitimate means. Failing that, attempts are made to attain these goals illegitimately through one or more types of criminal activities. In effect, drug use is an escape from failure. Cloward and Ohlin suggest that retreatists are **double failures** who have failed to achieve material success through either legitimate or illegitimate means (179–183).

Generally speaking, strain theory has not fared well as an explanation of drug abuse and addiction. Lindesmith and Gagnon (1964) challenged the efficacy of strain theory in explaining drug addiction. Although it may explain initial experimentation with heroin for some individuals, they argue, it falls short in explaining addiction. Indeed, the very lifestyle of the heroin addict precludes Cloward and Ohlin's scenario:

> If, as is commonly reported, the addict's habit costs him as much as from $10 to $50 a day [note this was written in the early 1960s] seven days a week, one may argue that it is no mean feat to raise these amounts. The user who supports himself by stealing finds that the value of stolen goods is heavily discounted by the fence, and if his habit costs him $25 per day he may have to steal goods worth from $75 to $100 to meet his daily expenses.... From this, one might reasonably argue that addicts are quite successful criminals. (Lindesmith and Gagnon, 1964, 176)

This observation is directly addressed by an early ethnographic study of drug users in New York, which found little evidence to support the ideas in strain theory. Examining the economics of the heroin-using lifestyle, Preble and Casey (1969) convincingly made the case that the heroin user is anything but a social dropout trying to escape an otherwise harsh existence:

> Heroin use today by lower class, primarily minority group, persons does not provide for them a euphoric escape from the psychological and social problems which derive from ghetto life. On the contrary, it provides a motivation and rationale for the pursuit of a meaningful life, albeit a socially deviant one. The activities these individuals engage in and the relationships they have in the course of their quest for heroin are far more important than the minimal analgesic and euphoric effects of the small amount of heroin available to them.... [T]he heroin user is, in a way, like the compulsively hard-working business executive whose ostensible goal is the acquisition of money, but whose real satisfaction is in meeting the inordinate challenge he creates for himself. (21)

Other ethnographic studies have also challenged the double-failure characterization of drug addiction (e.g., see Agar 1973; Biernacki 1979; Faupel, 1991). The weight of evidence from post-1960s ethnographic studies strongly suggests a very active and even criminally successful lifestyle among heroin addicts and users of other expensive drugs.

Strain theory languished for a number of years with the growing knowledge that crime is evident across all social classes, and as a result of the corresponding development of social process and social reaction theories. Strain theory reemerged through the work of Robert Agnew in the form of general strain theory. Agnew identifies sources of strain that are not class or economically based, but rather at the sociopsychological level (Agnew 1985, 1992, 2005 Agnew and White, 1992). He argues that criminal behavior is the result of negative attitudes and emotions that result from unpleasant social circumstances, such as: the failure to achieve positively valued goals such as wealth or academic success; the loss of positively valued stimuli such as unemployment or divorce; and the presence of negative stimuli such as emotional, physical, or sexual abuse (Agnew, 2004).

Drug use, crime, and delinquency are more likely to take place when these sources of strain are combined with opportunities for involvement in deviant behavior. For example, Hoffmann, Cerbone, and Su (2000) found that stressful experiences, particularly when coupled with lack of attachment to the family (which can influence opportunity), have a significant impact on adolescent drug use. Research testing general strain theory on drug use and delinquency demonstrates a marked impact on delinquency, but a more moderate effect on drug use (Agnew and White 1992; Mazerolle et al. 2000). Additional research by Paternoster and Mazerolle (1994) reveals that some strain factors—namely, negative relationships with adults, feelings of dissatisfaction with friends and school life, and encountering stressful events such as parental divorce or unemployment—are positively related to a composite index of delinquency that included two measures of drug sales. Still other research examined gender differences in the effects of strain and found that general strain theory variables affected the drug use of boys and girls in a similar fashion (Hoffman and Su 1997).

Because this perspective is extremely broad in scope, empirical testing has typically addressed specific aspects of the theory (e.g., Broidy 2001). Moreover, the theory has been tested primarily for its effectiveness in explaining delinquency generally, and when specific types of crimes are examined, they are usually violent and property offenses. Other areas, including drug and alcohol use, have received far less attention in testing this theory.

A Comment on Crime and the American Dream. In an important work in the sociology of crime, Messner and Rosenfeld (2007) correctly point out that strain (anomie) theory remains a work in progress. The authors argue (in reviewing the often-cited criticisms of the evolution of anomie theory from Durkheim to Merton) that strain theory provides insufficient information on how the structure of social institutions and the relationships between them can affect behavior. In addressing this issue, they look to American culture and society itself in an attempt to identify distinguishing features of it and, in doing so, conclude that America is "organized" (1) for crime. A major premise is that in the United States, compared with other developed nations, there is an inordinate emphasis on the economy at the expense of the other social institutions, such as the family, education system, and religion. Likewise, the authors point out that, according to this notion of the American Dream, success is viewed solely in universal, individualistic, and materialistic terms, resulting in an "ends justify the means" character of the culture. Although it gives little specific attention to drugs other than in the context of trafficking, this perspective provides valuable insight into how strain influences behavior.

Cultural Deviance Theories

Cultural deviance theories originated during the early part of the twentieth century with sociologists at the University of Chicago, who were attempting to understand patterns of urban crime and delinquency. In short, many of these scholars essentially concluded that cultural traditions often promoted crime. An early explanation was developed by Clifford Shaw and Henry McKay (1972; originally published in 1942) who asserted that drug use and other forms of delinquency are a consequence of life in "transitional neighborhoods" characterized by, among other things, residential turnover and lack of a strong community to encourage conventional values. Children living in these areas often lacked adequate supervision and were more likely to be influenced by delinquent gangs, a source of delinquent values. In later formulations of cultural deviance theory, gangs came to be characterized more as an example of a delinquent subculture.

The application of these ideas to subcultures of drug users received support from John O'Donnell (1967) in his research on addicts in the federal drug treatment facility in Lexington, Kentucky. Comparing drug addiction before and after passage of the Harrison Narcotics Act in 1914, which effectively criminalized the possession and distribution of narcotics, O'Donnell found evidence of the emergence of a drug subculture. O'Donnell suggested that with criminalization, continuing drug users experienced a common problem: how to maintain access to sources of drugs. Other problems also arose, such as learning criminal skills to support their habits and learning to avoid detection and arrest. He writes:

> When drugs were in short supply, they could be obtained from others. Information could be traded on where and how drugs could be obtained. Skills, which before had been unnecessary were not needed, and could be transmitted from one addict to another. These included criminal skills: how to commit burglaries or forge prescriptions; how to administer narcotics by the intravenous route; how to process paregoric so the residue could be injected; and how to "make" doctors. Addicts could support each other in the attitudes and values needed to maintain addiction in the face of mounting public disapproval. (1967, 78–79)

The criminalization of drug use, according to O'Donnell, arguably for the first time in American history resulted in the emergence of a distinct drug subculture.

Johnson (1973) also employs a subcultural perspective to explain marijuana use. He suggests that subcultures of marijuana use share a "conduct norm", essentially a mandate to smoke marijuana. Value and belief systems further reinforce the importance of the norm. Johnson explains that, regardless of the diversity of the marijuana subculture in other ways, such as social class or lifestyle, marijuana users recognize each other by virtue of marijuana use. Johnson (1980) later extended his theory to account for other drug-specific subcultures, arguing that distinct subcultures and special conduct norms exist for the alcohol abusers, people who inject heroin, and polydrug users. Each one possesses its own conduct norms, values, rituals, and vernacular that supports the use its particular drugs.

It should be pointed out that cultural deviance theory, particularly the work of Johnson, includes key features of social learning theory. Johnson acknowledges that it is typically within the subculture that individuals exhibit the norms associated with using drugs. However, the structural features of cultural deviance theories emphasize the importance of "social location" in relation to subcultures of crime and drug use.

An Integrated Structural Theory

In 1974, drug researcher and sociologist Charles Winick (1974a) proposed a theory that combined elements of both strain theory and cultural deviance theory. Winick contends that drug dependence is a function of three factors: access to drugs, disengagements from normative proscriptions against drug use, and role strain and/or role deprivation. Access to drugs refers to the various means by which drugs become available to users. Drug users can enhance access in a variety of ways, including connecting with wholesale dealers, learning new and more lucrative criminal skills, and by learning how to self-inject rather than being dependent on others (Faupel 1991).[3] Greater access to drugs provides more opportunities for getting high, which is posited as increasing the likelihood of abuse or dependence. Involvement in the drug subculture is a valuable asset in increasing availability to levels required for addiction to develop. Disengagement from proscriptions against drug use, Winick's second factor, refers to the process through which young drug users counteract conventional morality that, in varying degrees, places taboos on use of drugs. This element draws from Sykes and Matza (1957), who identify five *techniques of neutralization* used to disengage from conventional norms.[4] Similar techniques are used by drug abusers to provide a justification for behavior that at one time represented a violation of their own ethical standards. These techniques of disengagement are typically learned as addicts become immersed in the subculture of drug use.

The third element of Winick's theory is role strain and role deprivation. Role strain involves the perceived difficulty in meeting the obligations of a social position, and role deprivation refers to the termination of a significant and important position in the individual's life. Both increase the vulnerability to drug abuse and addiction, particularly if the first two elements of this theory are present. For example, Winick notes that physicians, whose work involves long hours and access to drugs, are subject to role strain and are also vulnerable to addiction. Physicians may also experience role deprivation in a number of ways, such as failing board exams or leaving the security of medical school to establish an individual practice. Faupel (1991) also identified the importance of role strain/role deprivation in what he terms the *life structure* of users, which is a critical element in predicting the level of drug use. Individuals who maintain a highly structured daily routine are better able to manage drug consumption than those who lead more chaotic lifestyles. With disruptions to life structure such as increased pressure from police, the loss of a job, the breakup of a relationship, or a particularly lucrative criminal event, the user is already well on his or her way to becoming, in Faupel's terms, a *free-wheeling addict* with little or no control over an escalating habit. Life structure features, including role strain and role deprivation, clearly play an important part in predisposing one to drug addiction.

Societal Reaction Theories

Societal reaction theories represent a fundamental paradigm shift with regard to explaining drug use and deviant behavior generally. The very question that we are trying to answer shifts from "Why do individuals (or categories of individuals) engage in problematic drug-using behavior?" to "Why does society respond to this particular type of behavior in the way that it does?" When discussing societal reaction theories, sociologists usually distinguish between labeling theory and conflict theory.

Labeling Theory

Labeling theory has its intellectual roots in the symbolic interactionist tradition. Interactionists such as George Herbert Mead and Herbert Blumer, among others, suggested early on that social reality is a constructed phenomenon. That is, although there are concrete social phenomena that may be observed and measured objectively, the meanings we assign to those phenomena are mediated by our social and cultural experiences.

We have addressed the issue of social construction of the reality of drug use in Chapter 1. There we learned that some drugs are defined as acceptable in American society. For example, drinking champagne or gourmet coffee can distinguish one as having an elegant palate. On the other hand, smoking marijuana or dropping LSD may render one a social pariah in his or her community. Yet it is difficult to make the case that one drug is intrinsically more damaging than another. These judgments are also social constructions. The recognition of the social construction of reality is, in part, the legacy of symbolic interactionism.

There are three basic questions that labeling theory asks in its attempt to understand drug use and addiction.

- Why are certain drug-using behaviors defined as deviant, and others not?
- Why do certain individuals who engage in these drug-using behaviors acquire a deviant label, while others who engage in the same behavior are not so labeled?

- What are the social and interpersonal consequences and implications of this labeling process?

We address each of these questions in the paragraphs that follow.

The Defining of Deviant Behavior. As we have already seen in Chapter 1, the social construction of drug use as a deviant behavior is rarely a rational process, if by *rationality* we mean that there is an objective assessment of the pharmacological dangers inherent in using particular drugs. Rather, according to labeling theory, the social construction is typically based on the vested interests and ideologies of those who have power and access to deviance-defining processes (such as legislative bodies or the mass media). Becker (1963) analyzed this process of moral entrepreneurship by tracing the initial criminalization of marijuana by the newly formed Federeal Bureau of Narcotics (the precursor of the Drug Enforcement Administration). The FBN, headed by Harry Anslinger, conducted a "reefer madness" campaign that was particularly instrumental in the legislation process and in the shaping of public opinion. Not coincidentally, the success of this criminalization effort led to a big increase in the FBN budget.

Gusfield (1963) explored this moral entrepreneurship process with regard to alcohol prohibition. He demonstrated that the prohibition movement and defining alcohol consumption as a socially unacceptable behavior was the end result of a political and public opinion battle between the more established and often-abstinent Protestant middle class versus the more recently immigrated Catholic working class. The latter group typically was comprised of ethnic minority, blue collar populations for which drinking was an acknowledged and accepted part of social life. More recently, Ruth Peterson (1985) performed a content analysis of the Comprehensive Drug Abuse Prevention and Control Act of 1970. Her analysis revealed a reduction in penalties for possession of certain types of drugs, particularly marijuana. Penalties were substantially increased however, for drug sales. Peterson's analysis suggests the legislation was intended to send a clear message regarding society's disapproval of drug use, but also to do so in a way that protected the privileged position of the "cream of American youth" from the full weight of the existing law, while singling out drug dealers who were perceived to be of more marginal social status (1985, 264).

Peterson's analysis of the legislative process of how drug-using and drug-dealing behaviors are defined has implications for the second question addressed by labeling theory: Why are some individuals singled out and labeled for certain behaviors, while others who engage in the same behaviors are not?

The Differential Labeling of Individuals. Labeling theory suggests that the primary factors determining who is labeled a criminal, a drug addict, or any other type of deviant are characteristics of the individual rather than of the acts in which they engage. Typically, those individuals most likely to be labeled and identified as drug addicts are those who are racial minorities, of lower socioeconomic status, or who have been otherwise marginalized by society. Peterson's (1985) analysis, discussed in the preceding section, suggests that the writers of the Comprehensive Drug Abuse Prevention and

Control Act of 1970 systemically, if not intentionally, singled out these marginalized segments of the population to bear the greatest impact of the law.

There is also controversy over the disparity in the way users crack cocaine versus powder cocaine are treated by the criminal justice system. These substances are not identical because of the way that crack is manufactured and ingested, but cocaine is the principle ingredient of both drugs, and the overall pharmacological effect of both drugs is very similar. The primary difference between these two drugs is not pharmacology, but rather the demography of the user. Crack cocaine is a preferred by minorities, younger users, and those with less means to purchase drugs. Powder cocaine, much more expensive per dose, is much more likely to be used by more mainstream members of society (Reiman 2007). In a recent Sentencing Project report, King (2008) suggests this aspect of the War on Drugs is the single largest contributor to racial disparity in the U.S. criminal justice system.

The Impact of Labeling. Much of the focus of labeling theory has been on the consequences of labeling for the individual labeled in some undesirable way. Once labeled, the individual takes on a new, devalued social identity. Goffman (1963) refers to this new deviant identity as a **stigma**. Similarly, Becker (1963) denotes it as the *master status*. Regardless of nomenclature, the public designation as a deviant—*pothead, junkie, crack whore,* or *drunk*—powerfully changes one's public identity. Moreover, consistent with the perspective of symbolic interactionism in which labeling theory is rooted, this public identity inevitably shapes one's self-concept. Schur (1971) suggests that a process of "role engulfment" is concurrent with public labeling. This phenomenon occurs when the deviant identity becomes the central feature of an individual's self-concept. Not only is the individual defined by others as a deviant, but the person now defines him- or herself as deviant.

Such self-definition has profound implications for subsequent behavior. According to labeling theory, individuals are likely to act in a way that is consistent with their self-concept. Edwin Lemert (1951) distinguishes between primary deviance and secondary deviance to capture this idea. **Primary deviance** consists of those rule violations that are often inadvertent and that most everyone engages in from time to time. These acts are not those of a career deviant or of one who thinks of him- or herself as a deviant; rather, they are the variety of indiscretions that, if detected and made public, could be the basis for labeling and role engulfment. When such a labeling process takes place and one's self-concept takes on a deviant character such as a pothead or dope fiend, subsequent behavior that conforms to the deviant self-identity is more likely. Lemert refers to this subsequent behavior as **secondary deviance**. Unlike primary deviance, which is usually occasional and sporadic, secondary deviance is routine and systematic as it reflects the new identity that the publicly labeled drug user has internalized. Rather than occasionally experimenting with drugs, or using them socially from time to time, the labeled user now uses on a regular basis. Drug-related activities and identities have now become a central focus.

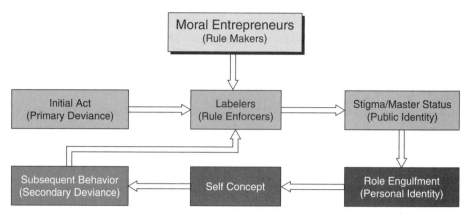

5.1 The Dynamics of Labeling Theory.

    Figure 5.1 depicts the sequence of events involved in the labeling process. Rule-making sets in motion a labeling process that typically begins following the commitment of an initial act of drug use (or other form of deviance).[5] Once labeled, a process of role engulfment takes place, and the self-concept begins a metamorphosis. According to labeling theory, the result is a much more systematic pattern of secondary deviant behavior. There are, moreover, labeling implications of secondary deviance itself. Such behavior serves to reinforce the perceptions of the labelers, whether teachers, police, other community agents, or even family members. The cycle of labeling then escalates, and the public identity of the drug user becomes even more firmly entrenched. Barring some form of external intervention, the dynamics of labeling theory suggest that drug-using and/or other deviant behavior patterns will eventually take the form of a full-blown, drug-using "career" in which an individual organizes major portions of his or her life around drug use and the activities associated with it. Labeling theory contains within it some profound policy implications, which will be discussed in the context of both the legal and therapeutic contexts of drug problems.

Conflict Theory

The decade of the 1960s provided sociologists with ample evidence that assumptions of the harmonious and fundamental fairness of American society may warrant further consideration. Our national complacency was shaken by racial protests and violence in urban areas from coast to coast. The Vietnam War was challenged by millions as imperialistic and unnecessary. Furthermore, many elites found that wealth and power could make them objects of scorn. These societal divisions resulted in many new ways of thinking about larger issues facing America, such as racism, poverty, abuses of political power, and deteriorating cities. A number of critical, macrosocietal arguments emerged under the rubric of conflict theory. As critical arguments, they challenged the legitimacy of American social institutions and of entrenched structures of power. As macro-level approaches, they examine the larger structural forces that affect communities and American society as a whole. These distinctions make them different from other sociological theories of drug use we have covered, which focus on how individuals are situated with American culture and social structures.

Elliott Currie (1985, 1993) is one sociologist who writes about social problems, crime, and drug abuse from a conflict perspective. Currie is primarily concerned with the abuse of crack cocaine and heroin in inner cities and how utterly destructive of families and communities it can be. In fact, conflict theory is most useful in explaining such forms of drug abuse, rather than,

5.2 Labeling theory asserts that when one is arrested or otherwise publicly exposed for deviant behavior such as drug use or possession, their identity as a drug user becomes an all-encompassing master status, which reinforces further drug use. (Photo: Associated Press/Joe Tabacca)

say, patterns of drinking and pot-smoking by affluent suburban teens. He says that higher rates of crack and heroin dependency are found in these urban centers because meaningful economic opportunities are scarce and because perceived powerlessness and alienation is so crippling. Going further, he argues that the dearth of economic options and the marginalization of entire communities is systematic and politically intentional. The War on Drugs conducted by government has done little to reduce these structural conditions, and hence has had little impact on the kinds of chronic drug dependency plaguing the cities (Currie 1993).

For conflict theorists, drug policy, to be meaningful, must attack the economic and political conditions that polarize us at a macro-societal level. It must be noted that social and political support for such a policy shift is not strong. Both major political parties, save for a relatively few legislators, would dismiss widespread economic restructuring as extreme or radical. Conflict theorists would not be surprised by this, given that the greatest harmful consequences of drug abuse are being felt by those who are most dissimilar demographically from the politicians themselves. The scourge of drug abuse most victimizes those who have the least clout and autonomy in our society. And the devastation of drug dependency helps to silence their voices more completely. Conflict theorists are pessimistic that this degrading cycle will be broken any time soon.

Summary

The theories that we have highlighted in this chapter are only a sampling of the most widely recognized explanations for drug use and addiction. While recognizing various approaches to understanding drug use and addiction, we have emphasized sociological theories in this chapter. This has been intentional. Drug use, perhaps more than any form of deviant or criminal behavior, has suffered from a very narrow, individualistic causal understanding among policy makers, practitioners, and in the popular media. Our intent is not to deny the reality of biological and psychological factors, but rather to expand our understanding of the etiology of drug use to include the cultural and structural factors that predispose certain categories of individuals to the use of drugs, or certain types of drugs, to which other categories of individuals are not so vulnerable. The sociological perspectives, we believe, are at least as important as biological and psychological dimensions for sound drug-use policies for the 21st century.

Key Terms

addictive personality
classical conditioning
differential reinforcement
double failure
operant conditioning
primary deviance
retreatist
scientific theory
secondary deviance
stigma

Thinking Critically...

1. Andrew Weil suggests that "the desire to alter consciousness periodically is an innate normal drive" and that drug use is grounded in this desire. Can you make the case that Weil's theory is scientific in nature. Explain why or why not.

2. Most sociological theories of drug use were formulated originally to explain crime and deviance generally. Can you make the case that drug use is just another expression of crime and/or deviance, and hence can be explained by these theories as well? Or would you want to make the case that there is something unique about drug-using behavior that requires special theories to explain it? To answer this question, consider the things that drug use has in common with other forms of crime and deviance. In what ways are these types of behavior different?

3. Most (not all) theories of drug use are premised on the idea that this behavior is abnormal, unhealthy, even pathological, and hence needs to be explained. Is it

possible to conceive that drug use (at least nonabusive drug use) is rational and perhaps even functional and healthy in that it provides personal, interpersonal, and social rewards? Would any of the theories discussed in this chapter be more responsive to this idea than the others? Explain.

4. Cloward and Ohlin make the case that drug users are double failures, meaning that they have attempted to succeed through conventional means such as employment and failed, and that they have also attempted to succeed through crime and failed there as well. So they drop out and simply get high on drugs. If you know people who use drugs on a regular basis (or perhaps you use), talk to these people about their lives. Does their drug use fit this pattern of a double failure?

5. If you had to pick one of the theories presented here as superior to all of the others in explaining drug use and/or addiction, which would it be? Explain your response by indicating what it could explain that the other theories cannot explain.

Learning from the Internet

1. Go to the website www.anonymousone.com. Click the hyperlink "Stories of Recovery." Among the many categories of stories, choose a story of recovery that seems interesting to you. (Most of these stories also tell of how the individual got involved in drugs/alcohol in the first place and of their pathway of addiction.) For the story that you have chosen, choose the theory you think best explains the person's story and discuss their experience through this theory.

2. Research any of the following drug theorists online. Find out as much as you can about their biographies and their theories of drug use: Alfred Lindesmith, John O'Donnell, Howard Becker, Andrew Weil, Ron Akers, Erich Goode, or Elliot Currie.

Notes

1. A tautology is an explanatory statement in which the explanatory variable (in this case, personality attributes) is the same or a very similar measure as the variable to be explained (in this case, drug-using behavior). Hence, when we suggest that marijuana use, a sensation-seeking behavior, is caused by a sensation-seeking personality feature, we have not explained much. It is, essentially, a circular reasoning.
2. At least one recent study by Durkin et al. (1999) does find support for control theory as a predictor of binge drinking among college students, but it seems to be an exception. This suggests that more research is needed to test the postulates of control theory among middle-class college students specifically with regard to excessive drinking behavior. There may be a different process at work here than what takes place when adolescents make the decision to use illegal drugs.
3. Learning how to inject one's self increases access in two ways. First, the individual does not have to wait for an experienced user's help and hence can use the drug whenever the felt need arises. Second, most experienced users demand drugs in exchange for their services, resulting in less drugs for the one needing this service.

4. The five techniques of neutralization as developed by Sykes and Matza are:
   - Denial of Responsibility
   - Denial of Injury
   - Denial of the Victim
   - Condemnation of the Condemners
   - Appeal to Higher Loyalties
5. The labeling process need not necessarily begin with an act of primary deviance. In many cases, the rule enforcers wrongly assume that an individual has committed a deviant act and publicly label them. The consequences are often the same: a public identity is established, thereby resulting in the formation of a deviant self-concept and, in turn, secondary deviance.

SOCIAL CORRELATES OF DRUG USE

CHAPTER **6**

Demographic Correlates of Drug Use

The term *demographic correlates* may be new for some of you, but it means simply population categories that have some relationship to drug use. We will be examining the four demographic correlates identified below. Each begins with basic statistical information, followed by a discussion of the dynamics of drug use particular to its population.

Demographics are an important part of any understanding of the dynamics of drug use. The fact is that drug use is *not* distributed evenly throughout any society. In the United States, for example, we know that younger people are much more likely to use illicit drugs than are middle-aged or older people. The elderly, by contrast, are much more likely to misuse prescription drugs. Similarly, the amount and types of drugs vary among different racial and ethnic groups. The demographic variation in drug use goes beyond the frequency and types of drugs used; the way individuals are introduced to drug use and the way they manage their drug use over time also varies. We will examine the following demographic categories, which have received a significant amount of attention in the literature: sex and gender, race and ethnicity, age, and social class.

Sex and Gender Correlates of Drug Use

We begin this section with an examination of drug use prevalence data for males and females. We make reference to both sex and gender because drug use affects men and women differently both because of physiological differences and because of differences in social expectations. When sociologists use the term *sex*, they are referring to the physiological characteristics of men and women. *Gender*, by contrast, refers to differences in the way men and women are expected to behave, to look, to feel, and so forth. Gender is *socially* derived, whereas sex is *biologically or physiologically* derived.

With regard to likelihood of drug use, Figure 6.1 reveals a clear pattern, namely that males are more likely to use drugs recreationally than are females. This pattern generally holds true for every age group, though among younger users, 12 to 17 years old, boys and girls use at more equal rates than older users (SAMHSA 2008). This pattern was also found by Lloyd Johnston and his colleagues in their samples of middle-school, high-school and college students (Johnston et al. 2008). The pattern is clear: men use more illegal drugs as well as more alcohol and tobacco than do women. This is consistent with our knowledge of deviant behavior in general: men are more often, and more seriously, involved in most deviant behaviors. The exception for the younger age category, however, does raise an important issue about onset of and early socialization into drug use.

Onset and Socialization into Drug Use among Males and Females

Data are somewhat mixed about the age at which men and women are first initiated into drug use. Most early studies of gender differences have suggested that men begin their careers earlier than women (Campbell and Freeland 1974; Eldred and Washington 1976; Moise et al. 1982). This has not been a universal finding, however, particularly for more expensive drugs such as heroin and cocaine (Inciardi 1979). Earlier research by Freeland and Campbell (1973) and Bowker (1977) suggests that males are more likely to be "carriers" of marijuana, meaning that they are more likely to introduce females to the drug for the first time. This is most often done in mixed-group settings or two-person settings involving romantic relationships. Similar findings were obtained by Brown and his colleagues regarding initiation into heroin (Brown et al. 1971), and more recently among crack cocaine users in Alabama (Lichtenstein 1997) and among Latino intravenous (IV) drug users in Harlem (Diaz et al. 2002). Moreover, Voss and Clayton (1984) find that transmission of drug use to new users typically takes place during the first two years of one's own use, what Voss and Clayton call the honeymoon period. If, as studies seem to

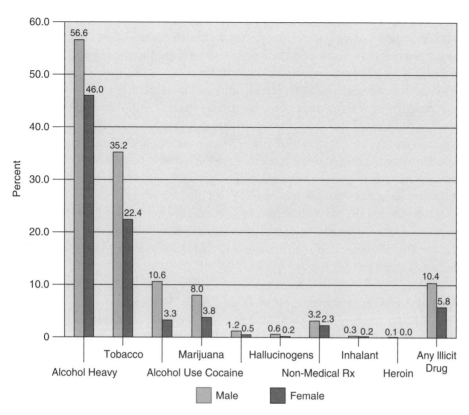

6.1 Percent of Men and Women Using Drugs in the Last 30 Days, 2007.

Source: Adapted from Substance Abuse and Mental Health Services Administration 2008. *Results from the 2007 National Survey on Drug Use and Health: National Findings.* Office of Applied Studies, NSDUH Series H-34, DHHS Publication No. SMA 08-4343. Rockville, MD: Substance Abuse and Mental Health Services Administration.

Available online: http://www.oas.samhsa.gov/nsduh.htm [Accessed September 22, 2008]

suggest, females are usually turned on by older males, this might account for why there are as many or more girls using in the 12–17 age group than boys.

The reasons that men and women first begin using drugs are consistent with the patterns of initial use. Research by Brown, Gauvey, Meyers, and Stark (1971) reveals that curiosity and the influence of friends and relatives are the two major reasons cited by both males and females for initiation. Females, however, are much more likely than males to indicate that the influence of others was a major factor. More recent research by Hser, Anglin, and McGlothlin (1987) finds that curiosity was a major reason for initial use of narcotics, though men were more likely to report this as a reason than women. Peer acceptance was also a reason given by men more than by women, although women were much more likely to report their spouse's use as a factor in their narcotics initiation. Additionally, the relief of pain was much more a factor for women than for men. Rosenbaum's research (1981b) also cites spousal use as a major factor in women turning on to heroin.

Although both women and men report similar motivations for their initial use, namely curiosity or peer pressure, women are much more likely to be drawn into continued drug use because of their reliance on a man. Women are more likely to be living with a spouse or common-law partner who is using narcotics than is the case with men (Anglin et al. 1987). It is commonly believed that women are coerced into drug use by male partners, but research by Payne (2007) among female drug users in the United Kingdom strongly challenges this notion. Payne reports that, although male relationships are pivotal in female initiation, this initiation is usually voluntary and conducted in the context of a relationship of trust. Women also report family problems as a reason for using heroin, probably not so much an escape from these problems, but as an effort to resolve them by using with their addicted spouses (Rosenbaum 1981b). Even more than this, females are much more likely than males to continue their drug use as a form of self-medication (Inciardi et al. 1993). The maladies that women attempt to mask or relieve through drugs are varied and will be discussed in the next section.

Special Problems Encountered by Drug-Using Women

There is a growing recognition backed by good scientific research that drug-using women encounter problems and issues that are unique to them and that pose serious consequences. The following problem areas are of particular significance to women: health issues, domestic issues, and stigmatization.

Health Issues

The use of legal *and* illegal drugs poses potential health risks for both men and women. We do not wish to minimize the risks to men by focusing on health risks to women. Indeed, we will be focusing in more detail on health issues for both men and women in Chapter 8. We focus on women in this section because women face risks that are unique to them, and because many of the health risks that women drug users encounter are generally much more consequential than those faced by men. Our examination of women's health issues looks both at how women's health affects their drug use and at how women's drug use affects their health. That is, we will look at health issues as both *antecedent to* (occurring prior to) and *consequences of* drug use (Gomberg and Nirenberg 1993).

First, examining antecedent health variables, an overriding health consideration is that women encounter more physiological cycles in ways that affect their well-being and sense of well-being than do men. These cyclical events and life stage markers include pregnancy and childbirth, lactation, menstruation, and menopause. All of these physiological events have profound hormonal impacts on women, which often result in depression and stress, leaving many women more predisposed to turn to drugs and alcohol (Gomberg 1982).

Psychiatric disorders commonly precede drug addiction and may be a causal factor in drug use, especially among women. Studies have also found higher rates of depression among female alcoholics than men, though it is difficult to determine which is the antecedent condition, alcoholism or depression (Reid 1998; Hesselbrock and Hesselbrock 1993; Schuckit 1986; Schuckit and Monteiro 1988). Emotional and psychological problems are also common among women who use opiates and other drugs, and at rates higher than their male counterparts (Giacomuzzi et al. 2005; Powis et al. 2000; Zilberman et al. 2003). Bray, Fairbank, and Marsden (1999) found that the stress experienced by military women as a result of their minority status on the bases was related to greater likelihood of cigarette smoking and illicit substance use.

Other areas of potential vulnerability for women are sexual dysfunction and eating disorders. A review of literature by Wilsnack (1984) suggests a high level of sexual dysfunction among alcoholic women, which seems to be antecedent to the onset of drinking problems (Wilsnack et al. 1986). Both clinical and cross-sectional studies have found that women who suffer from eating disorders such as bulimia or anorexia nervosa are more likely to use and abuse tobacco, alcohol, and marijuana, as well as stimulants, laxatives, and other drugs that are intentionally used to enhance weight loss. As is the case with depression, it is unclear whether some common causal factor drives both the eating disorders and the substance use, or whether eating disorders lead to and reinforce drug use. There is evidence to support both hypotheses (Krahn 1993). One thing is clear, however; doctors are much more willing to prescribe drugs to women than men who present health-related symptoms, resulting in generations of women becoming addicted to prescription drugs over the past century (Marsh 1982; Nellis 1980). According to Nellis and others, American women have been over-prescribed drugs by physicians who have been either less sensitive to physical and/or emotional symptoms presented by women than with men, and/or trained to address these symptoms by prescribing tranquilizers and other drugs. There is evidence, however, that this trend may be reversing. Goode (2008) points out that the number of prescriptions for barbiturates and amphetamines written today is only about 5 to 10 percent of the number written in the 1960s and 1970s.

The health consequences of drug and alcohol abuse to women are potentially immense. Perhaps the area of greatest concern is complications in pregnancy. Every year, approximately 500,000 infants are born who were exposed to illicit drugs in utero. Even more women use tobacco and alcohol during pregnancy (Reid 1996). A recent research initiative, *the Maternal Lifestyle Study*, revealed that pregnant women using drugs are significantly more likely to experience health complications including syphilis, gonorrhea, hepatitis, and AIDS than nonexposed women, as well as higher levels of psychiatric and emotional disorders (Bauer et al. 2002). Posing an even greater concern, however, are the health effects of maternal drug use on the developing fetus. Most drugs that a woman might use or abuse are capable of crossing the placental barrier to affect the fetus and, eventually, the newborn infant. When women abuse drugs and alcohol during pregnancy, they may give birth to infants displaying a number of symptoms—among them fetal alcohol syndrome, neonatal addiction, low birth weight (often due to premature delivery), spontaneous abortion—resulting in a greater likelihood of infant mortality than among infants born of non-drug-using women (Cuskey et al. 1972; Finnegan and Fehr 1980; Little and Wendt 1993; Rosett 1980). Additionally, infertility and other forms of sexual dysfunction have been noted in higher rates among women drug users than among nonusers (Lex 1993). A less dismal outlook is suggested by researchers with the Maternal Lifestyle Study, however, who followed prenatally exposed infants for three years. This research failed to find any significant impact of drug exposure on mental, motor, or behavioral impairment after controlling for birth rate and various environmental risks (Messinger et al. 2004).

Other health consequences have also been observed. Women who abuse alcohol more readily develop liver dysfunction than do men, contributing to a 50 to 100 percent higher liver dysfunction death rate among women than among men (Gomberg and Nirenberg 1993). A serious health issue that will be addressed at greater length is the risk for HIV/AIDS, particularly among IV drug users resulting from the sharing of dirty (infected) needles. Men and women both risk infection if they share needles; however women are especially vulnerable because in many cases they are dependent on a male, which means they are more likely to share his needle and to have unprotected sex with a man who may be infected (Breen et al. 2005; Fitzgerald et al. 2007; Lum et al. 2005). Unprotected sex is also a major risk factor among crack-using women. So-called crack whores who sell themselves sexually for crack run a great risk of acquiring gonorrhea, syphilis, hepatitis, and HIV/AIDS. Female crack users have substantially higher rates of sexually transmitted diseases than do male crack users (Metsch et al. 1996).

Domestic Issues

Like health issues, it is not always easy to determine whether the domestic issues that women drug users confront contribute to their substance abuse or are a consequence of that use. The answer seems to be that it is both. Women who come from troubled domestic backgrounds are more likely to use drugs, often as an attempt to escape from or possibly fix a domestic problem; ironically, this very drug use usually exacerbates their domestic crisis. We look first at what we know about how past domestic abuse and other problems contribute to drug abuse. Then we discuss how patterns of substance abuse by both men and women further complicate patterns of violence and other dysfunction in the family.

It has long been hypothesized that poor family relations contribute to substance abuse and, indeed, delinquency generally. Although the research is somewhat divided, it does seem that pathological family dynamics affect girls more than boys. Substance-abusing women consistently report coming from broken homes, sexual abuse, and other unfavorable home environments. In the now classic *The Road to H* (1964), Isidor Chein and his colleagues report that female addicts typically come from homes where the father is absent. Sexual abuse is also a common theme in the biographies of female drug addicts. Cuskey and Wathey (1982) found that more than 30 percent of the female (primarily) heroin addicts in their sample had been sexually abused as children, and nearly 35 percent had been physically abused. Among those who were sexually abused, about one-fourth reported rape as their first sexual experience. A similar pattern of childhood sexual abuse has been observed among alcoholics (Gomberg and Nirenberg 1993) and female crack users (Sterk 1999).

Female substance abusers suffer not only from early family histories of violence and abuse, but also frequently find themselves in abusive domestic relationships that contribute to their drug use (El-Bassel et el. 2005; Goldberg 1995; Martin et al. 2003). Sales and Murphy (2000), for example, find that women in violent partnerships often use drugs as a survival strategy, self-medicating to endure the violence. They further find that many women use drugs to appease a violent partner. These authors also find that women in violent partnerships frequently use drugs to give themselves a sense of control over their lives, a finding also reported by Young, Boyd, and Hubbell (2000).

Finally, both male and female drug abusers typically come from drug-abusing families. Nearly half of the women in Cuskey and Wathey's study (1982) reported alcohol abuse in their families of origin. Familial drug abuse was reported by 50 percent of the black women and 33 percent of the white women in their sample. Drug and alcohol use by parents and other significant adults normatively models this behavior for children, who learn to use these behaviors as responses to stressful circumstances.

Domestic relationships and dynamics also are profoundly affected by drug use and addiction. Once again, the impact of substance abuse on family life seems to be especially felt by women. Research indicates that substance abuse on the part of women may be a cause of violence against them by domestic partners (El-Bassel et al. 2005; Theall et al. 2004). Marsha Rosenbaum has signaled the corrosive impact of heroin addiction on the lifestyles of women in *Women on Heroin* (1981). Rosenbaum describes an initial honeymoon period, followed by a process of erosion of stability and structure in the female addict's life. She takes risks that eventually lead to a chaotic lifestyle and becoming overwhelmed by the demands of the heroin lifestyle. What began as a means of saving her marriage and family eventually undermines these relationships and the structure that sustains them (Rosenbaum 1981a, 1981b, 1981c). More recently, Powis and her associates (2000) report that opiate-using women often become careless in protecting their children from their drug habits, even purchasing and injecting heroin in the presence of their children. These same women, who would otherwise welcome treatment, refuse it because of the fear that their children will be taken from them.

Somewhat different dynamics are reported by observers of the crack scene. Ethnographic reports show that women are much more blatantly and overtly exploited for sex very early in their crack-using careers (Erikson et al. 2000; Inciardi et al. 1993; Pettiway 1997; Sterk 1999; Young et al. 2000). These reports suggest that women are more likely to experiment with crack cocaine out of curiosity than out of loyalty to a significant other. Moreover, the pharmacology and economics of crack overtake the user much more quickly than with heroin. Very soon after they begin using, these crack-using women are confronted with the difficult reality that they must find a way to support themselves and their habit. Most do not have a man to supply them with the drugs and very quickly learn to trade sex for drugs (Inciardi et al. 1993). It is not uncommon for crack-addicted women to lose their children because of their addiction and the lifestyle associated with it. Erikson and his colleagues (2000) report that crack-addicted women often voluntarily give up their children for adoption because they know that they cannot care for them properly.

The domestic consequences and dynamics of alcohol abuse by women more closely resemble heroin-addicted women than crack-addicted women. Some women become addicted to alcohol as adolescents, before they ever become involved in a domestic relationship (e.g., see Thompson and Wilsnack 1984). It is common, however, that female alcoholics become addicted *after* they are married and have established their own homes. Their alcoholism may develop from social drinking, a pattern not unlike Rosenbaum's portrayal of women who become addicted to heroin as a result of wanting to find a way to connect with their spouse. Other women develop a pattern of drinking in response to a sense of isolation from their spouses, and use alcohol as a way of masking loneliness. Regardless of the reason that women begin to use alcohol on a habitual basis, alcohol addiction profoundly affects a woman's relationship with her family. The female alcoholic may be able to mask her addiction for a sustained period of time if she does not have to work outside the home. Her drinking is usually very private and often not observed by others, except perhaps her husband and children. Eventually, however, the female alcoholic experiences a level of inundation similar to what Rosenbaum describes among female heroin users, and she fails to perform normal domestic duties, resulting in increased tension within her family. Violence is often part of domestic relationships, particularly if her spouse is also a problem drinker (Frieze and Schafer 1984).

Stigmatization

Substance-abusing women face society's disapproval to an extreme not encountered by men. It is certainly the case that when drugs and alcohol are abused, and when the user loses control over that use as is denoted in addiction, there is a level of stigma regardless if the user is a man or a woman. Moreover, the use of illicit drugs, specifically, places the user among the potentially stigmatized, regardless of gender. Beyond the general labeling attached to the perpetrators of deviant behavior, however, women who deviate are stigmatized in a manner that is far more scurrilous and destructive than that directed at their male counterparts. Society is much more tolerant of the misadventures of boys and even men than of girls and women. The adolescent boy who deviates is merely "sowing his wild oats"—a luxury that seems to be reserved for boys and, for the most part, middle-class boys. Girls engaging in the same behavior are generally cast as *sluts*, *whores*, *loose*, and all manner of sexual stigmatization, regardless of the nature of their indiscretion. Understandably, girls are much more vulnerable to a poor self-concept, which only increases the likelihood of drug and alcohol abuse and indiscriminate sexual activity.

Drug-using women are also stigmatized in a manner that far exceeds what men experience. Rosenbaum describes the nature and the consequences of this differential stigmatization:

> After having been addicted for several years, many women envision a heroin-free life, married to or living with a non-addicted man.... But there is an inherent obstacle to such relationships: Never-addicted men are generally not interested in becoming involved with a woman who has been a heroin addict, convicted of a crime, and probably a prostitute. Thus the option for a relationship with a man who is safe in terms of potential addiction or readdiction is reduced for the woman addict. In most cases, she is forced to limit her relationships to either addicted men or ex-addicts, which could led to recidivism for her.
>
> Men do not suffer the stigma of addiction as severely as women, especially in the area of interpersonal and sexual relationships. Addicted or formerly addicted men often develop relationships with non-addicted women, which is many times considered the road to abstinence for men; this rarely works in the reverse however. The woman who has been an addict seems to fall harder than her male counterpart; she alone is defined as "damaged goods." Differentiated societal mores pertaining to men and women are evident here: The man is seen as having temporarily transgressed, whereas the woman is defined as having permanently fallen. (1981a, 131–132)

A similar stigmatization takes place in the occupational arena. Although both men and women addicts or ex-addicts are stigmatized, the consequences for women are substantially more severe for men. Men, it seems, have an opportunity to redeem themselves through rehabilitation and are lauded by conventional society for their fortitude in beating their habits. Women are often not so well received. In some cases, she is given the status of a fallen woman. Part of the rehabilitation process that has been recognized by groups such as AA and others as an important step in the road to recovery is to share one's experiences with others. What is an important part of recovery and community acceptance for men, however, often results in rejection for women, as they attempt to reveal their identities outside of the therapeutic environment. Moreover, society has much higher standards for how women appear, and the physical wear and tear that the addicted woman experiences reduces her opportunities for employment and for social acceptance far more so than if she were a man. Her status in the community as an addict is much more difficult to leave behind than it is for her male counterpart. Friedman and Alicea (2001) point out that the use of heroin often begins as a statement of independence for women, an effort to take control of their lives, but as they move further into the heroin world, women heroin users become increasingly exposed to various forms of gender oppression. Indeed, Maher (1997) and Maher and Daly (1996) point out that the crack-using woman not only faces higher levels of discrimination in the conventional employment arena, but also encounters reduced economic opportunities within the drug world itself compared with her male counterparts. She is a member of a caste—an *out*-caste, to be sure—from which it is difficult if not impossible to escape.

The stigmatization process does not wait until a woman attempts to go drug free and live a conventional life. Drug-using women who are pregnant face especially strong vilification, including formal criminal charges (Goldberg 1995). As Maher (1990) points out, criminalization of drug use among pregnant women because of potential harm done to the fetuses they are carrying represents a new level of legal intrusion. *Robinson v. California* established that drug addiction is not a criminal offense, but it seems to be for women who are pregnant. Even if formal charges are not brought against a pregnant drug user, there is often a legal presumption that these women are guilty of child abuse or neglect (Maher 1992). This is a legal stigmatization not encountered by men.

Recent ethnographic evidence on crack-addicted women suggests a patriarchal culture that imposes a stigmatizing identity on them that far exceeds that experienced by heroin-using women. Sterk (1999) reports that the women in her sample of crack users were marginalized within the crack subculture. They were, to use a term borrowed from Lofland (1969), *unfit strangers* within the crack subculture itself. Most of these women were not able to maintain steady relationships with non-crack users, and any relationships with male crack users were often strained to the breaking point because of the common practice of trading sex for crack. Because of their marginalization within the subculture itself, women crack users often experience *ambient violence*, which Theidon (1995) describes as emotional and verbal (as well as physical) abuse in everyday encounters on the street with drug dealers, pimps, johns, and other men. There is what Hutton (2005) has called a *hegemonic masculinity* in the world of drug use, and this pattern of gendered power seems to be even more magnified in the world of crack cocaine. Crack-using women have been referred to as *toss-ups*, a term connoting that they are something to be used and then tossed away (Fullilove et al. 1990). They have also been pejoratively referred to as *skeezers* and *crack 'hos* (Fullilove and Lown 1992), *freaks, base whores, gut buckets, rock monsters* (Metsch et al, 1996), and *strawberries* (Elwood and Williams 1997).[1] Perhaps more than any other category of drug user, crack-using women suffer from what Goffman (1963) has referred to as a stigma of "blemishes of individual character."

Racial and Ethnic Correlates of Drug Use

Findings from the National Survey on Drug Use and Health (Figure 6.2) reveal both consistencies and inconsistencies with regard to recent drug use across ethnic categories. Native Americans are most likely to use drugs of all types, with the surprising exception of alcohol and cocaine (although they were most likely to report *heavy* use of alcohol). Asian Americans, by contrast, are the least likely to have used drugs within the last 30 days. Comparison among whites, blacks, and Hispanics, however, does not reveal a clear pattern. Whites are more likely to use alcohol and tobacco, as well as misusing prescription drugs such as tranquilizers. Blacks and Hispanics, by contrast, report a greater prevalence of hallucinogenic use, and Hispanics are more likely to report recent use of cocaine; blacks are more likely to have used one or more illicit drugs in the past 30 days than either whites or Hispanics. That there is not a

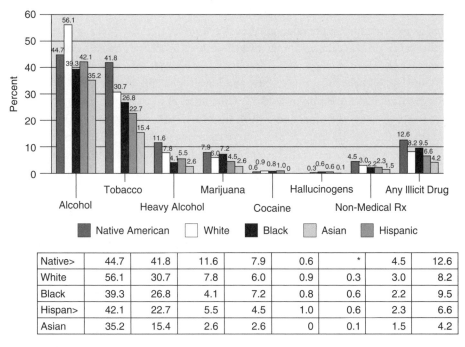

Native>	44.7	41.8	11.6	7.9	0.6	*	4.5	12.6
White	56.1	30.7	7.8	6.0	0.9	0.3	3.0	8.2
Black	39.3	26.8	4.1	7.2	0.8	0.6	2.2	9.5
Hispan>	42.1	22.7	5.5	4.5	1.0	0.6	2.3	6.6
Asian	35.2	15.4	2.6	2.6	0	0.1	1.5	4.2

6.2 Percent of Ethnic Groups Using Drugs in the Last 30 Days, 2007.

*= Low precision - no estimate

Source: Adapted from Substance Abuse and Mental Health Services Administration 2008. *Results from the 2007 National Survey on Drug Use and Health: National Findings.* Office of Applied Studies, NSDUH Series H-34, DHHS Publication No. SMA 08-4343. Rockville, MD: Substance Abuse and Mental Health Services Administration.

Available online: http://www.oas.samhsa.gov/nsduh.htm [Accessed September 22, 2008]

clear pattern suggesting that drug use is much more prevalent among ethnic minorities is probably somewhat surprising to many readers who intuitively see illicit drug use to be primarily a black problem (possibly with the exception of marijuana, which is commonly believed to be most heavily used among Hispanic populations, particularly Mexican-Americans).

Hispanic Drug Use Dynamics

The Hispanic population (also known as *Latinos)* in the United States is comprised of numerous subpopulations reflecting different countries of origin and certain distinctive cultural traits (Almog et al. 1993). The three dominant Hispanic populations in the United States are those from Mexico, Puerto Rico, and Cuba, in addition to Hispanics immigrating from Central and South America. Mexican Hispanics (commonly referred to as *chicanos* or the feminine *chicanas*) are located heavily in the Southwest area of the United States, in certain sections of the Midwest, and other locales where farming is prevalent; Puerto Ricans are found primarily in New York and other major cities such as Chicago; and Cubans are concentrated largely in Miami and other Florida communities. Generally, Puerto Ricans are most likely to have used drugs within the last 30 days (except for alcohol), and other Hispanic groups have very similar prevalence rates.

Research on the demographics of Hispanic users reveals certain patterns that distinguish them from white users: they have less education, lower rates of employment, are more likely to be on welfare, and have higher poverty rates (Anglin et al. 1988; Bourgois 1995; Bullington 1977; Chambers et al. 1970). Chicanos are also more likely to have been married and to be living with one or more other people than are whites (Anglin et al. 1988). These marriage and living arrangements highlight the elevated importance that Hispanics give to family, regardless of whether we are observing Chicanos or other Hispanic groups (Bullington 1977; Moore 1990; Glick 1990; Fitzpatrick 1990). Unfortunately, Hispanic immigrants encounter structural conditions that are disruptive to family life, as discovered by Bourgois (1995) among Puerto Ricans and by Page (1990) among Cuban Hispanics.

Drug use patterns among Hispanics also differ from those among whites. Anglin and his colleagues report that whites are much more likely than Chicanos to have used a variety of drugs, including hallucinogens, amphetamines, cocaine, tranquilizers, PCP, and narcotics other than heroin or street methadone (Anglin et al. 1988). Chicanos, by contrast, more narrowly focus on heroin use, though inhalants and alcohol are also popular drugs of choice (Almog et al. 1993). Alcohol use is also especially prevalent among Puerto Ricans (Singer et al. 1992). Anglin and his associates (1988) find that, except for heroin, Chicano men also tend to become involved in drugs at a later age than whites, a finding also reported by Almog and colleagues (1993).

It is not possible to understand fully the dynamics of Hispanic drug use apart from the cultural context in which this drug use takes place. Joan Moore (1978, 1991) provides a rich description of life in the barrios of Los Angeles, including drug using behaviors of the Hispanic youth there. She identifies three cultural traits especially relevant to understanding drug use in the barrio: machismo, personalismo, and carnalismo. *Machismo* broadly refers to everything from the aggressive hypermasculine image so commonly understood to the notion of "responsible adult manliness" (1978, 77). This translates rather directly to drinking behavior. Singer and colleagues (1992) report that drinking and masculinity are directly linked among Puerto Rican males, and that refusal to drink may even be interpreted as homosexuality. Research by Hardesty and Black (1999), by contrast, finds that Puerto Rican women attach a great deal of importance to motherhood, and that this status is an important lifeline in their attempts to recover from addiction. *Personalismo* refers to the ability to sustain long-lasting loyalties among friends and family, and *carnalismo* refers to the special "blood brother" bond that ties all Chicanos together. Related to the latter two cultural traits is a system of kinship known as *compadrazgo* that extends responsibility for child rearing beyond immediate blood-family to selected nonblood relatives (Bullington 1977). These cultural features may account in part for the higher rates of gang membership among Chicano addicts. It also accounts for a different economy of drug use in the barrios. Chicano youth gangs have been an instrumental part of the marketing of heroin and other drugs in the barrios of Los Angeles.

DRUGS AND EVERYDAY LIFE

Acculturation and Drug Use Among Hispanics

According to sociologist Scott Akins from the University of Oregon, and colleagues Clayton Mosher, Chad Smith, and Jane Gauthier, substance abuse increases among Hispanic immigrants as they replace their traditional cultural beliefs with those of white Americans, a process social scientists call *acculturation*. More specifically, acculturation involves the internalization of new cultural beliefs and social skills by an immigrant group, often replacing traditional beliefs and practices that they brought with them from their culture of origin. The study surveyed 6,713 adults in Washington and included 1,690 respondents who identified themselves as Hispanic. Akins restricted his study to the state of Washington precisely because there was not a sizable Hispanic population. Unlike other states such as California where there is a large Hispanic population, Hispanics in Washington are less likely to be able to maintain a strong traditional cultural lifestyle and are forced to adapt to surrounding cultural practices through this acculturation process.

Akins' results, presented at the 2007 annual meetings of the American Sociological Association and since published in the *Journal of Drug Issues*, caught the attention of the press. And for good reason. Acculturated Hispanics were nearly 13 times as likely to report using illegal drugs in the previous 30 days as their Hispanic colleagues who did not experience the acculturation process. The study reported that 6.4 percent of whites indicated that they used illicit drugs in the previous month, compared to 7.2 percent of acculturated Hispanics. However, less than 1 percent of nonacculturated, Spanish-speaking Hispanics reported such use in the same time period. According to Akins and his colleagues, recent immigrant groups are typically more conservative and have less tolerant views of drug and alcohol use. The authors further state that, although there are certain advantages to acculturation such as financial opportunities, it also brings with it "acculturation stress," which they define as "societal pressures that force immigrants to alter their lifestyles, behaviors, and the way they think about themselves as well as strains deriving from the disadvantaged social situation and environment facing recent…Hispanic immigrants" (Akins et al., 2008, 104). The authors note that because of this difficult acculturation process, substance use patterns tend to reflect those of the dominant culture to which they are acculturating.

The research further revealed that acculturated Hispanics were almost twice as likely as nonacculturated Hispanics to report binge drinking, and more than three times as likely to report continuous drinking for days in a row without sobering up, a practice known as *bender drinking*. The study controlled for several factors, including marital status, education, emotional health, and poverty level, among others.

Source: Akins et al. 2008.

Heroin addicts in the barrio are referred to as **tecatos**. Jorquez (1984) has described the tecato subculture as unique from non-Hispanic heroin subcultures. It has its own history, world view, rituals, and code of conduct. Jorquez suggests that Chicanos typically do not respond as well to mainstream treatment efforts because most treatment programs are not cognizant of these cultural differences. Fitzpatrick

(1990) has further pointed out that Puerto Rican families and communities do not generally ostracize their members when they become addicted. They remain connected, which makes it much easier for them to reenter Puertoriqueño cultural life when they attempt to go drug free.

This dynamic of a closely connected ethnic culture may explain why recent research has found higher levels of drug use among Hispanics who are more mainstreamed into American culture. Studies examining the effect of acculturation, as measured by language use, find that those individuals who grow up speaking primarily Spanish (or prefer to speak Spanish over English) report lower levels of illicit drug use than those preferring English (Delva et al. 2005; Epstein et al. 2001; Vega et al. 1998). Similarly Marsiglia's research focusing on ethnic labels and ethnic identity suggests that where there is a strong sense of ethnic pride and identification among Hispanic youth, drug use tends to be lower (Marsiglia et al. 2001, 2004). This body of *acculturation affects research* suggests that the culture of ethnic minority groups plays a protective role against initiation into drug use. This may not be unique to Hispanic culture, as such ethnic identity seems to affect African American youth in a similar way (Marsiglia et al. 2001). Hispanic culture may be especially effective in affording this protection, however, because of the inherent linguistic barrier. As young people of ethnic minorities become increasingly acculturated or mainstreamed into American culture—by becoming proficient in English, expanding peer networks to include more Anglophones, and becoming less attached to cultural and familial networks—they are exposed to the vices of American society including, among other things, illicit drugs, alcohol, and tobacco.

African American Drug Use Dynamics

There is perhaps no other ethnic category to which illicit drug use, particularly heroin and (crack) cocaine use, has been more closely identified in the popular media than African Americans. There is, to be sure, some historical basis for this, though perhaps more in the reporting than of the actual incidence of use. Although cocaine was initially used by professionals and others of the middle class in such concoctions as Mariani's Wine, Coca Cola, and various patent medicines, as well as through doctor's prescriptions, by turn of the century, the drug was commonly used by the laboring class. Its use was especially prevalent in New Orleans and other Mississippi Delta cities among dock workers, most of whom were black. Medical opinion at the time held that black workers were better able to endure hard physical labor and tough environmental conditions than whites. Cocaine was believed to increase this capacity even more and was welcomed by employers as a way of increasing productivity. It was also welcomed by the workers themselves for the stimulant effect that it had (Spillane 2000).

With the demographic shift in cocaine use came the inevitable concern for the criminalizing effect that cocaine might have (Morgan 1981). The identification of blacks as primary users of cocaine only exacerbated this concern, leading to highly sensationalized stereotypes regarding this drug. We have already pointed out in Chapter 2 that many southern police departments began issuing .38-caliber handguns to their officers because of the belief that .32-caliber bullets could not penetrate the skin of black men who were high on cocaine. A testimony to the Ways and Means Committee in 1910 further reveals the official attitude that linked black use of cocaine to exaggerated feats that posed a potential danger to society:

> The colored people seem to have a weakness for it [cocaine]. It is a very seductive drug, and it produces extreme exhilaration. Persons under the influence of it believe they are millionaires. They have an exaggerated ego. They imagine they can lift this building, if they want to, or can do anything they want to. They have no regard for right or wrong. It produces a kind of temporary insanity. They would just as leave rape a woman as anything else and a great many of the southern rape cases have been traced to cocaine. (U.S. House of Representatives 1910; cited by Morgan 1981)

A second historical event linking African Americans with cocaine use was the marketing innovation known as *crack*. Inciardi and colleagues (1996) note that the nation was first introduced to this new phenomenon on November 17, 1985, when, buried on the inside pages of Monday's edition of the *New York Times* was an article by journalist Donna Boundy on a local drug treatment program that almost inadvertently mentioned the use of a new form of cocaine called *crack*. From here, the new drug took on a life of its own as newspapers across the country became fixated on this new "threat."[2] Crack was perceived as a drug of choice among African Americans almost from the beginning. Its early users were identified in black inner-city neighborhoods, an ethnic and geographic pattern that subsequent research continued to confirm (Jacobs 1999). Crack is not, of course, limited to African Americans. An abundant literature now forthcoming reveals its prevalence among Hispanics and whites as well (Bourgois 1995; Riley 1996; Williams 1992). Nevertheless, the stereotype remains.

Despite this stereotype, empirical research on the cultural dynamics of drug use among African Americans is surprisingly sparse, though there has been some recent research Whereas numerous studies have included African Americans as all or part of their samples, and whereas many of these studies make certain demographic and other comparisons between whites and blacks, these studies do not provide a great deal of information on the social or cultural dynamics of drug or alcohol use among African Americans (Brown and Smith 2006; Herd 1987; Trimble et al. 1987).

Recent research has filled in some of the gaps in our knowledge of the social and cultural dynamics of African American drug use. An important factor appears to be social class, though research directly measuring social class and drug use is extremely sparse. Research by Barr, et al. (1993) demonstrated that social class is particularly significant in determining the level of substance use among black males. Poor black men are more than five times more likely to use drugs and/or alcohol than poor white men, though differences are minimal for higher-income males, a general pattern also reported by Herd (1987) for alcohol use. Research also shows a relationship between educational attainment and drug use. Both black and white heroin addicts tend to have dropped out of high school (Nurco et al. 1981); however, black males with lower educational attainment are much more likely to use drugs than are minimally educated white males (Barr et al. 1993). These data suggest that social class is a predominant factor contributing to African American drug use, though among the lower class, blacks are much more vulnerable to drug use than are whites.

In addition to expensive drugs such as heroin and cocaine, marijuana use has been used as part of a more general religious and political statement among some African Americans. Marijuana, or *ganja*, is a central ritual element among Rastafarians, (Campbell, 1980) who use it in much the same way as Christians partake of communion. It is believed that marijuana smoking enhances their spiritual awareness. This religious sect, which traces its origins to the election in 1930 of Ethiopian black nationalist leader Ras Tafari has distinct political overtones challenging the imperialism of the West, a theme that is especially pronounced in the writings of Marcus Garvey, a Jamaican apologist for black culture. Marijuana represents a direct repudiation of the mores of the dominant white culture. Marijuana use by African Americans is not limited to those who identify with Rastafarianism, of course, but the Rastafarian movement has provided an alternative cultural meaning to marijuana use among blacks that is not available to whites. This culture of drug use is discussed more fully in Chapter 7.

Native American Drug Use Dynamics

Native Americans comprise less than one percent of the population in the United States. Yet, probably no other ethnic group is more notorious for substance abuse, primarily in the form of alcoholism and alcohol abuse. The stereotype of the "drunken Indian" has been reinforced in the media and in our schools, and as with most stereotypes, a kernel of truth underlies it. Native Americans rank higher than any other ethnic minority with regard both to the percentage of their population reporting "heavy" use of alcohol over the past 30 days[3] and to higher rates of alcohol dependence than other ethnic groups (SAMHSA 2007b). We cannot fully understand the pathological features of Native American drinking patterns apart from the cultural and historical context in which these patterns are embedded. This is a truism, of course, in a text on the *sociology* of drug use, but it is especially critical that we understand this in the Native American context (Nichter et al. 2004). An extensive investigation commissioned by the American Indian Policy Review Commission has identified disruptive historical circumstances as a leading factor contributing to the high rate of alcoholism among Native Americans (Task Force Eleven 1976). Prior to the arrival of the Europeans, the use of alcohol (as well as peyote) was restricted primarily to religious ceremonies and spiritual contexts such as the Native American Church (discussed briefly below and in Chapter 7). The imposition of European culture on the native inhabitants of America resulted not only in geographical displacement from their land, but also in a certain cultural displacement that wreaked havoc on their way of life. Drinking patterns changed considerably. It has been suggested, for example, that the prohibition of alcohol sales to Native Americans from

1832 to 1953 may have been responsible for the "quick drinking" and "drink until it's gone" patterns of alcohol consumption that have come to be so identified with Native American alcohol use (Task Force Eleven 1976). Moreover, Native American culture is strongly collectivistic, as opposed to individualistic culture of the European settlers, a fact with profound implications for substance abuse (Pedigo 1983; Task Force Eleven 1976). Family and community peer pressure is strong in such a value system, leading to norms of sharing alcohol and drugs with friends, not turning down such offers, and normative prohibitions against confronting destructive alcohol- and drug-using behavior.

We must point out that, although alcohol abuse is more common among Native Americans because of these cultural and historical circumstances, this picture tells only part of the story. Native Americans do, indeed, report greater alcohol dependence; however, only 7 percent of that population report such dependence. This is a far cry from the broad-brushed stereotype of drunken comportment that seems to stigmatize the entire membership of this ethnic category! Moreover, it is also worth pointing out that Native Americans are more likely to report past year use of tobacco, marijuana, cocaine, and most other illicit drugs than all other ethnic groups (see Figure 6.2). The use and abuse of inhalant drugs among Native American has long been observed (Albaugh and Albaugh 1979; Pedigo 1983), and recent research reveals that this and other forms of substance abuse continue to plague Native American populations (Malcolm et al. 2006; Mosher et al. 2004). Yet, these native inhabitants are not stereotyped according to these dimensions of drug use.

One other area of drug use among Native Americans is addressed in Chapter 7, but worthy of mention here: the use of peyote as part of the religious ritual of the Native American Church. Peyote has been used by Native Americans in religious rituals for centuries without much attention. As the use of peyote in religious rituals spread throughout North America, it took different forms, some groups incorporated Christian elements, other groups were quite distinctly not Christian. Various of these groups joined together in what was eventually to become the Native American Church, which was incorporated in Oklahoma in 1918. The Native American Church became incorporated in other states and became international in 1954 with the incorporation of the Native American Church of Canada. Currently an estimated 250,000 people worldwide use peyote in their religious practice (Anderson 1996). The acceptance of the Native American Church, and especially the use of peyote, has not been well accepted by the American government over the years. Indeed, although the Native American Church has been officially recognized in several states, and the use of peyote is allowed, the drug remains banned in other states, even for religious ceremonial use.

Asian American Drug Use Dynamics
Our interest in drug use among Asian Americans is both historically and demographically based. The poppy plant, from which opium and other narcotics are derived, is grown in the Middle and Far East, and has been a part of Asian culture

for millenia. Moreover, as discussed in Chapter 2, it was the Chinese who introduced opium smoking to this country in the 19th century during the westward expansion, when tens of thousands of Chinese were imported into the United States to lay railroad tracks to the west. Narcotics use, especially in the form of opium smoking, has been part of the Chinese experience in America from the very beginning.

We recognize that the Chinese experience in America does not represent the broad spectrum of Asian Americans who trace their ancestry to the Far East, Southeast Asia, the Indian subcontinent, and Pacific Islands, and have been officially designated by the Census Bureau as Asian Pacific Islanders (API). This designation comprises more than 60 separate ethnic groups and subgroups (Harachi et al. 2001). The research on drug and alcohol use among Asian Americans has been relatively sparse, and what has been done has focused primarily on Chinese and Japanese. Figure 6.2 reveals that Asian Americans have the lowest prevalence rates of all ethnic categories reported, except for hallucinogens, where differences among ethnic categories are virtually nonexistent. Statewide surveys also reveal a similar low rate of use among Asian Americans (Harachi et al. 2001). This low rate is quite surprising, given the historical connection of Asians to opium use. In the paragraphs that follow, we speculate about the reasons for the low prevalence of substance use among Asian Americans.

Sue (1987) examines two possible factors that may account for lower rates of alcohol use and abuse among Asian Americans. First, a growing body of research suggests that genetic or other physiological factors predispose Asian Americans to an aversion to alcohol. These negative reactions include greater levels of flushing, higher pulse rates, and other uncomfortable symptoms. Sue also suggests that Asian Americans have strong cultural norms against excessive alcohol use. He suggests that a more collectivistic (rather than individualistic) value orientation gives Asian Americans a greater sense of responsibility to others, which restrains excessive drinking. Moreover, both Chinese and Japanese culture prescribe moderate alcohol use in certain social settings such as meal time. Alcohol is regarded as a substance promoting conviviality and good health in these cultures, rather than an avenue for achieving an altered state of consciousness.

A potential stress factor among immigrants is the process of acculturation. Asian Americans are among the most recent immigrants to America and are faced with integrating the values of the host culture even as they remain faithful to the values and lifestyles of their homelands (Oetting 1993). Intergenerational conflict often arises between first-generation immigrants who remain more loyal to traditional values and their children, whose loyalties are more likely tipped in favor of the new culture, which is their primary reference point. Given these dynamics, we would expect Asian Americans to have even higher rates of drug use than other minorities. But although these factors certainly play a role in the Asian American drug use that does occur (Bhattacharya 1998), other, protective factors mitigate substance abuse among these more recent immigrants. The family is the source of identity in Asian culture, and one's self-identity is integrated closely with the family system (Chung 1992).

Such strong family identification may be a powerful deterrent to drug use. Research has found, for example, that parents' disapproval of alcohol use was a particularly powerful predictor of lower prevalence of drug use among Asian Americans (Catalano et al. 1992; Gillmore et al. 1990) as compared with non-Asians. Similarly, strong parental involvement in children's lives was highly predictive of lower levels of substance use among Chinese and Southeast Asians (Catalano et al. 1992).

Our explanation for lower rates of drug use among Asian Americans remains speculative because the research on this ethnic category is limited. Most of the research on Asian Americans has focused on those of Chinese and Japanese descent. The few studies that have focused on specific subethnic groupings of Asian Americans suggest that this is a very heterogenous category. Whereas Chinese and Japanese have very low rates of substance use, for example, Pacific Islanders report rates nearly as high as other non-Asian populations (Austin 1999; Zane and Kim 1994). Moreover, there is virtually no research on how the cultural dynamics of Asian Americans relate to drug and alcohol use. More research is needed here as this is a growing and heterogenous segment of the American population.

Age Correlates of Drug Use

The age distribution of drug use represents an interesting but very logical pattern. Figure 6.3 portrays the percentage of five major age groups that have used each of five types of drug usage within the previous month. The drugs examined in this figure are alcohol (and "heavy" alcohol use), tobacco, marijuana, cocaine,[4] and prescription drugs. The age groups represented here correspond roughly to adolescence (12–17), college age (18–25), young adult (26–39), middle- aged baby boomers (40–64), and elderly (65 and over).

The age pattern for the drugs represented in Figure 6.3 is clear. A significant number of adolescents use these drugs, but adolescence is by no means the highest age group to be using either legal or illegal drugs during the previous month. Rather, it is the college age group (18–25) who are most likely to report drug use in the previous 30 days. The explanation for this pattern is quite straightforward: there is a good bit of experimentation with drugs during adolescence, but it is during the college years that both experimental and recreational use of most drugs takes place. As people get older their lifestyles change, and the use of both licit and illicit drugs are less and less a part of their lifestyles. Some cohort effects may also be at work; that is, people who are born at one time period may display a different pattern of drug use than those born during a different time period. Examining these trends across age categories does indeed suggest that certain age cohorts are more likely to use than others. Even within age cohorts, however, the pattern of modest levels of adolescent use, expanded college-age use, and gradually diminishing levels of use with increased age remains.

In this section, we will single out four specific age groups for closer analysis: adolescents, college students, the baby boomers, and the elderly. Research shows

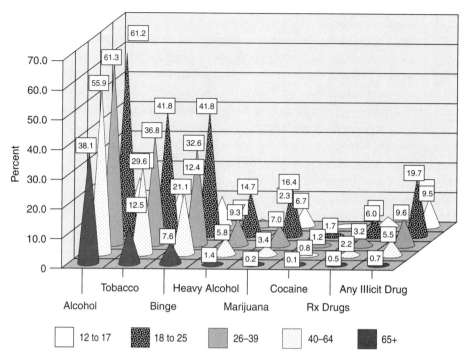

6.3 Percent of Age Categories Using Drugs in Last 30 Days, 2007.

Source: Adapted from Substance Abuse and Mental Health Services Administration 2008. *Results from the 2007 National Survey on Drug Use and Health: National Findings.* Office of Applied Studies, NSDUH Series H-34, DHHS Publication No. SMA 08-4343. Rockville, MD: Substance Abuse and Mental Health Services Administration.

Available online: http://www.oas.samhsa.gov/nsduh.htm [Accessed September 22, 2008]

that older people display certain drug use and abuse patterns, especially of prescription drugs, that set them apart from the rest of the population. The National Survey on Drug Use and Health does not, unfortunately, reflect the misuse of prescription drugs by the elderly since it is usually for medical purposes, even though it is often seriously detrimental to their health.

Drug Use among Adolescents

Adolescent drug use in the United States has been widely studied empirically since the 1960s and was originally the sole focus of the Monitoring the Future survey conducted by the University of Michigan's Survey Research Center. Recent data from the Monitoring the Future survey suggest reason for continued concern regarding adolescent drug use. Figure 6.4 reveals that recent illicit drug use has increased among 8th, 10th, and 12th graders throughout the 1990s, though we are witnessing a significant decline since the turn of the new millenium. When nearly 10 percent of 8th graders and approximately 25 percent of 12th graders have used illicit drugs in the previous month, parents, teachers, and public officials are understandably concerned about teen-age drug use.

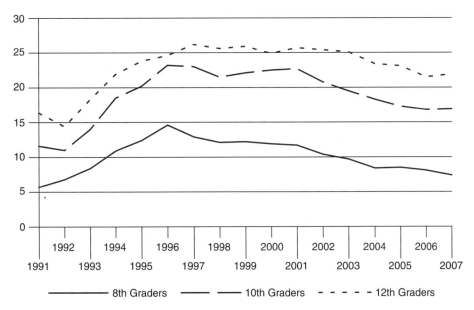

6.4 Percent of High School Students Using Any Illicit Drugs in the Last 30 Days, 1991–2007.

Source: Adapted from Johnston, Lloyd D., Patrick M. O'Malley, Jerald G. Bachman and John E. Schulenberg 2008, "Table 3: Trends in 30-Day Prevalence of Use of Various Drugs for 8th, 10th, 12th Graders" in *Monitoring the Future National Results on Adolescent Drug Use: Overview of Key Findings, 2007* (NIH Publication No. 08-6418). Bethesda, MD: National Institute on Drug Abuse.

Available Online: http://www.monitoringthefuture.org.

Before drawing any conclusions about levels of adolescent drug use, however, a couple of caveats are in order. First, most of the illicit drug use reported by these high school students is marijuana. This is not to suggest that adolescents are not also trying other illicit drugs. Nearly half of the students surveyed reported using other drugs as well. Use of illicit drugs other than marijuana, however, seems to be more sporadic. The second caveat is that even mid-1990 levels of illicit drug use are lower than what was reported in the mid- to late 1970s. In 1979, nearly 39 percent of 12th graders reported using illicit drugs during the previous month; in 2006, less than 22 percent reported such use. There was, in fact, a trend downward in teen drug use through the 1980s and early 1990s. This trend seems to have reversed in the mid-1990s, but resumed in the first decade of the new millennium, though not to the low levels of the early 1990s.

The trends for alcohol and tobacco are similar to that for illicit drugs. Monitoring the Future data reveal that 72 percent of 12th graders reported the use of alcohol in 1980, but that number declined through the 1980s and 1990s, and in 2001, only about 45 percent of high school seniors report using alcohol in the previous 30 days.[5] Tobacco use shows a slightly different trend, at least insofar as cigarettes are concerned. Approximately 30 percent of high school seniors smoked in the previous 30 days during the 1970s, decreasing only slightly through the 1980s, but rising again in the 1990s to even higher levels (36.5 percent in 1997) than in the 1970s. Once again, however, the last decade has shown a significant decline in tobacco use with less than 22 percent of America's high school seniors reporting cigarette use in the previous 30 days.

There is, furthermore, another tobacco form that appears to be attractive to young people, smokeless tobacco. Although cigarettes remain the most common form of tobacco use among teenagers, Monitoring the Future data reveal that in 1995 more than 12 percent of high school seniors had used smokeless tobacco in the previous 30 days (Johnston et al. 2008). A number of studies have confirmed the prevalence of smokeless tobacco use among young people. The National Youth Tobacco Survey, conducted jointly by the American Legacy Foundation and the Centers for Disease Control and Prevention in 1999, found that 4.2 percent of middle school boys and 11.6 percent of high school boys had used smokeless tobacco (CDC 2000). Tomar and Giovino (1998) reported that more than 20 percent of boys aged 11–19 had used smokeless tobacco, with 8 percent classifying themselves as regular users. They note that each day more than 2,200 young people first try smokeless tobacco and about 830 become regular users. Certain demographic patterns to smokeless tobacco use are discernible. This form of tobacco use tends to be a male phenomenon, and it tends to be higher among whites, with the possible exception of Native Americans (Arabi 2007; Nelson et al. 2006; Tomar and Giovino 1998). Athletes are more likely to use smokeless tobacco, which may be a result of role modeling among professional athletes (Arabi 2007; Tomar and Giovino 1998). Finally, it is worth noting that young people generally start using smokeless tobacco at a later age than they start using cigarettes (Arabi 2007). The good news is that smokeless tobacco use has been on the decline since the late 1990s. Monitoring the Future data reveal that only about 6 percent of seniors reported recent use in 2006 (Johnston et al. 2008), which represents a remarkable 50 percent decline since 1995. This trend is confirmed by the National Health Interview Survey (Nelson et al. 2006).

Another recent trend among young people is the smoking of *bidis,* imported cigarettes that are pleasantly flavored, and *kreteks,* clove-flavored cigarettes. The National Youth Tobacco Survey mentioned earlier found that more than 6 percent of high school boys and nearly 4 percent of high school girls reported smoking *bidis* (CDC 2000). Hrywna and colleagues (2004), utilizing the 2001 New Jersey Youth Tobacco Survey, reported almost double that of the National Survey, with 11.5 percent of high school boys reporting *bidis* use. The prevalence of *bidis* and *kreteks* use is even higher among those who smoke conventional cigarettes, and a particularly strong relationship emerges between these alternative cigarettes and cigar use (Hrywna et al. 2004; Soldz et al. 2003a). There is great concern among health officials because these forms of cigarettes seem to be targeted especially to young people with cherry, chocolate, and other candy flavorings, and there is a widespread (erroneous) belief that they are not as harmful as conventional cigarettes. Indeed, these imported cigarettes frequently do not even carry the legally required surgeon general's warning, and they are frequently sold to minors without checking for legal proof of age (Hrywna et al. 2004). The fact is that *bidis* and *kreteks* are very hazardous to health. Although the nicotine and tar content is slightly less in most cases, smokers of these products often take in more smoke for a longer period of time than smokers of conventional cigarettes (Malson et al. 2003).

This discussion of adolescent drug use would not be complete without a brief discussion of the use of so-called club drugs. These are drugs commonly used at rave parties, which have themselves taken on the character of a subculture (see Chapter 10). These drugs include MDMA (Ecstasy), ketamine, GHB, Rohypnol, LSD, and amphetamines, among others. Most research reports ecstasy to be the most commonly used of these drugs on the rave scene. Those who attend these events vary in age from 14 to 40 or older, but initiation into the use of these drugs quite typically begins during the teenage years (Hunt and Evans 2003). Monitoring the Future data suggest a declining prevalence of use among middle and high school students, and Krebs and Steffey (2005) observe that the age of onset into the use of these drugs has been decreasing over time. One reason for this is that rave parties are often advertised as "alcohol free," which allows promoters to lift any age restrictions and allays fears of otherwise concerned parents. The motivation and setting for using these drugs is almost always social in nature, with users reporting that they use for purposes of experimenting with drugs and to feel good and enhance social activities (Parks and Kennedy 2004).

Adolescent drug and alcohol use is of concern to officials not only because of the health and safety hazards that these drugs represent to these young people *as adolescents*, but also because we know that the use of these drugs as teenagers is highly predictive of continued use into adulthood (Mathers et al. 2006). There is also evidence that marijuana, and even alcohol and tobacco, may serve as "gateway drugs" to more expensive drug use as one becomes older (Gfroerer et al. 2002; Lessem et al. 2006). As we discussed in Chapter 2, this phenomenon is greatly misunderstood in the widespread belief that graduation to more serious drugs is somehow inevitable because of the pharmacological dynamics of addiction. This is not a correct understanding. However, we do know that the use of marijuana and, to a lesser extent, alcohol and tobacco positions young people in social networks that also encourage other drug use. For this reason, using drugs at an early age does indeed place young people at risk for more expensive drug use in their adult years.

Drug Use among College Students

College represents, for many young people, the establishment of their independence from their parents and, indeed, from adult authority in many areas of their personal lives. This is also a time when young people are exposed to many new pressures and influences. They are confronted in the classroom with challenges to the belief systems with which they grew up. They are confronted in the dormitories, fraternities, and sororities with lifestyles that are novel and perhaps a bit exciting. It should not be surprising, therefore, that this is a time of greatly expanded drug use for many young adults. Indeed, the National Household Survey reveals that the age group represented by college students, 18 to 25, reports the highest levels of all types of drug use within the previous month (see Figure 6.3).

The 1960s left an indelible mark on college campuses for later generations of college students. The country was in turmoil with civil rights unrest and, later in the decade, great disillusionment over the war in Vietnam. College drug-users of the 1960s and 1970s were defined by a distinct posture of protest, and drugs such as marijuana and LSD were a visible part of events such as Woodstock in 1969. Woodstock became a symbol of protest, and part of that symbolism was the open advocacy and use of marijuana and LSD. Experimentation with LSD was facilitated by its endorsement and use by Timothy Leary, a Harvard psychologist who was urging college students to "turn on" to LSD.

Certainly, reports of drug use and especially of the consequences of drug use were greatly exaggerated from time to time. The fact remains, however, that young people *were* turning on to drugs in far greater numbers than ever before. Moreover, these were largely the sons and daughters of middle-class families. America came to attention when the cream of its youth, those from middle-class families, were significantly represented among the ranks of drug users.

Lawmakers responded with haste to send a message to college students that drug use was not acceptable and that they would be punished accordingly. The real villains sought, however, were the drug dealers, who were believed to be responsible for turning a generation of young people on to deadly drugs such as marijuana, LSD, and cocaine. The most severe of sentences were reserved for the dealers who, it was believed, were not college students but inner-city entrepreneurs seeking to take advantage of innocent middle-class youth (Peterson 1985). Despite these efforts, college campuses continue to be a context for illicit drug use of various types, including marijuana, hallucinogens, cocaine, methamphetamines, and more recently drugs such as Rohypnol.

Most American colleges today are not characterized by protests, as in the 1960s or 1970s, but the effects of these protests, and the drug use that was part of them, remain. College campuses continue to be a place where many middle-class young people first begin experimenting with illegal drugs, often at rave parties that are also attended by younger high school students. Recent studies have also found increasing numbers of college students using cocaine, marijuana, and other drugs (Mohler-Kuo et al. 2003; Williams et al. 2006). However, illicit drug use on college campuses pales in comparison to alcohol consumption, much of it problematic. Figure 6.3 suggests that more than 60 percent of college-aged people are current users of alcohol, and studies focusing specifically on college populations report that more than 80 percent of college students report using alcohol in the previous 30 days (Bennett et al. 1999; Wechsler et al. 2002).

One review of research done on the topic of problem drinking concludes that most studies report between 20 and 25 percent of college students having drinking-problems (Berkowitz and Perkins 1986). One form of problem drinking that is quite common on college campuses is **binge drinking**. Binge drinking is generally defined as five drinks in a single drinking session for men and four for women.[6] A major study of students on 140 college campuses by Henry Wechsler and his associates at Harvard University found that more than 44 percent of students reported that they had engaged in binge drinking sometime in the two-week period prior to being interviewed (Wechsler et al. 2002). Durkin, Wolfe, and Clark (1999) found that 80 per-cent of the students in a

6.5 Binge drinking often takes place in festive atmospheres such as on spring breaks for college students. (Photo © iPhotoStock.com)

Maryland college reported binge drinking on at least one occasion during the prior semester. Figure 6.3 generally confirms these earlier studies, with more than 42 per-cent of college-aged (18–25) respondents reporting that they had engaged in binge drinking in the previous 30 days.

Binge drinking poses serious consequences for those students who participate, including relationship, academic, and health problems, and for many, eventual alco-holism, further illicit drug use, and problem behaviors associated with chronic heavy drinking. Powell, Williams, and Wechsler (2004) report that after the freshman year, *each drink* increases the probability of missing a class by 8 to 9 percent and increases the likelihood of getting behind in school by about 5 percent. This **secondary binge effect** extends beyond the drinker himself or herself to others, including nondrink-ers. Durkin and Clark (2000) report that, of their sample of students on one college campus, 35 percent reported driving a vehicle after a bout of binge drinking, 24 per-cent became involved in a fight, 23.3 percent engaged in unplanned sexual activ-ity, and 22.4 percent experienced a blackout. Hingson and colleagues (2005), using national data combining several data sources, similarly report more than 31 percent of college students drive an automobile while under the influence of alcohol, and among 18–24 year olds, 51 percent of traffic deaths are alcohol related. This same study also revealed an increase in alcohol-related nontraffic deaths among college students.

These numbers seem staggering, but we must remember that binge drinking is defined in these studies as drinking five (for men) or four (for women) drinks in a single drinking session (Wechsler et al. 1994). Europeans define binge drinking much more stringently. It is said that Italians consider eight drinks in a setting to be *normal* drinking! The fact that 80 percent of a student body drank five or four drinks in one session during the past semester is not nearly as dramatic as to suggest that 80 percent engaged in at least one episode of binge drinking. It is precisely the *normality* of drinking five or four drinks in a single setting the some scholars find objectionable about this definition (Dimeff et al. 1995), and others even find the term *binge drinking* without merit (Goodhart et al. 2003). Moreover, we also know that blood-alcohol content (BAC) depends on body weight, so having five or four drinks may produce some impairment of judgement for some people, others would not be affected by this quantity. The 5/4 threshold is, to be sure, a highly conservative threshold.

This interpretive caveat is not meant to diminish the potential alcohol-related problems that can occur on college campuses. Driving a car after 4 or 5 drinks *is* enough to make some drinkers illegal drivers and unsafe drivers to those around them (Wechsler and Austin 1998). And we know that many college students drink much more than this threshold level of binge drinking. Moreover, the data presented in Figure 6.3 suggest also that college-aged individuals are much more likely to be involved in "heavy drinking," which is more sustained than is binge drinking. We do suggest, however, that we be cautious when drawing conclusions, and that we not formulate policies and intervention strategies on these relatively rare extreme cases. College students who engage in threshold binge drinking are, in fact, engaging in *normative* behavior; nevertheless, they are easily labeled and stigmatized by zealous intervention efforts, a consequence that may be far more harmful than the drinking behavior itself.

Drug Use among the Baby Boomers

The baby boomers are that generation born after World War II, between the years 1946 and 1964. This generation has been regarded as somewhat unique among current demographic segments because of experiences they shared as a generation and because of the timing of historical events in their lives. During their formative years, these youngsters were confronted with the fear of nuclear holocaust at the height of the Cold War during the 1950s and early 1960s. The civil rights movement had a profound effect on the lives of this generation as they were teenagers and pre-teenagers when these events began to unfold. As they were turning 18, this country was at the height of the Vietnam War. This was not only a very unpopular war; it was also a bloody confrontation with an extremely high death toll. These young baby boomers faced a very uncertain future. Not surprisingly, this was a time of massive political unrest, which found expression in race riots, sit-ins, public demonstrations, and widespread drug use. The use of recreational drugs, particularly marijuana and LSD, was most certainly an expression of nonconformity among a dissident generation.

The baby boomers did not discontinue their drug use with the end of the Vietnam War or with the easing of race relations. Marijuana especially would continue to be a trademark of this generation. Data from the National Survey on Drug Use and Health reveal that 47.4 percent of adults between the ages of 40 and 64 (roughly the baby

Drugs: Myths and Reality

College Drinking and Drug Use: A Crisis?

The following extracts provide radically different views of drinking and drug use on college campuses *using the same data*. The second extract is a response to the report on which the first extract is based. Read the extracts and you decide.

Binge Drinking Widespread Among College Students: Little Progress Seen in Recent Years

Consumer Affairs

Nearly half of today's college student population is stumbling through the college year, either drunk or high on drugs, according to a new report by the National Center on Addiction and Substance Abuse at Columbia University. Forty-nine percent (3.8 million) of full-time college students binge drink and/or abuse prescription and illegal drugs, according to the report, "Wasting the Best and the Brightest: Substance Abuse at America's Colleges and Universities." The study also finds that 1.8 million full-time college students (22.9 percent) meet the medical criteria for substance abuse and dependence, two and one half times the 8.5 percent of the general population who meet these same criteria....

"It's time to get the 'high' out of higher education," said Joseph A. Califano, Jr., CASA's chairman and president and former U.S. Secretary of Health, Education, and Welfare. "Under any circumstances acceptance by administrators, trustees, professors and parents of this college culture of alcohol and other drug abuse is inexcusable. In

this world of fierce global competition, we are losing thousands of our nation's best and brightest to alcohol and drugs, and in the process robbing them and our nation of their promising futures," he said.

The report finds that from 1993 to 2005 there has been no real decline in the proportion of students who drink (70 to 68 percent) and binge drink (40 to 40 percent). However, the intensity of excessive drinking and rates of drug abuse have jumped sharply:

- Between 1993 and 2001 the proportion of students who binge drink frequently is up 16 percent; who drink on 10 or more occasions in a month, up 25 percent; who get drunk at least three times a month, up 26 percent; and who drink to get drunk, up 21 percent.
- Between 1993 and 2005 the proportion of students abusing prescription drugs increased:
  - 343 percent for opioids like Percocet, Vicodin and OxyContin;
  - 93 percent for abuse of stimulants like Ritalin and Adderall;
  - 450 percent for tranquilizers like Xanax and Valium;
  - 225 percent for sedatives like Nembutal and Seconal.
- Between 1993 and 2005, the proportion of students who:
  - Use marijuana daily more than doubled to 310,000.
  - Use cocaine, heroin, and other illegal drugs (except marijuana), is up 52 percent to 636,000.

Source: Excerpted from *Consumer Affairs*, "Binge Drinking Widespread Among College Students: Little Progress Seen in Recent Years." March 15, 2007. Available online: http://www.consumeraffairs.com/news04/2007/03/binge_drinking.html accessed May 26, 2008. Used with permission.

Drugs: Myths and Reality *(continued)*

Is There a College Substance Abuse Crisis?

Maia Szalavitz

Are things really getting worse or did Columbia's National Center on Addiction and Substance Abuse get the media's attention through the selective use of statistics?

Are we "Wasting the Best and the Brightest?" as the latest report on use of alcohol and other drugs by college students by Columbia's National Center on Addiction and Substance Abuse claims? Or is what Stats has dubbed the "Center for Abuse of Statistical Analysis" (and others have labeled the "Center for Alcohol Statistics Abuse") up to its old tricks?...

Careful readers of the report—a category which excludes almost all the journalists who reported its findings verbatim—may have wondered why CASA chose to look at trends in alcohol and other drug use from 1993 to 2005, rather than from the more obvious ten-year starting point, 1995—or from the 1970s, when statistics on the issue first began to be kept. Informed readers might also be curious about why the comparison point wasn't the highest level of drug use measured in teens (which occurred in 1979–81, depending on the particular drug); and they also might wish to know why the students were compared with the general population rather than with others their own age who do not attend college.

If such readers go to the source for most of CASA's data, the government's Monitoring the Future (MTF) and National Household Survey on Drug Use and Health (NHSDUH) studies, they will rapidly discover why.

Take, for example, the startling claim that in 2005 "almost one in four college students (22.9 percent) met the medical criteria for substance abuse or dependence, almost triple the proportion (8.5 percent) in the

general population." The source of this statistic appears to be a re-analysis of data collected for MTF or NHSDUH done by CASA.

This makes it appear as though college students are more likely to be addicts or alcoholics than non-college students, which is something that confounds common sense when you consider that the most severe cases of addiction start young and often result in failure to complete high school, let alone attend college—and that addiction itself often causes college dropout. (Note: "substance dependence" is the medical term for addiction; "substance abuse" is the medical term for use of substances that is potentially harmful but is not characterized by compulsion or long-term problems).

When you look at the NHSDUH figures for the general population age 18–25, you find a rate of substance abuse or dependence for 2005 of 21.8 percent. While this sounds equally as horrifying, the reason the rate is probably slightly higher for college attendees is that college binge drinking can often result in a "substance abuse" diagnosis: in other words, it's potentially dangerous but is not necessarily indicative of a long-term problem.

What CASA fails to point out (but is hinted at in the 8.5 percent substance abuse/dependence rate for the general population) is that the vast majority of college binge-drinking ends when graduates realize it is not compatible with employment that requires 9 A.M. cognitive clarity at work. The substance/abuse dependence rate for those over 26 is just 7.1 percent. In other words, stop the presses: many young people experiment with drugs and alcohol before they settle down and grow up.

CASA was forced to admit that college binge drinking itself has been steady between 1993 and 2005, so they problematized this as being an instance of "no significant decline" and pointed out minor changes

Drugs: Myths and Reality (*continued*)

in subcategories like a 16 percent increase in binge drinking "three or more times in the past two weeks." In the field, this is known as "data dredging:" Your main finding is not really that significant, so you parse enough subcategories in order to find something that looks scary or important....

Now we come to the curious choice of 1993 as the comparison year for the findings taken from Monitoring the Future. CASA notes that during that period the number of daily marijuana users more than doubled, going from 1.9 percent to 4 percent. If they had chosen 1995, however, the figure would have been 3.7 percent, which would have made the increase far less impressive. Even less scary would have been to note that in 1980, in the peak period of U.S. drug use, 7.2 percent of college students smoked marijuana daily and the nation did not collapse (in fact, this is the generation that produced the Internet boom)....

CASA says it wants to take the "high" out of "higher education;" but because college graduates are far less likely to have long-term substance misuse problems than those who do not attend or do not graduate, maybe it should focus more on keeping students in school rather than hyping fears about college drinking and other drug use. That college graduates remain less likely to get or stay addicted to alcohol or other drugs despite vastly expanded enrollment suggests that while "stay in school" may be a boring message, it may be the best widely applicable form of addiction prevention we have yet to develop.

Source: Exerpted from Maia Szalavitz, "Is There A College Substance Abuse Crisis?" Statistical Assessment Service (STATS), March 21, 2007. Available online: http://stats.org/stories/2007/is_there_college_crisis_mar21_07.htm (accessed May 26, 2008). Used with permission.

boom generation) has used marijuana (SAMSHA 2006a). Although people in their 20s report slightly higher percentages of lifetime use, it must be remembered that baby boomers were using at a time when marijuana use was not nearly as accepted in popular culture as it is today. Smoking marijuana in the 1960s and early 1970s was an act of defiance that involved great risk of serious sanction by the criminal justice system. That more than 47 percent of this generation report having smoked marijuana is extremely significant. Furthermore, although most baby boomers have stopped smoking marijuana with any sort of regularity, it is worthwhile pointing out that more baby boomers report current marijuana use than the use of diverted prescription drugs. Figure 6.3 reveals that 3.4 percent of 40- to 64-year-olds have smoked marijuana within the previous 30 days. There is, it seems, a small core of persistent marijuana users maintaining at least one of the symbols of Woodstock.

Marijuana is not the only drug in the baby boomer pharmacopeia. This generation also extensively used LSD, cocaine, and prescription pills, among others. Recent national surveys suggest that drug use of various types continues to be prevalent among the baby boomers, and may even be on the increase (Alcoholism and Drug Abuse Weekly 2006). Ethnographic research by Boeri, Sterk, and Elifson (2006) reveals a pattern of heroin and methamphetamine use by baby boomers similar to that found by Faupel (1991) among street heroin addicts. The central issues facing baby boomer drug use, according to these authors, are whether or not they are occupied primarily with conventional or unconventional role obligations and their ability to maintain control over their drug use. The baby boomers in their sample experienced phases of use ranging from *controlled users*, those with conventional role obligations who maintained strong control over their drug use, to *marginal users*, with conventional role obligations, but who were losing control over their drug use. Some of these marginal users would become *hustlers*, *dealers*, or *sex workers*, resorting to unconventional roles as a way of maintaining some control over their drug use; or they may become simply *junkies* who lost all meaningful social roles and control over their drug use.

The issues facing baby boomer users are not so different from users in other age categories in that their use is also facilitated and constrained by the social structure of which they are a part. Because baby boomers are more likely to be involved in meaningful jobs, family relationships, and so forth, controlling their drug use becomes much more of an issue than among younger people who are less likely to have these conventional role obligations. Baby boomers also face more potentially serious health issues related to their drug use than do younger users, which also makes their use more consequential. The reality is that the baby boom generation is a generation accustomed to using drugs, and there is some evidence to suggest that a substantial number of this generation have continued using various drugs recreationally.

Drug Use among the Elderly

Figure 6.3 reveals that illicit drug use among the elderly is extremely rare. Alcohol and tobacco use are more common for the elderly than illicit drug use, but less common when compared with other adult age groups. Use of prescription drugs for medical ailments is much more common, of course, as is the use of over-the-counter medication, which has been increasing in recent years, though largely ignored in the drug literature (Hanlon et al. 2001). Of primary concern with regard to drug use among the elderly is not so much the prevalence of use as the consequences and circumstances of use.

Consequences of Elderly Drug Use and Abuse

The aging process modifies the way in which the human body responds to drugs and alcohol, including the rate of absorption, how the drug is distributed through the body, and the rate and manner of excretion (Council on Scientific Affairs 1996). Hence, those who use pharmacological substances in their older years will almost certainly experience effects and consequences very differently than what they might have become accustomed to at an earlier time. Elderly drinkers, for example, generally have higher blood alcohol content because of lower levels of systemic water volume. Heavy drinking is much more likely to affect the intake of food, thus resulting in nutritional deficiencies (Breslow et al. 2003). Moreover, because elderly users are heavy users of prescription drugs, accounting for more than 30 percent of all prescription drug use (Willcox et al. 1994), they are especially at risk for overdose symptoms resulting from synergism of two or more drugs they may be taking, either legitimately or illegitimately. Recent research by Pringle and her associates (2005) found that some 77 percent of elderly prescription drug users were using drugs that interacted with alcohol, and that 19 percent of these drug users also used alcohol. Other research suggests even higher levels of alcohol consumption (Breslow et al. 2003). The results can be disabling or even deadly.

Elderly people experience other significant consequences of drug use. Longitudinal research by Fu, Liu, and Christensen (2004) revealed a decline in general health status that was directly related to inappropriate use of medications. Cognitive impairment is also commonly reported (Dealberto et al. 1997). Drugs have been identified as the cause of delirium in 11 to 30 percent of cases, according to various studies of elderly hospital patients (Moore and O'Keeffe 1999). Use of psychotropic drugs has also been linked to impairment of motor coordination (Kirby et al. 1999). Because the effects of drugs on the human body become more pronounced with age, negative health consequences will almost always be more severe than those experienced by younger users.

Circumstances of Elderly Drug Use and Abuse

If elderly individuals knowingly and voluntarily used drugs in an inappropriate manner, the consequences of elderly drug abuse might be more easily dismissed. The fact is, however, that many if not most elderly drug users and abusers are not aware that they engaging in drug abuse. We don't even call it drug abuse. Rather, we refer to it as "overprescription," "inappropriate medication," or "inappropriate drug prescribing." **Polypharmacy** is also used to describe the general practice of prescribing multiple drugs, though this term is most commonly defined as the concomitant use of four or more medications (Rallason and Vogt 2003). All these vocabularies tend to minimize the seriousness of this problem, which can result in several negative consequences for the patient, including nonadherence to the prescription because of the complexity of the drug regimen (Hughes 2004), adverse drug reactions including the potential for drug synergism, medication errors, and increased hospitalization (Rollason and Vogt 2003). Moreover, elderly drug users are at the mercy of medical professionals who all too often have little time or inclination to respond to their questions or concerns. Because it is easy to prescribe a drug for a particular symptom, elderly patients are often prescribed drugs unnecessarily or even inappropriately. Research by Willcox, Himmelstein, and Woolhandler (1994) revealed that nearly 25 percent of the residents in community living facilities were prescribed drugs that were *contraindicated*, meaning that they were not appropriate for a particular symptom. Indeed, Reid (1998) found that when female patients came in complaining of depression, most physicians don't even inquire about substance use patterns before prescribing sedatives.

The problem is not merely doctors asleep on the job, however. Much of the problem with overprescribing and inappropriate prescribing is a result of the increasing specialization of medicine today. Elderly people are especially likely to be under the care of numerous specialists who each prescribe drugs for particular conditions. The elderly patient may have several pharmacies at which prescriptions are filled, particularly when their specialists may practice in different communities (Mort and Aparasu 2002; Rollason and Vogt 2003). Unless the patient is alert to all of the medications that they are taking, it is very easy, indeed likely, that they will be prescribed medications that interact with each other to produce adverse effects. This is a problem that could be rectified with a central database, preferably organized on a national level, into which all prescriptions would be entered. Any doctor or pharmacist would only have to access the database to determine whether there were any potential untoward drug interaction effects. At present, however, we have no such program at the national level.

Finally, elderly individuals are also very likely to be using over-the-counter (OTC) medications in addition to prescribed medications. A review of research by Hanlon and colleagues (2001) revealed that between 31 and 96 percent of elderly Americans use OTC medications, with percentages varying by geographic region and ethnicity. Many of these medications contain alcohol. Because alcohol synergizes with other depressants, any prescription of sedatives, tranquilizers, or antihistamines to elderly patients could produce very severe consequences. Combine this with the fact that many elderly individuals drink alcohol, and symptoms of drug overdose are of especially great concern among a population whose bodies do not absorb, distribute, or excrete these chemicals as effectively as do the bodies of younger people.

Social Class Correlates of Drug Use

Social class is a very nebulous concept. There is no single measure of social class as there is for sex, ethnicity, and age. Consequently, research on the relationship between social class and drug use is both limited and ambiguous. Common-sense ideas about social class and drug use abound, of course. Illegal drug use has generally been associated with the lower class, though by the 1960s this image changed with regard to certain drugs. Notably, marijuana, hallucinogens, cocaine, and some inhalants came to be associated with the middle class, as these drugs were identified with college protests and a rebellious youth culture made up of children of middle-class parents. These drugs are generally not regarded as serious or dangerous. Sterk-Elifson (1996) has noted that drugs associated with the middle class are viewed as "good drugs which are used the right way" (64), which is to say they are either smoked or snorted compared with the "wrong" form of "bad" drug use by the lower class involving injection or smoking/inhaling crack cocaine vapors. Because we do not have any direct measure of social class, it is difficult to verify or falsify these popular stereotypes. Social class features have been used by various descriptive studies as a basis for sampling and identifying respondents (e.g., Buchanan 1993; Krebs and Steffey 2005; Sterk-Elifson 1996). These studies provide valuable information, typically of a qualitative nature, of the dynamics of drug use among middle-class women, for example, or lower-class youth. But even these studies are based either on the researcher's subjective determination of what constitutes social class or on some indirect measure of social class. Indeed, what we know about social class and drug use is built upon measures and observations about demographic characteristics of drug users that have some bearing on that social construct that we call *social class*.

Generally, when we think of social class, we think of economic standing, which can be measured in a number of ways. A very straightforward economic indicator is income. Studies show that drug use tends to be directly related to income, meaning that the higher the income, the greater the level of drug use (Parker et al. 1995; Petry 2000). The rationale for this is quite straightforward: drugs are a consumer commodity, and like any other consumer commodity, the level of consumption depends upon the level of available resources, which is provided by one's income. This rationale assumes that the demand for drug is elastic, that there is not an intrinsic need for drugs that leaves a user unable to adjust the amount of drugs that they use (Petry 2000). Research by Kandel and her associates (1995) qualifies these findings somewhat with their finding that income is positively related to drug use during the early part of one's career (until about age 30), but thereafter the relationship is reversed. These authors explain this pattern by suggesting that drug use has a delayed but cumulative effect on wages. It may be that higher wages at earlier ages encourages a lifestyle of drug use, but that over time, the use of these drugs becomes an impediment to opportunities for promotions and other incentives that would have the effect of increasing wage earnings.

Studies showing a positive relationship between income and drug use are contrary to other findings that people on welfare are much more likely to be drug users than those not on welfare (Delva et al. 2000; Lehrer et al. 2002). This research suggests that drug use may be an impediment to getting off welfare, which leaves drug users reliant on the meager assistance that they get from the government. Understood in this way, drug use is the determining factor in social class standing, rather than the other way around. The research on the relationship between drug use and welfare is not conclusive, however. Grant and Dawson (1996) found that rates of drug and alcohol use were relatively low among individuals on various welfare programs, and no higher than rates in the general population. Similar research by Yacoubian and Urbach (2002), using ADAM data from arrested populations, revealed close similarities between welfare-receiving and non-welfare-receiving arrestees.

Room (2005) suggests a much more intricate relationship in the fact that both poverty and substance use are morally stigmatizing conditions. He points out, for example, that under some conditions (e.g., toasting or celebrating) substance use may actually enhance an individual's standing, whereas under other conditions (addiction or loss of control) such use may be highly stigmatizing. Moreover, living in poverty may only exacerbate the problem of alcohol and drug use because of the stigmatizing nature of poverty. Using qualitative data, Luck, Elifson, and Sterk (2004) further point out that both drug use and being on welfare are symptomatic of women's position in society, both being the result of barriers, including lack of education, limited job skills, lack of meaningful employment opportunities, and the absence of affordable child care that prohibit many women from making a better life.

Employment is usually regarded as a contributing factor in the determination of social class because (1) it provides the basis for income, which is a direct measure of social class, and (2) one's job is, in and of itself, a source of standing and position in the community. Employment status might logically be linked to drug use in two very opposing ways. One might logically reason, for example, that drug use requires time for acquisition of the drug, use of the drug, and experiencing euphoria and other effects of the drug, none of which is compatible with maintaining regular employment. Seen in this way drug use is what Kaestner (1994b) calls a "time intensive" activity that will reduce the likelihood of employment. On the other hand, many drugs are expensive, requiring resources to acquire, which might make regular employment a necessity. In this way, drugs might be seen as a "goods intensive" activity (Kaestner, 1994b). Research on the relationship between drug use and employment is not clear. Research by Parker, Weaver, and Calhoun (1995) found that both drug and alcohol use was significantly higher among those who were employed. Zlotnic, Robertson, and Tam (2002), in research among homeless men, found quite to the contrary that recent drug users were 20 times as likely to be unemployed as non-drug users. Similarly, Reid and colleagues (2001) found that drug use is much higher in communities characterized by high unemployment rates. Other research is much less clear. Kaestner's research (1994b) reveals an idiosyncratic relationship between drug use and employment. Research by Atkinson and colleagues (2000) found that heroin users were not as likely to be employed, but other types of drug use did not seem to affect employment status. This research further revealed that the likelihood of legitimate employment was primarily determined by whether or not an individual had sources of income other than regular employment. The relationship between drug use and employment status is, in short, unclear. Most studies are not even clear, for example, about whether drug use should affect employment status, or whether employment status should affect drug use! It is also less than clear whether income affects drug use or drug use affects income. More important, perhaps, is an understanding of the conditions under which these social class variables affect or are affected by various types of substance use. Certainly, much more research is needed in this area.

Summary

We have, in this chapter, examined the question of whether certain segments of the population are more vulnerable to drug use and abuse than others. The answer to the question is that there are. We have seen, for example, that men are generally more likely to use drugs than women. We have also learned, however, that drug-using women face physical and relational complications from their drug use that go far beyond what most men experience. With regard to race, whites are more likely to report drug use than either Hispanics or blacks. We have also learned, however, that cultural, economic, and historical features of black, Hispanic and other ethnic communities contribute to unique experiences and problems associated with drug use. Drug use also varies in prevalence and type across different age groups. The motives for use and the consequences of use are quite different among adolescents, for example, than among the elderly. Finally, we have also identified factors related to social class, including income and employment status, that bear some relationship to alcohol and drug use. Research on the relationship between social class and drug use is much more limited, however, and that which has included social class variables does not present a clear picture of this relationship. Unlike the other demographic features examined in this chapter—sex, ethnicity, and age—it is not clear whether social class variables affect drug use or vice versa. Certainly, a plausible argument can be made either way.

This chapter on the demographic correlates of drug use should highlight an important sociological contribution to the study of drug use—namely, that the extent and nature of drug-using behavior varies by social categories. Whereas individuals exhibit certain unique drug-using qualities, there are also important similarities, at least broadly speaking, within population categories. These similarities, and the respective differences across categories, emphasized the importance of social as well as individual factors that account for patterns of drug use.

Key Terms

binge drinking
demographics
polypharmacy
secondary binge effect
tecatos

Thinking Critically...

1. What are some of the ways in which drug-using women are stigmatized? Why do you think that women who use illicit drugs are stigmatized more than drug-using men? How does this dynamic reflect differential patterns in the treatment of men and women in the larger society?

2. Besides being more vulnerable to stigmatization, discuss other ways in which women suffer from drug use disproportionately to men. Are these forms of victimization intrinsic to being female, or are they somehow the result of how society defines women? Explain

3. If it is true, as we suggest, that "whites are more likely to use drugs than either blacks or Hispanics," what do you think accounts for the stereotype that drug use is primarily concentrated among ethnic minorities?

4. Why is it that drug use is highest among young adults? Discuss the social factors that contribute to this demographic reality.

5. Speculate on the different social dynamics behind lower-class drug use and middle-class drug use. For example, are there likely to be differences in motivation for use? In the way individuals are introduced to drugs? In the consequences for drug use?

Learning from the Internet

1. Learn what you can about the special problems encountered by women drug users. The following sites may be helpful:

National Institute on Drug Abuse, http://www.nida.nih.gov/
Food and Drug Administration, http://www.fda.gov/womens/default.htm
You can also find information simply by using your search engine, using keywords "women's health" and "drugs."

2. Select any of the ethnic categories discussed in this chapter and research the cultural dynamics of drug use in that category. Search engine keywords might include, for example: *hispanic + drug use* or *chicano + culture + drugs*.

Notes

1. The term *strawberry* presumably came about as a description of the pursed lips of a woman prior to performing fellatio on a man. The term is now used to describe women (and men) who trade any number of sex acts for drugs (Elwood and Williams 1997).

2. It should be noted that there was an awareness of the presence of crack prior to the publishing of this *New York Times* article. Agar (2003) notes reports of crack cocaine circulating in subcultural and law enforcement circles as early as 1981.

3. *Heavy use* is defined as five or more drinks on the same occasion on each of 5 or more days in the past 30 days.

4. Cocaine use represented here does not include crack cocaine. The drugs represented here and the other drugs included in Figures 6.1 and 6.2 do not show complete data for age categories.

5. In 1993, the Monitoring the Future survey asked the question slightly differently, so that alcohol use involved "more than a few sips." Prior to that time, literally *any* use of alcohol was recorded as use. All other factors being equal, this change will result in a somewhat reduced percentage, but the reduction does not seem to be very much. In 1993, the question was posed both ways, and the difference was less than 3 percent (Johnston et al. 2000,. Table 2.

6. In February, 2004, the National Institute on Alcohol Abuse and Alcoholism issued the following statement defining binge drinking, which is generally accepted:

"A 'binge' is a pattern of drinking alcohol that brings blood alcohol concentration (BAC) to 0.08 gram percent or above. For the typical adult, this pattern corresponds to consuming 5 or more drinks (male) or 4 or more drinks (female), in about 2 hours" (National Institute on Alcohol Abuse and Alcoholism 2004, 3).

CHAPTER **7**

Institutional Correlates
of Drug Use

In the broadest sense, this chapter focuses on a number of institutional correlates of drug use. Newman defines a social institution as "patterned ways of solving the problems meeting the requirements of a particular society" (2008, 27). Examples of social institutions include the family, education, economy, politics and law, religion, health care, the military, and mass media (27–29). This examination will not be exhaustive of all social institutions. Some topics pertaining to particular institutions (e.g., the economy) are discussed elsewhere in the text. This chapter will pay particular attention to occupations and roles within key social institutions, showing how the structure and culture of an organization or group can influence alcohol and other drug use preferences and patterns.

We will also discuss how occupations and organizations are affected by the alcohol and other drug use of members and participants. The institutional contexts that we will examine in some detail in this chapter are: the medical profession, the military, law enforcement, religion, and sports. These institutions do not necessarily exhibit the most drug use; the entertainment industry, for example, almost certainly has higher levels of drug use than perhaps all of the contexts that we discuss here. Rather, this chapter focuses on those institutional arenas (1) where drug use has been identified as a significant issue, (2) where drug use represents a significant threat to the participants and/or the welfare of society generally, and/or (3) that represent the types of occupational dynamics that give rise to drug and alcohol abuse.

Much of what is contained in this chapter focuses on occupational dynamics that take place within the respective institutions we are examining. These occupational features are important for understanding drug use for several reasons. First, these institutions are the context for *work*, and working people spend a considerable amount of their time at the *workplace*, the geographical locale in which occupational activities are conducted. The workplace—usually a centralized location where others in the same or similar occupations interact in the production of particular goods or services—comprises the critical component of the institution of which it is a part which give rise to or is affected by drug and alcohol use of participants in those occupations. Different occupations will bring together different kinds of people to these institutional workplaces. Second, occupations vary in the demands imposed on those who hold various positions. Some occupations are inherently more stressful than others. Some have unique performance expectations that might be enhanced by the use of certain types of drugs. The occupational subculture of professional sports, for example, at least tacitly supports the use of steroids and other performance-enhancing drugs. Likewise, the structure and culture of both the military and law enforcement seems to increase the likelihood of alcohol or drug use, albeit unintentionally. Third, some occupations and associated workplaces provide greater access to certain types of drugs, a particularly important factor of the medical institution. For all of these reasons, the discussion of the institutional context of drug use cannot be separated from the occupational dynamics intrinsic to the institutions of which occupations are a part.

Drug Use Among Medical Professionals

Drug use is a major concern within the medical profession, in part because of the potentially catastrophic consequences of such use should a health care worker attempt to carry out his or her duties while impaired. Also, the job responsibilities of doctors, nurses, and other health care professionals include recognizing substance use (and its consequences) among patients (Baldwin et al. 2008). Medical personnel are able to obtain drugs in a variety of ways, but the most common methods involve theft from hospital pharmacies, falsely prescribing drugs for patients and diverting them for personal use, and diverting for personal use drugs that others legitimately prescribed to patients. Other means include obtaining drugs from an obliging pharmacist or "forgetting" to have a written prescription (Winick 1961). These practices are especially problematic because hospitals and medical oversight organizations historically have been reluctant to pursue reported cases of drug misuse (Banta and Tennant 1989).

The medical profession acknowledges that drug use occurs among its members, and it has implemented a number of efforts to reduce use and the various problems associated with it. In 1969 and 1971, Florida and Texas respectively passed pioneering legislation in the form of a "sick doctor statute," which made it easier to discipline doctors. Prior to these and subsequent acts in other states, physicians had to have committed specified acts of misconduct before being reported. These "sick doctor statutes" identify the inability of a doctor to perform with reasonable skill because of one or more enumerated illnesses (including drug abuse) as grounds for disciplinary action (Council on Mental Health 1973). Beyond these statutes, Banta and Tennant (1989) report that the Medical Association of Georgia has developed a program for drug-impaired physicians that identifies chemically dependent doctors and monitors their recovery. Some other states have implemented similar programs for monitoring physicians.

Patterns of Drug Use among Medical Personnel

Drug use among physicians was first brought to the attention of sociologists by Charles Winick in his now classic article, "Physician Narcotic Addicts (1961). Winick reported that approximately one of every one hundred physicians is an addict, a phenomenal rate of addiction when compared to the estimated rate (at the time) of one addict per 3,000 among the general population. Other early studies reported similarly high rates of use and addiction among physicians (Modlin and Montes 1964; Pescor 1942; Putnam and Ellinwood 1966). Most physician drug use in these early studies was for purposes of self-medication, primarily by narcotics and other depressants (Putnam and Ellinwood 1966; Valliant et al. 1970; Winick 1961). Early research on drug use by medical students also focused heavily on instrumental drug use. Unlike the early studies of physicians, however, which focused primarily on narcotics and depressant use, studies of medical students highlighted the use of stimulants and similar drugs primarily for the purposes of coping with stress and long hours (Blaine et al. 1968; Smith and Blachly 1966; Watkins 1970).

A second wave of research in the 1970s revealed a new pattern of recreational drug use, particularly of marijuana, among physicians and medical students. Marijuana was a visible part of youth culture during the late 1960s, and it is hardly surprising that this research interest emerged when it did. Lipp and Benson (1972) report that 25 percent of the physicians in their sample had tried marijuana, and 7 percent were current users. Moreover, most of the physicians in their sample (92 percent) used alcohol. Studies by McAuliffe and colleagues (1984, 1986) reveal that approximately 30 percent of the physicians surveyed in the New England area had smoked marijuana within the past year, and approximately 8 percent of these doctors were regular users (1984). In contrast, in 1985 an estimated 13.6 percent of the population in the United States had used marijuana within the past year, and just over 9 percent were current users (SAMHSA 1999c).

Research among medical students during this period reveals even greater levels of use. Generally, these studies have found that a substantial majority, approximately 70 percent, had at least tried marijuana. Moreover, a sizable minority, between 30 and 45 percent, report marijuana use within the past year (Mechanick et al. 1973; Rochford et al. 1977; Thomas et al. 1977; Conard et al. 1988; DeWitt et al. 1991; Maddux et al. 1986; McAuliffe et al. 1984, 1986). Similarly findings have been reported by Engs (1982) among medical students in Australia. Alcohol use was also high among medical students during this period, with 80 to 90 percent reporting current use of alcohol. Substantially fewer numbers of students were tobacco users. Indeed, in almost all cases, both current and lifetime marijuana use is higher than tobacco use among these future physicians. Other drug use patterns by medical students include cocaine use (Conard et al. 1988; McAuliffe et al. 1984), analgesics of various types, tranquilizers, narcotics, and increasingly, LSD and other hallucinogens (Baldwin et al. 1991; Maddux et al. 1986; Rochford et al. 1977).

More recent research suggests substantially lower use among physicians. A national study of 9,600 physicians reveals that less than 5 percent had used marijuana within the past year, and less than 1 percent had used cocaine, narcotics, or amphetamines in the one-month period prior to responding to the survey (Hughes, Baldwin et al. 1992. Self-reports suggest that only 3.3 percent of the physicians[1] in the sample reported using any illicit drugs in the previous year. This figure compares favorably with teachers (9.2 percent), social workers (19.2 percent), and lawyers and judges (19.1 percent) (Hoffman et al. 1996). Nurses, it seems, are substantially more likely to use illicit drugs and alcohol than are physicians. Among the nurses sampled, 12.1 percent report using illicit drugs during the previous year (compared with 3.3 percent of physicians), and 5.5 percent of the nurses reported current (previous 30 days) illicit drug use (Hoffman et al. 1996).

Finally, recent research has also investigated differences across medical specialties with regard to patterns of drug use. Alcohol use ranks high across all medical specialties, with over 90 percent of respondents reporting alcohol use (Hughes, Brandenburg, et al. 1992; Hyde and Wolf 1995). Psychiatry residents tend to have the highest levels of illicit drug use, ranging from 80 percent who have used marijuana to 11 percent who have used barbiturates. Emergency residents also reported high lifetime use of illegal drugs, particularly marijuana (79.7 percent) and cocaine (38 percent). Surgeons and pediatric and pathology residents, on the other hand, reported the lowest levels of illicit drug use (Hughes et al. 1992b).

Explaining Drug Use by Medical Personnel

A variety of reasons have been given for why physicians and other medical personnel self-medicate and in many cases become addicted to narcotic and depressant drugs. These include overwork, chronic fatigue, physical ailments, marital problems, personality disorders, disillusionment, poor self-concept, and mood enhancement and recreational use (Baldwin et al. 1991; Modlin and Montes 1964; Winick 1961, 1974b). Beyond these individualistic explanations, Holtman (2007, 543) notes that the organizational culture of the medical field encourages the use of drugs as a means of managing stress in the workplace. Two competing theories tend to dominate the discussion of why physicians and other medical personnel use drugs: the stress hypothesis and the availability hypothesis.

The **stress hypothesis** posits that compared to most other occupations, physicians are under exceptional stress. Physicians face life-and-death situations. A less than optimal performance can result in the death or permanent disabling of a patient. Moreover, long hours, working environment, and anxiety may contribute to fatigue (Leape and Fromson 2006) and result in role conflict by interfering with family obligations. Bressler (1976) identifies stress and role conflict as primary factors in physician suicide as well as drug use. Occupational stress is certainly consistent with many of the reasons that physicians give for abusing drugs, and it is also consistent with depressant use, and especially narcotic use. The stress hypothesis is also supported by Stout-Weigand and Trent (1981), who examined drug use and stress among a general sample of general practitioners, anesthesiologists, pathologists, dermatologists, and dentists. When the authors examined drug use in conjunction with reported stress levels, 23 percent of those who reported high stress levels also reported using drugs, whereas only 3 percent of physicians who reported low stress also reported drug use.

The **availability hypothesis** is predicated on the idea that medical personnel have greater access to controlled substances than most any other occupational group. Sociologist Charles Winick's (1974b) pioneering descriptive work among nurses reflects some of the same availability factors that he observed among physicians. For example, nurses who use drugs often request the night shift because there are fewer people to monitor their behavior and because patients are asleep, making it easier to divert medications or give a patient only a portion of a dosage and keep the rest. Still other nurses seek positions in nursing homes where chronic patients receive large dosages of narcotics and where complaints of pain are not as likely to be investigated. These are fairly elaborate strategies, and nurses who engage in such activities are almost certainly addicted to the drugs that they are using.

It seems likely that availability is a primary factor in the increased recreational drug use among medical personnel. Case studies conducted by McAuliffe (1984) reveal that much of the drug use among the health care professionals was recreational, not for functional purposes such as relieving stress. McAuliffe's work is partially supported by research among Quebec physicians, which concluded that it was not possible to identify a single type of physician addict. The so-called therapeutic addict, who has tended to dominate the literature on physician drug abuse, is but one type of addict. Other physicians much more closely resembled the street addict in the nature and purpose of their drug use (Wallot and Lambert 1984). Although numerous variables account for increased recreational use—not the least of which are cultural and philosophical shifts that have occurred over time—it would seem that availability factors may be more important than stress factors in accounting for increased recreational use.

Drug Use in the Military

Throughout history, accounts of substance use, particularly alcohol, by members of the military are common. The stereotypical image of toughness is related to one "holding his liquor" and has long been associated with soldiers; to that end, the military has long tolerated this tradition (Ames et al. 2007; Bachman et al. 1999). In the United States, contemporary concern for drug use among military personnel has its origin in the Vietnam War era. Robins' widely cited study, *The Vietnam Drug User Returns* (1974), chronicles the dramatic changes that occurred. Prior to Vietnam, these young men were highly experienced with alcohol and tobacco, less experienced with marijuana, and had almost no experience with other drugs. Only about 1 percent of these individuals had used any narcotic more than a few times, and only 11 percent had ever used narcotics. The Vietnam experience dramatically affected levels of drug use. Approximately 7 of 10 soldiers used marijuana and 1 of 3 tried narcotics, particularly opium and heroin. More importantly, approximately half of soldiers who used drugs while in Vietnam continued to do so after returning to the United States. Concerns over use following their return led to a number of changes in policy during the 1970s (Ames et al. 2007).

The post-Vietnam years have witnessed increasing attention to the problem of illicit drug and alcohol use in all of the branches of the armed forces. The military pioneered the practice of drug testing, which began on a sporadic basis for soldiers returning from Vietnam. Following a 1981 jet fighter crash into the deck of a nuclear aircraft carrier, which killed 14, injured 48 others, and resulted in over $2 million in damages, the Department of Defense (DoD) instituted mandatory urinalysis in all of the branches of the armed forces (Banta and Tennant 1989). There is convincing evidence that the mandatory testing in the military has been effective in reducing illicit drug use among personnel.

Since 1980, the DoD has sponsored nine surveys, the most recent conducted in 2005, to assess the level of substance abuse among active military personnel. In each of the survey years,[2] between 15,000 and 22,000 active military personnel answer questions about tobacco, alcohol, and illicit drug use, in addition to a host of other subjects such as health, diet, and exercise habits. In 2005, 16,146 active duty military completed the survey. As seen in Figure 7.1, use of illicit drugs precipitiously declined through the 1980s and leveled off through the next two decades. This decline reflects the corresponding downward trend in drug use among the general population since 1979. Tobacco use also declined substantially over the 25-year period, from 34.2 percent who described themselves as heavy smokers (20+ cigarettes daily) in 1980 to 11.0 percent in 2005. Heavy alcohol consumption generally declined in the 1980, with minor fluctuations since (Bray et al. 2006).

As mentioned previously, smoking and drinking have been encouraged among military personnel, at least informally (Bryant 1974; Ballweg and Li 1991). Cigarettes and alcohol are often available for reduced prices at base outlets. The DoD changed its posture in the 1980s, instituting mandatory drug testing and establishing policies to improve the health and quality of life of military personnel as a means of improving

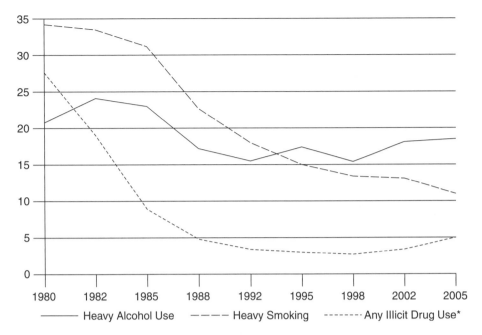

7.1 Trends in Substance Use in Military, 1980–2008.

* Because of difference in wording, 2005 data for any illicit drug use is not directly comparable to previous years.

Source: Bray, Robert M., Laurel L. Hourani, Kristine L. Rae Olmsted, Michael Witt, Janice M. Brown, Michael R. Pemberton, Mary Ellen Marsden, Bernadette Marriott, Scott Scheffler, Russ Vandermass-Peeler, BeLinda Weimer, Sara Calvin, Michael Bradshaw, Kelly Close, and Douglas Hayden 2006. *2005 Department of Defense Survey of Health Related Behaviors Among Active Duty Military Personnel: A Component of the Defense Lifestyle Assessment Program (DLAP)*. Research Triangle Park NC: Research Triangle Institute.

overall readiness (Bray and Hourani 2007; Bray and Kroutil 1995). These policies have been accompanied by programs to assist in quitting smoking and drinking, as well as quitting illicit drug use. However, some scholars suggest the effectiveness of these interventions is weakened by the inconsistent messages about substance use. Haddock and colleagues (2005) contend, for example, that advertising in military newspapers may send personnel mixed messages about the use of tobacco. Bray and Hourani (2007) suggest the same is true in regard to alcohol use. Moore, Ames, and Cunradi (2007) concur. They posit that efforts to address these inconsistencies should include price increases on alcohol and tobacco in base stores and clear messages to off-base bars that the sale of alcohol to underage people will not be tolerated.

A compelling argument can be made that the structural and cultural aspects of the military itself contribute to tobacco, alcohol, and drug use among its members. A number of authors suggest that one important factor is the heightened levels of stress associated with military life. Separation from family for extended tours, frequent relocation, maintaining a level of combat readiness, or the possibility of combat experience are all stressors that might predispose one to higher levels of substance abuse. To that end, the tradition of alcohol use as a means of dealing with stress or "blowing off steam" remains prominent (Bachman et al. 1999; Bray and

Hourani 2007). Similarly, Haddock and colleagues (2005) suggest that for some military personnel, alcohol use during off-duty hours is a "default" activity of sorts, in part because of the belief there is nothing else to do. The finding that most alcohol consumption occurs during off-duty hours (Moore et al. 2007) is potential support for this notion. Ames and colleagues (2007) assert that it is easier for the military to regard alcohol use as a matter of individual choice, as opposed to focusing on environmental and structural forces, a much more difficult task. Moore and colleagues (2007) suggest that until leadership genuinely emphasizes reducing the acceptability of alcohol use and conveys this message to subordinates, prevention efforts and programs will continue to be less than optimal.

Another and perhaps a more controversial area in which the demands of military life may encourage substance use lies in the approved use of controlled substances, most notably stimulants. Caldwell and Caldwell (2005), as well as Eliyahu and colleagues (2007), note that modern warfare has become a 24/7 venture in that operations can continue for extended periods of time. When these demands are viewed in the context of reductions in personnel and equipment, the strain on existing forces is pronounced. Simply put, there is no substitute for sleep, and fatigue can result in adverse consequences, including injury and death.

The military utilizes a number of tactics to alleviate problems associated with fatigue, including exercise, hydration, providing high protein meals at regular intervals, and taking advantage of limited opportunities for naps (Johnson 2007). Caldwell (2008) suggests the effectiveness of these approaches is limited. As a result, the U.S. military has authorized the use of stimulants when opportunities for sleep are not available. Caffeine and nicotine are classified as nutritional supplements, so there are no regulations on their use. On the other hand, Dexedrine (dextroamphetamine), a Schedule II substance, is also utilized on a limited basis. The use of Dexedrine has been approved for voluntary use by some personnel (usually pilots), provided dosages are monitored and regulated. However, this practice is not without controversy. For example, the Food and Drug Administration has not authorized the use of Dexadrine for this purpose (Caldwell et al. 2003). Furthermore, the United States is the only North Atlantic Treaty Organization (NATO) member that authorizes its use in these circumstances, and the ethics of this practice have been questioned (Caldwell 2008; Eliyahu et al. 2007). Caldwell (2008) contends this practice is ethical, so long as the use of Dexedrine is voluntary and its administration is appropriately monitored.

Controversy aside, this practice leads to an interesting question: Does the authorized administration and use of substances such as Dexedrine encourage other forms of drug use? Johnson (2007) notes that military pilots are extremely motivated individuals. For obvious reasons, this attribute is desirable among personnel in general, and military training emphasizes and encourages its development. However, does pressure to "Work through it!" result in a situation whereby failure to complete a task results in being viewed as weak? Previously, we discussed how ambivalent and sometimes contradictory messages may encourage substance use.

Caldwell (2008) acknowledges it is not surprising that the use of drugs to offset the effects of sleep deprivation and fatigue has generated debate, and it is unlikely this will be easily resolved.

However, it can also be argued that rates of substance abuse should be lower because of the recent military policy of zero tolerance along with programs to assist military personnel in reducing drug, alcohol, and tobacco use (Bachman et al. 1999; Bray et al. 1991, 1999). Prior to the policy shifts of the Department of Defense, military personnel were at least as involved as civilians in illicit drug use, but in the years subsequent to mandatory drug testing, the armed forces samples report substantially less drug use. Zero-tolerance policies or "coerced demand reduction" (Bachman et al. 1999, 676) seem to be reversing a previous trend toward greater drug and alcohol use. Nevertheless, Bray, Fairbank and Marsden (1999) report that stress experienced in military life is associated with substance abuse. The specific stress factors tend to be different among women than among men, however. Among males, specific stress factors at work and the tensions created in their families by military roles tend to correlate strongly with substance abuse. However, females are more likely to use illicit drugs and alcohol as a result of stress created by their minority status as a women in the predominantly male domain of the military.

Drug Use in Law Enforcement

If the literature on the subject is any indication, it would seem that *the* problematic substance in law enforcement is alcohol. A review of available literature on the subject published in 1986 revealed only two studies that even attempted to assess non-alcohol drug abuse among police officers (Dietrich and Smith 1986). Despite the small amount of quantitative data on the prevalence of alcohol use and abuse by police officers, department officials report that as many as 25 percent of police officers have a serious dependence on alcohol (Kroes 1976). If this is correct, and we define "serious dependence" as alcoholism, alcoholism is significantly higher among police officers than it is in the general population. Other studies tend to confirm these estimates. Van Raalte (1979) reports that 67 percent of police officers surveyed drank while on duty, and this study identified instances of off-duty drinking by officers that resulted in firearms injuries. Health problems have also been reported, including insomnia, memory lapse, and heart disease (Blau 1994; Territo and Vetter 1981). Mortality rates for cirrhosis of the liver, another indicator of problem drinking, has been found to be substantially higher for police officers than for the general population (Hitz 1973; Richmond et al. 1999).

Factors Contributing to High Rates of Alcohol Use by Police

Stress
Stress is perhaps the single most important factor in alcohol use by police officers. Lindsay (2008) contends that police officers are at greater risk for job-related stress

than perhaps any other group. A litany of factors contributes to police stress. Most people assume that law enforcement stress comes primarily from the life-and-death situations that police officers must face, in some cases on a daily basis. This vulnerability is, indeed, one source of stress among law enforcement personnel. But there are other factors that, taken together, exact a toll on law enforcement more than most occupational fields. These factors include: court scheduling problems, unfavorable court decisions, undesirable assignments, faulty equipment, lack of community support, rotating shifts, poor relations with supervisors, boredom, low pay, role conflict, public pressure and scrutiny, peer group pressure, lack of career development opportunities, excessive paperwork, inadequate rewards, distorted press accounts of police incidents, and exposure to human suffering (Blau 1994; Eisenberg 1975; Kroes et al. 1974; Territo and Vetter 1981).

These are but some of the many factors that contribute to police stress. A growing body of research suggests that alcohol use is a maladaptive coping mechanism through which law enforcement officers attempt to deal with stress. Furthermore, the identification of a situation as stressful is often related to coping abilities (Arrigo 2000; Haarr and Morash 1999). These factors are often compounded by the impact that they have on the families of police officers. The officer under stress brings his or her problems and frustrations home and often vents on his or her spouse. Additionally, erratic work schedules and 24-hour on-call availability can produce tremendous stress and conflict within a marital unit. For these reasons, law enforcement as an occupation has the dubious privilege of having one of the highest divorce rates in the country (Territo and Vetter 1981).

An examination of death certificates in Tennessee revealed that police officers are much more likely to die prematurely than individuals in most other occupations (Fell et al. 1980). It is also disturbing to note that numerous researchers have observed high rates of suicide among police officers (Allen 1986; Arrigo and Garsky 1997; Bonifacio 1991; Richmond et al. 1999; Territo and Vetter 1981; Wagner and Brzeczek 1983). Violanti (2004) offers the compelling suggestion that stress may increase the occurrence of post-traumatic stress disorder (PTSD) and related symptoms, which in turn affects alcohol use and thoughts of suicide.

It might be expected then that alcoholism and other forms of problem drinking (and other drug use) are affected by the high stress associated with law enforcement work. In a review of available literature, Dietrich and Smith (1986) concluded that the occupational stressors of police work do contribute to greater levels of alcohol consumption. One study (Violante et al. 1985) found that occupational stress is nearly 20 times more powerful in its impact on alcohol use than any of the other variables examined. Since Dietrich and Smith's study, a large and growing body of research provides support for the notion of a high level of alcohol use among law enforcement. However, this finding has been questioned somewhat. Lindsay (2008) suggests that results of localized and/or limited studies should be viewed with caution, as there has been no comprehensive study of this phenomenon in the United States. However, an example of one such study in Australia suggests that police are more likely to be moderate or heavy drinkers than are members of the general population (Smith 2007). Future research should seek to clarify this issue.

Occupational Subculture

The other set of factors contributing to greater than normal alcohol consumption by police is subcultural in nature. Law enforcement personnel share common experiences that distinguish them from other professions. They confront potential danger on a daily basis and confront public criticism more than most occupations. Moreover, many of the stressors that were identified earlier result in a strong sense of subcultural identification. The subculture of law enforcement not only tolerates higher than normal levels of alcohol consumption but actually encourages it. Drinking is a regular part of off-duty recreational time for many police officers.

Dietrich and Smith (1986) also cited literature that suggests that subcultural drinking may be used to test loyalty, trustworthiness, and toughness. The police subculture is largely, though not exclusively, a masculine domain, but some research suggests that females may mimic male colleagues' drinking behaviors to increase acceptance in the group (Richmond et al. 1999). Refusing to drink is seen as tantamount to rejecting fellow police officers. Moreover, the role that alcohol plays in the intense camaraderie of the law enforcement subculture often results in a blind eye to alcohol and drug abuse problems when they occur. Because drinking is such a part of the subculture of policing, fellow officers are often unaware when social drinking becomes problem drinking. Moreover, loyalty that is developed as part of these recreational activities precludes fellow officers from informing supervisors when they suspect a drinking problem with a colleague. Furthermore, the police subculture discourages officers with drinking problems from seeking help for their drinking and/or drug use problem. Doing so is a sign of weakness (Richmond et al. 1999).

Drug Use and Religion

The relationship between religion and substance use is quite complex. Upon examining the teachings of various faiths, mixed messages quickly become apparent (Robertson 2004). Across and even within faiths, attitudes toward alcohol and even drug use vary widely. For example, Judaism is more tolerant than Islam of alcohol use. In Judaism, wine is considered sacramental, and use by followers is quite common, whereas the opposite holds true for the Islam (Michalak et al. 2007; Miller 1998; Powell 2004). Research shows that if a religious belief system forbids the use of a substance, then followers are more likely to abstain (Michalak et al. 2007), particularly among those for whom religion has become a primary reference group (Chawla et al. 2007). On the other hand, among groups that tolerate use, defining acceptable limits is a difficult task. Bischke (2003, 276) employs the analogy of a tactic commonly used by parents when entrusting a child with a valuable possession: "Use it but don't break it."

Within Christianity for example, proscriptions toward alcohol in particular vary from total prohibition to open tolerance. As is the case with Judaism, some Christian

DRUGS AND EVERYDAY LIFE

Choir Practice

A vivid illustration of the stresses and strains of big city police work, and of how alcohol consumption is used as a stress reliever by officers, can be found in the novel *The Choirboys* by Joseph Wambaugh (1975). Wambaugh had been a Los Angeles police officer for some fourteen years, years where he experienced the violence and strains of police work first hand. During these years he also experienced the "blue curtain" of police fraternalism. To a great extent, the police believe that no one, save another cop, understands what they go through on the job. So when it comes time to wind down from work, they turn to each other and to alcohol, often in great quantity.

Wambaugh terms their group bacchanals "choir practices," wherein the officers gather late at night (or early in the morning, depending on one's point of view), in a public park, and sing drunkenly and howl at the moon. It is a catharsis for the choirboys,

serving both to relieve stress and to enhance fraternal bonds. It is ironic to refer to these officers as choirboys. They shake down liquor store owners for that night's booze, a practice more or less willingly engaged in by the merchants, as long as the cops don't become too greedy and exceed their agreed upon limit of two bottles per store per shift. When drunk—what a surprise—they act in rude and unprofessional ways, getting into fights, having adulterous and indiscriminate sex, acting anything but choirboy-like. Wambaugh's point is that big city officers should no longer be seen as one-dimensional figures of moral authority, but as flawed and fallible people, who generally work hard and play hard, and for whom alcohol abuse is both ingrained in the job and a source of negative consequences for the officers. Among these alcohol-related consequences are divorce, suicide, ill-health, and unrestrained rage. And these pathologies aren't limited to the officers in Wambaugh's fictional world, but for all too many flesh-and-blood policemen and policewomen bear the same burdens.

groups (e.g., Roman Catholics and some Anglicans) include the sacramental use of wine as part of their ritual (Miller 1998). Within Protestant denominations, attitudes vary, as reflected in the old joke, "What's the difference between a Methodist and a Baptist? A Methodist will speak to you at the liquor store" (Robertson 2004, 4). This oft-told joke reflects how various groups within Christianity may have somewhat differing opinions related to use of a substance, but at the same time it shows how individual responses to church teachings may vary. Most Methodist denominations are typically more tolerant of alcohol use than most Baptist denominations, but even within a denomination that promotes abstinence, individuals may follow the teaching to varying degrees. As a result, Conley and Sorensen (1971) suggest the church is simultaneously a cause and a cure for alcohol problems. Specifically, they state that because alcohol is frequently viewed as a "forbidden fruit" of sorts, use may increase anxiety and feelings of guilt and shame. Similarly, in commenting on the religious elements of Alcoholics Anonymous, Miller (1998) suggests that sobriety is best viewed when its spiritual realm is acknowledged and that for some people, alcohol and drugs may elevated to the status of "higher power," which would be viewed by some as idolatry.

However, the use of certain substances within the religious context has proven to be quite controversial. Hargrove (1989) notes that in many cases, mostly among primitive or non-Western religions, some drugs, particularly hallucinogens, are revered as sacred and incorporated into the worship experience. If a group believes that the divine can be found in nature, then the use of hallucinogenic plants as part of worship is not problematic. Aspects associated with the use of the drug may be interpreted within the context of religion. For example, the use of *ayahuasca*, a hallucinogenic plant, frequently results in nausea and vomiting. As will be discussed later in this chapter, groups that incorporate the use of *ayahuasca* into worship typically view the nausea and vomiting as a form of spiritual cleansing and detoxification (Halpern and Sewell 2005). In stark contrast, the Western viewpoint tends to regard nature and its status vis-à-vis religion in a very different manner. Even though the natural world was created by a deity, it is not divine. The sacred is found in holy documents and to a lesser extent in objects or relics (Gamble 2004).

The following sections will provide a glimpse of the sacramental use of psychoactive substances among groups that have a presence in the United States. In doing so, we will see that when the legal responses to these groups are compared, it could be argued that federal policy is at best awkward and possibly inconsistent.

Rastafarianism

Rastafari. The term evokes a number of images: the rhythmic beat and liberation message of reggae music (Spencer 1998); dreadlocks, the matted, shoulder-length hair that for some symbolizes African heritage and for others is believed to be an antenna of sorts for receiving divine messages (Johnson-Hill 1995); the sacramental use of *ganja* (marijuana) as a part of worship (Campbell 1980; Johnson-Hill 1995). Particularly in relation to the use of ganja, Rastafarianism, as a culture and a religious belief system, offers unique opportunities to examine the importance of behavior, identity, and the corresponding reactions to them.

At least in a symbolic sense, the origin of Rastafarianism can be traced to the countries of Ethiopia and Israel. The birth of the religion is generally linked with the 1930 coronation of a nationalist leader, Ras Tafari, as emperor of Ethiopia. Its development and early popularity occurred in Jamaica, however, promoted by Marcus Garvey, a Jamaican apologist for African culture whose views were widely read (Lewis 1998). During the decade of the 1930s, the economic and social conditions experienced in Jamaica have given rise to an intriguing yet controversial set of beliefs, primarily as a response to poverty and limited economic opportunity (Savishinsky 1998). The Rastafarian religion is closely intertwined with the culture itself. Although originating in Jamaica, Rastafarianism (also referred to as "Rasta") has spread abroad. In the United States, Rastafarianism began to receive increased attention during the 1970s, in part because a large number of Jamaicans had immigrated. It was also during this period that Rasta music, reggae, most notably the music of Bob Marley, increased in popularity (Taylor 1984). Largely through reggae, the tenets of the Rastafarian culture and religion (particularly pro-marijuana themes) attracted the attention of many, including the criminal justice system. The use of ganja by followers of Rastafari during worship reflects both symbolic and manifest responses to domination by those in power (Johnson-Hill 1995).

According to Rastafarianism, ganja is a sacramental herb, not a drug. Substance abuse (including alcohol) is discouraged. Ganja use is considered appropriate based on the principle of *ital livity*. This notion emphasizes a sense of naturalness in various aspects of life such as a vegetarian diet and the use of herbs for healing purposes (Hepner 1998).[3] The use of ganja is justified in part upon a reference to herbs in the Old Testament book of Genesis (Kitzinger 1969). According to belief, its use is sacramental in nature, being no different than the use of incense during a Roman Catholic mass (Kitzinger 1969; Lewis 1993). Used during individual meditation and group meetings, ganja is an integral element of worship (Johnson-Hill, 1995). Whether eaten, brewed into a tea, or smoked, ganja is believed to be a mechanism through which one can gain a greater understanding of God. Furthermore, ganja is believed to allow one to see through the distorted perceptions of God that has been corrupted by others (Breiner 1985–1986).

In some ways, the previously mentioned negative backlash was inevitable. Clearly, fundamental elements of Rastafarianism reflect the clash with the white, middle-class, capitalist establishment frequently referred to metaphorically by believers as "Babylon" (Johnson-Hill 1995). Breiner (1985–1986) notes that Babylon also refers to the location named Jamaica by Europeans, for the Rastafarian a place of captivity dominated by the West. Not only is the use of ganja offensive to the establishment, but according to followers, it assists the Rastafarian in realizing the many truths that are being withheld by Babylon (Kitzinger 1969; Johnson-Hill 1995). According to some, it is the mockery of capitalism and authority that has resulted in Rasta culture being defined as deviant and its followers becoming targets. Nonetheless, the use of ganja appears to be influential in this manner.

It is no surprise, then, that ganja use is a source of controversy. For example, a 1963 Jamaican press campaign implied that users of ganja were prone to violence (Campbell 1980). Hepner (1998) suggests that law enforcement and media portrayals perpetuate notions that violence and drug trafficking are key elements of Rastafarianism, both of which are strenuously disputed by followers. Such characterizations are remarkably similar to the "Reefer Madness" hysteria that led to the passage of the Marihuana Tax Act of 1937. Several observers, however, assert that a number of nonfollowers have adopted Rasta dress and mannerisms to "cloak" their violent and criminal activity within the context of a religion (Campbell 1980; Lewis 1989; Murrell 1998).

The extent to which Rastafarianism is a unified belief system is quite debatable, and even though official documents exist, doctrines are not formalized (Murrell and Taylor 1998). The following, adapted from Taylor (1984), identifies several basic elements that are generally agreed upon by most followers.

- Most central to the Rastafarian belief system is the acknowledgment of *Haile Selassie as the living God*. Haile Selassie, emperor of Ethiopia from 1930 to 1935, is generally regarded as a Messiah to most followers of Rastafarianism. During the 1930s, a number of impoverished Jamaicans turned to their African roots and looked to Selassie for deliverance from the Great Depression and oppression at the hands of Babylon (Lewis 1993). For some believers, the ascension of Selassie was viewed as fulfillment of Old Testament prophecies of the coming of the Messiah, whereas others view him as the incarnation of Jesus (Murrell and Taylor 1998).
- The black person is the reincarnation of the ancient Israelite. Followers view their situation of poverty and oppression as being similar to the ancient Israelites, who frequently experienced hardships at the hands of others. Particular emphasis is placed on the enslavement of the Israelite and their exile into Babylon. In fact, some contend that Haile Selassie is a descendent of King Solomon (Murrell 1998). The religious nature of Rastafarianism is enhanced because followers often consider themselves to be Israelites as well.
- Believers await the exodus to Heaven (Ethiopia) and the beginning of an age in which the black man (superior to whites) will eventually rule the world.

In light of these principles, Lewis (1989) correctly suggests it is rather ironic that in the United States, reggae music is popular among the white middle class.

Native American Church

Perhaps the most interesting example of drug use during worship can be found in the Native American Church. In the United States and Canada, current membership is estimated to be approximately 300,000 (Halpern 2004). Similar to Rastafarianism, the extent to which elements of Christianity are present differs by congregation. Generally speaking, church doctrine consists of a combination of Christianity and native beliefs. The sacramental use of peyote, however, is commonplace.

For thousands of years, Indian tribes in Mexico have utilized the peyote cactus during religious rituals (Institute for Substance Abuse Research 1990). Although the Native American Church was first incorporated in 1918 in Oklahoma, the use of peyote in North America is believed to have begun in the early 17th century (Peregoy et al. 1995). Following the Civil War, Native American religion experienced particularly acute oppression. Native American beliefs did not accommodate well to European cultural traditions. Because traditional Native American religion contained a plethora of spirits, calling upon these various spirits and seeing visions provided hope for these oppressed peoples and gave the shamans who received these visions extraordinary power. As the quest for visions became more important to Native Americans, they began to seek alternative ways of inducing them, including chemically through tobacco, jimson weed, the mescal bean, as well as through peyote, which had by now proliferated throughout many Native American reservations.

Peyote offered a more peaceful response to Native American oppression than earlier visionary movements, which promised the decimation of the white race, among other doomsday scenarios. As one anthropologist, Vittorio Lanternari, put it, "Peyotism, too, like the Ghost Dance, contained a messianic message; but whereas the Ghost Dance promised restoration of the past, Peyotism announced a new dispensation, and a renewal of Indian culture" (Lanternari 1965, 81; cited in Anderson 1996, 40). Peyote is harvested by removing and then drying the crown of the cactus. The crowns, whether left whole or cut into pieces, are frequently referred to as "buttons." The buttons from the peyote cactus contain the psychoactive substance mescaline that, when eaten, smoked, or brewed as a tea, can cause the user to experience hallucinations and kaleidoscope-like sensations. The effect of a typical dose of 4 to 12 buttons may last up to ten hours. Usually, the substance is consumed during dusk-to-dawn rituals that include prayer, singing, and dancing. It is during these ceremonies that users experience God through the intermediary of nature (Halpern 2004; Kiyanni and Csordas 1997; Liska 2004). In a symbolic sense, the use of the substance allows the believer to travel on what is frequently referred to as the "Peyote Road," which emphasizes respect for oneself, nature, and others (Kiyaani and Csordas 1997).

The Religious Freedom Restoration Act of 1993 effectively overturned a 1990 U.S. Supreme Court decision, *Employment Division of Oregon v. Smith* (1990), declaring that ritual use of peyote was not protected under the First Amendment. In *Smith*, followers of the Native American Church lost their jobs as a result of peyote use. Essentially, the act precludes the federal and state governments from prohibiting the use, possession, or transportation of peyote for legitimate religious purposes (Peregoy et al. 1995). Exclusive of the provisions pertaining to the Native American Church, peyote is a Schedule I substance under the Controlled Substances Act of 1970, and possession of it is a crime. Interestingly, these exclusions granted to the Native American Church are based on political, not religious grounds. The protection to use peyote during worship is based on the justification that because Indian tribes lived in this country prior to passage of the U.S. Constitution, an element of sovereignty is recognized for a practice that has existed for centuries (Lawrence 1990).

In the United States production and distribution of peyote for use during religious rituals is strictly monitored and controlled (Peregoy et al. 1995), and use and/or abuse by nonmembers is extremely rare (Julien 2001). The peyote cactus grows naturally in Mexico and in limited areas of Texas. Traveling to Mexico or Texas to obtain peyote is part of a lengthy and elaborate ritual (Ksir et al. 2008). Regulations include restrictions on both the user and the producer. As mentioned previously, ritual use of peyote is limited to members of the Native American Church only, and membership in the church is restricted to persons of at least one-quarter Indian ancestry. Presently, legitimate outlets for peyote are located in only four Texas counties, and only seven individuals are licensed distributors, or *Peyoteros*. Individuals who harvest and distribute peyote to members of the Native American Church are required to follow a myriad of both federal and state regulations, including annual registration (Lawrence 1990; *The Economist* 1999).

Drug Use, Religion, and the Law

The controversial practice of the ritual use of marijuana and other hallucinogens raises a particularly complex question: Does the guarantee of freedom of religion in the U.S. Constitution extend to situations in which drugs are used during worship? Legally speaking, the previous discussion shows the answer to this question is, Sometimes. The sacramental use of marijuana by Rastafarians or others is not permitted, in part because it is classified as a Schedule I substance in the Controlled Substances Act of 1970. Lawrence (1990) notes that the Ethiopian Zion Coptic Church, a Miami group whose beliefs are remarkably similar to Rastafarianism, failed in its attempt to obtain the right to use marijuana during worship (*Olsen v. DEA* 1986. This case is cited frequently as justification for the prohibition of ritual ganja use by Rastafarians. On the other hand, the Native American Church has the legal right to use peyote during religious services. In 1993, this practice became legally protected when President Clinton signed the Religious Freedom Restoration Act, overturning a 1990 Supreme Court decision that ritual peyote use was not protected under the first amendment (Peregoy et al. 1995).

The line between religious expression and exploitation is a fine one, and it is extremely difficult to distinguish between legitimate versus frivolous claims. Moreover, the previous discussion shows that the response of the U.S. government toward groups seeking to include the use of sacramental drugs as part of worship is somewhat inconsistent. A recent case further illustrates this point. In February 2006, the U.S. Supreme Court ruled in *Gonzales v. O Centro Espirita Beneficente Uniao do Vegetal* (2006) that the federal government could not prohibit the sacramental use of *ayahuasca* (Wellborn 2006). A number of groups, including Santo Daime, a Brazilian church that also has a presence in the United States, have benefitted from this decision (Halpern 2004).

Drug Use and Sports

When compared to the social institutions discussed so far, and certainly when compared to social institutions such as the family or the economy, the institution of sports, may in some ways seem trivial. However, it would be a mistake to discount the importance of this aspect of social life. Eitzen and Sage (2003) suggest that sport is a microcosm of society. A detailed discussion of this notion is unnecessary, but one can quickly identify examples that illustrate this point. The sport enterprise includes elements of bureaucracy, it is a business, the culture of sports includes tradition and ritual, and sport—in some ways similar to ethnicity and possibly religion—provides a source of identity for participants and followers alike (Eitzen and Sage 2003).

Furthermore, in the sections that follow, we will identify a number of ways in which sport and substance use have become intricately connected. In doing so, it will become apparent that sports can act as an influence on tobacco, alcohol, and drug use for athletes and others. Unconvinced? Remember that key elements of sport include competition and interaction with others. With this thought in mind, consider the following: How often do college students participate in drinking games? Research suggests that as many as six in ten college students participate in this activity (Grossbard et al. 2007). Also, consider the popularity of tailgating before and during sporting events. In a similar vein, the annual football game between the University of Florida and the University of Georgia has long been referred to as the "World's Largest Cocktail Party" (Abbott 2004).

Another example is found in a very popular form of automobile racing, NASCAR, whose origin is allegedly linked to bootleggers who utilized fast cars to escape law enforcement. In off hours, many of these individuals would race one another. Status within the group and financial gain provided motivation for the drivers. The potential for excitement and access to alcohol resulted in a following of spectators. Since its inception in 1949, NASCAR has grown exponentially, becoming one of the most popular spectator sports in the United States (Abbott 2004; Marcoplos 2006).

Doping[4]: Restorative and Additive Use

Drug use by athletes to improve athletic performance, commonly called **doping**, is a centuries-old practice. In the ancient Roman civilization, gladiators used stimulants prior to their deadly performances in the Colosseum (Putnam 1999). Other drugs used during these ancient games included alcohol, psychoactive mushrooms, and strychnine mixed with alcohol to bring about a stimulant effect (Voy and Deeter 1991). Canal swimmers in Amsterdam were charged with using drugs in 1865 (Voy and Deeter 1991), and in 1886, the first recorded drug-related death in sports occurred when a bicyclist collapsed after a long-distance race in Europe after taking a "speed ball," mixture of narcotics and cocaine (Putnam 1999).

Two broad categories of drugs are used by athletes. One, **restorative drugs**, are taken to facilitate healing from injuries or to reduce the pain of injuries, also to relieve hypertension and sickness. In short, these drugs are used to return an athlete to a state of normalcy as soon as possible. Drugs used in this way include pain killers, tranquilizers, muscle relaxants, anti-inflammatory agents, and in some cases, barbiturates. Both professional and amateur athletes misuse restorative drugs. Importantly, most drugs in this category are a legitimate part of the locker room pharmacopeia. Most drugs in this category are not absolutely prohibited when prescribed by a physician, but certain limits and conditions are placed on their use. For example, International Olympic Committee (IOC) rules allow only local or intra-articular injection of anasthetic drugs, and then only when medically justified. Similarly, most narcotic drugs are prohibited, but certain narcotics such as Darvon and codeine are permitted (IOC 2000).

Drugs: Myths and Reality

Doping in Sports

It is widely believed that "doping" in sports is a relatively recent phenomenon, as the level of competitiveness in Olympic and professional sports has increased over the past 30 years or so with razor-thin differences between winners and losers. As the general public has become aware of the use of steroids and other performance-enhancing drugs, a good-guy, bad-guy mentality that has pervaded amateur and professional sports. When Olympic medalists are investigated for doping, they are immediately vilified, even before the results are in.

Recent historical scholarship targets these commonly held ideas. In the opening chapters of his book *A History of Drug Use in Sport 1876-1976: Beyond Good and Evil* (2007), social historian Paul Dimeo challenges the notion that there ever was a "golden era" of drug-free sport, a myth that was constructed in the 1960s when the international sports world first began to take note of athletes using drugs to compete more effectively. Dimeo points out that the late nineteenth century saw a good bit of drug experimentation among athletes, unfettered by the stigma of cheating or by fear of health risks associated with drug use. There is the apocryphal story of Arthur Littleton, who in many accounts is described as the first victim of doping, alleged to have died as a result of his drug use in 1886. Littleton's death makes a good case for the antidoping entrepreneurs of the late twentieth century, except for the fact that careful historical research found him to be alive and well a decade after his alleged death.

Dimeo's research takes direct aim at the morality play that surrounds the drugs-in-sports controversy. He reveals that not until the late 1950s was a new ethic in which drug use by athletes was highly vilified and emotively charged. Dimeo's scholarship reveals that the strong antidrug measures that began in the 1960s were, in fact, part of a moral crusade against all that was thought to be wrong with sports as the institution was evolving at that time, including an ever-pervasive professionalization and commercialization of sport. This was not a grassroots concern, however; it was a top-down concern, with scientists and doctors being the main actors in the development of drug tests and corresponding regulations. Dimeo asserts that the new antidoping ethic was a white, professional, middle-class ethic imposed in a most patriarchal fashion without consultation or consent from athletes or others in the field of sport who were most affected by these regulations. The result for sports, says Dimeo, is an irrational system of regulations, unfairly applied, based on an unrealistic ideal of a level playing field even though the very point of training is, in Dimeo's words "to make the...field uneven" (129).

Sociologists have long recognized that when general social ills are deeply rooted in structural and cultural systems, there is a search for a scapegoat, an easy target to blame. Psychoactive drugs have frequently been the scapegoat for a plethora of social ills. Taking on the sins of all of society, drugs—and the people who use them—are vilified and caricatured as the personification of evil as they bear the stigma of a society's sins. This has been true of drug use in society generally, as we have shown in various chapters of this book. According to Paul Dimeo, it is also true of drug use in sports.

Many of these drugs are banned from use in amateur sports, but this type of drug use is not as much of concern to monitoring agencies such as the IOC and the National Collegiate Athletic Association (NCAA) as are the second, more controversial type of drugs, **additive drugs** (also called *ergogenic aids*). Unlike restorative drugs, these substances are used to allow the athlete to perform beyond what his or her healthy body is capable of doing on its own. Drugs that fall under this category can be divided into four types: stimulants, anabolics, beta-blockers, and diuretics.

Stimulants

Stimulants accelerate the activities of the central nervous system. Also called **ergogenic** (energy-producing) drugs, the stimulants include amphetamines, methamphetamines, caffeine,[5] and cocaine. Certain stimulants are permitted for athletes in the form of inhalers for treatment of asthma conditions but only with written notification of this condition by a recognized physician. There is some disagreement about how much stimulant drugs actually enhance athletic performance (Schwenck 1997; Voy 1991). However, Laties and Weiss (1981) point out that at the highest levels of competition even a 1 percent improvement can provide a significant edge. Stewart and Smith (2008) blame the culture of sport, in which success or winning is paramount. Despite differences of opinion regarding the competitive advantages of stimulants, there is almost no controversy over the fact that stimulants pose potential health risks to athletes. Amphetamines, methamphetamine, and cocaine are particularly potent. The health hazards of these drugs in the sports arena were made clear in 1986 when two athletes in their prime, Len Bias and Don Rogers, died as a result of cocaine use. Stimulants have been virtually banned from amateur sports, both because of the potential for enhancement, or at least the psychological confidence that they tend to produce, and because of the dangers that they pose to athletes using them (Ksir et al. 2008). Nevertheless, stimulants are used frequently in both amateur and professional sports.

Anabolics

Anabolics fall into three broad categories: proteins, steroids, and human growth hormones. Athletes use anabolic proteins to increase their stamina in events that require endurance, such as cycling and long-distance running. Artificially injecting these drugs not only provides an unfair competitive advantage, it can be dangerous as well. Athletes, who already have naturally high levels of anabolic proteins, run the risk of their blood thickening and developing clots, resulting in failure of vital organs. According to Liska (2004), these drugs are suspected in the deaths of some 18 cyclists in Holland and Belgium.

Another practice by athletes that produces an effect similar to the anabolic proteins is **blood doping**. Blood doping entails withdrawing amounts of blood (typically about two pints) two to three months prior to an event. This blood is frozen to preserve it, and by the time of the event, the body has replenished its own blood supply. The athlete will then infuse his system with the oxygen-carrying red blood cells from the blood that he or she has earlier withdrawn. The result is an extra supply of oxygen that will sustain the athlete through endurance events. Despite disagreement among sports doctors about whether this practice is truly drug use, it has been banned by the IOC since 1986 (Voy 1991).

Anabolic steroids are produced naturally by our bodies, but they can also be produced synthetically. Androgens contribute to sexual differentiation, the development of the reproductive system, and the development of muscle mass and the central nervous system (Pandina and Hendren 1999). Artificially produced steroids closely resemble testosterone, the male sex hormone. They are taken to build muscle mass and to repair muscle damage. These drugs are used by weightlifters, football players, and athletes in other sports that require muscle strength. Typically, steroids are used in the off-season and are administered on cycles ranging from 4 to 12 weeks in duration (Calfee and Fadale 2006). For some individuals, and when used in the proper circumstances, anabolic steroids can be utilized to achieve physical gains. However, research suggests the negatives outweigh the positives (Pandina and Hendren 1999). Chronic use of these drugs has serious health consequences including testicular atrophy for men; menstrual problems and the development of secondary male sex characteristics for women; and male pattern baldness, diminished sexual response, elevated cholesterol, increased risk of kidney disease, and heart attack for both men and women (Pandina and Hendren 1999).

Moreover, psychiatric problems that result from long-term steroid use have also been identified (Pope and Katz, 1994. Both affective (neurotic) and psychotic symptoms occur among athletes using steroids. Symptoms include severe mood swings, aggressiveness, irritability, and other behavioral disorders. The term **roid rage** is used to describe the increased hostility and aggression among steroid users. Citing various studies, Goldstein (1990) estimates more than a million steroid users in the United States, with perhaps as many as 96 percent of professional football players taking these body-building drugs. Their use begins even in high school. More than 6 percent of a national sample of 12th-grade males admitted to having used steroids (Buckley et al. 1988), and Goldstein estimates that 12 percent of high school football players use steroid drugs.

Human growth hormone (HGH), produced naturally in the pituitary gland, regulates human growth. It is widely believed among athletes (though there is controversy in the medical field) that HGH builds muscle mass and, when used in conjunction with anabolic steroids, enhances the effects of the steroids. This practice is potentially very dangerous. Growth hormones not only cause muscle enlargement but also can affect nearly every organ of the body. This potential, combined with the fact that growth hormones tend to reduce the fat protecting vital body organs, make their use especially risky in contact sports such as football.

Beta-Blockers
Beta-blockers have a depressant type of effect on the central nervous system and are prescribed by doctors for reducing blood pressure and slowing down the heart rate

7.2 The use of performance-enhancing drugs has become a major issue of concern in both professional and amateur sports. In the past few years, several Olympic athletes found to be using these drugs were forced to forfeit their medals. (Photo © iPhotoStock. com/shepophoto.com)

in patients suffering from conditions associated with hypertension. Because these drugs slow the heart rate, they are especially popular among athletes in precision sports such as archery and competition firearm events. By slowing the heart and respiration rate, these substances allow the athlete more time to aim and shoot between beats (thereby increasing accuracy). These drugs are generally banned for these sports.

Diuretics

Diuretics are among the more recent enhancement drugs to hit the sports world, and were first banned in Olympic competition in 1986 (Voy and Deeter 1991). Medically, they are used primarily to treat people with problems in fluid retention. Athletes discovered that they could use these drugs to lose weight. Some sports, such as amateur wrestling and boxing, impose weight limitations on participants. Another inducement to use these drugs is that they can be used to mask other drugs by speeding up the process of flushing drugs out of the body, which may decrease the likelihood of detection through drug testing. Other drugs also act as masking agents by blocking the release of drugs *into* the urine (Liska 2004). Like other additive drugs, diuretics pose health risks. Because they cause the elimination of fluids and the important vitamins and minerals contained in these fluids, particularly potassium, the use of diuretics disturbs the electrolyte balance in the blood. They have also been linked with cardiac arrhythmia and cardiac arrest (Voy 1991).

Recreational Drug Use by Athletes

Athletes are not immune from recreational drug use, but the frequency and prevalence of drug use by athletes has been debated. Part of the disagreement is a result of different methodologies used to estimate drug use by athletes. Some researchers base their estimates on drug tests. Drug testing generally reveals a very low rate of use, typically 1 to 2 percent of athletes testing positive (Leonard 1998). These findings are generally confirmed by Yesalis, Anderson, and colleagues (1990), who look specifically at anabolic steroid use. However, when unannounced tests with no punitive sanctions were conducted, about 50 percent of the athletes tested positive for steroids. Yesalis and colleagues conjecture that athletes have learned to stop using at the appropriate time prior to testing to avoid a positive result. Other researchers use self-report strategies, asking athletes whether they have used drugs (usually within a specified time period). Here again, responses indicate a rather low rate of drug use (Yesalis et al. 1988). A third technique is to ask athletes their perceptions of the prevalence of drug use in their particular sport. One researcher using this approach reported that, on average, respondents indicated that nearly 30 percent of athletes used steroids (Leonard 1998).

More recent research examining 1999 data collected in the Harvard School of Public Health College Alcohol Study (CAS), which surveyed students at 119 colleges across the United States, reveals that 52.4 percent of student athletes report current (previous two weeks) binge drinking, compared to 42.6 percent of nonathletes (Ford 2007a). Male athletes were more likely to report binge drinking (52 percent) than male nonathletes (49 percent). Similarly, 39 percent of female athletes (compared with 29 percent of female nonathletes) engaged in binge drinking. Athletes tended to be slightly less involved in marijuana and other illicit drug use than were nonathletes, however. Approximately 27 percent of male athletes reported marijuana use, as opposed to 31 percent of the nonathletes. There was little difference in marijuana use (approximately 25 percent) and other illicit drug use (approximately 12 percent) between female athletes and female nonathletes (Ford 2007b).

The previous discussion highlights the consistent finding that substance use, particularly alcohol use, is a significant issue on college campuses. Furthermore, it seems that college athletes are more likely to engage in problematic alcohol use than nonathletes. As mentioned previously, Stewart and Smith (2008) suggest the culture of sport, as a consequence of the emphasis on competition and success, promotes higher levels of use among athletes. It should not come as a surprise that college athletes are also more likely to participate in drinking games than are nonathletes (Grossbard et al. 2007). The culture of sport influences drinking behaviors of nonathletes as well. For example, research suggests that college students who are sports fans, when compared to students who are not sports fans, are more likely to engage in binge drinking and heavy drinking and are more likely to experience negative consequences as a result of alcohol consumption (Neal and Fromme 2007; Nelson and Wechsler 2003).

Summary

In this chapter we explored alcohol and drug use in a number of broadly defined occupational settings that are known for particular patterns of substance abuse. These are also very critical occupational areas for different reasons. The health professions are especially critical as we entrust our lives to the care of doctors and nurses. Impaired medical personnel can have a profound effect on health care delivery. Our national security is also of vital importance, and anything short of a sober, alert military force should not be acceptable to this society. Ironically, military men and women who serve their country face unique stressors that make them more vulnerable to drug and alcohol abuse. The same irony characterizes law enforcement. Sporting activities, when speaking of the participants, is a critical area because professional athletes in particular are highly emulated and serve as role models for our nation's youngsters.

Other critical occupational groups are vulnerable to substance abuse as well. We are increasingly aware of the problems caused by drug abuse in various sectors of the transportation industry, for example. Airline pilots, railroad engineers, bus drivers, and tractor-trailer drivers have all received attention for abuse of alcohol and drugs either in the popular media or in academic circles (e.g., Lund et al. 1989; Taggart 1989). Drug use among employees at critical utilities plants has also been addressed (Osborne and Sokolov 1989; Crouch et al. 1989). These are all vital occupational areas. We could explore still further: entertainers, college professors, people in the art and literary worlds, and even lumbermen have at some time or another been associated with abnormally high rates of alcohol and drug abuse. Our purpose in this chapter is not to be exhaustive in our identification and discussion of occupational correlates of drug abuse. Rather, we have identified these occupational arenas as representative of areas whose culture, structure, and dynamics give rise to substance abuse.

This chapter highlights an important sociological contribution to the study of drug use—namely, that the extent, nature, and context of drug-using behavior vary in a number of social domains. Using the examples of religion and sports, we identified additional examples of how the organization and practices of social entities can influence and even encourage alcohol or drug use. Although individuals exhibit certain unique drug-using qualities, there are also important similarities, at least broadly speaking, within institutional and occupational categories. These similarities, and respective differences across categories, suggest that social as well as individual factors account for patterns of drug use.

Key Terms

additive drug
anabolics
availability hypothesis
beta blockers
blood doping
diuretics
doping
ergogenic
restorative drugs
roid rage
stress hypothesis

Thinking Critically...

1. Identify two or three reasons why drug use is a significant issue in each of the institutional contexts we discussed in this chapter.

2. In addition to the institutional contexts discussed in this chapter, identify two or three other occupations or institutions in which drug use is a major issue. Discuss the nature of the problem or concern that each of these institutional contexts faces with regard to drug use. How are these institutions responding to drug use among their ranks?

3. The authors ask the question, "Does the guarantee of freedom of religion in the U.S. Constitution extend to situations in which drugs are used during worship?" The response to this question was, Sometimes. Give some thought to why the federal government does not allow the use of marijuana in Rastifarian rituals, but allows the use of peyote (by any measure a more potentially harmful drug) in the rituals of the Native American Church. Develop a well-reasoned argument either for or against this apparent inconsistency from what you have learned about the law regarding this issue.

4. The discussion of drug use in sports began with the statement that, compared to the other institutional contexts in this chapter, our concern with drug use in sports may seem trivial. Do you think sports is an important enough context to merit discussion in this chapter? Develop an argument for or against the importance of sports as an institutional context in a serious discussion of drug use in American society.

5. Compare and contrast law enforcement and the military as institutional contexts for drug use. Consider factors such as motives for using drugs, consequences of drug use, cultures of drug use, and any other important dimensions within and across these two social institutions.

Learning from the Internet

1. Learn what you can about the Native American Church and Rastifarianism from the multitude of sites on the web. The hyperlinks below will get you started, but there are many more.

   http://www.nativeamericanchurch.net/
   http://users.lycaeum.org/~iamklaus/native.htm
   http://altreligion.about.com/od/rastafarian/p/Rastafaq.htm
   http://en.wikipedia.org/wiki/Rastafari_movement

2. As we were writing this text, the Summer Olympic Games were being played in Beijing, China. The Winter Games will be played in Vancouver, Canada, in 2010. Find out what you can about drug use in the Olympic games, and how the International Olympic Committee prepares for and responds to such use. You

might begin your research by going directly to the IOC website at http://www.olympic.org/uk/index_uk.asp. Use other websites as well in your research. The following questions might guide your search:

What drugs are most frequently used?

What countries have the highest rate of use?

Are there differences between Summer and Winter Olympic Games regarding what drugs and countries are most frequently cited?

Notes

1. The category included physicians, dentists, optometrists, and podiatrists.
2. The survey was conducted in 1980, 1982, 1985, 1988, 1992, 1995, 1998, 2002, and 2005.
3. Or as noted by Johnson-Hill (1995), a diet that is consistent with the Deuteronomic and Levitical prohibitions regarding foods such as pork and scaleless fish.
4. The term *doping* has an interesting history. It apparently originated in South Africa centuries ago where the term *dop* referred to substances used in religious ceremonies. Over time, an *e* was added to form the word *dope*. When the word appeared in an English dictionary, it was defined as a narcotic, an opium mixture used for race horses (Voy 1991, 5). Over time, the term has come to mean different things in America. Among street heroin addicts, for example, *dope* refers specifically to heroin or other street narcotics (Faupel 1991). Among athletes, it has become a verb that refers to the process of using any variety of drugs to enhance athletic performance.
5. The NCAA and the IOC prohibit caffeine in excess of 15 and 12 micrograms per milliliter of blood, respectively.

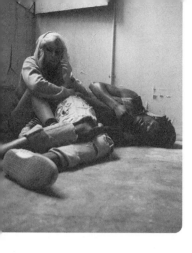

CHAPTER **8**

Health Correlates of Drug Use

No aspect of drug use may be more significant to a community or society than the health consequences of that use. Ultimately, we know that drugs can be fatal if not used properly. The Drug Abuse Warning Network (DAWN) reports that in the six states participating in state-wide reporting of mortality statistics, drug-related deaths ranged from 88 to 162 deaths per million population in 2003 (Office of Applied Studies 2005). Other potentially debilitating health consequences can also result from the careless or inappropriate use of drugs. DAWN reports that in 2005 more than 1.5 million emergency room visits were attributable to the abuse of drugs, and more than 800,000 of those involved illicit drugs (Office of Applied Studies 2007). The number of deaths and emergency room visits from drug abuse is but a small fraction of the total number of deaths and emergency room visits from other causes, nonetheless, these figures establish that drug use is a public health issue. We must recognize, of course, that many of the negative health consequences of illicit drug use are directly related to the legal status of these drugs, and indeed, this factor alone is possibly more debilitating to health than is the pharmacology of the drugs consumed. Due to the illicit nature of IV paraphernalia, for example, IV drug users often rent or borrow needles rather than carry their own for fear of being caught in possession. The result has been a rapid spread of AIDS and hepatitis among IV drug users, a consequence having nothing to do with the pharmacology of the drugs in question. We shall address this issue more fully in this chapter.

There is, furthermore, another side to the health consequences of drug use. Drugs can also be used to *promote* health among the population. We know, of course, that many drugs are routinely used in medicine precisely for this purpose: antibiotics, blood thinners, analgesics, and many others. There is, furthermore, an emerging voice for the use of certain other drugs, such as marijuana, and even heroin and alcohol, as valuable tools in promoting health and well-being.

This chapter will examine both types of consequences of drug use as well as some of the health and medical issues associated with these consequences. We begin the chapter with an examination of some of the potentially harmful health consequences of drug use, followed by a discussion of some of the recently emerging issues in the medical use of drugs.

Negative Health Consequences of Drug Use

Drugs can seriously affect and jeopardize the health and well-being of the user in many ways. One could fill a rather large volume discussing these potentially harmful effects. That is not our purpose in this section. Rather, we want to identify some of the major factors that contribute to ill-health among drug users. Within this context we will discuss some of the major health consequences associated with the use of chemical substances. Some of these consequences are **acute** in nature, meaning that they pose an immediate risk to the user at or around the time that they are used. The risk of overdose, for example, is acute because it is immediate in its effect. Other health consequences are **chronic**, meaning that they have a cumulative and long-term impact on the health of the user. The development of cirrhosis of the liver among long-term alcoholics is a chronic consequence of alcohol use as this is a condition that develops and gets worse over time. The major factors that we will address in this section are the pharmacology of drugs, synergism factors, and lifestyle factors that have implications for the health of the user.

Pharmacology of Drugs

Some ill-health effects of drugs are directly linked to the pharmacology of the drugs themselves. Moreover, certain types of drugs are more likely than others to cause health problems. This section examines problematic health consequences of the major categories of drugs discussed as part of the taxonomy in Chapter 3.[1] In addition, we address one additional drug category, steroids, which are of increasing health concern, especially in the world of sports as we discussed in Chapter 7.

Narcotics

There is perhaps no class of drugs more feared by the general public than the narcotics. Ironically, the narcotics are among the most benign of drugs in terms of their direct health impact pharmacologically. There are many allegations about how narcotics ravage the body, but most of these allegations are either exaggerations, confusions with other drug effects, a result of synergism with other drugs, or a result of lifestyle characteristics of those who use narcotic drugs. We will be discussing synergism and lifestyle characteristics later in this chapter. We do, however, want to discuss one important pharmacological feature of narcotics that can potentially affect the health of the user: their depressant effect on the central nervous system.

Narcotics, like the other depressants discussed below, slow down the activity of the central nervous system, which includes the respiratory and cardiovascular systems. This quality of the narcotics might put a user in danger of having insufficient oxygen delivered to the brain in an event called a heroin overdose, or simply OD, resulting in the respiratory and cardiovascular systems virtually shutting down. Overdose is perhaps the most feared consequence of heroin use. There is, however, a great deal of debate as to the risk of overdose. Erich Goode, in the seventh edition of his now classic work *Drugs in American Society*, claims that the lethal dose (LD) of heroin is only about 10 to 15 times higher than the effective dose (ED), the dose required to notice the effects of heroin (2008, 309). If this is the case, the potential for overdose is certainly high, if not the razor-thin difference that Goode suggests. Also, street heroin is more potent today than it was even 20 years ago. Furthermore, given the variable potency in street drugs, users often do not know the strength of the heroin that they are shooting.

Unfortunately, Goode does not provide the sources for this claim of a low ED: LD ratio. Other evidence suggests that the risk of overdose is much lower, and indeed, that most so-called overdose deaths do not result from overdose at all. Actually, the evidence against overdose being a major factor in what are typically identified as overdose deaths is quite compelling. Studies of overdose deaths tend to find that (1) morphine levels in overdose victims tend to be rather low, and (2) the typical overdose victim is an older, more experienced addict with a higher level of tolerance (Darke et al. 1998; Darke and Zador, 1996; Zador et al. 1996). Goode maintains a 10–15 ED:LD ratio, but other estimates place this at the very conservative end. Various studies suggest a range of 12 to 50 (adapted from Brecher 1972). A more middle-of-the-road, and probably more realistic, estimate would be 35–40, meaning that a lethal dose is 35–40 times greater than the effective dose.

Brecher's (1972) research revealed that a common practice among medical examiners has been to rule a death as an overdose in cases where more precise cause of death cannot be determined if there is circumstantial evidence that a victim has been using drugs or if he or she is a known drug addict. The reality of the overdose death, in most cases, is probably death due to synergism, what Brecher has called *Syndrome X*. We know that certain drugs, when used in combination with narcotics, produce a synergistic effect; that is, they produce a depressant effect many times the simple additive effect of the two drugs combined. Drugs that produce this effect are generally depressants category and include alcohol, barbiturates, and various tranquilizers. This explanation makes much more sense in light of the fact that reported overdose deaths increased greatly after World War II, and then again in the 1970s.

These were periods characterized by higher than normal use of alcohol and other tranquilizing drugs among addicts in the heroin subculture. Some may question the need to distinguish between overdose death and death due to synergism. It is important for several reasons. We often make policies based on the assumption that heroin or other narcotics have fantastically destructive powers (whereas the dangers of other drugs may be inappropriately minimized). Such policies will be fundamentally flawed if based on inaccurate fatality statistics. Also, treatment and educational efforts can be much more effective if we understand more completely the dangers associated with drug use patterns.

There are, however, other pharmacologically induced health problems associated with narcotics use. One such problem is lung disease, particularly pneumonia, as a complicating effect of the depressant action of narcotics on the respiratory system. Also, whereas sudden withdrawal from heroin is not particularly problematic from a health point of view for otherwise healthy adults, such rapid termination from heroin use can be fatal to the fetus of a pregnant woman (NIDA 2005). Use of narcotics by pregnant women is thus strongly discouraged, and for those women who are using narcotic drugs, withdrawal should be approached with great care. Still another consequence of narcotics use that has been noted with some concern is a decline in libido and sexual functioning. There is some conflicting evidence surrounding this issue, but the depressant action of the narcotics almost certainly has some impact on sexual functioning, much like alcohol and other depressants. Indeed, some addicts are reported to use heroin purposely to avoid the frustration of sexual arousal.

Depressants

The depressants share many of the same health consequences as the narcotics. Because of the inhibitory effect of these drugs on the central nervous system, depressants such as barbiturates, sedatives, and tranquilizers place the heavy user at potential risk for overdose and even death. Because these drugs have typically been diverted from pharmacies, the dosage is usually clearly indicated, and the user should be aware of the quantity and concentration of the drug that he or she is taking. Unfortunately, if a user is sufficiently under the influence, it may matter little how well dosages are marked. There is, moreover, the tendency to use depressants with other CNS inhibitors, particularly narcotics and alcohol. When this occurs, depressants synergize, and place the user in much greater danger of overdose.

A characteristic feature of non-narcotic depressants, which distinguishes them from the narcotics, is the potentially deadly effect of sudden withdrawal from these drugs. **Delirium tremens** (or DTs) is the term used to refer to the sudden withdrawal symptoms experienced by chronic alcoholics that include tremors, heavy sweating, insomnia, hallucinations, disorientation, and ultimately seizures. Although rare even for chronic alcoholics, under extreme conditions these symptoms can be fatal (Moak and Anton 1999). Other CNS depressants also produce potentially fatal withdrawal effects, though they do not necessarily have all of the effects of alcohol's delirium tremens (Brady et al. 1999).

Still another physiological feature of most of the CNS depressants is their ability to permeate the placental barrier during pregnancy. Regardless of whether the drug is alcohol, barbiturates, tranquilizers, or sedatives, pregnant mothers who consume these drugs put their infants at great risk of being born with the physiological symptoms of addiction. Moreover, these infants typically suffer from lower than average birth weight and other physical problems (Carroll 1989).

One depressant drug poses particularly troublesome health risks, alcohol. Alcohol is, ironically, a legal drug for adults in all of the United States, though pharmacologically it is one of the most dangerous of all recreational drugs. Among the several health risks posed by alcohol are liver dysfunction, cardiovascular problems, cancer, neurological problems, complications in pregnancy, accidental death and injury due to lack of motor coordination, and sexual dysfunction. We discuss these in the following paragraphs.

Liver Dysfunction. Alcohol directly affects the liver in several ways. One risk is the accumulation of fatty acids that can result in a *fatty liver*. This occurs because the liver burns fatty acids stored in it. Alcohol contains a high level of fatty acids, so these are used by the liver rather than the body's own fatty acids, resulting in an accumulation of such acids in the liver. If left unattended the cell membranes can rupture, resulting in the death of those liver cells. Another problem that can develop is *alcoholic hepatitis,* an inflammation of the liver causing impairment of liver function. This seems to develop where liver cells have died, but whether a fatty liver contributes to this condition is uncertain. The most serious liver problem is *cirrhosis*. There is by now a mountain of evidence that chronic alcohol use causes cirrhosis of the liver. When this happens, healthy liver cells are replaced by nonfunctioning fibrous tissue, resulting in a decrease in blood flow through the liver. The liver can function properly only with an adequate circulation of blood through it. Cirrhosis is the twelfth leading cause of death in the United States (Mathews et al. 2006).

Cancer and Heart Disease. Alcohol has also been linked to cancer and heart disease. In some cases, excessive alcohol use causes clogged arteries around the heart, known medically as *myocardial infarction*. This is a major cause of heart attacks. A similar symptom observed among alcoholics is the buildup of fat in the arteries, thereby limiting the blood supply to the heart. This condition is known as *angina pectoris*. Finally, excessive alcohol use has been linked with *cardiomyopathy*, a disease of the heart muscle itself (Moak and Anton 1999).

Neurological Dysfunction. Still another physiological consequence of long-term alcohol abuse is brain damage accompanied by psychosis. The name given to this symptom is *Korsakoff's psychosis*. This condition is commonly linked with a lack of thiamine (vitamin B_1, thiamine), a condition known as *Wernicke's disease.* These two conditions are so commonly found together that the condition is usually referred to as **Wernicke-Korsakoff syndrome** (Ray and Ksir 1999) or simply *wet brain*. Because many physicians are not familiar with many of the subtle symptoms of alcoholism, this condition is often underdiagnosed or misdiagnosed as Alzheimer's or other forms of dementia.

Complications in Pregnancy. Heavy use of alcohol by pregnant mothers can result in **fetal alcohol syndrome** (FAS). This condition, first formally identified in 1973, is recognizable by a number of possible symptoms including an abnormally small head, facial irregularities, heart and genital defects, and severe mental retardation among others (Liska 2004).[2] According to Ray and Ksir (1999) the three defining characteristics of fetal alcohol syndrome are: (1) growth retardation prior to and/ or following birth, (2) abnormal features of the face and head, and (3) CNS abnormalities resulting in mental retardation and abnormal neonatal behavior, among other things.

Coordination, Reaction Time, and Motor Vehicle Accidents. Another serious consequence of depressants generally is increased reaction time and loss of coordination. This feature generally has grave consequences when coupled with driving automobiles and running of dangerous equipment. The United States Department of Transportation (n.d.) reported 16,694 alcohol-related traffic fatalities in 2004—one every 31 minutes. Alcohol was involved in 39 percent of all traffic fatalities that year. The good news is that this represents a 20-percent decrease from the more than 22,000 alcohol-related fatalities in 1989. It has been estimated that there is 8 times the risk for a fatal crash per mile driven if one has a blood alcohol content of 0.10 or higher compared with a BAC of zero (Fell 1987), though Zador et al. (2000), using combined data from the Fatality Analysis Reporting System and the National Roadside Survey of Drivers, estimates that among drivers aged 35 and over, there is more than 11 times the risk for a fatal accident at BAC levels of 0.09. Drivers under 21 with BAC levels of 0.09 are more than 51 times as likely to have a fatal accident than sober adult drivers.[3] It is for this reason all 50 states, Washington, D.C., and Puerto Rico have adopted the more stringent 0.08 BAC level as the threshold of legal intoxication. Fell and Voas (2006), in a review of research, report that lowering the threshold from 0.10 to 0.08 has resulted in a substantial decrease in crashes and fatalities, with reductions ranging from 5 to 16 percent. They further estimate that drivers with BACs between 0.05 and 0.07 have a 4 to 10 times greater risk of being in a fatal accident than drivers with no blood alcohol content, and recommend lowering the legal threshold to 0.05 for adults (21 and over) and 0.02 for youth below 21.

Sexual Dysfunction. Still another consequence of chronic alcohol use is a decrease in libido. Contrary to popular opinion, whereas alcohol may decrease inhibitions and increase desire, it diminishes sexual function. Studies have found that chronic alcohol use results in decreased sperm count and atrophy of the testicles. Shakespeare apparently had it right when he said, "Lechery, sir, it provokes and unprovokes; it provokes the desire, but it takes away the performance" (Ray and Ksir 1999).[4]

Other Medical Problems. Another physiological response to alcohol use that is not commonly recognized is the dilation of peripheral blood vessels. Although not usually a serious medical condition, it can be fatal under certain circumstances. Under conditions of extreme cold, this response results in the body feeling warmer when drinking because the warm blood is flowing closer to the surface of the skin where nerve endings are located. Unfortunately, this takes away the necessary warmth from vital organs, which can be fatal (Ray and Ksir 1999). Other serious effects of alcohol include stomach ulcers and gastrointestinal problems generally. This occurs partly because of the direct irritant effect of alcohol on the stomach lining, but primarily because alcohol stimulates the secretion of excess acid (Liska 2004). Finally, alcohol use has been found to affect hormonal processes. Acute alcohol use sometimes results in low blood sugar levels (hypoglycemia) because of the inhibition of glucose metabolism. Chronic heavy drinking, however, often results in heightened blood sugar levels (hyperglycemia) and can be a major health risk for those individuals predisposed to diabetes (Moak and Anton 1999).

Stimulants

The principle pharmacological effect of the stimulants is that they accelerate the central nervous system function. This is not always bad, and indeed, stimulants are often used intentionally for this purpose, such as when college students consume many cups of coffee while studying for exams or writing papers. This quality of the stimulants becomes problematic to users when the user has a weak or defective cardiovascular system, and/or when the drug consumed is in extremely large quantities or great concentration.

The primary health impact of the stimulants that can be directly attributed to their pharmacology is the impact that they have on the cardiovascular system. Because stimulants elevate CNS function, it follows that the cardiovascular system will in some way be affected. Although all of the stimulants have potentially adverse effects on the heart and circulatory system, cocaine is particularly powerful in its CNS stimulant effect. Cocaine and methamphetamines have been found to constrict the vessels bringing blood to the heart, which can trigger chaotic heart rhythms called *ventricular fibrillations*. Moreover, cocaine, as well as other stimulants such as amphetamines and nicotine, causes an increase in both heart rate and blood pressure. As a result, users of these stimulants are at highly increased risk for heart diseases and strokes (NIDA 2004, 2006a, 2006b). It is estimated that about one-fifth of all deaths from heart disease can be directly attributable to smoking cigarettes. Moreover, nicotine use is linked to a greater likelihood of aneurysm (NIDA 2006b). Studies have also found that methamphetamine abuse can result in inflammation of the heart lining itself, placing the user at greater risk for heart disease (NIDA 2006a).

Research by Marc Kaufman and his associates (1998) has shed valuable light on the biology and pharmacology of heightened levels of strokes among cocaine users. Using magnetic resonance technology and double-blind comparison groups of individuals receiving cocaine a placebo (no cocaine), these researchers found that cocaine users experienced significantly more constriction of cerebral arteries than did the placebo group, and that increased dosages of cocaine produced even greater levels of vasoconstriction. Moreover, individuals with a history of cocaine use had more constriction than those without, suggesting a cumulative or chronic effect of cocaine use on the cardiovascular system. In addition to these findings, the research group found that the experimental (cocaine-using) group also had higher blood pressure and faster heart rates. So in addition to an increased level of cardiovascular activity and blood pressure, the constriction of blood vessels results in extreme pressure at certain critical areas. The results can be serious and even deadly, and can occur suddenly and without warning.

Heart disease and other cardiovascular problems are not the only direct pharmacological effects of stimulants. Research by Strickland and his associates (1993) suggests that mental functioning is seriously impaired in cocaine users as a result of vascular constriction in the brain. These researchers reported long-term attention and concentration deficits, memory loss, and other learning deficits among even casual and intermittent cocaine users, and even after the cessation of use (in this instance, a minimum of six months off the drug).

Another health hazard of the stimulants, particularly powerful stimulants such as cocaine and methamphetamine, is the extreme psychological reaction that they can produce. Schizophrenic-like reactions have been reported, including paranoia, and in the case of methamphetamines, hallucinations and **formication** (delusions of parasites or insects on the skin) have also been observed (Albertson et al. 1999; NIDA 1996a, 2006c).

Potential fetal and neonatal health consequences may result from stimulant use during pregnancy. Crack and cocaine use have received the most attention, though the research on effects of cocaine use on infants is not at all conclusive. Early studies alleged severe consequences of prenatal cocaine and crack use. According to early studies, infants born to cocaine-using mothers tended to have lower birth weight, delivered early, were less responsive to environmental stimuli, and showed higher than normal incidences of cardiorespiratory problems (Chasnoff et al. 1985; Chasnoff et al. 1989; MacGregor et al. 1987).

These effects can be explained in various ways. For example, blood vessels in the placenta become constricted, thereby restricting needed nutrients and oxygen to the fetus, which may result in a low-birth-weight infant. If the placenta becomes so damaged by blood vessel constriction caused by heavy cocaine use, much more severe consequences can result, including severe brain damage, or even spontaneous abortion. Moreover, like alcohol and the depressants, stimulants permeate the placental barrier, and cocaine and crack babies supposedly suffer consequences analogous to infants with fetal alcohol syndrome including low birth weight, incompletely developed internal organs, and smaller than normal head size. Cardiorespiratory problems may also develop, depending on what point in her pregnancy a mother was using cocaine (Brady et al. 1994; Metsch et al. 1996).

Research after about 1990, however, has found that most of the neonatal impact of prenatal cocaine use disappears when controlling for other lifestyle variables, other drug use, and especially alcohol use (Brown et al. 1998; Neuspiel et al. 1991; Richardson and Day 1994; Richardson et al. 1993). Many women who use crack or cocaine do not properly care for themselves nutritionally, which also has negative consequences for their fetuses. Similarly, crack-using women often live in older and substandard housing where there may remain lead paint and other environmental hazards (Metsch et al. 1996). Present research suggests that many of the adverse health consequences of infants previously attributed to mothers' use of cocaine is actually the result of a broader lifestyle that involves poor nutrition, alcohol use, and other unhealthy environmental attributes.

There is perhaps no stimulant—or other drug, for that matter—that is more damaging to health than tobacco, though many of the health hazards associated with tobacco use are not directly a result of the stimulant nicotine. In the United States, tobacco smoking caused an annual average 438,000 deaths from 1997 to 2001 (CDC 2005). This compares to approximately 75,000 deaths caused by alcohol in 2001 (CDC, 2004) and about 30,000 deaths due to all illegal drugs combined in 2004 (CDC 2007a). It should be stated at the outset that nicotine is a highly toxic substance. A single drop of pure, concentrated nicotine is a fatal dose. To place this in context, there is enough nicotine in a single cigar, if taken in concentrated form, to kill two people (Ray and Ksir 1999). The reason that smoking a single cigar is not lethal is that the nicotine is diluted enough and is not delivered to the smoker in a short enough time to deliver its fatal blow.

The effects of tobacco smoking go far beyond nicotine, however. It is estimated that cigar and cigarette smoke contains as many as 4,000 chemicals (Liska 2004), many of which pose health risks to the user. These chemicals include carbon monoxide, carcinogenic tars, and other particulate matter. About 90 percent of tars and other particulate matter are believed to remain in the lungs (Carroll 1989), which greatly increases the risk of cancer for the user. Cancer rates among smokers are approximately twice that of nonsmokers (four times greater among heavy smokers), and cigarette smoking has been linked to about 85 percent of all lung cancer cases (Ray and Ksir 1999). Other forms of cancer, including cancers of the mouth, larynx, esophagus, stomach, pancreas, cervix, kidney, and bladder, are also higher among tobacco users. Moreover, respiratory diseases such as chronic bronchitis and emphysema are linked to tobacco smoking (NIDA 2006b).

Tobacco smoking also has a deleterious effect on newborns. Nicotine readily permeates the placental barrier, and studies have found that nicotine concentrations in newborn infants have been as much as 15 percent higher than those found in the mother. Nicotine seems to concentrate in fetal blood, amniotic fluid, and breast milk, all of which contribute to high concentrations in infants. Also posing a risk, carbon monoxide in tobacco smoke lowers oxygen supply to the fetus (NIDA 2006b). For all of these reasons, fetuses of smoking mothers are much more likely to suffer spontaneous abortion than those of nonsmoking mothers, and if they survive to live birth, are more likely to be premature and underweight (Ray and

Ksir 1999). There is also heightened risk of sudden infant death syndrome (SIDS) among infants exposed to tobacco smoke either pre- or postnatally (Slade 1999; Ray and Ksir 1999).

Finally, a growing body of evidence holds that smoking poses health risks not only for smokers but for nonsmokers as well. **Environmental tobacco smoke** (ETS) is believed to cause approximately 3,000 lung cancer deaths annually among nonsmokers and plays some role in cardiovascular-related deaths of another 35,000 nonsmokers. Asthma sufferers are particularly vulnerable to "passive smoke," and infants in homes where there is smoking are more vulnerable to low birth weight, SIDS, asthma, and other respiratory problems (Aligne and Stoddard 1997; NIDA 2006b).

Hallucinogens

The hallucinogens have enjoyed both very positive and extremely negative publicity. Proponents of these drugs have claimed that they open the user to existential dimensions not possible otherwise. Opponents have claimed that they cause severe flashbacks and produce psychotic-like symptoms in the user, a charge especially leveled against LSD. Other claims, discussed in Chapter 3, include the allegation that LSD causes genetic damage in users. Both positive and negative claims are almost certainly greatly exaggerated. Despite the early claims of genetic damage and birth defects, subsequent research under carefully controlled conditions has failed to substantiate these allegations (Grinspoon and Bakalar 1979; Stephens 1999). The psychological effect of hallucinogens, whether their so-called mind-expansion properties or their ability to produce flashbacks, are subjective effects that result largely from the user's set and setting (see Chapter 1).

This is not to suggest that hallucinogens pose no direct health concerns. These are very potent drugs that, if taken in excessive dosages, can cause very extreme reactions that result in bizarre and dangerous behavior by the user. As we pointed out in Chapter 3, LSD is so powerful that dosages are measured in micrograms, rather than the standard milligrams: a milligram is 1,000 times stronger than a microgram. More recently, other hallucinogens such as ecstasy have become popular as "club drugs," commonly used at parties, concerts, and other recreational events that attract young people. Recent research sponsored by the National Institute on Drug Abuse (2006d) has found that MDMA (ecstasy) may indeed adversely affect brain functioning. Using positron emission tomography (PET), a brain imaging technique, researchers have discovered that individuals who use ecstasy showed significant reduction in serotonin transporters that seems to be a permanent or at least long-term effect. This loss was shown to result in loss of both verbal and visual short-term memory (Bolla et al. 1998; McCann et al. 1999; Mathias 1999).

Marijuana

Marijuana is a drug that has had a very checkered history in the American pharmacopeia. As noted in Chapter 2, it was legal until the 1930s in most states, and only a decade later it was vilified as a scourge on the American landscape. It is therefore quite understandable that numerous allegations have been made about the effects of marijuana, most of which have not stood the test of empirical scrutiny. At one time, for example, it was believed that marijuana caused chromosomal damage. Subsequent empirical investigation has failed to support that allegation. Marijuana has also been accused of causing cerebral atrophy lowered testosterone levels, and other serious effects—also not been supported by subsequent research (Goode 2008). However, the physiological and behavioral effects of marijuana have been substantiated empirically. We turn to these now.

Respiratory Problems. Perhaps most conclusively, marijuana affects the respiratory system of the user. In small to moderate amounts, marijuana has actually been found to benefit certain users, such as those with asthma, by causing the bronchial passageways to enlarge, an effect known as *bronchodilation*. Heavy use, however, has detrimental effects on the user, including inflamation or narrowing of the bronchial passageways known as *bronchoconstriction* (Liska 2004). Furthermore, Joy, Watson, and Benson (1999) report that marijuana smoking (as well as tobacco smoking) causes damage to the lining of the respiratory tract. Chronic marijuana use also significantly reduces pulmonary function.

Cancer. We mentioned in Chapter 3 that marijuana smoke contains some 400 chemicals. The consequences of marijuana smoking, therefore, go beyond those caused by THC, its active ingredient. Many of the chemicals found in tobacco are also found in marijuana. Various chemicals in marijuana smoke are also believed to be carcinogenic; indeed, on a per weight unit basis, estimates are that as much as four times the amount of tar is deposited in the lungs of marijuana smokers than in tobacco smokers. This is partly because marijuana cigarettes do not have filters, marijuana is usually inhaled more deeply than tobacco, the smoke is held in the lungs longer than tobacco smoke, and the marijuana cigarette is smoked more completely than a tobacco cigarette. On the other hand, it must also be remembered that tobacco is usually rolled much more tightly and that tobacco smokers typically consume many more cigarettes per day (Joy et al. 1999; Rickert et al. 1982). Caution is also called for when considering epidemiological studies because many marijuana smokers are also tobacco smokers (some 50 percent according to Stephens, 1999), and because lung cancer takes a long time to develop. Since widespread use of marijuana did not begin until the 1960s, large samples of users with long-term exposure are only now accumulating (Joy et al. 1999).

Memory Loss. There is also a growing body of evidence that marijuana smoking causes temporary and reversible short-term memory loss. This acute condition is especially critical among adolescents because the inability to recall for tests and other school requirements can have serious consequences for labeling and tracking by school officials. Only recently has the reason for this short-term loss of memory become clear. It appears that THC suppresses the activity of the neurons in the hippocampus, that part of the brain that is largely responsible for learning and memory. Researchers have discovered that learned behaviors that depend on the hippocampus deteriorate after sustained marijuana use (Joy et al. 1999).

Motor Function. Motor functioning is also affected by marijuana use. This evidence has been building for the last several decades and is now quite conclusive, though certainly more research is needed (Joy et al. 1999). Much of the evidence is based on laboratory simulations, but street driving and accident evidence also reveals that even a moderate amount of marijuana smoking can quite substantially affect perception and motor coordination (Mathias 1996; Ray and Ksir 1999). Although marijuana smoking may not cause a lack of coordination to the extent that alcohol does, it clearly impairs judgment and hence makes the user a worse driver than one who is sober and straight. The concern over marijuana's acute effect on motor functioning has been reinforced in recent years by investigations of accidents involving marijuana use, including a train accident in Maryland where the engineer was found to have been using marijuana hours earlier.

Addiction. There is growing evidence that marijuana may be addictive. This characteristic of marijuana was rejected for many years, especially by legalization advocates. We do know, however, that there are withdrawal symptoms associated with heavy marijuana use, including irritability, insomnia, profuse sweating, and gastrointestinal disturbance. There is also evidence, though disputed, that users develop a tolerance for marijuana. The tolerance seems to be fairly short acting, however, and does not necessarily lead to increased use (Joy et al. 1999).

Steroids and Human Growth Hormones

These drugs, used primarily by athletes, have very direct and potentially fatal consequences on the user, especially when used in large amounts or over a long period of time. We know that prolonged steroid use can result in testicular atrophy, impotence, kidney disease, and heart attacks. Emotional disorders, including increased aggressiveness and severe mood swings, are also linked to steroids (Liska 2004). Human growth hormone (HGH) also poses health threats. Growth hormones affect most organs of the body in some way. Recent evidence suggests that HGH is linked to *Creutzfeldt-Jakob*, a viral disease that, like the AIDS virus, takes years to incubate and can indeed be fatal. Complicating the problems caused by steroids and HGH individually, athletes often use these drugs in combination. Like so many other drugs, the synergism between these drugs compounds their effect (Voy 1991).

Synergistic Effects

Many of the so-called drug overdoses are really something called **synergism**, defined simply as the joint action of two or more drugs that produces an effect that is greater than the sum of their independent effects. In some cases, this combined effect is many times the sum of the independent drug effects. Innumerable drug combinations produce synergistic effects, and we will not even attempt to identify them all here. However, a couple of combinations are particularly relevant to recreational drug use.

One type of drug synergism is that which takes place between CNS depressants. Alcohol and barbiturates, when taken together, produce a powerful multiplier effect (Carroll 1989; Goode 2008). A similar synergism takes place between narcotics and other CNS depressants. Clinical tests also suggest that opioids may interact with drugs used to treat HIV patients resulting in toxic reactions (Stine and Kosten 1999). Another common drug combination that results in synergism is cocaine and alcohol. Cocaine is especially dangerous when taken in combination with alcohol because the two drugs synergize to produce something called *cocaethylene*, which has a longer duration in the brain and is more potent and toxic than the simple additive effect of these drugs (NIDA 2004).

We highlight these synergistic effects because they are most commonly observed among recreational drug users. Mixing of drugs is now commonplace among recreational drug users, and it is often done without any knowledge of how these drugs interact and what effect these drug interactions will have. Although commonly called "overdose," what is in fact taking place is a dangerous combination of drugs. We certainly do not want to downplay the health hazards of individual drugs that might threaten the well-being of the user, greater educational efforts need to be directed toward informing young people (as well as older people who use drugs both recreationally and medicinally) of the dramatic consequences of using certain drugs in combination and which drug combinations should be avoided.

Drug-Using Lifestyles and Health

It is our contention that most of the serious health hazards associated with recreational drug use are a consequence of the lifestyle milieu in which these drugs are taken. With this contention, we do not minimize the health hazards that result. Some of them are devastating, indeed fatal, and if Drug Abuse Warning Network (DAWN) emergency room and medical examiner data are any indication, these devastating consequences are affecting more Americans each year (Office of Applied Studies 2005, 2007). Direct pharmacological action does pose certain levels of risk, of course, depending on the drug in question and particularly when volatile combinations of drugs are used together. Even these risks, however, pale in comparison with the risks posed by other features of the lifestyles of many recreational drug users. In this section, we examine three areas of health concern that are primarily lifestyle-generated risks: infectuous diseases, nutrition and hygiene, and crime victimization.

Infectious Diseases

There is perhaps no more deadly risk associated with drug use than that of contracting HIV. As of 2005, more than 950,000 cases of HIV/AIDS in the United States were reported to the Centers for Disease Control and Prevention (CDC). Approximately 25 percent of these cases appeared to be the direct result of injection drug use. When sex with injecting drug users is considered, the total rises to more than 300,000 individuals (more than 30 percent of total cases) who have been infected with HIV either directly or indirectly as a result of IV drug use (CDC 2007b). Even these figures minimize the problem because they do not include the many cases of pediatric AIDS that result from pregnant women who have been infected. The CDC (2007b) report 9,101 pediatric AIDS cases in 2005; 93 percent of these cases are children who were put at risk through their mothers' infection or exposure to HIV.

Drug users contract the HIV virus primarily in one of three ways: (1) through infected needles, which is the most common mechanism, (2) through sexual contact with others who have the virus, and (3) through infected blood acquired in blood transfusions.[5] Intravenous drug users acquire the HIV virus largely through the sharing of needles, a practice common in the subculture of IV drug use. Because needles and syringes are illegal without a prescription in most jurisdictions, these "works" are at a premium. Consequently, there has developed a custom of sharing needles. Often, the individual who bears the risk of holding the needle will be rewarded with a portion of other participants' drugs. Bourgois and his colleagues (1997) have further found that among street addicts in San Francisco, the practice of sharing needles is necessitated by the broader economy of heroin use in that city. Those at the bottom of the underground hierarchy of street heroin users are forced to pool their resources with partners with whom they share their drugs and their works several times a day. Although they also make use of needle-exchange programs, these users are dependent on one another to get each other through the day without experiencing major withdrawal symptoms. The camaraderie is a necessity, forced by the economics of the heroin lifestyle.

Some entrepreneurs actually make a business out of renting needles, typically as part of a "shooting gallery" operation where drug addicts can go to buy drugs, rent a set of works, and shoot up away from view of potential undercover law enforcement operatives. The practice of needle-sharing would not be particularly risky if care were taken to sterilize needles between each use, but this is seldom the case. Inciardi and his colleagues (1995) report that between 5 and 15 percent of the syringes tested positive for HIV antibodies, depending on the day of the week tested. Even more alarming, they calculated that the average user who frequented Miami shooting galleries once per day could expect to test positive for HIV within 22 days. Those users who were careful not to use syringes with any evidence of blood in them could expect to test positive within 44 days. More frequent use of needles would, of course, shorten the time before one could expect to be infected.

The risk for HIV among IV drug users, however, is not confined to the use of infected needles. Because this disease is so prevalent among IV drug users, it is spread readily through sexual relations. One means of income for drug-addicted women and men is prostitution. This level of sexual activity increases both the prostitute's risk of contracting the disease from an infected client, as well as of her infecting a client. Moreover, many drug-using women will trade sex for drugs, a practice which has become especially common among crack users. Crack is viewed as an aphrodisiac,

Drugs: Myths and Reality

Crack House Sex

The following observation of activity in a Miami crack house by James Inciardi and his colleagues illustrates the casual but risky nature of the sexual exchanges that take place in crack houses.

There were 16 people in the room. Three men and four women were sitting or lying down by themselves, in various parts of the room....Only two were smoking crack; the others appeared to be resting, or waiting, or watching what was going on elsewhere in the room. In a corner farthest away from the entrance, two men were sitting at opposite ends of a couch. Both were smoking and receiving oral sex from two women. Periodically, one of the women would interrupt her "chicken-heading" to have a hit from the man's crack pipe. In another corner, two women were totally naked, with one straddling the other's face, receiving oral sex. They were "freaking" for crack. That is,

they were being paid in crack to perform. Close by, a solitary man was watching them intently, smoking a cigarette with one hand, masturbating with the other....

This scene continued for almost an hour. New customers would come and go—purchase crack, smoke crack, watch sex, engage in sex. Some would just look around and disappear into other rooms. The two men on the couch never spoke to each other, to the women, or to anyone else....The man who was masturbating and watching the two freaking women eventually got up and had vaginal sex with one of them—the one who had been on top, the straddler, the recipient. The other wiped her mouh, lit a cigarette, and watched—disinterested in all of the goings-on.

Source: James A. Inciardi, Dorothy Lockwood, and Anne E. Pottieger. 1993. *Women and Crack-Cocaine*. New York: Macmillan Publishing Company, pp. 70–71. Used with permission.

promoting sexual desire and intensity on a greater level even than other forms of cocaine. Hence, there is a ready market for sexual favors, and this is nowhere more apparent than in the crack houses themselves. Inciardi and his colleagues (1993) describe in very graphic detail the casual and anonymous nature of sexual contact in crack houses, a phenomenon that seems to be more prevalent than that experienced in other drug subcultures. An excerpt from their observations is reproduced in the "Drugs: Myth and Reality" feature of this chapter.

In research also conducted in Miami, McCoy, Miles, and Inciardi (1995) describe in more quantitative terms the risk inherent in this sex-for-drugs activity. Female crack users reported more than eight times the number of sexual partners as women who did not use crack, though they were more likely to insist on condom use. Nevertheless, they were nearly twice as likely to test positive for HIV than were non-crack users. Crack-using women were also much more likely to suffer from other forms of sexually transmitted disease such as syphilis, gonorrhea, genital herpes, and other genital sores.

The good news is that the incidence of HIV and AIDS have been declining over the past several years. Figure 8.1 reveals that the incidence of HIV/AIDS cases

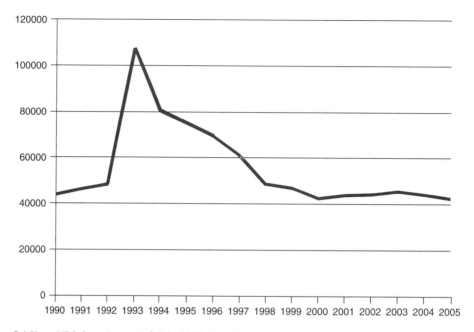

8.1 New AIDS Cases Reported, July 1989–June 2005.

Sources: Centers for Disease Control and Prevention, *HIV/AIDS Surveillance Report, 1991, 1993, 1995, 1997* [Table 1], *1999, 2001* [Table 2], *2003, 2005* [Table 14].

peaked in 1993 at more than 100,000 cases, but has greatly declined and then leveled off since.[6] Also encouraging are data from the Centers for Disease Control and Prevention (2007b) that injection drug users (IDUs) comprise a decreasing percentage of all new AIDS cases among adults and adolescents, from about 28 percent of all new cases in 1993 to 15 percent of all cases in 2005. This means, therefore, that as the incidence of AIDS is decreasing overall, the proportion of those cases that are transmitted via dirty needles is declining even more. This is a testament to the preventive and educational efforts that have been expended in this area, and this success should justify even more such effort.

Drug users are at risk for contracting and transmitting other infectious diseases as well, including various forms of hepatitis, some of which are especially toxic, even fatal. Because hepatitis exists in different forms, there is some confusion and misunderstanding regarding this disease. The most common form of hepatitis is Hepatitis A, which is primarily transmitted through water, food, or fecal material. This form of hepatitis normally has no long-term serious health consequences, and IV drug users are not much more at risk for it than the general population. A second type, *Hepatitis B Virus* (HBV), is much more serious and the form to which IV drug users are especially vulnerable. This is a virus transmitted largely through blood and sexual contact, and can also be transmitted to developing fetuses. HBV attacks the liver, often causing scarring and cirrhosis, and causes the death of approximately 5,000 Americans per year. The Centers for Disease Control and Prevention (2002a) have estimated that there are about 1.25 million Americans currently infected with this disease with some 73,000 new infections reported in 2000. The incidence of HBV is particularly problematic among intravenous drug users. The Centers for Disease Control and Prevention estimate that within five years after beginning injection, 50 to 70 percent of IDUs will become infected with HBV (2002a).

Another serious hepatitis strain is *Hepatitis C Virus* (HCV). This virus is also transmitted through blood and sexual contact as well as perinatally. Those groups most at risk are injection drug users, highly active and promiscuous sexual players, health care workers, and infants born to infected women. Like HBV, Hepatitis C attacks the liver, resulting in 8,000 to 10,000 deaths per year. The Centers for Disease Control and Prevention (2002a) estimate that approximately 3.9 million Americans have been infected with HCV, but that the incidence of new cases in 2000 was only about 30,000.

A final hepatitis virus that affects IV drug users is *Hepatitis D* (HDV), otherwise known as *Delta Hepatitis*. This virus depends upon the coexistence of Hepatitis B to replicate itself. When it occurs in conjunction with individuals with chronic HBV (known as a *superinfection*), the Delta virus is especially destructive. Long-term studies of chronic HBV carriers who acquire HDV in a superinfection suggest that 70 to 80 percent develop chronic liver disease with cirrhosis of the liver, compared with 15 to 30 percent of patients with chronic HBV alone (CDC 2007c).

We want to emphasize that the high prevalence and incidence of these diseases among drug users are only correlates of their drug use, not direct consequences. That is, the drugs involved—whether we are talking about heroin, cocaine, crack, or any other drug—do not cause these infectious diseases. Nor do these drugs cause higher rates of other sexually transmitted diseases such as gonorrhea, syphilis, or genital herpes. Rather, these diseases are a consequence of certain aspects of the lifestyles that these drug users lead (Rhodes 1996). Among heroin and IV cocaine users, for example, acquiring HIV and hepatitis is probably a result of the way in which they administer the drug (intravenously) and the care (or lack of it) they give to ensuring noninfected (clean) needles. Drug users can substantially reduce their risk of being infected in a number of ways: adopting alternative routes of administration (e.g., snorting rather than shooting), sterilizing their needles with bleach between each use, exchanging infected (dirty) needles in for clean ones where needle exchange programs are available, and refusing to loan or borrow needles from other addicts. These practices, if widely practiced, would both only reduce individual risks and curb the spread of these diseases substantially. Other lifestyle features also affect the spread of these diseases. Most significantly is the frequent and often indiscriminate sexual practices of some drug users. All of the infectious diseases that we have examined in this section can be transmitted sexually. Once again, reducing sexual activity, maintaining monogamous sexual relationships, and/or taking precautions when engaging in sexual activity are effective preventive measures. Recognition of the lifestyle dynamics of drug users is an important part of understanding the causal complex of the health issues that this population group confronts.

Nutrition and Hygiene

In 1962, the Supreme Court ruled in *Robinson v. California* that it was unconstitutional to punish people merely because they were addicted to narcotics. At least as well known as the decision of the court is this description of drug addiction presented in the court's opinion:

> To be a confirmed drug addict is to be one of the walking dead.... The teeth have rotted out; the appetite is lost and the stomach and intestines don't function properly. The gall bladder becomes inflamed; eyes and skin turn a bilious yellow. In some cases membranes of the nose turn a flaming red; the partition separating the nostrils is eaten away—breathing is difficult. Oxygen in the blood decreases; bronchitis and tuberculosis develop. Good traits of character disappear and bad ones emerge. Sex organs become affected. Veins collapse and livid purplish scars remain. Boils and abscesses plague the skin; gnawing pain racks the body. Nerves snap; vicious twitching develops. Imaginary and fantastic fears blight the mind and sometimes complete insanity results. Often times, too, death comes—much too early in life.... Such is the torment of being a drug addict; such is the plague of being one of the walking dead. (U.S. Supreme Court 1962)

This poignant description, which was intended to describe the heroin addict, paints a portrait of a rather pathetic individual who has worn down his or her body and is fraught with ailments, even impending death. Although there are certainly inaccuracies in this description, at least insofar as their application to heroin addiction, the attributes that do apply here have one thing in common: they are all a result of the lifestyles that heroin addicts lead, not a result of the pharmacological action of narcotic drugs. Moreover, much of what is described here is a result of a lack of proper nutrition and hygiene.

Even the most casual observer of the heroin subculture will note that, on average, heroin addicts tend to suffer from weight loss; some even appear rather emaciated. Heroin addicts participate in a rather frenetic lifestyle, continually looking for a "score" (drug purchase) and trying to "get over" (make money, usually illegally), all the while having to watch their backs to be sure that they are not identified by police or others who would take advantage of them. This lifestyle, commonly called "ripping and running," has been characteristic of post–Harrison Act years, since the recreational use of narcotics has been illegal. A now classic study conducted by Arthur Light and Edward Torrance in Philadelphia in the 1920s addresses the weight loss issue quite directly. A subsample of 100 heroin or morphine addicts were maintained in a hospital setting on adequate doses of morphine. At the end of the controlled maintenance period, only 4 of the subjects were grossly underweight— about the same percentage one would find in the general population. Furthermore, 6 of the 100 subjects were obese, and the remaining 90 were within the normal weight range. Yet these subjects had been taking the average of 21 grains of morphine or heroin per day, much more than the typical addict on the street would take (Light and Torrance, n.d.; cited in Brecher 1972). This study clearly suggests that it is not the pharmacology of heroin or other narcotics that results in physical deterioration, but rather the peculiar nature of addict lifestyles since the criminalization of narcotics for recreational use.

Other physical problems are also noted in the *Robinson v. California* opinion that bear some comment. The scarring and collapsing of veins and jaundiced skin reflect the hygienic conditions in which many IV drug users live. Dirty needles and blunt needles—in short, needles that are used far longer than intended—cause untold health consequences for addicts, including the spread of infectious diseases as well as the collapsing of veins (from blunt needles). Jaundiced skin is also related to poor hygiene, often a symptom of hepatitis.

One of the street heroin addicts interviewed by Faupel described the scene at the "crib" (home) of one of her acquaintances in New York City who was a "junkie broad":

> The baby was all pissy and messy laying in a rag all over the floor.... It was ridiculous for anybody to live like that ... [B]ecause of her being a woman, she could have got some kind of money some kind of way—if she had to whore, steal it, take it, or rob it—either way, she was supposed to feed those babies she had. (1991, 111)

This observation reveals an important truth about the subculture of heroin use, namely that there *is* self-respect among heroin addicts, a fact evidenced in the revulsion that this respondent experienced at the sight she saw. The other truth, however, is that when individuals become addicted, especially when they are desperately addicted, nutrition and hygiene take a much lower priority to the more urgent needs of securing drugs. Over time, this neglect of the physical body takes its toll.

Crime Victimization
Drug users, particularly illegal drug users, are more vulnerable to being victimized by crime than most of us. The reason for this is that they are, by their very act of using illegal drugs, criminals. This fact alone brings them into contact with other criminals who might victimize them. The connection between drug use and crime will be addressed in detail in Chapter 11. Much of what we have to say regarding the relationship between criminal offending and drugs has equal relevance to the connection between drug use and crime victimization. Hence, we will not explore that topic exhaustively here. We do, however, want to introduce research conducted by Paul Goldstein (1985) on the relationship between drug use and violence. Goldstein suggests three models to understand this connection. The first is a **psychopharmacological** model, which suggests that individuals on drugs engage in violent acts because their intoxication induces a loss of rationality and/or control. A second **economic-compulsive** model suggests that people become violent when they are desperate for drugs and do not have the resources to obtain them. At these times, they may engage in violent behavior to extort money for drugs. Goldstein's third model, the **systemic** model, suggests that violence is an intrinsic part of the culture

and economy of drug use, a dynamic that Goldstein later found to apply to the crack distribution network as well (Goldstein et al. 1989). It is this connection we will highlight in this chapter.

Violence is, to some degree, endemic to the lifestyle associated with illicit drug use. Goldstein (1985, 497) identifies several examples of systemic violence associated with the underworld of illicit drug use. Some of these include: disputes over territory between competing drug dealers; robberies of drug dealers in retaliation for perceived past unfair business practices, and typically a violent response by the dealer; punishment for failing to pay a debt; and retaliation against informers. Additionally, Goldstein points out that the HIV/AIDS epidemic has introduced still another source of violence, namely falsely representing a set of works to be clean or even new, when in fact they have been used by someone who is at risk for AIDS.

One final health risk that is directly connected with the criminal nature of the drug enterprise, and that broadly falls under Goldstein's systemic violence, is the tremendous risk of violence intrinsic to the production of some drugs, particularly methamphetamine. Once the near monopoly of a small number of "superlabs" located in Mexico and the southwestern United States, 237 superlabs were seized in 1999 by the DEA in several states, including states on the East Coast. Moreover, in addition to the superlabs, small, amateur, clandestine labs have sprung up in virtually every state in the union. Nearly 7,500 such labs were seized in 2006, which was fewer than the 17,000-plus seizures in 2003 and 2004 (DEA, n.d.). These labs are extremely dangerous—to the operators, to innocent people living in the immediate environment, and to law enforcement. Methamphetamine can be produced with over-the-counter ingredients, but the preparation process can be lethal. Chemicals used are corrosive, toxic, and highly combustible, often explosive when inappropriately mixed. So volatile are the chemicals involved in the manufacture of methamphetamine that law enforcement personnel are especially trained and provided full-body protective gear before entering a suspected meth lab. They are frequently met with armed resistance, which only exacerbates an already volatile situation (Koch Crime Institute 1999).

Potential Health Benefits of Drugs

We will, in this section, address three controversies that have arisen in recent years regarding the potential medical benefits of drugs normally used only for recreational purposes. The drugs in question are marijuana, which has been proposed as a medical response to several medical conditions; the extended use of stronger narcotics for terminally ill patients; and alcohol in moderate use as a means of enhancing health, particularly the heart and circulatory system.

Medical Marijuana
The use of marijuana for medical purposes is not new. The earliest reference to marijuana is found in a pharmacology book written nearly 5,000 years ago by the Chinese emperor Shen Nung, who recommended marijuana for a variety of ailments

including gout, rheumatism, malaria, and even constipation and absent-mindedness (Ray 1978). Other reports of the medical use of marijuana can also be found in ancient Greek writings (Guterman 2000). Grinspoon (2000) reminds us that marijuana was first recognized by Western medicine in 1839, when W. B. O'Shaughnessy discovered its usefulness as an analgesic, anticonvulsant, and muscle relaxant. Grinspoon and Bakalar (1995) have noted that since O'Shaughnessy's work, more than 100 articles on the medical use of marijuana were published by American and European medical journals, and more research continues each year. Marijuana was touted as therapeutic for tetanus, neuralgia, rheumatism, and asthma among other conditions. Indeed, marijuana use in the United States was primarily for medical purposes until the 1920s, when alcohol was prohibited and marijuana was sought as a functional alternative to alcohol. Simultaneously, medical interest in the drug was declining. Not until the 1970s was serious advocacy of marijuana as medicine reinvigorated (Grinspoon 2000).

Today, proponents of legalizing medical marijuana emphasize two specific health areas in which marijuana has been shown to be helpful. First, it has been quite effective in relieving the nausea associated with chemotherapy among cancer patients. Cancer patients began experimenting with marijuana in the 1970s as an *antiemetic* drug—to relieve the side effects of chemotherapy—and generally found it much more effective that other conventional medications (Grinspoon and Bakalar 1997; Joy et al. 1999). There is also some support among oncologists for the use of marijuana for cancer patients. A survey conducted among oncologists in 1994 revealed that, whereas only 12 percent of the physicians reported recommending marijuana to their patients, 30 percent indicated that they would do so if marijuana cigarettes were to be made legal (Schwartz and Sheridan 1997). An earlier survey by Doblin and Kleiman (1991) reported that 44 percent of oncologists indicated that they had recommended marijuana use to their chemotherapy patients. It is also noteworthy that more than 50 percent of the physicians in the 1994 survey had prescribed Marinol, the trade name for dronabinol, which is a synthetic tetrahydrocannabinol (THC), the primary active ingredient in marijuana (Schwartz and Sheridan 1997).

Still another potential medical use of marijuana is the stimulation of appetite, particularly among HIV/AIDS patients. Many patients suffering weight loss from AIDS have claimed that marijuana is the most effective and least toxic treatment for the nausea that caused their weight loss (Grinspoon 2000). The controlled research examining the effect of THC as an appetite stimulant has used dronabinol (Marinol). The research strongly suggests that THC is an effective appetite stimulant (Joy et al. 1999).

These are by no means the only medical uses that have been claimed for marijuana in recent years. In the 1997 revision of their classic book, *Marijuana: The Forbidden Medicine*, Lester Grinspoon and James Bakalar identify some 30 medical conditions for which patients have found marijuana useful. Included in these symptoms, in addition to the wasting associated with AIDS and the nausea associated with chemotherapy, are reducing intraocular pressure in glaucoma patients; easing

8.2 Currently, thirteen states have strongly worded statutes legalizing marijuana for medical purposes. The federal government, however, continues to prosecute major suppliers of medical marijuana, and even individuals are at risk for prosecution in these states for possession of marijuana. Advocates for the reform of state and federal laws to allow for legal distribution of medical marijuana can be found in just about all demographic segments of the population. (Photo: Associated Press/Lucy Atkins)

the symptoms of osteoarthritis, multiple sclerosis, and epilepsy; and relieving chronic pain from various causes (see also Joy et al. 1999).

There have been efforts to make marijuana legally available for medical purposes. Since the 1960s, the federal government has maintained a marijuana research plot at the University of Mississippi in Oxford, the fruits of which have been used since 1975 in carefully monitored medical cases. This program, called the Compassionate Investigational New Drug (IND) Program, has been used on an extremely limited basis, however. Among the many thousands of people who would benefit from this program, only 40 individuals throughout the United States have ever been approved. Moreover, only 13 people have actually received the government-cultivated cannabis, and the government has determined that they will not be providing cannabis to any new patients, not even to any of the 40 who have already been approved (Grinspoon and Bakalar 1993).

Attempts have been made in several states to make marijuana legally available since 1978. By 1991, 34 states had enacted legislation that would formally make marijuana legally available for medical use, and most recently, in 2003, Maryland was the 36th state to pass such favorable legislation. Most of these laws are grossly ineffective, however, because federal restrictions prevent doctors from prescribing marijuana. Hence, any state statute that includes the word "prescribe" is effectively neutralized by federal law because physicians are unwilling to place themselves at risk for federal sanctions. Furthermore, most of these bills provided no means to distribute marijuana legally, so marijuana patients would have to rely on illegal sources for their drugs. Maryland's law, although a step in the right direction, requires medical marijuana users to prove their medical condition in court to avoid criminal prosecution. Marijuana users still face arrest and up to $100 in fines in addition to court costs (Marijuana Policy Project 2006).

It was a 1996 referendum in California that represented a major shift in state medical marijuana laws. Underground distribution of marijuana for medical purposes had been going on for years in California, where marijuana has even been made available through vending machines (see "Drugs and Everyday Life"). A San Francisco organization called the Cannabis Cultivators Club first opened its doors in 1992, making marijuana available to some 12,000 medical users. City officials essentially turned a blind eye to what was going on, but in August of 1996, state narcotics agents raided the club and closed it down on marijuana possession charges. This resulted in a backlash by California voters who, with 56 percent of the vote, passed Proposition 215, otherwise known as the Medical Marijuana Initiative. Proposition 215 essentially made it legal to grow, possess, and smoke medical marijuana in California if it was recommended or approved by a physician (not "prescribed") (Rosin 1997; Marijuana Policy Project 2006).

A similar ballot initiative was passed in Arizona in that same year, and in 1998, three states—Washington, Oregon, and Alaska—voted at the ballots to legalize marijuana for designated medical purposes (Sager 1999). Maine passed a similar initiative in 1999, followed by Colorado and Nevada in 2000. Hawaii addressed the issue in a different way in 2000, by legislating the removal of criminal penalties for medical marijuana users rather than using a state-wide referendum (Marijuana Policy Project 2006). Montana, an extremely conservative state politically, voting to reelect George Bush in 2004 with 59 percent of the vote, voted by a 62 to 38 percent margin to legalize medical marijuana in Initiative 148 (Ferraiolo 2007). Rhode Island became the 11th state to pass an effective medical marijuana law in 2006, and in 2007, New Mexico became the 12th state to sign into law provision for the legal distribution of medical marijuana to authorized patients. Known as the Lynn and Erin Compassionate Use Act, Senate Bill 523 mandates the New Mexico Department of Health to develop rules governing the use and distribution of medical marijuana to authorized patients. These rules are to address specifically the creation of state-licensed "cannabis production facilities" among other things (NORML, n.d.a). Michigan was the most recent state to medicalize marijuana when, on November 4, 2008, 63 percent of the voters approved a medical marijuana initiative (Marijuana Policy Project 2008. Ferraiolo (2007) points out that from 1995 to 2005, no state has rejected any medical marijuana legalization initiative. Figure 8.2 shows those states with strong medical marijuana laws.

These new state laws do, of course, conflict with federal law that prohibits the possession and distribution of marijuana. Indeed, the federal response to the California referendum was almost immediate: any individual using marijuana, even if recommended by a physician, could face federal prosecution. Moreover, physicians recommending the drug could also be prosecuted as well as lose their licenses to prescribe medicine. Within a few months, the courts ruled that doctors could not be prosecuted, but left open the door to prosecute individual users. The case of *Conant v. McCaffrey* filed January 14, 1997, and heard in August of 2000 in Federal District Court, ruled that to prevent doctors from recommending the use of medical

DRUGS AND EVERYDAY LIFE

Medical Marijuana Vending Machines

The most recent innovation in drug marketing, perhaps, is not a new designer drug or an innovative brand name; it's a high-tech way of selling marijuana, one of the oldest drugs known to humankind. First appearing in Los Angeles, in January 2008, prescription vending machines (PVMs) make it easier for patients who have been approved (not "prescribed") to use marijuana for medical conditions that warrant its use. These new machines, referred to as "marijuana ATMs," are not exactly like the typical soda pop vending machines in hotel lobbies or freeway rest areas. The machines are carefully guarded with 24-hour security guards, allowing only those individuals who are authorized to use them. The machines require fingerprint identification a prepaid credit card, similar to an ATM card, containing all of their personal information, which is inserted into the machine. Only after the user is verified by a corroboration of the fingerprints and the information on the card is the marijuana dispensed.

The first of these machines appeared at the Herbal Nutrition Center in Los Angeles. Since that time, other machines have appeared throughout the city, including one on the campus of the University of Southern California. According to the inventor (and owner) of the machines, Vincent Mehdizadeh, the advantages of these machines are more convenient, 24-hour access, lower prices, and anonymity. Those patients who are registered

with Mehdizadeh's computer database as legitimate approved users can purchase the prepaid credit card.

It is not only the patients using the machines who find them to be an advantage. The dispensaries using the machines find them advantageous as well. Proposition 215 makes it legal to dispense medical marijuana in California, but the federal government doesn't quite see it that way. The DEA and other federal agencies have been intent on closing medical marijuana dispensaries wherever they can find them, including the highly publicized closings of the Cannabis Cultivators Club and the Oakland Cannabis Buyers' Cooperative in 1998. The Supreme Court ruled in favor of the federal government in 2001, giving them the right to close down the clubs, even though they were legal under California law. The PVMs are certainly advantageous to the dispensaries because they help to reduce the number of workers in the dispensary, should a raid occur, which did happen at the Herbal Nutrition Center in 1997. Furthermore, according to Mehdizadeh, the PVMs are more secure and hence more theft-proof.

What is the future of prescription vending machines? It depends on who you talk to. According to advocacy groups, the machine can be a real asset, especially for those who know exactly what kind of marijuana they need or want, though many may still want to feel or smell the marijuana or need the interaction with a real live person. Opponents of medical marijuana, however, such as the DEA, say it's just a matter of time until the government finds a way to shut them down.

marijuana was an abridgement of free speech and therefore was unconstitutional. Federal authorities then began to target distributors, especially larger clubs such as the Cannabis Cultivators Club (Sager 1999) and the Oakland Cannabis Buyers' Cooperative (OCBC). The Justice Department filed suit in January 1998 to close down the operations of these distributors and received a temporary injunction that

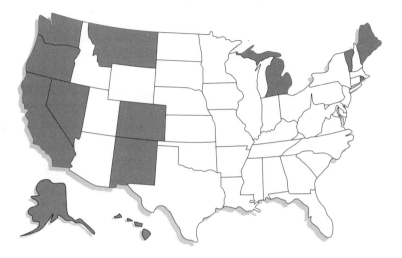

Thirteen States Have Legalized Medical Marijuana Use

(Select your state)

States That Have Passed Medical Marijuana Laws Since 1996:

Alaska, California, Colorado, Hawaii, Maine,
Michigan, Montana, Nevada, New Mexico,
Oregon, Rhode Island, Vermont and Washington

www.NORML.org

8.3 States with Strong Medical Marijuana Provisions.

Source: National Organization for the Reform of Marijuana Laws. http://www.norml.org [Accessed November 9, 2007] Used with permission.

Annotation: While many states have passed laws that would make marijuana legally available in those states. The wording of those laws in most of these states, however, has rendered these laws ineffective because of conflict with federal laws. A California referendum in 1996 initiated a shift in state legislation providing more effective state legislation. Since that time, a total of 12 states have passed laws which more effectively make medical marijuana legally available to patients.

closed the clubs down. One year later, however, the Ninth Circuit Court of Appeals ruled unanimously that "medical necessity" is a valid defense against federal law provided that the distributor can prove that a patient is seriously ill and that the marijuana is necessary. This was appealed to the Supreme Court by the Justice

Department, which ruled in its favor on May 14, 2001. The High Court ruled that the Controlled Substances Act did not recognize medical necessity, except when distributed through government-controlled research projects (*United States v. Oakland Cannabis Buyers Cooperative et al.* 2001).

Even more recently, in *Gonzales v. Raich*, the U.S. Supreme Court again overturned the Ninth Circuit Court of Appeals, which had ruled that enforcement of the Controlled Substances Act against *intrastate* medical marijuana distribution was unconstitutional because it did not affect *interstate* commerce, which was the legal justification for federal enforcement of drug trafficking under the Controlled Substances Act. Once again, the Supreme Court saw things differently and ruled that federal enforcement of even local distribution of medical cannabis within state boundaries was constitutional because such distribution was part of a "class of activities" (the national marijuana market) that could substantially affect interstate commerce. In essence, the Supreme Court ruled that states' rights pose no obstacle to the federal government's power to prosecute anyone for the cultivation, distribution, or possession of marijuana, even if for medical purposes (Beato 2007; U.S. Supreme Court 2005). The use of cannabis for medical purposes has, in effect, been rendered illegal throughout the United States on the basis of the federal Controlled Substances Act. The likelihood of federal arrest or prosecution of individual medical users is very small, however. Beato (2007) points out, for example, that despite the *Gonzales* ruling and the DEA raids that ensued, the number of distributors of medical marijuana in California increased from 20 to over 200 between 2000 and 2006. Moreover, approximately 99 percent of marijuana arrests in the United States are made by state and local authorities. Hence, in those states that have legalized marijuana for medical purposes, the statistical likelihood of arrest among patients using medical marijuana is only about 1 percent. "In fact, the federal government has declared its intention not to pursue patients who possess or use small amounts of marijuana for medical use" (Marijuana Policy Project 2006, 7).

In sum, the long history of medical use of marijuana is being rediscovered among contemporary Americans with a variety of ailments. There is strong clinical evidence that marijuana is an effective antidote to many of these maladies. The federal government has strongly opposed marijuana use for medical purposes and has stubbornly refused to move it from a Schedule I to a Schedule II drug, a designation that indicates a high degree of abuse potential, but nevertheless recognizes medical utility. Increasingly, however, voters and legislators in individual states are recognizing the legitimacy of marijuana use under certain medical conditions and are paving the way legally for people to access marijuana. This has created a tension between the federal government and the individual states that will likely be played out in the courts for some years to come. In contrast to the reticence of the United States to make medical marijuana legally available, Canada legalized marijuana for medical purposes on a national level in legislation introduced on June 14, 2001 (Canadian Government, 2001). We would urge that researchers and policy makers study the impact of this legislation for future policy initiatives in the United States.

Unrestricted Narcotics for Terminally Ill Patients

One of the consequences of advances in medicine is that people not only live longer, but are more likely to die of chronic, rather than acute diseases. Chronic diseases such as cancer often result in rather severe pain toward the end of a patient's life. Studies of outpatients have revealed that anywhere between 12 and 71 percent of dying individuals suffer severe pain in the last week of their life (Pantilat 1999). Indeed, for some patients, it is the excruciating pain that motivates them to seek suicide (Brown 1997). Many medical practitioners have decried this situation because they know that they have the ability to alleviate all or at least most of the pain that terminal patients experience through the use of opiates (primarily) and other pain-relieving drugs.

Physicians are hesitant to prescribe massive dosages of narcotics, however, for three reasons. First, they fear shortening the life span of the already terminal patient. Second, many physicians fear that to increase the dosages of narcotic medications will result in patients becoming addicted to these drugs. Finally, related to both of the preceding concerns, many physicians fear prosecution merely for prescribing these drugs in the large quantities necessary for pain relief because the scheduling of these drugs (typically Schedule II) places severe constraints on their use because of their addictive potential. Physicians also fear that they might be charged with assisting in suicide if it is believed that the narcotics they use shorten the lives of their patients. There seems to be a fairly broad consensus among medical practitioners and ethicists about the legitimacy and response to these concerns. We examine each of these concerns in the following paragraphs.

Shortening Life Span

It is commonly believed that narcotics, especially in heavy doses, so depress respiration that their use will prematurely end the life of a terminally ill patient. Extensive clinical evidence suggests that these concerns are unfounded (EAPC 1996). Furthermore, controlled research on 238 patients in a hospice unit showed no evidence for hastening of death. Patients who were given marked increases in opiates during their last 48 hours of life showed no significant differences in length of life from admission to the hospice, or in the frequency of unexpected death from those patients who were given no or only modest increases in opiates (Thorns and Sykes 2000). The World Health Organization (WHO n.d.) has developed an "analgesic ladder" designed to assist physicians in identifying the appropriate amount of medication to terminally ill patients. This three-step approach, initially developed in 1986, calls for increasing levels of pain relief beginning with Step 1, nonopiates such as aspirin or acetaminophen, which are often sufficient for low-level pain. Step 2 involves mild opiates such as codeine. Step 3 involves stronger opiates such as morphine, only if the previous two steps were not sufficient to relieve pain. The analgesic

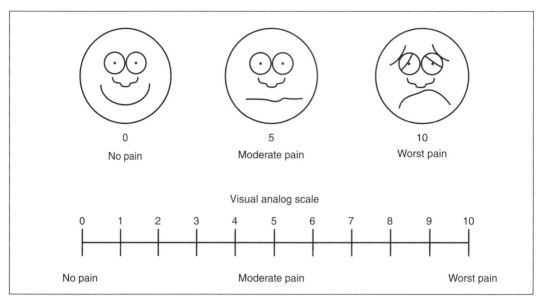

| 0 | 5 | 10 |
| No pain | Moderate pain | Worst pain |

Visual analog scale

0   1   2   3   4   5   6   7   8   9   10

No pain   Moderate pain   Worst pain

8.4 Visual Pain Scale.

Source: Pantilat, Steven Z. 1999. "Just Say Yes: The Use of Opioids for Managing Pain at the End of Life." *The Western Journal of Medicine*, 171, 4, pp. 257–259. Adapted and reproduced with permission from the BMJ publishing group.

ladder is often used in conjunction with a visual analog scale (see Figure 8.4) that has been found especially effective in helping patients accurately convey the level of pain that they are experiencing (Pantilat 1999). When opiates are administered with sensitivity to a patient's pain level, medical ethicists agree that overprescribing narcotics should not be a concern.

Addiction

Many doctors have been reticent to prescribe large dosages of narcotics, especially if these dosages must be maintained over a period of time, because of the potential for creating an addiction among their patients. Practitioners working in palliative care (care of dying patients) respond to this concern in two ways. First, it is argued that medical patients are not as vulnerable to addiction as are street users of narcotic drugs, do not experience the euphoria that a street user experiences, and do not have the same craving for the drug as is experienced by street users (Brown 1997). The logic of this argument might be a bit suspect in that the craving that street users experience typically come from the lack of the drug, a situation that medical patients with prescribed morphine do not typically experience. There is, however, some empirical evidence to back up this claim. Research using data from the Drug Abuse Warning Network reveals that the number of emergency room episodes involving the five opioids most frequently used in treating terminally ill patients (morphine, fentanyl, oxycodone, hydromorphine, and meperidine) decreased from 1990 to 1996. This decrease was observed despite the fact that physicians were actually increasing their prescriptions for the use of all of these drugs except for meperidine (Joranson et al. 2000). The concern over addiction does indeed seem unfounded. Moreover, many wonder why there is a concern regarding addiction, even if the use of these drugs does initiate or increase the level of addiction in patients. These patients are, after all, terminal. Their addiction, if indeed it occurs, allows them to lead useful and productive lives in their last days, an opportunity not available without the narcotics (Pelligrino 1998).

Concerns about Prosecution

The fact is that most physicians understand that the concern over shortened life span and addiction are not valid reasons to deprive dying patients of pain-reducing narcotics. Most physicians do not prescribe either because they are not alert to the level of pain that a patient is experiencing (Pantilat 1999), or more likely because they fear that they might be subject to criminal prosecution, especially under the Controlled Substances Act of 1970. Physicians fear criminal prosecution primarily on the grounds that the use of massive amounts of drugs may bring on the early demise of their patients.

This concern is, at one level, valid because a physician who is investigated by law enforcement or by medical examining boards is subject to public degradation that can have potentially catastrophic effects on his or her practice. Nevertheless, the need to provide adequate pain relief, even when it involves exceptionally large doses of narcotics (and in some cases barbiturates) overwhelms the prosecutorial risk, in our assessment. The fact is that the risk of prosecution is substantially limited for at least three reasons. First, as we have discussed above, medical evidence increasingly demonstrates that longevity is not appreciably shortened with the use of pain-killing drugs, and that those who use these drugs do not seek or crave them beyond what is needed to alleviate the pain associated with their medical condition.

Second, there are substantial regulatory and legislative efforts to protect physicians against unwarranted prosecution. The Federation of State Medical Boards approved a policy statement in 1998 known as *Model Guidelines for the Use of Controlled Substances for the Treatment of Pain*, which made three significant policy statements. First, they acknowledged that the use of controlled substances, including opiates, may be necessary for the treatment of both acute and chronic pain. Second, the *Guidelines* stated that a physician's treatment of a patient would not be judged by the quantity or longevity of drugs prescribed, which was a radical departure from previous policy. Finally, the *Guidelines* recognized the appropriateness of physicians treating chemically dependent individuals for pain with controlled substances (Federation of State Medical Boards, 1998; cited in Johnson 2003). Prior to the adoption of these guidelines, the American Society of Law, Medicine and Ethics had developed a model *Pain Relief Act* that would protect physicians who prescribed medication for the relief of pain against disciplinary action or criminal prosecution if they prescribed within acceptable guidelines (including those developed in the

Model Guidelines). The model *Pain Relief Act* has had an impact on statutes in several states. Prior to the model Act, only ten states had any statutes addressing treatment of intractable pain. As of 2003, some 23 states had enacted legislation providing for the treatment of pain that would protect physicians and other health care professionals from inappropriate disciplinary or criminal action (Johnson 2004).

Moreover, there have been efforts at the federal level as well. An early attempt, known as the *Pain Relief Promotion Act of 1999*, was first introduced in the house by Congressman Henry Hyde as HR-2260 (U.S. House of Representatives, 1999) and then in the Senate by Senator Don Nickles (S-1272). The bill stipulated that the dispensing of controlled substances as medically necessary to relieve pain is consistent with the Controlled Substances Act. The bill also called for education of law enforcement and health professionals on medically accepted means for alleviating pain. The House version of the bill passed with a strong majority in October of 1999, but it was not passed in the Senate. There are continued efforts to pass legislation at the federal level, however, including the *Conquering Pain Act*, introduced in 2001, which would formally acknowledge the undertreatment of pain and establish pain as a fifth vital sign. More recently, in 2007, the *National Pain Care Policy Act of 2007* was introduced, which would authorize an Institute of Medicine Conference on Pain Care to increase awareness of pain as a public health problem, in addition to providing for pain care education of physicians. All of these initiative are indicators of a growing awareness by both the government and the medical profession of the need for aggressive treatment of acute and chronic pain.

Finally, the administration of pain-relieving medication has long been defended ethically—which has usually translated into a legal defense as well—by a philosophy known as the "Doctrine of Double Effect." This is an old philosophy dating at least as far back as medieval Catholic theologians, which states that actions are morally permissible, regardless of the consequences of those actions, if it was not the intent of the actor to cause those consequences (Quill et al. 1997). The doctrine even allows for those consequences to have been foreseeable by the actor so long as he or she did not intend for those consequences to occur. Hence, when applied to the dispensing of opiates and other pain-relieving medication, *even if* addiction occurs or life is shortened by a physician's actions, the physician is justified in using these medications if his or her intent was to relieve the pain and suffering of the patient and not to cause addiction or death (Quill 1995). Generally, if an action on the part of a physician leading to a patient's death is to be regarded as morally acceptable under this doctrine, the action must conform to the following legal requirements:

- The medication must have a reasonable chance of reducing suffering or pain.
- The use of medication must be intended *primarily* to reduce pain and *not* to result in death.
- The use of medication cannot be for purposes of producing death as a means of relieving the pain and suffering.

- There must be enough reason to prescribe the increased medication to counterbalance any foreseeable risk of death. (Lieberson 1999)

Health professionals as well as law enforcement officials disagree about the appropriateness of applying this doctrine to the relief of pain in terminally ill patients. These usually come in the gray areas, such as sedating a person to a level of unconsciousness until their demise (Quill et al. 1997). Importantly, however, whereas recent Supreme Court decisions have upheld the principle of the sanctity of life above a patient's right to choose euthenasia,[7] our criminal law has consistently allowed for posing a risk to life if the expected benefits justify the risks. Such a risk is taken, for example, when high-risk surgery is performed to correct a serious medical condition (Quill et al. 1997). Schwarz (2004), on the other hand, notes that many clinicians and experts on pain management maintain that providing effective pain management to dying patients should need no further justification in the first place.

For all of these reasons, although the law is not crystal clear regarding the potential consequences for a physician administering opiates or sedatives to terminally ill patients, the risk of prosecution to physicians who are conscientious in their response to the pain of the terminally ill should be fairly minimal. Moreover, with the increasing effort to educate physicians on how to administer pain-reducing medications in an ethical and legal manner, we would expect to see greater use of these medications to reduce the pain and suffering of terminally ill patients.

Benefits from Moderate Drinking

We have discussed at some length, both in this chapter and in Chapter 3, some of the health hazards associated with alcohol consumption. Recent research, however, has revealed that when consumed in moderation, alcohol can actually enhance one's health. It has long been believed that alcohol has health benefits; indeed, its medicinal properties are mentioned in numerous places throughout both the Old and New Testaments. Only recently, however, have carefully designed studies scientifically supported such benefits. We should point out that there is controversy within the scientific community, and especially within the treatment industry, regarding the beneficial role that moderate alcohol consumption might have (Moak and Anton 1999).

It is, of course, important to define what we mean by *moderate* drinking. Typically, this is defined as a certain number of drinks consumed over a specified period. There is variation, however, in the amount of alcohol contained in different types of drinks, a problem that is especially apparent when examining cross-cultural alcohol consumption (Dufour 1999). Researchers have been developing more quantitative measures of levels of alcohol consumption (usually measured in the actual amount of alcohol consumed), and have developed equivalency tables for different types of beverages. Beer, for example, contains about 4.5 percent alcohol; wine, 12–13 percent; distilled alcohol, 40–45 percent. Hence, if a standard drink contains approximately 0.5 percent alcohol, one 12-ounce can of beer would be roughly equivalent to a 5-ounce glass of wine or a 1.5-ounce shot of distilled spirits. The question then becomes, What is moderation in drinking? Scholars vary in their assessment but generally agree that moderation consists of somewhere between one and two standard drinks per day (Dufour 1999; Klatsky 1999). Specific studies may use different definitions for moderation, but this definition is useful for purposes of this discussion.

Most of the research in this area has focused on the benefits of moderate drinking in lowering the risk of heart disease. A carefully designed meta-analysis of more than 40 experimental studies on this topic found a clear inverse relationship between moderate drinking and coronary heart disease (Rimm et al. 1999). On the basis of this analysis, it was estimated that 30 grams of ethanol consumption per day should lower one's risk of coronary heart disease by 24.7 percent (Rimm et al. 1999). Research by Michael Thun and his colleagues (1997), which analyzed 46,000 deaths in a prospective study of some 490,000 respondents, found that deaths due to cardiovascular disease were 30 to 40 percent lower among moderate drinkers than among abstainers.

Several types of heart disease seem to be positively affected by moderate drinking. A large-scale study in China, utilizing a sample of more than 18,000 middle-aged men, found that moderate drinkers had a 22 percent lower mortality rate than nondrinkers overall, and that they were 36 percent less likely to die from ischemic heart disease (Yuan and Ross 97), which involves a lack of blood flow (and hence oxygen) to vital body organs because of narrowed arteries. Most other studies of this type of heart disease also find lower risk among moderate drinkers (Klatsky 1999). The most common type of heart disease, coronary artery disease (CAD), is also reduced among moderate drinkers (Jackson et al. 1991; Rimm et al. 1991; Stampfer et al. 1988). Although why alcohol in moderation lowers CAD remains open to discussion, the most common hypothesis is that moderate alcohol use raises the level of high-density lipoprotein (HDL), commonly known as "good cholesterol." Several studies have confirmed that this mechanism is indeed operative in lowering CAD (Klatsky 1999; Rankin 1994). Other cardiovascular indications for moderate alcohol use include peripheral arterial diseases (PAD), which is a significant cause of death among the elderly (Camargo et al. 1997), strokes (Sacco et al. 1999), heart disease risk among diabetes patients (Howard et al. 2004; Senior 1999), and reducing mortality among individuals who have already had heart attacks (Muntwyler et al. 1998).

Although heart disease has received the most research attention, there is also some evidence that moderate drinking may offer health benefits in other areas as well. Mounting evidence suggests that moderate alcohol consumption may reduce cancer risk. The above-cited study of Chinese men (Yuan and Ross 1997) found a 15 percent lower cancer death rate among moderate alcohol users relative to lifetime nonusers—a substantive difference, though not statistically significant. Preliminary studies have also suggested possible benefits in reducing risk of dementia (Ruitenberg et al. 2002; Standridge et al. 2004), preventing bone loss and osteoperosis in women (Anonymous 2000; Standridge et al. 2004), and even reducing the likelihood of gallstones (Ashley et al. 2000). These findings, although not replicated in carefully controlled studies, are at least suggestive of a range of health benefits of alcohol use in moderation.

Summary

This chapter has set out to identify and describe some of the major health consequences of drug use. We want to emphasize two important things in this summary section. First, the psychoactive drugs *can and often do* pose real health risks to those who use them. Much of the risk, however, is related to factors other than the chemistry of the drugs themselves. Synergism and lifestyle factors account for much of the risk associated with drug use, especially illicit drug use. The recent scourge of HIV/AIDS and potentially fatal forms of hepatitis are exacerbated by the lifestyles of crack and IV drug users, a lifestyle which is encouraged by strongly repressive drug policies. Public health demands that we examine closely our drug policies and look for alternative approaches to addressing the problem of drug use in this country, and indeed, throughout the world.

Second, we want to emphasize that there are also positive health benefits to what might otherwise be considered recreational, or at least inappropriate, drug use. We have examined only three areas—medical marijuana, heavy doses of narcotics for terminally ill patients, and moderate alcohol consumption. The medical community has been very reticent to recognize the medical value of these and certain other drugs. Once again, there is a need to carefully examine both medical practice and culture, as well as legal constraints that would thwart medical practitioners from providing good medical care when it involves drugs that are generally associated with recreational use.

Key Terms

acute health consequences
chronic health consequences
delirium tremens
economic-compulsive violence
environmental tobacco smoke (ETS)
fetal alcohol syndrome (FAS)
formication
psychopharmacological violence
systemic violence
Wernicke-Korsakoff syndrome

Thinking Critically...

1. How is the concern in the media and elsewhere about heroin overdose a social construction? In thinking about this, consider whether so-called heroin overdoses are truly overdoses. Why might the media or agencies of social control want to depict drug-related deaths, or even deaths of drug users, whether or not the death was drug related, as overdose?

2. Why do you think alcohol is so widely tolerated, even legal, given the inherent dangers in this drug compared to the comparatively lower intrinsic dangers of other commonly identified illegal drugs such as marijuana or most narcotics?

3. If, as the authors maintain, it is the lifestyle milieu in which recreational drugs are taken that poses the most serious health risks to users, what does this suggest about how we should respond to recreational drug use? What sorts of policies might be most effective in combating and/or reducing these health risks?

4. Medical marijuana has recently emerged as a controversial policy issue in many states. What are the pros and cons of legalizing medical marijuana? What is your position on this issue?

5. If you were a medical doctor treating a patient in excruciating and chronic pain, would you continually prescribe narcotic drugs to relieve the pain, even if you knew there was a probability that your patient would develop a tolerance for the drug? Defend your decision either way.

Learning from the Internet

1. Learn what you can about the current status of medical marijuana laws throughout the United States. The following websites provide extensive information on this topic:

   National Organization for the Reform of Marijuana Laws, www.norml.com
   Drug Policy Alliance, http://www.drugpolicy.org

2. The use of narcotics and other drugs to ease pain is part of a general approach in medicine called *palliative care*. Find out what the medical profession recommends regarding the use of narcotics and similar drugs for palliative care. Are there disagreements among those in the medical profession? The following websites will help you get started:

   American Medical Association, http://www.ama-assn.org/
   Center to Advance Palliative Care, http://www.getpalliativecare.org/
   World Health Organization, http://www.who.int/cancer/palliative/en/
   Palliative Care Policy Center, http://www.medicaring.org/

Notes

1. We will not discuss mood- and performance-enhancing drugs in this chapter, except for a brief discussion of steroids. The major health consequences associated with these drugs and their potential for abuse have been discussed in Chapter 3.
2. Less serious than FAS is a condition known as *fetal alcohol effects* (FAE), which can manifest as low birth rate, spontaneous abortion, and less serious forms or partial features of FAS.
3. The comparison category for risk factors was male drivers aged 21 to 34. The risk of a fatal accident decreases with age, so for older drivers (35+), the increased risk factor of more than 11 is a conservative figure, but for younger drivers (16–21), the increased risk factor of more than 51 is slightly exaggerated.
4. William Shakespeare, *Macbeth*, Act 2, Scene 3.
5. HIV infections through infected blood transfusions were much more common in the earlier years. Implementation of careful screening techniques on the part of reputable organizations who collect blood has minimized the risk of HIV infection through this source.
6. We refer the student to Chapter 4 where we discuss the difference between incidence and prevalence. Although the total number of people with the AIDS virus (prevalence) continues to climb, the number of new cases diagnosed (incidence) has declined and now seems to be leveling off.
7. See *Vacco v. Quill* 521 U.S. 793 (1997) and *Washington v. Glucksberg* 521 U.S. 702 (1997).

CHAPTER **9**

Economic Correlates of Drug Use

The drug trade is big business. Philipson, Berndt, Gottschalk, and Sun (2008) contend that in the United States, the Food and Drug Administration (FDA) has regulatory authority over what amounts to approximately 20 percent of consumer spending. In the United States alone, it has been estimated that Americans spent as much as $140 *billion* per year on illegal drugs during the height of the crack epidemic in the late 1980s (U.S. House of Representatives 1988). Today that figure is considerably less, in large part because of declines in cocaine use and the availability of cheaper cocaine and heroin (ONDCP 2001a, 140, 142). However, the United Nations (2008a, 2008b) suggests that the recent production and use trends of decline (opium) or stabilization (coca) may be abating, although current levels still remain lower than during the late 1980s and early 1990s.

Moreover, legal drugs such as alcohol and tobacco have a profound impact on economies. Tax revenues, retail sales, health care costs, and employer liabilities such as absenteeism are but a few examples. It has been estimated that health care costs for smoking alone account for as much as 1.1 percent of the gross domestic product in high-income countries and almost that high in low-income countries as well (Lightwood et al. 2000). It has also been suggested that tobacco costs the global economy some $200 billion each year, when the economic benefits versus costs of health care, premature death, sick leave, and other effects are taken into account (Barnum 1994). Alcohol costs the U.S. economy nearly $220 billion each year (National Center on Addiction and Substance Abuse 2006), and this cost occurs in a number of ways. For example, Sommers and Sundararaman (2008) report that in 2001, the estimated cost associated with underage drinking was $2,207.00 for each person under the age of 21. Also, in a summary of research identifying the cost of various behaviors related to alcohol use, Wiese, Shlipak, and Browner (2000) suggest that hangovers result in approximately $2000 opportunity costs per working adult.

This chapter examines the economy of illicit drug and alcohol use from a number of perspectives. First, we examine the economic costs and benefits of drug use. We begin with an international perspective, examining the economic impact of the cocaine, heroin, and marijuana trade, with a particular emphasis on point-of-origin countries. Following that discussion, we examine the impact of drug use on the domestic economy. We do this both through a *macro*analysis, examining the large-scale costs of drug use to our economy—costs in health care, worker productivity, and so forth—and through a *micro*analysis, examining the impact of drug use on worker's likelihood of labor force participation, as well as how drug use affects income and wages. A second major section of this chapter examines, from cultivation to retail distribution, the underground economy of drug use. Finally, the last section of this chapter examines the dynamics of illicit drug and alcohol use in the workplace. This section begins by estimating the nature and prevalence of use in the workplace, followed by a discussion of workplace conditions that might affect the likelihood of drug and alcohol use by employees, and finally, how the government and employers are responding to drug and alcohol use by employees.

An Economic Cost-Benefit Analysis of Illicit Drugs

It is almost impossible to measure the amount of drug sales on a worldwide basis because of inconsistencies in reporting methodologies. According to the 2004 United Nations *World Drug Report*, the estimated value of the global illicit drug market at the retail level in 2003 was approximately $13 billion. The importance of the drug trade to the economies of nations is considerable. Clearly, the statement that "the drug business is big business" has enormous political and economic implications. Consequently, recent suggestions that the overall contribution of illicit drug monies to the gross domestic products is declining is viewed with cautious optimism (United Nations 2004).

The illicit drug trade is not only big business, but because of its size, it has a profound effect on the economies of many drug-producing and drug-using countries. Some of these economic consequences are extremely high, resulting in billions of dollars siphoned out of (or introduced into) countries, huge expenditures on law enforcement and drug treatment, and billions of dollars in business losses from diminished worker productivity.

An International Perspective

The drug trade is international in scope. At one time or another, nearly all psychoactive drugs have been bought and sold across sovereign borders. Tobacco, caffeine, marijuana, opium and its derivatives, and cocaine have all been traded on the international market. Today, the three categories of illicit substances that contribute the most to the international drug trade, at least as it relates to the United States, are cocaine, narcotics, and marijuana (United Nations 2008b).

International Cocaine Trade

Cocaine derives from the coca plant, which is grown primarily in the highlands of the Andes Mountains, especially in Bolivia, Peru, and Colombia, though it is also grown commercially in Pakistan, Bali, East Asia, and in the Caribbean. Native inhabitants of these areas have been chewing the coca leaf for centuries. Coca has long been part of the economy of these countries and has even been used as a medium of exchange (Brecher 1972). Although chewing coca leaf never became popular outside of its native countries, cocaine, the active ingredient in the coca leaf, has become an international commercial success.

During the late 1980s, at the height of the cocaine boom, Colombia, Bolivia, and Peru derived between 5 and 10 percent of their respective gross national products from the sale of the drug (United Nations 1997). Updated information for 2007 (see Table 9.1) shows that, particularly in the case of Bolivia, cocaine production and distribution remains an important element of the overall economy. Other countries are less dependent, but nevertheless receive sizable income from the sale of cocaine.

It has been estimated that from the late 1980s until the early 1990s, South American countries alone produced in excess of 200,000 metric tons of coca leaf per year (Bureau of International Narcotic Matters 1990). Between 1990 and 1998,

Table 9.1. Global cocaine production, 2007.

	Columbia	Peru	Bolivia
Coca leaf production (in hectares)	99,000	53,700	28,900
Coca leaf production (in metric tons*)	154,000	107,800	36,400
Cocaine producation (in metric tons*)	600	290	104
Percent of global production	55	30	16
Percent of national GDP	0.5	N/A	2.3

*Potential production.

Source: United Nations. 2008b.

production generally decreased, excluding a spike in 2001. Figures for 2007 reflect the highest levels of production since 2001 (United Nations 2008b). To place this figure in some perspective, note that the weight of coca leaf grown and harvested is not the same as cocaine produced. A number of steps are required to extract cocaine from the coca leaf. The leaf of the coca plant contains approximately one percent cocaine, so large amounts of the leaves are required (Inciardi 2002; Julien 2001).

From 1988 to 1999, the amount of cocaine shipped to the United States is estimated to have dropped by half, from approximately 600 to 300 metric tons. Changes in calculating production estimates make direct comparisons with pre-2004 data problematic, but it is estimated that in 2007, approximately 1,000 metric tons of cocaine were produced for worldwide distribution, with slightly less than half headed to the North America (United Nations 2008a). Generally speaking, price estimates for the retail, street value of cocaine are usually based on information from specific locations, and as such, they should be viewed with some caution. At the height of peak demand for cocaine, it sold at the street level for several hundred dollars per gram. As a result, it is estimated that in 1998, retail expenditures in the United States amounted to $39 billion (Rhodes et al. 2000). According to a recent National Drug Intelligence Center (NDIC, 2005) report, in 2005 cocaine sold for $25 to $110 per gram. It has also been noted that during the latter part of 2007, several U.S. cities experienced shortages of cocaine, most likely a consequence of increased eradication and interdiction. Subsequent production has increased slightly (which should increase availability to accommodate current demand), but sellers may use the threat of a shortage as a justification for increased prices (National Drug Intelligence Center 2007b; United Nations 2008a).

The impact of cocaine on the economies of producing countries can be measured in other ways. Substantial area is devoted to cocaine production. Virtually all of the world's supply of coca is grown in the countries of Colombia, Peru, and Bolivia. In 1990, there were approximately 220,000 hectares (540,000 acres) under coca cultivation. Excluding a spike between 1999 and 2000, when the total area under cultivation approached 225,000 hectares (555,000 acres), there has been a gradual decline since 1990. In 2007, due mostly to a 27 percent increase in Colombia, an estimated 181,600 hectares (449,000 acres) are under coca cultivation (United Nations 2008b, 67). The economic benefits of cocaine are not limited to producing countries. More than 75 percent of the global supply of cocaine originates in Colombia, but its distribution and processing is profitable to other countries in South and Central America, as well as in Mexico. For example, cocaine headed to the United States is usually routed through Mexico, where a large-scale distribution network is in place (NDIC 2007b). Approximately 55 percent of the cocaine entering the United States does so through the Central American–Mexican corridor, with locations in the state of Texas being the most likely point of entry. However, Colombia's unique geographic location—situated on both the Pacific Ocean and the Caribbean Sea and adjoining the Central American corridor, which connects to Mexico—it is likely that Caribbean, Pacific, and Central American routes will continue to be utilized (NDIC 2007b; United Nations 2008a, 2008b).

Although producing countries certainly reap economic benefits, they incur costs as well. A major cost to these countries is that the drug industry has provided a foothold for organized crime. Powerful organizations known as **cartels** often coerce farmers to grow the coca plant by threatening violence or by offering prices that greatly exceed potential earnings from legitimate crops. These cartels are also involved in trafficking, money laundering, firearms smuggling, and a host of other illegal activities. Civilian governments in South American cocaine-producing countries and in Mexico have become especially vulnerable to threats and control by organized crime groups (U.S. Department of State 2008; United Nations 1997). Perhaps more problematic in these countries, public officials can become corrupted by drug cartels seeking to ensure a favorable and predictable political environment from which they can conduct business (McCaffrey 1998). Moreover, because funds from illicit drug operations are typically laundered through a series of procedures involving several countries, the integrity of the financial systems of these countries is at risk. This often results in a loss of confidence in the legitimate economies of these countries, which can have devastating effects on their already fragile economies (U.S. Department of State 2008).

Still another cost to coca-producing countries is the direct impact that billions of dollars pouring in annually will have on monetary policy. In some ways, the impact of the illegal cocaine trade on the economy of Colombia is best described by the cliché of a "doubled-edged sword." Although earnings from illicit cocaine amounts to approximately $1.5 to $3 billion, or approximately 1 percent of the annual GDP, its overall impact on the economy is markedly negative. Allocation of resources to address issues related to national security, violence, consequences of the illegal drug trade on the legitimate economy, and foreign investments in the country have been affected (McLean 2003). Other drug-producing countries are victim to this paradox.

Typically, the producer country realizes a small increase in overall GDP as a result of illegal drug production and trafficking, but the dollar amounts are involved are staggering (United Nations 2004). When a country with a modest gross national product, such as Columbia or Bolivia, experiences an annual influx in the billions of dollars, it will almost certainly face the risk of excessive inflation (Keh 1996). Most of this money is controlled by drug cartels, but as these resources are introduced into the general economy through the construction or purchase of houses, hotels, resorts, and other consumer goods, the cost of living increases for everyone. Inciardi (1992) points out, for example, that during the early 1980s, the injection of large amounts of money into the economy created a sudden demand for automobiles and other luxury items. For example, small Chevrolet Chevettes were selling for as high as $25,000 in Columbia in 1981, when they were selling in the United States for about $4,000. Another example: hyperinflation in real estate made housing unaffordable for large segments of the population.

The agriculture of these countries is also affected by inflationary increases in the value of land. Because coca production dramatically increases the value of land, many farmers cannot afford to grow conventional crops. Simply put, growing the coca plant is more profitable than growing legal crops. There is great pressure to grow coca or to sell land at high prices to coca farmers. Farmers in lower-altitude regions, which are not suitable for coca production, are often lured to work in the higher-altitude, coca-production areas for higher pay because they cannot earn a sufficient living by growing conventional crops (Inciardi 1992). As a result, many people become dependent on this crop for their survival. The United Nations has initiated a concerted effort to promote alternative development and crop substitution (United Nations 2001).

International Heroin Trade

On a global level, the countries of Afghanistan, Myanmar (formerly known as Burma), and Laos are the largest producers of opium, followed by Colombia and Mexico. However, for many years Afghanistan has been and continues to be the single largest producer, responsible for an 90 percent of the global opium supply (U.S. Department of State 2008). For a number of years, most of the heroin coming into the United States also originated from Southern Asia; for example, over 90 percent of the heroin seized in the United States in 1989 originated in Southern Asia. This situation changed dramatically in 1993 when Colombian drug organizations expanded into the production and, in conjunction with Mexican traffickers, the distribution of heroin. The overwhelming majority of heroin produced in Colombia and in Mexico is destined for the United States. In part because of the influx of South American and Mexican heroin into the U.S. marketplace, the wholesale and retail price of the drug has decreased substantially since 1990. For example, in 1990, the estimated whole-sale and retail prices in the United States stood at $250 and $450 per gram, respec-tively, but by 2007, the estimated prices had dropped to less than $100 and $200 per gram (DEA 1999; NDIC 2007b; United Nations 2000, 2008a, 2008b).

The international economy of heroin production and distribution does share an important characteristic with the cocaine economy: the farmers who produce these drugs are very poor and dependent on the income that they derive from poppy production. They are also the most poorly paid. Farmers in Pakistan, for example, realize only about 6 percent of the entire profit from the opium trade emanating from that country. In contrast, the traffickers lay claim to approximately 90 percent of the profit. Despite their low position on the production-distribution hierarchy, poppy farmers realize profits of anywhere from 33 to 800 percent more for grow-ing opium than from legitimate crops such as onions, cabbage, wheat, and lentils. There is, therefore, great incentive to cultivate opium as a cash crop (United Nations 1997). The dynamics of the drug trade—from Southwestern Asia poppy grow-ing through Pakistani drug lords to German drug wholesalers and into European drug markets—was captured by the 1989 British television miniseries, *Traffik*. The outline of this six-hour masterpiece served as the basis for the popular 2000 movie entitled *Traffic*.

The economic and social cost to heroin-producing countries is very similar to that experienced by cocaine-producing countries. For example, it is estimated that approximately one-third of Afghanistan's GDP results from the opium trade. In 2007, the farm value of production is estimated to be $1 billion, with an approximate export value of $4 billion (U.S. dollars) (United Nations 2008b). In some instances, the substance is traded illegally with other countries for automobiles, food, electron-ics, and other goods. In some areas of the country, opium is used as a form of cur-rency. Furthermore, the fragile government is viewed as one of the most corrupt in the world (U.S. Department of State 2008). Organized crime is a part of the heroin trade, though it is much more involved in the refinement and distribution stages than in the growing stage. The heroin industry is not quite as vertically integrated as are the cocaine cartels. Whereas the cocaine cartels tend to control all stages of the industry, from production to consumer sales, the heroin industry tends to be some-what more loosely organized (United Nations 1997).

International Marijuana Trade

Varieties of the *Cannabis* plant can be found in most countries, whether naturally occurring or cultivated. For a number of reasons, it is far more difficult to compile information about the cultivation, production, and distribution of *Cannabis*. First, it is the most frequently consumed illicit drug. Secondly, *Cannabis* can be used to produce a number of products for use in various forms, such as marijuana, hash-ish, and hashish oil. Third, the sheer volume of the global trade makes it more dif-ficult to identify sources. Typically, estimates are in effect based on self-reported information from source countries. It is estimated the global marijuana (*Cannabis* herb) and hashish (*Cannabis* resin) production in 2006 consisted of approximately 41,400 metric tons and 6,000 metric tons, respectively (United Nations 2008b). Mexico is the leading producer of marijuana. Southwest Asia, particularly Morocco, has historically been the leading producer of *Cannabis* resin (hashish). However, recent declines in production in Morocco have coincided with a corresponding increase in production in Afghanistan (United Nations 2008a, 2008b).

There is some disagreement as to the extent to which marijuana used in the United States is imported or grown domestically, in part because of changes in the sources over the years. Prior to 1969, Mexico was a primary source for American Marijuana. That year, President Nixon launched **Operation Intercept**, a major border initiative that sought to prevent Mexican marijuana from entering the country. Most historians agree that Operation Intercept was a dismal failure in preventing the smuggling of marijuana, and in fact, it resulted in an increase in domestic production (Brecher 1972).

Nonetheless, it is estimated that approximately 25 percent of marijuana consumed in the United States is grown domestically (United Nations 2000). In order, the top marijuana-producing locations are California, Kentucky, Tennessee, Hawaii, Oregon, Washington, and West Virginia. Collectively, this group is sometimes referred to as the "M7 States" (NDIC 2007a). Furthermore, a number of Mexican, Asian, and Cuban trafficking organizations have begun to cultivate marijuana within U.S. borders, in both outdoor and indoor locations. A growing proportion of this outdoor cultivation is occurring in the western United States, particularly on national park and forest lands. These vast and remote areas provide a unique location for establishing, in some instances, quite elaborate operations. Indoor cultivation in general has also increased, in part because of law enforcement efforts to eradicate outdoor crops. Essentially, some domestic growers have moved operations indoors in an attempt to avoid detection by law enforcement (NDIC 2007a, 2007b). Marijuana is more frequently differentiated by THC content than by its country of origin. Generally speaking, marijuana grown in the United States is more potent than marijuana from Mexico (NDIC 2007a).

The Domestic Scene: A Macroeconomic Perspective

The previous sections outlined many of the ways in which drugs reach the United States. In this section and the one that follows, we will examine some of the costs associated with use and abuse of these substances in the United States. The economic impact of drug use in the United States is difficult to assess, in part because *cost* has been an elusive concept. Our first task must be to identify what is meant by *cost*. Perhaps the best way to do so is to elaborate the distinction between *private* cost and *societal* cost. Private costs refer to the immediate costs incurred by the drug consumer in the way of lost wages, cost of drugs, prison time, and so forth. We will discuss a number of these issues below when we talk about the impact of drug use on employment status and on other *micro*economic level costs. At this point, however, we are interested primarily in the *societal costs* of drug use.

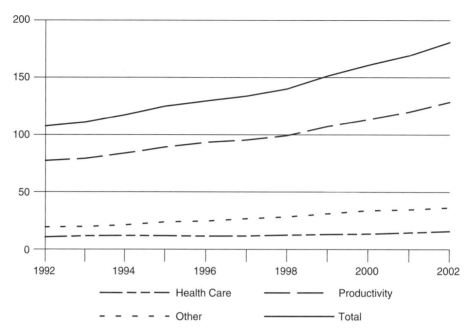

9.1 Societal Cost of (billions of dollars) Related to Drug Abuse (U.S.), 1992–2002.

Source: Office of National Drug Control Policy (2004). *The Economic Costs of Drug Abuse in the United States, 1992–2002.* Table IV-1. Analysis by the Lewin Group, 2004.

First, there are the direct economic costs associated with drug use including higher rates of absenteeism, poor work performance, and the costs of treatment and enforcement of drug laws. Criminal victimization has also been identified as a cost, though from a macrosocietal point of view, it has been argued to be a "forced transfer" rather than a genuine cost (Marks 1992).[1] Costs that are broader and more difficult to define include health care costs to spouses who are abused, children dependent on welfare because of drug-abusing parents, and health care costs for addicts suffering from complications of AIDS and other drug-and lifestyle-related illnesses. Collins and Lapsley have defined the economic costs of drug abuse as "the value of the net resources which in a given year are unavailable to the community for consumption or investment purposes as a result of the effects of past and present drug abuse, plus the intangible costs imposed by this abuse" (1996; cited in United Nations 1997, 104).

When defined in these terms, the cost of drug use in the United States is staggering. Overall, the estimated societal cost of drug abuse in the United States in 2002 was estimated at $181 billion. Figure 9.1 shows the estimated health care, productivity, and other costs for 1992 to 2002. During this period, total costs increased, on average, by just over 5 percent each year (ONDCP 2004b). We now examine more closely each of the categories of cost presented in Figure 9.1.

Health Care Costs

Approximately 10 percent of the overall societal costs of drug use in this country consists of health-related costs. In 2002, approximately $1.6 billion was spent on such items as hospitalization due to overdoses, poisoning, and drug-induced psychoses. Drug use often contributes to or exacerbates other illnesses or injuries, as well, resulting in longer hospital stays and pharmaceutical and ancillary medical expenses such as dental work. Most of these costs were responses to the deleterious consequences of drug and alcohol abuse. Cartwright states: "The medical consequences are broad and pervasive: infectious diseases, cardiovascular effects, respiratory effects, gastrointestinal effects, mental health effects, cancer, prenatal effects, other health effects, and mortality" (2008, 227). Recent data from the Centers for Disease Control and Prevention (2006) provide additional perspective: it is estimated that tobacco use results in over 430,000 deaths annually and approximately $76 billion in total health-related costs.

Some special medical conditions brought on by the substance abuse should be highlighted. For example, in 2002, the cost associated with infants exposed to drugs amounted to approximately $605 million, an increase from $407 million in 1992, or 4 percent each year. With this thought in mind, consider fetal alcohol syndrome and the health costs of drug-exposed infants. It has been estimated that approximately 2 of every 1,000 births show evidence of fetal alcohol syndrome. Estimates of the number of infants exposed in utero to illegal drugs vary, but one relatively conservative estimate from a study conducted in California suggests that at least 5 percent of newborns tested positive for illegal drugs (Harwood et al. 1998). In this particular study, the cost of treating alcohol and drug-exposed infants was estimated at $2.3 billion. It is possible to overestimate the costs of in utero drug exposure, as did occur with the so-called crack baby epidemic from the late 1980s and early 1990s, health consequences are an objectively real phenomenon. Cigarette smoking also poses potentially fatal risks for fetuses, and those that survive to term show a much higher prevalence of low birth weight from smoking mothers. Lightwood, Phibbs, and Glantz (1999) further estimate that each year low-birth-weight infants impose an additional $263 million in medical costs.

In some ways, the most sobering health consequence of illicit drug use is HIV/AIDS. It is estimated that just over a million people in the United States are infected with HIV. Slightly more than one in four cases are attributable to drug use, either directly through infected needles or indirectly through sexual contact with an IV drug–using infected person. In 1985, estimated costs of treating all HIV-positive people amounted to $630 million (Scitovsky and Rice 1987). That cost rose dramatically to $10.2 billion in 1992 (Hellinger 1992), but has since leveled to approximately $3.75 billion dollars in 2002, as treatment became less expensive and those with HIV are better able to avert AIDS with powerful drug cocktails that include protease inhibitors (Hellinger and Fleishman 2000).

In addition to the costly consequences of drug and alcohol abuse, there are medical costs associated with treatment and prevention. More than 11,000 treatment units in the United States provide various forms of treatment and rehabili-tative services to approximately one million addicts at any given time. Treatment, prevention, and training programs cost in excess of $9 billion in 2002.

Productivity Losses

The loss in human productivity as a result of drug and alcohol abuse, when stated in monetary terms, is without question the most costly consequence of widespread substance use. Each year, as a result of premature death, disability, and institution-alization, the American economy is debited more than $128 billion. It is estimated that in 2000, approximately 435 deaths were associated with tobacco use, 85,000 with alcohol use, and another 17,000 with illicit drug use (Mokdad et al. 2004). The monetary cost to premature loss of life is not easily measured. Economists have, however, been able to determine the cost of premature death by calculating the wages (including fringe benefits and taxes) that the average person would have made during their lifetime, assuming a normal life expectancy. For example, a male who dies at age 35–39 foregoes a calculated $700,000 in lifetime earnings, a female, about $500,000 (Harwood et al. 1998).[2] People who die at a later age have propor-tionately lower projected lost lifetime earnings.

Beyond greater-than-normal levels of premature mortality, substance abusers also suffer conditions that render them less productive in the workplace. Because of depression, withdrawal symptoms, overdose symptoms, and physical illness, people who are pharmacologically dependent do not perform as well on the job. Economists distinguish between two types of lost productivity caused by drug and alcohol abuse. One type of effect, sometimes called "internal effects" (Harwood et al. 1998), con-sisted of lower wages, unemployment, and unpaid absences from work experienced by addicts themselves as a result of symptoms and conditions related to their sub-stance abuse. There has been a great deal of research on the impact of substance abuse on wages (Berger and Leigh 1988; Gill and Michaels 1992; Kaestner 1994a, 1994b; Mullahy and Sindelar 1989, 1993) and on labor force participation (Kandel and Davies 1990; Mullahy and Sindelar 1991; Register and Williams 1992). We will examine these impacts in a later section in this chapter when we discuss the impact of substance abuse on employment. Some economists suggest that internal effects should not be considered a productivity cost because drug and alcohol users choose to use these substances and willingly accept the cost of lost wages and lower levels of employment in exchange for the benefits that they perceive from the consumption of drugs and alcohol. A second type of effect, sometimes called "spillover effects," refers to inferior job performance, high rates of absenteeism (which are costly to businesses), injuries on and off the job (which diminish performance), and the like.

Calculation of lowered productivity cost typically assumes that individu-als meeting the criteria for alcoholism or drug addiction will be impaired in their employability, wages, and/or overall earnings. The findings, however, are somewhat mixed. Generally (though with some exceptions), studies examining alcohol and drug *use*—as distinguished from *abuse*—suggest that there is little negative effect on labor force participation or wages and earnings (Berger and Leigh 1988; Kaestner 1991; Register and Williams 1992). Those studies that examine *abuse* of alcohol and other drugs such as marijuana and cocaine tend to report more negative effects on indicators of economic productivity (Gill and Michaels 1992; Kandel and Davies 1990). Harwood, Fountain, and Livermore (1998) confirm that problem drinking and drug abuse negatively affect economic productivity, most significantly when these problem behaviors are initiated early in life. Wage rates are similarly affected: early initiates make lower wages than nonusers or later initiates. Females are not as profoundly affected as males, though drug dependence was found to lower their employability significantly.

In addition to productivity costs from lowered employability or wages and earnings reduced by inability to perform, alcoholics and drug addicts who are institutionalized, whether in hospitals or in residential treatment programs, are removed from the arena of work. The Office of National Drug Control Policy (2004b) estimates that on any given day in 2002, approximately 1.1 million clients were in in-patient or residential alcohol and drug treatment programs. Another productivity cost that is often not considered by most people is the loss of work days by *victims* of drug- and alcohol-related crime. The value of time lost is based on the number of victimizations reported in the National Crime Victimization Survey, which estimated 5.25 million victimizations in 2002. Calculating only those victimizations that are drug- or alcohol-related (approximately 380,000), the Office of National Drug Control Policy (2004b) estimates approximately $1.8 billion in lost productivity of crime victims.

These components—premature death; lowered employability and wages; institutionalization of alcohol and drug addicts in treatment programs, hospitals, and prisons; and lost work by victims of crimes—are the primary elements that account for lost economic productivity in the United States.

Other Effects

We have indicated above that there were an estimated 33.6 million criminal victimizations in 1992, or about one victimization for every six Americans over 12 years of age (Harwood et al. 1998). Victims experience both physical and psychic injury as well as financial loss. There has, of course, been a debate in the literature about the nature of the relationship between drug use and criminal behavior, and particularly about whether alcohol and drug use actually *cause* criminal behavior. There is little debate, however, about the observation that drug users are much more heavily involved in crime than non–drug users.

Society, however also bears the cost of law enforcement, corrections, and other components of the criminal justice system that apprehend and punish drug-related criminals. It is estimated that more than $36 billion was spent in 2002 in criminal justice response to alcohol- and drug-related crime (and primarily to drug-related crime). Society also bears a heavy cost in providing drug abusers and alcoholics with social services such as disability insurance, Supplemental Security Income (SSI), Temporary Aid to Needy Families (TANF) (formerly known as Aid to Families with Dependent Children, AFDC), and food stamps. Grant and Dawson (1996) estimated that between 6.4 and 13.8 percent of social welfare recipients are heavy drinkers, and between 3.8 and 9.8 percent of those using these services are drug abusers. It is important to point out that these figures are not substantially different than the percentages of alcohol and drug users that we would find in the general population. They do, however, represent a substantial impact on our social welfare system. The United States spends an estimated minimum of $2.8 billion annually on social welfare benefits to drug and alcohol abusers (ONDCP 2004b).

Who Pays These Costs?

Victims and their families pay a substantial portion of the costs borne by society for substance abuse. It must be remembered that much of this cost burden is borne by innocent spouses and partners and children of the abuser. Cartwright (2008) suggests that non-drug users/abusers are responsible for 56 percent of the costs associated with drug use, and a majority of this amount is ultimately paid via increased taxes.

The Domestic Scene: A Microeconomic Perspective

This brief section examines the impact of drug and alcohol use on the economic behavior and productivity of individuals. Research in this area addresses two closely related questions: Does the use of drugs and alcohol affect labor force participation? Does the use of drugs and alcohol affect income and wages? The literature is decidedly mixed on both of these questions.

Theoretically, the most straightforward prediction is that drug and alcohol use should affect negatively both labor force participation and wages. Because of the potentially acute intoxicating effect of drugs and alcohol and the longer-term debilitating effects these substances can have on the human body, we would expect users to be more often fired and more likely unemployed. For these reasons, and because alcohol and drug use results in higher rates of absenteeism when workers are employed, we would expect that substance users (and abusers) would report lower wages than non-users. There is some empirical support for this line of reasoning. Kandel and Davies (1990) found that illicit drug use did adversely affect employment indicators among a subsample of nearly 7,000 males born between 1957 and 1964, drawn from the National Longitudinal Survey of Youth. The authors found that illicit drug use increased the likelihood of moving between jobs, gaps in employment, and longer terms of unemployment. Each of these, in turn, negatively affected wages. Research by Mullahy and Sindelar (1989, 1991, 1993) among alcoholics in the New Haven, Connecticut, area essentially confirms this view. They also found, however, that the impact of alcoholism varied by gender and by life cycle dynamics. Although alcoholism affects both men and women adversely, women are more severely affected economically as a result of their drinking. Moreover, alcoholism seems to affect those in the prime of their careers most negatively and most significantly. Differences between alcoholics and nonalcoholics were not significant among younger respondents; among older respondents, alcoholics actually earned *more* than nonalcoholics.

Mullahy and Sindelar's findings suggest another alternative: among younger age groups, alcoholics and drug abusers are more likely to have dropped out of school and have thereby established a longer work history than nonusers. This would theoretically result in greater probability of employment and therefore higher wages. Eventually, their lifestyle catches up with them, and their nonusing friends eventually overtake them economically. Moreover, in later years, nonusers might retire earlier, thus reflecting lower levels of employment and lower wages than those with a history of substance abuse, who must continue working full-time much longer. A number of studies support this contention (including Berger and Leigh 1988; Gill and Michaels 1992; Kaestner 1994a, 1994b; Register and Williams 1992).

The Underground Economy of Illicit Drugs

Because of the underground nature of the illicit drug economy, it is difficult to describe that economy with a great deal of precision. Furthermore, the nature of the underground economy varies somewhat with different drugs. Hence, we will highlight some of the broad features of this underground economy, as well as draw some comparisons between the illicit drug economy and features of the legitimate economy. Perhaps the best way to describe the underground economy of drugs is to divide it into various phases of production and distribution. These phases are crop cultivation, manufacture, importation, wholesale distribution, and retail distribution and will be discussed in the sections that follow.

Crop Cultivation

The cultivation of illicit drugs—especially opium, coca, and *Cannabis*, the three drug groups that make up most of the illicit drug economy—may take place either legally or illegally. For example, certain strains of *cannabis* are cultivated in some countries for industrial and nonpsychoactive purposes. Similarly, both opium and coca are used for legitimate medical reasons, and the cultivation of these plants for these purposes is legal. For example, approximately 12,000 hectares of coca are produced legally in Bolivia (United Nations 2008a). However, most of the cultivation of coca or the opium poppy is for illicit purposes. These illicit crops produce substantial profit margins, making it difficult for legitimate crops to compete. Moreover, coca can be grown where other crops cannot—on steep slopes with minimal soil fertility. Coca production is also dominated by highly centralized and powerful cartels that exert a great deal of pressure on farmers to produce coca. All of these factors contribute to a strong agricultural production of illicit drugs.

Manufacturing

The manufacturing process is a relatively simple procedure for marijuana, especially when compared with the cultivation stage. The leaves and flowering tops of the *Cannabis* plant are stripped and dried, in much the same way that tobacco is cured. Once fully cured, the dried leaves and flower buds are packaged for distribution.

The manufacture of opium and its derivatives and of coca products is somewhat more complex. Opium is typically converted into morphine at refineries that are usually proximate to the area where it is grown and harvested. The conversion of morphine to heroin involves a five-stage process to bind the morphine molecule to acetic acid (heroin's technical name is diacetyl morphine). Until the 1980s, heroin production was highly centralized, with most of the heroin in the world being refined at either Marseilles, France, or Hong Kong. More recently, however, heroin manufacture has become more decentralized, with refineries in the growing regions of Southeast and Southwest Asia as well as other parts of the world (United Nations 2008b).

The production of cocaine also begins in laboratories in close proximity to where the coca shrubs are grown. These laboratories soak the coca leaves with a mixture of several chemicals including alcohol, sulfuric acid, and benzol. A precipitate is formed with the addition of sodium carbonate, which is then washed with kerosene and chilled. This precipitate is called coca paste, which has up to a 90 percent concentration of cocaine (Inciardi 1992). Coca paste is refined further to produce cocaine hydrochloride, (powder cocaine) This substance is one of the two major forms that is then sold on the open market. The other common form is crack cocaine, which is produced by combining sodium bicarbonate (baking soda) with the powder cocaine.

Importation

Drugs enter the United States by land, air, and water. The route that an importer chooses depends upon a number of factors including the source country, the level of technological sophistication available, the drug in question, and the nature of law enforcement surveillance. Import operations range from small amateur operations in which individual entrepreneurs cross the border into Mexico to purchase and smuggle in quantities of marijuana, to large bureaucratic organizations that are centrally controlled and exert a tremendous amount of power and influence nationally and internationally. Such organizations include the infamous Cali and Medellin cartels of Colombia. These organizations often control production, manufacture, and importation operations. Because of heightened levels of law enforcement at U.S. borders, small entrepreneurial smugglers are increasingly rare.

Importation requires an increasing level of sophistication to outmaneuver the highly effective surveillance technology and techniques of the U.S. agencies (Adler 1985; Flynn 1997). Drug trafficking organizations often cooperate with one another to transport and distribute drugs for sale (NDIC 2007b). Smugglers now use sophisticated boats and aircraft with state-of-the-art radar and other detection devices.

Small but powerful jet planes are used for quick trips in and out of small secluded air-strips. Smuggling operations also use commercial vessels to stow and to ship drugs, and to provide false labels and documentation. **Mules**, individuals hired especially to take the risk by smuggling drugs on their person, are also used to import illegal drugs. Frequently, these individuals swallow cocaine and heroin in balloons or con-doms, or place them in the rectal or vaginal cavity to carry across the border and/or through customs.

Wholesale Distribution

Upon successful entry into the United States, drugs such as heroin and cocaine are typically sold to major wholesalers, who may supply an entire region of the country. Most synthetic drugs (such as methamphetamines, MDMA, and LSD) are manu-factured in the United States, so they begin their distribution journey within U.S. borders. Flynn describes the wholesale organization of the Cali cartel in New York:

> If a load of cocaine arrives at Kennedy International Airport or at the Port of
> Newark, one of the 10 to 12 Cali distribution cells in New York receives it. Each
> cell, made up of 15–20 Colombian employees who earn monthly salaries ranging
> from $2,000 to $7,500, conducts an average of $25 million of business a month.
> Each cell is self-contained, with information tightly compartmentalized. Only
> a handful of managers know all the operatives. The cell has a head, bookkeeper,
> money handler, cocaine handler, motor pool, and 10 to 15 apartments serving as
> stash houses. (1997, 153)

This account reflects a tightly controlled distribution system, and most wholesale drug distribution networks are not this highly centralized or controlled. Adler's (1985) ethnography, for example, describes dealing networks that are much more loose-knit and autonomous than that described by Flynn.

Normally, the heroin or cocaine that a wholesaler receives from an importer is very potent. Typically, the wholesaler will dilute or "step on" the drugs by adding an adulterant and thereby increasing the volume (and the profit). Each time these drugs are "stepped on," the volume is typically doubled and the potency thereby diminished by about 50 percent. Moreover, the wholesaler will probably also increase the price per diluted kilogram, which enhances the profitability to an even greater extent.

Retail Distribution

This level of distribution is very loosely organized. Those at the upper end of retail distribution, sometimes known as *dealers in quantity*, are entrepreneurs who sell for monetary profit. With heroin, these dealers typically deal in *bundles*, a quantity roughly equal to 25 street bags of heroin. Dealers with reputations for good heroin will often sell in concentrations that allow for still another cut or dilution, thereby providing the lower-level retailer an opportunity for still greater profits. The lower-level retailer is often a user as well, thereby earning the name of *juggler*. The modus operandi of the juggler is to buy a quantity of the drug, sell a small amount at a

Drugs: Myths and Reality

Gang Leader for a Day

What began as a casual stroll into Chicago's Hyde Park by aspiring sociologist and beginning graduate student Sudhir Venkatesh, culminated in a vibrant examination of gang and community life in what was at one time the nation's largest housing projects, Robert Taylor Homes. Venkatesh's introduction to Robert Taylor came almost accidentally, as is often the case among ethnographers studying deviant lifestyles. His research mission was to understand the causes and dynamics of urban poverty and, armed with surveys in hand, he ventured into one of the poorest sections of Chicago, only to be confronted by wary members of a gang known as the Black Kings (BKs). Into the tension strode J.T., leader of that segment of the BKs. Little did Venkatesh know at the time, but J.T. would become his closest ally for over a decade as he virtually lived with the BK gang members and other tenants who called Robert Taylor Homes their home. This experience would result in the publication of numerous articles and books, including his recent highly publicized account, *Gang Leader for a Day: A Rogue Sociologist Takes to the Streets* (2008).

The Robert Taylor housing project consisted of 28 high-rise (16-story) apartments, hosting a total of more than 4,300 individual apartment units in which some 27,000 people lived (officially or unofficially). It was home to J.T. and his branch of the Black Kings. J.T. oversaw a sizable crack distribution ring from the lobbies, stairwells, and grounds of several of the high-rise buildings on the grounds. Sudhir Venkatesh's chance meeting and subsequent friendship with J.T. provided a decade-long, intimate look into the heartbeat of an underground economy that included not only the distribution of drugs, but also sex, protection, housing perks, and even the sale of candy to children.

Venkatish learned early on that the drug market was a volatile one, and that the best business advice was to take a sure thing now, rather than hope for a bigger ship in the future. "You always take the sure bet in this game," J.T. advised him. "*Nothing* can be predicted—not supply, not anything. The nigger who tells you he's going to have product a year from now is lying. He could be in jail or dead. So take your discount now" (29; emphasis in original). He also discovered that despite the myth and the braggadocio, drug dealing is not nearly as lucrative as many are led to believe. Street-level "foot soldiers" in J.T.'s gang barely earned minimum wage, and many had to supplement their income with hourly work at fast food restaurants and the like.

J.T.'s gang controlled more than just the drug trade, however. The gang was also into pimping prostitutes, who were known as "affiliates." In return for a share of their profits, these prostitutes received protection from the gang and a place to ply their trade. "Independents" on the other hand, who were also allowed to work at Robert Taylor, were required to pay a fee for the use of vacant apartments, and it was known that they were assaulted much more frequently than the affiliates.

The BKs were not merely parasites, preying on the addictions of tenants and outsiders to drugs and sex. They contributed in important ways to the community life of Robert Taylor. They controlled the buildings and kept a watchful eye out for anyone who did not belong there. "[The BKs] acted as the de facto administration of Robert Taylor: J.T. may have been a lawbreaker, but he was very much a lawmaker as well. He acted as if his organization truly did rule the neighborhood, and sometimes the takeover was complete. The Black Kings policed the buildings more aggressively than the Chicago police did" (59). They did this in a number of ways. Strangers would be questioned and asked to

Drugs: Myths and Reality (*continued*)

leave if their answers were not satisfactory. In addition to the regular tenants, squatters would be allowed to sleep in the stairwells for a small fee. The Black Kings also bankrolled social events such as basketball tournaments. They provided financial support for day care, educational initiatives in the projects, as well as efforts to improve the physical conditions of Robert Taylor. Drug profits were behind virtually all of these community improvement efforts and everyone knew it. This was economic reality in the Chicago project.

Dominant as they were, the Black Kings were not the only players in the underground economy at Robert Taylor. A particularly important key player was Ms. Bailey, a mid-50s woman who served as the building president of the Local Advisory Council. Ms. Bailey got things done when nobody else could. But she was also an entrepreneur who understood the underground economy. Venkatish describes how she went about a clothing drive from various retail stores in the area. When he picked her up, she was carrying a large black plastic bag. She instructed Venkatesh, known to everyone in the projects as The Professor, to go first to the local liquor store. There, employees of the liquor store began loading the station wagon with cases of beer and liquor. She informed The Professor that she was given the liquor in exchange for directing her tenants to visit this store exclusively when they needed booze. But what did this have to do

with a clothing drive? The Professor was soon to find out. First stop, a grocery store. They were met by a friendly manager who gave them several heavy winter coats, the kind used by employees working in the freezer. Before they left, The Professor was directed to drop off three cases of beer. And so it was with all of the stores they visited. Through her unique underground entrepreneurial acumen, Ms. Bailey managed to accumulate coats and other winter clothing for young and old alike during the coldest days of a harsh Chicago winter.

There is something distasteful to most Americans about such an economic system that preys upon the weaknesses of drug addicts, prostitutes, and johns, and at the same time makes a profit in such an exploitive fashion on the basic needs of the poorest of the poor. It is not unique to Robert Taylor Homes, however. In a world that is largely ignored and overlooked by police, hospitals, housing authorities, and other social service agencies, residents of these neighborhoods have learned to get by in creative, if sometimes morally questionable ways. Whether we want to admit it or not, the drug trade, carried out by gangs such as the Black Kings, provides much of the economic infrastructure for these forgotten and overlooked neighborhoods.

Source: Venkatish, 2008.

highly inflated price, enough to pay for his own habit and usually a little more for spending money.

Retailing is the most risky enterprise in the entire underground drug economy. The retail distributor is typically selling to users or dealer/users who are, financially speaking, very unpredictable. Many times a customer will not have sufficient funds to purchase the desired quantity of drugs. The retail dealer may, of course, refuse to sell to the person. However, particularly if withdrawal symptoms are present, most dealers are usually not so cold as to send away the user. So, the drugs are sold with

the understanding that payment will occur at first opportunity, but the dealers frequently never see these individuals again and are thus cheated out of their money.
This type of encounter often results in violence between dealers and their patrons.
However, the risk does not stop here. Drug users and jugglers are often pressured
by police for information on higher-level connections. This tactic is called "flipping
an informant." Police on patrol in neighborhoods are quite aware of the users and
street-level dealers, so when a decision is made to crack down on drugs in an area, it
is very easy for police to gather information on local users and dealers and threaten
them with arrest if they do not cooperate. Consequently, the lower-level street juggler, as well as his or her connection, is at risk. No one in the distribution system of
illegal drugs is more vulnerable to arrest than those at the bottom of the hierarchy.
For that reason, teens and preteens are often used because they will avoid adjudica-
tion as an adult if arrested.

This reality, of course, reflects a pattern similar to the legitimate social stratification system. Those people situated at the bottom of the hierarchy are generally more
prone to arrest, more prone to health and accident risks in their jobs, and are the
least secure in the longevity of their positions. Indeed, the economics of illicit drug
distribution reflects, in many ways, the legitimate economy, and is rooted deeply in
it. Robert McBride states:

> [H]eroin use is the end result of certain characteristics of U.S. capitalism that
> generate both the market for the drug, and the system that supplies it. The
> demand for heroin is rooted in the class, race, and national conflicts of U.S.
> society. In turn, the heroin is marketed by an expanding distribution industry
> which is shaped by the underlying drive of capitalist enterprise to seize market
> opportunities in the quest for profit. (1983, 147)

At the retail distribution level, the underground economy of illicit drug distribution is especially reflective of our capitalist culture. Certain dealers, for example,
have developed a reputation for having "righteous dope" and attempt to capitalize on
this reputation by using marketing techniques that will be recognizable to potential
customers. Paul Goldstein and his colleagues (1984) examined the street marketing of heroin in New York City and found that these drugs were being distinctively
packaged and labeled as a marketing technique. Dealers sometimes stamp a symbol
onto the bag, use specially colored tape to make their drugs more recognizable and
noticeable, or simply stamp a number on the bag. Brand names are also given to the
drugs, and some of them very colorful. Goldstein and his colleagues were able to
identify over 400 different "brands" of heroin, including *Black Death, Cadillac, Down
and Dirty, Feel Like Dynamite, Good Pussy, Pink Panther, Not Responsible, Smoking Joe,*
and *Georgia Mud,* among many others. The proliferation of these "brands" reflects
broader capitalist economic sectors at early stages of development, not unlike the
relatively unregulated proliferation of Internet services and marketing techniques
in the early phase of Internet development and expansion. As industries develop,
control of the industries tends to be concentrated in the hands of a few major

corporations—something which may be happening at the top of the illicit drug importation and distribution hierarchy today.

Drugs in the Workplace

We have earlier examined alcohol and drug use patterns in five institutional contexts (Chapter 7). Earlier in this chapter, we also examined the economic costs of alcohol and drug abuse, much of which is borne by employers in the form of higher rates of absenteeism and generally lower productivity. Our focus in this section is the work setting itself. This section is divided into three broad sub-sections: the nature and prevalence of drug and alcohol use in the workplace; working conditions and other factors related to workplace drug and alcohol use; and responses to drug use in the workplace.

Nature and Prevalence of Drug Use in the Workplace

Most of the information that we have on drug use by employees in the workplace comes from the SAMHSA's (2008) National Survey of Drug Use and Health (NSDUH), which includes questions on level of employment (full-time, part-time, or unemployed) as well as information on occupational sectors in which workers are employed. Additionally, limited data are available from drug-testing procedures and employee assistance programs (EAPs), though these data are not very systematic.

The typical perception that people have of the alcohol abuser, and especially of those who use illicit drugs, is that of the street user—unemployed, often homeless and without purpose or direction. This picture is greatly distorted. Granted, the unemployed are more likely to be alcohol and drug users than are the employed. For example, according to 2007 NSDUH data, 8.2 percent of full-time employees used illicit drugs within the past 30 days, in contrast to 18.3 percent of unemployed people. However, by examining the employment status of alcohol and drug *users*, a different picture emerges. The 2007 NSDUH data reveal that in 2007, 75 percent of those who currently used illicit drugs (approximately 13.2 million people) were employed full or part time. Similarly, 79.4 percent of current binge drinkers (44 million people) report being employed full or part time, and 79.6 percent of current heavy drinkers (13.1 million) are employed full or part time Finally, 60.4 percent of adults who are substance abusers (12.3 million persons) report being employed full time in 2007 (SAMHSA 2008).[3]

The previous discussion is not intended to diminish the negative consequences of alcohol or drug use, but to shed light on one of the many misconceptions about drug users. Substance use in the workplace can result in serious consequences for the employee and others, and upon examining data related to alcohol and drug use and the workplace, we can reasonably conclude that users are less dependable and may cause more problems than nonusers. Typically, employees who use drugs miss more work days than nonusers, they are at a greater risk for on-the-job accidents,

DRUGS AND EVERYDAY LIFE

I Thought I Could Beat the System

I was convinced that I could beat the system. I was drinking and using drugs on the job, but I thought I was covering it well, and that no one would know. My "on the job" escapades began when I started working with FedEx in 2004 in Fort Collins, Colorado. The job started early in the morning and ended late at night. I had been drinking heavily, but I thought that the job would curb my appetite for booze. The first month or so, although I thought about drinking all day, I was able to wait until I got home to do so. The mental obsession for alcohol started to override my every thought. So, I decided that it would be okay to take a drink in the middle of the day to take the edge off. It escalated from there. I started drinking in the morning before work to deal with the hangover from the night before. I convinced myself that a bottle of Vodka on the truck was okay as long as I continued to do a good job. I started picking up the truck in the morning, headed back home, drank a six pack and picked up a liter of Vodka for the day. I had stopped caring about my performance at work. I started bringing cocaine to work with me on the truck to even out the drinking. Within a few months, I was drinking all day at work and using cocaine. Eventually, one of the customers called FedEx about a drunk driver. When they called me into the office, I denied any drug or alcohol use on the job. Before they gave me the drug test, I got mad and told them that it was unconstitutional. Needless to say, I lost that job.

I moved to Alabama and took a social work job for a private company in 2006. Amazing as it might seem, this job entailed working with therapeutic foster care children who had been removed from their families because of drug and alcohol use in the home.

I was found out quickly. My employer caught me drinking at nine in the morning and gave me the option of getting fired or going to AA. I chose AA, and attended faithfully for approximately 30 days. But I fell back into old patterns. Just like with the FedEx job, I decided a drink in the evening would take the edge off. Soon, I started taking pain pills in the morning. I preferred alcohol, but thinking myself pretty clever, I decided to use the pain medication in the mornings because I knew they would smell alcohol on my breath at the foster care family homes. That didn't last long. Soon, I had started drinking at lunch. It began to really get out of control when I started carrying a cooler of beer with me behind the seat, which I hid with a blanket. I actually believed chewing gum and cologne would cover up the smell. My reasoning became so affected that I convinced myself that for these kids to have a real high school experience, they would need to get drunk on the weekends occasionally. Furthermore, I reasoned, who better to initiate them into drinking than a caring social worker like me! So, I started bringing foster care kids back to my home to drink with me. It all fell apart when one night, I took a foster care kid out to dinner. I was so drunk, that I had forgotten my wallet, but proceeded to order six beers and six margaritas. I asked the child if he could pay for my meal and drinks. I believe he complied out of fear. This was my undoing because this teenager under my care now had an itemized receipt which showed a heavy bar bill. Three days later, as I stood in a Department of Human Resources office facing charges, I realized that I may have been careless. But even then, I quickly convinced myself that they would believe me and not him because, after all, I was the professional social worker! Not so. They did believe him and I was tied up in court for a year on neglect charges. Like a good drunk, I took the offensive and fought back by suing DHR

DRUGS AND EVERYDAY LIFE (*continued*)

for $1,000. Eventually, my lawyer convinced me to drop my law suit. DHR then agreed to drop a lawsuit that they had initiated against me. I would like to say that I learned a valuable lesson from these experiences. The story was not such a fairy tale, because alcohol had become my master. It is a struggle that I must wage one day at a time.

Brian
Personal Correspondence

and they are much more likely to file claims for workers compensation (Larson et al. 2007; United Nations 1998).

Relationship Between Work Conditions and Drug and Alcohol Use

Some interesting patterns emerge with regard to the nature of the workplace and its relation to drug and alcohol use. Figure 9.2 reveals an inverse relationship between the size of the workplace and the likelihood of employees using drugs. Beginning with the smallest workplaces, with 10 or fewer employees, 9.9 percent of the employees report drug use in the previous 30 days, as do 9.7 percent in workplaces with 10 to 24 employees, 8.2 percent in workplaces with 25 to 99 employees, 6.7 percent in workplaces with 100 to 499 employees, and 5.7 percent in the largest workplaces, with 500 or more employees. A similar inverse pattern emerges for current marijuana use as well as for heavy alcohol use. With few exceptions, as the size of the workplace increases, the percentage of employees reporting current use decreases (Larson et al. 2007).

The likelihood of drug and alcohol use also seems to vary with the type of occupation. Recall that Chapter 7 discussed occupational areas and the dynamics that seem to be involved in substance abuse in those work settings. In addition to these areas, drug and alcohol use appears to be highest among people in accommodations and food service and in construction. Pooled data for 2002–2004 reveal that among the former, 16.9 percent report drug use within the previous 30 days, 13.9 percent report marijuana use, and 12 percent report using alcohol heavily. Among construction workers, current drug, marijuana, and alcohol use is reported at 13.7, 11.7, and 15.9 percent, respectively (Larson et al. 2007). Generally speaking, blue-collar workers tend to have higher rates of drug use than do white-collar workers (Gleason et al. 1991).

Additional research has focused on the relationship between a number of psychological factors potentially related to substance use and abuse in the workplace, such as job satisfaction (Seeman and Anderson 1983; Seeman et al. 1988), job stress (Cooper et al. 1990; Martin and Roman 1996b; Pearlin and Radabaugh 1976; Roman 1978), and a sense of powerlessness in relation to work (Martin and Roman 1996a). A second line of inquiry, based on the social learning perspective, suggests that alcohol and drug use may be influenced by coworkers, especially where

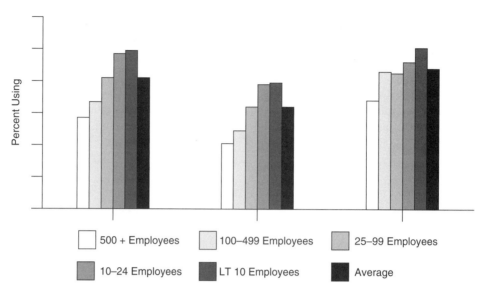

9.2 Percent of Employees Using Illicit Drugs, Marijuana, and Heavy Alcohol Use in the Past 30 Days by Company/Organization Size, 2002–2004 Average.

Source: Larson, Sharon L., Joe Eyerman, Misty S. Foster, and Joseph C. Gfroerer 2007. *Worker Substance Use and Workplace Policies and Programs*. DHHS # SMA 07-4273. Rockville MD: SAMHSA.

attitudes tolerant of or even encouraging use exist (Ames and James 1990; Cahalan 1970; Martin and Roman 1996a). However, the results of most of these studies have been either mixed or inconclusive. Additional research in these areas is needed to clarify questions that remain unanswered.

Due in part to the disparate findings of many of the studies that have examined the role of the workplace on alcohol and/or drug use, it has been suggested that drug and alcohol use are much more a function of the *workforce*. That is, characteristics of the employee, as opposed to the workplace, are better predictors of substance use and abuse. For example, Mensch and Kandel (1988), using data from the National Longitudinal Survey of Youth, examined both workplace characteristics (such as supervisor support, physical demands of the job) and workforce characteristics (such as marital status, education, race) for their effects on alcohol, tobacco, marijuana, and cocaine use. They found that job characteristics have little explanatory power among the subjects in their sample. However, certain individual characteristics do significantly predict drug use. Mensch and Kandel characterize the significant variables as those that suggest "a lack of conformity or attachment to social institutions" (1988, 181). These individual characteristics include having dropped out of school, having participated in delinquent activity, and being unmarried. Three other studies by Gleason, Veum, and Pergamit (1991), Hollinger (1988), and Steffy and Laker (1991) also find that demographic variables such as age, gender, and race more strongly predict substance abuse among workers than do workplace characteristics.

Consistent with findings of alcohol and drug use in general, younger workers, men, and Caucasians are most likely to be involved in drug and alcohol use.

Response to Substance Use in the Workplace

Historically, the response of most workplaces to drug and alcohol use by workers has been to ignore it. Until the 1970s, substance use and abuse has been seen as a problem of individuals, with little recognition or concern about company responsibility or response to drug problems in the workplace, except to terminate the employment of individuals who posed problems because of substance abuse. Scanlon (1991) points out that early responses focused mostly on alcohol use, and that prohibitionist organizations were strong influences in motivating industry to respond harshly to alcohol use. Some therapeutic programs existed even in the 1940s, such as the Occupational Alcoholism Program (OAP), but industry response was largely punitive in the sense of terminating employees who abused drugs and alcohol. The last 30 years has witnessed

9.3 The federal government has been actively been promoting a drug-free workplace since the enactment of the Drug Free Workplace Act in 1988. Promotional posters such as the one reproduced here are an important part of the government's strategy. (Photo: U.S. Department of Labor)

increased attention to this issue by both small and large businesses because of the adverse economic impact of drug- and alcohol-impaired individuals. This recent response represents both an extension of older punitive approaches and emerging therapeutic understandings of drug and alcohol abuse. Specifically, workplaces are adopting one or both of two responses to drug use among their employees: drug testing and employee assistance programs (Spell and Blum 2005). Both are related to an important piece of legislation known as the Drug-Free Workplace Act of 1988. We begin with a brief discussion of that legislation.

Drug-Free Workplace Act of 1988

In 1986, Congress passed the Omnibus Drug Act (ODA), which authorized $1.7 million for drug enforcement and education efforts in response to the growing concern with drug use in the United States. Other legislation would follow, and in 1988, President Reagan signed into law the Anti-Drug Abuse Act of 1988. A portion of this act, known as the **Drug-Free Workplace Act of 1988 (DFWA)**, applied specifically to drug use in the workplace. This act requires both federal contractors and grantees (such as universities receiving federal funds) to certify that they will provide a drug-free workplace. Private employers are not affected by the requirements of the DFWA, though many private employers subscribe to its principles.

A drug-free workplace is defined under these regulations as one in which employees are prohibited from manufacturing, distributing, dispensing, possessing, or using controlled substances (Scanlon 1991). Compliance with the Act requires that employers

1. Certify that they will maintain a drug-free workplace
2. Inform employees of the prohibition of drug-related activities at the workplace
3. Establish a drug-free awareness program, informing employees of the dangers of drug use at the workplace, and of sanctions that might be applied against them
4. Communicate to employees that they must inform the employer of any criminal conviction for a violation of a drug statute involving an incident at work
5. Report such convictions to the federal contracting or granting agency
6. Take appropriate personnel action against the employee, or require the employee to participate satisfactorily in a drug rehabilitation program
7. Make a good faith effort to provide a drug-free workplace by implementing the above activities, (Legal Action Center 1989; as quoted in Scanlon 1991)

These provisions of the DFWA do not require the establishment of either drug testing or employee assistance programs. Clearly, however, these provisions provide an important legal incentive for both drug testing and employee assistance programs among federally subsidized workplaces. Moreover, the legislation has raised awareness of the importance and value of the drug-free workplace generally. Companies have come to be aware of the tremendous costs associated with addicted and intoxicated workers. Whether it is difficult to assess how much the DFWA has directly raised awareness of the need for detection and prevention and treatment programs in the private sector, or whether it simply confirmed an awareness already present, it was almost certainly a catalyst for these programs, as they have sprung up like dandelions since the passage of this legislation.

Currently, the federal government's comprehensive drug-free workplace program is in place in more than 120 agencies and covers in excess of 1.8 million workers. It has been quite successful, according to those in the government who monitor the program. In 1997, only 0.5 percent of the more than 80,000 federal workers tested had positive results for illegal drugs. This compared with positive test rates in the private sector of approximately 5.0 percent of the 4 million tests done the same year (SAMHSA 1999e). According to the Drug Test Index, reported semiannually, the national rate of positive drug tests in the private sector has declined considerably over the years, from a high of 13.6 percent in 1988 to a low of 4.7 percent for the first half of 2000 (SAMHSA 2001).

Drug Testing

Drug testing in workplaces is almost totally limited to testing for *illicit* substances such as marijuana and cocaine, though alcohol testing may be included as well. These tests are conducted either as pre-employment screening or as post-employment periodic testing of employees. Post-employment tests may either be given with cause, such as following an industrial accident, or randomly as a deterrence mechanism. Drug testing has increased quite dramatically over the past 20 years. Hartwell, Steele, French, and Rodman (1996) note that participation in drug testing programs increased from 18 percent of Fortune 500 companies in 1985 to 40 percent in 1991, representing an increase of more than 100 percent in six years. Other studies report even higher levels of participation (Carpenter 2007; Harris and Heft 1992). By 2003, virtually all (98 percent) of Fortune 500 companies had implemented drug testing policies (Mosher and Atkins 2007).

Certain patterns can be observed in the types of companies that are more likely to utilize drug testing. First, testing programs are much more common among larger companies. Hayghe (1991) found that in 1990 only 2.6 percent of companies with fewer than 50 employees had drug-testing programs in place, whereas 45.9 percent of companies with 250 employees or more had such programs. Larson and colleagues (2007) utilize 2002–2004 pooled NSDUH data to show that the largest companies (500-plus employees) are much more likely to use both pre-employment screening and post-employment random testing. Implementation of drug-testing programs also tends to vary by type of industry or occupational category. Transportation, moving, and protective services report the highest rates of participation among occupational categories, whereas arts and design, entertainment, sports, and media report the lowest levels of random testing (Larson et al. 2007). Drug testing as a preventive response to drug use is discussed in some detail in Chapter 14.

Employee Assistance Programs

Employee assistance programs (EAPs) are, essentially, confidential, employer-financed programs to assist employees who are afflicted with any of a variety of psychological problems, including drug and alcohol abuse. Not only are the workers *afflicted*, but the workplaces are substantially *affected* by drug and alcohol abuse. As we have noted elsewhere, drug abuse is a social problem with enormous consequences, and one arena where the consequences are felt acutely is in the American workplace, with greater absenteeism and tardiness, more erratic work histories, several times more sick benefits, more on-the-job injuries (and more worker's compensation claims), and reduced productivity (Larson et al. 2007; SAMHSA 1991, 1999d; United Nations 1998).

Clearly, drug abuse has a number of potentially devastating economic ramifications, consequences that give workplaces a powerful incentive to help valued employees overcome their drug and alcohol abuse. The move away from punitive responses to employee drug and alcohol dependence and toward treating the issue constructively as a health concern, which is what Employee Assistance Programs do, emerged in the 1970s and spread rapidly during the 1980s. By 1990, there were more than 20,000 EAPs in place in companies of various types throughout the country (Scanlon 1991). Most EAPs are located in the company's human resources or personnel departments. Others may be located in the medical department or even the executive offices (Backer 1989). Like drug-testing programs, EAPs are much more prevalent in larger organizations. Not surprisingly, companies and organizations that utilize drug testing are more likely to have an EAP (Carpenter 2007; Spell and Blum 2005). Of workplaces with greater than 750 workers, 52 percent have them, compared with 15 percent of workplaces with 50 to 99 employees. Overall, just less than 33 percent of all American employees work for a company with an EAP (SAMHSA 1999d).

There is an increasing accumulation of evidence that EAPs are effective, both in terms of individual outcome measures (reduction in levels of drug and alcohol abuse, decreased absences, etc.) and in terms of the cost-benefit ratio to the employer. Blum and Roman (1995), in an overview of studies conducted since the 1970s, conclude that problems related to employee drug and alcohol abuse are reduced considerably in companies with EAPs. Moreover, the overall savings to these employers is substantial, with savings-to-investment ratios ranging from 1.5 : 1 to 15 : 1. Federal government assessments report that EAPs have assisted in the reduction of positive drug tests by 50 percent during the last decade, though they also credit drug-testing programs (SAMHSA 2001).

Summary

We have, in this chapter, attempted simply to sketch some of the broad economic dimensions of illicit drugs. At the macroeconomic level, the cultivation, production, and distribution of illicit drugs have profound effects on the broader economies of those countries involved. The cultivation of drugs such as cocaine, heroin, and marijuana preempts the growing of other agricultural products because they take up both land and labor resources that could be used in other agricultural pursuits. We have also seen that the high levels of money coming into certain drug-producing countries, while making a few people very wealthy, produces higher-than-normal inflation that negatively affects the ordinary citizens of those countries.

Drugs have an economic impact not only on producing nations, but also on consuming nations. Drug and alcohol consumption have an impact on the American economy through higher levels of absenteeism and lowered levels of productivity. There is some contradictory evidence about the impact of drug and alcohol consumption on family economics in terms of labor force participation and wage earnings, but overall the evidence seems to suggest that families also suffer negatively economic affects. Certainly, money that could otherwise go to buying food, clothing, and other necessities is instead being spent on drugs, alcohol, and tobacco. Our interpretation of the wage and labor force data further suggests that users of drugs and alcohol leave school and enter the labor force earlier, and remain in the labor force when nonusers are able to retire.

The underground, illicit drug industry further reflects, in many ways, the broader economic dynamics of the host society, particularly in relation to capitalism. The importation and distribution hierarchy resembles the distribution of other goods and services. At the retail level, the drug trade tends to resemble newly developing entrepreneurial areas. Competition—along with risk—is great, but so is the potential for profit. Higher-level distribution patterns, by contrast, more closely resemble more mature capitalist sectors. More control is exerted by a relatively small number of actors, resulting in fewer risks. And because of the greater level of monopolistic control, profits are guaranteed.

There are certainly ways in which the economy of illicit drugs is different from the larger economy. The very fact that these drugs are illegal introduces an element not present in the legitimate economy. Drug dealers at all levels must consider the risks and costs associated with running an illegitimate enterprise: the risk of arrest and incarceration; the risk that comes with dealing with individuals who work in the marginal sectors of society, such as greater levels of unpredictability; and the risk of violence, as these illicit entrepreneurs do not have access to courts to enforce agreements and contracts. Despite these differences, however, the similarities are instructive. Understanding that the illicit drug economy as a reflection of the larger economy helps to demystify what takes place in the world of drug importers, distributors, and street dealers.

Finally, drug use profoundly affects the workplace in ways that go beyond productivity and wages. Research on drug use in the workplace has revealed several factors that seem to be related to drug use, including size of the workplace, type of occupation, and factors such as job stress, worker morale, and alienation or powerlessness experienced by workers. Some have suggested, on the other hand, that it is the quality of the *workforce*, not the *workplace*, that determines the likelihood of drug use, including such factors as age, marital status, education, and race or ethnicity. Regardless of the reasons for drug use in the workplace, employers have responded with attempts to curtail employee drug use. They have done so through adopting drug-free workplace principles, drug testing, and employee assistance programs. The effectiveness of these programs has been debated, but evidence seems to suggest at least marginal, if not substantial, effectiveness of these initiatives.

Key Terms

cartel
Drug-Free Workplace Act of 1988 (DFWA)
employee assistance program (EAP)
mules
Operation Intercept

Thinking Critically...

1. What was Operation Intercept, and what did it teach us about international control of drugs?

2. The international drug trade provides a lucrative source of income for many farmers in developing countries. International drug control efforts seriously threaten that income. Carefully consider the costs and benefits of such international drug control efforts. On the basis of this analysis, what is your position on the advisability of international drug control efforts? What sort of policy might you suggest?

3. Do you think that drug and alcohol use in the workplace are more a result of characteristics of the *workplace* or of the *workforce*? Explain your answer by (1) identifying what is meant by each of these terms, and (2) providing comparative evidence supporting your position.

4. Assume that you are the CEO of a mid-sized business, employing about 150 people. It has come to your attention that some of your employees might have drug and/or alcohol problems. You have noticed that your absenteeism rates seem to be a little higher than normal, which is consistent with these reports. How would you respond to these reports? Answer this question by identifying the specific steps that you would take, and explain why you would take each of these steps.

5. Two responses that employers have had to drug use in the workplace is drug testing and employee assistance programs. What are the differences between these two approaches in terms of (1) their philosophy and (2) their goals? Do you think these two approaches are incompatible? Why or why not?

Learning from the Internet

1. The U.S. government has taken a leading role in international drug control efforts. Much of this effort is coordinated through the Office of National Drug Control Policy. Study their website at http://www.whitehousedrugpolicy.gov/. Describe the efforts of this agency and what the United States is doing to control international drug production and trafficking.

2. Several government agencies address the many concerns of drugs and drug use in the workplace, including the Office of National Drug Control Policy and the Department of Labor. Enter "drugs in the workplace" in your search engine. Go to the various government agencies that your search engine brings up. (Government websites will typically have a .gov designation, though this designation is also used for state government agencies.) Make a list of all of the *federal* government websites that you find, and describe the issues and concerns regarding drug use in the workplace that each agency addresses.

Notes

1. The reason that crime and victimization are not considered costs from a macrosocietal view is that the money or value of goods remains in circulation within the society (unless taken out of the country, of course). Hence, although the individual victim certainly incurs a cost, society at large still has the money and/or goods in circulation. Indeed, Preble and Casey (1969) have suggested that crimes by drug addicts serve as something of an underground welfare system, as stolen goods are made available to low-income people for prices that they can afford.

2. The calculation of foregone wages and productivity costs due to premature mortality uses a rather complex set of assumptions and procedures known as the "human capital approach." If you are interested in learning more about how productivity loss is calculated, you might consult one or more of the following sources: Harwood et al. 1998; Heien and Pittman 1989; Hodgson and Meiners 1982.

3. It must be remembered, of course, that the NSDUH will miss most homeless and all institutionalized populations. This figure, therefore, underestimates the percentage of unemployed drug users. Nevertheless, it is also clear that illicit drug users are heavily represented in the nation's workforce.

CHAPTER **10**

Cultural and Subcultural Correlates of Drug Use

Whenever drugs are used, there is a social context for that use, regardless of the type of drug that is being consumed. Alcohol, for example, is often used to celebrate festive occasions, from a wedding to the end of the work week. Coffee is typically consumed at mealtimes or during scheduled coffee breaks. Marijuana is often smoked at rock concerts or sitting around in a circle listening to music on a CD player. To suggest that there is always a social context for drug use certainly does not mean that drugs are always consumed in the physical presence of other people. Often they are deliberately used away from the presence of others, as witnessed by the lone alcoholic, the closet cocaine user, the independent Marlboro Man. Even in these instances, however, drug use has a social context. These drugs must be obtained from other people, whether on the street or in a grocery store. The use of these drugs contributes to the shaping of identities and reputations, and almost always affects the relationships that users have with others. All of these circumstances comprise the social context of drug use. Indeed, the understanding that drug use takes place in a social context is the very premise of the sociology of drug use and of this book.

The social setting in which *illicit* drugs are used is often quite different from that of legal drugs. It is not uncommon for illegal drug users to form **drug subcultures**—groups that are a part of the cultural mainstream and often share many of the values and goals of the cultural mainstream, but nevertheless maintain a distinctive lifestyle that is integrated around the use of illegal drugs. This chapter examines these unique social settings of drug use. The chapter is divided into three parts. The first describes the nature of drug-using subcultures by (1) exploring how and why these subcultures form and the functions they fulfill for users of illicit drugs, and (2) discussing some of the essential features of drug subcultures. The second section focuses on three specific subcultures of drug use: the rave subculture, the street heroin subculture, and the blunts subculture. The final part of the chapter focuses on the careers of drug users, primarily on heroin-using criminal careers, and how these careers are shaped by the subculture in which they develop.

What are Subcultures?

The subculture concept is widely used today and is found in nearly every introductory sociology text on the market. It is a concept of fairly recent origin, however, first introduced in the 1940s (Gordon 1947). *Subculture* usually connotes normative and ideological features of a segment of the population and frequent interaction among these individuals, which provide a basis for common identity. Commenting specifically on subcultures of drug use, O'Donnell (1967, 75) noted, "whatever else a subculture is, it implies contact between its members, learning from each other and recognition of oneself as a member of the group."

Deviant subcultures are those organized around behavior patterns that are to some degree in conflict with dominant cultural norms and values. Numerous deviant subcultures have been identified in the literature, including subcultures of prostitutes (Bryan 1966), gamblers (Hayano 1982), homosexuals (Harris 1973), and nudists (Weinberg 1966), among others. Drug-using subcultures are also deviant in nature and are organized around the use of one or more (usually illegal) drugs. Johnson (1973, 9) defines *drug subcultures* as "...those conduct norms, social situations, role definitions and performances, and values that govern the use of illegal drugs and the intentional nonmedical use of prescription drugs."

The Formation of Drug-Using Subcultures
Drug subcultures are generally found where drugs are illegal or at least strongly disapproved. It has been observed, for example, that heroin- and cocaine-using subcultures began to appear following the Harrison Act in 1914 (Lindesmith 1965; O'Donnell 1967). Similarly the subculture of marijuana use became evident following the Marijuana Tax Act in 1937 (Becker 1963; Brecher 1972), and the

psychedelic subculture of the 1960s was at least in part a response to strong public disapproval (Brecher 1972; Grinspoon and Bakalar 1979). Cross-cultural researchers have identified an analogous watershed in Jamaican history when, one morning in April 1963, all Rastafari in the country were made subject to arrest. Troops were even given authority to shoot anyone who resisted arrest. Marijuana, or ganja, was not only part of the Rastafari religion but had been part of Jamaican culture for many years. However, this shift in public policy led to a widespread media campaign that portrayed ganja users as potentially violent, thereby legitimating the arrest of thousands of Jamaicans. All of this only reinforced a core subculture of ganja users, many of whom were closely connected with Rastafarianism (Campbell 1980).

It is not a coincidence that drug subcultures tend to form under conditions where the use of these drugs are strongly disapproved. In what is now considered the classic explanation for the formation of deviant subcultures, Albert Cohen states: "The crucial condition for the emergence of new cultural forms is the existence, *in effective interaction with one another, of a number of actors with similar problems of adjustment*" (1955, 59; emphasis in original). Cohen maintains that all human behavior is essentially "problem solving" in nature, and when a number of individuals experience the same or similar problems, it is natural that they come together to find group solutions to their common problems.

Where drugs are made illegal or are socially disapproved, numerous problems are encountered by users: how to obtain drugs: how to obtain the money to purchase drugs, how to manage spoiled identities, how to avoid potential health risks, and how to avoid detection and arrest. Furthermore, users must maintain values and ideologies consistent with their behavior. These supports are not generally available in the larger culture where drug use and other associated behaviors are socially disapproved; hence, they must be found among others who share this lifestyle. In this way, the prohibition of drugs has itself contributed to the emergence and maintenance of drug subcultures, as Lindesmith (1965) and others have noted.

Recent research has documented the evolutionary character of the formation of subcultures by identifying "eras" of drug use (Golub et al. 2004; Golub and Johnson 1999, 2001; Golub et al. 2005a, 2005b). This research on "blunts" use in New York City identifies four distinct phases in the evolution of drug subcultures or drug eras. The first, the *incubation* phase, begins with a small subpopulation using certain types of drugs in fairly specific social contexts. The "heroin-injection era," for example, grew out of the specific context of the jazz music scene. This is followed by an *expansion* phase, which involves the introduction of the drug or drug-using style to a broader population base, which involves a "cultural diffusion" process. The *plateau* phase represents a subculture or era at its peak, when most people at risk for use have already begun (or have had the opportunity to begin) using a new drug or drug practice. Finally, the *decline* phase characterizes a typically gradual decline in the popularity of a particular drug or drug-using style. Golub, Johnson, and Dunlap (2005a) suggest that the various "drug eras" (which are broadly analagous to drug subcultures) are often tied to "drug generations," which is to say that certain types of drugs or styles of drug use wax and wane with generational eras and events. They use this model to examine the rise of a "blunts generation" in New York City and elsewhere in the 1990s. We examine the blunts subculture in more detail later in this chapter.

Characteristics of Drug Subcultures

Drug researchers have identified several characteristics of drug-using subcultures. Goode, for example, suggests that the following features tend to characterize drug subcultures:

1. Drug use is usually done in a group setting.
2. Others with whom one uses drugs are usually intimates, intimates of intimates, or potential intimates, rather than strangers.
3. One generally has long-standing and continuing social relations with others in the subculture.
4. There is a certain degree of value-consensus within the subculture.
5. A value-convergence will occur as a result of progressive group involvement.
6. Drug-using activity maintains the group's cohesion and reaffirms its social bond by acting it out.
7. Participants in the subculture view the activity as a legitimate basis for identity, defining themselves and others on the basis of whether they have participated in the activity. (1970, 21–22)

Goode's summary underscores the social and cultural basis for understanding drug-using behavior. Similarly, Fiddle (1963) identifies the following features of addict subcultures: (1) an ideology that justifies their behavior; (2) an expectation that new members will perpetrate the system; (3) specialized argot and cryptic means of communication; (4) an elaborate informational system; (5) rituals; and (6) strong personal relationships among addicts and a high degree of group identification. More recently, Smeja and Rojek (1986) suggest at least three principal components to a drug subculture, namely a drug-oriented value system, distinctive conduct norms, and special subcultural roles that define the rights and duties of each member and position in the subculture. Castro (2001) further suggests that drug subcultures are comprised of unique language, symbols, meaning systems, beliefs, and practices. These and other attempts at definition help to focus on the social and cultural features of the world of drug use.

In the following section, we examine three drug subcultures that feature the characteristics highlighted above. Each of these subcultures is unique with regard to the primary drug used. The rave subculture, which has recently emerged among high school and college students, is primarily focused on the use of ecstacy, though other drugs are used in rave settings as well. The street heroin subculture is organized primarily around the use of IV heroin, but includes a variety of other drugs (cocaine, crack, and prescription drugs, especially narcotics). The blunts subculture is made up of marijuana smokers. These subcultures also are comprised of different kinds of people demographically. Rave participants are usually young and quite typically middle class, blunts users are younger, and street heroin addicts are more likely to be lower class and typically minority youth and young adults. All of these groups, however, share features that set them apart from the larger culture and bond them to one another ideologically, symbolically, and normatively.

Three Subcultures of Drug Use

The Rave Subculture

A rave is defined as a dance party distinguishable by its music, clothing, paraphernalia, and in many instances drug use (NDIC 2001b). These parties originated in Europe during the 1980s as underground, often secret parties for a fringe subculture (McCaughan et al. 2005). Beck and Rosenbaum (1994), in an authoritative work on MDMA, or ecstasy, suggest that rave parties originated in something called the Acid House dance scene that was sweeping Europe in the 1980s. By the 1990s, these parties were widely popular in other parts of the world, including the United States (Marshall 2001). According to Hunt and Evans (2003) the rave subculture is truly a global phenomenon, enhanced through grassroots networking on internet web sites and chat rooms as well as through slick media promotions and packaging of international tours around club events. The rave scene has evolved from hot and overcrowded abandoned warehouses with strobe lighting strung up for effect to very sophisticated and highly commercialized events that are widely advertised (Hunt and Evans 2003; Martin 1999). Raving has become so extensive that one observer suggested that this phenomenon has become "the largest, most dynamic, and longest lasting youth sub- or counterculture of the postwar era" (Martin 1999, 77).

Certainly not everyone who attends rave parties uses drugs, but these substances are widely available. The drug most commonly associated with rave events is MDMA or ecstasy, otherwise known as *Adam, E, X,* and *eccie* (Martin 1999; Maxwell 2005; Yacoubian et al. 2004). Other substances commonly used tend to have stimulant and/or hallucinogenic properties, including Ketamine, GHB, and Rohypnol (Maxwell 2005). Use of these "club drugs," either singly or in various combinations, enhances the effect of the distinctive music played at raves. Moreover, club drugs possessing stimulant and/or hallucinogenic qualities are popular because they allow users to dance for hours without experiencing fatigue and dramatically enhance the visual and auditory sensations (NDIC 2001b). The music is usually electronically produced, is characterized as by a fast, repetitive beat, and is often accompanied by psychedelic lights, smoke, fog, and water sprayed to cool participants (Weir 2000), though other observers note more variation in musical style and beat (Hunt and Evans 2003; Martin 1999). Participants frequently dress in layered, loose-fitting, androgynous clothing that can be easily removed as they become overheated from dancing. Accessories and paraphernalia are usually brightly colored, and many "ravers" utilize lollipops or baby pacifiers as a remedy for the involuntary teeth grinding that often accompanies the use of club drugs (Weir 2001; NDIC 2001b).

Despite its reputation as a white, middle-class, youthful drug-using scene, the rave subculture is not homogenous with regard to participants. The typical attender is youthful (from teens to mid-twenties), but older participants are not uncommon. Hunt and Evans (2003) point out that chronological age is not nearly so significant within the subculture as is the length of time that one has spent in the rave scene. Ethnicity has not been widely researched, but a review of literature by Hunt and Evans (2003) suggests that raves attract varied ethnic groups, which may be a determining factor in the types of music, though ethnographic research by Thornton (1995) suggests that gatekeeping practices may keep ethnic minorities to a minimum at these events.

There are, moreover, status distinctions among ravers. The "inner circle" of ravers control the direction of these events and consist of the DJs, promoters, and club owners. Attendees tend to be stratified according to how long they have been part of the subculture and the extent of their participation in rave events (Martin, 1999). Further distinctions have also been identified. Hunt and Evans (2003) distinguish between "candy ravers," characterized as anyone who is young, wears bright colors, displays "candy" (bright colored, plastic) jewelry, uses ecstasy, and listens to upbeat music; and "jaded ravers," who have been in the scene much longer, are much less idealistic, less likely to use drugs, and are more critical of the rave scene. McCaughan and her colleagues (2005) identified several types of ravers in their research on the rave subculture in the Midwest. These types included "chemi-kids" who attended these events primarily as a means to obtain drugs, but are not otherwise active participants in the rave scene; "candy kids" who are typically new to the dance scene and characterized by bright candy-colored, jewelry; "junglists" who are much more jaded and have learned to hate the commercialization of raving in particular; "non-affiliated party kids" who see themselves as transcending all of the types and not belonging to any particular rave clique; and "old school ravers" who might be considered the "patriarchs" and "matriarchs" of the rave scene, those who have been raving for some time and are in a position to talk about "the way things used to be."

As raves have become more commercialized, most parties are advertised as alcohol free, so there are usually no age restrictions for admission and parents are less hesitant to allow teenagers to attend, although the cover charge, often more than $50, can be problematic. During the latter part of the 1990s, a number of popular media accounts highlighted the increasing popularity of raves, and rave parties were openly advertised using highly symbolic representations to stimulate interest in these events. Media reporting on these events often provided detailed accounts from party-goers of how drug use enhanced the experience. Information on the negative effects of these substance was minimal, and it was believed that if used "responsibly," club drugs posed little danger (NDIC 2001b).

In recent years, raves have come under increasing scrutiny because of concerns associated with drug use (Weir 2000). A number of studies suggest that use of club

10.1 Rave events are advertised through promotional materials such as posters and post-cards distributed at places like shopping malls and entertainment centers where young people gather. (Image: Alyssa Jolitz/The Gnarley Zombies)

drugs may result in a number of negative physical consequences, such as physical impairment, memory loss, and irreversible brain damage. Furthermore, death can result when club drugs are used in combination with other substances such as alcohol, cocaine, or heroin (NIDA 2000a).

The Street Heroin Subculture

The street heroin subculture is comprised largely (though not exclusively) of inner-city youth and adults who are also quite heavily involved in criminal activity to sustain their drug-using lifestyles. Contrary to popular belief, however, street heroin addicts are not indiscriminate in their criminal activities, nor can they be dismissed as "moral degenerates" who willingly abandon all ethical constraint in their pursuit of heroin. The lifestyle and behavior of heroin-addicted criminals can only be understood in the subcultural context in which they live their lives. Our discussion of the heroin subculture is organized around four broadly defined components that are consistent with the characteristics of drug subcultures made by those observers of the drug scene discussed in the previous section. These four components are: (1) boundary-maintenance mechanisms; (2) distinctive norms, values, and ideologies; (3) specialized knowledge and skills; and (4) a distinctive social organization that provides a basis for a social identity within the subculture.

Boundary-Maintenance Mechanisms

Wherever there are identifiable social groups, there are ways to distinguish between members of those groups and all others who are not members. We refer to these mechanisms for distinguishing between in-groups and out-groups as **boundary-maintenance mechanisms**. In a socially deviant world such as that inhabited by the street heroin user, these boundary-maintenance mechanisms become mandatory. Illicit drug users are often pariahs in their communities, despised by the respectable establishment, and subject to frequent surveillance and harassment by law enforcement agencies. Consequently, these individuals must be able to determine who can be trusted as a fellow member of the subculture. Two quite effective boundary-maintenance mechanisms have evolved among heroin users are the use of specialized argot and the assignment of monikers.

A specialized **argot** refers to the use of language in a way that is not shared by members of the larger culture. Johnson et al. (2006) distinguish between *argot* and two other forms of expression, *jargon* and *slang*. *Jargon* is a form of expression that communicates technical information, typically utilized by educated elites, usually formally taught, and conveyed in written as well as oral form. Practically every profession has its own jargon. Indeed, the field of drug research has its own technical jargon, such as *set* and *setting, drug scheduling*, and all of the technical names for drugs that we have discuss throughout this text. *Slang*, by contrast, is a language of sorts that is used in a very casual way, is often very short lived, and is used deliberately in place of normal words to drive home a point, pack a punch, or embellish a statement. Slang is a vocabulary that is understood and used by most members of society.

In contrast to both *jargon* and *slang, argot* is a comparatively secretive vocabulary whose use is, for the most part, restricted to a particular group or subculture. Among drug subcultures, such vernacular allows addicts to communicate with one another so that those who are not familiar with these specialized meanings—that is, those who are not in the subculture—are effectively excluded from meaningful interaction. The description of vernacular among blunts users (described in the "Drugs and Everyday Life" insert) vividly demonstrates how the specialized use of language can exclude outsiders from effective participation in the blunts subculture. Iglehart (1985) suggests that, while the pressures of stigmatization and threats by law enforcement necessitate the creation and use of argot, to be overheard using such argot by the uninitiated carries its own risk. Iglehart observes, in fact, that addicts often shift into standard English when interacting with outsiders.

Even more important than excluding outsiders, being able to converse in the subcultural vernacular provides a basis for cohesiveness among participants in the subculture. Street argot is often a metaphorical description of common experiences and problems faced by heroin users, and a short-hand means of communicating important information between them. In this way, the lexicon of the heroin subculture provides a basis for a common identity among street users.

Finally, it should be noted that just as there is regional variation in dialect and connotation in language in the straight world, such regional differences can also be observed in the drug-using world (Agar 1973), and among the commonalities of vernacular among drug users regardless of where they live and work are also many subtle differences. Agar (1973, 43) notes, for example, that the term *junkie* is commonly used throughout the United States to refer to a heroin addict (although even here, some restrict the use of *junkie* to an addict that is especially strung out). The term *jones*, on the other hand, is used to refer to a heroin habit in some places and to heroin itself in others.

Participants in drug-using subcultures often take a different name than that given to them at birth. These **monikers** or street names are not taken or assigned arbitrarily. They are typically applied to symbolize some aspect of a participant's personality, biography, physique, or other identifiable characteristic. Examples of such names include "Taxi-cab Mike," "Bent Over Bennie," "Put Your Lights Out Bernie," "Hanky-Panky Marie," and "Stone-Face Eddie."[1]

These appellations are not unique to drug-using subcultures. A similar process occurs among professional criminals (Inciardi 1975), religious cults (Zellner 2001), and in prisons and other total institutions (Irwin 1980). Indeed, most young boys and many young girls have had the experience of being given a nickname. These experiences are not unlike that of participants in drug subcultures who are given street names. Importantly, these street names provide the basis for a very special identity and attachment to the subculture of heroin use. The moniker not only symbolizes some physical or biographical feature of an individual, but represents acceptance into a very significant set of social relations. Street heroin users are known to each other primarily by these monikers, an identity they do not generally share with those who are not in some way associated with the subculture.

Distinctive Norms, Values, and Ideologies

In addition to the symbolic boundary-maintenance mechanisms discussed above, street heroin subcultures can be distinguished from the larger culture by special and often unique norms and values that guide the behavior of subcultural participants. All subcultures of drug use impose the expectation that their members will consume drugs. Some, including the street heroin subculture, also expect some level of criminal or quasi-criminal behavior, an activity commonly referred to as *getting over* (see Goldstein 1981). These subcultural norms clearly violate the normative code of most Americans who are not part of such a subculture.

The normative code of the heroin subculture is far more complex than merely demanding the consumption of heroin and engaging in illegal behavior. The subcultural participant is guided rather clearly about when and under what conditions it is appropriate to use drugs. It is regarded as highly inappropriate to shoot up in the presence of children or strangers (Faupel 1991). An offer to "turn on" a young child to heroin is even more strongly sanctioned. There are commonly understood rules for who makes an appropriate victim or *mark* when engaging in criminal hustles. One can observe a scale of social distance that is not so unlike that which can be found in the dominant culture. Contrary to popular belief, heroin addicts prefer not to steal from their own families or close friends to get their *copping* (drug purchasing) money. To the contrary, they are much more likely to target large, impersonal department stores if they are a shoplifter, or break into houses in a neighborhood across town if they are a burglar. Because their victims are not personally known to them, it is much easier for them to justify their criminal actions.

Fiddle (1963) has observed that one important element of drug subcultures is an "ideology of justification." This feature is especially pronounced with regard to the criminal activities of street heroin users. Heroin-using criminals justify their actions in many ways, some of which were reported to one of the authors of this book. One such justification might be called the "just desserts doctrine." Shoplifters frequently use this doctrine, legitimizing their actions against large department stores such as Macy's or Bloomingdales by complaining that these companies have been "ripping off" consumers for years. Hence, they (the companies) are only getting what they deserve. Sykes and Matza (1957) referred to such a justification as a "denial of victim." Another justification could be called the "drop-in-the-bucket doctrine," claiming that the amount of goods taken was insignificant in comparison to the large profits realized by the company. This technique, which Sykes and Matza call "denial of injury," plays on the theory that no one was victimized unduly. A related justification that plays on the same theory is that these merchants are insured for their losses anyway, so no one is hurt. Check forgers rationalize their crimes in the same way, claiming that neither the bank nor the individual depositor is victimized because both are insured under the FDIC. A check forger interviewed by one of the authors went so far as to say that he would only forge checks on banks that were insured by the FDIC, and he added that if the individual depositor was stupid enough not to take advantage of getting reimbursed by the FDIC, they deserved to be taken anyway (the just desserts doctrine or denial of victim).

In sum, contrary to the popularly believed dope fiend mythology (Lindesmith 1940), drug users do not suffer from an inevitable moral deterioration because of their addiction. Rather, they have adopted an alternative normative code that allows them to function in the social worlds of which they are a part. These normative codes come complete with ideologies and rationales to justify their behavior in the face of a critical and perhaps hostile cultural environment. The process by which drug users become socialized into this new normative system will be discussed in greater detail later in this chapter when we talk about drug-using careers.

Specialized Knowledge and Skills

Many observers of the street scene have noted that heroin users are skilled entrepreneurs who possess highly sophisticated talents and knowledge (Biernacki 1979; Faupel 1986, 1991; Hanson et al. 1985; Preble and Casey 1969). Simply considering the skills and knowledge required for consuming the drug, heroin addicts have to know where to *cop* (purchase) good quality heroin. Unless they are *snorting* (sniffing the drug through their nose), addicts must know how to blend the heroin powder with water and *cook* the heroin by heating it in a *cooker*, typically a twist-off soda bottle cap. Following this, it is necessary to draw the heroin into a syringe, filtering it for impurities with cotton or even a cigarette filter. Addicts who *mainline* (inject directly into the vein) must also learn how to *tie-up* to expose the vein. It is also a challenge for many to learn how to *bang* (inject) themselves properly, being sure to penetrate the vein wall without going all the way through both walls of the vein (in which case, of course, the heroin solution would not be deposited in the vein).

Because of the costly nature of heroin, most addicts have also cultivated criminal skills that are invaluable in helping them to support their habit. (See Chapter 11 for a discussion of the complex relationship between drug use and criminal behavior.) Ethnographers who study heroin addicts have long recognized the skillful and entrepreneurial character of the crimes that they commit (Biernacki 1979;

Goldstein 1981; Hanson et al. 1985; Preble and Casey 1969; Sackman et al. 1978; Waldorf 1973). Regardless of the type of criminal enterprise, certain skills must be mastered. Each type of crime presents its own challenges, of course; the skills that must be mastered by burglars, of *casing* and *breaking and entering* without detection, are not especially relevant to a prostitute or a check forger. Persons involved in these *hustles* must have developed a keen awareness of the behavior and body language of other people. Prostitutes, for example, must be able to distinguish undercover police officers from would-be *johns*. Similarly, they must be able to size up a john quickly to determine if he is a *freak* (one who will make outrageous demands on them, typically of a sado-masochistic nature) or, by contrast, if he will be a rather generous *trick*. Check forgers must be able to present a convincing facade when they present a bank teller with someone else's check, and then be able to read quickly the teller's reaction. Failure to do either may well result in their arrest.

Although most addict-criminals are probably not highly specialized professionals, many if not most street addicts develop a level of expertise that provides a basis for a reasonable income. Gould and colleagues suggest that

> the average, middle of the road dope fiend is much more successful than these losers. He usually has one or two hustles which he is fairly good at, but he knows enough about other hustles to be able to boost at Christmas time, work the parking lots in June when the universities are having graduation, and deal a little dope on the side to make ends meet. (1974, 52)

This observation suggests that, although addict criminals may not be highly specialized professionals, they do tend to gravitate toward some crimes more than others for their criminal income. This preference is what is meant when addicts speak of their *main hustle*. They may engage in any number of hustles from time to time, but they tend to fall back on one or two main hustles as their primary means of support.

Distinctive Social Organization

Drug subcultures resemble the dominant cultures of which they are a part in that work and other activities are organized and carried out according to broadly defined subcultural expectations. Just as we find specialization of work roles in the legitimate world of employment, there is a corresponding division of labor in street heroin subculture. As we have seen, addict-criminals tend to develop a main hustle, a criminal specialization that allows them to develop sophisticated skills for successfully carrying out their crimes. When this happens, they become identified with their specialties. They become known as a *booster* (shoplifter), an *ounce man* (middle-level drug dealer), or perhaps a *strong-arm man* (armed robber). Street heroin users may acquire other identities as well. They may be a *tout* or a *steer*, working for a dealer to identify potential customers, advertise the dealer's drugs (touting), and letting them know where they can obtain them (steering). They may play the part of a *bag man*, physically holding a dealer's drugs. (These individuals are hired by dealers to reduce their risk of getting caught.) Still others may act as *testers* for dealers, injecting small amounts of heroin into their bloodstream to determine the quality of the drug.

Sociologists refer to such a position in a social system as a *social status*. The behavioral expectations that are attached to the positions is called a *role*. How well people perform these roles provides an important basis for social identity, a fact of life in conventional society as well as in drug subcultures. Professors, for example, are evaluated on how well they perform, and as a result get the reputation as being "good" or "bad," "boring" or "interesting," "tough" or "easy." Drug users also occupy statuses within the social system of the drug subculture, and are expected to perform roles that are attached to those statuses (Smeja and Rojek 1986). Shoplifters know that when they work in pairs, one member of the team acts as a lookout for floorwalkers while the other performs that act of theft. Similarly, drug dealers must cop quantities of drugs from a wholesale dealer, cut these drugs by reducing the concentration of heroin in them, and finally bag the drugs for retail distribution. The challenge for the street-level drug dealer is to make as much money as he or she can, while maintaining a reputation as having, good quality *righteous* dope. Chapter 9 discussed the work of Goldstein and colleagues (1984) who described how dealers recognized the practical importance of maintaining a good reputation for having quality heroin, by assigning brand names to distinguish their drugs from other lower quality drugs being sold in the area. There is, furthermore, a system of social stratification in the street heroin subculture, which provides different levels of rewards to various statuses in the subculture. Weppner observed:

> There is a definite multilevel status hierarchy in subculture of addiction which runs from the high-class player, who is admired and emulated, to a garbage junkie, who is on the lowest end of the addict social ladder. The former is an individual who has a very lucrative hustle, such as pimping for a large number of prostitutes. He dresses expensively and may have a large bankroll, a flashy car, and body guards. The latter is the individual who can support his heroin habit only by providing a "shooting gallery" (a place to use drugs) and "works" (the hypodermics to administer them)....He is considered to have sunk very low on the status scale. (1973, 115)

Weppner's discussion of stratification in the drug subculture suggests an economic base. That is, those addicts who are self-supporting and have lucrative hustles, and who can afford to engage in conspicuous consumption activities (such as buying flashy cars) are accorded greater status in the subculture. Those who do not have these resources are likely to be regarded with disdain. Other researchers have identified hierarchies of drug dealing. One of the early attempts in this area was Preble and Casey's (1969) study of heroin distribution hierarchies in New York City, ranging from the importer at the top of the distribution hierarchy to the juggler at the bottom. Adler (1985) presents a similar hierarchy for marijuana and cocaine dealing. These hierarchies are more restricted to those who engage in the dealing enterprise, but nevertheless demonstrate the ever-present reality of social stratification in drug subcultures.

The Blunts Subculture

The 1990s witnessed the reemergence of a marijuana subculture, but in new wineskins—or perhaps it would be more appropriate to say in old tobacco skins. Marijuana smoking was clearly on the rise during the 1990s, as reported by the National Household Survey on Drug Abuse (later renamed the National Survey on Drug Use and Health), Monitoring the Future, and other sources. Nevertheless, the emergence of a new subculture of marijuana use was not recognized for several years until researchers began investigating the phenomenon more closely and discovered that marijuana was being used in a new form. Primarily smoked by young people, *blunts* are quite literally marijuana cigars, formed by removing the tobacco contents from a cigar and replacing it with marijuana. Golub and Johnson (1999) trace the emergence of the blunts generation to youth born in the 1970s who had witnessed the dangers of cocaine, crack, and heroin use. These drugs pose both observable health risks and social costs of apprehension and incarceration. According to Golub and Johnson, the new blunts generation is a direct response to these external forces.

The blunt subculture seems to have emerged in New York City during middle to late 1980s, born out of a marijuana-scarce market that required users to pool their resources to put together enough money to purchase the quantity necessary for filling the hollowed-out cigar known as the blunt (Sifaneck et al. 2003). Sifaneck and colleagues note that early users were primarily African Caribbean, African American, or Latino youth, often involved in the hip-hop subculture. Indeed hip-hop lyrics contains many references to blunts, even songs about how to roll and smoke them. The following lyrics from Red Man's "How to Roll a Blunt" (1992) are indicative of the way in which hip-hop gives expression to the blunts subculture:

> First of all, you get a fat bag of *ism*
> From uptown, any local store sells the shit friend
> Purchase a *phillie*, not the city of Philly
> Silly punk, I'm talking 'bout the shit called the Phillie *blunt*.

Over time, as the subculture has expanded (see the earlier discussion on the phases of subcultural evolution), the practice and culture of smoking blunts has moved far beyond New York City and into white middle-class suburban neighborhoods as well (Golub and Johnson 2001; Golub et al. 2005b; Kelly 2005). And although relatively new, research on the blunts subculture has revealed many of the broad features of the much more established street heroin subculture. Hence, we will use the same framework to examine the blunts subculture.

Boundary-Maintenance Mechanisms

As we have stated, subcultures utilize various strategies to maintain their distinctiveness from the larger culture of which they are a part. The blunts subculture has developed a very rich argot, some of which has been borrowed from the general marijuana subculture as well as other drug-using subcultures. Johnson and his colleagues

(2006) have compiled some 180 specialized words and phrases that are commonly used among blunts users. (Bardhi and Sifaneck, XXXX; cited in This argot ranges from generic references to marijuana such as *boom, trees, buds, broccoli*, and *spinach*; to references to law enforcement and the legal system such as *kj's (killa joys), jakes, cowboys, po-po, the Phillistines*, and getting *bagged*. We have included a partial list in the "Drugs and Everyday Life" insert in this chapter. Johnson and his colleagues (2006) maintain that the use of argot in the blunts subculture is not merely to maintain secrecy, which is a primary function of boundary maintenance. As we have suggested above with regard to the street heroin subculture, the rich argot of the subculture provides opportunity for subculture participants to express feelings and emotions that they experience as blunts users. Moreover, this argot provides a mechanism for readily identifying other subculture participants, as those who are not part of the subculture are not versatile with this language. Johnson and colleagues further state that such language allows subculture participants to communicate with each other effectively and efficiently, as these words contain rich meaning not otherwise conveyed. Finally, the argot of the subculture provides a valuable mechanism for integrating many aspects of the subculture.

Distinctive Norms, Values, and Ideologies

The blunts subculture shares many of the same normative expectations of participants that have been observed in the marijuana subculture that preceded it. Blunts users overwhelmingly prefer to smoke in groups (Dunlap et al. 2005), and indeed, one of the central values of the blunts subculture is social closeness and the maintenance of strong bonds of trust among participants. Anything that would threaten that closeness and trust is strongly discouraged.

The profoundly social character of blunts use begins when several users come together to raise the money to purchase the marijuana. All are expected to go in on a purchase by contributing an amount that, according to Dunlap and colleagues (2005) is usually about $10, though if a participant does not have the required $10, they are asked to contribute whatever they have. Participants who consistently come up short or fail to contribute are eventually excluded from participation and earn the label of *scavenger* (male) or a *hoover* (female) (Johnson et al. 2006). Use in social gatherings carries with it the further expectation to share the drug with other users, those who do not are looked upon disapprovingly, and repetitive violation results in stigmatizing labels such as a *hedgehog* or *bogart*. *Steamers*, on the other hand, are those who have a habit of taking more than the normative two puffs before eventually passing it along (Johnson et al. 2006). This "puff-puff-pass" conduct norm not only allows others to participate in the ritual but reinforces the value of self-control in marijuana use. Indeed, when users reach a desired high, they will often decline to participate the next time the blunt is passed to them rather than violate the commonly understood proscription against extreme inebriation.

Dunlap and colleagues (2005) identify other conduct norms that govern the social setting of blunts use. They note, for example, that particularly in *sessions*,

DRUGS AND EVERYDAY LIFE

Words and Definitions of Marijuana Argot in New York City in 2005

Compiled by Flutura Bardhi and Stephen Sifaneck

B-40—blunt dipped in 40 ounces of beer, left to dry, then smoked

back-yard boogie—bad marijuana

blazed—the act of being high from marijuana; having just had sex: "I just blazed it."

blunt head—one who smokes blunts chronically; similar to "pothead"

bogart—term for someone who doesn't pass the joint or blunt

boom—marijuana

broccoli—generic term for marijuana

Buddha—term for high-quality marijuana

buddha fest—uptown term for promarijuana rally and march (see " 'Weedfest")

burning trees—smoking marijuana

Chicago—when a joint or blunt is about to be smoked all the way down. A Chicago is taking a series of hits until it is out

clam-bake—the act of sitting inside a car or another enclosed space and smoking marijuana

climbing trees—getting high

coco-puff—mixture of cocaine and marijuana rolled in a joint or cigar shell; marijuana with cocaine sprinkled over it

coolie—blunt with marijuana and powdered cocaine, also called a whoolie/wooly

crunked—high and drunk at the same time (term made known by rapper, Lil Jon)

custies—customers

cypher/cipher—a small group formed to smoke marijuana and get high

dolo—smoking a blunt by one's self

euro—marijuana and tobacco rolled into a cigarette

faded—really drunk or really high on marijuana

flippin' tits—selling marijuana [or other illegal drugs]

free house—a house with no parents home; refers more to a house where both parents are at work or just out, not necessarily a home that has no permanent adult supervision

hedgehog—someone who won't pass the joint or the blunt

hoover—a girl who smokes marijuana for free, who never pays for marijuana

ism—marijuana

jakes—police

L—a blunt: "I have to L's."

m&m's—very good-quality marijuana

marijuana types—(street names/terms): Afghani, A-Plus, Arizona, Blueberry, Bubble Gum, Chocolate, Chronic, Colombian, Grapefruit, Gucci (Prada, Louis), Hawaiian Haze, Haze (Purple, Emerald), Honey Draft, Hydro (Candy, Vanilla), Jack Herer, Juicy Fruit, Mango Pina, Northern Lights, Orange, Regular Green, Skunk, Ses (Sensimilla), Snowbud, Sour Diesel, Strawberry, Sweet Diesel, Trainwreck, White Widow

"a one and a dutch"—a single cigarette and Dutch Master cigar; loosie cigarette smoked following a blunt

party/parties—a social gathering where many will smoke marijuana or blunts, as well as engage in other activities (drink alcohol, eat food, listen to music)

phat—good; adjective with positive connotation

pillow—a large amount of fluffy marijuana in a ziplock bag; a good value

Philistines—the police

Phillie Blunt—one of the earliest cigars used to roll blunts; sold in flavours (e.g. Strawberry, Vanilla, Chocolate); blunts derived its name from Phillie Blunt

DRUGS AND EVERYDAY LIFE *(continued)*

scavenger—someone who comes around to smoke other people's marijuana without ever contributing money for it

session—a planned gathering for purchasing and smoking marijuana/blunts

shotgun—the act of placing one's mouth around the lit end of a blunt or joint and having another person blow smoke directly into it; when one takes a hit of marijuana off a bong and blows it into the mouth of another person: "Mary and I were doing shotguns all night long and got really high."

shotty—putting a joint or blunt backwards in one's mouth and exhaling into someone else's mouth where that person will inhale; this intensifies the hit and is sensual/sexual: "I do shottys with shorties [females]."

steamer—one who takes more than the acceptable three puffs at a time from a blunt, joint or cigarette; being greedy; blunt/joint/cigarette gets very hot at the tip

steez—somebody's entire image, get-up, what they represent or are trying to convey in their style of clothing, attitude, body language, lingo, hairstyle etc.: "That kid doesn't really listen to hip-hop. That's just his entire steez."

trees—generic term for marijuana

walkers—police walking the streets

weed spots—places to buy marijuana, at bakeries, barber shops, beauty parlours, beauty supply stores, grocery stores, health food stores, juice bars, restaurants, 99-cent stores

Weedfest—nickname for the annual pro-marijuana rally held in May of each year in a New York City park, where there is talk of legalization and medical marijuana (see "Buddha fest")

Wet Daddy—weed soaked in PCP (Angel Dust)

whoola/woola—a blunt with crack added

whoolie—blunt with marijuana and powdered cocaine

Exerpted from Johnson, Bruce D., Flutura Bardhi, Stephen J. Sifaneck, and Eloise Dunlap. 2006. "Marijuana Argot as Subculture Threads." *British Journal of Criminology* 46, 1 (January), pp. 46–77 (72–77). Used with permission of Oxford University Press.

which generally last a considerable length of time (further discussed in the subsection on "distinctive social organization" below), it is expected that users will engage in a variety of behaviors other than smoking the marijuana. These behaviors may include watching a sporting event or a movie on television, dancing, talking, or playing cards. Arguments and other aggressive behavior are strongly discouraged and rarely occur. If participants are smoking at a larger planned *party*, they know to separate themselves from the larger gathering as it is understood that not everyone at the party is an active blunt smoker. For the most part, these and other conduct norms governing behavior at blunts gatherings are designed to reinforce overarching values of comradery, togetherness, openness, friendship, nonviolence, and mutual trust.

Specialized Knowledge and Skills

Howard Becker (1953, 1963) has eloquently described the process by which individuals learn to become marijuana users, including learning the techniques of deep breathing, holding the marijuana smoke in the lungs for a prolonged period of time, and learning to interpret the effects experienced from the drug as pleasurable (see Chapter 5). Blunts users must master all of these skills. Additionally, they must know where to *score* good marijuana. Generally, after everyone has contributed, one or two people who know local dealers will be entrusted with the money to make the purchase. Frequently, because they have these connections, they will be given a little more marijuana for the money (Dunlap et al. 2005).

Preparing blunts for smoking involves a different and more elaborate procedure than rolling joints. Blunt smoking involves the use of cigars as a delivery device, which may be one reason why young people who have smoked cigars previously are much more likely to smoke blunts than non-cigar smokers (Soldz et al. 2003b). The use of cigars as a delivery mechanism necessitates the identification, purchase, and adaptation of the cigar for marijuana use. Participants in the blunts subculture acquire a taste for particular brands of cigars to use as the carrier, though most accounts suggest that Phillies Blunt is the most common brand used (Sifaneck et al. 2005; Soldz et al. 2003b), which also accounts for the "blunt" appellation for the subculture itself. Over time, other brands have come into popular use, including White Owls, Optimos, and Dutch Masters. Marley, a female blunts user interviewed by Sifaneck and his colleagues, describes why she prefers Dutch Masters as her cigar of choice:

> [T]here's something about the Dutch Master, the extra step of having to do the leaf and everything that kind of makes it the thing to roll right now. With a Dutch Master rolling is more of a specialty; because you got to peel the outer layer first, then empty it and then repack it and then re-roll it. And it looks like an original cigar that you're smoking. (2005, 33)

Marley's rationale gives us a glimpse into the importance placed upon skill and competence required for preparing blunts. Dutch Masters are preferred because they require greater skill on the part of the user to prepare. Moreover, the fact that Marley is able to produce a blunt that looks like the original cigar gives testimony to her blunt-rolling skills.

The actual preparation of the cigar requires some level of expertise regardless of brand used. Once purchased, the cigar must be moistened and then slit from top to bottom, typically with a box cutter or other sharp cutting device. The cigar must then be pried open to empty the tobacco contents without breaking the outer shell. The shell is then moistened even more thoroughly to dissolve any adhesive that might remain and to make the shell more pliable for rolling (Sifaneck et al. 2005). The proper amount of marijuana must then be measured out and placed in the cigar leaf. The marijuana must be packed at just the appropriate density and the cigar leaf then wrapped around the packed marijuana (Kelly 2005). This process is briefly described in the "Drugs: Myths and Reality" insert in this chapter. When the blunts are successfully rolled, one of the participants who has gone in on the purchase of the marijuana will light the blunt, and the ritual of smoking begins.

Drugs: Myths and Reality

Blunts in the Burbs

I first knew Will smoked blunts when I had seen a telltale pile of cigar tobacco on the window sill next to his bed. We stopped into his bedroom one evening so he could don a "throwback" basketball jersey before meeting up with his friends and I headed home. "So, that's part of your cigar collection huh?" I said to him as he pulled the jersey over his head. "That?" he said with a laugh, "You know what that is." Indeed, I did. The following narrative describes the process of blunt creation and usage among Will and his friend Johnny.

Will's cell phone rang. "Yeah," he muttered into his cell phone before he turned to me and said, "Let's go." When we emerged from Will's mother's house, Johnny was waiting for us in his Japanese import car fitted with a racing muffler. Will and I had been watching basketball on T.V. earlier in the evening. As I climbed into the back seat, Will blurted out to Johnny, "Why are you late?" Johnny laughed. "What? Like there's something special going on tonight," he replied to Will. Then he turned to me and said, "Is this kid drunk already?" "Nah," I replied, "It's all good."

After Will lurched back into the front seat, Johnny drove off down the street. "If nothing interesting is going on, why did they convince me to go out with them tonight?" I wondered silently, realizing I should probably be in Manhattan at a club doing fieldwork for my "official" project instead of heading to a bar on Long Island with these guys. "So, what's the plan?" I asked them, hoping to get an idea of what was in store for me that evening. "What do you mean?" Johnny said. "Nothing. Never mind," I replied. "We're just going to a bar. Don't worry it's not far from the train [station]," Will interjected, perhaps sensing some of my uncertainty.

We eventually pulled into a parking lot and into one of the few remaining empty spaces. "Shit, I wish there was more light here," Johnny said. The nearest lamppost was about twenty feet away. "It'll do," Will said and pulled out a cigar from his pocket and handed it to Johnny. Johnny unwrapped the cigar from its cellophane and popped it into his mouth as he leaned back and reached into his front pocket with his right hand. He produced a small box cutter. "You always have that in your pocket?" I asked. "Yeah, why?" he replied as I remembered he works in a warehouse. I just shook my head. Will announced, "I gotta take a piss," and he hopped out of the car. Will left and walked over to a series of tall bushes lining one end of the parking lot.

While Will made use of his impromptu restroom, Johnny held the cigar lengthwise and slid the box cutter from one end to the other to open up the paper. He gently ran his thumbs along the tobacco shaft to make sure the split was complete. He then twisted his key counterclockwise in the ignition and lowered the automatic window on his side. As I sat back in the rear seat, Johnny leaned out the window with the cigar, split it open, and dumped the tobacco contents onto the ground. He wiped the remnants of tobacco off the cigar paper and sat back in the seat. Johnny raised his window and took his keys out of the ignition. By that time, Will was back in the front seat, having entered the car with an "Ahhhhhhhh, now that's more like it!"

As Will and I made idle chit chat about the basketball game, Johnny set to work licking the cigar paper. He moistened the paper so that he could roll a blunt for himself and Will. As he continued to lick the cigar paper I asked, "Doesn't that taste nasty?" "It's not too good," Johnny replied, "but it could be worse. You get used to it. Your tongue kind of gets a buzz." I still thought it was nasty.

He licked the cigar paper until it was pliable. Then Will produced a plastic bag of marijuana. He opened it and gave it a quick

Drugs: Myths and Reality (*continued*)

sniff before passing the bag over to Johnny. "Mmmm, smells tasty," he said to Johnny as he passed it over. Johnny emptied most of the bag onto the moist cigar paper sitting on his lap. He positioned the marijuana lengthwise in a long, half-inch-thick strip. Johnny then asked me to grab a piece of cardboard for him from the floor of the car by the backseat. He laid the cigar paper on the piece of cardboard and used the firm surface to begin rolling the blunt. He folded the short end of the cigar paper over the marijuana and then squeezed all along the bulge of marijuana and re-folded the end of cigar paper. He repeated this process a few times. The purpose of packing it in was to get a firmly rolled blunt. When he felt it was sufficiently tight, he continued rolling it along the longer end of the cigar paper. Johnny gave it a slight twist as he finished and ran the blunt lengthwise across his moist lips. Upon completing his masterpiece, he held it up to Will for approval. Will gave him a quick nod. Johnny then held the blunt at one end, flicked his lighter, and passed it lengthwise under the blunt a few times to dry out the damp cigar paper so that they could light and smoke the blunt.

Upon completing the several passes of his lighter under the blunt, Johnny sat forward and said, "Alright, time to go for a walk." We headed towards the other end of the parking lot, which was even less well lit than where we had parked the car. On our way, we talked about the Knicks, one of our usual topics. The regular season was in its final days and Will and Johnny argued about the Knicks and their playoff chances. Johnny went into a ramble about how the Knicks were ill equipped to go deep into the playoffs, so they were better off not going to the playoffs at all. This way, they would at least secure a better draft pick. After Johnny continued to ramble, Will interrupted him to remind him there was a more immediate task at hand. "C'mon, blaze that shit up," Will insisted as Johnny stood

there with the blunt in his hand. "Oh yeah," Johnny said as he cocked his eye and the left corner of his mouth edged up in a sly grin. The grin quickly disappeared, however, as he stuck one end of the blunt in his mouth and held his lighter at the other end until it was lit. He puffed on it a few times before sticking it out in my direction. I shook my head. "You sure?" he said, as he held it up in my direction. I nodded before replying, "Don't worry, I'll let you buy me some Grey Goose (their favorite brand of vodka) when we get into the bar. I won't let your hard earned paycheck go to waste." Will stuck his hand out, wiggled his fingers towards the blunt, and declared, "The Professor has spoken! Now give me the damn blunt." Will cackled out loud, as if his comment was funnier to him than it was to the rest of us.

Johnny just shook his head with a smile, then passed the blunt to Will and continued his rant. Not even seconds after the blunt left Johnny's right hand, his fingers were pulling a Marlboro out of the pack he had fished out of his pocket with his left.

As Will puffed the blunt and Johnny smoked what would be the first of two dozen cigarettes over the next couple of hours, we stood around that end of the parking lot for about ten to fifteen minutes, sometimes walking towards another spot or making ourselves look busy if a car happened to pass by. On one occasion, as an older man drove by slowly, Will cupped the blunt in his hand and lowered his arm behind his rear end as he nodded and smiled at the senior interloper. Johnny more emphatically and visually smoked his cigarette as if performing for the man in the car—which he clearly was. It was dark but they didn't want to draw any unneeded attention to themselves. They were simply getting their pre-alcohol buzz going.

Other friends waited, already drinking at a nearby bar. They expected Will and Johnny's arrival but were aware that the two

---

Drugs: Myths and Reality *(continued)*

probably had other things to do before heading inside. Will and Johnny passed the blunt back and forth seemingly with no rhyme or reason. Sometimes one of them held onto it for minutes at a time. When the other wanted another hit, he simply held out his hand for the blunt during the normal course of conversation. Though the centerpiece of our situation and the whole reason we were at this end of the parking lot away from the bar, Will and Johnny did not treat the blunt with any sort of significance. They merely smoked some when they wanted some.

When they were finished, some of the blunt remained. They didn't want to continue smoking the blunt and get higher than they felt they needed to be. Johnny meticulously

squeezed out a red ember from the front end of the blunt and then tapped his fingers against the front end of the blunt to make sure it was extinguished. He dropped it off into the ashtray of his car before we turned around and headed into the bar. By the time I left them to catch a train back to Manhattan, they had consumed several drinks in addition to the blunt they had smoked. They smoked no more marijuana beyond the parking lot blunt as of when I left.

Excerpted from Brian C. Kelly. 2005. "Bongs and Blunts: Notes from a Suburban Marijuana Subculture." *Journal of Ethnicity in Substance Abuse* 4, 3/4, pp. 90–93. Used with Permission of the publisher (Taylor and Francis, http://www.informaworld.com).

Distinctive Social Organization

The subculture of blunts smoking consists of a variety of statuses and roles, some of which we have already alluded to. There are individuals designated as the purchasers of the blunts, who also may play an informal leadership role in the blunts rituals. Some participants are more skilled at preparing the blunt. There are the newcomers, the dealers, and the recognized *scavengers* and *hoovers*. Possibly of even greater significance, however, is the type of social setting in which blunts are smoked.

Dunlap and colleagues (2005) identify three distinct types of settings for blunts use. The rituals as well as the normative expectations differ somewhat in each of these settings. The smallest of the settings is the *cypher*, which can begin with as little as one person smoking a blunt, who then encounters a friend who is invited to join. The cypher is formed very spontaneously and without any preplanning, usually involves a small number of people, takes place over a very short period of time, and no other activity is conducted while smoking the blunt. Cyphers almost always occur in a public place, which might include a club or a bar or an empty parking lot. Unlike larger planned events, discussed below, cyphers do not usually involve the ritual of collecting money for purchase of the blunt because one of the participants will probably already have it in his or her possession. One does not participate in a cypher unless invited, though having a blunt will usually guarantee an invitation. Once everyone has gotten high and the blunt is smoked, the group will usually dissolve.

The *session* is a deliberately planned event that forms when a group comes together for purposes of purchasing, preparing, and smoking blunts. Dunlap and colleagues (2005) identify five basic features of a session: (1) participants share in both the purchase and smoking of the blunt; (2) it is a planned event that usually takes place indoors, usually in an apartment or home, though sometimes in a club; (3) groups vary in size, but always involve at least three people; (4) they are much longer in duration than a cypher, as this is a social event and participants spend considerable time talking and socializing; and (5) they almost always involve nonsmoking activities such as watching a movie or sporting event, dancing, playing cards, and so forth. In the session, great emphasis is placed upon everyone contributing to the purchase of the blunt, and controlling one's consumption is also highly stressed.

The third type of setting in which blunt smoking takes place is the *party*. These are usually highly planned gatherings, often at someone's home, for some purpose other than smoking marijuana. Indeed, blunt smoking may be a fairly minor aspect of the overall party. The occasion may be a birthday party, people getting together to watch a sporting event, or something similar. Generally, the party is a larger gathering than either the cypher or the session. Alcohol is usually served, and not everyone at the party smokes blunts. Hence, blunts smokers will separate themselves from nonsmokers when it comes time to smoke. Typically participants will move back and forth between the blunts smoking and the rest of the party. Party norms do not necessarily require that a blunt smoker share in the purchase of the cigar. Attendees may share in other ways, such as bringing wine or beer to the party. Unlike the session, participants in the blunt smoking ritual at a party may not previously know one another. Furthermore, a great deal of socialization takes place between smokers and nonsmokers.

Drug-Using Careers

When we suggest that drug use and addiction can be understood as **careers**, it almost seems as though we are implying that the activities of drug users are comparable somehow to those of lawyers, doctors, nurses, truck drivers, and other people who work in the legitimate marketplace. In many ways, that is exactly what we are implying. The concept of the *career* was first used by sociologists studying occupations to refer to "the sequence of movement from one position to another in an occupational system by any individual who works in that system" (Becker 1963, 24). The term has also been used by criminologists and other sociologists for many years to understand deviant behavior as well. Goffman (1959, 1963) first introduced this concept to the deviance literature in his discussions of the moral careers of mental patients. Howard Becker (1963) would later extend the application of career to other forms of deviance including drug addiction (also see Coombs 1981; Faupel 1991; Fiddle 1976; Rubington 1967). This section examines career dynamics generally, followed by a special focus on the nature of drug-using careers and especially heroin-using careers.

Types of Careers

The concept of *career* is very inclusive, and has been used to examine everything from professional occupational careers such as medicine and law, to avocational careers such as volunteer, to deviant careers such as burglary, prostitution, and drug use. Hence, it might be helpful to differentiate between four broad types of careers on the basis of whether they are respectable or deviant and whether they are occupational or nonoccupational in nature.

Respectable vs. Deviant Careers

Respectable careers comprise those activities that are normatively acceptable or even encouraged in the larger culture. In this respect, doctors, lawyers, and other professions are respectable careers. Homemaking, hobbies, and volunteer activities can also be respectable careers. Deviant careers, on the other hand, consist of activities that violate social norms and consist of criminal behavior patterns as well as noncriminal lifestyles, such as nudism and mental illness, that nevertheless violate commonly accepted standards. These too can be understood as careers (see Bryan 1966; Faupel 1991; Goffman 1959; Wallace 1965; Weinberg 1966).

There are important differences between deviant and respectable careers. Luckenbill and Best (1981) point out that because of the deviant (and often illegal) character of deviant careers, these activities must often be carried out in secret or restricted to a small circle of acquaintances who share this lifestyle. Furthermore, the threat of punitive sanctions introduces an additional cost, or potential cost, to these activities, a calculation that does not have to be made by those pursuing respectable careers. Moreover, unlike many respectable careers, deviant careers are not usually carried out in a structured institutional environment. As a result, the sequence of statuses and roles is typically less predictable for those in deviant careers, making it more difficult to measure one's progress along the deviant career path. Unlike the upwardly mobile executive, for example, who measures his or her progress by increased responsibilities and periodic salary increases, this pattern of progression is not usually so clear with deviant careers. Indeed, the stigmatization that often accompanies deviant careers often results in what most outsiders would probably consider downward mobility. Drug addicts who become known by local law enforcement agents, for example, may be pressured to become informants. When this happens, it is difficult to maintain quality connections (dependable sources of drugs), and the addict may be forced to rely on low-quality "street dope," an indication of downward mobility in the street culture of hard drug use. On the other hand, having done time in a state penitentiary often contributes to the prestige that an individual enjoys on the street. The important feature of deviant careers illustrated here is that there is no clear line of progression in career mobility that most respectable careers enjoy.

Occupational vs. Nonoccupational Careers

We usually think of careers in terms of occupational pursuits, such as doctors, lawyers, truck drivers, and machinists. Generally, we might characterize these occupational careers as the sequence of statuses, roles, and activities that one engages in for the purpose of making a living—what we commonly call *work*. Sociologists have a much broader understanding of career than simply work or professional pursuits. Some 35 years ago, well-known sociologist Everett C. Hughes (1958) was careful

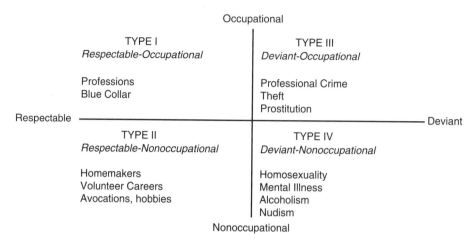

10.2 Types of Careers.

Source: Charles E. Faupel, 1991, *Shooting Dope: Career Patterns of Hard Core Heroin Users*, Gainseville, FL: University of Florida Press, p. 28. Reprinted with permission of the University Press of Florida.

Careers take many different forms. The two dimensions depicted in this figure are especially pertinent for understanding differences among careers. The respectability (vs. deviant) character of a career affects how openly individuals can engage in career activities and determines the risk of being scandalized or even arrested. The occupational (vs. non-occupational) character of a career is suggestive of whether a career is pursued as a means of income. Persons addicted to expensive drugs such as heroin or cocaine often pursue two types of careers: *Deviant–Non-Occupational* (Type IV) careers, which involve drug using activities, and *deviant-occupational* (Type III) careers, which involve criminal activities engaged in to obtain the finances to purchase the drugs.

to emphasize a broader understanding of career when he talked about homemaking and civic involvement as a career. Hence, we can also speak of nonoccupational careers, which include a host of activities around which people meaningfully organize their lives, even though these activities are not a means of livelihood.

Figure 10.2 illustrates four broad types of careers that can be identified on the basis of their normative (deviant vs. respectable) and occupational status. We can see from this figure that it is possible to think in terms of Respectable-Occupational (Type I), Respectable-Nonoccupational (Type II), Deviant-Occupational (Type III), and "Deviant-Nonoccupational" (Type IV) careers. Included in Figure 10.2 are some specific examples of careers that have been discussed by social scientists that represent each career type.

Drug Use and Career Types

The nature of drug-using careers is dependent upon, among other things, the type of drugs one uses and how one uses them. Marijuana, for example, is a relatively inexpensive drug that is affordable to a teenager on even a modest allowance. Hence, most individuals who use only marijuana on even a regular basis are probably pursuing Type IV (Deviant-Nonoccupational) careers. Research by Hathaway (2004) suggests that marijuana consumption careers proceed along one of four career trajectories: (1) steady increase from virtually no use to higher levels of use; (2) use over time remaining about the same; (3) use increasing, then decreasing after reaching a peak; and (4) use highly variable over time. The marijuana users interviewed by Hathaway suggested two factors that tended to determine their use patterns: levels of restrictive controls and/or levels opportunity for using marijuana, and the presence or absence of problems and stress levels that predispose users to smoke. Marijuana careers do not generally require special criminal skills such as might be characteristic of Type III (Deviant-Occupational) careers.

In contrast to the primarily consumer orientation of marijuana careers, users of expensive drugs or extremely frequent users of more inexpensive drugs (such as crack cocaine) often find themselves pursuing dual careers as a drug user and a criminal to sustain their habits. This distinction between what Goldman (1981) has called "consumer activities" and "income-generating activities" is important, for it suggests that such heavily involved drug users are typically pursuing these multidimensional careers of drug consumer and criminal. Importantly, for most of these individuals, criminal profits are not used merely to support a drug habit, although drugs certainly comprise a good share of their consumer budget. Criminal profits are also used to buy nice clothes, cars, and other consumer items. Successful drug-using criminals are, in short, making a living, not unlike those in respectable occupations. As one heroin-using criminal reported to one of the authors, "It was business to me then. My addiction was business. What I had to sell was business. I was very businesslike in manner too. Because it wasn't a game that I was playing." In this respect, many, perhaps most, individuals who use expensive drugs such as heroin or cocaine on a frequent basis are involved occupationally in criminal careers. Agar (1973) captures this quality of heroin careers in the title of his book *Ripping and Running*, a phrase that describes the frenetic pace the heroin-user's criminal lifestyle. Similarly, Biernacki (1979) describes "junkie work" as the criminal hustles that are the basis for the attribution of status in the addict subculture. Indeed Biernacki, and later Faupel (1986, 1991) have found that addicts tend to specialize in a "main hustle" at which they become quite adept in much the same way that individuals pursuing respectable occupational careers tend to specialize in some kind of work. It is, therefore, appropriate to characterize these criminally involved drug users as being engaged in Type III (Deviant-Occupational) careers.

There is, however, another aspect of drug-using careers that relates to the consumer activities of all drug users—those that develop around the acquisition and consumption of drugs. Drug users must learn to locate, purchase, and prepare the drugs that they use. They must also learn how to ingest the drug, whether mainlining, snorting, or smoking. Some mainline users even gain respect in the subculture of heroin use for being able to locate and hit veins readily. Of course, being able to ingest high-quality drugs—whether heroin, cocaine, marijuana, or any other drug—and still be able to function enhances the stature of a drug user in the subculture considerably. These features associated with drug use as a consumer activity predominantly reflect the dynamics of Type IV (Deviant-Nonoccupational) careers.

The Temporal Quality of Drug-Using Careers

Careers have a temporal quality, which means that they unfold over time and have distinctive characteristics at different periods. Studies of occupational careers, for example, have identified at least three periods, which can broadly be identified as career choice and entry (the early, initial period of careers), career mobility (the period throughout one's occupational lifespan), and career exiting (such as retirement).

Drug-using careers have a similar life span, although the terminology is different. Drug users, for example, do not speak of career choice or entry, but rather refer to their early drug-using activities as *turning on*, and will often experiment with several kinds of drugs before settling into their drug of choice. This early period of their careers is, for many, also a time of criminal experimentation until they ultimately settle into their main hustle. Having settled into a drug-using and perhaps a criminal lifestyle, these individuals experience many of the same ups and downs that occur in any occupational career, except that these fluctuations are usually much more extreme than that found in most Type I (Respectable-Occupational) careers. More than three decades ago, for example, it was observed that addicts go through several periods of abstinence and relapse throughout the course of their careers (Ray 1961), a pattern that has also been noted by other observers of the drug scene since that time (e.g., Akers et al. 1968; Coombs 1981; Waldorf 1971). Similarly, with regard to the criminal activities that sustain expensive drug-using activities, a pattern of frequent "occupational shifts" has been observed (Biernacki 1979; Fiddle 1976; James et al. 1976). Indeed, Marsha Rosenbaum (1981a), who has studied female drug use very extensively, describes the career of the female addict as "chaotic." Heroin addicts talk about *getting hooked* (becoming addicted), *jonesing* (withdrawing), developing a *main hustle*, and *getting busted*. This is all to suggest that careers in drug use are subject to conditions contributing to great fluctuation in ability to sustain one's lifestyle, what in conventional careers is referred to as upward and downward mobility.

Finally, although drug users do not usually characterize their leaving the drug scene as "retirement," this waning period is very much a part of most drug-using careers. To facilitate this process, many enroll in treatment centers, or in some cases seek to voluntarily scale down their drug use and criminal activity. This aspect of deviant careers has not been widely studied, though there has been some attention to this career phase in the literature (Sommers et al. 1994; Sommers 2001; Waldorf et al. 1991). Charles Winick (1962) described this process among heroin addicts as "maturing out." Waldorf (1983) found other patterns of "retirement" as well. Addicted users describe this process as *shaking the monkey* or *burning out*. Some become converts to religious or other social causes. Still others join the ranks of the alcoholic or the mentally ill.

We are more recently learning that many do not leave the lifestyle completely, but continue use beyond the age that most research has recognized. Tammy Anderson and Judith Levy have conducted research on active intravenous drug users between the ages of 50 and 68 (Anderson and Levy 2003; Levy and Anderson

2005) and have discovered that these aging IV drug users face career contingencies, related to their age status, that severely affect their lifestyles as drug users. Perhaps most obviously, the biological complications of age can profoundly interfere with their ability to procure drugs or the money for drugs. These older users also report finding it much more difficult to compete with younger users and criminals. This is due both to the biological limitations of age and to the fact that "new school" users (Anderson and Levy 2003) are tougher, more violent, and often have gang affiliations (Levy and Anderson 2005). These researchers further note that with increased age comes increased isolation, as ties with users and nonusers alike erode over time. The isolation from other users typically comes about because (1) their former associates in the subculture voluntarily leave the life; (2) mortality and morbidity take their toll, reducing the number of users in their age-cohort; and (3) forging relationships with younger users is difficult and even perceived as dangerous by these older users. In the words of Anderson and Levy, "Being an older injecting drug user...is to become marginal among the marginal" (2003, 762).

The temporal character of drug-using careers has been described in various ways by several observers of the drug scene. Most of these studies have focused on careers of heroin users. One of the first attempts to define drug use in terms of a career was that of Isidor Chein and his associates in their groundbreaking book, *The Road to H* (1964). This book was a study of black, Puerto Rican, and white teenage heroin users in New York City. They did not promote the term *career* for the sequence of involvement among the drug users they studied, they nonetheless identified four distinct stages of drug involvement among the teenagers they studied: experimentation, occasional use, regular use, and attempting to quit the habit. Chein and colleagues rely primarily on the euphoric effect of the drug and psychological characteristics of the users to explain why some teenagers in their study went from experimentation to occasional to regular drug use, and others did not. Shortly after the publication of *The Road to H*, Earl Rubington (1967) first applied the term *career* to these stages of addiction. Furthermore, Rubington attempted to understand these levels of drug involvement in the context of the addict subculture and describes some of the cultural contingencies that tend to shape these careers. He notes, for example, that experimentation with drugs is a special rite of passage for adolescents living in inner-city slum neighborhoods where there is a high level of drug use. Furthermore, the role redefinition that occurs after they successfully accomplish this rite of passage effectively blocks off other opportunities in the conventional world, and they are likely to become more deeply involved in the world of habitual drug use.

A similar career model has been developed by Coombs (1981), who identifies four distinctive phases to a drug using career: initiation, escalation, maintenance, and discontinuation and renewal. During the early initiation period, teenagers are motivated to experiment with drugs out of a need for independence from parental authority, a need for adventure, and a need for peer approval. This initiation period is an apprenticeship period during which the young drug user must establish the trust of others in the subculture. Successful initiation opens opportunities in the way of connections and criminal hustles that foster the escalation of drug using and criminal activities. The maintenance period, according to Coombs, is the mature period of addiction. Whereas during the experimentation and escalation periods, drug use was an exciting challenge, the maintenance period is one in which the addict's activities focus almost exclusively on obtaining supplies of the drug. Stated differently, "the pursuit of drugs is serious business, not fun and games" (Coombs 1981, 380). It is a matter of survival. Finally, one's drug use may be interrupted for any number of reasons ranging from involuntary incarceration or treatment, to voluntary abstention. Rarely, however, do addicts discontinue their drug use permanently, according to Coombs. They will resume their consumption after they get out of prison or treatment, or after they scale down their habit to more controllable proportions. Only those who have "burned out"—those who have failed, have lost their resources and social standing among their peers—are likely to consider leaving their career permanently. According to Coombs, this is the time in an addict's career when treatment programs can have their most significant impact.

More recently, Faupel (1991) has elaborated a model of heroin-using careers based on two important contingencies that he maintains are critical in explaining career patterns of heroin users. According to Faupel, the careers of heroin users are profoundly affected by levels of drug availability and life structure. *Drug availability* refers to all of the eventualities that make drug consumption possible. The term thus encompasses more than merely access to dealers who have quantities of the drug to sell, although this is certainly a part of what is meant by *availability*. In addition, the user must have resources to purchase the drug, whether money or various sorts of payment in kind such trading sexual services for drugs. It is not surprising therefore, that drug use increases considerably after addicts become adept at criminal behavior, as the proceeds of crime provide the necessary resources to enhance drug availability. Drug availability can also be enhanced through decreased costs, such as when a user connects with a wholesale dealer rather than relying on more expensive, retail street dope.

Life structure refers to the various roles played by drug users that establish a regular and predictable behavior pattern. It has been found, for example, the heroin addicts maintain reasonably predictable routines throughout most of their careers as drug users (Beschner and Brower 1985; Walters 1985). Many of these roles are conventional in nature and not very different from those of most nonusers. Many addicts work at conventional jobs, spend time with their families, go grocery shopping, get their children ready for school, and so forth. In addition, criminally involved addicts structure their days (and nights) through the criminal roles they perform. Shoplifters, for example, frequently establish regular sequences of stores and malls from which they *boost* (steal) during morning and afternoon hours, and *fence* (sell) what they have stolen during late afternoon hours.

Life structure is especially important to drug-using careers because it represents a degree of stability to one's lifestyle. The regularity of events in one's daily life defines one's routines and allows an individual to maintain control over his or her actions. It is within the daily structure of conventional and criminal routines that

Availability   Life Structure

	High	Low
High	The stable addict	The free-wheeling addict
Low	The occasional user	The street junkie

10.3 A Typology of Heroin-Using Career Phases.

Source: Charles E. Faupel, 1991, *Shooting Dope: Career Patterns of Hard Core Heroin Users*, Gainseville, FL: University of Florida Press, p. 47. Reprinted with permission of the University Press of Florida.

Careers typically involve a sequence of positions or "phases." This figure suggests a typical phase-sequence for heroin and other drug using careers. The sequence of these careers depends upon shifting levels of drug availability and life structure (level of routine) in an addict's life. Typically, users begin as *occasional users*, proceed to a *stable addict* phase, followed by a *free-wheeling addict* phase, and then to a down-and-out *street junkie* phase. Addicts may go through this sequence several times through the course of their careers.

heroin addicts *cop* and *shoot* drugs. Drug use is, in effect, scheduled as part of one's daily routine. Without such regularity, there is a lack of normative clarity by which to define appropriate actions, especially drug use. With large amounts of free, unstructured time on their hands, the addict does not have a daily routine to schedule drug use, and consequently, if the resources are there, he or she is likely to lose control over their drug consumption.

According to Faupel, heroin-using careers are patterned by the intersection of these two contingencies, drug availability and life structure. Figure 10.3 illustrates these career patterns.

The Occasional User

This period of drug use generally characterizes the beginning user, a period that Coombs (1981) refers to as *initiation*. Levels of drug availability are low because wholesale drug connections have not yet been established and because the beginning user has not yet learned a criminal trade to provide a lucrative income to purchase drugs. Early periods in drug-using careers are typically characterized by a comparatively high degree of life structure, according to Faupel. Young novices may be still in school, which occupies a considerable portion of their day. Those who are older when they become involved in drugs may be working at conventional jobs, engaged in domestic responsibilities such as homemaking and child rearing, or involved in any number of avocational interests that occupy their time. These conventional roles provide a strong basis for life structure among many beginning drug users.

Not surprisingly, Faupel found that during this early period of drug-using careers, criminal and drug-using skills were least developed. Interestingly, however, this was also the career period in which drug users most frequently violated the ethical code of the subculture. Novice occasional users frequently turned their nonusing friends on to drugs as one would share a cigarette with a friend. Similarly, this is a time when a young user is most likely to steal money for drugs from his or her family members.

This early period of drug-using careers may last days, weeks, months, or even years. Zinberg (1984) found many heroin users who never move beyond this limited and "controlled" use stage. Similarly, Waldorf, Reinarman, and Murphy (1991) found that many of their respondents maintained controlled levels of cocaine use for years at a time. For most addicts, however, the limited involvement of occasional users eventually gives way to more systematic and frequent drug use.

The Stable Addict

This career phase is characteristic of the mature, seasoned heroin user, a phase analogous to what Coombs (1981) refers to as *maintenance*. The basic skills necessary to maintain a drug-using lifestyle—knowing how to cop one's drugs, and in the case of heroin users, cooking and injecting, as well as the rudiments of criminal hustling— are learned during the occasional use period. The challenge of the stable addict period, in contrast, is to maintain a successful criminal-addict lifestyle. Criminal specialties, or main hustles, are cultivated during this period, which increase the level of one's income and therefore drug availability. Furthermore, by the time they become stable addicts, most heroin users have developed wholesale copping connections that can supply them with high-quality heroin at a reasonable price, a strategy that also increases drug availability through lowered cost.

The stable addict period is also characterized by a comparatively high degree of life structure, although the basis for this structure has changed dramatically. Whereas during the occasional use period, the beginning user was still involved in school, legitimate employment, or a myriad of other conventional roles that structured daily routine, the stable addict is immersed in a criminal lifestyle that provides an alternative basis for this life structure. Burglars, for example, typically "case" residential and commercial areas during the day as part of other activities in which they are engaged, then carry out the burglary at night. Shoplifters often establish one or more regular "runs," sequences of malls and shopping centers from which they steal. Their fencing, drug copping, and using are all part of a daily routine that is given structure by the patterns of their runs.

Other criminal specialties provide a similar structure, whether prostitution, drug dealing, armed robbery, or a combination of two or more such main hustles. The importance of criminal specialization during the stable addict career phase, therefore, is measured by both the increased level of drug availability it affords and by the daily structure that allows the addict to maintain some level of control over his or her drug consumption.

The Free-Wheeling Addict

This career phase is characterized by unprecedented levels of drug consumption. Unlike the stable addict period, where drug use may be heavy but always bounded by the structured routines that provide a basis for self-control, the free-wheeling addict has lost control over his or her habit. This period of heroin use may be brought on by any number of factors, such as the loss of a spouse, loss of a job, or even a temporary disruption to one's daily routine. Having developed a tolerance for heroin, the addict is extremely dependent on the external constraints to his or her consumption provided by a highly structured daily routine. When these routines are abandoned, the addict is at the mercy of the physiological cravings that are almost continuously present.

Most commonly, however, the free-wheeling phase of addiction is brought on by the *big sting*, an unusually lucrative score from (typically) some criminal action. When this occurs, the addict is not required to maintain a rigorous criminal life-style because he or she now has plenty of money to buy drugs without having to worry about getting more. Consequently, the addict who has just hit the big sting typically abandons his or her usual criminal routines and enjoys a rather extravagant, leisurely lifestyle. With no rigorous daily routine to gauge their drug consumption, free-wheeling addicts tend to let their habits escalate out of control. In his book, Faupel (1991) weaves the story of "Harry", a hard-working burglar who toiled almost daily as a burglar to maintain his heroin habit, as well as pay for gas for his car, clothing, and other incidental expenses. A friend of his dropped by one day with a roll of bills worth several thousand dollars and asked him to join him holding up grocery stores. Harry reports that the money was substantially better, needing only a three-day workweek. Harry's drug availability thus increased dramatically with his increased income, and the life structure provided by his daily burglary routines was abandoned. He reported that not only did his heroin use increase astronomically, but he started using cocaine on a regular basis and generally expanded his consumer lifestyle in an uncontrollable fashion. He was, in a phrase, living high on the hog.

The problem is that this free-wheeling phase cannot last forever. The money and the drugs eventually run out. At this point, if the addict has not severed all connections, he or she may return to a stable addict period. Often, however, free-wheeling dynamics set in motion a process of dissociation from fellow criminals and from wholesale dealers because the free-wheeling addict is not dependent on them for his supply. When this happens, the free-wheeling addict will probably find him or herself faced with the dilemma of the street junkie.

The Street Junkie

This period, characterized by little life structure and low drug availability, most closely approximates the stereotyped image that most people have of heroin addicts. It is as street junkies that addicts are most down and out and desperate for drugs, pathetically unkempt, and not able to maintain even the most rudimentary hygienic standards. They literally live a hand-to-mouth—or perhaps more appropriately, a hand-to-arm—existence.

This situation may be brought on by either an erosion of life structure, such as the loss of a job, death or divorce of a spouse, or other disruptions that erode the stable routines of a user. More typically, however, this street junkie career phase is brought on as a result of exhausting one's resources during a free-wheeling phase. Having developed an extremely large tolerance for drugs and having abandoned criminal hustling routines, it is not unusual for addicts in this situation to find themselves desperate, willing to do nearly anything for a fix. Because they have probably also severed their wholesale connections, however, they must typically pay top retail street prices for their dope, which only exacerbates their situation. Finding themselves in this situation, street junkies often abandon their own ethical codes in search of a bag. Such is the difficult dilemma of the street junkie.

It should be pointed out that the stereotypical image that most Americans have of heroin addicts is that of the street junkie. Faupel (1991) maintains that there is good reason for this. It is the street junkie who is most likely to seek out treatment centers, where researchers and the media have most ready access to populations of heroin addicts to do their stories. Similarly, it is the street junkie who is most likely to commit a crime on impulse because of an immediate felt need for dope and, because of this carelessness, is most likely to be caught. Consequently, the image of the heroin addict most visible to criminal justice officials is also that of the street junkie. Faupel cautions, however, that street junkie dynamics are only one small part of heroin-using careers. It is impossible to understand fully the dynamics of heroin addiction, he maintains, without understanding the other three career phases as well.

Summary

This chapter began with a pair of presuppositions about drug use that are unique to sociology and perhaps a handful of other social sciences such as anthropology. Those presuppositions are that (1) drug use and associated activities such as criminal behavior can be understood only in the social and cultural context in which they take place, and (2) when understood in this context, these behaviors are generally not pathological or abnormal, but are quite reasonable and understandable, reflecting a conformity to the social and cultural expectations of that context. This is so wherever subcultures of drug use have evolved, as illustrated by the three subcultures that we examined in this chapter. Indeed, we suggested that in most respects, drug-using lifestyles reflect similar dynamics as conventional lifestyles. Drug users, it was suggested, pursue careers that are defined by contingencies in the addict's cultural environment.

Because illegal drug use is criminal in nature, in some cases sanctioned severely by the criminal justice system, the activities associated with this lifestyle are not part of the cultural mainstream. Drug subcultures provide an alternative cultural and social environment that rewards rather than punishes these deviant behaviors. Furthermore, these subcultures provide valuable boundary maintenance mechanisms in the form of a specialized argot or unique street names that allow the participant a means of easily distinguishing between those who are and are not a part of the subculture. The drug subculture also provides a complex set of normative prescriptions and proscriptions that guide the behavior of the subculture participant. Similarly the drug subculture provides a valuable socialization function through the transmission of valuable knowledge and skills necessary to function effectively. Finally, not unlike the broader culture of which it is a part, there is a stratification system in the drug subculture that rewards some behaviors and participants more than others.

Illegal drug use is highly deviant in American society, and is understood as a pathology to be explained by most professionals and lay people alike. This chapter suggested an alternative perspective from which to interpret the lifestyle and behavior of drug users, a perspective that recognizes the rationality and goal-directed character of drug-using and criminal lifestyles that adheres to an alternative set of goals and normative expectations. It may well be that the subcultures that promote such activities are themselves abnormal and even pathological in character; the behavior of individuals within the context of these subcultures, however, cannot be regarded as pathological if understood from the social and cultural context in which it takes place. Drug users are, in this respect, not so fundamentally different from the faithful church- or synagogue-goer who engages in ritualistic behavior in response to group norms and expectations.

Key Terms

argot
boundary-maintenance mechanism
career
drug subculture
moniker

Thinking Critically...

1. How does the illegality or disapproval of certain forms of drug use lead to the formation of drug subcultures? What are the special problems faced by users of illegal drugs, and how do subcultures function to solve them?

2. Based on what you've read in this text, and any other reading that you may want to do, compare and contrast any two of the subcultures discussed in this chapter. What themes do all of these subcultures share in common? What are some important ways in which they differ? What do you think might account for any differences?

3. How does a "career" framework for understanding drug use change how you understand the nature of drug use?

4. This chapter presents an alternative to the prevailing notion that illegal drug use is best understood as a pathology, arguing that much drug involvement is a rational response to the users' cultural environment. If our society experienced such a perceptual shift, how might it change our social attitudes and responses

toward drug users? How might drug policies change in response to such an understanding?

5. This chapter described four characteristics of street heroin and blunts subcultures. Think of other subcultures that you are familiar with. (Examples might include subcultures of truck drivers or computer geeks.) How do these subcultures reflect the four characteristics of subcultures used to describe the subcultures in this text?

Learning from the Internet

1. Drug subcultures have arrived on the internet! Go to the following site:

   http://www.potsmokersnet.com/

   There are also other so-called underground drug sites on the internet. What do you learn about marijuana from this website? Is there information here that you might not find on other mainstream sites?

2. Research the middle-class drug subculture of the 1960s on-line. This drug subculture is commonly known as the *hippy* subculture. Many sites on line can be identified by simply typing "hippy" and "drugs" in your search engine. What were some of the subcultural features of this generation of drug users? How are these features similar to or different from contemporary drug subcultures, such as the rave and blunts subculture described in this chapter?

Note

1. These are actual street names of New York City heroin addicts collected by Edward Preble long-time street anthropologist doing research in New York City.

CHAPTER **11**

Violent and Criminal Correlates of Drug Use

Perhaps the greatest fear that many people have of illegal drugs is the association that these substances have with other forms of criminal behavior. These fears are continually reinforced in the media, where addicts are depicted as hopelessly enslaved to expensive and violence-causing drugs. In the minds of many Americans, crime is almost an inevitable consequence of drug use, and to be a drug addict is tantamount to being a criminal. The following quote from a San Francisco journalist captures the fear that many people have of the causal relationship between drug use and crime:

> He's after that money; he needs it to buy heroin. And he'll take it from you if
> you are his nearest and dearest friend, even if he has to kill you to do it. (in
> Silver and Aldrich 1979, 42)

More recently, allegations of the causal relationship between illegal drug use and crime have almost reached a feverish pitch as the media, lawmakers, educators, clergy, criminal justice personnel, treatment specialists, and others widely concur that drug use and related criminal behavior rank as one of the leading problems in the country today. Democrats and Republicans have both sought the high moral ground on this issue throughout the 1980s, 1990s, and into the new millennium. Hardly a day or week passes that one or more major newspapers or magazines do not offer commentary suggesting or at least implying that drugs are the cause of much crime in American society today. Former New York Senator Alfonse D'Amato has referred to drug addicts as "walking crime machines," proposing the death penalty for drug kingpins (U.S. Senate 1984).

This chapter examines the substance behind these allegations. We begin with an historical overview of how the relationship between drugs and crime was viewed, and how these views contributed to the drug policies in place today. Next is a description of three broad theoretical connections between drug use and crime: drug use cause crime; crime causes drug use; and "common-cause" explanations. Finally, the empirical evidence between drug use and crime is examined.

Historical Understanding of Drug Use, Crime, and Violence

The concern over drugs and crime is not unique to this generation, nor, for that matter, to the twentieth century. During the early seventeenth century in England, King James I was especially anxious to rid his country of tobacco. His strategy, not unlike what would be used centuries later, was to identify tobacco with evil foreigners who represented a threat to a civilized way of life. While not specifically suggesting that tobacco use causes crime, his implications were clear. According to the King, tobacco smoking belongs to:

> that sort of costumes, which having their original from base corruption
> and barbarity, doe in like sort, make their first entry into a Countrey, by an

inconsiderate and childish affectation of Noveltie.... For Tobacco ... was first
found out by some of the barbarous Indians, to be a Preservative, or Antidot
against the Pockes, a filthy disease, whereunto these barbarous people are (as
all men know) very much subject, ... so that as from them was first brought into
Christendome, that most detestable disease, so from them likewise was brought
this use of Tobacco, as a stinking and unsavourie Antidot, for so corrupted and
execrable a Maladie, the stinking Suf-fumigation whereof they yet use against that
disease, making so one canker or venime to eat out another.... Shall we ... that
have bene so long civill and wealthy in Peace, famous and invincible in Warre,
fortunate in both, ... shall we, I say, without blushing, abase ourselves so farre,
as to imitate these beastly Indians? ... Why doe we not as well imitate them in
walking naked as they doe? ... [Y]ea, why do we not denie God and adore the
Devill as they doe? (quoted in Corti 1931, 77)

Marijuana was another drug associated with antisocial behavior from time to
time. There is the legend of an eleventh-century Persian religious cult known as the
Assassins who committed murder for political reasons. Marco Polo is credited with
first spreading the legend of this group who used marijuana and, as the legend developed over history, committed murder and barbarous crimes after using the drug. The
tales of this cult were later popularized in Alexander Dumas' nineteenth-century work,
The Count of Monte Crisco. In 1931, Dr. A. E. Fossier wrote of this group, "this diabol-
ical, fanatical, cruel and murderous tribe ... under the influence of hashish ... would
madly rush at their enemies and ruthlessly massacre everyone within their grasp"
(1931, 247; cited in Grinspoon 1971). In retrospect, Grinspoon (1971) points out
that these tales were greatly exaggerated, and the causal link between the drug and
murders committed was not suggested until much later.

Alcohol has also been regarded as an evil menace causing a variety of types of
crime and other social ills. The temperance movements of the nineteenth and early
twentieth centuries played on and often exaggerated these tragedies. These reform
efforts sought to vilify alcohol, producing books and tracts that depicted it as a curse
on civilized society. One such publication, *The Curse of Drink: Or Stories of Hell's
Commerce* edited by prohibitionist Elton Shaw in 1909, is filled with tales of murder,
debauchery, abuse, and neglect brought on by the use of alcohol.

These early concerns over the potential criminal character and effect of using
drugs notwithstanding, the concern over drugs and crime as we know it today is a
phenomenon unique to the twentieth and twenty-first centuries. Never before has
crime been so intricately related to drug use in the minds of policy makers, practitioners, and the general public as it has in the last sixty or so years. One of the
earliest twentieth-century moral crusaders to fight drug use on this basis was a celebrated Navy captain, Richmond Pearson Hobson, who, as noted in Chapter 2, led
military-like crusades against alcohol and later narcotics use. Hobson's voice was
not as one crying in the wilderness. He touched a sensitive nerve in the consciousness of a morally receptive twentieth-century American society. Shortly after his

moral crusade against narcotics, in 1930, the Bureau of Narcotics was formed within the Department of Treasury under the leadership of Harry B. Anslinger. Anslinger launched a major antimarijuana campaign in the 1930s that depicted marijuana as "the Devil's Weed" and the "assassin of youth," causing violent and irrational behavior. Perhaps no other antidrug campaign before or since has played so loose with the facts in its attempts to create a moral climate of intolerance. The Bureau of Narcotics leaked several stories of alleged criminal incidences involving marijuana. The following story cited by Anslinger and Tompkins is an example of the type of information released by the Bureau:

> Del Rio, Texas. 1940. One Eleutero G. while allegedly under the influence of marijuana, shot to death two women and then committed suicide by literally slicing himself to bits about the abdomen, heart, and throat, in a manner which indicated that he was bereft of all reasoning.... It was the opinion of the doctor who saw G. just before he died that no one could so mutilate himself unless he was unable to feel "shock" and the only thing he knew that would produce such a condition, to such a degree, is marijuana. (1953, 23–24)

Perhaps most remembered in the drug education campaign of the 1930s was the movie *Reefer Madness*, which was produced as a documentary for purposes of warning parents of the evils of marijuana. The story is of a young man, Billy, raised in an upstanding family and doing well in school until he is introduced to the killer drug, *MARIJUANA*. His performance in school declines precipitously, and he becomes unfaithful to his girlfriend. While high on marijuana Billy is seduced by another marijuana user. During their love-making interlude he hears his girlfriend's voice. He dashes out only to find her being seduced by another older marijuana user in the room. A fight ensues, a gun goes off and accidentally kills his girlfriend. Billy, who has himself been knocked unconscious, wakes up to find a gun in his hand and (he thinks) himself responsible for his girlfriend's murder. In point of fact, he has been framed and is later exonerated. The moral that the movie is attempting to convey, however, is that marijuana is a killer drug that leads inevitably to a life of crime and debauchery.

By the 1940s there was a growing literature that depicted marijuana and other illegal drug users as morally degenerate, sexually violent, and criminally aggressive (Inciardi 1981a). These stereotypes, which one social scientist writing at that time referred to as the "dope fiend mythology" (Lindesmith 1940), became so firmly entrenched that they went virtually unquestioned by academicians and policy makers for the next three decades and beyond, in spite of a growing amount of evidence to the contrary (White and Gorman 2000).

By the late 1960s, however, marijuana was no longer depicted in terms of reefer madness. Indeed, rather than exciting the baser passions as was believed earlier, it was now understood to cause lethargy and laziness, a phenomenon commonly referred to as the *amotivational syndrome*. The drug that was targeted for its role in causing crime was once again heroin. The person most responsible for launching this new "war on drugs" in the 1960s was the governor of New York, Nelson Rockefeller. Rockefeller had been elected governor in 1958, but soon set his sights on the presidency. He lost his bid for the Republican nomination in 1964 to Barry Goldwater. Concerned with his image of being too liberal a Republican, Rockefeller recognized the need to court the more conservative wing of the Republican party while still not alienate the party's moderate to liberal constituency. He quickly seized upon the issue of drugs and crime, capitalizing on public opinion polls that were showing a growing concern of the American people toward drug use and crime (Epstein 1977).

Rockefeller worked diligently to establish a connection between drug use and crime in the mind of the American public, and to do so, he used some of the same strategies and vivid imagery of Richmond Hobson years earlier. Rather than argue a physiological basis for this connection as Hobson had done, however, Rockefeller suggested that as the user became physiologically dependent on drugs, he or she would be inevitably compelled to steal and commit other crimes to pay for this habit. Rockefeller cultivated what Epstein has described as a "vocabulary of fear" to launch "an all-out war on drugs and addiction" (1977, 268). Capitalizing on growing public sentiment, Rockefeller rushed a law through the legislature providing for the involuntary confinement of drug addicts for up to five years for treatment, regardless of whether they were guilty of any crime. In this, which has been described as "the nation's toughest drug law" (Joint Committee 1978) Rockefeller succeeded not only in appealing to both conservative and liberal elements in the Republican party, but also firmly reestablished the link between drug use and crime at the policy level.

Rockefeller's war on drugs took on national proportions under the Nixon administration. Edward Jay Epstein's book *Agency of Fear* (1977) chronicles the extended effort of the Nixon administration to wage this war on several fronts. During the 1970s the federal government undertook several initiatives to stop the flow of drugs into this country as well as to stop the distribution of drugs within our borders as part of an unprecedented "war on crime." So fully institutionalized was the presumption that drug use caused criminal behavior that these policies were being implemented in the absence of a strong body of empirical evidence for such a causal relationship. Indeed, when one study that was commissioned by the National Institute on Drug Abuse (Research Triangle Institute 1976) failed to find conclusive evidence that drug use caused crime, the National Institute on Drug Abuse (NIDA) refused to publish it (Clayton 1981).

The concern over drugs and crime has reached such a feverish pitch in the last decade that billions of dollars are being expended each year to fight this perceived menace. Correspondingly, a monumental amount of research has been conducted by many social scientists around the country attempting to understand more fully the nature of the relationship between drug use and criminal behavior. Along with some common areas of agreement, these studies have also produced many contradictory findings. The remainder of this chapter examines what we know and what we don't know about the relationship between drug use and crime. We begin by reviewing the theoretical and conceptual linkages between drug use and crime. We then review several empirical studies that examine this relationship. As we shall see, the relationship between drug use and crime is much more complex than the common-sense assumption that "drug use causes crime."

Theoretical Understanding of Drug Use, Crime, and Violence

It is generally accepted that drug users commit far more than their fair share of crime, if by "drug users" we mean regular users of expensive drugs such as heroin and cocaine. We must qualify this statement in two ways, however. First, not *all* drug users commit more than their fair share of crime. Many users of illegal drugs are otherwise law-abiding citizens. They use drugs on an occasional basis and do not let their drug use get out of control. These week-end "chippers" are what Norman Zinberg (1984) calls "controlled users." Second, even among those drug users who are involved in other types of criminal activity, it is not necessarily the case that drug use *causes* crime, as is commonly assumed. Stated in more scientific terms, a **correlation** between these two sets of behaviors (that is, where there is one, there is usually the other), does not imply **causality** (that one causes the other to occur). White and Gorman (2000) point out three possible ways in which we might conceive of the relationship between drug use and crime: (1) drug use causes crime; (2) crime causes drug abuse; and (3) both drug use and crime share common causes. This section broadly discusses these possible ways that drug use and crime might be related. Following this discussion, we will look closely at several studies that examine this relationship empirically.

Drug Use Causes Crime

It is most commonly believed that illegal drug use somehow causes criminal behavior. As we have discussed above, this belief has predominated throughout much of the twentieth century. This view has certainly not waned in the latter part of the twentieth century, as evidenced by the testimony of Senator D'Amato noted earlier. Generally, explanations for how drug use causes criminal behavior fall into two broad categories, pharmacological explanations and economic explanations.

Pharmacological Explanations

Pharmacological explanations suggest that criminal behavior is a direct effect of a drug's chemical qualities on the human organism. Understood in this way, a drug may cause a person to think irrationally and therefore act irrationally. Alternatively, drugs may lower one's ability to engage in self-control, resulting in impulsive criminal acts. The early moral entrepreneurs, such as Richmond Pearson Hobson and Harry Anslinger whom we discussed in previous paragraphs, generally adhered to this explanation for the drugs-crime connection. These views are generally not accepted today by most serious observers in regard to either heroin or marijuana, but the pharmacological explanation continues to be used to explain aggression associated with some types of drugs. Jeffrey Fagan (1990), in an extensive review of theoretical and empirical studies examining the relationship between drug intoxication and aggression, finds that certain drugs—such as alcohol, barbiturates, cocaine, amphetamines, and PCP—tend to be more strongly related to aggressive behavior than other drugs such as marijuana and heroin. Fagan suggests, however, that the link should not be viewed at face value as causal, as numerous variables mediate this association. This conclusion was confirmed in a review of the literature more than a decade later by Hoaken and Stewart (2003).

Several specific explanations have been offered for the aggressive behaviors that tend to accompany the use of these drugs. Studies conducted by medical and biological scientists tend to focus on neurological, hormonal, and/or genetic factors that are triggered by certain types of drugs. Some studies, for example, have sought to identify specific neural pathways and stimulus thresholds that provoke aggression (Moyer 1976). Other researchers have found a relationship between alcohol use and reduced testosterone levels (Cicero 1983). Schuckit (1988) found that prolonged use of anabolic steroids results in decreased levels of testosterone and reported feelings of aggressiveness and irritability. Still other studies (e.g., Maccoby and Jacklin 1974) have suggested a possible genetic predisposition toward aggressiveness. Recently, Elliott (2001) has begun harvesting DNA samples as part of his nationwide longitudinal National Youth Survey, which should be extremely helpful in understanding the genetic link between drug use and criminal behavior.

Another pharmacological explanation for drug use causing crime emerges primarily from psychology. This psychopharmacological perspective suggests that the use of certain drugs causes psychological impairment that, in turn, leads to violent and/or criminal behavior. Credited with formulating the first comprehensive psychopharmacological causal relationship between drug use and aggression was Abe Wikler, a pharmacologist and psychiatrist who worked for many years at the Federal Narcotics Hospital in Lexington, Kentucky (Mayfield 1983). Wikler compared the actions of alcohol and the opiates on human behavior using controlled experiments at the hospital. He found that opiates tend to reduce the primary drives, such as sex, hunger, and aggression. Alcohol, on the other hand, not only intensifies these drives, but also reduces the secondary drives, which constrain the expression of primary drives (Wikler 1952). This explanation, and variations on it, later came to be known as the **disinhibition hypothesis**, which is probably the most popular of the pharmacological explanations for aggressiveness associated with alcohol. The disinhibition hypothesis suggests that drug intoxication affects central nervous system functions that presumably control or inhibit aggression. Under the influence of such drugs, normal constraints and inhibitions on behavior are removed, resulting in antisocial behavior. This explanation has been most often used in relation to alcohol to explain both violence (e.g., see Collins 1983) and antisocial sexual behaviors (Langevin et al. 1988; Reinarman and Critchlow-Leigh 1987).

Other psychopharmacological explanations suggest that certain kinds of drugs activate underlying pathologies, causing heightened states of anxiety and even paranoia (Kramer 1983; Mayfield 1983). Still others point to an impairment of cognitive abilities while intoxicated (Fishbein 2000; Giancola 2000; Pernanen 1976). If this is the case, drug intoxication may reduce one's ability to engage in coping strategies in situations that may be deemed threatening (Collins 1983). Giancola (2007) suggests that alcohol has a "myopic" effect on attention that might facilitate aggression by focusing attention on more immediate provocative, rather than less obvious inhibitory, cues in hostile situations. Also, if drug intoxication reduces one's ability to function cognitively, communication is less effective, and other people's behavior that is normally rational and understandable might now be perceived as arbitrary and even irrational. These perceptual misunderstandings might understandably lead to aggressive behavior (Pernanen 1981).

Evaluation of Pharmacological Explanations. Pharmacological explanations for a causal connection between drug use and antisocial behavior are intuitively appealing. They are direct and can be corroborated by casual observation that people who are under the influence of drugs often act in an aggressive or otherwise antisocial manner. There are a number of problems with these explanations, however, which merit careful review. First, it is important to recognize that these explanations are generally restricted to a limited number of drugs, typically alcohol and other depressants such as barbiturates, certain stimulants such as cocaine, amphetamines, and more recently crack, and a few other drugs such as phencyclidine (PCP) (Goldstein 1985). These explanations are not generally applied to drugs such as marijuana, heroin, sedatives, and tranquilizers, or many of the hallucinogens. Furthermore, pharmacological explanations are generally applicable only to crimes of violence, which are usually of an expressive nature; that is, crimes not oriented toward some ulterior end such as making money. Finally, the empirical evidence suggests that direct, pharmacologically based violence is rare (MacCoun et al. 2003).

Beyond these general caveats, pharmacological explanations also suffer in that, despite their popularity, the causal mechanisms that trigger violent behavior remain elusive. White and Gorman (2000) point out that how alcohol and other drugs act on the nervous and endocrine systems to produce aggressiveness is not well understood. Perhaps this should not be surprising, for as Mayfield (1983) points out, we do not even know the precise biological mechanisms by which alcohol causes drunkenness!

Most extensively criticized, perhaps, is the disinhibition hypothesis. Ironically, it is also perhaps the most widely accepted explanation, at least among the general public. Despite the popularity of this explanation, there has yet to be any scientific research that biologically and pharmacologically accounts for such disinhibition (Woods and Mansfield 1983; Fagan 1990). As noted by Sutherland, Cressey, and Luckenbill (1992, 145), some individuals may become aggressive or act violent, just as others are likely to "sing, exchange dirty stories, or cry." In this regard, it has been suggested that disinhibition effects may be socially learned rather than pharmacologically induced (see Taylor 1983). According to proponents of this learned disinhibition hypothesis, people who consume large amounts of alcohol may simply behave consistently with their expectation that intoxication will result in disinhibition, and in turn aggression and otherwise disapproved sexual behavior. Related to this, others point out that normative expectations for behavior are relaxed for intoxicated persons. There is a disavowal of responsibility while under the influence of alcohol that, within reasonable limits, is regarded as socially acceptable. According to this perspective, drinking may be an excuse to engage in otherwise antisocial behavior (Collins 1983; Fagan 1990).

In sum, although pharmacological explanations have a broad-based appeal and provide important clues about the relationship between some types of drug use and some types of criminal behavior, these explanations are less than complete. Social scientists point out that the pharmacology of drug use takes place within a social context that may profoundly affect the way in which drugs and human behavior interact. As Mayfield points out, "we ... see the 'maudlin drunk,' the 'amorous drunk,' the 'gregarious drunk,' the 'belligerent drunk'" (1983, 142). If chemistry alone is responsible for antisocial behavior, we should expect to find a much more predictable response to such intoxication. Hence, we must look beyond these immediate pharmacological and biological mechanisms if we are to understand the drugs-crime connection.

Economic Explanations

It is possible that drug use may cause criminal behavior in a less direct way. Perhaps drug intoxication does not produce irrational or aggressive states pharmacologically, but rather, users of these drugs commit crimes to pay for an expensive habit. This explanation, which Goldstein (1985) calls the "economic-compulsive" model, is premised on two important assumptions: illegal drugs are *expensive*, and illegal drugs are *addicting*. It is important to note that both of these premises are directed toward *illegal* drugs. It is not true, of course, that all illegal drugs are expensive. Marijuana, for example, is relatively cheap, as are LSD and many illegally used prescription drugs such as Valium. Hence, those arguing that the causal linkage between drug use and crime is an economic one are generally referring to more expensive drugs such as heroin and cocaine.

The problematic character of these drugs is not only that they are expensive, however. They are also addicting, or at least strongly reinforcing. It is assumed (though not well documented empirically) that once users of drugs like heroin and cocaine become dependent on them, they will not be able to control their need for them. As Collins and colleagues (1985) describe it, these dependencies create an "inelastic demand." Furthermore, because these drugs are addictive, the user develops an increasing tolerance for the drug, requiring ever greater amounts to experience the same effect. This spiral of addiction to drugs that are already expensive thus makes it necessary for the user to engage in crime to feed his or her habit. These two factors—the expensive nature of the drugs and their addictive qualities—are a sure recipe for crime according to advocates of this perspective. This is why Goldstein (1985) has called this the "economic-compulsive" model.

Evaluation of Economic Explanations. We begin this evaluation of the economic-compulsive model by questioning one of its core assumptions, the compulsive nature of drug use. More specifically, it is not at all clear that use of and addiction to expensive illegal drugs creates the inelastic demand that forms the basis for the economic-compulsive explanation. The fact is that with heroin, cocaine, and other expensive drugs, users frequently lower the level of their use to accommodate unfavorable circumstances. A review of the literature by MacCoun, Kilmer, and Reuter (2003) reveals that addicts are very sensitive to the price of drugs and may respond to rising prices either by voluntarily withdrawing or by seeking treatment, rather than compulsively engaging in property crimes to feed the same habit.

The economic-compulsive model has fueled the policy agendas of the last four presidential administrations, and indeed, some empirical studies, which we describe in more detail in a later section on empirical research on drugs and crime, provide some support for such a model (Anglin and Speckart 1986, 1988; Anglin and Perrochet 1998; Ball et al. 1981, 1982, 1983; Speckart and Anglin 1986a). The series of studies conducted by John Ball and his associates was especially instrumental in the shaping of public policy, as it was formally reviewed in the senate hearings on alcoholism and drug abuse (U.S. Senate 1984). Despite the important character of these studies, it would be premature to conclude that drug use causes crime in the fashion that they suggest. In the first place, these studies were based on either arrestees or, in the case of the Anglin and Speckart studies, of methadone patients. We must be careful about making generalizations from such captive samples, as these individuals are not necessarily representative of the addict population at large. They are in trouble or are having difficulty coping with their habit, which is why they were arrested or entered a methadone maintenance program in the first place. Chaiken and Chaiken (1985) found, for example, that among incarcerated offenders, those who are arrested frequently are either emotionally disturbed and inept offenders who commit very few crimes but get caught nearly every time they do, or they are frequent users of drugs who commit crimes frequently, but get caught because they do not carefully plan their crimes to avoid detection. These studies do point to one important truth: people who use drugs with great frequency are more likely to be arrested than people who use infrequently. We should not infer from this, however, that high-frequency drug use causes the behavior that results in arrest. People who use drugs less frequently may commit just as many crimes, but they may also be more careful in how they commit these crimes.

It is also important not to confuse correlation with causation. Research by Ball and colleagues and by Anglin and Speckart demonstrate a *correlation* between drug use and criminal behavior among the addicts in their samples. It is quite tempting to assume from such data that drug use causes the criminal behavior. It is just as plausible, however, to conclude the inverse, that crime causes the drug use. This does not mean that people feel some overwhelming compulsion to use drugs as a result of committing crime. However, as we shall describe below, it is possible that crime is functionally related to subsequent use of drugs in a more or less causal way.

Alternatively, it is possible that both drug use and crime are the result of still other factors in the environment of the criminal addict. This possibility is discussed in greater detail in the section entitled "Common-Cause." The point we want to make here is that, although it intuitively makes sense to infer that drug use causes crime when higher levels of drug use are accompanied by more criminal activity, such judgements are premature. The relationship between drug use and criminal behavior is much more complex than this, and most research fails to demonstrate a clear, unambiguous causal relationship between drug use and crime. (See Chaiken and Chaiken 1990 and Hunt 1990 for reviews of this literature.) We now examine other ways in which the relationship between drug use and criminal behavior might be interpreted.

Crime Causes Drugs Use

Empirical research on the drugs-crime connection conducted by social scientists over the past four decades has led many observers of the drug scene to reevaluate the assumption that drug use causes criminal behavior. Studies conducted since the 1950s have quite consistently found that initial involvement in criminal activities begins substantially prior to experimentation with drugs for most users (Chaiken and Chaiken 1982; Greenberg and Adler 1974). Moreover, although increased levels of crime tended to accompany higher levels of expensive drug consumption, research by Faupel (1991) suggests that changes in the levels of drug use were typically *preceded* by increased criminal activity, as measured by criminal income. This suggests that the demand for drugs is quite elastic depending on the resources available, in contrast to the commonly held inelastic demand model (see Collins et al. 1985; Fields and Walters 1985). If this is the case, it does indeed make sense to suggest that perhaps crime causes drug use in some way.

The ethnographic evidence suggests one way in which crime may, in a sense, cause drug use. Several researchers have reported that various types of drugs may actually be used to facilitate the commission of crimes (Faupel 1991; Goldstein 1979) or that certain drugs are often used to celebrate a particularly successful criminal score (Faupel 1991; Walters 1985). Goldstein (1979) reports, for example, that it is common for prostitutes to turn to alcohol or other drugs as a means of coping with the sometimes harsh demands of their trade. Faupel (1991) also reports that drugs are used for quite functional reasons in committing other crimes. Armed robbers sometimes use alcohol and barbiturates to place them in a more belligerent frame of mind. Others reported taking amphetamines to provide the necessary energy to sustain an active criminal lifestyle. Most of the addicts interviewed by Faupel also used heroin at one or more times in their careers to help them in the commission of their crimes. Moreover, research by Collins and Messerschmidt (1993) suggests that the criminal lifestyle itself is often conducive to periods of partying and other leisure activities involving drinking and drug use.

These data suggest that, insofar as there is a causal relationship between drug use and crime, it may be opposite the expected direction. As experienced by the addicts in the respective studies of Goldstein and Faupel, drugs are often used to support and maintain a criminal lifestyle, not vice versa. At the same time, the proceeds of crime are also used to pay for the drugs that these addicts consume. These studies reflect a growing body of literature suggesting a reciprocal relationship between drug use and crime (see White and Gorman 2000).

Common-Cause Explanations

Social scientists are increasingly of the opinion that it does not make sense to speak in simple causal terms when describing the relationship between drug use and criminal behavior. Both behaviors, they argue, are inextricably interwoven with the broader subculture of which they are a part. That is, crime cannot be understood simply as a response to a drug craving, nor can drug use be understood simply as an accessory to crime. These are mutually supportive activities, and both are linked with other variables that encourage criminal behavior and drug use. The relationship between drug use and crime is, in this sense spurious.

A **spurious relationship** is one that appears causal, but in fact both variables are related in the same way to a third variable. The result is a *correlation* between the two variables in question. Observers of the drug scene note that most drug-using criminals begin committing crimes at an earlier age than they begin using drugs, or at least expensive drugs such as heroin or cocaine that are purported to cause crime because of their addictive and costly nature. Rather than interpret this sequence to mean that crime causes drug use, however, the common-cause explanation understands both drug use and criminal behavior to be products of a cultural system that promotes and rewards these behaviors. Studies have found, for example, that many factors such as delinquent peers, which are strongly related to delinquency, are also related to drug and alcohol use (Elliot et al. 1989; Goode 1972; White et al. 1987, 1999). Other variants of this common-cause model hold that drug use and criminal or delinquent behavior are merely coincidental, that they serve similar functions for individuals who engage in them, or that both behaviors are manifestations of a single, underlying attribute or characteristic. A growing body of research supports this notion, particularly for serious offenders. The following sections examine two types of common-cause explanations. The first, which we have labeled the "problem behavior syndrome" (see Jessor and Jessor 1977), identifies factors in the biographies and experiences of drug-using criminals that account for both types of behaviors. The second common-cause explanation focuses specifically on subcultures of crime and drug use.

Problem Behavior Syndrome as a Common Cause

Jessor and Jessor (1977) suggest that both delinquency and drug use are two of a number of nonconforming expressions of independence from adult authority figures that function to assist youth in identifying with delinquent peer groups. The authors refer to the recurring, persistent presence of delinquent behaviors as a **problem behavior syndrome**, which includes alcohol and drug use, delinquency, and being sexually active (Donovan and Jessor 1985). Subsequent research provides support for this argument, finding that these various dimensions of unconventional behavior reflect a more general dynamic at work, that being the need for peer acceptance (Donovan et al. 1988). In that regard, Huizinga and Jakob-Chien (1998) show in particular that drug use among these juveniles is associated with serious delinquency.

Other research, not necessarily based upon the Jessor findings, clarifies a number of elements associated with this relationship among serious offenders. Research among club drug users by Krebs and Steffey (2005) reveals that they are much more likely to come from families with a criminal history and more likely to have been a victim of violence than are nonusers. Similar to findings from the Jessor studies, these users are also more likely to engage in other high-risk behaviors such as carrying weapons, or having unprotected sex. Osgood, Johnston, O'Malley, and Bachman (1988) propose that the simultaneous occurrence of drug use and delinquency/crime illustrates the phenomenon referred to as "generality of deviance." Their research suggests that behaviors such as alcohol and drug use, delinquency, sexual promiscuity, poor school performance, among others, are all reflections of this single attribute. The authors contend that the debate over whether drug use precedes delinquency or vice versa is irrelevant for these offenders because both activities tend to be mutually reinforcing. Similarly, Gottfredson and Hirschi's (1990) influential work proposes that substance use and other manifestations of deviant and delinquent behavior are characteristics of people with low self-control. Finally, Terrie Moffitt (1993, 1997) provides a compelling argument that delinquency and drug use during adolescence reflects the desire to mimic adult behavior. Moffitt distinguishes between adolescence-limited delinquency and "life-course persistent" offending. For the former, experimentation with drug use, delinquency, and sexual activity is in some ways a natural occurrence during the transition from childhood to adult status. As these youths enter adulthood, delinquent behavior decreases substantially or altogether because they begin taking adult roles and responsibilities. On the other hand, life-course persistent offenders exhibit antisocial behavior at early ages and continue into and throughout adulthood.

Drug-Crime Subculture as a Common Cause
Still others have identified a more general subcultural context promoting both drug use and criminal behavior. Street drug subcultures tend to encourage both drug use and crime in a number of ways. (See also Chapter 10 on drug-using careers.) In the first place, these subcultures provide a network of friends and associates who possess drugs or have means of obtaining drugs. It is thus quite natural for young people with acquaintances who use drugs to experiment themselves. Moreover, it is often these same acquaintances that introduce the would-be drug user to a criminal lifestyle. Life history data obtained by Faupel (1991) reveals that early experimentation with delinquency and crime is usually pursued with others who are often experimenting with drugs and crime themselves.

Drug subcultures not only provide a network of drug-using and criminal acquaintances, but with them a vehicle for transmitting the necessary knowledge for successfully maintaining a criminal and drug-using lifestyle (Biernacki 1979; Faupel 1986, 1987a, 1991; Gould et al. 1974; Sackman et al. 1978). The ability to acquire a sufficient income to support a drug habit requires some degree of criminal sophistication, whether one's crime is shoplifting, prostitution, burglary, robbery, or any of a number of crimes that users of expensive drugs rely on for income.

Still another important component of subcultures of drug use and crime is a stratification system that confers status and prestige on those who can acquire and consume large amounts of drugs, and who demonstrate a mastery of the skills described above (Biernacki 1979; Faupel 1991; Rosenbaum 1981a). Accompanying this system of stratification is a set of norms that define appropriate means for pursuing criminal and drug-using activities (Faupel 1987b, 1991; Hanson et al. 1985; Sutter 1969). Together, the normative and stratification dynamics operative in drug-using subcultures encourage drug use and crime among subcultural participants.

The subculture of drug use also provides the context for understanding violent behavior among drug users. In a now classic article, Paul Goldstein (1985) attempts to explain violence among drug users by suggesting a "tripartite conceptual model" that includes three possible explanations for violent behavior in this population. The first two explanations—a direct pharmacological effect and an economic-compulsive effect—correspond to the two explanatory models we summarized earlier in the "Drug Use Causes Crime" paradigm. Goldstein's third explanation, which he has termed *systemic violence*, suggests that violence is an intrinsic part of the culture and economy of drug use, and that it is endemic to the underground economy of illicit drug use. Violence arises for various reasons, including territorial disputes between dealers, or robberies of drug dealers in retaliation for being shorted in the past—a response that might result in even further retaliation from the victimized dealer. Violence may also be inflicted on an informer or on a user who repeatedly comes up short and fails to pay a mounting debt to a dealer. In all of these cases, violence is used as a means of settling disputes because the courts are not available as an avenue to achieve justice in the world of illicit drugs. Subsequent research by Goldstein and his colleagues (1989, 1991) provides evidence for systemic violence, as well as the more commonly understood pharmacologically induced violence among cocaine and crack users.

Evaluation of Common-Cause Explanations

All common-cause explanations share a focus on extraneous variables that affect both drug use and criminal behavior. Drug-using criminals do not exist in a vacuum but live their lives in a broader social context that affects their behavior, both drug use and crime, in profound ways. Problem behavior syndrome explanations point to dynamics such as the need for peer acceptance or establishing independence from adult authority figures. The subcultural perspective understands the drugs-crime connection in the context of a broader cultural and interactional framework that defines and encourages both sets of activities. Seen in this way, it does not make sense to speak of "cause" when considering the relationship between drug use and crime. Goode summarizes the subcultural position on the relationship between marijuana use and crime, an observation that might be applied to other types of drug use as well:

> We are led overwhelmingly to the conclusion that *marijuana users tend to be somewhat more likely to commit crimes solely because they are part of a drug-using subculture*; the actual properties of marijuana appear to be completely unassociated with criminal behavior. Anyone (*whether he uses marijuana or not*) who makes friends and becomes involved with others who use drugs— especially others who use drugs in addition to and aside from marijuana—stands a higher likelihood of committing offenses, simply because this segment of the population tends to be more lax about obeying the law. It is merely because marijuana users tend to associate with others who are part of this subculture that their crime rate is somewhat higher. In other words, the marijuana-crime relationship—in terms of the causal or effects model—*is completely spurious*. (1972, 451; emphasis in original)

11.1 Regular users of expensive drugs rely on a variety of criminal enterprises such as burglary, the proceeds of which are used for the purchase of drugs. The question before researchers and students of drug use is whether or not addiction to drugs actually causes crime, whether crime facilitates drug use, or whether both drugs and crime are a function of other factors such as the influence of drug subcultures. (Photo © iPhotoStock.com)

Common-cause explanations are both profoundly sociological in their understanding of the relationship between drug use and crime. They are sociological because they implicitly recognize the broader social context in which these behaviors occur. This is not to suggest that no causal mechanisms link crime with drug use. Causal mechanisms, however, cannot offer a complete explanation for the correlation that we see between drug use and criminal behavior.

Empirical Understanding of Drug Use, Crime, and Violence

The relationship between drug use and criminal activity has been extensively studied by social scientists, indeed perhaps more so than any other topic in the field. Furthermore, this is a relationship about which there is very little consensus, as we have seen in the previous section. The purpose of this section is to examine more closely the empirical evidence regarding the drugs-crime connection. This review does not attempt an exhaustive literature review, as literally hundreds of studies have examined this question (see Gandossy et al. 1980; Greenberg and Adler 1974; Speckart and Anglin 1986b; and White and Gorman 2000 for more extensive literature reviews). Rather, we shall discuss a small number of studies that represent the variety of methodologies used and results obtained by social scientists doing research in this area.

Empirical Evidence from Official Sources

Official sources of data on drug use and crime include primarily prison and arrest statistics. Data from each of these sources is discussed below.

Prison Statistics

The most widely distributed data on drug use and crime using prison statistics are disseminated by the Bureau of Justice Statistics, a division of the National Institute of Justice in Washington, D.C. These data are drawn from thousands of inmates in state prisons and local jails who constitute a representative sampling of the population of jail and prison inmates in the United States. These inmates are then interviewed regarding their drug use history. Some 83 percent of inmates in state prisons used drugs on at least one occasion, and about 70 percent used on a regular basis at some point in their lives. The data further reveal that more than half used during the month prior to the offense for which they were incarcerated, and nearly a third used drugs at the time of their offense (Mumola and Karberg 2006). These percentages are substantially higher than for the general population, where 59.2 percent of those aged 18 to 34 (the highest drug-using age group) reported using illicit drugs at some time, and only 19.4 percent reported any such use during the previous month (SAMHSA 2005). It is also worthwhile to also point out that approximately half of the state prison inmates reported that they were under the influence of drugs at the time they committed the offense for which they were incarcerated.

These data make it clear that incarcerated offender populations have much higher rates of drug use than the general population. Statistics such as these suggest, preliminarily at least, that drug use may play a role in criminal behavior. Indeed, the finding that approximately one-third of the inmates sampled reported being under the influence of drugs at the time they committed their offense provides some support for the pharmacological explanation discussed above. Care must be taken in the interpretation of these data, however. As we emphasized in the previous section, the fact that incarcerated offenders report higher rates of drug use than the general population does not necessarily mean that the use of these drugs *caused* the user to commit the crimes in question.

Arrest Statistics

In Chapter 4, we introduced the Arrestee Drug Abuse Monitoring Program (ADAM). You will recall that sampled arrestees participate on a voluntary basis, providing a urine sample and agreeing to an interview with an ADAM staff person. The urinalysis provides objective evidence of whether or not one has been using drugs within one to two days prior to arrest, in the case of most drugs, and within a month prior to arrest in the case of PCP or marijuana. In addition, the interviews ask arrestees about their prior use of drugs, means of administration, and so forth (Wish and Gropper 1990).

ADAM data reveal that approximately 74 percent of arrestees test positive for one or more drugs at the time of arrest (Zhang, n.d.), though some offense types are more highly represented than others. Offenses claiming the highest percentage of drug positives are drug offenses and property crimes, typically about 80 and 70 percent, respectively. Drug positives are less represented among violent offenders, though in most cities, more than half of violent arrestees tested positive (ADAM 2000).

The high percentage of arrestees testing positive for drugs, regardless of the offense for which they are arrested, further confirms the strong correlation between criminal behavior and drug use. Again, however, we must be cautious in how we interpret these data. ADAM results are often misinterpreted as providing evidence for a causal link between drug use and crime. The urine test results simply do not provide the definitive evidence necessary to draw a conclusion about the role of drug use on crime. The drug use may have occurred prior to the crime, after the crime, just before arrest, or even after arrest while in detention. The test, therefore, indicates nothing about whether the drugs, or the need for drugs, was a motive for the crime. In addition, the test results say nothing about whether the arrestee was a chronic user or a casual experimenter. The results do indicate the types of drugs recently used by arrestees in a jurisdiction and changes in use trends (Wish and Gropper 1990, 369). Hence, although these data are dramatic and are often used as the strongest evidence yet for the causal role of drug use and addiction in criminality, other approaches are required to assess more adequately the drugs-crime relationship.

Empirical Evidence from Self-Reports

In an effort to measure more precisely the relationship between drug use and crime, research efforts have come to rely increasingly on self-report methodologies. Self-reporting carries recognized problems with under-reporting and other potential sources of bias, but there is a general consensus among researchers using this method that it is possible to mitigate most sources of bias through careful choice of interviewers, developing validity checks within questionnaires (typically by asking the same question in different ways and locations in the interview), and comparing results with findings from other researchers as well as with official data (called *triangulation*). These safeguards, which have been developed over several decades of self-report studies, have provided reasonable assurance to all but the most skeptical that the advantages of self-report methodologies in allowing more detailed and directly focused data far outweigh the potential disadvantages that may occur as a result of potential under- or misleading reporting.

Numerous specific self-report methodologies have evolved to examine the relationship between drug use and crime. Four broad types of methodologies are described here: correlational studies, sequence studies, longitudinal studies, and ethnographic studies. The differences among these methodologies are not always sharply defined, and some individual studies may appropriately be considered under more than one of these categories.

Correlational Studies

Correlational studies compare the level of crime among samples of drug users with criminal activities of those who do not use drugs. (Alternatively, these studies may compare the level of drug use among criminal and noncriminal samples.) These studies generally, though not universally, find that drug users are much more criminally involved than nonusers. Harrison and colleagues (2001) find, for example, that alcohol, marijuana, and cocaine use are all strongly correlated with violence. James Derzon and Mark Lipsey (1999), in a meta-analysis of marijuana use and delinquency, found that current marijuana users were much more likely to engage in nonviolent forms of delinquency than were nonusers. Interestingly, however, when examining this relationship over time, prior marijuana use was not related to later delinquency, though prior delinquency was predictive of later marijuana use. Other studies of delinquents, however, found that as individuals progress from using only alcohol and marijuana to using other drugs, they also tend to become more involved in delinquency (Elliot et al. 1989; Fagan et al. 1987). Research among young people using club drugs is less clear. Krebs and Steffey (2005) find that club drug users are more likely to engage in violent crime as well as drug dealing. Research published at the same time by Hendrickson and Gerstein (2005), however, suggests a contradictory pattern: ecstasy use was actually higher among the general population than among a sample of arrestees.

Studies conducted among adults generally suggest a correlation between drug use and criminal behavior. Such correlations are found among heroin users (Hammersley and Morrison 1987; Inciardi and Pottieger 1998), cocaine and crack users (Johnson et al. 1994), and alcohol users (Collins and Messerschmidt 1993; Zhang et al. 1997). It should be noted that, especially among cocaine and crack users, much of the criminal activity consists of drug dealing and other crimes related to drug distribution.

It must be remembered that studies finding a correlation between drug use and criminal behavior are just that, *correlational*. Correlation does not establish causation, and when it comes to the relationship between drug use and criminal behavior, we have already pointed out that it is quite plausible to suggest that the causal connection might go the other way (criminal involvement leading to drug use), or even more likely, that both drug use and crime are related to other common individual, social, and cultural factors. Self-report research has attempted to overcome the limitations of correlational methodologies by establishing a temporal ordering of drug use and crime. We examine this research next.

Sequence Studies

Studies that use what we call the "sequence" methodology represent a higher level of sophistication in understanding the causal relationship between drug use in crime, in our view. This is done by examining the *sequence of initiation* into drug use and criminal activity. Respondents are asked to indicate when they first began using drugs and when they first committed a crime. The logic behind this kind of questioning is that if drug-using criminals began using drugs before they committed their first crime, there is a stronger basis for drawing a causal connection between the two behaviors. If, on the other hand, one's first crime is committed prior to the time they first began using drugs, the common-sense assumption that drug use causes crime must be reexamined. In either event, by ascertaining the sequence of initiation into drug use and crime, researchers have been able to move beyond simply establishing a correlation between drug use and crime. Establishing that one set of activities occurs before or after the other provides at least a rudimentary basis for drawing some conclusions about the causal relationship between drug use and crime.

One of the most extensive studies utilizing self-report data from street respondents (those not incarcerated or in treatment) was conducted by James Inciardi over a several-year period beginning in the1970s. Inciardi and his colleagues interviewed street heroin addicts in several major cities throughout the country. These street addicts were asked a series of questions regarding their drug-using and criminal histories. They were asked how old they were when they first began using each of a list of some 20 different drugs, including alcohol. In addition, they were asked to indicate how old they were when they committed their first criminal offense, as well as when they began to use drugs and commit crimes on a regular basis.

Table 11.1 presents the median ages at which the street addicts from Inciardi's Miami sample began to commit crimes and to use various drugs. Table 11.1 reveals that the only drug use that preceded the first crime committed by the male addicts in Inciardi's sample was alcohol and, for female addicts, marijuana. Other types of drug use, however, which are more expensive and usually suspected in criminal behavior, did not begin until some two to four years following the first crime committed by these addicts.

It should be pointed out that these data were collected prior to the introduction of crack cocaine. Inciardi and his colleagues did, however, do follow-up studies among crack users (Inciardi and Pottieger 1994; McCoy, Inciardi, et al. 1995). Their findings nearly mirrored the sequence found in the earlier study among heroin users, except that the ages for all initiation experiences of the crack users were one to three years earlier than the 1970s heroin users. These findings are also reported in Table 11.1. Inciardi's findings raise some perplexing questions about the drugs-crime connection. They preclude any simplistic causal explanation that involvement with drugs directly causes one to begin committing crimes. Indeed, these data provide stronger support for the idea that involvement in criminal activities has a causal effect on eventual drug-using behavior.

Table 11.1. Sequence of initial drug use and crime among heroin and crack users in Miami, Florida.

	Median age			
Activity	1970s Heroin study		1990s Crack study	
	Males (N = 236)	*Females* (N = 117)	*Males* (N = 114)	*Females* (N = 84)
First alcohol use	12.8	13.8	10.0	10.0
First alcohol intoxication	13.3	13.9	—	—
First crime	15.1	15.9	14.0	14.0
First illicit drug use	15.2	15.2	14.0	14.0
First marijuana use	15.5	15.4	14.0	14.0
First arrest	17.2	18.3	15.0	15.0
First barbiturate use (pill)	17.5	17.0	15.0	15.0
First heroin use	18.7	18.2	17.0	16.5
First continuous heroin use	19.2	18.4	—	—
First cocaine use	19.7	18.7	16.0	16.0
First crack use	—	—	21.0	20.0

Sources: Adapted from Inciardi, 1979; Inciardi and Pottieger, 1994; and McCoy et al., 1995.

One approach to understanding the causal relationship between drug use and crime is to determine the sequence of initiation into drug use and crime. This is typically done by asking drug-using criminals the age at which they first used various drugs and the age at which they first committed crime. If drug use causes crime, it must be established that drug use began *prior* to criminal activities. As these data by Inciardi and his colleagues show, criminal activities begin substantially prior to first experience with most types of drugs other than alcohol. Such data such thus fail to support the contention that drug use causes crime.

Another study using a slightly different methodology for establishing the sequence of initiation into drug use and crime was conducted by Jan and Marcia Chaiken in the early 1980s for the RAND Corporation (Chaiken and Chaiken 1982). The Chaikens surveyed some 2200 male inmates in Michigan, California, and Texas prisons. They found, first, that 35 percent of their respondents reported that they had never used drugs. Among those who were drug users, however, their data suggest that the onset of crime is just as likely to precede first drug use as vice versa. Just over 20 percent of the drug-using sample (10 percent of the total sample) reported that their drug use began prior to their first crime, but more than 26 percent (12.5 percent of the total sample) reported that they began committing crimes at an earlier age than they began using drugs. More than 52 percent of the drug-using sample (25 percent of the total sample) reported that they began using drugs and crime about the same time.

Chaiken and Chaiken's findings further call into question both the pharmacological and economical drugs-cause-crime hypotheses. Although approximately 20 percent of their sample reported earlier drug use involvement, the overwhelming majority of these inmates began using drugs either coterminously with or substantially after they began engaging in criminal activities. Moreover, when inmates were further asked about their motivations for committing crimes, only 26 percent of those using "hard" or expensive drugs cited a need for money for drugs as one of the primary reasons for their first crime. Indeed, less than half (46 percent) indicated that needing money for drugs was an important or very important reason for later criminal activity, and only 2 percent cited their drug involvement as the only important motive for later criminal activity.

One final study examining the sequence of initiation into drug use and crime, using still a different methodology, is the National Youth Survey, an extensive study of more than 1,700 youth who were aged 11 to 17 in 1976 and were interviewed seven different times over a 10-year period. At each interview, these youth were queried regarding their participation in minor (nonindex) crimes, major (index) crimes, alcohol use, marijuana use, and polydrug use. These responses were then compared to determine the sequence of initiation into each of these sets of behaviors.

Results from these surveys have been extensively reported by Delbert Elliot and colleagues (1989). They report a substantial history of criminal behavior before the onset of drug use for most of the youth in their sample. Among those youth for whom it was possible to ascertain a temporal ordering (a temporal ordering was not ascertainable if the first reporting of both sets of behaviors occurred in the same interview period), these researchers found the following:

- Involvement in minor (nonindex) offenses:
  - preceded first alcohol use in 63 percent of the cases
  - preceded first marijuana use in 93 percent of the cases
  - preceded first polydrug use in 99 percent of the cases

- Involvement in major (index) offenses:
  - followed first marijuana use 63 percent of the cases
  - preceded polydrug use in 67 percent of the cases

Collectively, studies that focus on the sequence of initiation into drug using and criminal behavior provide quite convincing empirical evidence that criminal behavior on the part of drug users cannot be explained by the simple cause-effect relationships that have commonly been forwarded. These data provide no evidence whatsoever that young people somehow get seduced into using drugs, develop a habit, and are then forced to commit crimes to pay for that habit. The only types of drug use that precede criminal behavior in the biographies of most drug-using criminals are alcohol and marijuana. Neither of these are the sorts of expensive and addictive drugs that are depicted as having the power over addicts to cause them to engage in criminal activities. Studies examining the sequence of drug use and crime initiation clearly and consistently call for a rejection of this rather simplistic understanding of the relationship between drug use and criminal behavior. As we shall see below, however, the causal relationship between drug use and crime may be understood in more complex terms than the sequence studies are able to address.

Longitudinal Studies

Partly in response to the implications suggested by findings such as those described above, a number of researchers have argued that it is not sufficient merely to determine the sequence of initiation into drug use and criminal behavior. Rather, they argue, it is necessary to examine the relationship between drug use and crime over time throughout the careers of addict criminals. These researchers correctly point out that, although the onset of criminal behavior patterns may precede experimentation with drugs, or at least with expensive drugs, it may well be that over the course of their careers, as addicts develop more sizable habits, the tolerance that they develop for these drugs makes a criminal lifestyle increasingly mandatory. Hence, although the hypothesis that drug use causes crime is necessarily rejected as applied to the early, experimental stage of drug-using and criminal careers, this hypothesis may have more plausibility when considered with respect to the overall careers of addicts. Studies examining the relationship between drug use and crime over a more extended period of time, longitudinal studies, generally attempt to identify periods at various times in an addict's biography wherein levels of drug use and crime are compared. This section examines three such studies, each which utilizes a slightly different methodology to ascertain the relationship between drug use and crime over time.

A widely cited series of studies was conducted by David Nurco, John Ball, and their associates among arrested addicts, initially in the Baltimore area (Ball et al. 1981, 1982, 1983) and later in New York (Nurco et al. 1988; Hanlon et al. 1990). The research team interviewed addicts in these areas extensively about their drug use and crime over their lifetimes. Specifically, these researchers identified biographical periods when the addicts in their sample were at risk, meaning that they were not in prison or in an institutional setting, and found that, on average, these addicts were on opiates 61.6 percent of the time they were at risk (Ball et al. 1981). Addicts were closely questioned regarding levels of crime during times that they were addicted (which they defined as using regularly over a period of at least a month) and during times when they were not addicted. Rather than calculate the total number of criminal events, the researchers simply recorded the number of *days* that one or more criminal events took place. In this way, their study sought to compare the regularity with which criminal activity took place during addicted and nonaddicted periods.

Their results are quite remarkable, given the findings of the studies described in the preceding section: the number of crime days per year was substantially higher during periods of addiction. Indeed, they were more than six times as likely to have committed a crime on any given day while they were addicted. Later research by Kinlock, O'Grady, and Hanlon (2003) used the same basic methodology of crime days to examine the impact of drug use on crime in the six-month period immediately prior to incarceration. This research found that the total number of crime days leading up to incarceration was significantly affected by the frequency of cocaine and opiate use, as well as by the number of different types of drugs used. These data thus strongly suggest that, although drug use may not precede crime in the sequence of initiation, criminal activity picks up dramatically when addicts are using expensive drugs on a daily basis.

A slightly different methodology was employed by Anglin, Speckart, and their colleauges as they attempted to gauge the relationship between drug use and crime over time among methadone patients in California (Anglin and Speckart 1986, 1988; Anglin and Hser 1987; Speckart and Anglin 1986a). These researchers attempted to identify critical points in time in the biographies of the 671 male addicts they interviewed: when narcotic drugs were first tried, the onset of addiction (as defined by the first time narcotics were used daily for a period of at least 30 days), and the termination of addiction. They then queried their respondents regarding the number of arrests during each of these periods, as well as the percentage of their time involved in property crime, the average number of crime days (see Ball et al., described above), and the average number of crime dollars for each period (Anglin and Speckart 1988). Similar to the Ball and Nurco research, Anglin and Speckart found that the addicts in their sample were substantially more involved in crime when they were using narcotics on a daily basis, whether measured by percentage of time spent on crime, crime days, or criminal income.

These findings reinforce the Baltimore and New York findings of Ball, Nurco, and their colleagues. Although there is certainly evidence for preaddiction criminality, there is also a substantial increase in criminal activity after the onset of addiction. Regardless of the measure of criminality employed, these differences are dramatic and significant. Anglin and Speckart concur with the conclusion by Ball and colleagues that there is a causal relationship between narcotics use and criminal behavior.

While the Baltimore–New York and California research discussed above was under way, Bruce Johnson and his associates were devising a rather novel strategy in New York City (Johnson et al. 1985). Their methodology was unique in that they did not question addicts regarding their drug use and criminal behavior over their entire career, as the two studies discussed above had done. Rather, the Johnson team interviewed several cohorts of addicts who were using varying levels of drugs at the time of interview. These New York addicts were interviewed daily for a period of five days, followed by weekly interviews over the next four weeks. During each session, respondents were asked to relate specifically what crimes they had committed and what drugs they had used *that day* or *during the preceding week*. Similarly, they were asked to indicate whether they used any of a list of drugs each day/week they were

Table 11.2. Average number of crimes per year and average annual criminal income of street addicts in New York City.

Type of activity	Heroin use group		
	Irregular	Regular	Daily
Average number of crimes			
Non-drug crimes[a]	116	162	209
Drug business crimes[b]	245	823	880
Miscellaneous drug activity[c]	95	177	283
Minor crimes (non-cash)[d]	59	54	76
Total crimes	515	1,217	1,447
Average annual income			
Non-drug crime income[a]	$2,885	$5,719	$8,540
Drug business income[b]	1,566	1,402	2,752
Miscellaneous drug income[c]	1,417	3,965	7,418
Minor crime income (non-cash)[d]	136	117	110
Total criminal income	6,004	11,203	18,820

[a]Includes robbery, burglary, shoplifting (for resale), "other larcenies," forgery, con games, prostitution, pimping, and "other illegal."
[b]Includes drug sales, steering and touting (for money), copping (for money).
[c]Includes drug thefts, steering and touting (for drugs), copping (for drugs), avoided expenditures for drugs.
[d]Includes shoplifting (for own use) and fare evasion.
Source: Johnson et al., 1985, Tables 7-2 and 7-4. Reprinted with permission of the publisher.

interviewed. In this way, the Johnson team was able to avoid the problems of respondents not being able to remember crime and drug use from months or even years earlier. The sample was then divided into three user groups, based on the frequency of their heroin use: "irregular users" used heroin two or fewer days per week; "regular users" used three, four, or five days per week; and "daily users" used six or seven days per week. The level of criminal activity for the three groups was then compared.

The findings of the Johnson team are not quite as dramatic as those reported by the Ball and Nurco team or by the Anglin and Speckart research, but the trends are nevertheless consistent with the Baltimore and California studies. Table 11.2 compares both the average number of crimes committed and the average dollar value of these crimes across the three user groups. Overall, daily users committed nearly three times the number of crimes than irregular users. Furthermore, the average annual criminal income of daily users was more than three times that of the irregular users.

Johnson and colleagues also discovered that heroin addicts are much less criminally involved, at least in the traditional sense, than is commonly believed. Rather, they rely on a number of quasicriminal activities to enhance their access to drugs. The addicts in their study reported that much of their income derived from such activities as *touting* and *steering* (directing potential customers to fellow dealers), renting their works, *hitting* (injecting) less-experienced users, and testing drugs for local dealers. Typically, they would be remunerated for these services with heroin or other drugs rather than with cash. Hence, by interviewing addicts on a daily and weekly basis regarding their drug-using and criminal activities, Johnson and his colleagues demonstrated that addicts are able to maintain a drug-using lifestyle in many ways, including but not limited to predatory criminal activities.

Using the same methodology (except that interviews were conducted over eight weeks rather than four), Goldstein and colleagues (1991) examined the relationship between cocaine use and violence. The results of this study once again reveal the complexity of the relationship between drug use and crime. It was found that whereas the frequency of cocaine use bears no relationship to violence, the volume of cocaine use was accompanied by higher levels of violence among males, though not among females. Women who used large amounts of cocaine were, however, more likely to be victims of violence.

The longitudinal studies that we have reviewed here portray a dramatically different picture of the relationship between drug use and criminal behavior than did the earlier studies, which sought to establish the sequence of initiation into drug use and criminal behavior. How do we account for these findings, which seem so diametrically opposed? First, we must recognize that the sequence studies and the longitudinal studies are, in fact, measuring two very different phenomena. Studies using the sequence methodology seek only to determine patterns of initiation into drug use and crime. Any statement of the causal relationship between these two activities is limited to whether or not drug use plays a role in an individual becoming involved in crime in the first place. The answer is that it does not. The longitudinal studies, on the other hand, seek to determine whether, once addicted, greater levels of criminal activity are required to maintain a drug-using lifestyle than would be the case if the addict were not using drugs or using them less extensively. The answer is that increased levels of drug use are clearly accompanied by increased levels of criminal behavior.

Despite their greater level of methodological sophistication, however, the longitudinal studies fail to establish causality definitively. That is, although they demonstrate that higher levels of criminal activity correspond to periods of daily use or addiction, such an analysis remains correlational in nature. These studies fail to demonstrate which came first, for example, an increase in the level of drug use or an increase in the level of criminal activity. Again, it is assumed that addicts increase their criminal involvement in response to the demands of their addiction. However, as we have demonstrated in the theoretical discussion earlier, it is also plausible to suggest that the level of one's drug consumption increases only after one's income (typically acquired through criminal means) expands sufficiently to support such a habit. To assess adequately the relationship between drug use and crime over time, methodologies are needed that are more sensitive to the temporal dynamics of addict careers, such as those employed by more qualitatively oriented ethnographers.

Ethnographic Studies

Beginning in the late 1960s, a number of researchers began seriously to question many of the common-sense notions about drug addicts and addiction, such as the idea that drug addicts suffered from addiction-prone personalities, or that they were retreatists and double failures who preferred to drop out of society rather than to compete in it. These researchers argued that it was necessary to attempt to understand the world of drug addiction from the perspective of the addict himself or herself. To gain this subjective understanding, it was necessary to utilize a methodology that allowed the addict to frame the issues, in essence, to permit the respondent to do the talking. Most ethnographic accounts have not focused specifically on the relationship between drug use and criminal behavior as we have discussed it here. Rather, the general lifestyle dynamics of drug users are described, including both criminal and drug-using activities. Among the first to describe the lifestyles of street drug users was the urban anthropologist Edward Preble (Preble and Casey 1969). In this groundbreaking article, Preble and Casey depict the lifestyles of heroin addicts in rather revolutionary terms. They maintain that the heroin addict is not a sick, pathological individual suffering from an addictive personality, or a retreatist or double failure who drops out because he is not able to succeed in the conventional world of work. In their view, the heroin addict is a skillful entrepreneur who successfully meets the challenges of a lifestyle of addiction:

> Heroin use today by lower class, primarily minority group, persons does not provide for them a euphoric escape from the psychological and social problems which derive from ghetto life. On the contrary, it provides a motivation and rationale for the pursuit of a meaningful life, albeit a socially deviant one. The activities these individuals engage in and the relationships they have in the course of their quest for heroin are far more important than the minimal analgesic and euphoric effects of the small amount of heroin available to them. If they can be said to be addicted, it is not so much to heroin as to the entire career of a heroin user. The heroin user is, in a way, like the compulsively hard-working business executive whose ostensible goal is the acquisition of money, but whose real satisfaction is in meeting the inordinate challenge he creates for himself. (21)

The insights that Preble and Casey provided were soon echoed by other ethnographers (Biernacki 1979; Hanson et al. 1985; Rosenbaum 1981a; Sackman et al.

DRUGS AND EVERYDAY LIFE

Manny's Story on Drug Use and Crime

Robbery worked for me for such a long time for two basic reasons. First, I was lucky. God must take care of dope fiends. Because for almost two solid years, while on a constant heroin run that cost on the average of 150 dollars per day to maintain, I pulled off robberies almost daily. Seldom a week went by without at least one or two major robberies. In all this time I was only busted once—at the end of the run. The sun shines on the just and the unjust; I believe it!

Second, robbery worked for me because it is a swift, and relatively sure, method of criminal endeavor. I mean, in between fixes and noddings I could venture forth from my apartment, meet my partners, pull the caper off, and return to my pad—sometimes within fifteen minutes! New York is wall-to-wall people, sidewalks are crowded with folks doing their thing. It is a simple matter to step out four or five blocks, step in to one of a thousand or so neighborhood shops, score, and go home. People don't have the slightest idea how simple it is....Other times we'd just walk out the door, find a likely place that had cash, hit it, and hole up for a few hours until the local cops changed shifts. When nobody is killed on a robbery, shift change at the station house usually kills the investigation. They got so many unsolved robberies in downtown

New York they could paper the county with them. Sometimes people don't even report it when they're hit, especially if they don't carry insurance or haven't paid it up.

After we'd been together for a while I turned my friends onto robbing connections and bookies. I figured, what the hell. The bookie's money is just as good as the grocer's. And I knew where a thousand nag parlors and numbers shops were located. Sometimes there's more money in cigar stores and shoeshine joints than in the local bank. And they bend easy. They don't want to get blown away for mere money. You can always score money in the underworld, but you only live once regardless of your game. Bookies don't like to get hit, but what can they do if they can't kill you? Can they call the cops? No. Can they spend a a lot of time looking for you if they don't know who you are? No. So they usually just mark it off and go on taking care of business....

Yes, it's a kick! You know, it's really a choice thrill to pull off a caper against the other underworld operator. It's like a game. It doesn't do violence to the "underworld code of honor" either, the way I figure it. It's like legitimate competition, sort of like manifest destiny or the survival of the fittest.

Source: Excerpted from Richard P. Rettig, Manual J. Torres, and Gerald R. Garrett. *Manny: A Criminal-Addict's Story.* Boston: Houghton Mifflin Company, 1977, pp. 59–61. Reprinted with permission.

1978; Sutter 1969). These studies portray street heroin users as highly skilled entrepreneurs, actively engaged in a meaningful criminal lifestyle. This character of addict criminality is depicted by the street term *main hustle* that implies a criminal specialization of sorts, whereby addicts develop the requisite skills and expertise to maintain a successful criminal lifestyle. Much of the proceeds of these crimes is spent on drugs, but the ethnographic evidence strongly suggests that throughout much of their careers, criminal addicts are not driven to crime by their habits, as the drug-use-causes-crime hypothesis might suggest. On the contrary, criminal involvement provides its own rewards in the sense of accomplishment and increased stature in the subculture when one is successful in his or her criminal endeavors.

A small number of ethnographic studies have directly examined the relationship between drug use and crime. All of these studies reveal that this relationship is much more complex than either drug-use-causes-crime or crime-causes-drug-use, or for that matter, that both drug use and crime are somehow caused by a common set of variables. Smith and Stephens' 1976 study of 30 recently institutionalized addicts in New York State examined the sequence of (1) scoring (making money, typically through criminal means), (2) levels of drug use, and (3) subsequent criminal activity during their last month on the street (prior to their institutionalization). The authors found a total of 28 different patterns among their respondents, although most criminal/drug-using events fell into one of three patterns. The first, and most common pattern was that of an "average" score, "average" drug use, and "average" levels of subsequent criminal activity. This was the most "routine" pattern as illustrated by the following recollection of one of their respondents whom they called "Ron":

> I was workin' seven hours everyday...over at this numbers hole....I used to get a quarter and stretch it out over three days...that was enough to keep me right [i.e., to avoid withdrawal symptoms]. Everyday it was pretty much the same routine. The hours were regular...I 'd tighten up in the morning and be over there by 11 A.M., before the first drop, and stay there until 2 P.M. Then I'd leave...take care of myself again and be back by 5 P.M. and stay there until 9 P.M....I come back later for an hour or so and then I'm finished for the day. I had enough to use what I needed if I didn't get greedy, which I didn't...and I had some change in my pocket too...to get some good shoes and things. (Smith and Stephens 1976, 161)

A second dominant pattern was a "high" score, "high" drug use, followed by "low" or no criminal activity. Here, the proceeds of their scoring were so high that addicts were able to cease their criminal activity for a period of time before resuming normal "average" hustling routines. Finally, a third pattern depicts a "low" score, "low" to "average" levels of drug use, followed by "average" hustling activity. Respondents reporting this pattern generally experienced difficulty scoring, which resulted in their having to scale down their drug consumption. Because they did not have access to large amounts of drugs, they immediately commenced engaging in subsequent hustling activity.

Smith and Stephen's findings suggest, first, that there is not a monotonic relationship between drug use and crime, as suggested by Anglin and Speckart above. Quite to the contrary, the relationship between drug use and crime is very elastic. Indeed, Smith and Stephens go on to point out that these sequences are also affected by numerous confounding factors. Second, these findings suggest that levels of drug consumption are largely a function of available resources (scores), which are usually derived from criminal activities. Furthermore, when these resources are more limited, the level of drug consumption decreases accordingly. Their research thus suggests that drug use is much more elastic, and that drug users are much more capable of adjusting to lower amounts of drugs than characterized by the longitudinal studies discussed previously. In this way, drug use is portrayed to be primarily a function of the level of criminal activity rather than vice versa.

Research conducted by Goldstein (1979) examining prostitution and drug use also presents a complex drugs-crime connection. With regard to initiation into drug use and prostitution, Goldstein found some instances where drug use preceded prostitution, other instances where prostitution preceded drug use, and still others where initiation into both drug use and prostitution occurred at about the same time. Beyond the sequential relationship between drug use and prostitution, however, Goldstein finds that drug use may be related to prostitution in a number of ways. First, the relationship may be *economical,* as when women turn to prostitution to support a drug habit. Second, it may be *psychoactive,* as when girls or women find themselves providing sexual services while they are in an altered state of consciousness. Third, it may be *functional,* as when women find that the use of drugs facilitates their prostitution. Finally, it may be *subcultural,* as when women in a drug-using subculture respond to peer pressure to engage in prostitution (or vice versa).

Other ethnographic research has emphasized the fact that drug users are active agents in their own destiny, and that both drug use and criminal activity are rational choices that addicts make. Fagan (1994) and Sommers, Baskin, and Fagan (1996) identify human agency as a critical factor among women crack and cocaine users. Rather than being limited to traditional roles for women in the street drug economy (typically prostitution), the women they studied took advantage of an expanding drug market with new entrepreneurship opportunities not available to women in earlier eras, particularly opportunities to deal drugs at relatively high levels. These women fashioned careers in dealing and other illegal entrepreneurial activities.

The concept of *career* to understand the dynamics of drug use and crime was directly and extensively applied by Faupel (1991).[1] Faupel maintains that the relationship between drug use and crime is variable over the course of an addict's career. Four career phases are identified as they relate to levels of drug availability and life structure. During the early, "occasional use" period of their careers, when drug availability is low and life structure is high, the use of drugs and criminal behavior have no causal connection with each other whatsoever. Insofar as they are related, they are both a product of a common subcultural experience. In terms of the theoretical models presented earlier in this chapter, therefore, the common-cause or subcultural explanation best explains this early period of initiation into drugs and crime. As addicts move into the "stable addict" phase of their careers, drug availability increases, and both drug consumption and criminal activity escalates dramatically. Faupel maintains, however, that this escalation of the criminal lifestyle is not in any way caused by heightened addiction. Indeed, it is quite the other way around. As young heroin-using criminals become more adept at crime, they make more money,

Drugs: Myths and Reality

Does Drug Use *Really* Cause Crime?

Contrary to the "drugs-cause-crime" hypothesis, which suggests that increases in the level of heroin consumption are necessarily followed by stepped-up criminal activity, the dynamics reported by the addicts in this study are quite the opposite: increased heroin consumption is *preceded* by increased criminal activity as measured by estimated criminal income. This does not necessarily imply a greater frequency of crime, for...stable-addict status usually brings with it greater sophistication in skill and technique, often resulting in higher proceeds per criminal event.

These life history data also reveal, however, that the relationship between drug use and crime is much broader and more complex than simple causality....[I]ncreased criminal income not only enhances drug availability but also provides the basis for an expanded life structure, an alternative daily routine. Because these criminal routines

usually provide greater flexibility than do most forms of legitimate employment, they free the addict from prohibitive roles and social contacts that may be imposed by more rigid schedules. Drug-using activities are certainly facilitated under these more flexible routines. Nevertheless, criminal routines do impose certain constraints on the addict life-style. Moreover, they provide an important structure to one's drug-using activity. It is in this respect that Old Ray likened the routine of dealing drugs to legitimate employment: "When you're working, the world has its rhythm, its time clock. You have your eight-to-five time clock. Well, it's the same way with dealing drugs." The result is a curious paradox. Criminal activity not only enhances availability, thereby providing for heavier drug consumption, but also places broad limits on the amount of heroin consumed by providing some semblance of structure and routine.

Source: Charles E. Faupel. *Shooting Dope: Career Patterns of Hard-Core Heroin Users*. Gainesville, FL: University Presses of Florida, 1991, pp. 73–74. Reprinted with permission of the University Press of Florida.

which provides them the basis for increased drug consumption. One of the respondents in that study explained this relationship as follows:

> The better I got at crime, the more money I made; the more money I made, the more drugs I used. I think that most people that get high, the reason it goes to the extent that it goes—that it becomes such a high degree of money—is because they make the money like that. I'm saying if the money wasn't available to them like that, they wouldn't be into drugs as deep as they were. (Faupel 1991, 73)

The "free-wheeling" phase of addiction, when addicts indulge in seemingly uncontrolled, hedonistic drug consumption, is also usually brought on by criminal activities, often in the form of the big sting. This occurs when an addict makes a criminal score so big that he or she does not have to resort to their usual criminal routines for a period of time. Hence, with seemingly unlimited resources and no need to engage in the daily routines of hustling, addicts easily let their habits get out of control. When this occurs, they develop a rather high tolerance for heroin that will eventually necessitate further criminal involvement. Importantly, however, the free-wheeling period itself comes about, typically, because of the unusual success that one has enjoyed as a criminal. Hence, both the stable and free-wheeling phases of addiction are most accurately characterized as "crime causes drug use."

It is when addicts reach the last "street junkie" phase of their addiction that they become desperate for drugs. Having developed a tolerance for heroin as free-wheeling addicts and eventually running out of the money that permitted that level of drug use, street junkies must rely on whatever means they have available to supply them with their next fix. This is the period in an addict's career when he or she will commit desperate acts for drugs, often violating their own subcultural code of ethics and often getting arrested. This is the only period of an addict's career, Faupel maintains, of which we can truthfully say that "drug use causes crime."

Faupel's research, like earlier ethnographies, therefore cautions us not to be overly simplistic in our understanding of the relationship between drug use and criminal behavior. This relationship is a much more complicated and dynamic one, and changes over the career of an addict.

Drug Use, Crime, and Victimization

This chapter has addressed the relationship between drug use and criminal behavior from the standpoint of the perpetrator; that is, we have asked the question, How is drug use related to the *commission* of crime? Before leaving this topic, we want to address briefly the question, How is drug use is related to being a *victim* of crime? This was discussed briefly in the chapter on health correlates of drug use, but we want to address it more systematically here. There is a fair amount of research documenting a connection between drug use and victimization. The nature of this relationship, however, is complex, and like the relationship between drug use and crime perpetration, it has been suggested that drug use causes victimization; that victimization causes drug use; and and that both drug use and victimization are caused by other variables, including subcultural dynamics that produce both drug use and victimization.

Drug Use Causes Victimization

There is by now mounting evidence that drug use, especially alcohol use, is causally linked to crime victimization. A half-century ago, Marvin Wolfgang (1958) recognized the potential effect of alcohol intoxication on victim-precipitated homicides. We have also known for decades that alcohol is a major factor in domestic violence, and research suggests that the use of other drugs by domestic partners considerably increases the risk for assault within the home (Willson et al. 2000). The most direct way in which a *victim's* drug use induces their own victimization is through the intoxicating effect that drugs and alcohol can have on an individual, leaving them vulnerable to violence or property crime victimization. This happens, for example, when women are given rohypnol, or "roofies," in their drinks to induce temporary amnesia. This is an issue of concern, both in the United States and other countries, though research suggests that only a small minority of date rapes or acquaintance rapes are due to such involuntary drug use (Hindmarch and Brinkmann 1999). More commonly, such rape occurs following *voluntary* consumption of alcohol and other drugs, leaving the victim in an intoxicated state and less able to resist overtures from perpetrators. Horvath and Brown (2007) report that, in the majority of rapes in which alcohol or drugs are involved, the victim has voluntarily self-intoxicated. Ramisetty-Mikler and colleagues (2006) similarly report that among high school students, early onset of alcohol use doubles the risk of being a victim of sexual assault and date rape. This finding is consistent with research by Krebs and Steffey (2005) that young people who use club drugs generally engage in other high-risk behavior that may lead to victimization.

More indirectly, drug use may induce victimization as a result of living in crimi-nogenic neighborhoods. Neighborhoods characterized by high levels of drug use and drug dealing are typically high in other types of crime as well, including burglary and various forms of larceny in addition to violent crimes such as robbery and assault. Drug users living in these areas are therefore much more vulnerable to criminal vic-timization. Ford and Beveridge (2006) find that the visible presence of drug sales is especially predictive of victimization rates for all of the types of property crimes that they examined, suggesting an economic basis for crime victimization.

Victimization Causes Drug Use

It is a traumatic experience to be victimized by crime. When the crime is violent in nature such as rape, assault, or armed robbery, victims are left with personal viola-tion that leaves deep scars. Researchers have identified numerous symptoms of post-traumatic stress syndrome among victims of rape and spousal abuse. Symptoms include flashbacks and nightmares, which can themselves be quite devastating. Victims of personal crimes experience fear, anxiety, depression, anger, and self-de-structive impulses, often resulting in maladaptive behavior (Karmen 2007). Such behaviors might include aggression, withdrawal, suicide attempts, or early sexual experimentation.

We also know that victims of crime, under certain circumstances, are more likely to use drugs and alcohol. Cross-cultural research in Belgium, Russia, and the United States revealed that even witnessing violence resulted in an increase in the likeli-hood of substance use (alcohol, tobacco, marijuana, and/or hard drugs). Moreover, drug and alcohol use increased as the severity of the violence witnessed increased (Vermeiren et al. 2003). Similar findings were observed among California students (Weiner et al. 2005) and native Hawaiians (Austin 2004).

There is perhaps no form of victimization more traumatizing than sexual abuse and violence, and research has found that sexual assault is more strongly related to post-traumatic stress and other morbitity factors than any other form of victimiza-tion (Boudreaux et al. 1998). Among those factors is an increased risk for substance use and dependency (Kaukinen and DeMaris 2005). Alcohol and drugs are often used to cope with the trauma that victims experience, or perhaps to alleviate anxiety and increase a sense of control over their lives following such an experience that leaves one feeling so vulnerable. When this trauma occurs at a young age, the consequences are likely to be especially serious because victims are in their formative years. Research by Kaukinen and DeMaris (2005) among white and minority women reveal that sexual assault during childhood significantly increases the likelihood of prescription drug use later in life. These researchers found some differences between white and minority women in their sample with regard to illicit drug and alcohol use. White women were more affected in this way by childhood and adolescent sexual assault, whereas among minority women, adult sexual victimization was a much stronger predictor of illicit drug and alcohol use. Kaukinen and DeMaris suggest that the recency of victimization may be more consequential because of the vividness of the trauma, which is temporarily alleviated through drug and alcohol use.

Regardless of the nature of the victimization, drug and alcohol use and abuse are one mechanism that victims of crime use to cope with the trauma of the criminal event forced upon them. The problem with this response, of course, is that use of chemical substances as a coping mechanism often exacerbates the problems in their lives resulting from the victimization, as well as creating other problems. This difficult situation in which victims of crime so often find themselves has not gone unnoticed. The importance of early intervention programs and strategies has been stressed by academics and policy makers alike for many years, and over the past couple of decades, implementation efforts have greatly increased.

Common-Cause Explanations

Crime victimization may also result from more general common cause, notably subcultural and lifestyle factors that include but go beyond drug use. Goldstein (1985) identifies *systemic violence* as violence that is endemic to the subculture of drug use. Violence or the threat of violence is used to enforce agreements and as retribution for failure to comply with normative understandings within the subculture. Violence is also endemic to the kinds of work in which subculture participants must engage. Sex workers, for example, are at risk for greater levels of violence victimization, a finding reported by Metsch, McCoy, and Weatherby (1996) among crack-using women in American cities and by Wechsberg, Luseno, and Lam (2005) among drug-using prostitutes in South Africa.

Subculture participants both perpetrate violence and are victims of violence. Lana Harrison and her colleagues (2001) found that American and Canadian youth involved in binge drinking and in cannabis and cocaine use were more prone to violence victimization than were nonusers. Drug-using youth were also more likely to be perpetrators of violence than nonusers. It is understandable that those involved in the commission of violent crime are also more susceptible to victimization. The finding that marijuana use is associated with higher levels of violence was surprising, given the reputation of cannabis as a "peace" drug. Harrison and her colleagues explain their findings by suggesting a "general deviance syndrome" among a small number of violence-prone youth that also accounts for increased drug use, including marijuana use. McElrath, Chitwood, and Comerford (1997) use routine activity theory to explain the systemic violence of the subculture. Injection drug users (IDUs), they argue, are much more highly exposed to a larger pool of motivated offenders, and drug users are seen as attractive targets by these offenders because they are likely to have either drugs or cash on their person, and because they have relatively little by way of protection against such victimization (what routine activities theorists refer to as a "lack of capable guardians"). Ramos-Lira, Gonzalez-Forteza, and Wagner (2006) point to a similar dynamic among Mexican middle school students by suggesting that both drug use and violence victimization result from exposure to opportunities common to both experiences. Youth living in deteriorated areas of the city are exposed to higher levels of drug availability. These areas are also characterized by high incidence of broken homes, unemployment, a transient population, and stress, all of which are related to violence and being a victim of violent acts.

Summary

It is commonly assumed in American society that drug use causes users to commit crimes. This idea is not an entirely new one, with casual references to crime and other antisocial behavior resulting from the use of one form of drug or another appearing well prior to this century. The pervasiveness of this belief, and its reflection in public policy decisions, however, is uniquely a twentieth-century phenomenon. In this respect, compared with earlier times, twentieth-century America truly has had a preoccupation with and fear of drugs as a crime-causing agent.

The scholarly literature addressing the relationship between drug use and crime typically falls into three distinct theoretical categories. That literature suggesting that "drug use causes crime" is usually stated either in terms of the *pharmacological* or psychoactive effect that drugs have on users, limiting their ability to think clearly or to control their impulses; or in terms of the *economic* demands placed on users as a result of being addicted to expensive drugs such as heroin or cocaine. A second theoretical argument is that "crime causes drug use," which suggests that only as individuals become involved in delinquent and criminal lifestyles do they begin to participate in drug-using activities. According to this perspective, crime either provides financial resources to spend on drugs, a consumer expenditure that would not otherwise be made, or that drugs play valuable functions in the successful completion of a criminal act. Finally, it has been suggested that both drug use and criminal behavior are the result of a "common cause," either a common syndrome of personality and behavioral characteristics or involvement in a subculture that rewards these behaviors.

Social scientists have been empirically examining the relationship between drug use and crime for several decades. A number of research methodologies have been employed, including the use both of prison and arrest statistics and of self-reports of drug use and crime. This research provides no conclusive evidence about any single relationship between drug use and crime—it is much more complex than that. Studies of arrestees and prison inmates reveal that these populations are much more likely to have used drugs than the population as a whole—a finding shared by self-report studies that compare drug-using and non-drug-using sample populations. Interestingly, however, research that attempts to establish the sequence of initiation into drug use and crime almost invariably finds that delinquent and criminal behavior commence prior to initiation into serious drug use. Hence, in terms of initiation into drug use and crime, both these studies and the ethnographic research over the past 20 years fail to support the idea that young people get hooked on drugs, which then forces them into a life of crime that they might otherwise have avoided. Generally, the empirical research supports the idea that both drug use and crime are initiated through common subcultural associations.

The issue of initiation into drug use and crime tells only part of the story, however. We can also ask, is there a causal relationship between drug use and crime later in one's drug-using career? Longitudinal studies comparing levels of criminal behavior during periods of addiction or daily use with periods of less frequent or no use provide very clear and convincing evidence that addicts are much more criminally active when they are using drugs on a daily basis. These studies conclude that, as the level of one's drug consumption increases, drug use plays a causal role in criminal behavior. This interpretation has been questioned by ethnographers, however; whereas they agree that both drug use and crime might increase over the career of an addict, they do not necessarily agree that the increased drug use *caused* the increased crime. Indeed, Faupel's (1991) research suggests that, in fact, throughout much of an addict's career, it is increased criminal income that facilitates increased drug use. Only when an addict has developed an uncontrollable tolerance and is without a stable means of supporting such a level of drug use, as a street junkie, does his or her addiction actually cause them to commit acts of crime.

Finally, this chapter examined the relationship between crime victimization and drug use. Some evidence suggests that drug use may lead to victimization through the intoxicating effects that many drugs have, leaving an individual much more vulnerable to victimization. We also know that having being victimized by crime, particularly by violent and sexual crimes, leaves one vulnerable to drug use as a coping mechanism. Furthermore, a body of research suggests that both drug use and victimization are functions of the general lifestyle and subculture in which drug users participate.

Taken as a whole, the empirical literature fails to support exclusively *any* of the theoretical positions on the relationship between drug use and crime described in this chapter. Rather, each of these descriptions accurately describes the drugs-crime connection in different ways and at different times in an addict's career. This literature further suggests that it is not possible to explain any single relationship between drug use and crime, because there are several ways in which these two sets of behaviors are related. It might rather be appropriate to describe the relationship between initiation into drug use and criminal behavior, or between the escalation of drug use and crime, or perhaps even between the maintenance of drug-using and criminal lifestyles. In sum, the empirical research, when taken collectively, suggests that we must move beyond a simple cause-and-effect understanding of the relationship between drug use and criminal behavior.

Key Terms

causality
correlation
disinhibition hypothesis
problem behavior syndrome
spurious relationship

Thinking Critically...

1. The authors open this chapter by stating that "perhaps the greatest fear that many people have of illegal drugs is the association that these substances have with other forms of criminal behavior." What do you suppose is meant by this statement? What are some of the drugs most feared? What perceptions do most people have regarding their affect on human behavior, particularly in causing crime? Based on your reading of this chapter, which of these fears are realistic? Which are not realistic?

2. Thinking about Chapter 2 with regard to our concerns about drug use and crime, how might our understanding of history affect how we respond to allegations regarding the fears that people have of how drugs cause crime and violent behavior? For example, what lessons does our experience with *Reefer Madness* have for us with regard to how we should respond to allegations about the consequences of drug use?

3. Using the "Typology of Heroin-Using Career Phases" in Chapter 10 (Figure 10.2) describe how the relationship between drug use and crime might change over the career of an addict.

4. Assume that you have been asked by your governor to head up a study on drug use and its relationship to crime in your state. Based on the information in this chapter and in Chapter 4, how would you organize such a study? Include here how you would select the sample of people to study, the sorts of questions to ask, how you would ask them, and so forth.

5. Perhaps the most commonly cited reason for the "war on drugs" is that drug use causes criminal behavior. Based on the information in this chapter, what sort of a "war" on drugs would you devise in response to the connection that seems to exist between illegal drug use and criminal behavior?

Learning from the Internet

1. The media usually presents a particular slant on the relationship between drug use and criminal behavior. Get a sense of media portrayals of drug use and crime by going to three or more newspapers online and read stories addressing this issue. Most newspapers have an internal search engine. Simply type "drugs" and "crime" in the search engine. Major newspapers should have several stories. Below are listed several regional and national newspapers. Feel free to also read stories in local newspapers if you have URLs for them.

> New York Times, www.nytimes.com
> Boston Globe, www.boston.com
> Miami Herald, www.miamiherald.com
> Los Angeles Times, www.latimes.com
> San Francisco Chronicle, www.sfgate.com
> Philadelphia Enquirer, www.philly.com
> Chicago Sun Times, www.suntimes.com
> Detroit Free Press, www.freep.com
> Atlanta Journal-Constitution, www.ajc.com

2. The government publishes material, including statistics, on drug use and crime. Go to the following websites published by various agencies of the United States government. What do they tell you about the relationship between drug use and crime? In what ways must you be cautious in your interpretation of these statistics?

> Bureau of Justice Statistics, www.ojp.usdoj.gov/bjs/drugs.htm
> Office of National Drug Control Policy, http://www.whitehousedrugpolicy.gov/publications/factsht/crime/index.html
> Federal Bureau of Investigation, Uniform Crime Reports, www.fbi.gov/ucr/cius2007/index.html
> Arrestee Drug Abuse Monitoring Program, www.ncjrs.gov/pdffiles1/nij/193013.pdf

Note

1. The reader is referred to Chapter 10 for a more complete discussion of Faupel's application of *career* to the lifestyle of drug users.

SOCIETAL RESPONSE TO DRUG USE

CHAPTER **12**

Legal Responses to Drug Problems: Prohibition, Legalization, and Decriminalization

This chapter takes a close look at the possible legal responses to drug use and abuse in the United States. As the title of this chapter suggests, three major policy alternatives have been discussed by scholars and researchers, policy makers, politicians, practitioners, and social commentators: prohibition (or criminalization), legalization, and decriminalization. Each of these approaches to the drug problem will be addressed in detail in this chapter. Despite the fact that the authors of this book have our own policy preferences, the purpose of this chapter is not to convince the reader of the advisability of one policy option over the others. Rather, we seek to discuss each of these approaches as objectively as possible, review historical experience with each, and consider the advantages and disadvantages offered by each. At the end of this chapter and in Chapter 15, we will offer a fourth option for workable drug policies for the twenty-first century, an alternative known as *harm reduction*.

The Importance of Policy to Understanding Drug Use in America

You may wonder why it is important to understand these larger policy options in the first place. After all, drugs may be quite harmful to the individuals who abuse them, as well as to those around them, and to do anything other than prohibit these dangerous substances seems not to make sense. Besides, how does understanding these larger policy questions contribute to our knowledge about why people use drugs in the first place, what kinds of people use drugs, the relationship between drug use and crime, and a host of other issues that we have already addressed in earlier chapters of this book? We contend that *all* of these aspects of drug use in American society are affected by the legal and political climate in which these drugs are used.

Let us look at one set of examples that illustrates how such broad drug policies affect many aspects of drug use. Tobacco is a drug that has enjoyed widespread popularity throughout much of the twentieth century, and to this day it is a legal drug in every state and jurisdiction, restricted only to minors and by local ordinances prohibiting smoking in certain places. Even then, the penalties for smoking where prohibited are minimal. Tobacco is one of the most harmful recreational drugs used today, but because of its legal status, tobacco is not *perceived* to be as dangerous as, for example, heroin. Furthermore, because tobacco is a legal drug, it is a drug of choice across a broad spectrum of the population, including upper-, middle-, and lower-class individuals, men and women, young and old, all races and ethnicities. Narcotics such as heroin, on the other hand, are used more often by lower-class, minority males between 18 and 35 years old. This is no coincidence. This segment of the population has comparatively little stake in the conventional social order. Most do not own their own homes. Many do not have jobs, and if they are employed, it is likely not a high-paying professional position that offers them standing in the community at large. It is not surprising that this is the segment of the population most likely to use prohibited narcotics, which, as an added benefit, dull the pains of an otherwise harsh existence. Furthermore, this is the segment of the population most likely to be involved in street crime, and hence we can observe at least an apparent link between drug use and crime among those who use illegal drugs (see Chapter 11 for a lengthy discussion on this issue). This linkage is not reported among users of tobacco. Similarly, there is no subculture of tobacco users as is found among heroin users. As we have seen, the highly prohibited nature of heroin is fertile ground for the development of a heroin subculture (see Chapter 10).

We are arguing, in short, that we are concerned about policy issues because we cannot fully understand all of the other aspects of drug use without knowing something about the legal and social context in which drugs are used. Hence, in the sections that follow, we look at four broad policy approaches to drugs. The first three—prohibition, legalization, and decriminalization—have dominated discussions and debates among policy makers and practitioners throughout the twentieth century. Harm reduction, the final approach discussed, is a relative newcomer to the formal debate, advocating strategies that would minimize the harm resulting from drug use and from society's reaction to that use.

Prohibition

Prohibition refers to a policy of criminalization, whereby the production, manufacture, growing, selling, and/or possession of drugs are violations of one or more criminal statutes. This is the policy response to most substances that are commonly considered drugs, including marijuana (in most states), heroin, cocaine, crack, methamphetamine, among others. Drugs that fall under a policy of prohibition, although different in their pharmacological effects, share one important feature in common: they are illegal, and those who use these drugs are potentially criminals. The primary agency of societal response to drug use under a policy of prohibition is the criminal justice system.

Mark Kleiman (1985) identifies five strategies of enforcement of prohibition statutes. One approach is to reduce the amount of illegal drugs produced in the first place, a strategy known as **source reduction**. This involves a number of possible strategies, depending on the drug in question. In the case of heroin, cocaine, and other drugs that are not grown or manufactured domestically, this policy involves working with other governments in eliminating drug crops. Drugs that are grown or manufactured domestically, are source-reduced by gathering intelligence information, making arrests, and confiscating or destroying the drugs and/or drug manufacturing equipment. There is a certain logic to source reduction. Drug marketing, like most marketing strategies, is typically organized in a hierarchal, pyramid fashion, with a smaller number of actors at the top. Because fewer people are involved at the top end of the pyramid, enforcement actions should be most effective here.

However, in the case of the international drug trade, such as with heroin or cocaine, any action at this level involves imposing on sovereign governments. In many cases, the cultivation of the poppy plant is a staple agricultural export grown by many farmers. One strategy of the U.S. government has been to implement crop substitution programs to provide an alternative source of income for local farmers. These programs have met with only limited success (Kaplan 1983). Recent experience South America suggests that alternative crops simply do not provide enough income for impoverished farmers without substantial international subsidies (United Nations 2006). Indeed, Vargas (2005) suggests that the reason these programs, which he calls "alternative development programs," have not succeeded is that the U.S. government provides only limited support for them, preferring instead eradication programs that produce quicker results for less cost. This approach, Vargas notes, fails to address the social and economic roots of illicit drug production.

A second strategy, border **interdiction**, seeks to prevent illegal drugs from entering the United States after leaving the borders of producing nations. Like source reduction, interdiction is usually accomplished at the federal law enforcement level. The primary agencies involved in border intervention are the U.S. Coast Guard (at sea) and the U.S. Customs and Border Protection[1] (at ports of entry), though other agencies such as the Immigration and Naturalization Service, the Federal Bureau of Investigation, and the Drug Enforcement Agency become involved from time to time. A recent statement by the U.S. Customs and Border Patrol claims seizures of more than 1.7 million pounds of narcotics in 2007, representing nearly 3,500 arrests by this agency alone (U.S. Customs 2007). For its part, the U.S. Coast Guard reported 234,000 pounds of cocaine and 9,000 pounds of marijuana seized in 2006, which represents a doubling of cocaine seizures since 1997, but a mere 10 percent of marijuana seizures a decade ago. The value of cocaine seizures by the Coast Guard alone over the past decade was nearly $50 billion (U.S. Coast Guard 2007). The sheer volume of traffic entering the United States makes drug interdiction an extremely difficult operation. Although their seizures are impressive, these figures should make obvious the difficult challenge of stemming the flow of drugs into the United States.

A third strategy of enforcement is disruption of distribution networks of illegal substances. This strategy is targeted at high-level domestic trafficking operations and is typically carried out by the

12.1 Interdiction of drugs on the high seas and at our borders is one of the key elements of our current prohibitionist drug policy. (Photo: Associated Press/Kent Gilbert)

DEA and FBI. At state and local levels, comprising the fourth and fifth strategies of law enforcement, agencies focus on targeting wholesalers (middle-level dealers in charge of large distribution rings in a city or region) and street dealers. In 2005, 1,846,351 drug abuse violation arrests were reported in the Uniform Crime Reports, representing an 11.5 percent increase from 10 years earlier, and about a 200 percent increase from 1980.

Street-level enforcement strategy uses a variety of tactics. One tactic involves using undercover operatives over a sustained period of time to get to high-level dealers controlling large distribution rings. The theory behind this approach is that by closing down a major distribution ring, the supply of drugs is seriously curtailed in a given area. There are problems with this approach, however. It is much more vulnerable to police corruption. It is also extremely time consuming, and months or even years of undercover work may ultimately yield nothing. Moreover, even if a major operation were shut down, either new or existing organizations would likely fill the drug vacuum (Kleiman and Smith 1990).

Because of the difficulties in going after the heads of major distribution rings, many law enforcement agencies are focusing more on street-level retail markets. Strategies vary. In some cases, merely flooding a drug-infested area with uniformed police officers can cut down on the amount of illegal drug dealing that takes place there. Police departments have long used informants to make drug buys, which are later prosecuted on the strength of their informants' testimony in court. Needless to say, problems with the truthfulness of informants and their credibility in court has limited the effectiveness of this enforcement strategy. More recently, many departments have gone to a strategy known as *buy-busts*, in which undercover operatives or informants buy drugs from local dealers using marked money. Officers who are

Drugs: Myths and Reality

Arrests of the Rich and Famous

The U.S. government, primarily law enforcement agencies such as the Drug Enforcement Administration (and its predecessor, the Bureau of Narcotics and Dangerous Drugs), since the 1930s have championed the arrests of famous citizens as a show of force, resolve, and as a supposed deterrent to marijuana use.

America is a celebrity driven culture. *Both* sides of the contentious debate over marijuana law reform realize this and often try to exploit America's fascination with "celebrity culture." . . .

The following list is comprised of celebrities from the world of theater, music [and] sports.

Movie and TV Stars:

Robert Mitchum—Famous actor and one of the first celebrity victims of marijuana prohibition. Mitchum was arrested in a 1948 stakeout in Laurel Canyon, CA.

Source: *High Times*

Bob Denver—Played lovable character "Gilligan" on popular 60s television show *Gilligan's Island*. Arrested in 1998 after a package containing two ounces of marijuana was delivered to his West Virginia house.

Source: *Associated Press, Princeton, WV*

Oliver Stone—Filmmaker of renowned movies *JFK*, *Platoon*, and *Born on the Fourth of July*, pulled over by police officers for driving erratically and subsequently arrested when hash and painkillers were found in his car.

Source: *San Francisco Chronicle*, August 25, 1999

Matthew McConaughey—Actor in such popular movies as *Dazed and Confused* and *Amistad* busted in his Texas home after numerous noise complaints from neighbors. Officers saw him dancing naked and playing bongos. He was arrested and booked on suspicion of possession of marijuana and paraphernalia.

Source: *Houston Chronicle*, October 26, 1999

Brad Renfro—Actor in 1994 movie *The Client* arrested on marijuana (and cocaine) charges.

Source: *The Associated Press*, April 6, 1999

Musicians, Singers and Performers:

Whitney Houston—Grammy-winning pop diva was busted boarding an airplane in Hawaii. Officers found 15.2 grams in her bag.

Source: *Boston Globe*, January 17, 2000

Ray Price—73-year-old country music singer was arrested in his Texas home for possession of marijuana.

Source: *San Francisco Chronicle*, March 26, 1999

James Brown—Godfather of Soul busted on marijuana and other charges.

Source: *Reuters*, Aiken, SC, January 29, 1998

The Rolling Stones—Band members were busted several times in 1967.

Source: *High Times*

Willie Nelson—Busted in Texas in 1995 with pot in his car. Charges were dropped

Drugs: Myths and Reality *(continued)*

later when search was determined to be illegal.

———————

Source: *High Times*

Louis Armstrong—Legendary trumpeter busted in 1931 outside of an LA jazz club.

———————

Source: *High Times*

The Grateful Dead—Their infamous house at 710 Ashbury was raided in 1967. Band members Bob Weir and Pigpen were arrested. Amazingly the police didn't find the pot hidden in a kitchen pantry.

———————

Source: *High Times*

Gene Krupa—Jazz drummer arrested in 1943 in San Francisco after LA narcotic officers followed him. They seized the pot and he spent 84 days in jail.

———————

Source: *High Times*

Carlos Santana—Legendary Grammy award winning guitar player busted at Houston Airport in 1991 for transporting five grams of marijuana from Mexico.

———————

Source: *High Times*

Freddy Fender—Tex-Mex pop star busted in Louisiana in 1960 for less than six grams of pot.

———————

Source: *High Times*

———

Athletes:

Kareem Abdul-Jabbar—Former Lakers star busted at Pearson International Airport in Toronto Canada with six grams of marijuana by U.S. Customs officials. Paid $500 fine. Jabbar claims to have used marijuana for years to successfully treat severe migraine headaches.

———————

Source: *Associated Press*, Toronto, March 20, 1998

Robert Parish—Boston Celtics star arrested in 1991 when police intercepted two ounces of pot being shipped Federal Express to his Massachusetts house. He paid a $37 fine.

———————

Source: *High Times*

Ferguson Jenkins—Pitcher and Cy Young award winner busted in 1980 for possessing hash.

———————

Source: *High Times*

Orlando Cepeda—Former San Francisco Giant and MVP award winner in 1967, charged with smuggling 160 pounds of marijuana from Puerto Rico to Miami in 1976.

———————

Source: *High Times*

Vernon Maxwell—Former Houston Rocket busted in Texas in 1995 after running a red light. Police found a gram of pot in a baggie on the floor of his car.

———————

Source: *High Times*

Isiah Rider—Former Portland Trail Blazer's guard arrested in 1996 when officers observed him in a car attempting to smoke marijuana from a soda can. He was charged with possession of less than one ounce of marijuana.

———————

Source: *Eugene Register-Guard*, December 10, 1998

Drugs: Myths and Reality *(continued)*

Mookie Blaylock—Atlanta Hawks star busted in 1997 when drug-sniffing dogs uncovered marijuana on him in a Vancouver Canada airport.

Source: *Wire reports*

Todd Marinovich—Former USC and Raiders quarterback arrested for growing one pot plant in his house in 1996.

Source: *High Times*

Source: Excerpted from National Organization for the Reform of Marijuana Laws. n.d.b. *Arrests of the Rich and Famous*. Available online: http://www.norml.org/index.cfm?Group_ID=4439 (accessed May 31, 2008). Used with permission.

directly in the vicinity make an immediate arrest. This strategy is more effective because usually an officer witnesses the transaction, and the marked money, seized at the time of the arrest, verifies the officer's testimony. Still another approach is to establish police mini-stations in active drug-dealing areas. This provides a greater presence of law enforcement in these areas, which is hypothesized to have a deterrent effect.

Retail-level t strategy, or what Kleiman and Smith (1990) call "street sweeping" is not without problems. Perhaps most problematic is the great potential for abuse of authority—harassing innocent citizens, brutality in making arrests, and even planting evidence to make a bust. Moreover, because of the high demand for drugs, successful sweeps in one area typically send drug operations into nearby neighborhoods. This has been referred to as the *pop-up* phenomenon: suppression in one area is followed by distribution networks popping up in other areas. Recent research by David Weisburd and his colleagues (2006), however, offers more optimistic implications for the effectiveness of street level enforcement efforts. These researchers found that when focused crime prevention efforts were implemented in neighborhoods, the pop-up or displacement effect did *not* take place in adjacent neighborhoods. Indeed, surrounding neighborhoods benefitted by decreased criminal activity, especially when the targeted crimes were drug dealing or prostitution.

Source reduction, interdiction, and domestic enforcement are all **supply-side strategies**. *Supply-side* refers to the focus of these efforts on the *supply* of drugs. Supply-side strategies have been the principal weapons of prohibition policy throughout the twentieth century. Prohibition policies also make use of **demand-side strategies** that attempt to reduce the *demand* for drugs. They include treatment and drug education programs that may be ordered by the court or as an alternative to a prison sentence. These strategies are discussed in Chapters 13 and 14.

Advantages of Prohibition

Prohibition has at least two important advantages over the other policy alternatives. First, it results in fewer people using substances that may be potentially very harmful to them and those around them. Second, and related to the first point, such a policy sends an important symbolic message about virtues valued by Americans such as sobriety and self-control. These arguments are found not only in the scholarly debate, but in the public debate as well (MacCoun et al. 1993). We examine each of these advantages in this section.

Limits the Number of Users

The rhetoric and the debate over legalization often obscure the fact that policies of prohibition do, in fact, limit the number of people who use a particular drug (Goldstein and Kalant 1990; Inciardi and Saum 1996). Our experience with alcohol has demonstrated the repressive effect that a policy of prohibition can have on drug use. Currently, two of every three Americans consume alcohol. The social cost resulting from alcohol use is twice that of all other illegal drug use combined. And as Goldstein and Kalant (1990) correctly point out, many illegal drugs *are* potentially dangerous, and hence any policy that reduces the potential number of users is, on the face of it, virtuous. Citing evidence from the National Household Survey on Drug Abuse, Kleber (1994) suggests that, indeed, prohibition strategies *are* working to reduce the level of drug use in this country.

Opponents of prohibitionist policies claim that although criminalization of drugs may reduce the overall number of drug users and quantity of drugs consumed, they do so at great cost to health, social well-being, and civil liberties (Nadelmann 1988). The prohibition of alcohol, for example, substantially lowered levels of alcohol use but gave rise to certain other social problems such extending the domain of organized crime. These concerns, discussed more fully below, are well founded, and for that reason, sober consideration of alternative policies is warranted as we look to the future. Nevertheless, because of the potentially destructive effect that drug use can have on users and those around them, the advantage of reducing overall levels of drug use must not be ignored as we consider future drug policy. James Jacobs notes:

> The drug-legalization movement is urging us to consider the transformation of American society from an alcohol culture to a poly-drug culture in which a wide range of psychoactive drugs...would instantly be made the legal equivalents of alcohol. These drugs would become as widely available as alcohol and would spawn commercial industries promoting and celebrating their use. It would be as if the United States had decided to multiply its alcohol experience many times over with dozens of new drugs. The impacts of such a revolution would surely be felt in every niche of our society and culture. (1990, 41)

This is a sobering observation that weighs in heavily as we consider the relative value of a policy of prohibition over other policy alternatives.

Reinforces Values of Sobriety and Self-Control

The second advantage of a prohibitionist policy, which is closely related to the first, is that such a policy reinforces the moral value that our culture places on sobriety and self-control. We are not talking here merely about the instrumental effect of the law on public attitudes toward drug use (which one hopes would result in fewer people using less drugs). The symbolic function of prohibitionist drug policies is that they reinforce deeply held values and traditional virtues that have served our society quite well over the years. Gusfield (1967) states that such laws express support for one set of norms over others. They give legitimacy to one way of life over another. Gusfield was talking about the prohibition of alcohol, but this principle is valuable when considering nonalcohol drug laws as well. They provide a normative and institutional support structure for behaviors and lifestyles that society claims to value. The other side of that coin, of course, is that these laws lose their symbolic value and perhaps even their ability to curtail behavior substantially if they do not, in fact, reflect dominant social values. Insofar as the symbolic function of prohibitionist drug laws are concerned, therefore, it would seem that an important task of social scientists and policy makers alike is to assess accurately the values and the beliefs that Americans hold with regard to the use of recreational drugs.

Disadvantages of Prohibition

American prohibitionist drug policies have been suqjected to numerous critiques. Among the most often cited is a pair of articles authored by a leading advocate of drug policy reform, Ethan Nadelmann (1988, 1989). In addition to his contention that prohibitionist policies have failed, Nadelmann argues that serious social and economic costs of these policies must be carefully weighed.

Costs to the Taxpayer

Nadelmann (1988) notes that between 1981 and 1987, federal expenditures for the enforcement of drug laws more than tripled, from less than a billion dollars per year to approximately $3 billion. That figure increased to nearly $19 billion in 2002 (Reuter 2006). The drug law enforcement agencies have received massive budgetary increases over the past 30 years. The Drug Enforcement Administration budget has increased from $65.2 million in 1972 to more than $2.3 *billion* in 2007, a nearly 40-fold increase. Other drug enforcement agencies such as the FBI, the U.S. Marshal's Service, Coast Guard, and the U.S. Custom's Service also received hefty increases. Nadelmann (1988) estimated the total expenditure for drug law enforcement in the United States in 1987 to be $10 billion. By the middle of the current decade, this figure quadrupled to some $40 billion annually (Caulkins and Reuter 2006).

Yet these statistics do not reveal the totality of the financial burden to American taxpayers. Increased arrests have clogged court dockets, creating a need for more judges, prosecutors, and in many cases more courts, including special drug courts. Many of the defendants in these cases also require the use of public defenders, again at great cost to taxpayers. Moreover, the demand for new prisons because of prison overcrowding from mandatory sentencing provisions is at an all-time high. All of these are direct economic costs to taxpayers. Advocates of legalization argue that not only could these costs be reduced greatly if drug were legalized, but the government could actually reap great economic benefits through the tax revenues that could be collected from the sale of these substances. We will address this issue more fully in a later section.

Costs in Increased Crime

As we have seen in Chapter 11, the relationship between drug use and crime is a complex one that defies simple cause-effect analyses. Critics of America's prohibitionist policies reject the simplistic assumption that drugs intrinsically cause criminal and violent behavior through some sort of pharmacological mechanism. If that were so, reducing the level of drug use would automatically reduce the level of crime and violence in the United States. Critics of prohibition do, however, fall back on an equally simplistic understanding of the relationship between drug use and crime when they argue that prohibitionist policies inflate the price of drugs, thus requiring those addicted to these drugs to commit crimes to sustain their drug habits. Nadelmann notes, for example:

> [M]any illicit-drug users commit crimes such as robbery and burglary, as well as drug dealing, prostitution, and numbers running, to earn enough money to purchase the relatively high-priced illicit drugs. Unlike the millions of alcoholics who can support their habits for relatively modest amounts, many cocaine and heroin addicts spend hundreds and even thousands of dollars a week. If the drugs to which they are addicted were significantly cheaper—which would be the case if they were legalized—the number of crimes committed by drug addicts to pay for their habits would, in all likelihood, decline dramatically. (1988, 17)

Recent evidence showing a positive association between the number of drug arrests and the crime rates for New York's 62 counties lends some support to Nadelmann's claims (Shepard and Blackley 2005). We noted in Chapter 11, however, that drug users do not necessarily engage in higher levels of crime because of an increase either in the level of their use or in the price of their drugs. Most addicts begin their criminal careers before they become involved in expensive drugs, and they frequently expand their criminal activity before their drug consumption picks up. Furthermore, it is not uncommon for drug users to lower their drug consumption at least temporarily to accommodate lower levels of availability. In short, as Boyum and Kleiman (2003) point out, drug consumption is not as inelastic as Nadelmann's argument implies, but varies greatly both up and down as drugs become more or less available.

Two connections between drug use and crime, however, *are* directly linked to prohibitionist policies. The first of these is definitional, namely, the buying, selling, and possessing of illegal substances. Because these activities are defined as criminal under prohibitionist policies, these policies can be said literally to cause the crime. This is not to say that the policies cause the *behavior* (i.e., buying or selling of drugs); but the buying or selling of drugs is a *crime* directly because of the policy. Hence, by criminalizing drugs, we automatically increase the level of crime in a society. This is significant because much of the taxpayer expenditure for drug-related crimes is precisely for these crimes-by-definition. As a result, the criminal justice system is required to process drug offenders, placing a heavy burden on overloaded courts and correctional systems. Boyum and Kleiman (2003) point out that 20 percent of all incarcerations are for drug-related offenses, and that drug-related incarceration has increased by 80 percent over the past decade.

A second linkage directly resulting from prohibitionist policies is what Goldstein (1985) referred to as *systemic violence* resulting from the operation of illegal drug markets. Systemic criminal acts involve such things as disputes over territories between rival drug dealers; punishment for failing to come good on a debt; retaliation for selling adulterated drugs; the intimidation or elimination of informers; or the robbery of dealers who may have sold "short" (less than the full amount) or diluted drugs. All of these crimes are virtually unheard of in legitimate markets because parties who have been treated unjustly in a financial transaction have legal courses of action to seek redress. One can file suit in a small claims court, notify the Better Business Bureau, or seek legal injunctions on competitors violating franchise boundaries. None of these mechanisms are available to dealers and consumers of illegal drugs (or any other illegal product or service) *precisely because they are illegal* and to use these mechanisms would reveal one's identity as a criminal (Miron 2001). These sorts of crime do not comprise even close to a majority of all drug-related crimes, but they are not an insignificant proportion either. These crimes are a true cost of our current "war on drugs" in that they result directly from prohibitionist drug policies.

Costs of Corruption

Police officers responsible for narcotics law enforcement are particularly vulnerable to corruption for a couple of reasons. First, violation of narcotics laws, particularly when it involves large amounts of expensive drugs such as heroin and cocaine, carries with it very severe sanctions. Drug dealers have a large incentive to bribe narcotics officers handsomely to look the other way. Second, because of the high profit margins that drug dealers enjoy, they can afford to pay off officials who might stand in their way. Finally, both drug dealing and bribery are "victimless" offenses which, carry with them little incentive for either party in the crime to report the wrongdoing. Therefore, narcotics officials can be on the take with virtual impunity (Barnett 1987; Nadelmann 1988). Even the most idealistic individuals are corruptible given the amounts of money involved.

Costs to Public Health

The prohibition of drugs poses certain public health risks both to users and to the rest of society. Prohibitionist policies create risks to users and addicts in several ways. First, because possession of drugs with intent to sell is a serious offense, distributors and manufacturers are motivated to produce and distribute drugs that are highly concentrated, taking up less bulk thereby reducing the visibility of their trafficking. It has been argued that this factor is largely accountable for the shift from less potent opium smoking to more potent and potentially toxic injectable drugs. Stephen Magura (2007) even contends, in what he calls the "iron law of drug prohibition," that prohibition policies tend to be effective in curtailing weaker types of drugs, but increase the availability and use of more potent and dangerous drugs. Furthermore, because prohibitionist policies effectively render the government impotent to regulate and monitor drug quality, addicts really do not know what they are getting in terms of purity and potency; drug concentration and potential contaminants are not consistent.

In addition, many states also prohibit the possession of needles and syringes, which are the "works" required to inject drugs. This has resulted in an addict using the same needles over and over again, and to sharing needles with other addicts. Indeed, entrepreneurial drug dealers have learned that they can make a good profit on renting needles, often as part of a larger shooting gallery operation where addicts come to get out of sight of the police while they inject their drugs (Inciardi et al. 1995; Murphy and Waldorf 1991). This phenomenon has led to widespread increases in hepatitis-B and HIV among IV drug users. The spread of HIV could be dramatically curtailed among IV drug users with the ready availability of clean needles and syringes.

The public health threat is not limited to current users. Sexual partners of infected addicts are directly exposed to hepatitis and HIV, and to a lesser extent children and others living in their households might also be affected. The public health is also threatened through the crimes, particularly violent crimes, that addicts might perpetrate against them. Still another health casualty of prohibition policies are those who have legitimate medical needs that Schedule I drugs might provide. The medical benefits of marijuana are increasingly accepted by individual medical practitioners, if not by major medical associations such as the American Cancer Society (Schwartz and Sheridan 1997). Yet, in most places, patients cannot obtain these drugs legally. Terminal patients often have difficulty obtaining adequate prescriptions for morphine and other narcotic analgesics because of fears by doctors that they will be perceived as feeding an addiction. Although technically legal to prescribe these drugs in such situations, our prohibitionist policies cast suspicion upon doctors who prescribe large amounts of narcotics to their patients. Cocaine is also an effective anesthetic in dealing with acute pain yet is effectively precluded under current policy.

Good drug education is another casualty of our current policies. A wealth of public health information is not made available to would-be drug users. Drug education programs are limited in the kinds of information they can convey under prohibitionist policies. The only acceptable content is, "Abstain." Some are reached by these messages, and we do not dispute that our current drug education programs may be effective in convincing *some youngsters* not to use drugs. Those young people who choose to experiment with drugs despite this admonition, however, have no authoritative guidelines for responsible experimentation. Such individuals are left with nothing but the informal knowledge and wisdom of peers as they embark on their pharmacological journeys. Treatment efforts are also constrained by such an abstinence-only model, which may discourage some highly addicted users from seeking treatment (Magura 2007). This is, of course, a controversial issue because many believe that such information may actually encourage or at least lend symbolic support to drug use as a way of life. These concerns are part of the balancing act required in identifying what sort of drug policy we want for the twenty-first century.

Costs to Civil Liberties

Critics of prohibition suggest that the assault on civil liberties may be the greatest cost associated with prohibition (Nadelmann 1988, 1989; Wisotsky 1986). The use of wiretapping and other forms of technological surveillance, compulsory drug testing, and forcible entering of suspected drug dealers' homes are some of the many ways in which the privacy of citizens are threatened. Police are pressured to make busts, which results in unreasonable searches and seizures of innocent people and their homes (Barnett 1987). More than 80 percent of the 1,839 court-authorized wiretaps in 2006 (and more than 93 percent of court-ordered wiretaps by federal agencies) were for suspected narcotics violations—percentages that have been creeping up through the years (U.S. Courts Administrative Office 2006, 19).

Wisotsky (1986), in an especially probing look at drug legislation, identifies many of the sources of attack on civil liberties. Among these is the Comprehensive Crime Control Act of 1984, which effectively denied bail to drug defendants on a finding by a judge that the defendant posed a danger to the community—a finding that could be applied even to drug dealing. There has also been a loosening of the exclusionary rule for drug cases. Wisotsky discusses how search-and-seizure procedures have been interpreted to get around otherwise constrictive exclusionary rule requirements:

> The law does not regard the dog's sniffing as the equivalent of a search on the theory that the odor of contraband is an exterior olfactory clue in the public domain. As a result of this theory, no right of privacy is invaded by the sniff, so the police do not need a search warrant or even probable cause to use the dog on a citizen. If the dog alerts, moreover, that fulfills the probable cause requirement, and the police may then search the driver or vehicle for drugs. (1986, 128)

The prohibitionist war on drugs has challenged heretofore protected liberties in other ways as well. Recently, we have witnessed an increase in the use of *profiling*, the practice of selectively detaining automobiles and drivers who fit a profile of a typical drug runner. This proactive law enforcement effort attempts to interdict more systematically shipments of drugs en route to their destinations. Unfortunately, the typical profile involves being black or Hispanic and male, a fact that results in the observation that it is not safe to be DWB, driving while black (a word play on the charge DWI, driving while intoxicated). One writer has charged that this practice has resulted in "the Fourth Amendment's death on the highway" (Harris 1998), and another has referred to this practice and others that disproportionately target minorities as "the new Jim Crow" (Glasser 2000). Most of those stopped because of profiling have no contraband in their possession, resulting in great numbers of innocent citizens—disproportionately those of color—being inconvenienced and subjected to the humiliating experience of being detained for possible drug law violations.

Prohibitionist policies have also inflicted costs on our civil liberties through the Comprehensive Forfeiture Act (CFA) that allows officials to seize all assets related to a drug enterprise, including contraband, tools to facilitate transport and promotion of contraband (e.g., automobiles and aircraft), and both direct and indirect proceeds of drug enterprises. The intent of these statutes is to make it truly costly for drug dealers and distributors to operate. Normally, assets seized are cash and automobiles, but personal items and even homes have been seized as alleged indirect proceeds under the CFA. These assets are normally retained by local law enforcement agencies, which provides an incentive for departments to seize property with only minimal evidence that they may be contraband or proceeds of drug trafficking. There have been numerous allegations of innocent third parties having their property seized under this statute. Once the property is seized, it then becomes the responsibility, and expense, of the alleged conspirator to prove his or her innocence to get their property returned. Clearly, this is a reversal of the normal presumption of innocence.

Maintaining a policy of prohibition clearly offers benefits. Some of these are real, measurable benefits, such as minimizing the number of people who use potentially dangerous substances. Some cannot be directly measured, such as the unequivocal statement of the value that our culture places on sobriety and drug-free lifestyles. There are, however, sobering costs to what many have called the great American experiment with drug prohibition. These costs are not trivial; they challenge some of our core values of privacy, health, and even law and order itself. These costs demand a sober look at alternatives to our current policies of prohibition. We turn to those alternatives now.

Legalization

The second major policy alternative is **legalization**. Legalization involves the lifting of all criminal and civil prohibitions and sanctions. Legalized drugs become commodities that are available in the legitimate market place, whether through prescription, through private or state-run specialty outlets, or generally over the counter. Legalization is often presented as synonymous with decriminalization, but these are two very distinct policy approaches, and we discuss them separate here. (Decriminalization is addressed in the following section.)

Legalization itself is not a unitary policy option. Indeed, one of the criticisms of legalization is that it is not always clear what its advocates mean by the term. The impetus for legalization comes primarily from two sources: civil libertarians and public health advocates. Advocates are generally concerned for either civil liberties or public health, but usually not both. We see, on the one hand, people such as the late conservative talk show host William Buckley and conservative economist Milton Friedman advocate a policy of legalization based largely on civil libertarian grounds. Their concern is with the inappropriate interference of government into the affairs of private citizens. Others, such as George Schultz, former Secretary of State under Ronald Reagan, Baltimore Mayor Curt Schmoke, and Gary Johnson, former governor of New Mexico, have advocated a policy of legalization because it allows for greater government control in the way of quality oversight to help ensure that the public health is not as jeapordized. Legalization is a policy position that clearly unites people with very different political and social goals. It should come as no surprise, however, that the kind of legalization policy proposed by these two groups is very different. Hence, it is worthwhile, before discussing the benefits and costs of legalization, to describe briefly the general models that have been put forth. It should be noted that all models that have been seriously proposed would allow access only to adults. These approaches to legalization are the laissez faire model, the limited distribution model, and the medical model.

Laissez-Faire Model

This is the most extreme of all legalization models. This approach to drug legalization most closely resembles the way in which tobacco is distributed today. Drugs would be available through a variety of outlets, including drug stores, grocery stores, vending machines in restaurants, and so forth. Minors would be prohibited from purchasing drugs, but if our experience with the sale of tobacco products is any indication, this prohibition would be almost impossible to enforce.

The laissez-faire model is the one most strongly advocated by civil libertarians. These voices base their position on their understanding of human nature and of the founding political principles of the United States. Civil libertarians generally believe that human beings are blessed with the gift of free choice and rational decision making. Indeed, they point out that our criminal justice system itself is based on this understanding of human nature. The notion of mens rea (criminal intent), for example, implies the freedom to choose between right and wrong. Steven Wisotsky, who argues primarily from a civil libertarian perspective, suggests that the current direction of prohibitionist drug policies totally ignores this premise:

> The impasse in the War on Drugs thus finds its anchor in this unexamined, unconscious denigration of the human capacity for responsible choice and self-control in the matter of drugs and consciousness. Ironically, that meta-conception violates the fundamental moral premise of our political, economic, and legal systems: that the individual is competent to order his life, to vote, to manage his own affairs and be responsible for whatever results he produces in life. (1988, 201)

This understanding of human nature is closely linked with a laissez-faire political philosophy that is committed to preserving the freedom of individual choice. An architect of this philosophy was John Stuart Mill, whose position on this issue was nearly absolute:

> The only purpose for which power can be rightfully exercised over any member of a civilized community, against his will, is to prevent harm to others. His own good, either physical or moral, is not a sufficient warrant. He cannot rightfully be compelled to do or forebear because it will be better for him to do, because it will make him happier, because, in the opinions of others, to do so would be wise, or even right. These are good reasons for remonstrating with him, or reasoning with him, or persuading him, or entreating him, but not for compelling him.... [Furthermore] [m]ankind are greater gainers by suffering each other to live as seems good to themselves, than by compelling each other to live as seems good to the rest. (Mill 1975/1859, 14–15, 18; cited in Glasser 2000, 715)

The laissez-faire model, in its most pure and uncompromising form, proposes no restriction on the sale and availability of any form of substance, with the exception of restricting access to children. The model is one of unrestrained, free-market capitalism. Although philosophically compelling to some, it is not taken seriously by most practitioners and lobbyists who are working to take practical steps toward legalization, or at least away from current repressive prohibitionist policies.

Limited Distribution Model

This model is a variant of the laissez-faire model. Like laissez-faire advocates, proponents of limited access advocate free access to mind-altering substances for those legitimately entitled to such access, namely adults who are not impaired in their ability to make rational decisions. The major difference between those who advocate laissez-faire and those who advocate limited access is in the concern and emphasis placed on preventing unwarranted access to drugs, particularly in limiting access to children. For this reason, limited access advocates propose carefully regulated sales either through government outlets (similar to state-run liquor stores), or through private outlets with special licenses and subject to close government regulation and monitoring. The closest model that we have to a limited distribution approach are state-run liquor stores and gambling enterprises. Jacobs (1990) points out that there is very little difference between these operations and private retail outlets except that prices are higher, hours are shorter, and (in the case of gambling) the odds are stacked more favorably for the house. It is questionable how effective a limited distribution model would be in limiting access to sectors of the population deemed unsuitable.

Medical Model

This model is the most restrictive of the three legalization models. Essentially, a medical maintenance approach to legalization calls for the legalized distribution of drugs either (1) to people with medical conditions who could benefit from currently prohibited drugs, and/or (2) to current addicts for purposes of preventing withdrawal symptoms. Most proponents of the medical model focus on the legal distribution of maintenance dosages to addicts. Since we discussed the medical use of certain drugs, particularly marijuana, in Chapter 8, our focus here will be on medical maintenance. Proponents of this model call for drugs to be distributed through physicians or medical clinics, and addicts would be monitored in much the same way as a patient receiving any other kind of medication. They would be required to come into the clinic or doctor's office, where they would be questioned and perhaps provide urine and/or blood samples before having their prescriptions continued.

Proponents of medical maintenance look to the British model for maintaining addicts. When the Harrison Act was passed in the United States in 1914, the British passed a similar act, the Dangerous Drugs Act, which essentially limited the distribution of narcotic drugs to physicians, pharmacists, and other medical personnel. The Harrison Act stated that medical personnel could supply narcotics to patients only "if in the practice of his profession"; the Dangerous Drugs Act allowed physicians to dispense "So far only as is necessary for the practice of his profession" (cited in Kaplan 1983, 156). These qualifying phrases, which are almost identical, would be the basis for differences in how the British and American systems evolved. U.S. Supreme Court decisions in the United States subsequent to the Harrison Act effectively ruled that the prescription of narcotics to addicts for purposes of maintenance was *not* in accord with "the practice of his profession." Hence, by the mid-1920s, addict maintenance was illegal except for the use of morphine at the Federal Public Health Service Hospitals in Lexington and Fort Worth, and in other select clinics across the country. Britain, however, never interpreted its legislation in the same restrictive sense, and physicians were free to prescribe heroin and other narcotics to addicts that came through their offices. In effect, Great Britain approached the issue of addiction as primarily a *medical* problem requiring medical solutions, whereas the United States approached it primarily as a *criminal* matter.

The British model worked well throughout much of the twentieth century. Among social scientists, an early American proponent of the British model was Edwin Schur, who noted in 1965 that addiction in Great Britian was "remarkably benign" (154). Schur went on to say that there were less than a thousand addicts in all of Britain, and that there was almost no illicit trafficking in narcotics because addicts were not only able to obtain them legally, but could purchase them at very low cost because these drugs are subsidized under the National Health Service. These early reports have led to a great deal of support for a similar system in the United States. Critics and other observers have pointed out, however, that since the time of Schur's writing, the situation has changed dramatically in Britain. Indeed, Britain has all but abandoned this system of narcotics distribution. When it began, those who were being treated in the British clinics and doctor's offices were primarily middle-class addicts who became addicted while being treated for pain. However, as awareness of the availability of heroin in Britain became more widely known, it attracted more individuals who were committed to the use of heroin for pleasure, and it was not long before doctors and clinics were overwhelmed with requests for narcotics, much of which was later diverted to other subcultural users (Kaplan 1983). Kaplan points out that between 1961 and 1969, the number of addicts in Britain increased by at least 500 percent, and more importantly, the demographics of addicts changed from the primarily middle-class, medically induced to younger and less stable. These changes resulted in severe restrictions on heroin distribution and the withdrawal of freedom of most private physicians to prescribe heroin at all (Kaplan 1983).

According to critics, the British model did not work in Britain, and we should not expect it to work here either. Moreover, Jacobs (1990) points out that even if it were an effective policy here, its effectiveness is restricted to heroin and the narcotics. Control of drugs such as cocaine and crack, LSD, methamphetamines, marijuana, and many other drugs of concern would not benefit from such a model. These are recreational drugs usually taken for the pleasure of effect rather than avoidance of withdrawal symptoms, because they are not addicting in the classical sense of producing physical tolerance. There is no maintenance dose for most of these drugs, and it is not even appropriate to talk about medical maintenance for anything other than narcotics, according to Jacobs.

Advantages of Legalization

Most of the benefits of legalization are in reducing the costs of prohibition. The advantages of legalization are generally stated in terms of economic benefits, moral benefits, and public health benefits.

Economic Benefits

Advocates of legalization point to the dramatically escalating economic costs of a prohibitionist policy that is, by most standards, not working very well. We have already discussed the 16-fold increase in taxpayer dollars being spent on supply-side efforts to curb the availability of drugs in this country. Nadelmann (1988) and other legalization advocates would have this money put to much more productive use. Beyond the money saved, a policy of legalization also allows for taxation of drugs in much the same way that alcohol and tobacco are taxed today. Hence, rather than spending billions of dollars annually to curtail drug importation and distribution, federal, state, and local governments could be the recipients of stronger tax bases. Treatment and drug education programs could be the beneficiaries of much of this money, thereby focusing on demand reduction and recognizing drug use and addiction as a medical issue requiring education and treatment rather than punishment.

Moral Benefits

We use the term *moral benefits* in its broadest sense to refer to the answers legalization provides to the moral dilemmas posed by prohibition. One of the dilemmas that we have discussed is the widespread corruption observed among police officers in narcotics units. Legalization should reduce the level of police corruption considerably. In the first place, the underground market that creates the need for corrupt officials should be substantially reduced. Moreover, legal drug enterprises do not require corruption of officials to operate profitably. The expectation of legalization proponents is that for both of these reasons, corruption would not be a major issue if drugs were made legal.

Another moral dilemma created by our current system of prohibition is the hypocrisy of a policy that heavily penalizes the possession and use of some drugs (e.g., marijuana), while other drugs that are by just about any standard more socially and personally harmful (e.g., alcohol and tobacco) are permitted and even promoted. Such an inconsistent policy sends mixed and confusing messages to children and young people. There comes a time for many, if not most, young people watching their parents use alcohol, tobacco, and prescription drugs, to reject the legal distinction as an irrelevant moral distinction in the choices that they make.

This reality suggests another difficulty with current policy that could be answered by legalization: the inability to reach young people who have already made the decision to use drugs. Drug education must be an all-or-nothing proposition under a policy of prohibition: "Drugs are bad. You shouldn't use them. Here are the reasons why." That is the only message that can be communicated. Ethan Nadelmann states, with regard to current marijuana policies,

> It's still impossible . . . for any government official to speak out publicly about
> the difference between responsible and irresponsible use of marijuana, as they
> would with alcohol. All marijuana use is defined as drug abuse—notwithstanding
> extensive evidence that most marijuana users suffer little if any harm. That
> position may be intellectually and scientifically indefensible, but those in
> government regard it as politically and legally obligatory. (1997, 51)

Young people who experiment with drugs and discover that the effects prophesied did not occur are likely to reject any future efforts to educate them by anyone in authority. Moreover, those who have already rejected this message have no moral or practical guidelines for their drug use. If we were to legalize drugs, educators would have more options for reaching current users. We are using such an approach with alcohol with messages such as "Friends don't let friends drive drunk." The message defines appropriate and inappropriate use of alcohol, and assigns responsibility for appropriate use. The opportunity for moral and practical influence greatly expands when drugs are legalized.

The other moral benefit of a policy of legalization is the potential restoration of civil liberties that have been seriously imperiled by our expanding war on drugs. These threats were discussed in the earlier section on prohibition. Although legalization is not expected to eradicate entirely the underground market for drugs, and hence not completely eliminate the need for repressive law enforcement strategies, such a policy should certainly reduce the threats to civil liberties that we now experience.

Public Health Benefits

The public health benefits to a policy of legalization come in several forms. First, only through a policy of legalization can the government truly regulate the quality of drugs distributed. Many of the toxic reactions to drugs result from either wide variations in purity or the use of toxic materials to dilute the drugs. Marijuana, for example, can be laced with *angel dust* (PCP) and other potent substances like embalming fluid (a combination known as *fry*). If the user is unaware of this, severe reactions could result (Nadelmann 1989). Similarly, although heroin is usually diluted with milk sugar and perhaps quinine, both inert substances, dealers have been known to cut their drugs with strychnine and even rat poison, which can produce toxic and even fatal effects.

Additionally, legalization facilitates the distribution of clean needles, thereby substantially reducing the risk of contracting the HIV and hepatitis viruses. The Drug Policy Alliance (2002) reports that more than one-third of all AIDS cases in the United States and a majority of HIV-infected women, children, and infants are directly linked to illegal IV drug use.

A third public health benefit is that access to certain drugs for medical uses will be enhanced. Certainly, it is possible to make exceptions to general prohibition policies for medical use of certain drugs such as marijuana to treat glaucoma or nausea related to chemotherapy, but in reality, there is great resistance to these exceptions. It is difficult for glaucoma or cancer patients to gain legal access to marijuana. It is virtually impossible to access cocaine for anaesthetic purposes, and doctors are extremely hesitant to prescribe narcotic medications for at-home pain relief, even though such drugs are often called for.

A final and more indirect benefit of legalization is that it squarely defines addiction as a *medical* issue and provides the political base to support a stronger effort at treatment and drug education. Although both drug treatment and drug education have been given some attention under our current prohibition policy, there are serious constraints on their effectiveness. The United States has never seriously waged a treatment and education campaign, at least not with the same degree of commitment that we have waged supply-side efforts of law enforcement, the "war on drugs."

Disadvantages of Legalization

Opponents of legalization have challenged the proposed benefits of legalization and have identified additional problems with a policy of legalization as set forth by legalization champions. Other than government officials such as former drug czars William Bennett, General Barry McCaffrey and John Walters, there has been perhaps no more outspoken critic of legalization than James A. Inciardi, director of the University of Delaware's Center for Drug and Alcohol Studies. Inciardi has identified numerous problem areas with drug legalization, which we highlight here.

Insufficient Development of Legalization Proposals

Perhaps the greatest criticism that Inciardi and others level at legalization advocates like Ethan Nadelmann is that they have not really provided us with meaningful legalization proposals (Inciardi and McBride 1989; Jacobs 1990). These critics point to many areas of insufficient policy development in the legalization agenda. First, it is not clear whether all or only some drugs should be legalized, and if only some, which ones? What potency limits should be established? What about minimum age limits? What type of distribution model should be established—a laissez-faire, limited access, or medical maintenance model? Where could the drugs be sold—in supermarkets? On-premise use only, such as serving alcohol in bars? What about cultivation, and where would it take place? Should advertising be permitted? These and other questions need to be addressed in a well-conceived proposal for legalization. In the absence of these details, these critics maintain that legalization is not worthy of serious policy consideration.

Increased Use and Public Health Costs

Legalization would almost certainly result in increased use of the legalized drugs. Although some advocates of legalization have questioned this likelihood, both our historical experience with alcohol prohibition (and its lifting) and the logic of classical economics affirms it. Even a massive increase in drug consumption would not be of particular concern if drugs were, in fact, benign substances that did no harm to users or to others around them. However, not even the most ardent supporters of legalization make the claim that drugs are completely harmless. Even marijuana, once considered virtually harmless, especially when compared with tobacco, is now recognized as containing hundreds of chemicals, many of which have unknown or potentially serious health effects. Cocaine, thought in the late 1970s to be benign and nonaddictive, is now known to have a physiological basis for addiction, albeit a different basis than the narcotics. We also know that cocaine is potentially dangerous to those with heart conditions and is especially toxic when combined with alcohol.

Given the potential harm caused by these drugs, we must ask ourselves if we are willing to put more citizens at risk by legalizing them, since critics rightfully note that the numbers of users would climb post legalization. More specifically, we must ask ourselves if the public health benefits described above outweigh the public health costs of many times more people being exposed to the physiological and psychic risks that these drugs pose. This is an important question, because although legalization advocates claim that we are losing the war on drugs, the best survey research indicates that overall drug use has actually declined since the 1970s and has leveled off after a slight rise in the 1990s among high school students (Johnston et al. 2007b). If current prohibition policies have not eliminated drug use, at least they seem to have contained it.

Costs of Going Against Public Opinion

This argument against legalization closely parallels the position that prohibition sends an important symbolic message about the value of sobriety. The fact is, according to legalization opponents, the American people do not want to see drugs legalized. Even marijuana, the most tolerated of currently illegal drugs, has little support for nonmedical legalization. Recent Gallup Poll data indicate that about 60 percent of Americans oppose the legalization of marijuana, though that number has declined from about 80 percent in the early 1970s (Carroll 2005). Opposition to legalization varies directly with age, with only about 50 percent of 18- to 29-year-olds and some 80 percent of those over 65 years of age opposing legalization of marijuana (Carroll 2005). It should also be pointed out that there is strong support for legalization of marijuana for medical purposes when prescribed by physicians. Those who oppose prohibition on the basis of civil liberties, public health, or moral arguments will not be impressed with public opinion as the basis for policy, but the practical problems of implementing a policy that is contrary to what more than two-thirds of the population believes desirable are immense.

Decriminalization

Decriminalization is a policy alternative that is similar to legalization, but with some very important differences. Many people understand decriminalization as some sort of compromise policy, half-way between prohibition and legalization. This is perhaps the reason that marijuana has been decriminalized but not legalized in a number of states; legislators are more willing to take this seeming half-way step than to legalize. This conception of decriminalization as something short of legalization could not be further from the truth, however. Decriminalization is, in fact, a third policy option that, although similar to legalization in some ways, is quite unique.

Decriminalization is a policy that removes criminal sanctions from the activity in question. In the case of drugs, the activity targeted for removal of criminal sanctions is usually the possession of small amounts of a drug. This does not mean that the activity in question is legal. In most states that have decriminalized marijuana, possession of even small amounts of marijuana is still a violation of the law, but not of the criminal law.[2] Typically, such possession is regarded as a civil infraction, much like exceeding the speed limit, and is subject to civil penalties, usually fines, but no jail time or other restriction of liberty can be meted out.

Decriminalization of marijuana has been established as policy in thirteen states (see Table 12.1). This policy option did not come to pass suddenly or without precedent, however. Starting in the mid-1960s, individual states began to reduce the criminal penalties for marijuana possession such that by 1972, simple possession of less than an ounce of marijuana was classified as a misdemeanor in all but eight states (Bonnie 1980). Currently, all 50 states have either reduced the charges for possession of small amounts of marijuana to a misdemeanor, or have decriminalized such possession. Also in 1972, the National Commission on Marijuana and Drug Abuse (which was created by the same legislation that enacted the Controlled Substances Act of 1970) issued the first of two reports, entitled *Marihuana: A Signal of Misunderstanding*. This report called for a drastic change in policy regarding possession and "casual distribution" (not for profit) of marijuana. The Commission called on federal and state governments to remove these low-level offenses from the list of criminal offenses, though the public possession and use could result in fines (National Commission on Marihuana and Drug Abuse, 1972). States soon

Table 12.1. States that have decriminalized marijuana.

State	Quantity Involved	Penalty
Alaska*	0 to 1 ounce	None
California*	0 to 1 ounce (28.5 grams)	$100 fine
Colorado	0 to 1 ounce	$100 fine
Maine	0 to 1.25 ounce	$350 to $600 fine
Massachusetts	0 to 1 ounce	$100
Minnesota*	0 to 1.5 ounce (42.5 grams)	$200 fine
Mississippi*	0 to 1 ounce (30 grams)	$100 to $250 fine
Nebraska	0 to 1 ounce	$100 fine
Nevada*	0 to 1 ounce (if over 21 years)	$600 fine
New York	0 to 1 oz. (25 grams)	$100 fine
North Carolina*	0 to 0.5 ounce	30 days suspended, $200 fine
Ohio*	0 to 3.5 ounces (100 grams)	$100 fine
Oregon*	0 to 1 ounce	$500 to $1000 fine

*States that maintain misdemeanor status on possession for personal use, but do not arrest or suspend sentences for cooperative defendants.
Source: NORML 2004.

responded. Oregon was the first state to decriminalize in 1973, with a statute stating that unlawful possession of one ounce or less of marijuana was a "violation" and punishable at that time by not more than $100.[3] Other states followed suit. These states and their penalties associated with the use and possession of small quantities of marijuana are listed in Table 12.1.

The impact of decriminalization on levels of drug use has been closely monitored over the past 25 years. According to Thies and Register (1993), marijuana use in Oregon increased from about 24 percent prevalence (of 18- to 29-year-olds) in 1974 to 30 percent prevalence in 1977. Similar increases were reported following decriminalization in California (Cuskey et al. 1978). It should be noted, however, that the prevalence of marijuana use was increasing nationwide during this period of time. Cross-cultural research by Trebach (1987) suggests a slight decline in drug use in Holland following decriminalization there. Although cross-cultural data must be interpreted with great care, it seems safe to conclude, considering the growing body of data from the United States, that the impact of decriminalization of marijuana on the prevalence of use will be minimal at most. What is not so certain, however, is the impact of decriminalization of other drugs, such as heroin or cocaine, on the prevalence of their use. Marijuana is a drug that is already quite widely available, even in those jurisdictions where it is criminally prohibited. We would not expect decriminalization to have as much of an impact where a substance is already relatively easy to obtain. Drugs such as heroin, cocaine, crack, and other substances with much more restricted distribution would likely experience a substantial increase in prevalence.

Advantages of Decriminalization over Legalization

When compared to prohibition policies, decriminalization carries many of the advantages and disadvantages of legalization. There are, however, some unique benefits and costs to this policy option that distinguish it from legalization. Let us look first at some of the advantages.

Stronger Base of Public Support

The very fact that several states have decriminalized marijuana suggests that the public is much more willing to endorse a policy of decriminalization than one of legalization. Moreover, all 50 states have reduced simple marijuana possession to a misdemeanor—again suggesting public support for constraining criminal law in this area.

Maintains Stronger Symbolic Message

Many drug policy experts are much more comfortable with a decriminalization model because, in their view, it does not represent wholesale support, symbolically, of drug use. Rather, it is a recognition that for certain drugs, particularly marijuana, harsh criminal offenses are doing more harm than good and, indeed, more harm than moderate drug use itself. Hence, although not endorsing the use of these drugs, decriminalization is believed to lessen the damaging consequences of using them.

Maintains Criminal Sanctions for Trafficking

This advantage over legalization is the counterpart to maintaining a stronger symbolic message. Those who believe that marijuana use is potentially very destructive argue that there must be mechanisms in place to punish severely large-scale traffickers. Decriminalization allows for such punitive action.

Disadvantages of Decriminalization over Legalization

Decriminalization is politically advantageous over legalization, but given the mood of the country with regard to drugs and drug use, there are nevertheless several ways in which decriminalization is not as attractive an alternative to drug prohibition.

Public Health Disadvantages

All of the public health costs associated with prohibition essentially remain under policies of decriminalization. Because decriminalized drugs are not made legal, there are no mechanisms by which the government can systematically monitor or regulate the production and quality of these substances. Users are still at the mercy of an underground market and the questionable ethics associated with that method of distribution.

Crime and Corruption Disadvantages

Decriminalization will probably not have much impact as legalization on the level of crime and corruption. High-level dealers of decriminalized drugs remain subject to major penalties and continue to have incentive to corrupt public officials. The cost of decriminalized drugs is also governed by illegal market dynamics, so the economic link between drug use and crime remains.

Limited Cost Savings

Decriminalization does indeed represent some cost savings to law enforcement, in that enforcement efforts can focus on major dealers and distributors. Courtroom dockets are not as deadlocked with casual users, and prisons may be less overcrowded. Decriminalization does not, however, allow the public treasury to recoup any associated costs through taxation. Hence, decriminalization continues to be a drain on public funds rather than a source of renewal.

Still a Criminal Justice Model

Many advocates of legalization urge the movement toward a medical model of drug addiction. The argument is that addiction is a disease and should be treated in the same way as alcoholism. It is impossible to embrace fully a medical model of addiction with a policy of decriminalization. Indeed, decriminalization does not move us any closer to a medical model than does prohibition, except perhaps to make the electorate more accepting of the use of otherwise illegal drugs for special medical purposes.

Limited Applicability

Decriminalization has been reasonably successful in those states that have decriminalized marijuana. Studies have shown no substantial rise in the prevalence of marijuana use in these states (Thies and Register 1993). This does not mean, however, that decriminalization is a viable policy option for most illegal drugs today. Because of the highly reinforcing effect of some drugs such as heroin and cocaine, and to the hysteria associated with so many illegal drugs, a policy of decriminalization of any amount of these drugs will likely result in quite different consequences than has our experience with marijuana. Under a policy of marijuana decriminalization, for example, an individual may be more likely to experiment a few times than would otherwise be the case, and may even go on to use occasionally. If the same increase in levels of experimentation with more dependency-producing substances such as cocaine or heroin were to take place, it is likely that decriminalization would result in a substantial population of addicts whose habits would require them to become involved in drug sales to sustain their consumption levels. These newly created addicts would be forced to deal in higher-level volume than would be acceptable under most decriminalization statutes. Hence, even if decriminalization is a workable policy option for marijuana, it cannot be simply transposed to other drugs.

Harm Reduction: An Alternative Framework for Drug Policy

Harm reduction generally shifts the goal of drug policy from that of eliminating or even decreasing drug use (which is the goal of current policy) to reducing the harm that is caused by both drug use and drug policies (Massing 1999; Nadelmann 2004). Clearly, abstinence and reduced levels of drug use on a societal basis are laudable goals and should be pursued whenever it is possible to do so without risking greater harm to the user and/or to society. However, our current policies of prohibition in and of themselves pose risks. Harm reduction proponents advocate a weighing of the risks of drug use against the policies that attempt to curtail this use. Harm reduction, in its essence, embodies President Jimmy Carter's challenge to congress in 1977: "Penalties against drug use should not be more damaging to an individual than the use of the drug itself. Nowhere is this more clear than in the laws against possession of marijuana in private for personal use." The harm reduction approach is grounded in the supposition that drug use will never be totally eliminated, and that we can expect recreational drug use to remain a part of society indefinitely.

European Roots

Harm reduction as a formalized approach to drug policy evolved in the late 1980s, though many of the strategies embodied in harm reduction were being implemented in the underground drug culture and literature of the 1960s and 1970s. Recreational users and addicts were informed through comic books and other media how to avoid the pitfalls associated with the use of a variety of drugs (Nadelmann et al. 1997). There were other voices in the wilderness, including the earlier cited *Marihuana: A Signal of Misunderstanding*, which called for lowering of penalties and decriminalization for possession of small amounts of marijuana (National Commission on Marihuana and Drug Abuse, 1972). A similar proposal known as the Le Dain Report was issued in Canada (Le Dain Commission 1972).

Harm reduction was first promoted as a serious policy approach in European countries and Australia, the culmination of what is seen by many as a series of failed attempts at international drug control (Bullington 2004; Carstairs 2005). The Netherlands responded by the early 1970s with the designation of "approved dealers" who were allowed to distribute small amounts of marijuana in youth centers under carefully controlled conditions (Bullington 2004). The impetus for the strong

DRUGS AND EVERYDAY LIFE

A Harm Reduction Manifesto

- [W]e...bring a different moral calculus to bear on drug policy, starting with the basic notion that there is nothing inherently immoral or unethical about consuming psychoactive drugs absent harm to others.
- We believe that people should not be punished simply for what they put into their bodies.
- We see no legitimate basis for discriminating between the moderate and responsible alcohol user and the equivalent user of marijuana, cocaine, Ecstasy, methamphetamine, or any other illicit drug.
- We similarly see no basis for discriminating between an individual who is addicted to alcohol and one who is addicted to an illicit drug. The only

legitimate discrimination is between those drug users who do no harm to others and those who do.
- Most of us see this as a basic issue of human rights, grounded in a human being's right of sovereignty over one's mind and body, and analogous to principles of nondiscrimination on the basis of race, raith, gender, sexuality, and so on.
- [W]e view the legal and popular presumption that people can and should be coerced to refrain from particular drugs (but not others) as the principal reason why U.S. drug control policies have wreaked such havoc on dozens of countries, thousands of communities, millions of lives, and most of the core values of a free society.

Source: Excerpted from Ethan Nadelmann. "Criminologists and Punitive Drug Prohibition: To Serve or to Challenge?" *Criminology & Public Policy* 3, 3 (July 2004), p. 445. Used with permission of the American Society of Criminology.

push toward more systematic harm control strategies in many European countries was the AIDS crisis and the recognition that IV drug users were a primary risk group for acquiring and spreading HIV. While the United States maintained strong prohibitionist policies in response to this crisis, many European countries, as well as Australia, turned to a public health model incorporating harm reduction principles. Germany, for example, shifted its focus away from strong prohibitionist policies with stiff sentences to public health policies such as providing clean needles to addicts and an increased emphasis on treatment (Körner 2004). Spain responded with needle exchange programs and increased availability of methadone maintenance (Gamella and Rodrigo 2004). More recently, several countries including Australia, Switzerland, Germany, Spain, the United Kingdom, and Portugal, have established safe injection sites that are clean and sanitary, and where addicts can obtain clean needles, without fear of police harassment (Carstairs 2005).

Harm reduction has emerged globally as a strong policy option to abstinence and prohibitionist policies, despite resistance to such strategies led by the United States. As harm reduction has increased in world-wide stature, it has broadened in scope as well. Once concerned almost exclusively with containing the spread of diseases and other public health concerns, HIV and hepatitus in particular, harm reduction now incorporates new models for drug education, addresses the human rights concerns of users, and incorporates legal drugs such as alcohol and tobacco.

It has been suggested that harm reduction is no longer a single, unitary policy option, but as it has matured, distinctive fractions have developed within the movement. Tammi (2004) identifies these fractions as: (1) the professional public health fraction, which is the oldest, emerging directly out of the HIV/AIDS crisis and relying on professional medical and scientific experts to address public health concerns and recommend ways of reducing harm; (2) the mutual self-help and identity movement fraction, which has its roots in the more general self-help movement and emphasizes user involvement in the development and implementation of harm reduction policies; and more recently (3) the global justice fraction, which emphasizes global justice concerns and sees harm reduction as a social justice and human rights movement, presenting themselves in solidarity with other human rights movements. Even as harm reduction has been evolving in these ways, it remains fundamentally a policy reform agenda that opposes the United States–dominated policy of prohibition and abstinence-only that, as Bullington (2004) states, lurks as the "elephant in the closet."

Harm Reduction Strategies

Harm reduction strategists identify several approaches to harm reduction. Nadelmann, McNeely, and Drucker (1997) offer what is perhaps the most systematic approach to articulating a harm reduction strategy, conceptualizing three levels of prevention, each with its own specific strategies, as summarized in Table 12.2.

Primary prevention strategies focus on discouraging drug use where possible. Abstinence might be viewed as an ideal, but it is only one of several approaches to avoiding the problems currently associated with drug use. Among those who have already chosen to use drugs, primary prevention efforts are directed at warding off addiction. At the primary level of prevention, harm reductionists seek to encourage responsible patterns of drug use, limiting drug use to occasional or recreational levels if possible, or at least manageable levels of more frequent use. A major component of a harm reduction strategy is to eliminate the necessity of purchasing drugs in the illegal market place. Users who are forced to become involved with the illegal subculture of drug use run much higher risks of addiction as they become more and more immersed in this subculture. Risk of addiction is enhanced because, as friendship patterns develop in these subcultures, there are greater pressures to conform to the drug-using lifestyles of peers. Access to drugs is also enhanced through contacts with dealers and wholesalers. Furthermore, the public labeling and degradation of identity that results from being arrested, tried, and punished helps to set in motion a process that makes one vulnerable to addiction. According to labeling

Table 12.2. Three levels of intervention in harm reduction.

Level of intervention	Definition	Policy responses
Primary prevention	Prevention of drug use where feasible, and especially of addiction	Marijuana decriminalization Drug education Medical legalization
Secondary prevention	Limiting severity, and consequences to community, of drug addiction	Needle exchange programs Drug zones Safe injection sites
Tertiary prevention	Limiting consequences of addiction to user	Treatment

Source: Adapted from Nadelmann et al., 1997, Table 4.1. Reprinted with permission.

and symbolic interactiontheorists, the public labeling of one as a deviant only reinforces the deviant self-concept, and we tend to act in a way that is consistent with our self-identity.

There are, of course, other social and public health problems associated with the illegal drug market such as uncertain quality of drugs, crime, and infectious diseases that harm reductionists would seek to avoid. Hence, a major harm reduction proposal is to decriminalize, if not legalize, certain drugs with lower potential for addiction. Marijuana is the drug most targeted for decriminalization or legalization, but other drugs are candidates as well. The legalizing of marijuana for medical purposes has been especially targeted in recent years, as more and more physicians are recognizing and speaking out on the potential benefits of marijuana in the treatment of glaucoma, nausea resulting from chemotherapy, and the wasting syndrome common among AIDS patients.

Another strategy, which is not always identified as part of a primary prevention strategy but is consistent with it, is a focus on drug education. Current education efforts are not sufficient to reach those who have already chosen to use drugs. The only message that is contained in D.A.R.E., Partnership for a Drug-Free America, and other educational initiatives in the United States is abstinence. Harm reduction educational efforts put safety first by providing such information as: What kind of drug combinations should be avoided because of synergism and other interactive effects? What subjective effects should one expect from various drugs, and what sorts of behaviors should one avoid while using these drugs? What hygienic practices ensure safer drug use? How can one pace his or her drug use? What are ways to cope with symptoms of withdrawal? This is all information that drug users need to avoid the pitfalls of addiction and the harmful consequences of use and addiction should addiction occur. Much of this information is, indeed, an important part of secondary prevention efforts.

Secondary prevention is directed primarily at those individuals who might already be characterized as addicted. At the secondary level, harm reduction policies seek to reduce the length and severity of addiction- and drug-related disorders. Many of the education elements suggested as part of primary prevention are also aimed at minimizing the severity of drug addiction to addicted individuals. These educational efforts often go hand-in-hand with **needle exchange** programs, which are also a central part of secondary prevention efforts. These programs seek to reduce the spread of HIV and hepatitis by providing addicts with clean and sterile needles in exchange for used needles to minimize the prevalence of dirty needles available to addict users (Singer et al. 1991). Needle exchange programs also typically provide condoms to addicts to help reduce the spread of HIV among IV drug users through sexual contact. Many of these programs also provide educational materials to addicts, including instructions on how to sterilize needles, information about safer sexual practices, and assistance in linking addicts with needed medical services. Some of these programs are quite aggressive in their efforts to reach addicts, using vans and buses to get the word out, while others operate as drop-in centers (Nadelmann et al. 1997).

The need for these programs was recognized by addicts long before the HIV/AIDS epidemic; some such programs were operating underground by the early 1970s. Early programs for needle exchange were established in the Netherlands in 1984. Public distribution of clean needles did not begin in the United States until 1986 when Jon Parker, a former injection drug user working on his master's degree, began distributing needles to drug users. Parker had a professor who publicly declared that addicts should not be the focus of prevention efforts in the spread of AIDS because they would not change their behavior anyway. Angered, Parker began meeting with local area addicts, and out of those discussions, he launched the first known public needle exchange effort in this country. Two years later, Tacoma, Washington, established the first community-supported needle exchange program in the United States (Lane 1993). Unfortunately, the political climate at the federal level has presented many hurdles to the successful establishment of needle exchange efforts (Sherman 2006), and a corresponding NIMBY (not in my backyard) mentality at the local community level has severely limited needle exchange efforts in the United States (Strike et al. 2004).

Another strategy, employed with mixed success primarily in European cities, is the provision of specially zoned areas for drug users to congregate and not be subject to harassment or risk of arrest from police. The principle behind this idea is the same as that which governs red light districts and pornography shops in large cities: containment within a delimited area to avoid the spread of these unwanted activities in other commercial and residential areas. The first well-known designated drug locale was in the Zurich, Switzerland, neighborhood of Platzspitz, commonly known as Needle Park. Needle Park was deemed a success early on, as heroin addicts and other drug users did indeed congregate here rather than in various isolated pockets throughout the city. The enthusiasm waned, however, as Needle Park soon became a haven for thousands of outsiders who would flock to Zurich, creating a strain on the system and threatening surrounding neighborhoods. The park was shut down in 1992 (Bullington 2004).

The efficacy of special zones for drug activity continues to be debated, some jurisdictions have adopted the more restricted proposal of safe injecting rooms for addicts (McKeganey 2006). These safe injecting rooms consist of small centers where drug users can get clean needles and condoms, obtain basic medical care, and even use drugs in a hygienic environment. These centers are not without controversy and have prompted heated debate in some European countries where they have been established, as they are believed by many to encourage injection drug use (McKeganey 2006; Skretting 2006). On the other hand, according to harm reduction strategists, these policies are consistent with other policing practices in both the United States and Europe that seek to contain other marginal behavior, including sex, drinking, and gambling establishments (Nadelmann et al. 1997).

Tertiary prevention is directed primarily at established addicts and seeks to minimize the medical and social consequences of their addiction to themselves and to others with whom they have contact. The distinction between secondary and tertiary intervention efforts is by no means sharply delineated. Much of what is identified as secondary prevention is clearly aimed at reducing the spread of HIV and containing crime—clearly efforts to reduce social and medical consequences. As articulated by Nadelmann and his colleagues (1997), however, tertiary prevention is reserved primarily for greater access to treatment, particularly drug maintenance treatment.

Methadone maintenance is the most widely used form of drug treatment for hard-core heroin addicts in the United States today. Harm reduction strategists such as Nadelmann and colleagues urge the proliferation of methadone maintenance as a means of reducing higher-risk drug injection. Rather than limit methadone distribution to government-controlled clinics, harm reductionists urge the integration of methadone maintenance into mainstream medical practice so that private physicians could prescribe methadone to their addicted patients. Such a policy would increase the availability of noninjectable drugs (methadone is usually taken orally), thereby reducing the necessity of relying on illegal, perhaps toxic, injectable heroin. Moreover, because of an expansion in the potential number of methadone providers, such a system is more effective in linking addicts with other needed medical services (Nadelmann et al. 1997).

Harm Reduction: A Viable Approach?

Contrary to what popular belief, many if not most harm reductionists are not favorable to legalization for any of several reasons. Although harm reduction has indeed been embraced by most legalization advocates, it is also believed by many staunch prohibitionists to represent workable solutions to some of the most serious costs of prohibition policies. These harm reduction strategies are believed by many (though certainly not all) prohibition advocates to be workable within a more general prohibitionist framework (Nadelmann 1998). Indeed, insofar as illicit drug use continues to be a politically charged issue—which, by all indications, it will continue to be—harm reduction can be effective in the United States only if it can work within a prohibitionist framework. Despite the initial rush to decriminalize marijuana in the 1970s, there has been no corresponding enthusiasm on the part of the state and federal legislatures toward either legalization or further decriminalization. Insofar as harm reduction strategies are politically or publicly linked with a policy of legalization or decriminalization, it is highly unlikely that they will ever be adopted on a widespread basis in the United States. It is somewhat foreboding that John Walters, former director of the Office of National Drug Control Policy under President George W. Bush, continues to oppose the use of needle exchange programs, a harm reduction approach that holds potential to curtail the spread of HIV/AIDS among IV drug users. It is, at the same time, encouraging that this rigid stance is being questioned by high-ranking members of Congress such as Henry Waxman, chair of Committee on Oversight and Government Reform (2008). Despite this increased high-level attention, it would seem that until harm reduction can be articulated in terms that do not diminish the goal of prohibition—to reduce drug use—its adoption in the United States will be limited.

Harm reduction is, we predict, a policy alternative that will overshadow both legalization and decriminalization. Indeed it already has, as evidenced by the fact that such ardent legalization advocates as Ethan Nadelmann now insist on a self-identity of "harm reductionist" (Nadelmann, 2002). Harm reduction appears to offer a potential meeting ground for old prohibitionists and old legalization advocates to develop a sound drug policy agenda for the twenty-first century.

Summary

In this chapter we have endeavored to provide a balanced assessment of the major policy options that involve legal responses to American drug problems. Prohibition, legalization, and decriminalization models represent distinct policy responses to drug use with consequences and implications, benefits and costs, that should be taken into consideration by anyone planning drug strategy. Drug policy makers in this country have often been unwilling to be thoughtful, even rejecting and disparaging clear scientific evidence, which has resulted in a collection of policies that are at times contradictory and ineffective. Political expediency and moral entrepreneurship, rather than a sober and balanced approach, have led to the implementation of policies that at times do more harm than good. Harm reduction, a policy orientation born out of grave concern over the spread of HIV/AIDS and other infectious diseases among both users and non users, often gets crowded out in the drama of political rhetoric. Public opinion on a host of legal response issues is similarly swayed by ideas and beliefs that, although popular, are not grounded in the empirical research on policy alternatives. Our current situation cries for a humane policy grounded in objective research, particularly cross-cultural research, assessing the impact of creative policy strategies implemented by other countries that have seriously struggled with practical solutions to their drug problems.

Key Terms

decriminalization
demand-side strategies
harm reduction
interdiction
legalization
needle exchange
primary prevention
prohibition
secondary prevention
source reduction
supply-side strategies
tertiary prevention

Thinking Critically...

1. Develop a case for either prohibition, legalization, or decriminalization. Be sure to consider all of the costs and benefits of each policy orientation, and then explain why the policy you choose is superior.

2. If you were asked by your governor to write a drug policy based on principles of harm reduction for your state, what would that policy look like? Identify as many components as possible, and provide a rationale for each of those components based on harm reduction principles.

3. The authors stated in this chapter that the impetus for legalization comes generally from two sources, civil libertarians and public health advocates. How do these two perspectives differ in their vision of what a good legalization policy might look like? Which of the three models of legalization do each of these advocates generally favor?

4. Discuss specific examples of primary, secondary, and tertiary policy strategies. In your opinion, which of these strategies should receive the greatest emphasis in our response to drug use and addiction? Explain.

5. The authors ask the rhetorical question, How does understanding these larger policy questions contribute to our knowledge about why people use drugs in the first place, what kinds of people use drugs, the relationship between drug use and crime, and a host of other issues that we have already addressed in earlier chapters of this book? After reading this chapter, and thinking about the other chapters

your have read and the other materials that you have encountered in this course, how would *you* answer this question? Be specific.

Learning from the Internet

1. The Drug Policy Alliance generally supports a policy of harm reduction. Go to their website at http://www.drugpolicy.org/homepage.cfm and read through various materials presented there, especially articles specifically addressing harm reduction issues. Summarize some of the specific policy options that the Drug Policy Alliance advocates, either directly or implicitly, under the banner of harm reduction.

2. NORML is an acronym for "National Organization for the Reform of Marijuana Laws," found at http://www.norml.org/. Study their website. Based on your careful reading of the materials on their website, how does NORML want to see marijuana laws reformed?

Notes

1. U.S. Customs and Border Protection was created in 2003 within the Department of Homeland Security by merging the U.S. Customs Service, the Border Patrol, and the inspection functions of the Immigration and Naturalization Service and the Agriculture and Plant Health Inspection Service (APHIS).
2. Some states that are considered to have decriminalized small amounts of marijuana technically maintain criminal statutes. Enforcement of these statutes, however, is conducted as though it were a civil offense, by imposing fines rather than jail time.
3. Oregon has since increased the fine to $500-$1000. See Table 12.1.

CHAPTER **13**

Therapeutic Responses to Drug Problems: Drug Treatment

This chapter addresses varied approaches to the treatment of drug addiction. Among the range of treatment philosophies, the concept of *treatment* implies at least two things that all have in common. First, it assumes that excessive drug use is itself a problem, and moreover that it is an individual problem in need of correction. Second, it implies that these problems can, in fact, be corrected. These presuppositions might seem to be obvious to anyone even casually familiar with drug use as a social issue. However, as we have pointed out early in this book, there is no universal agreement that drug use, even high levels of drug use, necessarily represents an individual problem. As discussed in Chapter 12, many scholars and observers of the drug scene suggest that the problem is society's punitive response toward drug use and not drug use itself. Furthermore, it has not always been assumed that drug abuse and addiction are treatable. As recently as the 1960s it was often believed, even by professionals in the field, that "once an addict, always an addict." As the phrase was interpreted then, there was a sense of hopelessness for the abuser who had gone too far into addiction. Today, it more often is taken to mean that, although the biochemical alterations caused by addiction remain, the individual does not have to be an active, using addict.

The discussion that follows must be understood with these considerations in mind. We begin by briefly sketching the history of drug treatment efforts in the United States. This section is followed by a discussion of the major treatment modalities, or approaches to treatment, and the philosophies that undergird these approaches. We will then discuss the effectiveness of treatment, and finally, we identify some of the major issues in treatment today.

History of Treatment for Drug Addiction

Early societal responses to both drug and alcohol abuse were moralistic and mostly punitive. The drug user—one who used pharmacological substances that were socially disapproved—was viewed as morally depraved. This was at least partially the response of the twentieth-century prohibitionist movement to the user of alcohol as well, who was characterized as a drunkard or a sot. At least one author of the time referred to the sale of alcoholic beverages as "hell's commerce" (Shaw 1909.

By the early twentieth century, moralistic rhetoric began to wane. Drug addicts and alcoholics were increasingly seen as redeemable, and a treatment industry began to emerge. It should be noted that the treatment of drug abuse in the United States, until recent years, was oriented primarily to alcohol and narcotics abuse. Alternative treatment methodologies for other types of drugs would eventually come, but the dominant treatment methods have been shaped by efforts to treat alcohol and narcotics addiction. It is also important to point out that treatment for alcohol and narcotics addiction followed separate paths. Researchers and practitioners working in these treatment fields remained largely segregated, resulting in separate but parallel research and programmatic efforts at treatment.

History of Alcohol Treatment

Although early responses to alcohol abuse were heavily moralistic in nature, it was also recognized that the alcoholic suffered from a malady, a disease that was beyond his or her control and required treatment. An early proponent of what would eventually be understood as a disease model of alcoholism was Dr. Benjamin Rush, who saw chronic inebriation as an addiction. Indeed, Schneider (1978) suggests that the early prohibitionist movement in the nineteenth century explicitly recognized inebriety as a disease. There were also "inebriates' institutions" in the nineteenth century, which were intended to remove the alcoholic and alcohol abuser from jails and lunatic asylums so that their problems could be more effectively addressed (Baumohl 1986). These institutions and the treatment effort they represented did not last long. Baumohl suggests that they were all but extinct by the time of Prohibition in 1920.

Alcoholics Anonymous

In 1935, soon after the end of national alcohol prohibition, two alcoholics by the name of Bill Wilson and Bob Smith met in Akron, Ohio, to offer support to each other in their desire to achieve and maintain sobriety. This would later be recognized as the very first Alcoholics Anonymous meeting, the start of a spiritually based self-help form of alcohol treatment that in its history has helped millions live sober lives. As it developed, Alcoholics Anonymous drew heavily from two ideological sources. First, AA accepted the idea that alcoholism was a disease over which the alcoholic had no control. This medical understanding of alcoholism was combined with a spiritual focus, originally a specifically Christian teaching regarding sinful humanity, the necessity of confession of sin, and the redemption of sinful humanity through the power of God. Especially influential was a movement formed in the 1920s known as the Oxford Group, which held to conservative Christian teaching but rejected the institutional character of religion. This group met in homes and hotels rather than in churches and cathedrals, had no organized board of officers, and called itself an "organism" rather than an "organization." Bill W. and Doctor Bob, as they are widely known in the AA fellowship, attended meetings of the Oxford Group and based their Twelve Steps on the tenets of this movement. Although AA has been criticized for its distinctly Christian roots, it has been praised by many for its role in saving millions of lives. In 1999, *Time Magazine* named Bill W. one of its twenty "heroes and icons" of the twentieth century, a group that *Time* describes as "the nearly sacred modules of humanity with which we parse and model our lives. (*Chua-Eoan* 1999). The program of Alcoholics Anonymous received similar end-of-the-century recognition.

E. M. Jellinek and the Yale Research Group

Also shortly after the repeal of Prohibition, the Research Council on Problems of Alcohol was formed at Yale University. This council was made up of physicians and scientists interested in identifying the causes of alcoholism. The Council pushed the concept of alcoholism as a disease and invited Elvin M. Jellinek to direct a multidisciplinary Yale Center for Alcohol Studies. Jellinek published numerous articles promoting the idea of alcoholism as a disease, culminating in his *The Disease Concept of Alcoholism* in 1960. Here, Jellinek proposed a four-stage progression of alcoholism, which he identified as *alpha, beta, delta,* and *gamma* alcoholism. Gamma alcoholism is characterized by an increased tolerance to alcohol, adaptation of cell metabolism, withdrawal symptoms, and an inability to control how much one drinks at any given time, despite obvious physiological consequences including cirrhosis of the liver (Schneider 1978). The disease model of alcoholism was officially endorsed by the World Health Organization in 1951 and by the American Medical Association in 1956. The American Psychiatric Association also formally promoted this idea in 1965 following Jellinek's influential work, and by the late1970s, the DSM-IIR (*Diagnostic and Statistical Manual of Mental Disorders*) listed "alcohol dependence syndrome" as a treatable psychological illness (Hobbs 1998).

The successful promotion of alcoholism as a disease resulted in the establishment of a very profitable treatment industry. These efforts began with simple **detoxification**, a term drawn from medicine that refers to the process of ridding toxins (poisons) from the body. Alcohol and other chemical substances are viewed as poisons that have accumulated in the body and must be purged. *Detoxification* is a term that continues to be widely used in the treatment industry, which is perhaps somewhat unfortunate because it implies that once the human organism is detoxified, the person is "cured" of the addiction. Nothing could be further from the truth. In the first place, drugs are not poisons as we normally understand this term. Moreover, addiction to alcohol and other psychoactive substances involves far more than a physiological dependence. Psychological, spiritual, and social forces combine to bring individuals to a place of addiction. Any attempt to conquer the power of addiction will require that we address all these factors. The treatment industry has recognized this, and treatment efforts have since expanded in complexity. Residential programs such as the Betty Ford Foundation in California and Hazeldon in Minnesota and Florida draw heavily on the disease model, while recognizing the multifaceted nature of addiction.

History of Narcotics Treatment

Early Treatment Efforts

Addiction to opium and other narcotics was also interpreted through a moral lens prior to the twentieth century. By the 1890s, the physiological basis for opiate addiction was recognized, though by no means fully understood, by the medical profession. Treatment was simply detoxification, and the primary debate was whether sudden, rapid, or gradual withdrawal from opium and morphine was the most effective (Terry and Pellens 1928). Cure was equated with a drug-free blood system, regardless of how short-lived that condition might be. There was a great deal of experimentation at this time, as some experts recommended withdrawal over the course of a year or more, while others recommended sudden withdrawal over a matter of days. Drugs used to help patients withdraw gradually also varied. It was believed in the latter nineteenth century that cocaine was effective as a cure for narcotics addiction. When heroin was introduced by Bayer Pharmaceuticals in 1898, it was believed to be nonaddictive and was advocated both as a method of withdrawal and as a cure for morphine dependency (Lipton and Maranda 1983). With the passage of the Harrison Narcotics Act in 1914, this debate ended as most medical professionals understood the Act to prohibit supplying narcotics to addicts. Local health departments responded in 1920 by providing maintenance dosages of narcotics to addicts—a measure that was, interestingly enough, initially endorsed by the Treasury Department. This endorsement did not last long, however. Abuses led the government to shut down the maintenance programs, closing the last program in 1924.

Establishment of Narcotics Institutions

Serious treatment efforts for narcotics addicts did not begin until the establishment of the Federal Public Health Service Hospitals, commonly known as "narcotics farms," in the 1930s. Like the inebriates' institutions before them, these hospitals represented an effort to separate narcotics addicts from the general federal prison population for purposes of treatment and treatment experimentation. Voluntary walk-ins were also treated in these institutions, but most were court-ordered patients. Treatment consisted primarily of gradually weaning patients from heroin with decreasing dosages of morphine, though methadone was used later. The hospitals closed within four decades after they started, another experiment in drug treatment coming to an end when the Lexington, Kentucky, hospital was transformed into a minimum-security federal prison in 1973. The federal hospitals provided researchers with a great deal of data on narcotics addiction and its treatment, much of which continues to be cited today.

Synanon and the Therapeutic Community

There was very little in the way of treatment innovation for narcotics or other drugs until 1958, when former alcoholic Charles Dederich founded a program in California that he called Synanon.[1] Synanon represented a new approach to drug treatment that used an environment insulated from outside influences, 24 hours a day, and emphasized confrontation and shock therapy to break down the addict's psychological defenses. Additionally, these programs provided educational and vocational opportunities. This approach was more generally referred to as a *therapeutic community*, and Synanon's model was replicated throughout the country starting in the early 1960s.[2] The therapeutic community was and still is a rather controversial treatment modality, but it continues to find widespread support for treatment of various forms of addiction.

Methadone Maintenance

A major breakthrough in treatment for narcotics addiction came in 1965 when Drs. Vincent Dole and Marie Nyswander introduced the first methadone clinic in New York City. Methadone, a synthetic narcotic that can forestall an addict's physiological craving for heroin, had been synthesized in the 1940s but was not recognized as an approach to addiction treatment until Dole and Nyswander's pioneering efforts. Initially, the goal of the methadone clinics was to detoxify heroin addicts gradually with decreasing dosages of methadone, much in the way that morphine had been used earlier in the century. Over time, the goals and purpose of the methadone clinics have evolved; proponents of this treatment approach generally acknowledge that most addicts treated with methadone will remain dependent on narcotics, and they now advocate continued maintenance of addicts on methadone. By the 1970s, **methadone maintenance** was accepted as a major mode of treatment for narcotics addiction, an appeal largely because it is relatively inexpensive and there are very quick and observable results in terms of lowered levels of criminal activity.

Criminal Justice–Related Programs

The 1960s also witnessed another innovation in drug treatment—linking drug treatment with the criminal justice system. In 1961, the state of California established the California Civil Addict Program, the first major effort at involuntary commitment of (primarily) narcotics addicts for treatment. Essentially a diversion program administered by the California Department of Corrections, it presented an alternative to incarceration through which addicts would serve their time in treatment rather than prison. A similar program was established in New York, though it was short-lived. The federal government also established a civil commitment program, authorized by the Narcotic Addict Rehabilitation Act of 1966. This, too, was a rather short-lived effort. The 1960s also witnessed the introduction of treatment programs within state and federal prisons. These programs were based on a general therapeutic community model and were very popular throughout the 1970s (Anglin and Hser 1990).

Since the 1960s the general trend in drug treatment has been twofold: (1) recognize the differences among individual addicts—particularly between men and women—and the necessity of a multiple treatment approach to address the variety of individual treatment needs; and (2) broaden the scope of treatment to address addiction to drugs other than narcotics and alcohol. The following section identifies the major treatment modalities in place today, including the programs presented in this historical overview.

Major Treatment Modalities

The literature of drug abuse treatment identifies broad **treatment modalities** or general approaches to treatment, representing fundamentally different strategies for treating drug addiction. We identify four general types, representing the broad range of treatment options: medical and pharmacological approaches, residential drug-free programs, out-patient drug-free programs, and self-help programs. Specific treatment programs may integrate two or more of the approaches above; indeed, these integrated efforts are often among the most successful.

Medical and Pharmacological Approaches

There are two basic types of pharmacological approaches to treatment for drug addiction. The first of these comprises programs of drug substitution, either to maintain the addict or to gradually withdraw the addict from dependence on the drug. Throughout treatment history, numerous efforts have been made to treat substance abuse with alternative drugs believed to be less addicting and/or less harmful to the user. Indeed, as already noted, heroin was initially proposed as a substitute for morphine addiction because it was believed to be less addictive. We now know, of course, that this was not the case! The most widely recognized programs of this type are methadone maintenance or methadone detoxification. More recently, buprenorphine, a drug recently approved for treatment by the FDA, has been quite widely used. The second type of pharmacological approach involves using antagonists that either block the effect of the addict's drug of choice or produce highly uncomfortable counter-effects.

Methadone Maintenance

Because methadone is a synthetic narcotic (see Chapter 3), its use in drug treatment is limited to narcotics addiction. Methadone programs today are driven by two broad and somewhat contradictory philosophies that Graff and Ball (1976) call the metabolic and psychotherapeutic models. The metabolic model understands drug addiction as a metabolic disease resulting from a biochemical deficit or imbalance. As a consequence, those who adhere to this model do not believe that the addict is capable of functioning without narcotics or a narcotics substitute. Eventual **abstinence**, total cessation of narcotics use, is not deemed a realistic goal, and long-term maintenance on methadone is assumed. Certain forms of psychotherapy and other therapeutic initiatives are seen as useful, but they are ancillary to the central form of treatment, namely the daily dosage of methadone.

The psychotherapeutic model, by contrast, understands drug addiction to be primarily a psychiatric or emotional disorder. Rather than ancillary, psychotherapy is the primary method of treatment, and methadone is used only for stabilizing the addict so that he or she can more effectively benefit from the psychotherapy. The ultimate goal of treatment for those adhering to the psychotherapeutic model is abstinence. Hubbard and colleagues (1989), in their comprehensive study of treatment programs in the United States, note that despite an increasing trend toward the psychotherapeutic model, most programs are still of the metabolic variety.

The treatment experience of an addict in methadone maintenance is highly variable, depending on the treatment philosophy of the program, how bureaucratically it is structured, the adequacy of funding, and a host of other factors. Since retention in the methadone program is an important component of success, the nature of the addict's treatment experience is highly relevant. Methadone maintenance, whether short or long term, is a central feature of all methadone programs. Methadone is advantageous over other narcotics because it is taken orally and it has a longer effective dose, ranging from 24 to 36 hours. The addict is initially assessed with regard to his or her tolerance, which is usually done over a period of several days, gradually bringing the addict up to a maintenance-level dosage. During this period, the addict may also be assessed for psychotherapeutic and other rehabilitative needs, and an individualized treatment plan ideally is developed (Hubbard et al. 1989). Most methadone programs are outpatient in nature, meaning that during the maintenance phase, the addict comes into the clinic on a daily, sometimes weekly, basis to obtain their allotment of methadone. All of the clinics in the Hubbard study allowed at least some of their patients take-home dosages of methadone after they had been in the program for a specified length of time. The client is subject to urinalysis to detect for heroin use, which is prohibited while on methadone maintenance. A successful urinalysis would be defined as test results that are methadone positive and morphine negative (heroin is also known as diacetyl morphine and breaks down into morphine in the bloodstream).

Methadone maintenance is the most widespread form of government-supported treatment for narcotics addiction in the United States today. As of 2005, more than 1,000 methadone clinics throughout the United States treated more than 235,000 patients at any given time (SAMHSA 2006b.). Advocates for methadone and buprenorphine maintenance such as the Drug Policy Alliance claim that it is effective at reducing illicit and unhealthy drug use, drug-related crime, and death and disease. They would like to see government restrictions on methadone use lifted and greater funding for these programs so that more heroin abusers (and by extension, society as a whole) can benefit from access to methadone. They also advocate doctors being able to prescribe methadone for individual patients, something not currently permitted, and for pharmacies to carry methadone, which they view as a life-preserving drug. One last area of advocacy involves the destigmatization of methadone treatment centers and their clients. Planning for methadone clinics frequently suffers from the NIMBY ("not in my back yard") phenomenon, where neighborhoods either deny that narcotics addiction is a problem in their locale or they attempt to block treatment centers because of fear that the clientele will be a threat to the area. Such fear, advocates say, prevents an important solution to a serious public health problem.

In October, 2002, buprenorphine, an alternative drug to methadone, was approved by the FDA as a Schedule III drug specifically for use in treatment of narcotics addiction. It is currently marketed under the tradenames Suboxone or Subutex and is often administered in conjunction with the narcotic antagonist naloxone. This treatment innovation holds promise for a couple of reasons. First, it does not cause as severe a respiratory depression as methadone, thereby rendering addicts less vulnerable to overdose and less subject to severe withdrawal discomfort. Moreover, buprenorphine can be effective when taken every other day or even less frequently, unlike methadone, which must be taken daily. In addition, as a Schedule III drug and with special provisions of the Drug Addiction Treatment Act of 2000, buprenorphine can be administered and prescribed by private physicians who have been trained and approved to do so—something that physicians have not been able to do for over 40 years (Jones 2004; Maxwell 2006). This allows many addicts access to treatment who might not otherwise be accepted into methadone clinics, as many of these clinics require that a potential client be addicted for at least a year to qualify for services (Leshner 2003). Finally, because addicts would have more control over treating their addiction would face less stigmatization, they would be encouraged to seek help and to comply with their treatment plans. So successful has buprenorphine been that in February 2008, experts converged on Washington, D.C., for the Third Buprenorphine Summit, the first being convened in 2003. The purpose of the summit was to assess the successes, progress, and continued barriers to access to opioid treatment with buprenorphine.

Smoking Reduction Efforts

Another area where drug substitution has been effective is in smoking reduction efforts. Today, there are about 45 million smokers in the United States (nearly 21 percent of adults), of whom more than 70 percent want to quit, and some 19 million (44 percent of smokers) actually attempt to give up smoking each year, according to the Centers for Disease Control and Prevention (2002b, 2007d), though only a fraction of these succeed for any appreciable length of time. It is this high failure rate that led former U.S. Surgeon General C. Everett Koop to declare that nicotine was a more powerfully addicting drug than was heroin. Various nicotine substitution products have been approved and marketed widely to assist smokers in quitting. These products come in four different forms: chewing gum, transdermal patches, nasal sprays, and inhalers. These products deliver decreasing doses of nicotine into the bloodstream, thus easing withdrawal symptoms when smokers attempt to quit, but do not contain the harmful tars and carbon monoxide that are responsible for some of the most serious health consequences of cigarette smoking. Studies on the effectiveness of these replacement products are promising, though they are not effective for everyone.

Chemical Antagonists

Chemical **antagonists** are drugs that either block the effects of an addictive substance or produce highly unpleasant side effects if the addictive substance is used.

Unlike methadone, these are not drug substitutes, though methadone has been called a narcotic antagonist. Although methadone blocks any further effect of heroin or morphine use, methadone is a synthetic narcotic and as such, it is a substitute for heroin, morphine or other narcotics.

Two narcotic antagonists that have been used in the treatment of narcotics addiction are cyclazocine and naltrexone (also called Trexone). These drugs are not themselves addicting and actually induce a withdrawal syndrome. However, if these antagonists are taken after one has already withdrawn and is no longer physically dependent on narcotics, the antagonists prevent euphoria and dependence if the recovering addict relapses, thereby serving as an effective behavior modification agent. Another class of narcotic antagonists, most notably naloxone or better known as narcan, is used to induce rapid reversal of opiate overdoses. The federal government has promoted research on narcotic antagonists, especially naltrexone. There is not a strong, unequivocal body of research that suggests its effectiveness. Antagonists do seem to reduce the craving for the drug in the period immediately following detoxification, but once the antagonist is discontinued, craving for narcotics returns. This reinforces the ideas stressed in Chapter 5 that addiction is much broader than a physical dependence.

A second chemical antagonist is Antabuse® (generic name, disulfiram). Unlike the narcotic antagonists, however, which simply block the effects of narcotic drugs, Antabuse produces a heightened sensitivity to alcohol that results in a highly unpleasant, often severe reaction in the presence of alcohol. Some of the symptoms include flushing, throbbing in the head and neck, difficulty in breathing, nausea and vomiting, chest pains, heart palpitation, vertigo, and blurred vision (Internet Mental Health n.d.). Antabuse has been used for many years in the treatment of alcoholism and shows some promise, but Doweiko (1990) points out several drawbacks to its use. First, the interaction effects can be extremely severe, requiring emergency hospitalization. Second, antabuse requires up to 30 minutes to react to the presence of alcohol, so its aversive conditioning value may be limited. Third, the drug must be administered on a daily or nearly daily basis for optimal effect, so effectiveness would be highly affected by a patient's willingness to continue using the drug. Finally, because Antabuse does not recognize the source of the alcohol, use of over-the-counter products containing alcohol will produce the same untoward side effects as beverage alcohol. For all of these reasons, Antabuse has not been a major treatment approach in alcoholism.

Residential Treatment Programs

Residential treatment programs are, by definition, drug-free programs except where short-term chemical substitution is required for gradual withdrawal from certain drugs. Generally, participants in residential treatment have been detoxified and stabilized medically before admission. Residential programs involve 24-hour care. These programs vary on the length of stay recommended, though higher success rates are generally correlated with longer stays.

Therapeutic Communities

The **therapeutic community** (TC) is a fairly broad term that encompasses some 650 treatment programs across the United States, according to the website of Therapeutic Communities of America, the national organization representing TCs. As we mentioned earlier, the genesis of residential treatment is generally traced to a California program founded in 1958 by Charles Dederich called Synanon. Treatment in the TC is governed by a treatment philosophy that mandates a comprehensive change in an addict's lifestyle, a resocialization process. Physical dependency is the first of many lifestyle problems to be addressed if the addict is to live successfully in the outside world. The goal of the TC is, therefore, not only the cessation of drug use, but also seeing that the addict leads a productive life with legitimate employment, healthy family and social relationships, and an absence of criminal activity. TCs vary in the details of their approach to treatment. Those modeled after Synanon tend to be long-term programs, at least 15 months in length. These programs are typically divided into three phases: residential, reentry, and aftercare. Each phase has its own goals and processes, briefly described below. Modified TCs are not as comprehensive and usually involve a shorter duration. These programs do not place as much emphasis on the reentry or aftercare phases of treatment (Hubbard et al. 1989).

Accomplishment of program goals involves a variety of therapy approaches, including confrontation and encounter therapy, educational opportunities, and aid in job placement. The heart of the therapeutic community, however, consists of the group therapy sessions led by former drug abusers and often confrontational in nature. During the residential phase, addicts are confronted with their former destructive way of life and challenged to change their focus. These confrontations, sometimes called *haircuts*,[3] can be harrowing, almost brutal, to the addict being confronted. Yablonsky describes this process as it was practiced in Synanon: "This form of verbal attack employs ridicule, hyperbole, and direct verbal onslaught....An important goal of the 'haircut' method is to change the criminal tough guy pose. The self-image held by newcomers is viciously attacked and punctured in the 'haircut'" (1965, 241). These verbal attacks are designed to bring a resident to a breaking point, at which time the group is also there to encourage and build them up in their efforts to embody positive values and lifestyles.

As individuals progress through the program, they are gradually given more and more responsibilities. At some point in the program, usually after at least 12 months, the addict is considered ready for reentry. This phase involves spending time outside of the program, usually working a full- or part-time legitimate job. The recovering addict is still tied very closely to the program during this phase. Hawkins (1979) points out that a central task of the reintegration phase of treatment is to assist the addict in developing meaningful bonds with individuals and institutions in conventional society. Aftercare is the logical extension of reentry. During this phase, the addict has formally "graduated" from the program. The program remains available to him or her, however, as a resource when encountering difficult terrain. Occasional counseling sessions or job placement services may be necessary. The program is available to the recovering addict for these purposes. These last two stages, reentry and aftercare, have received much less emphasis in some treatment programs, but some attempts have been made to foster reintegration into the local community.

The Minnesota Model

The **Minnesota Model** is discussed here to represent comprehensive, though usually shorter-term, approaches to drug addiction and especially alcoholism. Minnesota has

13.1 The Betty Ford Center in Rancho Mirage, California, is possibly the most well-known drug and alcohol treatment facility in the United States. This program is a residentially based program that normally treats clients over a thirty-day period. (Photo: Getty Images)

long been a leader in alcohol intervention programs, and by the early 1980s the state had more than 3,800 beds and 1,000 outpatient slots for alcoholics (Laundergan 1982). The formal name for this model is the Minnesota Model for Chemical Dependence Intervention and Treatment, which had its beginnings in the late 1940s. The model was based on the Twelve Steps of Alcoholics Anonymous, which were applied initially in two small treatment programs, Pioneer House (in 1948) and Hazelden (in 1949). Over time, addiction professionals were added, treatment wards were unlocked allowing freedom of activity for patients, and lectures and group and individual therapy sessions were added to the program. Today, Minnesota-style programs have a mix of professional and nonprofessional staff; among the professional personnel are medical practitioners, psychiatrists, psychologists, clergy, and social workers.

The Minnesota Model is best represented by Hazelden facilities located in Minnesota and Oregon (in addition to outpatient centers in Chicago and New York City), which hold to the philosophy that alcoholism and drug addiction are progressive and incurable medical diseases that can be arrested through treatment. Treatment at Hazelden is an approximately 30-day program involving a variety of therapeutic approaches (though many addicts are referred subsequently to extended care residential facilities). Initially, most patients go through detoxification. This is not regarded as a primary therapy so much as a prelude to group and individual therapy strategies. Early in the treatment process, the patient is exposed to group therapy, where he or she is confronted by others with the nature of their condition. About one-third of the way through the program, the patient is exposed to the Twelve Steps of AA (or NA, Narcotics Anonymous), and overcoming the patient's resistance to attending such groups is given a lot of attention. Participation in Twelve Step programs is seen as essential for successful long-term recovery. The more the patient embraces the Twelve-Step way of life voluntarily, the greater the chance of success (Miller and Hoffman 1995; McCrady and Delaney 1995). The spiritual dimension of recovery is highly emphasized, and clergy are a visible part of Hazelden's program (Laundergan 1982). Aftercare is also emphasized, and the facility is available at any time to graduates of the program. Hazelden and the Minnesota Model have been replicated and/or adapted by numerous programs throughout the country. Perhaps the most well known, for its celebrity connections, is the Betty Ford Center in Rancho Mirage, California, now with a children's program in Irving, Texas, as well.

Out-Patient Drug-Free Programs

This category of programs is comprised of a host of local treatment facilities that generally provide either chemical detoxification services or individual and group therapy or both. Both of these types of services are included in comprehensive residential programs such as Hazelden and the Betty Ford Center as discussed above. **Detoxification** is a central component of these programs. The process of detoxification varies, depending on the substance involved. Detoxification from narcotics is generally accomplished without the use of drugs and is often done "cold turkey"— that is, suddenly, over a period of a few days. Other drugs, such as alcohol, barbiturates, and most tranquilizers, may require a more gradual process, as there is a risk of seizures and other medical complications. Detoxification as a formal treatment process is done under the watchful eye of a physician, though of course many addicts detoxify on their own. Detoxification addresses only one's physiological dependence on a drug. Insofar as drug addiction involves psychological and social components, the long-term prospects for an addict who has been through detoxification without any further treatment is not very bright. Indeed, many addicts go through detoxification not so much to assist them in leading a drug-free life as to lower the level of their dependence on heroin, alcohol, or other drugs and thereby lessen the financial or health burdens of their addiction.

Individual, family, and group therapy programs are what we usually think of when we talk about out-patient drug-free treatment. In some cases, programs are little more than crisis centers where individuals call or drop in to get them through acutely distressful situations. Other programs range from informal drop-in *rap centers*, which typically use peer relationships along with other structured and unstructured activities to help refocus youth and younger adult addicts, to highly professional counseling centers (Kleber and Slobetz 1979). Behavior and family therapy are common therapeutic strategies. In their treatment typology, Cole and James (1975) identify two broad approaches to out-patient drug-free treatment: "change-oriented" and "adaptive." Change-oriented approaches seek a more comprehensive identity transformation similar to the resocialization process that takes place in therapeutic communities. Adaptive approaches, by contrast, are a much less radical approach and seek to lessen the dependence of an individual on alcohol or drugs so that they can function more effectively in their lives. Hubbard and colleagues (1989) found that among the out-patient drug-free programs in their study, about half were change oriented. Most used individual counseling rather than group counseling strategies. Because most out-patient drug-free programs are very small and locally governed, often with only the most meager record keeping, very little research has been conducted on the effectiveness of these programs.

Self-Help Groups

The model that most self-help groups pattern themselves after is Alcoholics Anonymous AA, which was started in 1935 in Akron, Ohio, by two alcoholics, Bill W. and Bob S. Although their full names are known now, the truncation of their last names is significant, as Alcoholics Anonymous and those programs which borrow their philosophies from AA emphasize anonymity. Meetings often close with the admonition, "Who you see here, what you hear here, when you leave here, let it stay here." Twelve-Step groups are spiritually oriented, and their primary principle is that the alcoholic or drug addict is powerless over his or her addictive disease and dependent upon God (or one's "Higher Power") for the resources to maintain sobriety. Addiction is regarded as a disease that has spiritual as well as physical and psychological dimensions. Sobriety, rather than controlled drinking, is the goal of AA, because it is believed that alcoholism is a permanent disease requiring continual and daily awareness of one's dependence on God Who in many AA groups is simply referred to as one's Higher Power. Self-examination and accountability to others are also fundamental principles of AA, as are making amends for the wrongs done to others and being ready to assist other alcoholics along the Twelve-Step path.

Today, there are more than one million members of AA worldwide. A general survey of the United States population revealed that about 9 percent of American adults have been to at least one AA meeting (Room and Greenfield 1993). Over the years, the basic structure and content of AA meetings have not changed much, though the membership has changed substantially. Whereas members were at one time primarily comprised of middle-class white men, women and various ethnic groups are now quite highly represented (McElrath 1998). The AA model has also been adapted and applied to populations using other substances, as well as those experiencing nondrug addictions such as gambling, overeating, and compulsive sexual activity.

What sets AA and its clones apart from the treatment approaches we have discussed thus far is its explicit acknowledgment of a spiritual dimension to addiction and recovery. While recognizing physiological, psychological, and social dimensions to substance abuse, the spiritual dimension is a separate though inextricable part of all of them. Morever, the nature of our spiritual selves is such that we recognize that we are part of a larger cosmic order than what is empirically observed and that we are dependent upon the Creator of that order. It is for this reason that, even with the broader, revised wording that describes this Higher Power (or a "God of one's understanding"), some atheists and agnostics have a difficult time with the precepts

DRUGS AND EVERYDAY LIFE

Ten Hut!

Everyone; At Ease.

I am sergeant Central Nervous System and you are in Alcohol Withdrawal Boot Camp.

Here we learn how to attack the enemy; Alcohol, within the body, and drive it out. As you know we have a limited amount of troops in this body. The only way we can be defeated, is by our body consuming more parasites of alcohol.

As in the past, that has killed many of our troops and fowled our efforts to bring complete recuperation to our body. We have become merciless in our efforts. You all know the strain alcohol has caused us. How the battle is lost when our body has overindulged and we are submerged with the shakes, tremors, and hysteria. Some of our troops have never made it back. I spoke with "Sister Liver of Saint Organ", and she agreed that even she cannot tolerate the constant abuse of alcohol after a long periods of time. She spoke of other sisters who just "gave up" and quit!

The outcome to the body was not a pleasant one. So back to business. Our job is to eliminate! compensate! and repair! our body as soon as possible once it has been ceased. Remember that not every body will respond in the same manner, so we must allow for individual circumstances and enforce different strategies as we go to war.

Your schedule will be as follows: After the first 24 hours since our body has last consumed the enemy, alcohol, and have positioned themselves in their sleeping quarters, I need two troops to attend to the brain and eyes. I need constant stimulation to the brain! I want excess! I want information overload! Whatever it takes you keep that brain stimulated. I want thoughts! Thoughts of the 12 steps! I want Insomnia! We are going to drive those alcohol parasites out with principals. They can't go on destroying the body forever without back up, and the only way they will get back up, is if our body isn't thinking correctly.

So shove those 12 steps up their cerebral cortex and do it now! In the meantime I need the other troops to hold those eyelids open. I want a visual!! Don't give me that slack half-drooping eyelid stuff! I want them up! Up! Up! And fully alert!! Remember, "Insomnia"! They will sleep when I tell them they can sleep. Now, after they are asleep, I need four troops to go to the legs, grab those muscles and s t r e t c h. I want to hear those leg cramps from our body! Don't give me no Mickey Mouse little "ouch." I want to hear bellows of pain! Let our body know we are here, doing our job! Then I want the rest of you troops to do a ten-mile hike throughout the body. We must create as much sweat during their sleeping hours as possible. I want them to wake up totally saturated! I want to flush out those parasites. Let's hear it! "Leave no pore dry! Leave no pore dry!" Good!

Okay troops, that is enough for the first night. Now, if we did our duty, then our body should wake up feeling extremely tired, sweaty and exhausted. But give me an hour and I'll get them alert. They will feel better than they have in years! They will have more clarity, they will feel at ease instead of disease. They will have put last night behind them. Now troops, this is a two-week training session. It will depend upon our body. Once it is over we will once again live in our body in good health, peace and serenity.

I am making light of what is very real for me on a nightly basis. But to those who are contemplating sobriety, don't let this scare you. I welcome these symptoms. I know each morning when I wake up from one of these nights that my body is recuperating from years of abuse. I am healing and it is only a temporary war. So hang in there, it's worth it, as you can tell it hasn't ruined my sense of humor.

Gyorgyi M.

Source: Anonymous One, n.d.

of the AA model (Horowtiz 2000). The importance of the spiritual dimension has been long recognized in the medical profession, however, and more recent academic literature on drug addiction and treatment has recognized its importance (Green et al. 1995), though others interpret what goes on in AA meetings strictly in clinical psychological terms (Khantzian and Mack 1994).

Effectiveness of Drug Treatment

When evaluating the effectiveness of drug treatment programs, we need to keep in mind several things. First, many if not most drug addicts eventually quit on their own. Referring to narcotics addiction, Winick (1962) has called this "maturing out" of addiction. Waldorf refers to the same process as the "natural recovery" from addiction (Waldorf 1983; Waldorf and Biernacki 1981). However labeled, when it comes to heroin addiction, most addicts seem to cease or at least seriously curtail their drug use by the time they reach middle age. It has therefore been suggested that those who seek treatment (or are compelled to seek treatment) may be the most resistant to change (Goode 2008). Furthermore, many addicts seeking treatment are not even attempting to go drug free; they want to lower their tolerance to a drug so their habit will not be as costly, or so they may slow down the rat race of their lives temporarily (Faupel 1981). Effectiveness statistics must be interpreted in light of these realities. On the other hand, addicts who *are* ready to exit the drug-using lifestyle may seek treatment to assist them in this process. Many of these are individuals who would probably be successful in a "natural recovery" anyway, and it is not clear how much one's lifestyle change can be credited to the treatment program itself or to other factors working in an addict's life to motivate him or her to quit using drugs. For all of these reasons, we must be careful in how we interpret treatment effectiveness statistics.

Indicators of Treatment Effectiveness

Historically, studies have used three indicators to assess the effectiveness of drug treatment: (1) abstention from (or reduced) drug use, (2) abstention from (or reduced) crime, and (3) indicators of mainstream success such as employment, enrollment in school, or conventional domestic roles (Sells 1979). Multiple indicators such as these are used because it is recognized that drug use is multifaceted in both cause and effect. An effective treatment program designed for hard-core drug addicts should address at least these fundamental areas: reduced drug use, reduced crime, and increased conventional productivity.

Assessment of treatment effectiveness is not an easy task and is affected by a number of methodological considerations, including:

- Is total abstinence from drug use (or crime) necessary to consider a program successful, or are we willing to consider *reduced* drug use (or crime) an indicator of success?
- For *how long following treatment* must a client be drug free (or reduced in usage) to be considered successful?

Drugs: Myths and Reality

Natural Recovery from Addiction

It is widely believed that addiction to psychoactive drugs is such a powerful force that once an individual becomes entangled in the seductive web of addiction, he or she is at the mercy of others for recovery. Even though recidivism rates in drug treatment programs are high, these programs tout themselves as an addict's last and only hope. The drug treatment industry makes this appeal with slogans such as, "The path from drug rehab to recovery starts at Lakeview's Addiction Treatment Center" (http://www.lakeviewhealth.com/). Clearly, good treatment programs can facilitate recovery from addiction, and we contend that more public monies should be spent on treatment than is currently the case.

It is quite another matter, however, to make the case that drug treatment is *necessary* for recovery. Observers of heroin users—a population addicted to one of the most addictive drugs known to human kind—have been reporting natural recovery from heroin addiction for nearly half a century. Charles Winick (1962) identified this phenomenon in the early 1960s as what he termed "maturing out" of narcotics addiction. Later, sociologist Dan Waldorf more extensively examined this process of "natural recovery" from narcotics addiction (Waldorf 1983; Waldorf and Biernacki 1981.) Waldorf and his colleagues would later note a similar process among cocaine addicts (Waldorf et al. 1991).

Robert Granfield and William Cloud (1996) identify several factors that facilitate this natural recovery process. They suggest that individuals who have a "stake in conventional life" are more likely to recover from addiction on their own than those who do not. These researchers found that those who naturally recover tend to have people in their lives who provide support for quitting, such as family or non-using friends. Most who recovered on their own reported that they had not yet "burned their social bridges" with the conventional community, so they were able to rely on that community to help them in the recovery, thereby making it unnecessary for them to seek out the alternative community of drug treatment centers. Granfield and Cloud further reported that successful self-recoverers also voluntarily abandoned the drug-using community of which they had been a part. In some cases, they even moved across country to facilitate this separation. Finally, those successful in the natural recovery process reported that they built alternative support structures. They deliberately set out to become involved in community social groups such as churches, health clubs, dance companies, and the like. Some decided to go back to school, others took up hobbies that brought them into frequent contact with non-users.

The research on natural recovery reveals an important truth about recovery from addiction. This is a profoundly *social* process. Because the social basis of addiction itself is frequently not recognized, it should not be surprising that we too often fail to see that recovery from addiction will also require an alternative social environment. Those who are successful in recovery—whether on their own or facilitated by specialized treatment programs—engage in a process of resocialization whereby they become involved in an alternative (non-drug) community that reinforces what is for them a radically new drug-free life style.

- What point in an abuser's addictive career *prior to starting treatment* do we use as the comparison point for evaluating treatment effectiveness?
- Where reduction in criminal activity is used as a measure, how is it measured: Arrests? Charges? Convictions? Self-reported behavior?
- How is productive conventional activity measured? Is it appropriate to use the same measures for everyone, and if not, on what basis do we compare levels of productive behavior? For example, many drug addicts have regular jobs but underperform because of active drug abuse. This is substantially different from the addict who has never had steady legitimate work.

Studies of treatment effectiveness have not been consistent on any of these dimensions, so assessment of the effectiveness of treatment have produced varied results (Faupel 1981). Despite the methodological difficulties, numerous independent efforts have been made to assess the effectiveness of treatment. Four efforts are particularly important for what they tell us about treatment effectiveness: the Drug Abuse Reporting Program (DARP); the Treatment Outcome Prospective Study (TOPS); the Drug Abuse Treatment Outcome Studies (DATOS); and the National Treatment Outcome Research Study (NTORS) conducted in the United Kingdom. We will briefly examine each of these sources of information with regard to what they tell us about the effectiveness of the various treatment modalities.

Drug Abuse Reporting Program (DARP)

DARP was the earliest attempt to collect data on treatment effectiveness on a national level. Data were collected on some 44,000 addicts entering treatment between 1969 and 1972. A total of 52 federally funded agencies were represented in the study, comprising 139 separate treatment programs. DARP collected data on clients entering methadone maintenance, therapeutic communities, out-patient drug-free programs, and simple detoxification programs. Clients were followed up over the next 12 years to determine treatment effectiveness. The evidence suggests that treatment does have a positive impact on drug use and criminal behavior. Among the nearly 75 percent of the sample who reported one or more relapses in opiate use in the 12 years of the study, only 41 percent reported a continuous relapse for two years or more. Moreover, 75 percent of the sample had not used daily for at least a year (61 percent had not used at all for the previous year). Arrest rates, which were used as a measure of criminality, also declined by about 50 percent following treatment (Simpson and Sells 1990), and employment improved following treatment (Simpson et al. 1982).

Treatment Outcomes Prospective Study (TOPS)

This national study conducted by Hubbard and his associates (1989) collected data from more than 11,000 clients admitted to treatment between 1979 and 1981. A total of 41 treatment programs in 10 cities are represented in these data. TOPS data comprise methadone maintenance programs, therapeutic communities, and out-patient drug-free programs. TOPS data reveal that the percentage of clients who reported engaging in *regular* (daily or weekly) drug use declined for all types of drug use. Cocaine was least responsive to treatment, whereas heroin and nonmedical psychotherapeutic drug use were most strongly affected. Hubbard and colleagues further found that cocaine was least affected by such factors as time spent in treatment and treatment services offered. With regard to treatment modality, methadone maintenance had a stronger impact on heroin use, whereas residential treatment and out-patient drug-free programs more strongly affected other types of drug use. Because methadone maintenance explicitly focuses on opiate use, this result should not be surprising. Therapeutic communities also are geared toward narcotics use; however, the treatment methodology is not as narrowly focused and is effective for other types of addiction as well. Hubbard and his colleagues found, consistent with many other studies, that the length of time spent in treatment is among the strongest predictors of reduced drug use following treatment. De Leon, Wexler, and Jainchill (1982) found that among those who graduated from Phoenix House, a leading therapeutic community, 75 percent remained abstinent through five years of follow-up observation, whereas among dropouts from the program, only 31 percent remained drug free.

Clients in all of the modalities examined by Hubbard and colleagues (1989) reduced the level of their criminal involvement during and following treatment. The most significant drop was among those enrolled in residential treatment programs, but methadone maintenance and out-patient drug-free programs also contributed to substantially reduced criminal activity among their clients. These generally positive findings are consistent with what other researchers have found as well (De Leon et al. 1982; Faupel 1981; Hser et al. 1988). One thing that must be remembered when interpreting data such as these is that addicts often enter treatment when their drug use and/or criminal behavior is escalating, and therefore the baseline in these studies may be atypically high. Hence, we should expect to see such a reduction—a reduction that may occur eventually even without treatment (Faupel 1981, 1991).

The impact of drug treatment on productive, legitimate employment is less clear than the other indicators of treatment success. Methadone clients were less likely to be employed full time three to five years after treatment than they were prior to entering the treatment program. Both out-patient drug-free programs and residential programs saw more of their clients obtaining full-time employment following treatment. This difference among the treatment modalities may result from the fact that legitimate employment is more likely to be a part of the treatment goals in these modalities, or in the case of out-patient drug-free programs, clients may be more likely to have been generally employed but, because of their drug abuse problems, temporarily unemployed when they entered treatment.

Drug Abuse Treatment Outcome Studies (DATOS)

This, the third series of national studies in the United States, was launched in 1990 and is on-going. The treatment modalities included in these studies include methadone maintenance, long-term residential programs (such as therapeutic

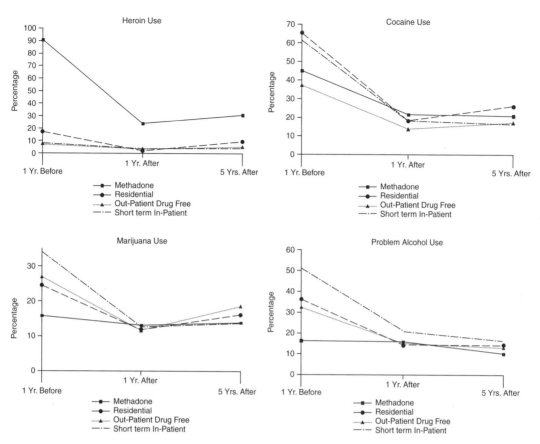

13.2 Prevalence of Regular Drug Use Before, During, and After Treatment among DATOS Clients.

Source: Hubbard, Robert L., Gail Craddock and Jill Anderson. 2003. "Overview of 5-Year Followup OUtcomes in the Drug Abuse Treatment Outcomes Studies (DATOS)" *Journal of Substance Abuse Treatment* 25, Table 2, p. 129.

communities), short-term inpatient programs, and out-patient drug-free programs. More than 10,000 clients in 96 treatment programs, located in 11 United States cities were initially sampled. Both one-year and five-year follow-up studies were conducted (Hubbard et al. 2003). These data, like the TOPS data, are encouraging in what they suggest about the potential effectiveness of drug treatment.

Hubbard, Craddock, and Anderson (2003) note major reductions in drug use among DATOS clients, regardless of treatment modality, as shown in Figure 13.2. With the exception of marijuana, drug use prevalence decreased by approximately 50 percent across the treatment modalities over the five-year follow-up period. Predatory crime was also substantially effected, decreasing by 60 percent or more in all four of the treatment modalities examined (see Figure 13.3). Finally, as revealed in Figure 13.4, the effectiveness of drug treatment in promoting full-time employment is somewhat mixed. Long-term residential treatment is most effective here, with employment increasing by more than 200 percent over the five years that these clients were followed. The other modalities were less effective, though short-term

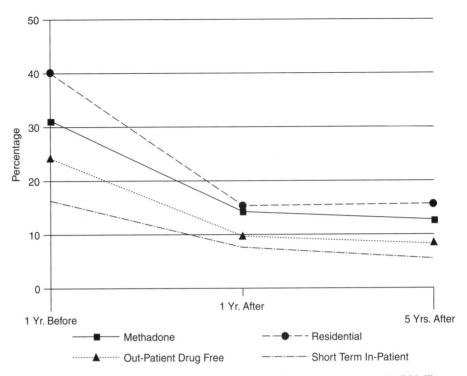

13.3 Prevalence of Predatory Crime Before, During, and After Treatment among DATOS Clients.
Source: Hubbard, Robert L., Gail Craddock and Jill Anderson. 2003. "Overview of 5-Year Followup OUtcomes in the Drug Abuse Treatment Outcomes Studies (DATOS)" *Journal of Substance Abuse Treatment* 25, Table 2, p. 129.

in-patient treatment was the only modality that showed little increase in employment. This is partly because a relatively high proportion of these clients were already employed full time during the year prior to their treatment.

National Treatment Outcome Research Study (NTORS)

NTORS is based in the United Kingdom and was was conducted over five years, from 1995-2000, in response to a request from the British Minister of Health to examine the effectiveness of treatment services in the United Kingdom, rather than to rely on the early American-based treatment outcome studies discussed above (Gossop et al. 2000; Hall 1997). Data collection for NTORS began in 1995, targeting clients in 54 treatment programs comprising four treatment modalities. Gossop and colleagues (2003) identify two of these as residential modalities—(1) specialist in-patient programs, targeting opiate addiction and usually located in medical facilities such as hospitals, and (2) residential rehabilitation programs, including 12-step programs, Minnesota Model programs, and therapeutic communities—and two as methadone based—(3) methadone *maintenance* programs, and (4) methadone *reduction* programs.

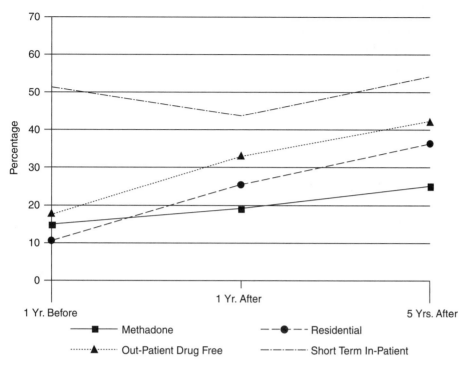

13.4 Prevalence of Full-Time Employment Before, During, and After Drug Treatment among DATOS Clients.

Source: Hubbard, Robert L., Gail Craddock and Jill Anderson. 2003. "Overview of 5-Year Followup OUtcomes in the Drug Abuse Treatment Outcomes Studies (DATOS)" *Journal of Substance Abuse Treatment* 25, Table 2, p. 129.

The NTORS data of treatment effectiveness are very encouraging. Over the five-year follow-up period, heroin use declined by some 50 percent across all modalities. Nonprescription methadone and tranquilizers were also substantially reduced regardless of modality. Understandably, cocaine and amphetamine use responded much more to residential treatment than to methadone treatment, declining by some 50 percent among residential treatment clients. Alcohol was least responsive to all of the treatment modalities. Criminal activity was also profoundly affected; both residential and methadone modalities reported more than 60 percent reductions in criminal activity (Gossop et al. 2003).

Summary of Treatment Effectiveness

Because of the methodological differences in research efforts examining treatment effectiveness, there is some variation in the reporting of treatment outcomes. Moreover, we must be careful that we do not incorrectly assume a causal relationship between treatment efforts and positive changes in indicators of treatment success. As we have suggested above, it may well be that many individuals entering treatment were ready to change their lifestyles and would have eventually reduced their drug use, reduced their criminal participation, and found employment regardless of treatment participation. However, whereas the *degree* of effectiveness varies from study to study, the *fact* of improved lifestyle during and following treatment is nearly universal across the research done on this issue. Recent research conducted in the United Kingdom provides added cross-national confirmation of the positive impact of drug treatment. This very fact is important and should be noted by policy makers when making funding decisions. Treatment shows great promise in our efforts to reduce drug use and the untoward behaviors associated with it, yet remains relatively underfunded by the federal government.

Contemporary Issues in Treatment

As treatment for drug addiction has evolved, several issues or treatment alternatives have emerged that bear on the effectiveness of treatment. We address five of these issues below: drug treatment efforts linked to the criminal justice system, including compulsory and court-ordered treatment, drug courts, and prison-based treatment programs; gender issues in treatment; community reintegration after treatment; the British Model of drug treatment; and rapid opiate detoxification.

Drugs and the Criminal Justice System

A variety of issues face the criminal justice system today as increasing numbers of drug users find themselves caught up in the machinery of criminal justice. In this section we address three issues of particular relevance today. First, we consider the general issue of compulsory treatment, the philosophical debate concerning forced treatment, and its effectiveness. Next, we discuss a recent trend in the criminal justice processing of drug offenders, the use of specialized drug courts. Finally, we discuss the effectiveness of prison-based treatment programs.

Compulsory treatment is a general term that refers to the nonvoluntary participation of addicts in treatment programs and includes both drug courts and the prison-based programs described below. Moreover, compulsory treatment is not a special type of treatment modality, and indeed, both nonvoluntary and voluntary clients are often treated within the same programs. The term *compulsory treatment* refers to required drug treatment and a variety of legal and quasilegal incentives for such treatment. It might refer to a probation officer's recommendation to enter treatment, a judge's order to enter treatment as a condition of probation, the option provided by a judge of entering treatment as an alternative to prison, or a mandatory treatment program while in prison (discussed below). Moreover, a variety of terms have been used, often interchangeably, to refer to this process: coercion, mandated treatment, involuntary treatment, legal pressure, and criminal justice referral (Anglin et al. 1998). Leukenfeld and Tims (1990) suggested that the term *compulsory treatment* replace them all.

Compulsory treatment is based on the philosophy that most drug addicts are not intrinsically motivated to seek treatment, or to stay in treatment once being admitted, and hence must be forced to do so for their own benefit but especially the benefit of the community. Those opposed to compulsory treatment argue that effective rehabilitation requires that the addict be committed to change, a commitment that can not generally be externally imposed. If this is the case, compulsory treatment would not be particularly effective, and might even be counterproductive as addicts forced to undergo treatment would resist and undermine treatment procedure and goals (Hartjen et al. 1981). Others opposed to compulsory treatment have raised both ethical and constitutional issues regarding involuntary commitment of drug abusers (Platt et al. 1988; Rosenthal 1988). Because of these concerns, researchers and policy experts have been especially interested in whether or not such efforts to induce treatment have been effective. To the extent that coerced clients are as effectively rehabilitated as voluntary clients, compulsory treatment is justifiable, it is claimed, on the grounds that more addicts can be reached.

Compulsory treatment is not a new concept among American responses to drug abuse. Earlier in this chapter we learned that Congress authorized the establishment of the U.S. Public Health Service Hospitals, which were hardly hospitals at all but were alternative forms of incarceration specifically designed for narcotics addicts (Inciardi 1988). California instituted a large-scale civil commitment program in 1961 that provided for compulsory treatment of addicts for up to seven years without being convicted of a criminal offense. This program was followed up by a similar program in New York in 1966, and nationally by the Narcotic Addict Rehabilitation Act of 1966 (NARA), which provided for compulsory treatment of addicts *charged* with nonviolent federal offenses, treatment instead of imprisonment for addicts *convicted* of federal crimes, and voluntary commitment of addicts not currently in the criminal justice system (Inciardi 1988).

More recently in the early 1970s, a program entitled Treatment Alternatives to Street Crime (TASC) was established in the state of Delaware, eventually operating at some 200 sites in 30 states (Inciardi 2004). Under this program, which is now officially known as Treatment Accountability for Safer Communities, nonviolent offenders with drug or alcohol addiction were referred to community-based treatment programs as an alternative or supplement to other criminal justice procedures. TASC clients are monitored for compliance with individually tailored treatment plans, which ultimately entailed goals of abstinence and improved social functioning and employment (Cook and Weinman 1988).

Research shows that individuals referred by the criminal justice system stay longer in treatment than voluntary referrals (Hubbard et al., 1989), a factor that has been associated with treatment success (Anglin and Hser 1990; De Leon 1998; Simpson and Friend 1988). There is simply more time to apply therapeutic techniques, and perhaps to overcome client resistance as well. Research on the effectiveness of the TASC initiative, which is now growing, suggests that compulsory treatment is effective in reducing drug use (Anglin et al. 1999; Hubbard et al. 1989). It seems that the interruption of drug-use patterns early in a drug-using career, which the TASC program seeks to do, is instrumental in long-term drug use reduction.

The effect of compulsory treatment on predatory criminal behavior is not as clear, though recent research on TASC programs in the midwest suggests some reason for optimism here as well (Ventura and Lambert 2004).

There is also evidence that compulsory treatment is efficacious for the treatment of alcohol abuse. Rosenberg and Liftik (1976) found that convicted drunk drivers who were required to attend a treatment clinic as a condition of probation had much better and longer attendance rates than voluntary admissions. Using a much larger base of 1,055 subjects collected through the Washington State Alcoholism Monitoring System, Dunham and Mauss (1982) found that not only did involuntary patients stay in treatment longer, but they were more successful in maintaining abstinence than were voluntary patients; indeed, court-ordered referrals were more than twice as likely to remain abstinent as were voluntary referrals.

Criminally involved, hard-core drug abusers are at the core of many of the social pathologies found in our society. Linking drug treatment with criminal justice services makes sense, because we are able to hold addicts accountable for their criminality while offering them support for changing their behavior and their lifestyles. For nonviolent offenders, this can occur as an alternative to prison. One response that is becoming increasingly popular throughout the United States is the establishment of separate specialized drug courts to process and monitor criminal offenders with substance abuse problems.

Drug courts are specialized courts that handle drug cases either as an alternative to and separate from the criminal court system or as part of the court system in the sentencing and/or probationary stage. The first drug court was established in Dade County, Florida, in 1989, in an effort to address the high levels of recidivism among drug offenders in the Miami area while reducing the burden on the existing court and prison system (Berman and Feinblatt 2001). This program quickly received national attention and gained the favor of the federal government. The White House has hailed the drug courts as "one of the most promising trends in the criminal justice system" (White House 2004, 6). Since 1989, the Office of Justice Programs has awarded millions of dollars to fund drug courts. As of November, 2008, more than 2000 drug courts were active in the United States (Bureau of Justice Assistance 2008).

Because drug courts are locally established, what they look like and how they operate varies across the country. Some, for example, see themselves as primarily a diversion agency, funneling clients into treatment programs prior to any involvement in the courts. Other jurisdictions may refer cases to drug courts after trial but prior to sentencing. Still others may use the drug courts as a probationary tool following sentencing. Despite these differences, drug courts do share broad goals. The National Association of Drug Court Professionals (1997) identified ten key components, are listed in Figure 13.5. Taken together, these common components of drug courts seek to integrate the criminal justice system with treatment delivery options in the most effective way while protecting both the interests of the community and the due process rights of the drug court participants.

Because the drug courts are so varied in the specific implementation strategies that they employ, evaluation of their effectiveness at the national level is difficult.

#1:	Integration of drug treatment services with criminal justice case processing.
#2:	Promotion of public safety and participants due process rights, using a non adversarial approach.
#3:	Early identification and placement of eligible participants.
#4:	Provision of access to a continuum of alcohol, drug, and other treatment related services.
#5:	Monitoring of alcohol and drug use through testing.
#6:	Coordination of various agencies in responding to compliance or noncompliance.
#7:	On-going judicial interaction with each drug court participant.
#8:	Monitoring and evaluation of achievement of program goals to measure program effectiveness.
#9:	Continuing interdisciplinary education to promote effective drug court planning, implementation, and operation.
#10:	Forging of partnerships between drug courts, public agencies, and community-based organizations to generate local support and enhance program effectiveness.

13.5 Ten Key Components to Drug Courts.
Source: National Association of Drug Court Professionals, *Defining Drug Courts: The Key Components,* 1997. Washington, DC: U.S. Dep't of Justice.

Studies conducted in individual jurisdictions have been quite promising, however (National Institute of Justice 2006). Early studies in Miami, for example, found significantly fewer re-arrests among drug court defendants than among comparable defendants not processed through drug courts (Goldkamp and Weiland 1993). More recent research in San Mateo County, California, was more cautionary, finding no significant differences in re-arrest rates between participants in the drug courts and nonparticipants; however *graduates* of the program were significantly less likely to be re-arrested than nongraduates, at 19 vs. 53 percent (Wolf et al. 2002). These results are encouraging overall, and indeed, it would seem to make sense to expand the coordination of programs and agencies even more. Cooper (2007) points out, for example, that even in drug court jurisdictions, welfare benefits are still generally denied to those convicted of drug charges, as are educational loans, public housing benefits, and voting rights.

For serious offenders, the drug courts may not be an option, and prison sentences will be required. If these individuals are to be reached therapeutically, drug treatment will be needed while they are incarcerated—a separate though related issue in substance abuse treatment to which we now turn.

Prison-based treatment programs have been controversial in part because of the high cost of such programs and because of the perception among some that these and other rehabilitation programs should not be the responsibility of the taxpayer.

This is a short-sighted point of view, as most criminals with drug-abusing histories will eventually be returned to the community. Relieved of their compulsive substance abuse, they are a substantially reduced threat to those same taxpayers. Moreover, many of these individuals have other mental health problems that call for a therapeutic response, and Wexler (2003) notes that prison-based programs are now beginning to address these co-occurring substance abuse and mental health issues. Most prison-based treatment programs model themselves after community-based therapeutic communities. Most are isolated from the rest of the prison population to provide a 24-hour treatment environment, and frequently many of the treatment staff are themselves former addicts, such as is found in community-based treatment communities.

Studies of prison-based programs in New York and Oregon by Wexler and colleagues (1992) and Field (1992), respectively, demonstrated an inverse relationship between how long prisoner-clients were in these programs and recidivism rates; that is, the longer prisoners were in the prison-based program, the less likely it was that they would recidivate. Indeed, Andrews and colleagues (1990) report that at least 40 percent of the carefully designed evaluation studies report positive effects of prison-based rehabilitation programs generally (both drug and non-drug programs). Their meta-analysis of the literature in this area revealed that the effectiveness of prison-based treatment was dependent upon the appropriateness of treatment for the specific needs of the client.

Compulsory treatment—whether court-ordered, out-patient, or prison-based—on balance, seems to have a positive impact on post-treatment outcomes. The fact that clients can be coerced to stay in treatment for a longer period of time is almost certainly the primary reason. Although a motivated client would seem to be the best candidate for treatment success, even clients who are not motivated initially may learn the motivation in the process of treatment. We have emphasized in several chapters that drug use is a learned behavior. *We must therefore emphasize here that, for those who have become addicted to drugs, living a drug- and crime-free lifestyle is also learned.* Hence, even court-ordered treatment entrants may learn to accept the value of being drug-free and may come to participate as willingly as voluntary participants.

Moreover, we must be careful not to assume that all compulsory clients are necessarily nonwilling, nor that all voluntary clients are necessarily willing. That is, although compulsory clients are required to enter a treatment program by the criminal justice system, some or even many may be ready for such an experience (Anglin et al. 1998). For some, especially those early in their criminal and drug-using careers such as TASC clients, the criminal justice encounter may be the attention-getter needed to motivate them to change their lives. On the other hand, so-called voluntary clients may be under threat of eviction or loss of a spouse if they do not enter treatment (Maddux 1988). Such an entry is hardly willing, though technically considered voluntary. One thing we do know: compulsory clients are usually in treatment for a substantially longer period of time, and this time spent in a therapeutic environment has been demonstrated to be effective in producing a changed lifestyle, particularly in reducing the level of drug use.

Gender Issues in Treatment

Until the 1970s, almost no attention was given to treatment for women addicts. Virtually all of the research on drug treatment—and drug addiction generally for that matter—was conducted among male addicts under the wide and mistaken believef that knowledge gained in studying male addicts would apply to women as well. Research supported by the National Institute on Drug Abuse, as part of their initiative "Drug Addiction Research and the Health of Women," shows that "gender differences play a role from the very earliest opportunity to use drugs, that women and men tend to abuse different drugs, that the effects of drugs are different for women and men, and that *some approaches to treatment are more successful for women than for men*" (2000b; our emphasis).

In 1973, the First National Conference on Women and Drug Concerns was held in Washington, D.C., where women raised concerns about the need to understand women as a special drug-using and treatment group. This conference was soon followed by special programs for women's concerns established by the National Institute on Drug Abuse, and in 1976, Public Law 94-371 was passed, giving priority consideration to prevention and treatment programs for women (Beschner and Thompson 1981). Although no universal definition exists of what constitutes substance abuse treatment for women, it is generally agreed that such programming should include at least the following core components (Brady and Ashley 2005):

- Ancillary services, such as child care or transportation services, to increase access to treatment by women clients
- Services to address special and unique needs of women, such as prenatal care, mental health services to address women who have been abused, and so forth
- Women-only programs providing women a unique treatment environment free from the potentially threatening environment of men.

In their study, Brady and Ashley found that nearly 30 years after this legislation, only about 37 percent of treatment facilities across the United States offered *any* special programs for women.

Female addicts share many of the circumstances, experiences, and needs of their male counterparts, but some treatment needs are unique to women. Numerous problems specific to women or more often encountered by women in treatment or seeking treatment have been noted in the literature over the past 30 years. We address some of the major issues that have been raised in this section.

Lack of Child Care Facilities

Lack of child care facilities has long been noted as an obstacle to women entering drug treatment (Rosenbaum and Murphy 1981; Laign 1987). Research has consistently noted that a majority of women seeking treatment, between 67 and 75 percent, have one or more children for whom they are responsible (Beschner and Thompson 1981; Brady and Ashley 2005; Hanke and Faupel 1993). Furthermore, research by Faupel and Hanke (1993) found that although 67 percent of the women who have ever been in treatment had at least one child, *98 percent of the women who have never been in treatment have at least one child*. Clearly, many drug-abusing mothers are deterred from seeking treatment because of a lack of child care. Yet, nearly 30 years after Public Law 94-371 was passed, only 13 percent of treatment facilities in the United States offer child care services (Brady and Ashley 2005).

Counseling Needs

Because most treatment programs are oriented toward men or have grown out of male-oriented models, women entering treatment are likely to encounter a male-dominated treatment process. Male domination manifests itself in a variety of ways. Residential programs, particularly therapeutic communities, frequently use ex-addicts as counselors. They are typically male. Male counselors are often counter-productive in treating addicted women, who have been physically and/or sexually abused by men (Boles et al. 2005; Gil-Rivas et al. 1997). Also, residential treatment programs typically use confrontive therapy, such as the "haircut" discussed earlier in this chapter. This can be a very effective approach in breaking down the "tough guy" image that men often present, but can be devastating to a woman addict who already suffers from emotional, physical, and/or sexual abuse at the hands of men. Reed (1987) suggests that these tactics may cause women who have developed a "learned helplessness" to feel even more out of control.

Still another way in which the counseling needs of women are not met in traditional programs is the ratio of male to female clients in these programs. Because of the abusive experiences they have had with men, the therapeutic environment needed by many drug-using women is an all-female environment. Yet, only 6 percent of treatment programs in the United States today serve women only (Brady and Ashley 2005). Some mixed-sex programs have separated men and women for therapy purposes, but the majority do not according to Brady and Ashley. Where mixed-sex programming occurs, males usually dominate. Reed (1987) reports that most women in treatment were in programs with anywhere from a 2 : 1 to a 10 : 1 ratio of men to women. Research from a variety of fields has demonstrated that men are more outspoken and assertive than women in mixed group settings. Such domination by men makes it likely that the women in these programs are not able to address their issues and concerns, at least not in group therapy sessions.

Sexism

Friedman and Alicea (2001) in a recent study of women in methadone treatment programs identified sexism as a major obstacle encountered by women seeking treatment. Counselors regarded these women as poor mothers, and those on the outside, family and friends, did as well. The demeaning interactions they encounter discourage many women from seeking treatment, opting to try to get by as best they can on their own. It has been quite widely documented that treatment staff often view women as inherently "sicker" than men (Palm 2007). Whereas men's problems are typically centered around lack of motivation and/or skills training, women are believed to have deeper problems. Consequently, many of the services available to men such as job training skills and the like are not offered to women because it is believed that either they could not benefit because of other psychological problems, or that such job skills are not necessary for women (the assumption being that they will be supported by a man). NIDA-supported research (2000b) backs up the notion that female treatment clients often have a greater range of other problems (such as physical ill health, physical and sexual abuse, history of attempted suicide), that should not be used to exclude them from a full range of programs that might benefit them.

Unique Physical Needs of Women
Women coming into treatment often have physical symptoms or needs different from men. Studies have found that women are more likely than men to cite physical symptoms a motivators for treatment (Beschner and Thompson 1981). Many women entering treatment have prostituted themselves for drug money and bring with them such attendant physical problems as gynecological and urinary infections, venereal disease, and HIV/AIDS. Pregnant women pose particular needs and concerns, and the number of women seeking treatment who are pregnant is significant. Pregnancy is often a motivator to seek treatment, as these women do not want to give birth to addicted children. Many treatment programs will not admit pregnant women at all (Karan 1989), and most programs that do admit women do not provide adequate care for women who are pregnant. Brady and Ashley (2005) report that only 12 percent of treatment programs provide any prenatal care whatsoever.

Community Reintegration
Perhaps the most neglected aspect of drug treatment has been follow-up services designed to assist clients in maintaining a drug free lifestyle after the structured environment of treatment. Following treatment, addicts face the difficult challenge of integrating into a community that, for many, is rather foreign. Many addicts have lived their lives on the streets in inner city areas, have relied on criminal activities to support their habits and lifestyles, and have developed friendship networks that are primarily comprised of other addicts. This is the *setting* of their addiction. If treatment is to be successful in the long term, a change of setting will almost certainly be required (Faupel 1985). Former addicts seeking to live a drug- and crime-free lifestyle need legitimate employment. They also need friendship networks that are supportive of a conventional lifestyle. Broken family relationships need repair. If such a supportive community is not available to recovering addicts, the only recourse for many is to return to the streets from whence they came, with all of the influences and triggers that led them into a lifestyle of drug use and crime in the first place. Treatment programs of a number of different types warn against the people, places, and things that will lead one back to abusing drugs. Steering clear of them may require not only changing one's attitude but one's "latitude" as well.

The word that is used to describe the shift in *setting* from the nonconventional and drug-using milieu of the streets to a more conventional context is **reintegration**. This is probably a misnomer, because at least for many recovering addicts, this will be the first time they have ever been a part of a conventional community. Reintegration is quite typically initiated by placing the addict in a **halfway house**. Halfway houses are transitional living facilities that serve as a bridge between the treatment program and the conventional community. Here, the addict lives with other addicts in a therapeutic environment with some, though not all, of the structure of the treatment program, and is encouraged to seek work and build relationships in conventional society. Several problems have been identified with halfway houses. Perhaps most problematic is that communities are resistant to hosting them. Ideally, halfway houses should be located in communities that are free of drugs and crime and that might be a catalyst for helping integrate the former addicts into conventional society. Kubrin and Stewart (2006) found that offenders released from prison to higher socioeconomic neighborhoods were much less likely to reoffend than those returning to disadvantaged neighborhoods. Yet, these are the very neighborhoods most resistant to halfway houses (Dembo et al. 1983). Residents in these communities do not understand addiction and have a fear of the unknown, the same NIMBY mentality mentioned with methadone clinics. There is also the fear of a reduction of property values as a result of such facilities (Dembo et al. 1983).

Employment is a major need of recovering drug addicts. Strong evidence has emerged that meaningful conventional employment is important to the post-treatment success of recovering addicts (Kemp et al. 2004). Unfortunately, many employers are hesitant to hire ex-users, which is understandable in light of their often shaky work history while using drugs. Some efforts have been made to facilitate work opportunities for recovering addicts. Related to employment, many addicts need vocational and educational skills before they can even begin work (Kemp et al. 2004). Educational institutions can be very intimidating to ex-addicts; problems in school were often catalysts for them becoming involved in drugs and crime in the first place. Programs that encourage and help to facilitate educational pursuits are therefore needed.

There are other important points of reintegration as well. Families of addicts may be seriously strained or broken from the addiction. Friendship networks need to be established, whether informally or formally through organizations such as churches and synagogues, neighborhood associations, family counseling, and others. Indeed, social support networks following treatment have been found even more important to ultimate recovery than what takes place while in treatment (Broome et al. 2002). Unfortunately, the groups and organizations most capable of offering such support are often resistant to helping recovering addicts, or may not be especially knowledgeable about how to do so. The common theme in all of the obstacles to reintegration is the need to educate the community regarding the nature of addiction and the positive contribution that recovering addicts can make to an organization, neighborhood, or community. The obstacles to successful reintegration lie not only with the addict or with the aftercare component of treatment programs. They especially lie within us as residents and members of would-be host communities and all of the social service groups contained therein. The unspoken skepticism of most Americans regarding the rehabilitative potential of recovering addicts too often results in a self-fulfilling prophecy: we generally expect that recovering addicts will relapse or underperform, yet it is our very resistance to community reintegration that most likely brings about such a result.

The British Method: Heroin Maintenance

Since the years immediately following the Harrison Narcotics Act of 1914, and reinforced more recently by the Comprehensive Drug Abuse Prevention and Control Act of 1970 (both discussed in Chapter 2), heroin maintenance has been precluded legally in the United States. Heroin is a Schedule I drug, which means that it has no officially recognized medical utility, and hence is illegal for all medical purposes in this country. That includes use for relief of severe or chronic pain and for keeping addicts comfortable. In addition, after 90 years of antiheroin sentiment, and a raft of media messages that heroin may just be the devil incarnate, Americans are not likely to be open to a discussion of heroin as legitimate medicine. Yet *heroin maintenance*—widely known as the **British Method** or the British System—is used in several European countries, and its efficacy and desirability as a treatment modality for heroin addiction in this country has been debated for more than 30 years, particularly in the 1970s.

The British are credited by name because they were the first to use heroin maintenance as part of drug abuse policy. Starting in the 1960s, addicts who had tried unsuccessfully to kick their heroin habits by other means could register with the government and the National Health Service to have heroin prescribed for them.[4] As with other NHS programs, the heroin was provided free of charge in amounts geared to the level of the addict's habit. Thus it was fairly unprofitable for them to divert their heroin to the black market, a major concern of those who challenge such a plan (Kaplan 1983, 158–183). The focus of the heroin maintenance policy is not a punitive one, designed to stamp out drug abuse, but rather is on public health and is designed to mitigate the damage that drug abuse does (Nadelmann 1995). (We discuss such an approach under the rubric of *harm reduction* in Chapter 15.) One of the reasons why heroin maintenance might reduce the consequences of heroin addiction is that the heroin being provided is legal (and free or inexpensive) and is of known purity. Hence, the addict need not worry about being arrested, need not steal or prostitute to afford his or her drug of choice, and is unlikely to suffer a drug overdose. It should also be mentioned that heroin, when administered under healthful conditions, is a relatively benign medicine, meaning that it doesn't damage the body's ability to function as many other drugs, including many legal pharmaceuticals, can do. Most of the deaths associated with heroin arise from its illegality not its inherent toxicity.

The popularity of heroin maintenance as an alternative drug abuse treatment policy rose in the early 1990s in some circles with the realization that new cases of HIV and hepatitis infection were increasingly found in IV drug–using populations. Concern about public health led the governments of Switzerland, the Netherlands, and Denmark to offer legal heroin to addicts (Nadelmann 1995; Sheldon 1997). The Swiss experience since 1994 is quite instructive. They sell heroin at state-run clinics to addicts who meet rigid qualifications: at least two consecutive years of active addiction, plus criminal records or health problems (other than addiction) or both. Addicts come to the clinic one to three times a day, pay 15 Swiss francs each time (about 10 U.S. dollars), and inject on site under antiseptic conditions. The addicts are also enrolled in free comprehensive health, social, and psychological services. The program is monitored by the World Health Organization of the United Nations (Nadelmann 1995).

The results have been quite impressive. Ribeaud (2004) reports that over some four years, crime decreased by nearly 70 percent among those in the Swiss heroin maintenance program, or what has become known as "the Swiss heroin trials." Nadelmann (1995) reports that from 1994 to 1997, new HIV and hepatitis infections dropped to almost zero, and employment jumped from 30 to 60 percent. It is easy to see why some government officials proclaimed it a huge success. Others, however, who believe that abstinence is the only true success in drug policy disagree that this is success. They proposed a constitutional amendment that would disallow heroin (and a host of other drugs) to be used medically, a proposal that was rejected by Swiss voters in 1997 (Sheldon 1997).

We are a long way from adopting a heroin maintenance policy in the United States. Not only must numerous practical issues be addressed (Staton and Leukefeld 2002), but American policy makers continue to be locked in a drug war mentality that is not compatible with heroin maintenance as a harm reduction measure. We, your textbook authors, would welcome open discussion of heroin maintenance as an example of "thinking outside the drug war box."

Rapid Opiate Detoxification

We have mentioned previously that the detoxification process is often a necessary first stage in overcoming drug addiction. It allows the addicts, typically over five to seven days, to cleanse themselves of the drug(s) in their system, which reduces physiological drug craving and allows them to benefit from therapy groups and other modes of treatment. **Rapid opiate detoxification** shortens the detoxification process and reduces its discomfort. It was developed by European physicians in the 1980s and refined by an Israeli physician, Dr. Andre Waissman, in the early 1990s. Under heavy sedation or general anesthesia, the opiate receptors in the patient's brain are blocked by a drug like naltrexone, while other medications speed up the physiological reactions to hasten drug elimination. The result is that the patient awakens without having experienced withdrawal symptoms (Cucchia et al. 1998). Depending on the method and drugs employed, the process can take as little as four to six hours (called *ultra-rapid detox*) or 12 to 24 hours. The addict is then prescribed naltrexone, a narcotic antagonist, to reduce the likelihood of post-procedure relapse. The extended use of narcotic antagonists has been increasingly recommended, and some suggest that it might be more appropriate to refer to this procedure as *rapid antagonist induction* (Streel and Verbanck 2003).

Rapid detoxification has its critics in the medical, scientific, and legal fields. Some question its effectiveness, claiming relapse rates of 80 percent within six months of detox (Cucchia et al. 1998). This does not come as a surprise to those who have spent time in the drug treatment field. Detoxification does *not* constitute a cure. Addiction is a lifestyle that has been learned over a period of, often, many years. Rapid detoxification does not address the lifestyle issues that must be unlearned, nor the social context of addiction and recovery that has been recognized by those emphasizing the importance of effective community reintegration, as discussed earlier. Critics are also quick to point out that patients have died soon after having the procedure—seven patients (over four years) in one New Jersey physician's out-patient practice alone. The doctor in question, Lance L. Gooberman, himself a recovering drug addict, argues that they had underlying heart conditions that he and others had not detected (*Alcoholism and Drug Abuse Weekly* 2001). In response, many in the medical community assert that the procedure is too stressful for the bodies of addicts ravaged by years of drug abuse (Marshall 2001; Associated Press 2000). The death of a patient in the United Kingdom and the subsequent trial of Dr. Gary Gerson raised still another perplexing issue: that rapid detoxification may by unduly motivated by commercial interests. Dr. Gerson was the director and shareholder of a company called Medetox Ltd., which performed ultra-rapid opiate detoxification commercially (Badenoch 2002). It is important to note that, although the procedure has been approved for use by the American Society of Addiction Medicine, experts agree that more research is needed.

Summary

Drug treatment programs, also known as therapeutic approaches to the problem of drug dependency, use a variety of methods or treatment modalities to help those who are dependent on legal or illegal drugs and no longer desire to be. The drug(s) people are dependent on, their physical and mental health, their commitment to change, and their financial resources and support systems all influence which type of treatment they might seek. Drug treatment assumes that addiction is a medical illness or condition capable of being arrested, if not outright cured. Most experts contend that addiction affects one physically and emotionally (and perhaps spiritually as well). Therefore, the most effective drug treatment programs are comprehensive and multifaceted, including some combination of the following: detoxification and medical stabilization, drug counseling and drug education, individual and group therapy, and aftercare planning including relapse prevention and help with a support network.

Drug treatment works. For many addicts, therapeutic intervention—the application of an appropriate treatment modality at the right time—allows them to give up a habit and a way of life that is self-destructive and harmful to others. This doesn't mean that treatment is any kind of a guaranteed cure for drug dependency; frankly, it is unsuccessful for many and is unnecessary for others. We are aware, and have argued in this chapter, that claims of success, particularly from treatment programs themselves, need to be examined with a critical eye. We are likewise cognizant of the fact that some researchers claim a failure rate of 70 to 90 percent. Those seeking drug treatment are more likely to be hard-core abusers who have been unsuccessful at stopping on their own and who have not been helped by the criminal justice system's punitive responses. These hard-core abusers consume a disproportionate amount of illegal drugs, and their impact on our social institutions—the family, the economy, health care, and criminal justice among them—is enormous. Anything that can ameliorate these considerable consequences is worth considering. We argue that treatment works because we choose to focus on those it helps, to whatever degree it helps, regardless of the particular form the treatment takes.

We are not alone in this position. Our federal government concurs, though as we have noted, actual funding for drug treatment has lagged behind spending on law enforcement. Consider the following from statement from the Office of National Drug Control Policy, essentially, the "drug czar's" office: "[N]umerous studies support the logic and rationale of providing treatment for drug users. The research reveals that the societal costs of untreated addiction, such as violence, crime, poor health, and family breakup far exceed the costs of providing treatment" (ONDCP 2001b). We concur—drug rehabilitation can be costly, but we believe that the costs of *not* treating hard-core drug and alcohol dependency can cost our society much more. Former Delaware Governor Russell W. Peterson calls our current emphasis on imprisonment over treatment for the addicted "an immoral offense that threatens our way of life." In his view, we have two options: continue our bankrupt strategy, or invest enough in drug treatment to ensure decent lives for as many as we can help (Peterson 2000).

Key Terms

abstinence
antagonist
British Method
compulsory treatment
detoxification
drug courts
halfway house
methadone maintenance
Minnesota Model
prison-based treatment programs

rapid opiate detoxification
reintegration
therapeutic community (TC)
treatment modalities

Thinking Critically…

1. Early understanding of alcoholism and drug addiction by treatment specialists was that these were quite literally diseases involved toxins that needed to be detoxified. In what ways do current treatment efforts reflect this disease model of addiction? In what ways have treatment efforts today departed from this model?

2. Some have suggested that the therapeutic community is more sociological in its approach to understanding addiction and treatment than any other type of treatment. Discuss the basis for this claim.

3. The British Method, at least in its earlier years, made heroin easily available to addicts through physicians and clinics. The rationale for this approach is that addiction is a disease and that, insofar as there is no "cure," physicians should be free to treat the symptoms of that disease (withdrawal distress). The United States rejected this model but uses methadone, which is also a narcotic that some have argued is much more troublesome than heroin in its effects on users. The rationale for rejecting the British Method is that heroin use is a crime, therefore it would be improper to prescribe heroin to addicts. Do you agree with this logic? Which approach do you think makes more sense? Why?

4. A major divide separates drug treatment specialists regarding the purpose and goals of treatment, resulting in further differences of opinion regarding the proper techniques for accomplishing these goals. Some argue that the purpose and goals of treatment should be to make the drug addict completely drug free, and that treatment should consist of drug-free methods of accomplishing this task. Others argue that treatment should facilitate the addict's effective functioning in society, not necessarily make an individual drug free. Reflect on this philosophical divide and articulate what you think should be the proper goals and technique of drug treatment.

5. Alcoholics Anonymous and its counterpart Narcotics Anonymous are widely acclaimed self-help systems for addicts that base their efforts heavily on spiritual restoration. What role do you think spirituality and faith have in recovery from addiction?

Learning from the Internet

1. Several large residential treatment programs in major cities throughout the United States consider themselves therapeutic communities. There is even a national organization to promote this concept in treatment known as Therapeutic Communities

of America. Go to its website at http://www.therapeuticcommunitiesofamerica.org/ and click the hyperlink called "members." This link will list first individual board members, followed by organizational members that consist of individual TCs in various cities. Most of the organizations listed have hyperlinks to their home pages. Go to several of these TC home pages and learn what you can about their philosophy and methods of treatment. Identify the key points to their philosophy (collectively) and summarize the major strategies they use to implement this philosophy.

2. Alcoholics Anonymous and its counterparts (such as Narcotics Anonymous) are by most accounts the most successful self-help organizations in the area of alcohol and drug treatment. Go to AA's website to learn more about this organization: www.aa.org. You will have to navigate around the website a bit, but learn what you can about the history and philosophy of the organization. Identify what you believe to be some of the important things in its history and philosophy that have made AA so successful.

Notes

1. The word *synanon* originated with one of the early residents of the program. Attempting to say two words in the same breath, *symposium* and *seminar*, he managed to come out with a badly garbled rendition that sounded like *synanon*. From this point forward the organization was known as Synanon (capital S), and the group seminars known as synanons (small s). The history of this group is more fully described in Yablonsky (1965).

2. Some of the more well known therapeutic communities include Phoenix House, Odyssey House, and Daytop Village, all in New York City, and Gateway Foundation in Chicago.

3. The haircut is usually a systematic verbal attack on an individual by others in the group in response to misbehavior or inappropriate attitudes. This process received its name in the original Synanon community, however, to refer to actual haircuts: individuals in the group would chop the hair of the wayward resident as a symbol of their disapproval (Yablonsky 1965).

4. The British amended this system in 1968, setting up heroin maintenance clinics as part of the National Health Service. Private patients with the financial means may still go to their own physicians for prescriptions of heroin.

CHAPTER **14**

Preventive Responses to Drug Problems: Drug Education and Drug Testing

The third mode of societal response to the problem of drug abuse in America is prevention. Unlike drug treatment, which addresses the problem of drug abuse *after* it has affected individuals, the two responses considered in this chapter—drug education and drug testing—generally attempt to intervene *prior* to the development of a drug abuse problem. Preemptive responses are fairly recent newcomers in society's arsenal of responses to drug use. This is surprising, given the recognition in medicine that it is better to prevent a disease than to treat it once it has already occurred. It is all the more surprising given that treatment efforts to date have not had a consistent track record. Moreover, although federal spending on prevention efforts, which are usually identified as drug education efforts, increased through the 1990s, the have declined in more recent years. The proposed budget for Funding Year 2009 is $1.5 billion for prevention efforts, down more than 15 percent from the $1.85 billion budget in 2007 (ONDCP 2008). This figure represents a mere 10.7 percent of the overall federal drug budget, also down from the 14 percent of the budget that prevention represented in the 1990s.

Drug prevention is a demand-side response to the problems associated with drug use. Both drug education and drug testing represent efforts to reduce the number of individuals who use drugs and/or the amount of drugs that people use. As we suggested in Chapter 12, practitioners and policy makers often distinguish between primary, secondary, and tertiary prevention strategies. Primary prevention is geared toward preventing the initial, or at least chronic, use of drugs by individuals, which is the goal of most drug education programs. Secondary prevention focuses on early identification of drug use and intervention prior to the development of major drug-related problems and full-blown addiction. Most drug testing is conducted with this purpose in mind. Tertiary prevention is directed at those who are already addicted, and although referred to as a prevention strategy, it actually focuses on rehabilitation (Bukoski 1991). The major tertiary prevention is drug treatment, which was addressed in Chapter 13.

Drug Education

Drug education has a fairly long history in the United States, even though it has only recently been emphasized in drug policy strategies. Perhaps the earliest drug education programs emerged from the prohibitionist movement and the efforts of the Women's Christian Temperance Union (WCTU) to eradicate alcohol and the problems it caused (Bordin 1981). Early efforts at drug education were profoundly ideological in nature, often making exaggerated claims that would fail to hold up to empirical investigation. Perhaps the most well-known early education effort was the film *Teach Your Children*, which was originally produced as a drug-education film in 1936 by the Federal Bureau of Narcotics. It was later released under the title *Reefer Madness*. The film depicts an upstanding, middle-class high school boy getting turned on to marijuana and becoming a sexually aggressive, rather crazed and violent person who is eventually charged with a murder he did not commit. The information it presented is clearly exaggerated but was widely believed at the time. The problem with this kind of information, of course, is that when claims about the effects of these drugs do not materialize, the credibility of the message and the messenger is compromised. This can have unfortunate consequences. Marsha Rosenbaum quotes a heroin addict who, when asked how she became addicted to heroin, replied,

> When I was in high school they had these so-called drug education classes. They told us if we used marijuana we would become addicted. They told us if we used heroin we would become addicted. Well, we all tried marijuana and found we did not become addicted. We figured the entire message must be b.s. So I tried heroin, used it again and again, got strung out, and here I am. (1999, 1)

When drug education is mentioned today, what immediately comes to mind for most people are high-profile programs such as DARE (Drug Abuse Resistance Education) or the many commercials sponsored by the Partnership for a Drug Free America. These are, indeed, drug education programs, but they represent a narrow slice of the broad spectrum of approaches to drug education in the United States today.

Through the years, there have been numerous approaches to classifying drug education programs. Perhaps the most helpful typologies are those which characterize the nature of the message communicated to the audience. Ellickson (1995), among others, distinguish between the informational model, the affective model, and the social influence model, a typology that we have found most useful for our discussion. After discussing each of these models and their effectiveness, we will examine an emerging approach that falls under the more general approach to drug policy, harm reduction.

Informational Model

The **informational model** is probably most familiar to baby boomers who went through public schools in the 1960s and early 1970s. This traditional approach is designed simply to convey factual information about the nature of drugs and how they affect the human body in the short and long term. Drugs and their effects were always presented in negative terms, and the consequences of drug use were often exaggerated. Typical of these programs was the use of scare tactics with a method of presentation that allowed little opportunity for student interaction or engagement.

Informational programs are typically implemented through the schools, but other media are also used, especially the general mass media. Among the first organizations to provide drug educational material through the mass media were the American Cancer Society and the American Heart Association. These organizations targeted cigarette smoking. Studies of the effectiveness of these campaigns suggest that they were quite successful in reducing smoking (Flay 1987; Pisani 1995). Alcohol has also been the target of mass media advertising. The object of this advertising has not been so much abstinence as responsible drinking, and especially not driving if drinking. These ads have been sponsored by Mothers Against Drunk Driving (MADD), the

Ad Council, and by beer companies themselves (Pisani 1995). Jacobs (1989) points out that these educational attempts have been less than effective in changing behavior, namely drunk driving. There are numerous reasons for this, including the fact that strong pro-drinking messages are also broadcast, and that the transfer of knowledge to behavior is often difficult when it comes to drinking and driving.

Perhaps the most visible antidrug information to be disseminated through the mass media, however, is that sponsored by the Partnership for a Drug-Free America. The Partnership was conceived in 1986 by Phil Joanou, chairman of the Dailey Advertising Agency. It is a nonprofit, private sector coalition consisting of representatives from advertising, public relations firms, and media companies (Pisani 1995). The messages were initially directed primarily at preteens who had not yet begun to experiment with drugs, and their content was powerful. Few will forget the frying pan image with "This is your brain. This is your brain on drugs." More recently, the Partnership has been targeting parents and caregivers. Research conducted by the Gordon S. Black Corporation, examining drug attitudes and behavior from 1987 to 1992, suggests that the advertising campaign of the Partnership for a Drug Free America may have had some impact, though many variables may have combined to produce a downward trend in use, and it should also be noted that drug use has fluctuated since (Pisani 1995).

In 1998, the United States Congress approved funding for a national media campaign under the auspices of the Office of National Drug Control Policy (n.d.) to reduce and prevent drug use among young people. Known as the National Youth Anti-Drug Media Campaign, it was launched in 1999 in collaboration with the Partnership for a Drug Free America and other private and public corporations. The Campaign progressed in three phases. Phase I consisted of a 12-city pilot test of ads addressed to various ethnic groups, followed by audience awareness surveys and focus groups. Phase II took the Campaign national with TV, radio, print, and internet advertising. In September 1999, Phase III focused on ages 9 to 18, but primarily on the "tween" years of 11 to 13 (Eddy 2006). The authorizing legislation for the Campaign requires that its effectiveness be evaluated, a task assigned through the National Institute on Drug Abuse. The effectiveness of this campaign, discussed more thoroughly below, has been disappointing.

One other type of informational program that has found widespread acceptance is what are commonly called "drunk driving schools." Based upon a model developed in Phoenix, Arizona, in response to the high number of drunk-driving-related fatalities in that area, these classes are designed for DUI arrestees to provide extensive information on things such as how driving skills deteriorate at various blood alcohol content (BAC) levels, the fallacy that alcohol effects can be counteracted with coffee or cold water, and the penalties for driving under the influence. These educational courses also include sessions that are more reflective in nature, such as keeping diaries, and life activities inventories that address issues of personal and social adjustment (Jacobs 1989).

Effectiveness of Information-Based Programs

Evaluation studies of the impact of informational drug education programs have generally revealed disappointing results. A review of the evaluations of the drunk driving schools by Jacobs (1989) revealed that the recidivism rate for individuals graduating from these schools was about the same as a control group that received no education. School-based programs do not fare much better. The *National* Youth Anti-Drug Media Campaign has also proved disappointing. The final evaluation, which assessed the effectiveness of the Campaign from its inception of Phase III in 1999 through June 2004, examined three areas of effectiveness: recall of campaign messages, effect on parents, and effect on youth drug use. The campaign was shown to be quite effective in terms of recall, with about 72 percent of parents and 77 percent of youth recalling antidrug messages. The campaign also had a favorable effect on parents, as measured by behaviors such as talking to their children about drugs, monitoring their activities, and doing fun activities with them. There was little evidence, however, for the effectiveness of the campaign on marijuana use

14.1 Drug education efforts use the mass media in disseminating information about drugs and their effects. The leading informational campaign in recent years has been the National Youth Anti-Drug Media Campaign conducted under the auspices of the White House Office of National Drug Control Policy. (Photo courtesy of www.theantidrug.com)

by youth, the primary drug targeted in the ad. In fact, the month prior to the survey showed an increase in marijuana use between 2000 and 2002, with a slight decline from 2002 to 2004. There was, furthermore, no evidence that current users discontinued their use, another stated goal of the Campaign (Orwin et al. 2006).

Meta-analyses, (which analyze the results of previous studies) of studies of school-based programs reveal that whereas these programs may be quite effective in affecting the *attitudes* of youth toward drugs, they are not especially effective in changing their *behavior* (Tobler 1986; Tobler and Stratton 1997; White and Pitts 1998). Moreover, Tobler (1986) found that "knowledge only" programs (that is, information-based programs) were inferior to other programs, particularly those that involve peer resistance. Information-based programs are highly didactic in nature and allow for very little interaction. She also found that multimodal programs were more effective than those using a single modality. In her 1997 follow-up, conducted with Howard Stratton, Tobler found that "interactive" programs were much more effective than "non-interactive" programs. Finally, of 62 evaluations included in their review, White and Pitts (1998) found only 18 studies that suggested program effectiveness, but of those, only two provided verification for lack of drug use; the remaining 16 were based on self-reports.

The conclusion that we draw from these evaluations is that information-oriented drug education programs are not effective for deterring drug use. It is generally acknowledged that these programs are quite effective in increasing levels of knowledge about drugs and their effects, and even that they have an impact on attitudes about drug use. Knowledge and attitudes do not, however, automatically translate into desired behavior. One might speculate that the reason for such ineffectiveness is the greatly exaggerated claims about drugs and the damage that they do. We know that these claims have damaged the credibility of antidrug authorities, as evidenced by the quotation by the heroin addict that was included at the beginning of this section. If this were the only problem, it would easily be solved: we would simply cease making exaggerated claims. The more fundamental problem with information-based programs is that they include no mechanism to translate *cognitive changes* into *behavioral changes*. Because of these failures, practitioners have sought to develop other approaches to drug education that address emotional and behavioral levels as well as cognitive levels of understanding.

Affective Model

Programs using the **affective model** seek to improve communication skills, decision-making ability, and self assertion, all which are believed to underlie a predisposition toward drug abuse (Botvin and Griffin 2006; Ellickson 1995). The affective model emerged in the early 1970s in response to a growing recognition that certain "risk factors" were associated with vulnerability to drug use. Such risk factors include everything from genetic and congenital conditions to personality characteristics to the socioeconomic conditions of one's family and neighborhood (Gerstein and Green 1993). It is, of course, impossible to address all of these predispositions in a drug education program, but some factors can be addressed. A widely used curriculum using the affective model is *Reconnecting Youth: A Peer Group Approach to Building Life Skills* (Eggert et al. 1995). Oriented to high school students, this curriculum was first developed in 1984 and seeks to enhance self esteem, teach decision-making skills, and develop communication skills. These are all factors that, when absent, are believed to predispose young people to drug use and abuse, as well as other maladies such as depression and suicide. Students who are poor academic achievers are targeted for the program, which is a semester-long, daily curriculum that is interactional in nature. It includes social activities that seek to build positive friendships and develop positive attitudes toward school. It is believed that by developing social, communication, and decision-making skills, all which should result in enhanced self-esteem, many at-risk students will be prevented from becoming drug abusers. The logic behind this program is a direct application of the principles of social control theory, which suggest that drug use and other forms of delinquency result from a lack of social bonds connecting young people with conventional society. These activities can be prevented through programs that establish strong social and emotional bonds between children and parents, teachers, and other conventional adults. Furthermore, positive social bonds provide young people with a favorable attitude toward school and other conventional institutions, which in turn, make drug use and other antisocial behavior less appealing. (For more discussion of social control and its implications for drug use and abuse, see Chapter 5.)

Another program which also draws upon social control theory is *Families that Care: Guiding Good Choices* (GGC, formerly Preparing for the Drug-Free Years). This program focuses especially on the establishment of positive bonds within the family, which include opportunities for involvement in family activities, development of skills to accomplish tasks and solve problems, and a healthy system of rewards and punishments within the family (Haggerty et al. 1999). Unlike the Reconnecting Youth program, GGC targets families with children in grades 4 through 8. Moreover, this program targets the *parents and guardians* of children in this age range rather than the children themselves. The program does not address any specific substances of abuse. Rather, the idea is to train parents to be proactive in developing bonds with their children, thereby insulating their children from the pull toward drug abuse. Parents are typically invited to participate in five two-hour sessions that address issues such as setting clear expectations regarding drug and alcohol use, learning how to identify risk factors associated with drug use, managing family conflict, and establishing family bonds. The earlier PDFY was piloted during the mid-1980s in ten public schools in Seattle, Washington, before being distributed as a video-assisted program for broader dissemination in 1987. Other field tests were conducted with a health maintenance organization and in a program involving the broadcast media. The program was revised and renamed in 2003, and is now marketed by a for-profit corporation. Since its inception, Guiding Good Choices has been implemented in more than 30 states and in Canada, training more than 120,000 families.

A very recent drug education effort on the part of the British government has been underway since 2003. This program, known as Blueprint, was initially launched in 23 school districts in England. It involves a multicomponent approach to drug education that includes classroom activities for students, instruction for parents, media outreach, health policy, and a general community component (Stead et al. 2007). The target population are young people 11 to 13 years old. The classroom activities involve ten lessons for students in 7th grade and five follow-up lessons for 8th grade. These lessons include factual information about drugs and drug use, small-group discussions that focus on prevalence of drug use, discussion of values regarding drug use, strategies for making decisions about drug use, and even board games to reinforce these ideas. The parental component addresses issues that include parent-child communication, dealing with conflict, and drug and drug use information. The media component of Blueprint seeks to obtain the cooperation of the media to disseminate fact-based information about drugs and drug use. Finally, Blueprint also includes a policy component that seeks to increase the effectiveness of laws restricting the sale of alcohol and tobacco to minors (Baker 2006). Blueprint is an extremely comprehensive approach to drug education.

Effectiveness of Affective Programs

Affective programs have shown some promise, although the effectiveness of these programs is not altogether clear. An evaluation of the Reconnecting Youth program conducted by the developers of the program showed a favorable impact (Eggert et al. 1990; Eggert and Herting 1991). Controlling for other factors, the researchers found that participation in the program significantly reduced drug use among these high school participants. Independent research by Halifors and her colleagues (2006), however, is less optimistic. These researchers point out that the original evaluations conducted by the developers of the program demonstrated the *efficacy* of the program, meaning that results were favorable under controlled and optimal conditions. *Effectiveness* is a more rigorous test, however, in which evaluations are made under real-world conditions. In the case of school-based programs, for example, larger classes conducted by regular school personnel is more likely the context of delivery for a drug education program. Under these conditions, the Reconnecting Youth curriculum did not produce significant effects (Halifors et al. 2006).

As with the Reconnecting Youth program, evaluation of the parent education program GGC conducted by the developers also shows promising results. Most of the evaluation research on this program was conducted in rural Iowa communities. The results of these studies include the following:

- Alcohol and drug use were significantly more delayed among children of program participants than among children of a control group (Park et al. 2000; Spoth et al. 1999; Spoth et al. 2002).
- Depression symptoms, which typically rise during adolescence, rose less among program participants (Mason et al. 2007).
- The cost-benefit ratio for program participation is extremely encouraging, with $5.85 saved for every dollar invested in the program. It is further estimated that the net benefit to participating families is nearly $2,700 (Spohl et al. 2002).

The effectiveness of the Blueprint program has not yet been evaluated. Preliminary evaluations of teacher response, however, suggest that they have responded well to the training component of the program, and believe it to be critically important to the ultimate success of the program (Stead et al. 2007), This is encouraging, as are the evaluations of the other affective programs. We remind the reader, however, that most of these studies have been conducted by those who have been instrumental in developing or implementing the programs, and those conducted by independent researchers are not so optimistic. Moreover, there are limitations to these studies. The GGC (PDFY) evaluations, for example, were conducted primarily among rural families. There are many conditions and pressures in urban areas toward drug use that may not be as present or powerful in rural areas. Moreover, we do not have evidence for the long-term impact of these programs. These evaluations usually are not carried out over more than one year, though some have followed up for as long as three years. It must also be remembered that these programs have a broader focus than simply reduction in drug use, though this is certainly a central goal. Reconnecting Youth also has as its stated goals reduction in depressive episodes and suicides among youth, as well. Hence, a fair evaluation of these programs must consider all their stated goals.

Social Influence Model

The **social influence model** is the most recent, and according to some, the most promising approach to drug education (Ellickson, 1995). Sometimes referred to as **drug resistance education**, this model seeks to prepare young people to resist the pressures by peers toward drug use. Adolescents are particularly vulnerable to peer pressure, and smoking, drinking, and other forms of drug use are often perceived as avenues to peer acceptance. The theoretical bases for the social influence model are drawn from social inoculation theory developed by William McGuire (1964) and from social learning theory, particularly as developed by Albert Bandura (1977). Inoculation theory argues that as one is confronted by persuasive arguments and pressures toward a particular activity, he or she becomes "inoculated" against the effect of those pressures. This idea views peer pressure as a cultural equivalent of germs: if we expose a young person to a weaker and more protected dose of these germs (persuasive arguments), antibodies (resistance) to the real-world pressures should develop. Social learning theory, as developed by Bandura, stresses the importance of imitation and reinforcement of preferred behavior. Hence, by presenting young people with the arguments for using drugs, typically in a simulated situation, and then modeling how one might resist that pressure and positively reinforcing proper responses to that pressure, young people should be better equipped to resist the pressure to use drugs.

Some of the earliest attempts to use the social influence model were employed in the 1970s to prevent smoking among junior high youth (Evans et al. 1978; Hurd et al. 1980; McAlister et al. 1979; Murray et al. 1984). These programs were aimed at 7th graders because it was believed that until that age, most young people do not face serious pressures to smoke. The earliest of these studies were conducted by Richard Evans and his associates in Houston area schools (1978). They exposed students to nonsmoking peers on film and provided information about short-term health hazards of smoking. The Houston research found a significantly lower onset of smoking among those students exposed to the smoking information than among a control group not exposed to this information.

Later, researchers at the Harvard University School of Public Health and the Stanford University Heart Prevention Program began delivering the same messages, but using older, live role models and introducing role playing to help build resistance. This research also found significantly lower rates of smoking among students exposed to older role models than among the control group. After the academic year in which the program was offered, nearly 10 percent of the control sample reported smoking within the past week, whereas only 5.6 percent of the experimental group reported smoking behavior (McAlister et al. 1979). Minnesota researchers presented factual information as well as using both same-age peer opinion leaders and adult (teacher) leaders who led student discussions in response to films depicting short-term consequences of smoking. This research also demonstrated a significant effect of antismoking education on smoking behavior. Two components of this education had a particularly strong deterrent effect: an emphasis on immediate consequences of smoking (especially social consequences), and a personalization of the course materials by using peer role models and role playing (Hurd et al. 1980; Murray et al. 1984).

With the success of smoking resistance education programs, the model was soon applied to other drugs as well. Project SMART (Self-Management and Resistance Training) began as a demonstration project at the University of Southern California. This study targeted the three so-called gateway drugs—tobacco, alcohol, and marijuana—among 7th graders. The study used interactive instructional techniques for resisting peer and media influences, as well as parental pressures and role modeling. Both affective and social influence strategies were employed. Results generally favored the social influence model over the affective model in delaying the onset of use of these drugs. A similar project, ALERT (Adolescent Learning Experiences in Resistance Training), headed by Phyllis Ellickson at the Rand Corporation targeted 7th and 8th graders. This program addressed beliefs about the consequences of drug use and developed drug resistance strategies for students at this vulnerable age. Students are taught a variety of ways to say no and provided opportunities to practice identifying the internal and external pressures toward drug use (Ellickson 1995). Other programs of a similar nature include Project STAR (Students Taught Awareness and Resistance) in the midwest and AMPS (Alcohol Misuse Prevention Study) focusing specifically on alcohol misuse (Ellickson, 1995).

The most well-known drug resistance education effort, project DARE (Drug Abuse Resistance Education), was implemented jointly by the Los Angeles Police Department and the Los Angeles public school system in 1983. Today, DARE boasts that it is reaching some 26 million students in 75 percent of the nation's schools. It also claims to be disseminating information to more than 50 countries around the world (Rosenbaum 2007a). The DARE program is targeted primarily to grades 5 and 6, but includes components that are used throughout K through 12, as well as special education and parent components (Bureau of Justice Assistance 1995). DARE differs from all of the other social influence curricula in that materials are presented primarily by police officers rather than by teachers (though teachers are often involved in ancillary educational activities). The curriculum is typically divided into 17 one-hour lessons, which are delivered one day each week of a semester. The curriculum is quite typically integrated into a school's curriculum as part of health, science, social studies, or other subject areas as appropriate. The primary focus in these sessions is on peer pressure resistance: teaching students to recognize peer pressure and suggesting alternative ways to resist that pressure. It is believed that using police officers to deliver the content of the DARE curriculum lends credibility to that content. Other actors are also used as well, including teachers and older high school students as role models (Clayton et al. 1991).

The DARE program came under increasing criticism during the 1990s because of the failure to demonstrate effectiveness (discussed below). DARE was not about to give up easily and a highly contentious political struggle began involving DARE officials, government bureaucrats, politicians, academic researchers, and the media. The controversy was aired on natinal news and took place behind the scenes as D.A.R.E. America threatened to sue anyone who criticized the DARE program on the allegation that they were making false statements about the program (Rosenbaum 2007a). This controversy resulted in a meeting facilitated by the Department of Justice and the Department of Education that brought the conflicting parties together to air their differences and to explore ways to improve the DARE program. The result of the controversy led to a revamped DARE, variously called the New DARE, DARE Plus, or Take Charge of Your Life. This new curriculum is targeted primarily at 7th grade students. Police officers are still used, though much more in the role of a coach than of a lecturer providing information to students. Students in the New DARE are taken through a 10-week course dealing with issues of self-respect, medical issues related to substance abuse, communication, decision-making and assertiveness training, and controlling anger, among others (National Center for Mental Health Promotion and Youth Violence Prevention n.d.).

The University of Akron has been awarded a multimillion-dollar five-year grant from the Robert Wood Johnson Foundation to evaluate the effectiveness of the New DARE, Take Charge of Your Life. The program is being evaluated among a large cohort of approximately 19,000 students attending 83 high schools (coming from 122 feeder middle schools) in six cities in the United States. The revised DARE curriculum is also being implemented and evaluated in Minnesota under the name of DARE Plus (Perry et al. 2000, 2004). The Minnesota studies comprise more than 6,000 students who were attending 24 middle schools in the state during academic year 1999–2000. Studies of the effectiveness of the revised DARE curriculum are limited, but the results to date suggest that the New DARE may be somewhat more effective than the original curriculum.

Effectiveness of Social Influence Programs

Prevention programs using the social influence model have been shown to be comparatively more effective than either the information or affective models discussed earlier. Early studies of such programs for deterring smoking show a significant deterrent effect as measured by the amount of time until the onset of smoking (Arkin et al. 1981; Evans et al. 1978; Hurd et al. 1980; Murray et al. 1984). All of these studies also found that stressing short-term physiological consequences was more effective than focusing on long-term consequences of smoking. Project SMART data collected by William Hansen and his colleagues at the University of Southern

Drugs: Myths and Reality

Project Dare: Ineffective Scientifically, Popular Ideologically

For many if not most of you, your first exposure to drug education in any form was Project DARE, which you initially encountered in elementary school. We know this because of DARE's amazing success at being selected as the drug education program of choice in 75 percent of school districts nationwide (and in some 50 other countries around the world) (Rosenbaum 2007a). You met the police officers who came into your classroom; you wore the T-shirts with the red DARE logo; your parents drove you around in cars festooned with DARE bumper stickers, paying for gas with their DARE affinity credit. As one expert noted, "It was the only game in town."

Project DARE, which stands for Drug Abuse Resistance Education, was created in 1983 by the Los Angeles Police Department in response to, among other things, the moral entrepreneurship of then–First Lady Nancy Reagan and her "Just Say No" campaign. Indeed, much of what DARE does is teach young students that drugs are dangerous and teach them the eight ways to say "No." Self-esteem building is also part of the curriculum. At very simple levels it contains an informational component, an affective component, and a peer resistance component. Through the 1980s and 1990s, DARE solidified its position as the drug education program politicians love to fund, perhaps because elected officials like rhetorical campaigns that make complex issues seem easily manageable.

From the beginning, the simplistic nature of the program drew criticism from a wide range of experts who pointed out flaws in the program's intention and in its design (Cohn 2001). Indeed, more than thirty research studies that evaluated the program largely agreed that the program was ineffective in changing student drug-using behavior and in improving peer resistance (Zernike 2001). The most comprehensive of these studies, by Clayton and associates (1996), concluded that "it was clear...DARE has no sustained effects on adolescent drug use." Indeed, as we mention elsewhere, adolescent drug use increased during much of the 1990s. Critics of the program gained momentum. By the year 2000, several cities had jettisoned the program, including Salt Lake City, where it had been in place for a decade, but whose mayor declared it a "poor substitute" for effective drug education and "a complete fraud on the American people" (Janofsky 2000). The surgeon general, who is the country's chief medical officer, and the National Academy of Sciences likewise gave DARE a thumbs-down. Of greatest consequence was the decision of the U.S. Department of Education, distributor of $500 million of the $2 billion dollars in federal drug education grants, to ban schools from using its money on the DARE program because it lacked scientific validation (Zernike 2001; Cohn 2001). For their part, DARE and its supporters in government and law enforcement had responded consistently that the program had no flaws, accomplished its goals, and that its critics represented disgruntled groups bent on decriminalizing drug use (Zernike 2001).

So it came as somewhat of a public relations surprise when the head of DARE admitted in February of 2001 that his program has not been sufficiently effective and that DARE had been reinventing itself for two years with the help of a $13.7 million grant from the Robert Wood Johnson Foundation (Rosenbaum 2007a). In short, they were acknowledging the validity of long-leveled criticisms and of research studies showing the program to be an ineffectual failure. But they were being given another opportunity by politicians who felt that it would be cheaper

> ## Drugs: Myths and Reality *(continued)*
>
> to fix the broken DARE than to try to match with a new program the 75 percent penetration that DARE had achieved. The "new and improved" DARE focuses on an older cohort of students and largely replaces lecturing by police officers with discussion groups and role-playing to lead the students themselves
>
> to conclude that they do not need to use drugs or give in to peer pressure to do so. Currently, both the old and the new DARE programs are being used, with the curricula to be evaluated side-by-side through surveying middle school and high school students, grades 7 through 11.

California revealed that the social influence programs were also much more effective in delaying the onset of marijuana, tobacco, and alcohol use than were affective programs. Indeed, they found that students in the affective programs had an earlier onset than controls (Hansen et al. 1988). Project ALERT, also targeting tobacco, alcohol, and marijuana, substantially decreased tobacco and marijuana use, though its impact on alcohol use was much more limited (Ellickson et al. 1993). Finally, meta-analyses of existing research on drug education programs of all three types alone and in combination reveal that social influence programs produce the highest effects on subjects' knowledge, attitudes, drug use, and life skills (Tobler 1992). Peer-based programs were found to be nearly three times more effective in delaying or reducing drug use than were the affective programs, and some 13 times more effective than information-only programs (Tobler 1992).

The one exception to this pattern, ironically, is the DARE program. One study that evaluated the results in 36 Illinois schools revealed that DARE had no effect on subsequent tobacco or alcohol use as compared to a control group (other drug use was not tested), though some very short-term effects were noted (Ennett et al. 1994). Other studies found a similar pattern of a short-lived impact on drug use. Examining the impact of DARE programs in Lexington, Kentucky, schools over a five-year period, University of Kentucky researchers found no appreciable difference between DARE and control students (Clayton et al. 1996). Similar findings were reported by Lynam and his colleagues (1999), who followed DARE students over a 10-year period. A meta-analysis of eight studies by Nancy Tobler and her colleagues found that, unlike other social influence programs, DARE made virtually no significant impact on subsequent drug use. Although knowledge of and attitudes about drugs were favorably affected, drug *use* was not (Ennett et al. 1994).

The New DARE, however, holds some promise. The University of Akron reports that after four years, the New DARE, Take Charge of Your Life is effective in reaching adolescents who are at an elevated risk for substance use, as indicated by risk predictors. The revised curriculum seems to have the strongest impact on normative beliefs about drug use (Carnavelle Associates 2006). The DARE Plus programs in Minnesota were also more effective than the earlier DARE programs, particularly among boys. DARE Plus boys were less likely to show increases in alcohol, tobacco, or drug use as they moved into high school (Perry et al. 2003). Perry and colleagues suggest that the role models in the programs may have been more effective for boys. They also point out that boys had higher baseline levels of substance use than girls, which may partially account for why they showed lower levels of increase into their high school years.

Are social influence (otherwise called *resistance education*) programs effective? The evidence is, to be sure, mixed. Project DARE has consistently failed to demonstrate any appreciable impact on drug use. Other programs, including the New DARE, have been more promising, particularly when compared with information-only and affective-only curricula. Gorman (1998) makes the case that none of the drug education efforts have been substantially effective, and that our efforts at drug education have continued despite the negative evidence only because such programs are compatible with prevailing political and ideological winds. Other reports, such as *In Their Own Voices* (Brown et al. 1995) based on the experience of students and teachers in California's drug education programs, have also raised serious questions about how effective these programs are. Although there is clear evidence of some level of effectiveness, critics have challenged abstinence-only approaches generally.

Harm Reduction Model

The admittedly modest effectiveness of social influence programs, though more favorable than information and affective models, has led some scholars to suggest an alternative approach to drug education. Critics of existing drug education efforts point to several questionable assumptions underlying all of these efforts: (1) abstinence for all adolescents is a realistic goal; (2) drug *use* is synonymous with drug *abuse*; (3) the stepping stone theory, that one form of drug use inevitably leads to another; (4) understanding the risks associated with drugs will automatically deter young people from experimenting; and (5) children are not able to make responsible decisions about drug use on their own (Rosenbaum 1996). These critics further observe that, despite decades of drug education efforts, drug use has not appreciably declined among our nation's youth. Hence, they are calling for a more "reality-based" approach (Rosenbaum 1999) based on principles of harm reduction and generally known as a harm reduction model.

Harm reduction as an approach to substance abuse is not at all new in practice, though it has not always been recognized as a formal policy approach until the late 1980's. With regard to drug education, harm reduction strategies have targeted alcohol use for about 30 years, with messages encouraging "responsible" alcohol use among adults. Responsible alcohol use involves things such as using designated drivers; maintaining awareness of how much alcohol one is consuming, facilitated by the proliferation of "standard serving" information; pacing one's drinking; finding alternative ways to cope with problems; and finding recreational activities other than drinking alcohol, to name just a few (Riley 1993).

Harm reduction directly specifically at drug education began to get notice in the 1980s. One attempt by Andrew Weil and Winifred Rosen in 1983 was taken off the shelves of drug education curricula almost as soon as it appeared because it approached drugs and drug use in a dispassionate and factual way. This text, *From Chocolate to Morphine: Everything You Need to Know About Mind-Altering Drugs*, provided comprehensive, objective information to students about the nature of drugs and stressed achieving nonabusive relationships with drugs if any relationship was to be achieved (Rosenbaum 1996). An earlier attempt by David Duncan in 1972 was successful in reducing adverse reactions to "huffing" in a southwestern urban locale. Duncan and his colleagues developed the harm reduction program, which encouraged abstinence, but also provided information about how to engage in these activities safely, if they were going to do it (Duncan et al. 1994). Despite its success, this program was not widely disseminated.

More recently, other model programs have been developed, including a British-based program, Harm Reduction Drug Education (HRDE), which advertises itself as a "secondary" prevention approach in that its goal is not to prevent drug use per se, but rather to recognize the reality of drug use and attempt to prevent drug abuse. This program has received only limited support in the United Kingdom (Rosenbaum 1996). A second program was developed in the United States in 1982 by Sandee Burbank, an Oregon mother who was dissatisfied with the nature of drug education in the schools in Oregon. This program, Mothers Against Misuse and Abuse (MAMA), addresses the potential abuses of licit and illicit drugs and seeks to provide factual information about these drugs. MAMA's primary approach is to present factual information through the use of pamphlets and other written materials. Other organizations to sponsor a harm-reduction approach include The Center for Educational Research and Development in Berkeley, California, The Harm Reduction Coalition in New York, and DrugEdNet in Melbourne, Australia.

According to Rosenbaum (1996, 1999), a harm reduction approach to drug education, which Rosenbaum refers to as *safety first*, is based on four assumptions. First, *drugs* include both legal and illegal substances that can be abused. Legal drugs can be dangerous when used inappropriately, and illegal drugs can be used comparatively safely under appropriate conditions. Second, harm reduction education recognizes that abstinence is not realistic for all young people. Third, the *use* of drugs does not necessarily constitute *abuse*. Drugs *can* be used in a responsible manner according to harm reductionists. Finally, the *context* of drug use is a primary factor in safe drug use. The context includes both the psychological state of the user (drug *set*) and the social context of use (drug *setting*). Based on these assumptions, harm-reduction education has a number of specific goals (Rosenbaum 1996, 1999, 2007b):

1. Provide objective factual information about legal and illegal substances. Such information should include facts about the physiological effects of drugs, as well as risks and benefits. Presentation of this material must distinguish between real and imagined dangers of drugs.

2. Incorporate the experiences of the youths themselves. Because children are often the experts in certain aspects of drug use, their experiences should be a part of any drug education program.
3. Incorporate role models into drug education materials. Rosenbaum suggests using older peers who have used, but not abused, drugs as role models.
4. Encourage moderation, if youthful participation in drug use persists.
5. Promote an understanding of the legal and social consequences of drug use.
6. Promote safety through personal responsibility and knowledge.

The harm-reduction model is not generally accepted by government or schools because it departs from the abstinence-only mindset attached to illicit drugs. This is understandable. It is difficult to advocate for *responsible* use of illegal drugs. Indeed, we must ask, is *any* illicit drug use responsible, given the potential social consequences? It is one thing to advocate responsible alcohol use, for example, which is a legal substance and one is not likely to be arrested for possession of it. Otherwise responsible use of illicit drugs such as marijuana, cocaine, or heroin, however, can have very serious consequences that can destroy the life of the user in today's repressive prohibitionist social and legal environment. The required context for an effective harm-reduction approach to drug education, it would seem, is a broad drug control policy that is built upon principles of harm reduction.

Drug Testing

Drug testing can take many forms ranging from crude observational techniques such as looking for needle tracks or pupil constriction to examining urine samples for traces of drugs in a process known as **urinalysis** to even more sophisticated analysis of blood and hair samples. Drug testing has been used for a variety of purposes, including reducing drunk driving, insuring fair competition in athletic events, cutting down on drug use in the military, and screening potential employees as well as testing current employees for drug use. Professionals in this field frequently distinguish between drug testing and drug screening. **Drug screening** is a less precise process that involves a qualitative analysis of a sample to determine whether particular drugs are present. Drug testing is a more precise process that involves a quantitative analysis of body tissue or fluids to determine with greater precision the concentration of a particular substance in an individual (Montagne et al. 1988a). These two processes have broadly similar goals and indeed frequently use the same technology. Hence, we do not distinguish between drug testing and drug screening here, and use the term *drug testing* to refer to both.

History and Prevalence of Drug Testing
Drug testing has been conducted in one form or another in the United States since at least the nineteenth century through observational techniques such as slurred

speech in the case of alcohol intoxication to constricted pupils among narcotics users (Ackerman 1991). Drug testing as we understand it today, however, is a distinctly twentieth-century phenomenon. We will examine the history of drug testing in the United States as it came to be used in an ever expanding number of social contexts.

Drug Testing in Law Enforcement and the Criminal Justice System

The first biochemical testing for drugs took place in the 1920s in response to concern over alcohol intoxication. Any manufacture or distribution of alcohol was prohibited under the Eighteenth Amendment, and intoxication certainly implied the manufacture and distribution of alcohol. Because alcohol is metabolized rather quickly and expired through the lungs, the only ways to test for the presence of alcohol is in the blood or on one's breath. Some police departments made use of kits that provided a rather crude analysis for the presence of alcohol in the blood of motorists suspected of driving under the influence. The technology to analyze breath, a far less invasive form of testing using a device commonly known as a *Breathalyzer*, was developed in the 1930s (Ackerman 1991; Montagne et al. 1988a).

Drug testing of arrestees began on a systematic basis in 1987 with the establishment of the Drug Use Forecasting System (DUF), which in 1997 evolved into the Arrestee Drug Abuse Monitoring System (ADAM) (see Chapter 4). Interviews are conducted and drug specimens collected over a two-week period, four times per year. Urine specimens provide a valuable validity check on self-reported drug use, and are used to confirm 10 categories of drugs: amphetamines, barbiturates, benzodiazepines (Valium), cocaine, ppiates, PCP, methadone, marijuana, propoxyphene (Darvon), and methaqualone (Quaaludes and other sedatives).

In addition to law enforcement, other criminal justice agencies such as correctional institutions also test for drugs. Parolees, probationers, and others on community release are also frequently tested. Some jurisdictions utilize an intensive supervision probation (ISP), involving a reduction in caseloads for probation officers to enable them to maintain closer surveillance on clients, including testing for the use of drugs (Mieczkowski and Lersch 1997). Finally, it should also be pointed out that drug testing of criminal justice personnel is increasingly commonplace. Though not without controversy, the practice has been upheld as constitutional by the United States Supreme Court in several rulings including *Policeman's Benevolent Association v. Washington Township* (1988), *Guiney v. Roach* (1989), and *National Treasury Employee's Union v. von Raab* (1989) (Walsh and Trumble 1991).

Drug Testing in Sports

Drug testing in sports began in the 1930s, though at this time, it was not human athletes who were being tested. The testing, rather, was for race horses suspected of having been given morphine, which was known as a performance enhancer. The method used to test the horses involved injecting mice with the saliva from the horse. If the mouse's tail became rigid, this meant that the horse tested positive and was disqualified from the race (Ackerman 1995).

Drug testing among human athletes did not begin until the 1960s when the International Olympic Committee (IOC) began screening the urine of Olympic athletes. The impetus for the Olympic Committee's testing program was the death of a cyclist who had been using amphetamines to enhance his performance (Zemper 1991). The IOC did not comprehensively test Olympic athletes until the 1972 games, however; the primary reason for testing at this time was to ensure an even playing field among all of the amateur athletes participating. Committee officials were particularly concerned about the use of stimulants, but in 1976, the IOC began testing for anabolic steroids, which were recognized as performance enhancers (Montagne et al. 1988a). Other drugs would also be banned because of concern for the safety and health of the athletes (Ackerman 1995). Collegiate sports were not systematically subjected to testing until 1986, when the National Collegiate Athletic Association (NCAA) first developed and implemented a drug testing policy.

Professional sports have been much slower to adopt drug testing, particularly mandatory testing, because of strong resistance on the part of players' unions. Nevertheless, drug testing does occur in professional sports albeit in a rather patchwork fashion. Some sports, such as tennis, have provisions for mandatory testing. Others, such as football, provide for testing with cause; that is, if a player demonstrates behavior that might suggest that he is on drugs, that individual player can be tested. The National Hockey League was the last of the four major professional sports (baseball, football, and basketball being the other three) to require mandatory drug testing in 2006. Insofar as drug testing does take place in professional sports, the purpose is not so much to promote fair competition as to provide positive role models for youngsters who follow these sports (Wagner 1987). Chapter 7 provides more information on drug use and control of drug use in sports.

Drug Testing in the Military

Drug use among military personnel has been recognized as a problem at least since the Civil War, when thousands of soldiers became addicted to morphine, which was indiscriminately used as an analgesic for war wounds and to treat dysentery. The frequency of soldiers returning home addicted from this and subsequent wars was substantial, and addiction to morphine came to be known as *soldier's disease* or *army disease* (Ksir et al. 2008). It was not until soldiers began returning home from the Vietnam war addicted to heroin that the government became concerned enough to begin testing for drug use. The military drug testing effort was only sporadic, however, until the early 1980s. In a survey of some 20,000 military personnel in 1980, the Pentagon found that 27 percent of Navy personnel under age 25 reported using drugs (Ackerman 1995). Then, in 1981, a tragic crash of a jet fighter on the deck of the nuclear aircraft carrier *Nimitz* killed 14 people and injured 48 others. Six of the deck crew who were killed were found to have used illegal drugs within the past 30 days (Ackerman 1995; Banta and Tennant 1989). This led the Department of

Defense to institute mandatory urinalysis in all branches of the armed forces. The Navy conducts the most extensive drug testing program, screening for amphetamines, barbiturates, cocaine, marijuana, opiates, and PCP. The Navy's testing program has become a model for rigorous procedures to ensure valid and reliable results, performing some 1.8 million urinalyses annually, with only a handful of reversals of disciplinary action because of faulty reports (Ackerman 1991).

Drug Testing in Schools

Testing for drugs in schools has a very recent history and remains controversial today. The procedures used for drug testing are regarded as invasive of human privacy (see "Constitutionality of Drug Testing" later in this chapter), and children and youth have always been a high priority for protection against such intrusions. A recent survey of physicians reveals that 83 percent of those surveyed oppose the testing of students in schools (Levy et al. 2006). As drug use has affected young people at earlier and earlier ages, however, and as this use was believed to affect school performance, pressure began to mount for student testing as a deterrent.

The first constitutional test of this procedure involved athletes using drugs. Officials in the Vernonia, Oregon, school district became concerned with what they believed was a growing problem among athletes and instituted a Student Athlete Drug Policy that called for the random urinalysis of all athletes in the district. One of those athletes, James Acton, refused to take the drug test on grounds that it violated his Fourth Amendment rights against unreasonable search and seizure. This case went all the way to the United States Supreme Court in 1995, whose finding for the school district was premised on three points: (1) athletes in school are under state control during school hours and hence are subject to greater control than are free adults; (2) the privacy invasion is minimal, since the urinalysis involves procedures that are no more invasive than relieving one's self in a public restroom, and the results would be viewed only by limited authorities; and (3) the government's concern over the safety of minors overrides the minimal invasion of privacy involved (Oyez Project 1995, 2002). As the popularity of these policies grew, school districts began to implement these procedures for nonathletes as well. Extending the Vernonia decision to nonathletes came to a head in 2002 in the case of *Board of Education of Independent School District No. 92 of Pottawatomie County v. Earls*. This case challenged the constitutional right of school districts to test students involved in any competitive extracurricular activity (for example, debate teams). Once again, the Supreme Court ruled in favor of the school district that random drug testing was constitutional under these circumstances.

Despite the removal of constitutional obstacles, school districts have been somewhat slow to implement drug-testing policies. A 2003 University of Michigan study revealed that only 5 percent of schools randomly tested student athletes for drugs, and only two percent tested participants in extracurricular activities (Miller 2005). A major disincentive is the costly nature of such testing, which the federal government is attempting to alleviate. Almost immediately after the *Earls* decision in 2002, the Office of National Drug Control Policy issued a pamphlet entitled "What you Need to Know about Drug Testing in Schools" (2002b) in which the Office clearly endorsed the policy. President Bush, in his 2004 State of the Union Address, credited random drug testing for the recent decline in drug use among teenagers and proposed an additional $23 million for schools opting to utilize random testing. This was immediately followed by a bill introduced by Rep. John Peterson (R-PA) that would provide grants under the Safe and Drug-Free Schools and Communities Act to schools implementing random drug testing for *all* students (Rosenbaum 2004). This, of course, has not yet been ruled constitutional but is nevertheless being pursued by several school districts. Massachusetts, for example, recently unveiled a plan to give local school districts the option of random testing for all students provided a parent gives consent (Miller 2005). Clearly, the government is encouraging such policies with its incentive grants, which will likely result in an increase in random drug testing. This is all taking place despite little evidence that drug testing deters student drug use. The government is, according to some, "selling student drug testing with slippery science" (Brendtro and Martin 2006, 78).

Drug Testing in the Workplace

Problems with alcohol abuse in the workplace were recognized by nineteenth-century industrialists who hired investigators to probe the off-work drinking habits of their employees (Hanson 1993). The toll of drug and alcohol abuse on the American workplace has been widely recognized since the 1960s. Preemployment drug screening was recommended by the early 1970s as a response to the cost of drug abuse in accidents and absenteeism. Costs to employers in absenteeism and lowered productivity the United States for alcohol alone is estimated at $148 billion annually (Weiss et al. 2000).

Private industry did not begin to test for drug use among its employees until the 1980s, following the lead of the United States military. Among the first in the private sector to initiate testing programs were the transportation and utilities industries. Task forces were organized among companies in these industrial sectors as early as 1982 to look into testing employees for drug use, though some companies, such as Greyhound, had already been testing by that time (Walsh and Trumble 1991). Then in 1983, the National Transportation Safety Board issued a report implicating alcohol or drugs in seven train accidents involving several fatalities and more than $17 million in property damage between June 1982 and May 1983. This resulted in more routine testing in the public transportation industry and in other public safety–related industries.

A major impetus for drug testing in the workplace was the signing of Executive Order #12564 on September 15, 1986, by Ronald Reagan. This order established the goal of a Drug-Free Federal Workforce. Less than one year later, in July 1987, Congress enacted legislation implementing the executive order and effectively established drug testing procedures in the agencies of the federal government (NIDA 1989). This legislation mandated testing only for federal agencies, but private sector companies were not long in developing their own workplace testing policies.

Workplace drug testing today generally takes one of three forms: (1) applicant screening, (2) random testing of current employees, and (3) reasonable suspicion testing. Additionally, larger firms with employee assistance programs (EAPs) may require drug testing as a follow-up to counseling or rehabilitation services.

Drug testing is now quite routine among many large corporations and even smaller businesses. Hartwell and his colleagues (1996) reported that more than 48 percent of workplaces, representing 62 percent of America's workforce, test for drug use. Among smaller work sites (50–99 employees), 40.2 percent reported testing, and 70.9 percent of employers with more than 1,000 workers tested for drug use. Workers are less likely to be tested for alcohol use than for drug use, with only 23 percent of work sites reporting alcohol testing programs. Recent research by Larson and colleagues (2007) is slightly more conservative, suggesting that 42.9 percent of the workforce are employed in firms that conduct prehire screenings, and 29.6 percent of the full-time workforce reporting random drug testing at their place of employment. Even this more conservative estimate is a statement of the level of concern that exists over illegal drug use in light of the fact that alcohol is far more prevalent and alcohol-related accidents far more numerous than drug impairment in the workplace.

Development of Drug Testing Technology

Laboratory testing was first introduced in the 1920s in the form of crude analysis of blood samples for alcohol intoxication (Ackerman 1991). Breathalyzers replaced blood testing in the 1930s as a less invasive detection technique. Use of Breathalyzers was not widespread, however, until the 1960s when growing concerns about highway safety resulted in the passage of the National Highway Safety Act in 1966. This statute provided for alcohol testing and has been a standard weapon in the arsenal of law enforcement since (Ackerman 1995).

Testing for drugs other than alcohol would not take place until the 1950s. At that time, an observational test, the nalorphine pupil test, emerged as a standard technique to detect narcotics use by parolees. This test used a narcotics antagonist, nalorphine, which caused the pupils of people under the influence of narcotics to enlarge (Montagne et al. 1988a). Studies have indicated, however, that this test has a high rate of both false negatives and false positives (DeAngelis 1976). Urinalysis is the most common means of drug testing today, and actually dates to ancient times when Hippocrates recommended examining urine to help make medical diagnoses (Ackerman 1991). That was a visual test only, of course, and it wasn't until the microscope in the nineteenth century that urinalysis came to be a standard diagnostic aid. Urinalysis would not be used as a means for testing for drug use, however, until the middle of the twentieth century. The discussion that follows examines six broad types of testing, a typology based on the bodily source of evidence: breath tests; blood, urinalysis, saliva, and sweat tests; and hair analysis.

Breath Tests

Breath tests are used exclusively for testing for alcohol intoxication. There is a direct relationship between the concentration of alcohol in the blood with the concentration of alcohol in the breath, a ratio of 2,100 to 1. That is, 2,100 milliliters of breathed air contain an equivalent amount of alcohol as one milliliter of blood (Freudenrich 2000). Hence, breath tests can produce a reliable reading of blood alcohol content (BAC) and have the advantage of being less invasive and a cost-effective alternative to blood testing for alcohol concentrations. Three types of devices can determine alcohol levels in breath. The most commonly used method is *gas chromatography*, commonly known as the Breathalyzer. Though a proprietary name for a specific breath testing device, the Breathalyzer has become virtually synonymous with breath tests generally. A second device for measuring alcohol on the breath is called an Intoxilyzer, also a proprietary name, which uses infrared spectroscopy to identify types of molecules on the basis of how they absorb infrared light (Freudenrich 2000). Finally, *fuel cell detectors* use two platinum electrodes with an acid electrolyte material that measures electrical current produced by oxidized alcohol molecules (Freudenrich 2000). This technology has an advantage over the other two in that it can be manufactured as a portable unit (Montagne et al. 1988a).

Blood, Urine, Saliva, and Sweat Tests

Testing for drugs in blood, urine, saliva, and sweat utilizes the same basic techniques, regardless of the bodily fluid tested. Before discussing the techniques, however, we would like to point out some things regarding each of these fluid sources. First, testing for drugs in the blood stream has disadvantages that have made it a very unpopular means of drug testing. Extracting samples of blood is highly invasive, and when less invasive techniques were developed, they became very popular. Use of blood samples also heightens the risk to test administrators of contracting HIV/AIDS and other communicable diseases. Finally, evidence of drugs in the bloodstream is temporary, and hence is not of great use for determining past drug use. Blood tests are, however, considered the most reliable for detection of current evidence of drug use and are often used in accident investigations and, in some cases, in conjunction with urine samples for confirmation purposes (Potter and Orfali 1990).

Urine is by far the most common bodily fluid used for drug detection today. Collection is relatively noninvasive, and it has an advantage over blood specimens because drug concentrations remain in urine for an extended period of time, resulting in greater concentrations and allowing for assessing past as well as current drug use. Urine sampling, also known as *urinalysis*, is limited, however, in that it cannot measure current levels of toxicity or concentration and thereby cannot assess whether one is currently impaired as a result of drug use. Urinalysis as a method for determining whether drug use was the cause of an accident, for example, is quite unreliable.

Even less invasive than urinalysis is saliva testing, which has been used with increasing frequency in recent years. This fluid has the added advantage of providing more current readings on drug intoxication than does urine, and it may be used to test for the presence of most drugs.

A very recent innovation in the arsenal of drug testing is the sweat patch. This device consists of a gauze pad covered by a protective membrane and resembles a large bandage. The patch is typically affixed to the upper arm and worn for 7 to 10 days, then sent to a laboratory for analysis. The sweat patch is becoming increasingly popular in probation departments to monitor for drug use, and has found favor with federal courts to monitor individuals on federal probation. Proponents of the sweat patch point out that because the patch is worn over a period of days, it allows continual monitoring and thereby serves as a deterrent to drug use. Opponents point to the high risk of false positives caused by contamination from a variety of sources, including the possibility of drug residues on the skin (even if the subject has not actually ingested a drug) or drugs in the environment seeping through a drug patch (particularly if it is wet). Both sources of contamination can be caused by untrained technicians applying and removing the patch. Furthermore, opponents argue that no one really knows the proper dose-response relationship of sweat tests, which refers to the relationship between the test results and drug content in the body.

Testing for drugs in blood, urine, saliva, and sweat is conducted using one of two broad types of methods. The first, chromatography, is the oldest laboratory method of drug detection. The basic principle behind chromatography is that different chemicals have varying affinities for other chemicals. Generally, the process involves forcing sample material (blood, urine, saliva, sweat) that is mixed with other liquids or gases through a medium that separates the individual parts of the sample material at different rates. Because the sample material may contain several chemicals, each with its own unique level of affinity and style of interaction with the medium, each will separate at a different times and place in this process. A detection technique is then used to determine the concentrations of each chemical (drug) present after the separation process.

A significant development in the technology of drug detection came in the 1970s with the introduction of immunoassays, the second method used to separate and measure the presence of drugs in bodily fluids. Immunoassays utilize antibodies produced by animals injected with antigens consisting of drug-protein compounds. These antibodies are specific to particular drugs and will attach to them when exposed in urine or blood media (DeAngelis 1976). Several immunoassay techniques have been developed, but the most widely used is the enzyme multiplied immunotechnique (EMIT). The immunoassays, and particularly EMIT, are very popular because they are inexpensive to administer and provide very quick results. They are limited, however, in that they are prone to cross-reactivity, meaning that the antibodies of the immunoassay will sometimes interact with substances chemically similar to the drug that the test was designed to measure (Montagne et al. 1988a). Hence, when positive results are found using these methods, reputable testing centers will usually use more precise techniques such as sophisticated chromatography procedures to verify them.

Hair Analysis

The principle behind hair analysis is that the hair follicle absorbs the drug from the bloodstream and deposits it in the hair as it grows. Hence, by analyzing hair at different points of growth, it is possible to identify approximately when drugs were used and even the level of use at that time, as strands of hair lock in the record of drug use (Holden 1990; Montagne et al. 1988a). Typically, hair to be analyzed is taken from the head, which normally grows at a rate of about 1 to 1.3 centimeters per month, so hair that is 12 centimeters long will provide a record of drug use for between 9 and 12 months. The test used to determine the presence of drugs in the hair is normally radioimmunoassay (RIA), with gas chromotography/mass spectronamy (GC/MS) used to confirm RIA results (Fay 1991; Holden 1990).

Hair analysis has the advantage of preserving the evidence of drug use for a much longer period of time than is possible through the other techniques, thereby allowing investigators to go back months and perhaps even years in determining the presence of drugs. The pioneer of this method, Werner Baumgartner, was able to analyze a lock of hair that once belonged to the poet John Keats and found evidence of opiates preserved there. More importantly, however, because hair keeps a permanent record of drug use, as well as other trace metals, it is possible to trace prior drug use in living individuals to a time many months earlier (in contrast to urine, which maintains a record of most drugs for only about 72 hours). There is, however, a downside to this technology. Some have suggested that RIA has not yet proven itself accurate for hair analysis (Holden 1990). Moreover, unlike urinalysis, hair analysis does not allow for precise time-frame identification for drug use. When it is necessary to identify whether drugs were used on a particular day or even a narrow window of days, hair analysis does not offer a necessary level of precision to make such determinations (Fay 1991).

Effectiveness of Drug Testing

It is difficult at this point in time to assess the effectiveness of drug testing programs. For one thing, organizations have various goals when doing drug testing and screening. Hanson (1993) identifies various goals of drug testing:

- Identification of drug users in an organization
- Deterrence of potential drug abuse
- Improvement of worker morale
- Increased productivity
- Decreased workplace accidents
- Overall cost-effectiveness.

Hence rather than asking *Is* drug testing effective?, we might better ask *In what ways* is drug testing effective? Even the answer to that question remains somewhat elusive, because there is not a great deal of good, systematic information regarding effectiveness at this time (Krauthamer 1998; Maltby 1999). Nevertheless, some scattered research has addressed this question.

Identification of Drug Users

Hanson (1993) attempts to evaluate the effectiveness of drug testing for identifying users by comparing national epidemiological data with results of testing programs. The 1988 National Household Survey on Drug Abuse estimated that about 8 percent of full-time employees reported drug use within the past 30 days (Kopstein and Gfroerer 1991). Studies conducted at the same time examining workplace drug use by employees and applicants as revealed by drug tests report similar percentages (Bureau of Labor Statistics 1989; Zwerling et al. 1990). The fact that there appears to be consistency between anonymous self-report data and drug-testing data would suggest that this goal of drug testing may be effectively met.

Deterrence

Research on the deterrent effect of drug testing has been limited (Larson et al. 2007), but among the small number of studies addressing this issue, some examined trends in positive drug tests over time as an indicator of the deterrent effect of drug testing programs. A national study of postal employees suggests that drug prevalence among applicants was somewhat lower than that for the general population. Although other factors may account for some of this difference, researchers suggest that awareness of preemployment drug testing probably had some deterrent effect (Normand et al. 1990). Lange and colleagues (1994) more rigorously tested for the deterrent effect by comparing applicants testing positive prior to instituting a drug testing program with applicants two years following the establishment of a drug screening program. Applicants for employment at a major teaching hospital (Johns Hopkins) were tested over a two-month period in 1989 to provide a baseline aggregate indicator of positive drug tests. A drug screening program was then established. The original data were compared with applicants who applied two years later, during the same two-month window. Those applicants testing positive had decreased from 10.8 to 5.8 percent—nearly a 50 percent decrease.

The deterrent effect of drug screening has also been tested with military personnel. The military has a dual policy of mandatory random drug testing and zero tolerance. Mehay and Pacula (1999) found that prior to the implementation of mandatory drug testing by the military in 1981, rates of drug use by military personnel corresponded closely with that of civilian personnel, as revealed by self-reports. Ten years after mandatory testing was introduced, drug use decreased from 27.6 percent (1980) to only 3.4 percent in 1992, a rate significantly below that of the civilian workforce.

More recently, French, Roebuck, and Alexandre (2004) examined the deterrent effect of drug testing by analyzing data from more than 15,000 households to determine whether workplace drug testing influenced the likelihood of drug use by employees. Their research revealed a projected 24 percent lower rate of drug use among employees at worksites with drug testing programs, and 38.5 percent lower rate of *chronic* drug use among drug-tested employees. These results reinforce the findings of earlier studies that find a lower proportion of drug use positives over time.

Researchers examining and reviewing the data on the deterrent effect of drug testing urge caution in our interpretation of these data. As drug testing is increasingly conducted on a more random basis (as opposed to testing for cause), for example, the larger general samples alone will reduce the percentages testing positive (Hanson 1993). Others suggest that declining rates in firms that test for drug use is simply reflective of an overall decline in drug use in the general population (Maltby 1999). Moreover, recent research suggests that those who use drugs are not as likely to work or apply for employment at firms that test for drugs (Larson et al. 2007), suggesting that drug testing might simply result in a shuffling of drug-using employees to companies that do not test. Despite these cautions, the evidence seems to indicate that drug testing may have at least some deterrent effect.

Impact on Worker Morale

There is great concern that drug testing will negatively affect worker morale (Maltby 1999). These concerns are not taken lightly by employers because low morale inevitably affects worker productivity, absenteeism, accident rates, and so forth. The impact on morale is not entirely clear, but research suggests that this should not be an overwhelming concern to employers if such testing is conducted appropriately. LeRoy (1991) found that most unionized workers (76.6 percent) generally favored drug testing as long as the tests are carefully controlled for privacy. Similarly, Larson and colleagues (2007) report that 46 percent of the workers in their national sample indicated that they would be more likely to work for employers who conducted prehire drug screenings, and another 49 percent indicated that it would not affect their decision one way or the other. These researchers further found that nearly 40 percent of full-time workers indicated that they would prefer working for employers that conducted *random drug tests*. Only 8.7 percent indicated that they would prefer not to work in companies conducting random drug tests. The research that we have would seem to suggest that employers should not be particularly concerned that drug screening or random testing might have a widespread negative impact on worker morale.

Impact on Productivity

An intuitive argument can be made about the effectiveness of drug testing on productivity. On the one hand, it has been argued that drug users would likely be less attentive, have higher rates of absenteeism, and hence be overall less productive than nonusers. Moreover, it might be argued that highly productive workers prefer to work in companies that weed out drug users, resulting in a self-selection process whereby companies that test for drug use get the best and most productive employees. This argument is based on the premise that drug use impairs functioning and productivity, an assumption that has not been well documented in the literature. It can be argued, on the other hand, that drug tests are time consuming (as well as expensive) and distract workers from performing their jobs as effectively. Moreover, when workers are fired because of positive tests, and replacements hired, the learning curve lowers the overall level of productivity in a company. Finally, insofar as morale problems are associated with drug testing, it is plausible that workers might act in a passive-aggressive manner by maintaining lower levels of productivity.

Research offers some minimal support for the idea that drug testing might improve productivity. Zwerling, Ryan, and Orav (1990) found an absentee rate higher among those who tested positive for marijuana or cocaine than among those who tested negative. These authors note, however, that the differences are not as great as one might expect. Moreover, research by Shepard and Clifton (1998) challenges the assumption that drug testing should result in higher levels of productivity. Examining 63 companies in the computer and communications fields, Shepard and Clifton compared net sales divided by the number of employees—a proxy measure for productivity—of companies that do and do not test for drug use. The authors also examined the impact of preemployment drug testing and random employee drug testing independently. They found that companies that utilized either preemployment screening or random testing had *lower* levels of productivity than did those companies that did not. More research is needed in this area, using various measures of productivity as well as a variety of organizational settings. The limited research that we do have, however, does not indicate a strong positive effect on productivity.

Impact on Accident Rates

Drug testing has been imposed on certain industries precisely because of safety concerns associated with drug use on the job. High-profile accidents in which drugs are allegedly involved often result in a clamor for drug testing of employees in positions that involve public safety—industries such as public transportation, law enforcement, and medicine. The evidence is not entirely clear about how effective drug testing is in reducing accidents, but testing programs do seem to have a favorable impact. Research in Houston by Fay (1996) reveals that worker compensation claims decreased by more than 63 percent over a four-year period among companies that utilized both preemployment screening and random drug testing, significantly more than the 19 percent reduction over the same period among companies that did not utilize these testing procedures. Fay also found a significant reduction in the amount of compensation payment in companies that tested: companies that did not test experienced an increase in compensation payments over the same period.

Zwerling, Ryan, and Orav (1990) found that on-the-job accidents and injuries among postal employees were higher among those testing positive for drugs, suggesting that if drug testing does deter drug use, accident rates might go down as a result of testing. This was found to be the case in the construction industry, according to Gerber and Yacoubian (2001), who reported a 51 percent decline in accident rates over a two-year period among companies implementing drug testing programs. Drug testing in the trucking industry also provides some evidence for effectiveness in reducing accidents. Jacobson (2003) reports a 9 to 10 percent reduction in truck accident fatalities following the implementation of mandatory drug testing for commercial drivers. Similarly, Swena and Gaines (1999) found that among commercial truck drivers, the number of accident fatalities per 100 million miles declined significantly in the first two years following the establishment of a random drug testing program for interstate carriers in 1989. After the first two years, however, the impact was negligible, so there would appear to be a waning of the impact of drug testing on accidents, or at least fatal accidents, over time. Once again, more research is needed to examine various types of industries using various measures to assess the effectiveness of drug testing programs for increasing worker and public safety.

Cost Effectiveness

When asked, most managers who utilize drug testing believe that their programs are cost effective (American Management Association 1992). Yet, millions of dollars are spent to identify a relatively small number of drug users in workplaces across America. Although drug testing does appear to be effective in identifying and weeding out drug users as potential employees, seems to have something of a deterrent effect, and would appear to cut down on serious accidents, companies must ask whether the overall benefits outweigh the burdensome cost of testing. The answer probably depends on the level of drug use in a particular area or potential employee pool. Zwerling, Ryan, and Orav (1992) report that drug screening would have saved the Postal Service in Boston $162 per applicant hired. They note that this benefit is based on 12 percent of the applicant pool testing positive for drugs, and a cost of $49 per urine sample screened. Others have suggested a much lower rate of drug use in the population. Anglin and Westland (1989) report that only about 1 or 2 percent of drug samples sent to commercial testing laboratories in California test positive. Under such conditions, drug testing is not cost effective. Furthermore, drug testing may cost much more than the $49 per sample assumed by Zwerling and his associates, again limiting its cost-effectiveness. It would seem, based on the evidence that we have, that drug testing is only marginally cost effective at best, at least from a financial point of view.

Controversies Surrounding Drug Testing

Drug testing has not been without controversy. The major objections to drug testing have been the reliability of the tests and the constitutionality of testing itself. We discuss these issues below.

Reliability of Drug Tests

A major concern that critics of drug testing programs have is the potential for false positives. The most popular test used, the EMIT test discussed earlier, has great potential for false positives. All immunoassay techniques hold the potential for false positives because of cross-reactivity, which occurs when the antibodies that detect certain drugs also detect chemicals that are similar to the target drug (Montagne et al. 1988a). The problem with false positives, of course, is that these non-targeted chemicals detected by the antibodies may not be illegal substances. The consequences can be devastating, including losing a job, being disqualified from sporting events, or even arrest.

Because of problems with cross-reactivity, most organizations that test or screen for drug use will follow up on all positive tests with more sophisticated tests before making any final judgements or taking any action against individuals who test positive. Typically, this will be done with a chromatography technique such as gas chromatography, which has a much greater level of specificity in distinguishing among various types of drugs. The problem, of course, is that not all companies conduct such confirmatory analyses, though more and more companies are recognizing that they are advisable for legal purposes (Montagne et al. 1988b).

There remains, however, one further problem, namely, that most drug testing techniques do not measure the current level of drug use or impairment but rather simply provide evidence of drug use in the past (Faley et al. 1988). Hair analysis is capable of storing information for a year or longer depending on the length of hair strands available. Urine and saliva samples also provide evidence of past drug use, which in most cases takes place during one's personal time. Many have argued that it is not appropriate in most cases to be infringing on the private activities of individuals (discussed as a constitutional issue in the next section). Beyond this argument, however, when such tests are used for cause, such as determining the cause of an accident, they are used inappropriately, and reputations can be inappropriately harmed as a result. Only blood tests (and breath tests for alcohol use) can provide information about immediate levels of toxicity (Potter and Orfali 1990), and there is evidence that the courts recognize the advantages of blood tests over urine tests (Faley et al. 1988).

Constitutionality of Drug Testing

Perhaps the major objection raised to programs of involuntary drug testing is that they represent a violation of the Fourth Amendment, which guarantees protection against unreasonable search and seizure of one's person. It is argued that drug testing represents a most invasive practice, the extrapolation and examination of bodily fluids. According to critics, this procedure is even more invasive than searching one's home, which is typically the focus of the Fourth Amendment protections. The practice was so reprehensible to some that as early as 1972, drug testing came to be dubbed "chemical McCarthyism" (Lundberg 1972). Moreover, to ensure that urine is not switched or otherwise tampered with, the process of collecting urine itself can be invasive, involving monitors to ensure against cheating.

Drug testing certainly involves search and seizure, the seizing of body fluids for purposes of searching for illegal substances. The constitutional questions are (1) whether this practice involves unreasonable search and seizure, and if it does, (2) who is restricted from engaging in drug testing. Supreme Court and numerous lower court rulings have generally recognized that mandatory drug testing without cause constitute unreasonable search and seizure. Testing for cause or because of suspicious behavior, however, has generally not been regarded as unreasonable (Montagne et al. 1988b). Furthermore, the courts must balance the rights of individuals to be free from unreasonable search and seizure against the safety and well-being of the community. Hence, the courts have generally upheld the constitutionality of mandatory drug testing where the safety and well-being of the public is at stake; that is, even without suspicion, mandatory drug testing is not considered unreasonable when the state has a *compelling interest* to do so (Ackerman 1991, 1995).

Two Supreme Court cases, decided together in 1989, were especially instrumental in defining the compelling interest argument. The first was *Skinner v. Railroad Labor Executive's Association (NLEA)*. The Federal Railroad Administration (FRA) had established regulations requiring the testing of train employees involved in train accidents. The high court upheld the constitutionality of these regulations, even though any given individual was not under suspicion, because safety on the nation's railroads constituted a compelling interest that justifies a departure from normal probable cause requirements. The second case was the *National Treasury Employee's Union (NTEU) v. Von Raab*. This case involved slightly different circumstances. In 1986, the U.S. Custom's Service, under the direction of Commissioner William Von Raab, implemented a drug testing program for employees who either carry firearms, are involved in drug interception at the borders, or are in high-level positions with access to classified information. Even though public safety was not directly an issue here, the court concluded that a compelling interest of the government was at stake, that being minimizing the drug trade. Hence, normal search and seizure precautions were not necessary. A third case decided in 1995, *Vernonia School District v. Acton*, extended this exception to high school athletes on the basis of ensuring the safety of minors under governmental supervision. More recently, in 2002, in *Board of Education of Independent School District No. 92 of Pottawatomie County v. Earls*, the high court further extended the exception to the unreasonable search and seizure clause to any student who participated in competitive extracurricular activities. These latter cases represent a new institutional context in which drug testing is now commonplace, namely the school.

A major distinction recognized by the courts, however, is that between private sector and public sector organizations. All of the cases cited above involve government agencies or organizations. Mandatory drug testing by private employers is generally not considered a violation of the Fourth Amendment because such testing does not constitute governmental search or seizure. The problem, however, is that the distinction between public and private sector employment is not always clear. Public utilities, which are regulated by the federal government, for example, may be subject to constitutional restraints even if they are privately owned, as we saw in *Skinner v. RLEA*. Similarly, private companies that are under contract to the federal government may be subject to the same constraints as public organizations (Ackerman 1995; Montagne et al. 1988b).

The Fourth Amendment is not the only constitutional basis for objecting to drug testing. The Fifth Amendment, which protects a defendant against self-incrimination, has also been argued as a constitutional basis for the illegality of drug testing. The logic behind this argument is that by making urine or other bodily fluids available for testing, positive test results are a form of self-incrimination. The courts have generally

DRUGS AND EVERYDAY LIFE

Constitutionality of Drug Testing in Schools

Board of Education v. Earls

Facts of the Case

The Student Activities Drug Testing Policy adopted by the Tecumseh, Oklahoma, School District (School District) requires all middle and high school students to consent to urinalysis testing for drugs to in order to participate in any extracurricular activity. Two Tecumseh High School students and their parents brought suit, alleging that the policy violates the Fourth Amendment. The District Court granted the School District summary judgment. In reversing, the Court of Appeals held that the policy violated the Fourth Amendment. The appellate court concluded that before imposing a suspicionless drug-testing program, a school must demonstrate some identifiable drug abuse problem among a sufficient number of those tested, such that testing that group will actually redress its drug problem, which the School District had failed to demonstrate.

Question

Is the Student Activities Drug Testing Policy, which requires all students who participate in competitive extracurricular activities to submit to drug testing, consistent with the Fourth Amendment?

Conclusion

Yes. In a 5–4 opinion delivered by Justice Clarence Thomas, the Court held that, because the policy reasonably serves the School District's important interest in detecting and preventing drug use among its students, it is constitutional. The Court reasoned that the Board of Education's general regulation of extracurricular activities diminished the expectation of privacy among students and that the Board's method of obtaining urine samples and maintaining test results was minimally intrusive on the students' limited privacy interest. "Within the limits of the Fourth Amendment, local school boards must assess the desirability of drug testing schoolchildren. In upholding the constitutionality of the Policy, we express no opinion as to its wisdom. Rather, we hold only that Tecumseh's Policy is a reasonable means of furthering the School District's important interest in preventing and deterring drug use among its schoolchildren," wrote Justice Thomas.

Source: Oyez Project 2002. Used with permission.

rejected this reasoning, however, maintaining that the Fifth Amendment applies to testimonial evidence, not to physical evidence (Montagne et al. 1988b).

Finally, the opponents of drug testing have invoked the Fourteenth Amendment in challenging the legality of the practice. Section 1 of the Fourteenth Amendment states that the government shall not "deprive any person of life, liberty, or property, without due process of law; nor deny to any person within its jurisdiction the equal protection of the laws." Two challenges are contained herein, commonly called the *due process clause* and the *equal protection clause*. Due process is not clearly defined in the constitution, and the courts are left to define its meaning within the context of the cases that it hears. In cases of drug testing, due process involves, at a minimum, confirmatory testing and documenting chain of custody for samples, which simply means tracking the location of the sample from initial collection to storage (Ackerman 1995; Montagne et al. 1988b).

The equal protection clause has been used to challenge refusal of employment to methadone patients because most methadone patients in the jurisdiction in question (New York) were either black or Hispanic. The court agreed with this line of argument in the 1979 case *New York City Transit Authority v. Beazer*, finding that the Transit Authority violated the equal protection clause of the Fourteenth Amendment. The equal protection clause has also been invoked to define drug and alcohol dependency as a handicap. Although the language of the Federal Vocational Rehabilitation Act of 1973 does not specifically identify drug addiction or alcoholism as a disability, subsequent court cases tended to interpret the act as though past drug addiction was protected as a disability (Bompey 1986). More recently, the Americans with Disabilities Act of 1990 specifies that individuals with a past history of addiction (not casual use or current addiction) are protected under the act. This does not necessarily affect drug testing, but it does constrain organizations in how they can respond to positive tests.

The constitutionality of drug testing will continue to be challenged. The organization taking the lead in this area is the American Civil Liberties Union (ACLU). This organization is challenging drug testing on several fronts, including drug testing of students and teachers in schools, workplace issues, and drug testing among recipients of public assistance.[1]

Summary

This chapter has addressed two types of societal response to drug use, which have one important characteristic in common—both are preemptive efforts to prevent drug use and/or abuse. Beyond that important characteristic, drug education and drug testing have relatively little in common. Drug education is oriented primarily to the prevention of drug *use*; drug testing targets current drug users to prevent *abuse*. Drug education typically targets younger people 10 years old and even younger; drug testing typically targets older youth and adults. The context for most drug education is in the school; drug testing is carried out in a variety of environments, probably most commonly in the work place. Finally, although not a stated objective, drug testing is often used in a punitive way—loss of one's job, failure to get a job, removal from athletic competition, or even arrest if one tests positive. Drug education is purely preventive in its focus.

There is, furthermore, a great deal of controversy over how to implement these policies. Very few people would dispute the value of good drug education programs. What constitutes good drug education, however, is widely disputed. Scholars and practitioners not only disagree on the kinds of content that should be included in drug education programs, but even on what the goals of drug education should be. Ostensibly the goal for most drug educators is to prevent drug use. Yet, when effectiveness of drug education programs is measured, drug-using behavior is often a very minor part of the outcome measures. Highlighted instead in many of the evaluation studies are change of attitude and level of knowledge. These are hardly indicators of behavior. Moreover, a growing body of researchers and practitioners suggest that abstinence is not a realistic goal, and that we may be doing more harm than good by putting all of our emphasis there. Rather, harm reductionists argue that we need to provide reliable information to young people (and parents and other adults) about the effects of drugs so that people can make responsible choices.

Drug testing also is laden with controversy. There are, of course, the technological and cost issues that cause debate among drug experts, but beyond these there are the fundamental questions: Should we be testing for drugs in school, work, sports, and elsewhere? What should we do with the results of drug tests? What do we want to accomplish by testing? These fundamental questions need answers. Otherwise, as is the case with so many areas, our ability to test with ever increasing precision will result in more and more motivation to do so, even at the expense of precious and long-held cultural values, particularly the sacred respect of one's privacy.

Key Terms

affective model
drug education
drug resistance education
drug screening
drug testing
informational model
social influence model
urinalysis

Thinking Critically...

1. Of the three broad approaches to drug education, the social influence model has generally been found most effective. The one glaring exception to this record of success, however, is DARE. This is, of course, ironic because DARE is also the most popular. Consider the following questions: (1) Why do you think DARE, a social influence model program, has been so ineffective while other social influence model programs have been comparatively effective in accomplishing their goals? (2) Why do you think DARE continues to be so widely used despite its demonstrated ineffectiveness?

2. Harm reduction, as an approach to drug education, questions the assumptions made by existing drug education efforts. Carefully consider the assumptions identified as questionable by harm reduction strategists. Utilizing your knowledge of the sociology of drug use gleaned thus far in this course, engage in a dialogue with the harm reductionists on these points.

3. Attempt to develop an integrated drug education approach that would combine elements of the informational model, the affective model, and the social influence model. In your integrated model, are you able also to include some of the major components of a harm reduction model as described in this chapter?

4. Drug testing has been challenged on both practical and constitutional grounds. Consider the legitimacy of these challenges. After careful consideration, answer the question, Under what conditions, if at all, should drug testing take place?

5. We have identified drug testing as a preventive response to drug use in American society. Consider whether drug testing is truly a preventive response or merely a punitive response. Provide evidence and arguments to support your position.

Learning from the Internet

1. The National Youth Anti-Drug Media Campaign, under the auspices of the Office of National Drug Control Policy, has launched a major effort at disseminating information on the effects of drug use through the media. Go to their website at http://www.mediacampaign.org/. In the right-hand column of the website, you will see a section called "Ad Gallery" with TV, radio, print, and banner (internet) ads. Go to several of the ads. Identify the themes that the campaign seems to be emphasizing. Do you agree with the messages that are communicated in these ads? Which ones do you question? Why?

2. The United States Supreme Court has made numerous decisions regarding the constitutionality of drug testing in the United States. Through the efforts of the Oyez Project, it is now possible to find both summaries and complete arguments of Supreme Court Decisions from the past several decades. The Oyez Project website is located at www.oyez.org.

   a. Prior to going to the website, make a list of all of the Supreme Court Cases cited in this chapter. (You may also be aware of some other cases concerning drug testing that are not listed here.)
   b. Now go to the website, and near the top of the page on the left, click the "cases" button." Then, go to the search engine for the site (located near the top of the page on the right), and type the name of the case (or a key word in the case). After a moment, you will see the name of the case appear in hyperlink, with an extremely brief summary of the case next to it.
   c. Click the hyperlink to see a more detailed summary of the case. Read the summary carefully.
   d. Now go to the "opinions" for each case. The opinions can be found on the left side of the page that provides the summary, under the heading "Case Basics." Opinions are much longer than the summary, but they provide much more insight into the thinking of the judges.
   e. Do this for each of the cases cited in this text. Write down the highlights and other things that jump out at you as you read these summaries and opinions.

Does reading the legal thinking behind these decisions help you to understand the rationale behind these Supreme Court decisions? Do you care to argue with any of the judges on any of these issues?

Note

1. More information pertaining to the work of the ACLU can be found on their website, www. aclu.org.

CHAPTER **15**

Drug Policy for the Twenty-First Century

Throughout this text, we have represented issues related to the study of psychoactive drugs from a range of perspectives so that you, the student, will have a broad base of information necessary to think critically about drugs and drug policy in American society. This chapter, by contrast, is much more partisan in nature; we are using it as a platform to develop general policy recommendations on some of the key drug-related issues that have been raised throughout this text. It should come as no surprise that we, as college professors and researchers in the field, have some firm beliefs about what direction drug policy should take in the next decade and beyond.

Our Guiding Philosophy

Our general philosophical position is two-pronged. First, we urge that drug policies and governmental practices be primarily empirically based. Good empirical evidence is methodologically sound, based on the systematic collection and analysis of data, and is not selected simply because it backs up an a priori theoretical or moral position. Policies lacking solid evidential support need to be reevaluated; either the empirical evidence for them needs to be stronger, or the basis for the moral positions and/or traditions that guide them must be challenged. What is not helpful, in our view, is to maintain policies that are strongly dissonant with the weight of empirical evidence simply because "it has always been this way." We concur with Ethan Nadelmann (1998, 111) when he writes that "U.S. drug policy...has preferred rhetoric to reality, and moralism to pragmatism." And in the main, this has made American drug policy ineffective and counterproductive much of the time.

Second, we are guided by an ethic of harm reduction. This philosophical position holds that drug policies should be aimed at reducing the many costs—to physical health and emotional well-being, to social relationships and roles, and to economic stability—associated with drug abuse. This strikes us as good, common sense. Who wouldn't want to reduce the harm that drugs, and misguided drug policies, do?

Robert Westermeyer (n.d.) suggests that the harm reduction approach to drug abuse and other addictive behaviors rests on three central tenets: (1) Drug-related behaviors should be seen as a continuum from high risk to minimal risk, rather than an all-or-nothing phenomenon. (2) Changing addictive behavior should be approached in a step-wise fashion, with abstinence being the final step. (3) Sobriety is not for everybody. What Westermeyer is saying, first, is that we must not be content to see drug use simple as dangerous, but that we must recognize there are varying levels of involvement, different types of drugs that represent different levels of danger, different modes of ingestion with different levels of risk, and differing lifestyle factors—all of which result in a continuum of risk. We must acknowledge this continuum, identify high-risk drug-using behaviors, and make those the highest priorities in our drug policies. Second, it is not realistic to expect that we can "cure" drug addiction by some magic bullet. Addiction is a complex process in its development, and its undoing is also a complex process taking place one step at a time. Finally, he suggests that it is important to recognize that abstinence from drugs is not for everyone. This means a couple of different things, which may be seen by some as controversial. He argues that we should not set a goal of eradicating all drug use; it isn't going to happen. Some compulsive drug users are going to be unable to stop using, "choosing" drug involvement over sobriety. More controversial, certainly, is the interpretation that people should be able to choose to experience psychoactivity or intoxication. In fact, some forms of chemically altered consciousness are allowed by our society, moderate recreational drinking being the most obvious example. And as stipulated elsewhere in this text, there are other, currently illegal drugs such as marijuana that may be used in a similar manner.

We believe that the philosophical basis of harm reduction is compelling, yet acknowledge that there is room for disagreement among observers of the drug scene about what policies and practices might best accomplish this purpose. Indeed, the authors of this text have some differing opinions about policy emphases, though they are admittedly few and not terribly significant.

Supply-Side Policies and Demand-Side Policies

Drug scholars and policy makers distinguish between supply-side and demand-side strategies for addressing problems associated with drug use and abuse in American society. Supply-side strategies are directed at curtailing supplies of drugs that might otherwise be made available to users in the population. Demand-side policies, by contrast, focus on reducing the need or demand that users or potential users have for drugs. Primary supply-side strategies employed by the United States include:

- *Source reduction* works toward eliminating supplies of drugs where they are grown or manufactured. This often involves international politics, working with other governments to provide incentives for farmers not to produce the raw materials for drugs, or to employ sanctions against those who continue to do so.
- *Border interdiction* involves the interception of supplies of drugs moving from growers and manufacturers to dealers after they leave other countries and before they enter the United States. These activities often take place directly at the borders, on the high seas, or in coastal waterways, but may also be carried out in rural, uninhabited areas where planes with drugs land and dispose of their cargo.
- *Curtailing domestic distribution* endeavors to break the supply chains between drug suppliers within this country, as drugs move from the hands of large-scale importers to local street dealers. These strategies are carried out by federal, state, and local officials, depending on the size of the operation and whether or not drugs are being transported across state lines.

One additional supply-side strategy is fundamentally at variance with the above: to change the legal definition of drugs through legalizing or decriminalizing drugs. Legalization and decriminalization policy proposals vary from a carte blanche, laissez-faire approach, to very selective conditions for changing the legal status of any individual drug. A very selective approach would be, for example, the legalization of marijuana for medical purposes. Legalization and criminalization are normally not considered supply-side drug strategies because changing the legal definition of drugs generally makes drugs more rather than less accessible. Yet they are policy alternatives that affect the supply of available drugs, so we feel it is appropriate to consider them as supply-side strategies. And they are strategies that work well with a number of demand-side approaches, to which we now turn our attention.

Demand-side strategies include two basic approaches, often used in conjunction with one another—drug education and drug treatment. Each of these strategies comprise a number of approaches and philosophies to reducing the demand for illegal drugs. Drug education seeks to target young people before they begin using drugs, or drug users of all ages before they become abusers of or, addicted to, habit-forming drugs. One approach to education appeals to the powerful emotion of fear, depicting the potential consequences of drug use in the most extreme form. This has been the general approach taken by the Partnership for a Drug-Free America, a private organization that has worked closely with federal antidrug agencies for a couple of decades. We believe that this is of limited usefulness, working only with the very youngest of targeted audiences, and then only for a few years at best. Other approaches, such as the police officer presentations of the DARE program, target the reality of peer pressure in the lives of adolescents and teach children how to resist the pressure to use drugs. We discussed this program's popularity despite its general ineffectiveness in a previous chapter. Still other approaches are primarily information-based, providing basic information about drugs and how they affect the human body. This approach is more common in health education courses that are a part of a school's general curriculum.

We feel strongly that drug education must provide information that meets three criteria:

- It is of age-appropriate intention, complexity, and depth. For example, simple moral messages are acceptable for six-year-olds but not for preteen and older students.
- It is based on current and empirically derived knowledge, presenting drug risks honestly and without exaggeration.
- It is aimed at reducing the harm done by drug abuse in our society. Appropriately informed students will usually avoid drug use or, if not, will generally be safer drug consumers.

Drug treatment, by contrast, intervenes in the demand cycle after an individual has already become addicted to drugs and is living a drug-dependent lifestyle with deleterious consequences to health or social roles. These programs have varied and sometimes competing philosophies about treatment, which makes sense because drug dependency is not a one-size-fits-all phenomenon. The long-term, chronic addict who has gone through many attempts at getting clean only to relapse repeatedly is a more intransigent case than an addict whose life has not yet begun to revolve totally around the phenomenon of addiction. Methadone maintenance, perhaps appropriate for the first type of heroin addict but certainly not for the latter, understands addiction to be a function of biochemical alteration of basic brain functioning, one that demands a chemical component to a multifaceted approach. Other modalities, grounded more solidly in the social sciences, understand addiction as primarily a social and psychological process. Long-term treatment centers, group and individual therapy, and self-help groups address individual and environmental factors within the addict's control. These groups adopt abstinence as their goal and encourage a drug-free lifestyle. Certainly, the recent addict would be more appropriately placed here, though we wish to stress that many people who decide to stop abusing drugs and suffering consequences are able to do so without formal drug treatment. There are, in addition, approaches to treatment that are spiritually based. These are primarily self-help groups such as Alcoholics Anonymous, and its counterparts targeting other substances and compulsive behaviors, which have no membership fees and advocate a drug-free lifestyle (though AA remains tolerant of caffeine and nicotine use). Literally millions of Americans and many others around the world have achieved and maintained sobriety within these fellowships. For addicts who are willing to consider spiritual solutions, we endorse them unreservedly.

Although these demand-side approaches to the problem of drug use and addiction vary widely in their philosophies and approaches, they share in common a commitment to reducing the level of marketplace demand for illicit substances. As long as there is a market for these drugs, they argue implicitly, suppliers will go to great lengths to ensure supplies and maximize their profits. Short of transforming our society into a police state, no level of law enforcement can effectively curtail supplies to a drug-hungry and drug-desiring market.

Evaluating Supply- and Demand-Side Policies

An assessment of the worthiness of prohibitionist-based supply-side strategies depends a great deal on one's political and ideological point of view. There is little doubt that these policies have curtailed the availability and ultimate consumption of recreational drugs beyond what would be the case if drugs were allowed to be freely distributed. Although some have argued that prohibitionist policies have produced a "forbidden fruit" mentality that ultimately creates a greater demand for drugs (e.g., Friedman 1972), we see convincing evidence that prohibitionist policies do curtail the overall level of drug use.

The policy of prohibition, however, comes at a heavy cost. Most obvious is the economic cost. Nadelmann (1998) notes, for example, that in 1980 the federal budget for drug control was $1 billion, and state and local budgets were two to three times that. These numbers had increased to approximately $16 billion in 1997. Estimates for 2009 were approximately $14 billion dollars, not because the drug problem had demonstrably lessened, but because federal funds were being diverted elsewhere.

The costs of drug prohibition extend far beyond dollars and cents, however. As noted earlier, prohibitionist policies have created or at least expanded the context for law enforcement corruption, as police officers face great temptation either to extort money and drugs from drug dealers and other criminals or to accept bribes for non-enforcement. There is no way to quantify this cost to society because it goes so far beyond the value of the money or drugs changing hands. Police and criminal justice corruption deeply affects the morale of a department and undermines the credibility of the criminal justice system itself.

We have also discussed public health costs that can be attributed directly to prohibitionist drug policies. Of urgent concern at this time is the rapid spread of HIV/AIDS among the injectable drug-using population. Approximately one-third of HIV-positive men and boys and one-half of HIV-positive women and girls contracted the disease through drug abuse. It is, unfortunately, not only the drug user who may be victimized by infected needles, but spouses and others with whom an infected person has intimate or quasi-intimate relations.

Finally, we have identified civil liberties costs that are attached to prohibitionist policies. Wiretaps, surveillance, and mandatory drug testing are all intrusions into the private lives of individuals. Americans have so far been willing to sacrifice privacy rights to help reach the goal of drug-free neighborhoods and workplaces. This cost has questionable returns given the impossibility of the goals these prohibitionist practices have intended to accomplish.

Supply-side policies rest on three fundamental premises regarding drug use. The first assumption is that availability of drugs in communities and neighborhoods creates users, which creates addicts. Second, addiction to drugs creates an inelastic demand for drugs. That is, the addict requires the addicting drug, in amounts that typically increase as tolerance for the drug sets in. Third, because the demand for the drug is inelastic, and illegal drugs such as heroin are very costly, addicts will be forced to commit crimes to support their habits. Consequently, supply-side theorizing goes, the very availability of drugs is the critical factor in determining the extensiveness of addiction and the antisocial behavior associated with it. Most supply-side policies are focused on reducing levels of availability so that, in the most optimistic yet unlikely scenario, it will be impossible for addicts to get drugs, which will result in a reduced demand for drugs. Interestingly, drug legalization also accepts the same presuppositions as prohibitionist strategies, but argues that by making drugs legal, addicts with inelastic needs and demands for drugs can purchase drugs that will be both cheaper and less harmful to one's health, thereby eliminating the need to commit crimes. Levels of drug use will remain high, but without the associated social costs.

Decades of research seriously challenge the assumptions upon which supply-side intervention strategies are based. The first assumption—that the availability of drugs reliably creates a population of addicts—is highly questionable. Addict populations certainly develop where there are drugs available. This is hardly surprising. Yet we have seen that addiction among health professionals—doctors, nurses, and medical students—is not substantially higher than in the general population, and in the case of physicians, it is actually lower. Clearly, availability alone cannot account for the high rates of drug use in inner cities and other high-drug-use locales. Moreover, the assumption that once an individual begins using drugs on an occasional basis, he or she will necessarily progress to addiction has not been supported by research. We know that there are many people who use drugs like heroin and cocaine on an occasional basis for years without becoming addicted. Although availability is certainly an important variable in levels of drug use, there is no causal connection between levels of availability and addiction.

The second assumption of supply-side policies—that addiction produces an inelastic demand for drugs—is also questionable. The fact is that addicts frequently reduce their level of drug use, sometimes voluntarily, sometimes involuntarily. During panics, periods when drugs are not as accessible, most users simply lower their consumption and/or turn to other legal or illegal drugs. Heroin users report that they will cut down on their level of heroin consumption during times when they have to abort their normal criminal activities because of police surveillance (Faupel 1991). Periods of incarceration or forced treatment represent involuntary periods of elasticity in an addict's level of use. The empirical reality is that addicts are not marionettes on strings. Drug addicts, like consumers of other goods, make choices including the choice to lower the level of their use. Insofar as levels of drug consumption are elastic, the third assumption—that drug use or addiction causes crime and other antisocial behavior—is also questionable. Indeed, as we have discussed, it is often the case that criminal activity is a precursor to increased drug use.

The assumptions on which supply-side proposals are predicated are questionable in our view. Our concerns are reinforced by the limited successes of a decades-long War on Drugs that has escalated to a cost of many billions of dollars per year, yet drug supplies remain plentiful, with purity levels quite high and costs to the addict lower than they were two decades earlier.

Demand-side policies begin with a fundamentally different premise, namely that demand drives supply, rather than vice versa. That is, where there is a demand for a product, such as a drug-hungry market, suppliers will respond to that demand. This is a different starting point than supply-side strategies, which assume that supplies create the demand. If it is the case that demand for drugs fuels the illicit drug industry, then it makes sense to address problems associated with drug use (crime, drug abuse, health problems, and so forth) by attempting to curtail the demand for these drugs. Demand-side approaches also bring different assumptions about the nature of addiction. Rather than an inelastic demand, these approaches recognize that individuals largely choose to use drugs. Choices are also made following addiction, including the choice to forego food for drugs, to commit crime, and so forth. Drug addicts can also choose to use alternative drugs or engage in alternative behaviors that do not involve the use of drugs. Indeed, the two demand-side approaches—drug education and drug treatment—emphasize these alternative behavior choices. Proponents of these approaches suggest that only by assisting young people in finding modes of expression other than initiating drug use through various educational approaches, and/or by helping current users to quit using drugs through treatment, can we significantly address the problem of drug abuse. Drug abuse cycles can be stopped through educational and treatment efforts, providing addicts and would-be addicts the tools to exercise their choice to resist drug use today and in the future.

Unfortunately, drug education and drug treatment programs have not had much more success in realizing their goals than have supply-side strategies. The effectiveness of drug treatment is highly variable across treatment modalities, partly because the various modalities define their goals differently. The goal of drug-free treatment programs is nothing less than a lifestyle of abstinence, and in some cases success is further defined as having productive employment and a cessation from criminal activity. Methadone maintenance (and more recently buprenorphine maintenance), by contrast, seeks only to eliminate illegal drug use, while providing heroin addicts with a safer and legal alternative drug. Methadone maintenance has been reasonably successful from the standpoint of its own success criteria—most notably that addicts remain heroin (morphine) free and test methadone positive instead—and this success has led harm reduction strategists to tout methadone maintenance as a major thrust of their policy promotion package (Nadelmann et al. 1997).

We have been cautious in our critique of drug education and drug treatment, however, because we believe that our society has not made a strong commitment to demand-side policies. Despite promises that things will be otherwise, relatively minuscule (and shrinking) amounts of federal dollars are spent on drug education and treatment efforts as compared with the massive amounts of funding to law enforcement organizations for supply-side initiatives. It is our considered opinion that the equation needs to be reordered, with the bulk of our financial resources steered away from law enforcement programs and commited to demand-side policies. As long as we continue to view the phenomena of drug abuse and addiction as primarily criminal justice issues, rather than public health issues, progress will be modest at best and will come at great social and economic cost.

Specific Policy Issues and Recommendations

As we recommend specific policy options, we remind the reader that our discussion is governed by principles of harm reduction. This means that we are not governed by the lofty yet unreachable goal of zero drug use in American society. Only political rhetoricians, those trying to convey their "toughness" on the subject for their own political gain, promise the utterly unattainable. We do believe, however, that it is a reasonable goal to reduce the level of drug use. Ultimately, however, from a harm reduction standpoint we are committed to reducing the harm caused by drugs and drug use. Drug use reduction and harm reduction are related, but not necessarily identical goals.

Drug Legalization

Drug legalization and decriminalization are both supply-side policy recommendations that are promoted out of concern for the social and personal harm that has been caused by the strong prohibitionist policies of the twentieth and early twenty-first centuries. Most serious scholars concur that drug policy in the United States since the Harrison Narcotics Act of 1914 has resulted in extremely heavy economic, health, and civil liberties costs for individuals and for our society as a whole. Proponents of legalization, however, must demonstrate convincingly that abandoning prohibition would be less costly before any serious-minded legislature will entertain such a proposal. Beyond convincing evidence, many decades of ideological resistance to altering punitive drug policy must also be overcome. Much of the theoretical arguments for or against legalization or decriminalization have been speculative, not scientific. Advocates of decriminalization of marijuana argue that these policies should cause, at most, a small increase in the number of users and the frequency of use. Any increase would be counteracted, they say, by individuals abandoning alcohol, cocaine, and other more harmful forms of drug use for marijuana, which they contend has less serious consequences. Opponents of altering marijuana policy generally predict a considerable increase in marijuana and other types of drug use, arguing that decriminalization symbolizes public acceptance of drug use. Who's right?

Empirical evidence in this area by Thies and Register (1993), using sophisticated econometric techniques, suggests that decriminalization has not resulted in large increases in use of marijuana and other illegal drugs, as its opponents claim. Clearly, lifting criminal sanctions in the dozen states that have done so since 1973 has not had the drastically negative consequences that opponents project. The advantages of decriminalization are less clear, though considerable evidence suggests that decriminalization has allowed law enforcement to focus more resources on other, more serious forms of drug use and crime.

Decriminalization does not allow for government regulation or taxing of marijuana commerce, which is a potential benefit of legalization (but is also a source of concern for those who do not want the drug trade to be regulated according to government whim). We do not know what untoward effects legalization would have on drug use, but the best evidence that we have based on decriminalization research casts serious doubt on the claims made by prohibitionists. There are, moreover, compelling arguments for legalization of drugs from both public health and economic perspectives. Legalizing drugs would allow for the effective regulation of drug quality, which should ameliorate public health problems associated with the variable purity of illegal street drugs. Such regulation would be costly, but these costs could be more than offset with tax revenues generated from the sale of formerly illegal drugs. Legalization of drugs would, additionally, provide more options for treatment and drug education. If drug education did not have to preach pure abstinence, as is currently the arrangement, we might reach experimenting teenagers or those on the invitational edge of use more effectively. These individuals would need an educational approach that provides important and valuable information about how drugs might affect them, about drug interaction effects, and about how to avoid contracting HIV and other contagious diseases. Drug treatment programs might also benefit from legalization by gradually taking polydrug users off of currently illegal drugs to presumably safer substitutes in the detoxification process.

Despite these potential advantages, we are not advocating for full legalization of psychoactive drugs. What we are calling for is open and honest dialog among scholars, practitioners, and politicians. A climate that would foster this does not currently exist and will not as long as we allow morally based rhetoric, absent scientific backing, to predominate. Drug policy is highly politicized, with distrust causing erosion of the commonsensical middle ground. Our first goal in developing workable solutions is to break the impasse in the rhetoric and practice of the drug war.

We would hope that out of these dialogues would emerge a recognition of the need for thoughtful consideration of creative solutions, with implementation strategies and teams given responsibility for overseeing them. Such strategies must include working with states and localities who wish to develop creative responses to problems of drug abuse in their jurisdictions. The one-size-fits-all national drug control policy simply hasn't worked. Currently, the federal government attempts to squelch any efforts by states or localities to legalize Schedule I drugs for any purpose. The Drug Enforcement Administration and the Office of National Drug Control Policy threaten those who challenge the established orthodoxy with losing federal funding or with using the federal courts to override state initiatives. A new posture must be adopted by federal authorities, a posture of first listening to grassroots concerns and responding creatively to them. This would be possible through a bipartisan dialogue such as that suggested above.

Finally, alternative policies that have been proposed by scholars and experts on the front lines of drug abuse prevention—ranging from decriminalization or legalization of certain drugs to limited legalization for medical purposes—need to be carefully evaluated, however politically unpopular that might prove to be. Do these policies result in more widespread drug use? Do they decrease or increase the economic, social, and/or public health costs of drug use? Nearly three decades ago, James Inciardi (1981b) called for a research agenda to evaluate the impact of marijuana decriminalization. We strongly concur, not merely for marijuana decriminalization but for other proposed policies as well. Such research should be part of an assessment process, the results of which would be available to other states and locales, and indeed the federal government itself, prior to adopting these policies. It is critical, we believe, that any change in existing policy be made only on the basis of good objective empirical research. To obtain such data, pilot programs need to be implemented in real life situations, with jurisdictional limits and a prescribed probationary period. What we don't know can kill us or harm us in a number of ways.

Legalization of Medical Marijuana

According to the Marijuana Policy Project (2008), thirteen states have effectively legalized marijuana for medical purposes, ranging from reducing nausea associated with chemotherapy in cancer patients, to helping prevent wasting syndrome among AIDS patients, to relieving intraocular pressure among glaucoma patients. Most states that have legalized medical marijuana have done so via voter referendum. During the Clinton and George W. Bush years, the federal government was quick to react to the state laws, initially targeting doctors who recommended marijuana to their patients. The federal government has also targeted individual users and the clubs that distribute marijuana to authorized medical patients. In the *United States v. Oakland Cannabis Buyers Cooperative et al.* (2001), a locally hailed program that provided truly ill individuals an opportunity to purchase medicinal marijuana, with the support of California voters and local law enforcement officials, was declared in violation of federal law. The government's attempts to close down the cannabis collectives has been challenged in ongoing state and federal court battles. Yet in other situations, the federal government has been frustrated in its attempt to negate these state laws by the federal courts in such cases as *Conant v. Walter* (2002), which ruled that to prevent doctors from recommending the use of medical marijuana was an abridgement of free speech and therefore was unconstitutional.

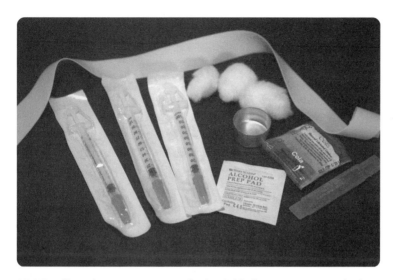

15.1 Needle exchange programs and other initiatives to promote safe drug use have been implemented in several countries, but with only limited success in the United States, largely because of the federal government's opposition to such programs. (Photo: Todd Huffman)

It is precisely this combative approach to grassroots policy that is detrimental to effective drug policy. Oncologists, physicians who specialize in the diagnosis and treatment of cancer and tumors, are strongly (though not universally) supportive of the use of marijuana to reduce the nausea associated with cancer chemotherapy. There is also broad-based support in the medical community for the medicalization of marijuana for AIDS and glaucoma patients. This is clearly a public health issue and not a criminal justice issue, a distinction that gets buried by antidrug hysteria. Physicians should be the primary consultants for federal as well as state and local policy regarding the use of marijuana to treat medical conditions. There is a sufficiently long history of the use of marijuana medically to evaluate the social and economic impact of those policies. A federal response of tolerance and a willingness to study the impact of these state initiatives should be implemented. Coordinating federal policy with state policies would provide strong guidelines for other states that might be wanting to move in the direction of making marijuana medically available to patients who need it.

Legalization of Needles and Needle Exchange

Making needles legally available is another variant of the legalization theme. Such a policy neither implies nor requires the legalization of drugs of any form and hence lacks an important feature of supply-side policies, namely, addressing the level of availability of drugs in a given area. Neither advocates nor opponents of the legalization of needles suggest that they will significantly affect the availability of heroin or other injectable drugs. Indeed, these programs may be more likely to affect demand in that treatment referral and educational services are often built into many current needle exchange programs, which if successful, may lower the demand for injectable drugs. On the other hand, if opponents of these programs are correct in their argument that legalizing needles sends a moral message that drug use is an acceptable behavior, the demand for these drugs may increase slightly. Because needle exchange and the legalization of needles generally involves a legalization process, we are considering it here.

Any controversy regarding legalizing needle access revolves around the moral message that such a policy would send, and the supposition that a subsequent increase in drug use because of greater access to needles would occur (Burack and Bangsberg 1998). Where restricted access or illegal needles remains, the moralizers have dominated the conversation, forcing public health concerns to take a back seat in policy discussions. This is unfortunate, because, as we have noted elsewhere, a substantial proportion of new HIV infections result from sharing tainted paraphernalia or from having unprotected sex with those who share needles. The empirical evidence is clear and quite unequivocal. Wherever access to clean needles has been legitimized, the frequency of needle sharing has declined and the spread of HIV/AIDS dimished. A metastudy commissioned by the Centers for Disease Control to evaluate the impact of needle-exchange programs in California concluded that 10 of 14 credible studies documented a reduction in the frequency of needle sharing among IV drug users (IDUs) (Lurie et al. 1994). Research by Watters and colleagues (1994) in San Francisco revealed a 47 percent reduction in needle sharing after the introduction of a needle exchange program there. Conversely, Broadhead, Hulst, and Heckathorn (1999) reported a 118 percent increase in the reuse and sharing of dirty needles after a needle exchange program was closed in Connecticut. Similar results have been reported elsewhere in the United States and around the world (Burack and Bangsberg 1998). Research by Des Jarlais and his colleagues (1996) in New York City found that IDUs who did not avail themselves of needle exchange programs were 3.3 times more likely to test positive for the HIV virus. Studies of Hepatitis B transmission have also documented a downward trend following the introduction of needle exchange programs (Burack and Bangsberg 1998). We also point out that those studies which addressed the issue found little or no increase in drug use in locales that established needle exchange programs (Burack and Bangsberg 1998).

The empirical evidence regarding the public health benefits of legally available syringes is overwhelming. The appropriate question is not *whether* we should make clean needles and syringes available to injecting drug users but rather *how* that process should take place. Two broad models might be adopted: one is a laissez-faire model, which would make needles and syringes available over the counter at local pharmacies. This model has certain advantages. First, needles will be more readily available to addicts wherever they might be, rather than having to travel some distance to a needle exchange program and risk being discouraged in the process. An addict in withdrawal distress could more easily access sterile equipment through this model. A second advantage is that such a model might be less likely to create a "needle park," a gathering place for addicts that might be undesirable for residents of local neighborhoods.

The second model, more restrictive and typical of the needle exchange programs that exist today, requires a one-for-one exchange, at least until an addict has established a dependable track record. One-for-one means that an addict is given one clean needle and syringe for every dirty needle and syringe turned in.[1] This model has a number of advantages. First, it allows for a system of monitoring the distribution of needles specifically to addicts. Second, and perhaps more importantly, this model has a built-in mechanism for getting dirty needles off the street, thus affecting nonenrolled addicts or nonusers who might accidently wound themselves. Finally, needle exchange programs provide a valuable educational and treatment referral forum. Many needle exchange programs offer educational materials on how to avoid HIV transmission through both needles and unprotected sex. Some include knowledgeable counselors to answer questions that clients might have. Addicts who want assistance in getting off drugs can also get referrals to methadone or other treatment programs. Needle exchanges that occur with mobile vans that park in various areas of a city on a set schedule reach even more addicts.

We strongly recommend, as a first step, that states establish enabling legislation that would (1) remove all criminal penalties for possessing needles and syringes and (2) establish the principles for needle exchange programs. The restricted model embodied by needle exchange programs permits access in a public health setting, either by clinic or van, not in a free market setting. Needle access is an urgent public health issue, not a criminal justice issue; indeed, it should not even be considered a moral issue, except insofar as saving lives is a moral imperative. It should not be overtly politicized, and this is best accomplished through bipartisan legislative support of such programs at both state and federal levels.

Drug Testing

Drug testing has been a controversial policy primarily because many argue that however effective it might be, it contravenes the protections against unreasonable search and seizure afforded by the Fourth Amendment to the U.S. Constitution. The Fourth Amendment states:

> The right of the people to be secure in their persons, houses, papers, and effects, against unreasonable searches and seizures, shall not be violated, and no Warrants shall issue, but upon probable cause, supported by Oath or affirmation, and particularly describing the place to be searched, and the persons or things to be seized.

Opponents of drug testing contend that extracting bodily fluids for purposes of testing for the presence of illegal substances violates the principle of being secure in one's person, especially when there is no probable cause to suspect an individual of illegality or impermissible drug use. Such a practice, opponents argue, is considerably more invasive than other practices prohibited by the Fourth Amendment. Indeed, some states have provisions in their constitutions that make public sector drug testing illegal except when there is a compelling interest of the state to conduct such testing. Federal government employees, with the exception of the military and certain other critical positions such as the secret service, are protected against random drug testing. The private sector, however, has embraced occupational drug screening much more readily.

Like other policy proposals, we evaluate drug testing policies from a harm reduction perspective. Both costs and benefits are associated with drug testing and screening programs. The potential costs of drug testing are (1) invading one's person; (2) violating one's right to private conduct, particularly that which does not affect public roles; and (3) the potential for false positives stemming from imprecise measurement. We have already addressed the constitutional basis for privacy concerns. Privacy, and the concomitant right to be secure in our households (and indeed our own bodies), is a fundamental tenet of American values and justice. This is a right that should not be trampled upon for anything less than compelling interests of the collective. Moreover, as we have discussed in Chapter 14, the most common test procedure (EMIT) that is used to test for drugs in urine is known to have a high rate of false positives. Many, but not all, employers will routinely subject positive reports to other tests. Consequently, not only are the privacy rights of individuals violated by drug tests, but they may unjustly lose their jobs and means of livelihood.

Before dismissing drug testing as a violation of personal and civil rights, however, we must also recognize the important benefits that testing provides. We know that alcohol and drug abuse account for a great deal of absenteeism and workplace accidents. Workers under the influence of drugs not only threaten their own safety and company productivity, but may also threaten the safety of other workers and the general public as well. Current policy distinguishes between random testing and testing for cause. Random testing means that all employees or organizational members (or those in certain occupational categories) are subject to testing at the discretion of the organization. Testing for cause means that an individual can be tested only if reasonable cause can be demonstrated, typically erratic behavior or other performance-related observations. The guiding principle here is the search and seizure clause of the Fourth Amendment, which states that unreasonable searches shall not be made and that such searches require that probable cause be established. This is an important principle, though it is subject to certain exemptions.

First, existing policy distinguishes between high-risk or highly sensitive occupations and those that do not pose such a risk to collective welfare: for example, *Skinner v. Railway Labor Executives' Association* (1989a) and *National Treasury Employees Union v. Von Raab* (1989b). These two cases, one involving testing of transportation employees, the other of Secret Service personnel, explicitly recognize the special nature of these occupations and the overriding public interest that is served by testing employees in these strategic occupations. The court has ruled testing employees in such occupations is inherently reasonable because of the state's compelling interest in ensuring a drug-free workforce in these occupations. Many lives depend upon the good clear judgement of transportation personnel, and in the case of the military, Secret Service, and similar organizations, national security is potentially at stake. This is sound policy and is not only constitutionally justified, as interpreted by the Supreme Court, but is also consistent with harm reduction principles as we interpret them.

A second distinction apparent in existing policy is the distinction between public and private organizations. Public organizations, particularly federal government agencies and organizations that are funded by the federal government, must adhere to a strict interpretation of the Fourth Amendment and are not allowed to conduct drug testing without cause except in the high-risk occupations discussed above. Private companies, however, are given much more latitude in drug testing. Private employers routinely administer periodic mandatory random testing. The motive is usually stated in commercial terms: drug-using employees have higher absentee rates and perform less well on the job. Commercial interests have never been recognized by the courts as a compelling interest to justify exemption from constitutional provisions. We feel strongly that there is no defensible reason why the protections of the Fourth Amendment should be extended only to public employees. The provisions and protections of the Constitution should not be denied private employees any more than they should be denied racial minorities or women. If indeed the Supreme Court has found that random drug testing for federal and public employees violates the intent of the Constitution, then random testing of private employees violates it as well. Private employers find drug testing to be a valuable tool in weeding out bad employees, but such intrusive mechanisms should be challenged. Indeed, we argue that good job performance monitoring can accomplish the same goals more effectively and with less chance for inappropriate dismissal than drug tests. With the exception of occupations that carry public safety and national security ramifications—occupations such as airline pilots, air traffic control operators, the military, and so forth—random drug testing poses a far greater risk to the public well being than the good it sets out to achieve. We recommend, therefore, that the restrictions currently applied to public workers also be applied to the private sector.

Drug Education

Research has failed to demonstrate that drug education has had a great impact on drug use in the United States. Drug education *as it has been implemented* has been expensive and ineffective. In fact, it seems that the more popular and widely funded the program, the less effective it has proven to be. We must recognize that different types of educational approaches are more effective for some individuals but less effective for others. There are, especially, age-appropriate pedagogies, but also approaches with differential appeal depending on gender, race, and social class. Furthermore, current drug users should be targeted with different approaches than nonusers or those who are only experimenting. Current users have already made the decision to use drugs and adopt attendant lifestyles. They need information about how to avoid or minimize the risks associated with drug use. This need not conflict with or undermine an abstinence message, but simply recognizes that some will choose not to abstain.

We urge that drug education efforts be developed and coordinated more systematically than in the past, and that they rely on empirical evidence of what works and why. Rather than the piecemeal efforts developed by various types of agencies and professional niches, a streamlined strategy analogous to what takes place in general education should be pursued. Professional drug educators should be leading, developing, and implementing the nation's drug education program, with input from psychologists, sociologists, criminal justice specialists, and public health personnel. Moreover, drug education should be fully integrated as part of the curriculum throughout the K–12 experience, rather than something artificially inserted just for the sake of doing something.

Finally, as part of the nation's drug education program, we suggest that the nature and effect of drug use be presented in a realistic fashion. Scare tactics making greatly exaggerated claims of the effects of drug use have no place in any educational curriculum. Drug education, like any other education, must be about providing students with accurate information and engaging them to integrate that information into their cognitive, emotional, moral, and behavioral lifestyles. Emotional appeals that employ dramatic and exaggerated claims about the hazards of drug use represent a rather desperate circumvention of empirical data. It is an understandable response when one is playing a losing hand, but it holds potential for much greater harm as young people learn for themselves—either through their own experience or from their peers—that these claims are exaggerated, if not completely manufactured. This discovery results in a cynicism toward all representations made by authority figures, including teachers, parents, pastors, police, and counselors. Our nation's drug education program must be, above all, credible to the population that we are attempting to reach.

Drug Treatment

Supply-side advocates frequently point to the high recidivism and relapse rates of clients in treatment programs as evidence of the failure of drug treatment and of demand-side policies generally. This is surely a glass-half-empty response that carries with it an unrealistic expectation of what success means in the battle against drug dependency. In truth, if those who relapse after treatment are given second and third opportunities to stay abstinent, the success rate grows. This takes patience as well as a greater commitment to funding drug treatment. The amount of public money spent on treatment has been a pittance compared with that spent on law enforcement and other supply-side approaches to drug reduction. The federal government spends more than twice as much on supply-side strategies as on demand-side strategies, and that ratio grew more lopsided between 2002 and 2008. State and local governments, in most cases, are even more one-sided in their funding of law enforcement over treatment efforts.

The naysayers are premature in their contention that drug treatment is a failure. Drug treatment explicitly recognizes drug addiction as a public health problem rather than a criminal justice issue. Drug addiction is much more complex than merely the rational choice to use drugs, which is the philosophical premise of our criminal justice system. Addiction is an intricate web of physical, psychological, and indeed social pathologies that necessitates a strong public health commitment from two sets of actors. The first are the potential funding sources for treatment programs. The core of such funding, we contend, must be the federal government itself, followed by state government, local government, private foundation funding, and individual payment for services—in that order. Some of the best treatment available today is funded by private sources, typically by clients themselves or third-party insurance underwriters, though since the mid-1980's private foundations have had some involvement as well (Renz 1990; Renz and Lawrence 1998). Heavy dependence upon for-profit treatment denies this opportunity to many of those who need it most. Although private treatment still has a place for those who can afford it and prefer the amenities that these facilities offer, public treatment facilities should not be inferior in quality or availability for those who cannot afford the luxury of private treatment.

The second set of actors is the professional drug and alcohol treatment community itself. Treatment approaches vary; the various modalities are born out of deeply differing philosophies about the nature and causes of addiction, as well as differences in the definition of success. These differences of perspective should not be cause for cynicism or territorial in-fighting. The time has come to move beyond the parochialism of defending turf to working together toward a comprehensive drug treatment strategy in the United States. This effort must involve treatment professionals from all of the leading modalities working toward strong public health policy in this area. Many types of programs have an important role to play in a coordinated and comprehensive treatment strategy that puts public health first and reduces the harm that drug abuse and drug dependency does.

Summary

We have expressed serious reservations with both the past and current direction of American drug policy. The war on drugs has been counterproductive and rhetorically overheated. Built on questionable assumptions about drugs and drug users, and oriented toward absolutely unreachable goals, it has increased the costs of the drug problem to our society. Our hopes for the future of drug policy, one that we feel is sane and likely to produce demonstrable benefits, are expressed in this chapter. The issues discussed herein are not exhaustive. More specific policy concerns—such as using racial profiling in making drug arrests, habitual offender statutes that saddle repeat drug offenders with ridiculously long sentences and clog our correctional systems, and the use of highly sophisticated but privacy-trampling surveillance equipment—are also important areas for public drug debate that must be addressed in a realistic fashion in the years ahead. The policy areas that we have addressed here, however, are some of the pivotal policy concerns, both in their importance and urgency for our time and because how we respond to them now will almost certainly indicate how we respond to other drug policy issues in the future.

The perspective from which we must evaluate drug policy in the twenty-first century is harm reduction. Policies that would, on balance, reduce the overall level of harm to individuals, communities, and societal institutions should be pursued;

policies that would not reduce or might even increase levels of harm should be abandoned. Also to be abandoned is the oft-stated goal to have a "drug-free America by the year 2---." Erich Goode captures this well: "The only realistic approach to the drug problem is to develop methods not to eliminate drug use or even reduce it drastically, but to live with it and make sure that drug users do not seriously harm themselves and others" (1999, 413). Harm reduction is a broad concept whose benefits will not always be easy to quantify. It strives to improve individual and public health, reduce the economic cost of our expensive "war," and reverse the trampling of civil liberties. Establishing good drug policy for the twenty-first century requires assessing the economic and social costs of current policies and realizing the cost reduction inherent in proposed policies. This is a monumental task for social scientists, the quantification of a reality that is not readily quantifiable. It also involves the ability to make correct assumptions about how policies may change behavior. This is why we suggest taking advantage of jurisdictions that have made policy changes and evaluating the impact of those changes. Social scientists have attempted to make good, reasoned assessments of the impacts of current and potential drug policies, and have come to very different conclusions. This work must continue until we arrive at a sufficient consensus to make sound recommendations to our policy makers.

The second task that must be accomplished is quite out of the range of social scientists: to rank the areas of harm. Unfortunately, because of the multifaceted nature of harm reduction, reducing harm in one of area may increase risks and potential harm in other areas. For example, a policy of legalization might reduce economic costs, civil liberties costs, and even perhaps individual and public health costs, but such a policy might well exacerbate domestic conflicts and moral dilemmas in our culture. Some of these questions, of course, require good measurement, but we must also make evaluative decisions about what kinds of costs to individuals and to society are of greatest priority for harm reduction. This question must be addressed by moral philosophers and others who might construct arguments about the societal good, so it is beyond the scope of this text. It is, however, work that must be done as we develop the architecture for drug policy in the coming decades.

Thinking Critically...

1. In the "Our Guiding Philosophy" section at the beginning of this chapter, the authors argue for drug policies and programs to be based on good empirical evidence rather than rhetoric or politics or morality alone. Why? Why do you think that policy has not often been based on quality research to date?

2. How are the assumptions and goals of drug policies based on harm reduction fundamentally different from those of a war on drugs? Make a strong case for one set of assumptions and policies over the other.

3. Assess the relevance to drug policy of the maxim, Think globally (or nationally), but act locally. Provide some examples of how this maxim might be carried out.

4. What evidence is presented to support the contention that drug policy to date has made drug problems worse rather than better?

5. How have your own experiences as a recipient of drug education efforts shaped your personal position on drug use for you and your peers? If you found it to be a positive experience, what, in particular, worked for you? If you found it ineffective, what do you wish you had been taught? Consider both the approach used and the specific messages imparted to you.

Learning from the Internet

1. A strong advocate of harm reduction policies is the Drug Policy Alliance, discussed in Chapter 12. Go to their website once again at http://www.drugpolicy. org/homepage.cfm. Identify harm reduction proposals made by the Drug Policy Alliance that go beyond proposals discussed in this chapter.

2. The federal government takes a very different position on drug policy than does the Drug Policy Alliance. One of the agencies charged with developing the nation's drug policy is the Office of National Drug Control Policy, which operates out of the White House. Go to their website at http://www.whitehousedrugpolicy.gov. What is your sense of the policies proposed here?

3. White House policies are set forth each year in an annual National Drug Control Strategy. The NCDS for 2008 can be found at http://www.whitehousedrugpolicy.gov/publications/policy/ndcs08/. (Other years can usually be found simply by replacing "ndcs08" with "ndcs09", "ndcs10," etc.) Identify some of the specific strategies outlined for 2008 (or whichever year you choose to examine).

Note

1. It should be noted that many public health advocates, especially those administering needle exchanges, prefer a one-for-one plus five model, if not a one-for-one plus ten model, such as are available in some big cities like Philadelphia. In these models, addicts receive five or ten needles for every one they turn in. This potentially increases the number of needles in a community, but it also increases the likelihood that sterile needles will be employed.

GLOSSARY

abstinence—total cessation of drug use, often considered an unrealistic goal, particularly among long-term narcotics users.

acute health consequences—health consequences of drug consumption that affect the user at or around the time that a substance is used.

addictive personality—term used to describe the notion that addiction is more likely to occur among people having an inadequate personality. This concept is unsupported by most research.

additive drug—drugs used to enhance performance, typically athletic performance, at levels considered to exceed normal limitations of the body.

affective model—modality of drug education, based on the assumption that some individuals possess an underlying predisposition to drug abuse, that seeks to improve communication skills, decision-making, and self assertion—all of which are believed to be related to this predisposition.

amotivational syndrome—alleged personality changes associated with marijuana use, such as laziness and decreased motivation.

anabolics—substances that artificially build muscle and body mass.

antagonist—drug that blocks the effect of another drug or causes uncomfortable side effects if a particular drug is used.

antagonistic effect—process through which one drug cancels the effect of another.

Anti-Drug Abuse Act of 1988—broad legislation dealing with various aspects of drug and alcohol use that increased the penalties associated with various substance-related activities, among other provisions.

argot—nonstandard or specialized language associated with a particular group or subculture that distinguishes that group from the outside world.

availability hypothesis—notion that persons having easy access to drugs are more likely to use them (e.g., physicians and pharmacists).

beta blockers—substances that are designed to lower blood pressure and the heart rate; often used to treat hypertension.

binge drinking—the consumption of five or more alcoholic drinks on one occasion for men, and four or more drinks on one occasion for women.

blood-alcohol content (BAC)—the concentration of alcohol in the blood, measured in grams of alcohol per 100 milliliters of blood.

blood doping—introduction of red blood cells into the blood supply for the purpose of increasing endurance by increasing the oxygen-carrying capacity of the circulatory system.

boundary-maintenance mechanism—various ways in which members of a group (in-group) can distinguish themselves from non-members (out-groups).

British method—controversial treatment modality whereby registered narcotic addicts are dispensed heroin via a legal prescription.

career—a sequence of activities around which an individual organizes some aspect of his or her life, including drug use and/or criminal behavior.

cartel—term for drug trafficking organizations operating primarily out of Central and South American countries.

causality—term denoting the relationship between two variables in which one variable causes the other to occur (e.g., the claim that drug use causes crime).

chronic effect—effects of drug use that accumulate over time as one continues to use or abuse a particular substance.

chronic health consequences—health consequences of drug consumption that are cumulative and long-term.

classical conditioning—the pairing of a conditioned stimulus such as a bell, a location, or contextual factor with an unconditioned stimulus such as alcohol or drugs.

CNS stabilizers—central nervous system stabilizers; category of drugs that stabilize mood and/or behavior.

compulsory treatment—non-voluntary participation in drug treatment, often court ordered.

Controlled Substances Act of 1970—sweeping legislation that superceded U.S. drug laws following the Harrison Act and provided a classification scheme (schedules) of drug categories.

correlation—an association (not necessarily causal) between two variables.

dark figure—proportion of total crimes committed that are not brought to the attention of the police.

decriminalization—policy that removes criminal sanctions associated with an activity or behavior (as opposed to removing all restrictions, or legalization).

delirium tremens—severe withdrawal symptoms associated with alcoholism, such as hallucinations, disorientation, or seizures, that can, in extreme circumstances, result in death.

demand-side strategies—refers to a variety of programs and efforts, including treatment and education, that serve to reduce the demand for drugs.

demographics—characteristics used to distinguish individuals from one another, such as age, gender, race, ethnicity, socioeconomic status, and so forth. Of particular importance is how behavior such as drug use differs across one or more of these categories.

depressants—substances that slow the action of the central nervous system and the physiological processes dependent on it, such as respiration, heart rate, and reaction time.

detoxification—refers to the processes through which the body rids itself of poisonous (toxic) substances; applied to drugs and alcohol, the process of ridding the body of the physical presence of drugs.

differential reinforcement—according to Akers' social learning theory, the balance of actual or anticipated rewards and/or punishments associated with past, present, and future behavior.

disinhibition hypothesis—notion that alcohol or drug use interferes with the internal control mechanisms of the central nervous system, or that use affects the recognition of external controls (i.e., possibility of arrest), resulting in antisocial behavior.

diuretics—substances that flush liquids out of the body.

doping—the use of drugs to improve athletic performance.

dose—the amount of a substance taken on one occasion.

double failure—according to differential opportunity theory, a person who is unable to achieve "success" through both legitimate and illegitimate means.

drug—a substance that, once ingested, may alter the structure or functioning of a person; sociologically, something that has been defined by society, or certain segments of society, as a drug.

drug abuse—the use of a substance or substances in such a way that leads to unintended (and usually negative) personal, interpersonal, or social consequences.

drug addiction—condition characterized by the physical need for a drug, commonly accompanied by physical symptoms when the drug is withdrawn.

drug courts—specialized courts that handle drug cases, either as an alternative to the criminal court system or as part of the court system in the sentencing and/or probationary stage.

drug dependence—condition characterized by the physical, psychological, or behavioral need for a drug.

drug education—broad term referring to measures to prevent and/or reduce drug use by providing information on, among other things, the impact of and negative consequences of use.

Drug-Free Workplace Act of 1988 (DFWA)—federal law requiring that federal contractors and grantees implement policies providing for a drug-free workplace.

drug interaction—effect of one drug on another when both are consumed.

drug resistance education—an approach to drug education that uses simulated settings to teach children and adolescents how to resist peer pressure to use drugs; more generally known as a *social influence model* for drug education.

drug schedules—classification criteria outlined in the Controlled Substances Act of 1970 that categorize drugs based on the characteristics of medical use and potential for abuse.

drug screening—qualitative analysis of a blood or urine sample to identify the presence of a drug.

drug subculture—groups that are a part of the cultural mainstream and often share many of the values and goals of the cultural mainstream, but nevertheless maintain a distinctive lifestyle that is integrated around the use of illegal drugs.

drug testing—quantitative analysis of body tissue or bodily fluids to determine the concentration of a particular substance; more precisely measures level of drug concentration than drug screening.

drug tolerance—resistance to the effect of a drug that develops over time, resulting in greater amounts being necessary to achieve the same result.

drug use—use of any chemical substance that act acts like a drug or that is believed to act like a drug.

economic-compulsive violence—that violence committed in an attempt to secure drugs or the money to purchase them.

effective dose—dose most often necessary for the effect one wishes to achieve.

employee assistance program (EAP)—confidential, employer-financed programs and services designed to address a number of issues related to productivity in the workplace, including alcohol and drug use.

endorphin—an opiate produced in the body that functions as a neurotransmitter.

environmental tobacco smoke (ETS)—smoke in the air, whether in trace or large amounts, that is inhaled by nonsmokers; also called *passive smoke* or *second-hand smoke*.

epidemiology—in medical fields, the study of the spread and distribution of diseases; used in social sciences to refer to study of the spread and distribution of social phenomenon such as drug use and crime.

ergogenic—the effect of certain drugs, such as stimulants and steroids, to increase the capacity of the human body to engage in physical and mental labor.

ethnography—research methodology in which researchers spend time in the natural habitat of the subjects they are studying.

etiology—the study of the causal factors associated with a phenomenon.

fetal alcohol syndrome (FAS)—refers to a number of birth defects that are attributed to the children of women who consumed alcohol while pregnant.

formication—a delusion or hallucination associated with stimulant use and characterized by the belief that insects, reptiles, or spiders are crawling on or under the skin.

functional alternative—the substitution of one drug for a similar drug to achieve the same action or effect.

gateway drug—drug that is believed to lead to the use of other, more dangerous or addictive substances.

halfway house—transitional living facility that serves as a bridge between a residential drug treatment program and reintegration into the community.

hallucinogens—substances that produce extreme subjective effects in users, such as physical distortion of reality, often resembling hallucinations.

harm reduction—drug policy approach that focuses on reducing the harm or negative consequences associated with drug use.

Harrison Narcotics Act of 1914—legislation that in effect criminalized the non-medical use of narcotics and cocaine.

idiosyncratic effect—when one's sensitivity to the effect of one drug is greatly enhanced by the presence of another.

incidence—from a social science perspective, the frequency of engaging in an activity or behavior (i.e., How many times have you…?).

informational model—drug education philosophy that provides information emphasizing various negative consequences of alcohol or drug use.

interdiction—law enforcement measures designed to prevent illegal drugs from entering their intended destination; typically engaged at the borders of a country.

intoxication—behavioral and mental dysfunction caused by the effect of alcohol or drug use on the central nervous system.

legalization—the removal of all criminal and civil penalties associated with an activity or behavior.

lethal dose—the amount of a drug that results in death.

Marihuana Tax Act of 1937—federal legislation that placed severe restrictions on the cultivation, sale, and distribution (and ultimately the possession) of marijuana.

methadone maintenance—treatment program for narcotic abuse whereby methadone, a synthetic narcotic, is substituted for heroin to prevent withdrawal symptoms.

Minnesota model—treatment modality originating in Minnesota based on the assumptions that addiction is a disease that can be treated through counseling and therapy.

moniker—slang term or nickname used to refer to someone who is a member of a subculture.

moral entrepreneur—individuals or groups who argue that they are the ones who should define the reality of drugs and their users.

mules—individuals who smuggle illegal drugs by concealing them on or in the body.

N, n—statistical symbol used to denote the size of a population (N) or sample thereof (n) under study.

narcotics—natural derivatives of the opium poppy or a synthetic substance that is, chemically speaking, similar to it. These highly addictive substances produce euphoric and/or analgesic effects.

National Prohibition Act of 1919 (Volstead Act)—legislation which implemented the Eighteenth Amendment to the U.S. Constitution, which prohibited the manufacture, sale, and distribution of alcohol. The Twenty-First Amendment (ratified in 1933) repealed prohibition and rendered the National Prohibition Act unconstitutional.

needle exchange—harm reduction program in which people who inject cocaine or heroin may exchange used hypodermic needles for unused ones in an attempt to reduce the spread of HIV and other communicable diseases.

neurotransmitter—chemical mechanism through which impulses are transmitted from one nerve cell to another.

objective drug effect—drug effects that result from being under the influence of a substance and that can be measured reliably.

official statistics—data on drug use that are gathered as a function of the day-to-day procedures and functions of the government or of other agencies cooperating with the government.

operant conditioning—the reinforcement of behavior resulting from actual or perceived rewards associated with engaging in that behavior.

Operation Intercept—initiative of the Nixon administration (1969) that sought to curb marijuana trafficking from Mexico into the United States. Considered by most to be a failure, this operation had the effect of increasing domestic production of marijuana.

overdose—the result of consuming too highly concentrated and/or excessive amounts of a particular drug; the specific effect on the body varies with the type of drug. Overdose is often confused with *synergism*, which is the joint action of two or more drugs which produces an effect greater than the sum of the effects of individual drugs.

patent medicine—medications, tonics, or elixirs containing alcohol, cocaine, morphine, or cannabis that were readily available in the nineteenth century at medicine shows or over the counter.

pharmacology—study of how drugs affect the structure and function of the body.

polydrug use—ingestion of multiple substances near enough to each other that their effects interact.

polypharmacy—practice of prescribing multiple drugs, usually four or more, to a single patient; often used in discussions of overprescribing, inappropriate medication, or inappropriate drug prescribing.

potency—strength of a drug.

prevalence—in the social sciences, the number of individuals who have engaged in a particular activity or behavior, such as crime or drug use (i.e., Have you ever...?).

primary deviance—norm violations that are often inadvertent and not the result of a deviant self-concept.

primary prevention—policies and preventive efforts designed to discourage the onset of drug use.

prison-based treatment programs—drug treatment programs located within prisons and specially designed to treat prisoners with drug addiction; typically modeled after *therapeutic communities* (*see below*).

problem behavior syndrome—the notion that among persistent juvenile delinquents, various forms of nonconformity (i.e., delinquency, drug use, being sexually promiscuous) are expressions of some underlying characteristic.

prohibition—the ideal of abstinence as it relates to alcohol or drug use; also refers to general policy initiatives known as "criminalization" whereby the production, manufacture, growing, sale, and/or possession of drugs are violations of one or more criminal statutes.

Prohibition—the period between 1920 and 1933 during which the legal manufacture, sale, and distribution of alcohol was prohibited in the United States (*see also* National Prohibition Act of 1919).

psychedelic—term originating in the 1960s to characterize more positively the use and effects of hallucinogenic drugs.

psychoactive drug—substances that affect thoughts, perceptions, mood, and behavior through their impact on the central nervous system.

psychopharmacological violence—situation in which an individual engages in violent behavior as a consequence of being under the influence of a drug.

psychopharmacology—study of how drugs affect the function of the central nervous system

Pure Food and Drug Act of 1906—broad legislation that placed a number of restrictions on the production and distribution of both food and drugs. Of key importance is the requirement that ingredients be listed.

purity—percentage of a substance consisting of the drug itself.

rapid opiate detoxification—controversial treatment program utilizing various drugs to accelerate the detoxification and withdrawal from narcotic addiction.

rate—the number or frequency per unit of population; e.g., Uniform Crime Reports are based on population units of 100,000, so the rate is calculated as (incidents/total population $\times$ 100,000).

reintegration—the shift in setting from the nonconventional and drug-using milieu of the streets to a more conventional context, following a prolonged period of treatment typically in a residential program.

restorative drugs—drugs used to reduce the pain of injuries or to accelerate recovery from them.

retreatist—in Merton's anomie theory, an individual who rejects both the goals of society and the accepted means of achieving them; drug addicts generally fall in this category.

roid rage—the increased aggressiveness and hostility associated with use of anabolic steroids.

route of administration—method through which drugs are introduced into the body.

scientific theory—an explanation for the relationship between two or more phenomena that is written in such a way that it can be falsified with empirical evidence.

secondary binge effect—consequences of binge drinking that affect people other than the user (e.g., unwanted sexual advances from or an automobile accident caused by someone who has been binge drinking).

secondary deviance—norm violations in response to the consequences of primary deviance. Secondary deviance reflects ones' self-identification as deviant.

secondary prevention—policies and measures intended to reduce the severity of the consequences associated with drug use after it has begun.

serotonin—a neurotransmitter involved in regulating a number of basic yet important bodily functions, including mood.

set—the psychological state of the individual at the time of drug use, including one's expectations or emotional mood.

setting—the environment in which drug use occurs.

social construction—the process through which reality is influenced as a consequence of individuals interacting with one another and with social groups or organizations; in the case of drugs and drug use, the process that leads the public to label a substance as a drug, or drug use as a problem behavior.

social influence model—an approach to drug education that uses simulated settings to teach children and adolescents how to resist peer pressure to use drugs; sometimes referred to as *drug resistance education*.

source reduction—a number of strategies designed to reduce the amount of illegal drugs produced, including crop eradication, confiscation, seizure of equipment, among others.

spurious relationship—when the believed relationship between two variables can be explained only by the presence of a third variable.

stigma—a deviant identification associated with some type of discrediting behavior.

stimulants—the category of drugs that stimulate or increase the action of the central nervous system.

stress hypothesis—the notion that alcohol and drugs are utilized as a means of dealing with excessive stress, particularly that which is related to employment.

subjective drug effect—drug effects that are grounded in the experiential reality of the user and cannot be measured on a consistent scale.

supply-side strategies—a variety of efforts designed to curtail, control, or regulate the available supply of drugs.

synapse—the microscopic space between two neurons across which electrical impulses are transmitted by neurotransmitters.

synergy, synergistic effect—the joint action of two or more drugs that produces an effect greater than the sum of the independent effects of each interacting drug.

synesthesia—an effect of hallucinogen use characterized as a blending of the senses (e.g., smelling colors, seeing sounds).

systemic violence—violence that is related to the nature of the illicit drug trade and culture.

taxonomy—classification or categorization based on some attribute or characteristic of the object under consideration.

tecatos—slang term used to refer to an addict in the Hispanic heroin subculture.

temperance—the philosophical position that alcohol may be used in moderation.

tertiary prevention—policies and measures aimed at individuals who are already addicted, designed to minimize the medical and social consequences of addiction for the addicts themselves and for those associated with the addict (i.e., family, coworkers, etc.).

therapeutic community (TC)—a comprehensive, residential-based treatment program that emphasizes confrontation followed by resocialization.

therapeutic dose—the amount of a drug necessary to achieve an intended medical effect.

treatment modalities—broad or general approaches to treatment of alcohol or drug abuse and addiction.

unofficial statistics—data gathered by researchers for the purpose of identifying drug users, learning relevant information about them, and estimating incidence and prevalence of use.

urinalysis—drug testing that uses samples of urine.

Volstead Act—*see* National Prohibition Act of 1919.

Wernicke-Korsakoff syndrome—brain damage attributed to excessive alcohol consumption, believed to be related to the way in which alcohol interferes with the absorption of vitamins, particularly thiamine.

withdrawal symptoms—physiological symptoms accompanying cessation of drug use; specific symptoms vary with each drug.

BIBLIOGRAPHY

Abbott, Gary L., Sr. 2004. "Southern Comfort: Indulgence and Abstinence in the South." In C. K. Robertson (ed.), *Religion and Alcohol: Sobering Thoughts*, 195–208. New York: Peter Lang.

Ackerman, Deborah L. 1991. "A History of Drug Testing." In Robert H. Coombs and Louis Jolyon West (eds.), *Drug Testing: Issues and Options*, 3–21. New York: Oxford University Press.

———. 1995. "Drug Testing." In Robert H. Coombs and Douglas Ziedonis (eds.), *Handbook on Drug Abuse Prevention: A Comprehensive Strategy to Prevent the Abuse of Alcohol and Other Drugs*, 473–489. Boston: Allyn and Bacon.

ADAM. *See* Arrestee Drug Abuse Monitoring Program.

Adler, Israel, and Denise B. Kandel. 1981. "Cross-Cultural Perspectives on Developmental Stages in Adolescent Drug Use. *Journal of Studies on Alcohol* 42: 701–715.

Adler, Patricia A. 1985. *Wheeling and Dealing: An Ethnography of an Upper-Level Drug Dealing and Smuggling Community*. New York: Columbia University Press.

Agar, Michael. 1973. *Ripping and Running: A Formal Ethnography of Urban Heroin Addicts*. New York: Seminar Press.

———. 2003. "The Story of Crack: Toward a Theory of Illicit Drug Trends." *Addiction Research and Theory* 11 (1): 3–29.

Agnew, Robert. 1985. "A Revised Strain Theory of Delinquency." *Social Forces* 64 (1): 151–167.

———. 1992. "Foundation for a General Strain Theory of Crime and Delinquency."

Agnew, Robert, and Helene Raskin White. 1992. "An Empirical Test of General Strain Theory." *Criminology* 30 (4): 475–499.

Akers, Ronald L. 1969. *Deviant Behavior: A Social-Learning Approach*. Belmont, CA: Wadsworth.

———. 1992. *Drugs, Alcohol, and Society: Social Structure, Process and Policy*. Belmont, CA: Wadsworth.

Akers, Ronald L., Robert L. Burgess, and Weldon T. Johnson. 1968. "Opiate Use, Addiction and Relapse." *Social Problems* 15 (4; Spring): 459–469.

Akins, Scott, Clayton Mosher, Chad L. Smith, and Jane Florence Gauthier. 2008. "The Effect of Acculturation on Patterns of Hispanic Substance Use in Washington State." *Journal of Drug Issues* 38 (1; Winter): 103–118.

Albaugh, Bernard, and P. Albaugh. 1979. "Alcoholism and Substance Sniffing among the Cheyenne and Arapaho Indians of Oklahoma." *International Journal of the Addictions* 14: 1001–1007.

Albertson, Timothy E., Robert W. Derlet, and Brent E. Van Hoozen. 1999. "Methamphetamine and the Expanding Complications of Amphetamines." *The Western Journal of Medicine* 170: 214–219.

Alcoholism and Drug Abuse Weekly. 2001. "Trial Puts Spotlight on Rapid Opiate Detox Procedures." *Alcoholism and Drug Abuse Weekly* 13 (3; January 15): 6–7.

———. 2006. "Substance Abuse among Older Adults Growing." *Alcoholism and Drug Abuse Weekly* 17 (2; January 9): 7.

Alger, Mrs. H. A. 1860. *New York Times*, December 4.

Aligne, C. Andrew, and Jeffrey J. Stoddard. 1997. "Tobacco and Children: An Economic Evaluation of the Medical Effects of Parental Smoking." *Archives of Pediatric and Adolescent Medicine* 151: 648–653.

Allen, Scott H. 1986. "Suicide and Indirect Self-Destruction Behavior among Police." In James T. Reese and Harvey A. Goldstein (eds.), *Psychological Services for Law Enforcement*, 413–417. Washington, DC: National Symposium on Police Psychological Services, FBI Academy, Quantico, VA.

Almog, Yishai J., M. Douglas Anglin, and Dennis G. Fisher. 1993. "Alcohol and Heroin Use Patterns of Narcotics Addicts: Gender and Ethnic Differences." *American Journal of Drug and Alcohol Abuse* 19: 219–238.

American Cancer Society. n.d. "Great American Smokeout" Available online: http://acsf2f.com/gaso/aboutgaso.html (Accessed March 25, 2009).

American Management Association. 1992. *AMA Survey on Workplace Drug Testing and Drug Abuse Policies*. New York: American Management Association.

Ames, Genevieve, M., Carol B. Cunradi, Roland S. Moore, and Pamela Stern. 2007. "Military Culture and Drinking Behavior among U.S. Navy Careerists." *Journal of Studies on Alcohol and Drugs* 68: 336–344.

Ames, Genevieve, and Craig Janes. 1990. "Drinking, Social Networks, and the Workplace: Results of an Environmentally Focused Study." In Paul M. Roman (ed.), *Alcohol Problem Intervention in the Workplace: Employee Assistance Programs and Strategic Alternatives*, 95–111. New York: Quorum Books.

Anderson, Edward F. 1996. *Peyote: The Divine Cactus*. Tucson, AZ: The University of Arizona Press.

Anderson, Tammy L., and Judith A. Levy. 2003. "Marginality among Older Injectors in Today's Illicit Drug Culture: Assessing the Impact of Aging." *Addiction* 98: 761–770.

Andrews, D. A., Ivan Zinger, Robert D. Hoge, James Bonta, Paul Gendreau, and Francis T. Cullen. 1990. "Does Correctional Treatment Work? A Clinically Relevant and Psychologically Informed Meta-Analysis." *Criminology* 28: 369–404.

Andrews, George, and Simon Vinkenoog (eds.). 1967. *The Book of Grass: An Anthology of Indian Hemp*. New York: Grove Press.

Anglin, M. Douglas, and Yih-Ing Hser. 1987. "Addicted Women and Crime." *Criminology* 25 (2): 359–397.

———. 1990. "Treatment of Drug Abuse." In Michael Tonry and James Q. Wilson (eds.), *Drugs and Crime*, 393–460. Chicago: University of Chicago Press.

Anglin, M. Douglas, Yih-Ing Hser, and W. H. McGlothlin. 1987. "Sex Differences in Addict Careers 2: Becoming Addicted." *American Journal of Drug and Alcohol Abuse* 13: 59–71.

Anglin, M. Douglas, Douglas Longshore, and Susan Turner. 1999. "Treatment Alternatives to Street Crime: An Evaluation of Five Programs." *Criminal Justice and Behavior* 26 (2; June): 168–195.

Anglin, M. Douglas, and Brian Perrochet. 1998. "Drug Use and Crime: A Historical Review of Research Conducted by the UCLA Drug Abuse Research Center." *Substance Use and Misuse* 33 (9): 1871–1914.

Anglin, M. Douglas, Michael Prendergast, and David Farabee. 1998. "The Effectiveness of Coerced Treatment for Drug-Abusing Offenders." Paper presented at the Office of National Drug Control Policy's Conference of Scholars and Policy Makers, Washington, DC, March 23–25.

Anglin, M. Douglas, Timothy M. Ryan, Mary W. Booth, and Yih-Ing Hser. 1988. "Ethnic Differences in Narcotics Addiction I: Characteristics of Chicano and Anglo Methadone Maintenance Clients." *The International Journal of the Addictions* 23: 125–149.

Anglin, M. Douglas, and George Speckart. 1986. "Narcotics Use, Property Crime, and Dealing: Structural Dynamics across the Addiction Career." *Journal of Quantitative Criminology* 2: 355–375.

———. 1988. "Narcotics Use and Crime: A Multisample, Multimethod Analysis." *Criminology* 26 (2): 197–233.

Anglin, M. Douglas, and C. A. Westland. 1989. "Drug Monitoring in the Workplace: Results from the California Commercial Laboratory Drug Testing Project." In Steven W. Gust and J. Michael Walsh, *Drugs in the Workplace: Research and Evaluation Data*, 81–96. NIDA Research Monograph #91. Rockville, MD: National Institute on Drug Abuse.

Anonymous. 2000. "Moderate Drinking Prevents Bone Loss in Older Women." *Better Nutrition* 62 (12; December): 20.

Anonymous One. n.d. Gyorgyi M., "Ten Hut!" Available online: http://www.anonymousone.com/story72.htm (accessed March 20, 2009).

Anslinger, Harry J., and Courtney Ryley Cooper. 1937. "Marihuana: Assassin of Youth." *American Magazine* 124: 19, 150–153.

Anslinger, Harry J., and William F. Tompkins. 1953. *The Traffic in Narcotics*. New York: Funk and Wagnalls.

Arabi, Ziad. 2007. "An Epidemic that Deserves More Attention: Epidemiology, Prevention, and Treatment of Smokeless Tobacco." *Southern Medical Association* 100 (9; September): 890–894.

Arkin, Rise Morgenstern, Helen F. Roemhild, C. Anderson Joyhnson, Russell V. Luepker, and David M. Murray. 1981. "The Minnesota Smoking Prevention Program: A Seventh-Grade Health Curriculum Supplement." *The Journal of School Health* (November): 611–616.

———. 2000. *ADAM: 1999 Annual Report on Adult and Juvenile Arrestees.* Washington, DC: National Institute of Justice.

———. 2003. *ADAM: 2003 Annual Report on Adult and Juvenile Arrestees.* Washington, DC: National Institute of Justice.

Arrigo, Bruce A. 2000. *Introduction to Forensic Psychology: Issues and Controversies in Crime and Justice.* San Diego: Academic Press.

Arrigo, Bruce A., and Karyn Garsky. 1997. "Police Suicide: A Glimpse Behind the Badge." In Roger G. Dunham and Geoffrey P. Alpert (eds.), *Critical Issues in Policing: Contemporary Readings,* 609–626. Prospect Heights, IL: Waveland Press, Inc.

Ashley, Mary Jane, Jurgen Rehm, Susan Bondy, Eric Single, and James Rankin. 2000. "Beyond Ischemic Heart Disease: Are There Other Health Benefits from Drinking Alcohol?" *Contemporary Drug Problems* 27 (Winter): 735–777.

Associated Press. 2000. "Two Doctors May Lose Licenses Over Fast-Detox Method Medicine." (December 31). Available online: http://www.doctordeluca.com/Documents/UROD_MDs_License.htm (accessed June 2, 2008).

Atkinson, John S., Isaac D. Montoya, Roberto A. Trevino, and Alan J. Richard. 2000. "Labor Force Participation in a Sample of Substance Users." *American Journal of Drug and Alcohol Abuse* 26 (3): 355–367.

Austin, A. Aukahi. 2004. "Alcohol, Tobacco, Other Drug Use, and Violent Behavior among Native Hawaiians: Ethnic Pride and Resilience." *Substance Use & Misuse* 39 (5): 721–746.

Austin, Gregory A. 1999. "Current Evidence on Substance Abuse among Asian American Youth." In *Current Evidence on Substance Abuse among Asian American Youth,* 169–219. DHHS Publication No. SMA 98-3193. Washington, DC: U.S. Government Printing Office.

Bachman, Jerald G., Peter Freedman-Doan, Patrick O'Malley, Lloyd D. Johnston, and David R. Segal. 1999. "Changing Patterns of Military Drug Use among US Military Recruits Before and After Enlistment." *American Journal of Public Health* 89 (5): 672–677.

Backer, Thomas E. 1989. "Drug Abuse Services and EAP's: Preliminary Report on a National Study." In Steven W. Gust and J. Michael Walsh (eds.), *Drugs in the Workplace: Research and Evaluation Data,* 224–244. NIDA Research Monograph 91. Rockville, MD: National Institute on Drug Abuse.

Badeneoch, James. 2002. "A Death Following Ultra-Rapid Detoxification: The General Medical Council Adjudicates on a Commercialized Detoxification." *Addiction* 97 (5; May): 475–477.

Baker, Paul James. 2006. "Developing a Blueprint for Evidence-Based Drug Prevention in England." *Drugs: Education, Prevention and Policy* 13 (1; February): 17–32.

Baldessarini, Ross J., and Leonardo Tondo. 2000. "Does Lithium Treatment Still Work? Evidence of Stable Responses over Three Decades." *Archives of General Psychiatry* 57: 187–190.

———. 2001. "Long-Term Lithium for Bipolar Disorder." *The American Journal of Psychiatry* 158: 1740.

Baldessarini, Ross J., Leonardo Tondo, and John Hennen. 1999. "Effects of Lithium Treatment and Its Discontinuation on Suicidal Behavior in Bipolar Manic-Depressive Disorders." *Journal of Clinical Psychiatry* 60: 77–84.

Baldessarini, Ross J., Leonardo Tondo, John Hennen, and Adele C. Viguera. 2002. "Is Lithium Still Worth Using? An Update of Selected Resent Research." *Harvard Review of Psychiatry* 10: 59–75.

Baldwin, Dewitt C., Jr., P;atrick H. Hughes, Scott E. Conrad, Carla L. Storr and David V. Sheehan. 1991. "Substance Abuse Among Senior Medical Students." *JAMA* 265 (16; April 24): 2074–2078.

Baldwin, Jeffrey N., R. Ellen Davis-Hall, Edward M. DeSimone II, David M. Scott, Sangeeta Agrawal, and Thomas P. Reardon. 2008. "Survey of Attitudes and Behaviors toward Alcohol and Other Drug Use in Allied Health and Physician Assistant Students." *Journal of Allied Health* 37 (3): 156–161.

Ball, John C., Lawrence Rosen, John A. Flueck, and David N. Nurco. 1981. "The Criminality of Heroin Addicts: When Addicted and When Off Opiates." In James A. Inciardi (ed.) *The Drugs-Crime Connection*, 39–65. Beverly Hills, CA: Sage Publications.

———. 1982. "Lifetime Criminality of Heroin Addicts in the United States." *Journal of Drug Issues* (3): 225–239.

Ball, John C., John W. Shaffer, and David N. Nurco. 1983. "The Day-to-Day Criminality of Heroin Addicts in Baltimore: A Study in the Continuity of Offense Rates." *Drug and Alcohol Dependence* 12 (1): 119–142.

Ballweg, John A., and Li Li. 1991. "Trends in Substance Use by U.S. Military Personnel." *Armed Forces & Society* 17: 601–618.

Bandura, Albert. 1969. *Principles of Behavior Modification*. New York: Holt, Rinehart and Winston.

———. 1977. *Social Learning Theory*. Englewood Cliffs, NJ: Prentice Hall.

Banta, William F., and Forest Tennant. 1989. *Complete Handbook for Combating Substance Abuse in the Workplace*. Lexington, MA: Lexington Books.

Barbey, J. J., and S. P. Roose. 1998. "SSRI Safety in Overdose." *Journal of Clinical Psychiatry* 59 (Supplement): 42–48.

Barnett, Randy. 1987. "Curing the Drug-Law Addiction: the Harmful Side Effects of Legal Prohibition." In Ronald Hamowy (ed.), *Dealing with Drugs: Consequences of Government Control*, 73–102. Lexington, MA: D.C. Heath.

Barnum, Howard. 1994. "The Economic Burden of the Global Trade in Tobacco." *Tobacco Control* 3: 358–361.

Barr, Kellie E. M., Michael P. Farrell, Grace M. Barnes, and John W. Welte. 1993. "Race, Class, and Gender Diffrences in Substance Abuse: Evidence of

Middle-Class/Underclass Polarization among Black Males." *Social Problems* 40: 314–327.

Bauer, Charles R., Seetha Shankaran, Henrietta S. Bada, Barry Lester, Linda L. Wright, Heidi Krause-Steinrauf, Vincent L. Smeriglio, Loretta P. Finnegan, Penelope L. Maza, and Joel Verter. 2002. "The Maternal Lifestyle Study: Drug Exposure During Pregnancy and Short-Term Maternal Outcomes." *American Journal of Obstetrics and Gynecology* 186 (3; March): 487–495.

Baumohl, Jim. 1986. "On Asylums, Homes, and Moral Treatment: The Case of the San Francisco Home for the Care of the Inebriate, 1859–1870." *Contemporary Drug Problems* (Fall): 395–445.

Beato, Greg. 2007. "Pot Clubs in Peril." *Reason* 38 (9; February): 26–36.

Beck, Jerome, and Marsha Rosenbaum. 1994. *Pursuit of Ecstasy: The MDMA Experience.* Albany, NY: State University of New York Press.

Becker, Howard S. 1953. "Becoming a Marijuana User." *American Journal of Sociology* 59: 235–242.

———. 1963. *Outsiders: Studies in the Sociology of Deviance.* New York: The Free Press.

———. 1967. "History, Culture and Subjective Experiences: An Exploration of the Social Bases of Drug-Induced Experiences." *Journal of Health and Social Behavior* 8: 163–176.

Bennett, Melanie E., Joseph H. Miller, and W. Gill Woodall. 1999. "Drinking, Binge Drinking, and Other Drug Use among Southwestern Undergraduates: Three-Year Trends." *American Journal of Drug and Alcohol Abuse* 25 (2): 331–350.

Berger, Mark C., and J. Paul Leigh. 1988. "The Effect of Alcohol Use on Wages." *Applied Economics* 20: 1343–1351.

Berger, Peter. 1963. *Invitation to Sociology: A Humanistic Perspective.* Garden City, NY: Anchor Books.

Berkowitz, Alan D., and H. Wesley Perkins. 1986. "Problem Drinking among College Students: A Review of Recent Research." *Journal of American College Health* 35: 21–28.

Berman, Greg, and John Feinblatt. 2001. "Problem-Solving Courts: A Brief Primer." *Law & Policy* 23 (2; April): 125–140.

Beschner, George M. and William Brower. 1985. "The Scene." In Bill Hanson, George Beschner, James M. Walters, and Elliot Bovelle (eds.) *Life with Heroin: Voices from the Inner City,* 19–29. Lexington, MA: Lexington Books.

Beschner, George, and Peggy Thompson. 1981. *Women and Drug Abuse Treatment: Needs and Services.* Rockville, MD: National Institute on Drug Abuse.

Bhattacharya, Gauri. 1998. "Drug Use among Asian-Indian Adolescents: Identifying Protective/Risk Factors." *Adolescence* 33 (Spring): 169–184.

Biederman, J., T. Wilens, E. Mick, T. Spencer, and S. V. Faraone. 1999. "Pharmacotherapy of Attention-Deficit/Hyperactivity Disorder Reduces Risk for Substance Use Disorder." *Pediatrics* 104: e20.

Biernacki, Patrick. 1979. "Junkie Work, 'Hustles' and Social Status among Heroin Addicts." *Journal of Drug Issues* 9: 535–551.

Birmingham, Karen. 2001. "Dark Clouds over Toronto Psychiatry Research." *Nature Medicine* 7: 643. Available online: http://www.nature.com/nm/journal/v7/n6/pdf/nm0601_643.pdf (accessed May 21, 2008).

Bischke, Paul M. 2003. "Pleasure Drugs and Classical Virtues: Temperance and Abstinence in U.S. Religious Thought." *International Journal of Drug Policy* 14: 273–278.

Black, J. R. 1889. "Advantages of Substituting the Morphia Habit for the Incurably Alcoholic." *Cincinnati Lancet-Clinic* 22: 537–541.

Blaine, Jack D., Carl M. Lieberman, and Joseph Hirsh. 1968. "Preliminary Observations on Patterns of Drug Consumption among Medical Students." *The International Journal of the Addictions* 3: 389–396.

Blau, Theodore H. 1994. *Psychological Services for Law Enforcement.* New York: John Wiley and Sons, Inc.

Blum, Terry C., and Paul M. Roman. 1995. *Cost-Effectiveness and Preventive Implications of Employee Assistance Programs.* Rockville, MD: Substance Abuse and Mental Health Services Administration.

Board of Education of Independent School District No. 92 of Pottawatomie County v. Earls, 536 U.S. 822 (2002). Available online: http://www.oyez.org/cases/2000-2009/2001/2001_01_332/ (accessed April 4, 2009).

Boeri, Miriam Williams, Claire E. Sterk, and Kirk W. Elifson. 2006. "Baby Boomer Drug Users: Career Phases, Social Control, and Social Learning Theory." *Sociological Inquiry* 76 (2; May): 264–291.

Boles, Sharon M., Vandana Joshi, Christine Grella, and Jean Wellisch. 2005. "Childhood Sexual Abuse Patterns, Psychosocial Correlates, and Treatment Outcomes among Adults in Drug Abuse Treatment." *Journal of Child Sexual Abuse* 14 (1): 39–55.

Bolla, K. I., U. D. McCann, and Ricaurte, G. A. 1998. "Memory Impairment in Abstinent MDMA ("Ecstasy") Users." *Neurology* 51: 1532–1537.

Bompey, Stuart H. 1986. "Drugs in the Workplace: From the Batter's Box to the Boardroom." *Journal of Occupational Medicine* 28: 825–832.

Bonifacio, Philip. 1991. *The Psychological Effects of Police Work: A Psychodynamic Approach.* New York: Plenum Press.

Bonnie, Richard. 1980. *Marijuana Use and Criminal Sanctions.* Charlottesville, VA: The Michie Company.

Bonnie, Richard J., and Charles H. Whitebread. 1970. "The Forbidden Fruit and the Tree of Knowledge: An Inquiry into the Legal History of American Marijuana Prohibition." *Virginia Law Review* 56. Available online: http://www.drugtext.org/library/reports/vlr/vlrtoc-3.htm (accessed May 30, 2008).

Booth, Martin. 1998. *Opium: A History.* New York: St. Martin's Press.

Bordin, Ruth. 1981. *Woman and Temperance: The Quest for Power and Liberty, 1873–1900.* Philadelphia: Temple University Press.

Bostic v. McLendon, 650 F. Supp. 1507 (N.D. Ga. 1986).

Botvin, Gilbert J., and Kenneth W. Griffin. 2006. "Drug Abuse Prevention Curricula in Schools." In Zili Sloboda and William J. Bukoski (eds.), *Handbook of Drug Abuse Prevention: Theory, Science and Practice*, 45–74. New York: Kluwer Academic/Plenum Publishers.

Boudreaux, Edwin, Dean G. Kilpatrick, Heidi S. Resnick, Connie L. Best and Benjamin E. Saunders. 1998., "Criminal Victimization, Posttraumatic Stress Disorder, and Comorbid Psychopathology Among a Community Sample of Women." *Journal of Traumatic Stress* 11 (4): 665–678.

Boundy, Donna. 1985. "Program for Cocaine Abuse Underway." *New York Times*, November 17. Late City Final Edition, Section 11 WC, Page 12.

Bourgois, Phillippe. 1995. *In Search of Respect: Selling Crack in El Barrio*. Cambridge, U.K.: Cambridge University Press.

Bourgois, Phillippe, Mark Lettiere, and James Quesada. 1997. "Social Misery and the Sanctions of Substance Abuse: Confronting HIV Risk among Homeless Heroin Addicts in San Francisco." *Social Problems* 44: 155–173.

Bowker, Lee. 1977. *Drug Use among American Women, Old and Young: Sexual Oppression and Other Themes*. San Francisco: R & E Research Associates, Inc.

Boyce, P., and F. Judd. 1999. "The Place for the Tricyclic Antidepressants in the Treatment of Depression." *Australian and New Zealand Journal of Psychiatry* 33: 323–327.

Boyce, S. S. 1900. *Hemp, A Practical Treatise on the Culture of Himp for Seed and Fiber with a Sketch of the History and Nature of the Hemp Plant*. New York: Orange Judd.

Boyum, David, and Mark A. R. Kleiman. 2003. "Breaking the Drug-Crime Link." *The Public Interest* 152 (Summer): 19–38.

Brady, Joanne P., Marc Posner, Cynthia Lang, and Michael J. Rosati. 1994. *Risk and Reality: The Implications of Prenatal Exposure to Alcohol and Other Drugs*. Available online: http://aspe.os.dhhs.gov/hsp/cyp/drugkids.htm (accessed June 3, 2008).

Brady, John C., II. 1985. *Substance Abuse and Treatment in Silicon Valley—A Cost Analysis, July*. Milpatas, CA: Psychology Management Systems.

Brady, Kathleen T., Hugh Myrick, and Robert Malcolm. 1999. "Sedative-Hypnotic and Anxiolytic Agents." In Barbara S. McCrady and Elizabeth E. Epstein (eds.), *Addictions: A Comprehensive Guidebook*, 95–104. New York: Oxford University Press.

Brady, Thomas M., and Olivia Silber Ashley. 2005. *Women in Substance Abuse Treatment: Results from the Alcohol and Drug Services Study (ADSS)*. DHHS Publicatino No. SMA 04-3968, Analytic Series A-26. Rockville, MD: Substance Abuse and Mental Health Services Administration, Office of Applied Studies.

Bray, Robert M., John A. Fairbank, and Mary Ellen Marsden. 1999. "Stress and Substance Abuse among Military Women and Men." *American Journal of Drug and Alcohol Abuse* 25: 239–251.

Bray, Robert M., and Laurel L. Hourani. 2007. "Substance Use Trends Among Active Duty Military Personnel: Findings from the United States Department of Defense Health Related Behavior Surveys, 1980–2005." *Addiction* 102: 1092–1101.

Bray, Robert M., Laurel L. Hourani, Kristine L. Rae Olmsted, Michael Witt, Janice M. Brown, Michael R. Pemberton, Mary Ellen Marsden, Bernadette Marriott, Scott Scheffler, Russ Vandermaas-Peeler, BeLinda Weimer, Sara Calvin, Michael Bradshaw, Kelly Close, and Douglas Hayden. 2006. *2005 Department of Defense Survey of Health Related Behaviors among Active Duty Military Personnel: A Component of the Defense Lifestyle Assessment Program (DLAP).* Research Triangle Park NC: Research Triangle Institute. Available online: http://www.ha.osd.mil/special_reports/2005_Health_Behaviors_Survey_1-07.pdf (accessed November 6, 2008).

Bray, Robert M., and Larry A. Kroutil. 1995. "Trends in Alcohol, Illicit Drug and Cigarette Use among U.S. Military Personnel: 1980–1992." *Armed Forces & Society* 21: 271–283.

Bray, Robert M., Mary Ellen Marsden, and Michael R. Peterson. 1991. "Standardized Comparisons of the Use of Alcohol, Drugs, and Cigarettes among Military Personnel and Civilians." *American Journal of Public Health* 81: 865–869.

Brecher, Edward M. 1972. *Licit and Illicit Drugs.* Boston: Little, Brown and Company.

Breen, Courtney, Amanda Roxburgh, and Louisa Degenhardt. 2005. "Gender Differences among Regular Injecting Drug Users in Sydney, Australia, 1996–2003." *Drug and Alcohol Review* 24 (July): 353–358.

Breiner, Laurence A. 1985–1986. "The English Bible in Jamaican Rastafarianism." *Journal of Religious Thought* 42 (2): 30–43.

Brendtro, Larry K., and Gordon A. Martin. 2006. "Respect Versus Surveillance: Drug Testing Our Students." *Reclaiming Children and Youth* 15 (2; Summer): 75–81.

Breslow, Rosalinda A., Vivian B. Faden, and Barbara Smothers. 2003. "Alcohol Consumption by Elderly Americans." *Journal of Studies on Alcohol* 64 (6; November): 884–892.

Bressler, Bernard. 1976. "Suicide and Drug Abuse in the Medical Community." *Suicide and Life Threatening Behavior* 6: 169–178.

Broadhead, Robert S., Yaël Van Hulst, and Douglas D. Heckathorn. 1999. "The Impact of a Needle Exchange's Closure." *Public Health Reports* (September–October): 446–447.

Broidy, Lisa M. 2001. "A Test of General Strain Theory." *Criminology* 39 (1): 9–36.

Broome, Kirk M., Dwayne Simpson, and George W. Joe. 2002. "The Role of Social Support Following Short-Term Inpatient Treatment." *The American Journal on Addictions* (11): 57–65.

Brown, Barry S., Susan K. Gauvey, Marilyn B. Meyers, and Steven D. Stark. 1971. "In Their Own Words: Addicts' Reasons for Initiating and Withdrawing from Heroin." *The International Journal of The Addictions* 6: 635–645.

Brown, Edwin W. 1997. "Why Suffer from Chronic Pain?" *Medical Update* 21 (2): 1–2.

Brown, Emma J., and Frances B. Smith. 2006. "Drug (Ab)use Research among Rural African American Males: An Integrated Literature Review." *International Journal of Men's Health* 5 (2; Summer): 191–206.

Brown, Joel H., Marianne D'Emidio-Caston, Karen Kaufman, Teddy Goldsworthy-Hanner, and Maureen Alioto. 1995. *In Their Own Voices: Students and Educators Evaluate California School-Based Drug, Alcohol, and Tobacco Education (DATE) Programs*. Sacramento, CA: California State Department of Education.

Brown, Josephine V., Roger Bakeman, Claire D. Coles, William R. Sexson, and Alice S. Demi. 1998. "Maternal Drug Use During Pregnancy: Are Preterm and Full-Term Infants Affected Differently?" *Developmental Psychology* 34: 540–554.

Bryan, James H. 1966. "Occupational Ideologies and Individual Attitudes of Call Girls." *Social Problems* 13 (4; Spring): 441–450.

Bryant, Clifton D. 1974. "Olive-Drab Drunks and GI Junkies: Alcohol and Narcotic Addiction in the U.S. Military." In Clifton D. Bryant (ed.), *Deviant Behavior: Occupational and Organizational Bases*, 129–145. Chicago: Rand-McNally.

Buchanan, David R. 1993. "Social Status Group Differences in Motivations for Drug Use." *Journal of Drug Issues* 23 (4; Fall): 631–644.

Buckley, William E., Charles E. Yesalis, K. E. Freidl, William A. Anderson, A. L. Streit, and James E. Wright. 1988. "Estimated Prevalence of Anabolic Steroid Use among Male High School Seniors." *Journal of the American Medical Association* 260: 3441–3445.

Bukoski, William J. 1991. "A Definition of Drug Abuse Prevention Research." In Lewis Donohew, Howard E. Sypher, and William J. Bukoski (eds.), *Persuasive Communication and Drug Abuse Prevention*, 3–19. Hillsdale, NJ: Lawrence Erlbaum Associates, Publishers.

Bullington, Bruce. 1977. *Heroin Use in the Barrio*. Lexington, MA: D.C. Heath.

————. 2004. "Drug Policy Reform and Its Detractors: The United States as the Elephant in the Closet." *Journal of Drug Issues* 34 (3; Summer): 687–722.

Burack, Jeffrey H., and David Bangsberg. 1998. "Epidemiology and HIV Transmission in Injection Drug Users." *HIV InSite Knowledge Base*. Available online: http://hivinsite.ucsf.edu/InSite.jsp?doc=kb-07-04-01&page=kb-07 (accessed October 29, 2008).

Bureau of International Narcotic Matters. 1990. *International Narcotics Control Strategy Report*. Washington, DC: U.S. Department of State.

Bureau of Justice Assistance. 1995. "Drug Abuse Resistance Education (D.A.R.E.)." *Bureau of Justice Assistance Fact Sheet*. Washington, DC: U.S. Department of Justice.

————. 2008. *Summary of Drug Court Activity by State and County*. BJA Drug Court Clearinghouse Project. Available Online: http://www1.spa.american.edu/justice/documents/2150.pdf (Accessed April 3, 2009).

Bureau of Justice Statistics. 1992. *Drugs, Crime, and the Criminal Justice System: A National Report from the Bureau of Justice Statistics*. Washington, DC: U.S. Government Printing Office.

Bureau of Labor Statistics. 1989. *Survey of Employer Antidrug Programs.* Washington, DC: U.S. Bureau of Labor.

Bureau of Narcotics. 1932. *Traffic in Opium and Other Dangerous Drugs for the Year Ended December 31, 1931.* Washington, DC: U.S. Treasury Department.

———. 1936. *Traffic in Opium and Other Dangerous Drugs for the Year Ended December 31, 1935.* Washington, DC: U.S. Treasury Department.

———. 1937. *Traffic in Opium and Other Dangerous Drugs for the Year Ended December 31, 1936.* Washington, DC: U.S. Treasury Department.

Burkett, Steven R., and Bruce O. Warren. 1987. "Religiosity, Peer Associations, and Adolescent Marijuana Use: A Panel Study of Underlying Causal Structures." *Criminology* 25: 109–131.

Bush, George. 2004. *State of the Union Address.* Available Online: http://www.c-span.org/executive/transcript.asp?cat=current_event&code=bush_admin&year=2004 (accessed April 4, 2009).

Cahalan, Don. 1970. *Problem Drinkers: A National Survey.* San Francisco: Jossey-Bass.

Caldwell, John A. 2008. "Go Pills in Combat: Prejudice, Propriety, and Practicality." *Air and Space Power Journal* 22 (3): 97–104.

Caldwell, John A., and J. Lynn Caldwell. 2005. "Fatigue in Military Aviation: An Overview of U.S. Military-Approved Pharmacological Countermeasures." *Aviation, Space, and Environmental Medicine* 76 (7): C39–C51.

Caldwell, John A., J. Lynn Caldwell, and Kecia K. Darlington. 2003. "Utility of Dextroamphetamine for Attenuating the Impact of Sleep Deprivation in Pilots." *Aviation, Space, and Environmental Medicine* 74 (11): 1125–1134.

Calfee, Ryan, and Paul Fadale. 2006. "Popular Ergogenic Drugs and Supplements in Young Athletes." *Pediatrics* 117 (3): e577–e589.

Camargo, Carlos A., Jr., Meir J. Stampfer, Robert J. Glynn, J. Michael Gaziano, JoAnn E. Manson, Samuel Z. Goldhaber, and Charles H. Hennekens. 1997. "Prospective Study of Moderate Alcohol Consumption and Risk of Peripheral Arterial Disease in U.S. Male Physicians." *Circulation* (95): 577–580.

Campbell, Horace. 1980. "Rastafari: Culture of Resistance." *Race & Class* 22: 1–22.

Campbell, Richard S., and Jeffrey B. Freeland. 1974. "Patterns of Female Drug Use." *International Journal of the Addictions* 9: 289–300.

Canadian Association of University Teachers. 2001. "Academic Freedom in Jeopardy at Toronto." *CAUT-ACPPU Bulletin* 48 (May). Available online: http://www.cautbulletin.ca/ (accessed May 21, 2008).

[Canadian Government.] 2001. "Controlled Drugs and Substances Act-Marijuana Medical Access Regulations." SOR 2001-227, PC 1146.

Capehart, Tom. 1998. "Outlook for U.S. Tobacco." Economic Research Service. Washington, DC: U.S. Department of Agriculture.

Carnavale Associates. 2006. *A Longitudinal Evaluation of the New Curricula for the D.A.R.E. Middle (7th Grade) and High School (9th Grade) Programs: TAKE*

CHARGE OF YOUR LIFE: Four Year Progress Report. Gaithersburg, MD: Carnevale Associates LLC.

Carpenter, Christopher S. 2007. "Workplace Drug Testing and Worker Drug Use." *Health Services Research* 42 (2): 795–810.

Carroll, Charles R. 1989. *Drugs in Modern Society*, 2nd ed. Dubuque, IA: William C. Brown.

Carroll, Joseph. 2005. "Who Supports Marijuana Legalization?" Gallup News Service. Available online: http://www.gallup.com/poll/19561/Who-Supports-Marijuana-Legalization.aspx (accessed March 7, 2008).

Carroll, Rebecca. 1991. *A Rhetorical Biography of Harry J. Anslinger, Commissioner of the Federal Bureau of Narcotics 1930–1962.* PhD Dissertation, University of Pittsburgh.

Carstairs, Catherine. 2005. "The Stages of the International Drug Control System." *Drug and Alcohol Review* 24 (January): 57–65.

Carter, Jimmy. 1977. Message to Congress (August 2). Cited in NORML, "Special News Bulletin," June 15, 1999. Available online: http://norml.org/index.cfm?Group_ID=3381#point2 (accessed March 8, 2008).

Cartwright, William S. 2008. "Economic Costs of Drug Abuse: Financial, Cost of Illness, and Services." *Journal of Substance Abuse Treatment* 34: 224–233.

Castro, Russel A. 2001. "Drug Use, Cultures, and Subcultures." In Clifton Bryant (ed.), *Encyclopedia of Criminology and Deviant Behavior*, Vol. 4, 294–296. Philadelphia: Taylor and Francis.

Catalano, Richard F., Diane M. Morrison, Elizabeth A. Wells, Mary R. Gillmore, Bonita Iritani, and J. David Hawkins. 1992. "Ethnic Differences in Family Factors Related to Early Drug Initiation." *Journal of Studies on Alcohol* 53 (3; May): 208–217.

Caulkins, Jonathan P., and Peter Reuter. 2006. "Reorienting U.S. Drug Policy." *Issues in Science and Technology* 23 (1; Fall): 79–85.

CDC. *See* Centers for Disease Control and Prevention.

———. 1992. *HIV/AIDS Surveillance Report, 1991.* Atlanta, GA: Department of Health and Human Services, Centers for Disease Control and Prevention.

———. 1994a. "Preventing Tobacco Use among Young People: Report of the Surgeon General. Atlanta, GA: Centers for Disease Control.

———. 1994b. *HIV/AIDS Surveillance Report, 1993*, Vol. 5, No. 4. Atlanta, GA: U.S. Department of Health and Human Services, Centers for Disease Control and Prevention.

———. 1995. *HIV/AIDS Surveillance Report, 1995*, Vol. 7, No. 2. Atlanta, GA: U.S. Department of Health and Human Services, Centers for Disease Control and Prevention.

———. 1997. *HIV/AIDS Surveillance Report, 1997*, Vol. 9, No. 2. Atlanta, GA: U.S. Department of Health and Human Services, Centers for Disease Control and Prevention.

CDC. 1999. *HIV/AIDS Surveillance Report, 1999*, Vol. 11, No. 2. Atlanta, GA: U.S. Department of Health and Human Services, Centers for Disease Control and Prevention.

———. 2000. "Tobacco Use among Middle and High School Students—United States, 1999." *The Journal of the American Medical Association* 283: 1134–1142.

———. 2001. *HIV/AIDS Surveillance Report, 2001*, Vol. 13, No. 2. Atlanta, GA: U.S. Department of Health and Human Services, Centers for Disease Control and Prevention.

———. 2002a. *Viral Hepatitis and Injection Drug Users*. Atlanta, GA: U.S. Department of Health and Human Services, Centers for Disease Control and Prevention.

———. 2002b. "Cigarette Smoking among Adults—United States, 2000." *Morbidity and Mortality Weekly Report* 51 (29; July 26): 642–645.

———. 2003. *HIV/AIDS Surveillance Report, 2003*, Vol. 15. Atlanta, GA: U.S. Department of Health and Human Services, Centers for Disease Control and Prevention.

———. 2004. "Alcohol-Attributable Deaths and Years of Potential Life Lost—United States, 2001" Available online: http://www.cdc.gov (accessed April 6, 2009).

———. 2005. "Annual Smoking-Attributable Mortality, Years of Potential Life Lost, and Productivity Losses—United States, 1997–2001." *Morbidity and Mortality Weekly Report* 54 (25, July 1): 625–608.

———. 2006. *Sustaining State Programs for Tobacco Control: Data Highlights 2006*. Available online: http://www.cdc.gov/tobacco/data_statistics/state_data/data_highlights/2006/00_pdfs/DataHighlights06rev.pdf (accessed November 15, 2008).

———. 2007a. "Deaths: Final Data for 2004." *National Vital Statistics Reports* 55 (19; August 21): 1–120 Atlanta, GA: U.S. Department of Health and Human Services, Centers for Disease Control and Prevention.

———. 2007b. *HIV/AIDS Surveillance Report, 2005*, Vol. 17, rev. ed. Atlanta, GA: U.S. Department of Health and Human Services, Centers for Disease Control and Prevention.

———. 2007c. *Viral Hepatitis*. Available online: http://www.cdc.gov/ncidod/diseases/hepatitis/index.htm (accessed November 8, 2007).

———. 2007d. "Cigarette Smoking among Adults, United States, 2006." *Morbidity and Mortality Weekly Report* 56 (44; November 9): 1157–1161.

———. 2008a. "Targeting Tobacco Use: The Nation's Leading Cause of Death." Atlanta, GA: Centers for Disease Control. Available online: http://www.cdc.gov/nccdphp/publications/aag/pdf/osh.pdf (accessed May 21, 2008).

———. 2008b. *Healthy Youth! YRBSS: Youth Risk Behavior Surveillance System*. Available online: http://www.cdc.gov/HealthyYouth/yrbs/index.htm (accessed June 4, 2008).

Chaiken, Jan M., and Marcia R. Chaiken. 1982. *Varieties of Criminal Behavior*. Santa Monica, CA: Rand.

———. 1990. "Drugs and Predatory Crime." In Michael Tonry and James Q. Wilson (eds.), *Drugs and Crime*, 203–239. Chicago: University of Chicago Press.

Chaiken, Marcia R., and Jan M. Chaiken. 1985. "Who Gets Caught Doing Crime?" Discussion Paper. Washington, DC: Bureau of Justice Statistics.

Chambers, Carl D., Walter Cuskey, and Arthur D. Moffett. 1970. "Mexican American Opiate Addicts." In John C. Ball and Carl D. Chambers (eds.), *The Epidemiology of Opiate Addiction in the United States*, 202-221. Springfield, IL: Charles C. Thomas.

Chasnoff, Ira J., William J. Burns, Sidney H. Schnoll, and Kayreen A. Burns. 1985. "Cocaine Use in Pregnancy." *New England Journal of Medicine* 313: 666–669.

Chasnoff, Ira J., Carl E. Hunt, Ron Kletter, and David Kaplan. 1989. "Prenatal Cocaine Exposure is Associated with Respiratory Pattern Abnormalities." *American Journal of Diseases of Children* 143: 583–587.

Chawla, Neharika, Clayton Neighbors, Melissa A. Lewis, Christine M. Lee, and Mary E. Larimer. 2007. "Attitudes and Perceived Approval of Drinking as Mediators of the Relationship Between the Importance of Religion and Alcohol Use." *Journal of Studies on Alcohol and Drugs* 68: 410–418.

Chein, Isidor, Donald L. Gerard, Robert S. Lee, and Eva Rosenfeld. 1964. *The Road to H: Narcotics, Juvenile Delinquency and Social Policy*. New York: Basic Books.

Chitwood, Dale D., James E. Rivers, and James A. Inciardi. 1996. *The American Pipe Dream: Crack Cocaine and the Inner City*. Fort Worth, TX: Harcourt Brace.

Chua-Eoan, Howard. 1999. "Heroes and Icons." *Time Magazine* (June 14). Available Online: http://www.time.com/time/magazine/article/0,9171,991272,00.html. Accessed April 3, 2009.

Chung, D. K. 1992. "Asian Cultural Commonalities: A Comparison with Mainstream American Culture." In S. M. Furuto, R. Biswas, D. K. Chung, K. Murase, and F. Ross-Sheriff (eds.), *Social Work Practice with Asian Americans*, 27–31. Newbury Park, CA: Sage.

Cicero, Theodore J. 1983. "Behavioral Significance of Drug-Induced Alterations of Reproductive Endocrinology in the Male." In E. Gottheil, K. A. Druley, T. E. Skoloda, and H. M. Waxman (eds.), *Alcohol, Drug Abuse and Aggression*, 203–226. Springfield, IL: Charles C. Thomas.

Clayton, Richard. 1981. "Federal Drugs-Crime Research: Setting the Agenda." In James A. Inciardi (ed.), *The Drugs-Crime Connection*, 17–38. Beverly Hills, CA: Sage Publications.

Clayton, Richard R., Anne Cattarello, L. Edward Day, and Katherine P. Walden. 1991. "Persuasive Communication and Drug Prevention: An Evaluation of the DARE Program." In Lewis Donohew, Howard E. Sypher, and William J. Bukoski (eds.), *Persuasive Communication and Drug Abuse Prevention*, 295–313. Hillsdale, NJ: Lawrence Erlbaum Associates, Publishers.

Clayton, Richard R., Anne Cattarello, and Bryan M. Johnstone. 1996. "The Effectiveness of Drug Abuse Resistance Education (Project DARE): 5-Year Follow-Up Results." *Preventive Medicine* 25: 307–318.

Cloward, Richard, and Lloyd Ohlin. 1960. *Delinquency and Opportunity.* New York: Free Press.

Cohen, Albert K. 1955. *Delinquent Boys.* Glencoe, IL: Free Press.

Cohen, Maimon M., Michelle J. Marinello, and Nathan Back. 1967. "Chromosomal Damage in Human Leukocytes Induced by Lysergic Acid Diethylamide." *Science* 155: 1417–1419.

Cohn, Jason. 2001. "Drug Education: The Triumph of Bad Science," *Rolling Stone,* May 24: 41–42.

Cole, Steven G., and Lawrence R. James. 1975. "A Revised Treatment Typology Based on DARP." *American Journal of Drug and Alcohol Abuse* 2: 37–49.

Collins, David J., and Helen M. Lapsley. 1992. *The Social Costs of Drug Abuse in Australia in 1998 and 1992.* Report prepared for the Commonwealth Department of Human Services and Health, Canberra, Australia.

———. 1996. *The Social Costs of Drug Abuse in Australia in 1998 and 1992.* National Drug Strategy Monograph Series No. 30. Canberra, Australia: Australian Government, Department of Health and Ageing. Available Online: http://www.health.gov.au/internet/main/publishing.nsf/Content/health-pubhlth-publicat-document-mono30-cnt.htm (accessed April 6, 2009).

Collins, James J., Jr. 1983. "Alcohol Use and Expressive Interpersonal Violence: A Proposed Explanatory Model." In E. Gottheil, K. A. Druley, T. E. Skoloda, and H. M. Waxman (eds.), *Alcohol, Drug Abuse and Aggression,* 5–25. Springfield, IL: Charles C. Thomas.

Collins, James J., Robert L. Hubbard, and J. Valley Rachal. 1985. "Expensive Drug Use and Illegal Income: A Test of Explanatory Hypotheses." *Criminology* 23: 743–764.

Collins, James J., and Pamela M. Messerschmidt. 1993. "Epidemiology of Alcohol-Related Violence." *Alcohol Health and Research World* 17: 93–100.

Committee on Oversight and Government Reform. 2008. Letter by Henry A. Waxman, Chairman of the Committee, and Barbara Lee, Member of Congress, to John P. Walters, Director of the Office of National Drug Control Policy, dated February 15, 2008. Available online: http://oversight.house.gov/documents/20080219093736.pdf (accessed March 13, 2008).

Conant v. McCaffrey. 2000. United States District Court for the Northern District of California No. C 97-00139 WHA.

Conant v. Walters, 309 F.3d 629 (9th Cir. 2002).

Conard, Scott, Patrick Hughes, DeWitt C. Baldwin, Karl E. Achenbach, and David V. Sheehan. 1988. "Substance Use by Fourth-Year Students at 13 U.S. Medical Schools." *Journal of Medical Education* 63: 747–758.

Conley, Paul C., and Andrew A. Sorensen. 1971. *The Staggering Steeple: The Story of Alcoholism and the Churches.* Philadelphia: Pilgrim Press.

Consumer Affairs. "Binge Drinking Widespread among College Students: Little Progress Seen in Recent Years," March 15, 2007. Available online: http://www.

consumeraffairs.com/news04/2007/03/binge_drinking.html (accessed May 26, 2008).

Consumer Reports. 1993. "High Anxiety." *Consumer Reports* 58,1(January): 19–24. Yonkers, NY: Consumer's Union of U.S., Inc.

Cook, L. Foster, and Beth A. Weinman. 1988. "Treatment Alternatives to Street Crime." In Carl G. Leukefeld and Frank M. Tims (eds.), *Compulsory Treatment of Drug Abuse: Research and Clinical Practice,* 99–105. National Institute on Drug Abuse Research Monograph Series #86. Washington, DC: U.S. Government Printing Office.

Coombs, Robert H. 1981. "Drug Abuse as Career." *Journal of Drug Issues* 11 (Fall): 369–387.

Coombs, Robert H., and Douglas M. Ziedonis. 1995. *Handbook on Drug Abuse Prevention: A Comprehensive Strategy to Prevent the Abuse of Alcohol and Other Drugs.* Boston: Allyn and Bacon.

Cooper, Caroline S. 2007. "Drug Courts—Just the Beginning: Getting Other Areas of Public Policy in Sync." *Substance Use & Misuse* 42 (2–3): 243–256.

Cooper, M. Lynne, Marcia Russell, and Michael R. Frone. 1990. "Work Stress and Alcohol Effects: A Test of Stress-Induced Drinking." *Journal of Health and Social Behavior* 31: 260–276.

Correia, Christopher J. 2005. "Behavioral Theories of Choice." In Mitch Earlywine (ed.), *Mind Altering Drugs: The Science of Subjective Experience,* 3–24. New York: Oxford University Press.

Corti, Count Egon Ceasar. 1931. *A History of Smoking.* London: George C. Harrap and Company.

Cotton, N.S. 1979. "The Familial Incidence of Alcoholism. *Journal of Studies on Alcohol* 40, 89–116.

Council on Mental Health. 1973. "The Sick Physician: Impairment by Psychiatric Disorders, Including Alcoholism and Drug Dependence." *Journal of the American Medical Association* 223: 684–687.

Council on Scientific Affairs. 1996. "Alcoholism in the Elderly." *Journal of the American Medical Association* 275: 797–801.

Cox, W. Miles. 1985. "Personality Correlates of Substance Abuse." In Mark Galizeo and Stephen A. Maisto (eds.), *Determinants of Substance Abuse: Biological, Psychological and Environmental Factors,* 209–246. New York: Plenum Press.

Cowan, Richard. 1986. "How the Narcs Created Crack." *National Review,* December 5, 30–31.

Crothers, T. D. 1902. *Morphinism and Narcomanias from Other Drugs.* Philadelphia: W.B. Saunders & Co.

Crouch, Dennis J., Douglas O. Webb, Lynn V. Peterson, Paul F. Buller, and Douglas E. Rollins. 1989. "A Critical Evaluation of the Utah Power and Light Company's Substance Abuse Management Program: Absenteeism, Accidents and Costs." In Steven W. Gust and J. Michael Walsh (eds.), *Drugs in the Workplace: Research and Evaluation Data*, 169–193. NIDA Research Monograph 91. Rockville, MD: National Institute on Drug Abuse.

Crowley, Thomas J. 1981. "The Reinforcers for Drug Abuse: Why People Take Drugs." In Howard Shaffer and Milton Earl Burglass (eds.), *Classic Contributions in the Addictions*, 367–381. New York: Brunner/Mazel.

Cucchia, A. T., M. Monnat, J. Spagnoli, F. Ferrero, and G. Bertschy. 1998. "Ultra-Rapid Opiate Detoxification Using Deep Sedation: Short and Long Term Results." *Journal of Drug and Alcohol Dependence* 52 (3): 243–250.

Currie, Elliott. 1985. *Confronting Crime: An American Challenge.* New York: Pantheon Books.

———. 1993. *Reckoning: Drugs, the Cities, and the American Future.* New York: Farrar, Straus, and Giroux.

Curtis, Richard. 1999. "The Ethnographic Approach to Studying Drug Crime." In Office of Justice Programs, *Looking at Crime from the Street Level*, 13–15 (November). Washington, DC: National Institute of Justice.

Cuskey, Walter R., Lisa H. Berger, and Arthur H. Richardson. 1978. "The Effects of Marijuana Decriminalization on Drug Use Patterns: A Literature Review and Research Critique." *Contemporary Drug Problems* (Winter): 491–532.

Cuskey, Walter R., T. Premkumar, and Lois Sigel. 1972. "Survey of Opiate Addiction among Females in the United States between 1850 and 1970." *Public Health Reviews* 1: 6–39.

Cuskey, Walter R., and Richard B. Wathey. 1982. *Female Addiction.* Lexington, MA: D.C. Heath.

Darke, Shane, Wayne Hall, Don Weatherburn, and Bronwyn Lind. 1998. "Fluctuations in Heroin Purity and the Incidence of Fatal Heroin Overdose." *Drug and Alcohol Dependence* 54: 155–161.

Darke, Shane, and Deborah Zador. 1996. "Fatal Heroin 'Overdose': A Review." *Addiction* 91: 1765–1772.

Darrow, Clarence, and Victor Yarros. 1927. *The Prohibition Mania: A Reply to Professor Irving Fisher and Others.* New York: Boni and Liveright.

DAWN. *See* Drug Abuse Warning Network.

DEA. *See* Drug Enforcement Administration.

Dealbarto, Marie-Jose, Gail J. McAvay, Teresa Seeman, and Lisa Berkman. 1997. "Psychotropic Drug Use and Cognitive Decline among Older Men and Women." *International Journal of Geriatric Psychiatry* 12: 567–574.

DeAngelis, Gerald G. 1976. *Testing and Screening for Drugs of Abuse: Techniques, Issues and Clinical Implications.* New York: Marcel Dekker.

De Fiebre, Christopher M. and Allan C. Collins. "Exploring the Genetic Commonality of Alcohol and Tobacco Abuse." *Science Blog* (June). Available Online: http://www.scienceblog.com/community/older/2002/G/2002156.html (Accessed March 27, 2009).

De Leon, George. 1998. Prison Based Therapeutic Community Treatment: What We Know, and Where We Should Go. (March 19). Remarks to the Office of National Drug Control Policy. Available Online: http://www.ncjrs.gov/ondcppubs/treat/consensus/deleon.pdf (Accessed April 3, 2009)

De Leon, George, Henry K. Wexler, and Nancy Jainchill. 1982. "The Therapeutic Community: Success and Improvement Rates 5 Years After Treatment." *The International Journal of the Addictions* 17: 703–747.

Delva, Jorge, Yehuda D. Neumark, Carolyn D. M. Furr, and James C. Anthony. 2000. "Drug Use among Welfare Recipients in the United States." *American Journal of Drug and Alcohol Abuse* 26 (2): 335–342.

Delva, Jorge, John M. Wallace Jr., Patrick M. O'Malley, Jerald G. Bachman, Lloyd D. Johnston, and John E. Schulengerg. 2005. "The Epidemiology of Alcohol, Marijuana, and Cocaine Use among Mexican American, Puerto Rican, Cuban American, and Other Latin American Eight-Grade Students in the United States: 1991–2002." *American Journal of Public Health* 95 (4; April): 696–702.

Dembo, Richard, James A. Ciarlo, and Robert W. Taylor. 1983. "A Model for Assessing and Improving Drug Abuse Treatment Resource use in Inner-City Areas." *The International Journal of the Addictions* 18: 921–936.

De Quincy, Thomas. 1850. *Confessions of an English Opium-Eater*. Boston: Ticknor, Reed, and Fields.

Derzon, James H., and Mark W. Lipsey. 1999. "A Synthesis of the Relationship of Marijuana Use with Delinquent and Problem Behaviors." *School Psychology International* 20: 57–68.

Des Jarlais, Don C., Michael Marmour, Denise Paone, Stephen Titus, Q. Shi, Theresa Perlis, B. Hose, and Samuel R. Friedman. 1996. "HIV Incidence among Injecting Drug Users in New York City Syringe Exchange Programmes." *Lancet* 348 (October 12): 987–991.

de Wit, Harriet. 2005. "Relationships Between Personality and Acute Subjective Responses to Stimulant Drugs." In Mitch Earlywine (ed.), *Mind Altering Drugs: The Science of Subjective Experience*, 258–274. New York: Oxford University Press.

DeWitt, C. Baldwin, Jr., Patrick H. Hughes, Scott E. Conard, Carla L. Storr, and David V. Sheehan. 1991. "Substance use among Senior Medical Students: A Survey of 23 Medical Schools." *Journal of the American Medical Association* 265: 2074–2078.

Diaz, Theresa, David Vlahov, Vincent Edwards, Sally Conover, and Edgar Monterroso. 2002. "Sex-Specific Differences in Circumstances of Initiation into Injecting-Drug Use among Young Adult Latinos in Harlem, New York City." *Aids and Behavior* 4 (2; June): 117–122.

Dietrich, Joseph F., and Janette Smith. 1986. "The Nonmedical Use of Drugs Including Alcohol among Police Personnel: A Critical Literature Review." *Journal of Police Science and Administration* 14: 300–306.

Dimeff, Linda A., J. Kilmer, John S. Baer, and Alan G. Marlatt. 1995. "Binge Drinking in College" (letter). *Journal of the American Medical Association* 273: 1903–1904.

Dimeo, Paul. 2007. *A History of Drug Use in Sport 1876-1976: Beyond Good and Evil.* London: Routledge.

Doblin, R., and M. A. R. Kleiman. 1991. "Marihuana as Anti-Emetic Medicine: A Survey of Oncologists' Attitudes and Experiences." *Journal of Clinical Oncology* 9: 1275–1290.

Dole, Vincent P., Marie E. Nyswander, and Alan Warner. 1968. "Successful Treatment of 750 Narcotics Addicts." *Journal of the American Medical Association* 206 (December 16): 2708–2711.

Donovan, J. E., and R. Jessor. 1985. "Structure of Problem Behavior in Adolescence and Young Adulthood." *Journal of Consulting and Clinical Psychology* 53: 890–904.

Donovan, J. E., R. Jessor, and F. M. Costa. 1988. "Syndrome of Problem Behavior in Preadolescence." *Journal of Consulting and Clinical Psychology* 56: 762–765.

Doweiko, Harold E. 1990. *Concepts of Chemical Dependency.* Pacific Grove, CA: Brooks/Cole.

Drug Abuse Warning Network 2002. *Drug Abuse Warning Network: Development of a New Design. Methodology Report.* Washington, DC: Office of Substance Abuse and Mental Health Services Administration, Office of Applied Studies.

———. 2005a. "New DAWN: Why It Cannot Be Compared with Old DAWN." *The New DAWN Report* (September).

———. 2005b. *Drug Abuse Warning Network, 2003: Area Profiles of Drug-Related Mortality.* Washington, DC: Office of Substance Abuse and Mental Health Services Administration, Office of Applied Studies.

Drug Enforcement Administration (DEA). n.d. *Maps of Amphetamine Lab Incidents.* Available online: http://www.usdoj.gov/dea/concern/map_lab_seizures.html (accessed November 9, 2007).

———. 1999. *DEA Briefing Book.* Washington, DC: U.S. Government Printing Office.

———. 2005. *Drugs of Abuse.* Washington, DC: U.S. Government Printing Office. Available Online: http://www.usdoj.gov/dea/pubs/abuse/1-csa.htm#Formal (accessed June 24, 2008).

———. 2008. *Maps of Methamphetamine Lab Incidents.* Available online: http://www.usdoj.gov/dea/concern/map_lab_seizures.html (accessed May 20, 2008).

Drug Policy Alliance. 2002. "Effectiveness of the War on Drugs." Available online: http://www.drugpolicy.org/library/factsheets/effectivenes/index.cfm (accessed 2/28/2008).

Dufour, Mary C. 1999. "What is Moderate Drinking?" *Alcohol Health and Research World* 23 (1): 5–14.

Duncan, David F., Thomas Nicholson, Patrick Clifford, Wesley Hawkins, and Rick Petosa. 1994. "Harm Reduction: An Emerging New Paradigm for Drug Education." *Journal of Drug Education* 24: 281–290.

Dunham, Roger G., and Armand L. Mauss. 1982. "Reluctant Referrals: The Effectiveness of Legal Coercion in Outpatient Treatment for Problem Drinkers." *Journal of Drug Issues* (Winter): 5–20.

Dunlap, Eloise, Bruce d. Johnson, Ellen Benoit, and Stephen J. Sifaneck. 2005. "Sessions, Cyphers, and Parties: Settings for Informal Social Controls of Blunt Smoking." *Journal of Ethnicity in Substance Abuse* 4 (3–4): 43–80.

Durkin, Keith F., and Gregory A. Clark. 2000. *Binge Drinking in a Sample of University Students: Prevalence, Consequences and Correlates.* Lake Charles, LA: McNeese Community Coalition to Prevent Underage Drinking.

Durkin, Keith F., Timothy W. Wolfe, and Gregory Clark. 1999. "Social Bond Theory and Binge Drinking among College Students: A Multivariate Analysis." *College Student Journal* 33: 450–462.

Duster, Troy. 1970. *The Legislation of Morality: Law, Drugs, and Moral Judgment.* New York: Free Press.

EAPC. *See* European Association for Palliative Care, Expert Working Group.

Eaton, Danice K., Laura Kann, Steve Kinchen, Shari Shanklin, James Ross, Joseph Hawkins, William A. Harris, Richard Lowry, Tim McManus, David Clyen, Connie Lim, Nancy D. Brener, and Howell Wechsler. 2008. *Youth Risk Behavior Surveillance–United States, 2007.* Morbity and Mortality Weekly Report (MMWR) 57 (SS-7; June 6): 1–131.

Economist. 1999. "A Field Full of Buttons." *The Economist* 351 (8113): 27.

Eddy, Mark. 2006. "War on Drugs: The National Youth Anti-Drug Media Campaign." *CRS Report for Congress* (July 3). Available online: http://italy.usembassy.gov/pdf/other/RS21490.pdf (accessed April 30, 2008).

Eggert, Leona L., and Jerald R. Herting. 1991. "Preventing Teenage Drug Abuse." *Youth & Society* 22: 482–524.

Eggert, Leona, Liela Nicholas, and Linda Owen. 1995. *Reconnecting Youth: A Peer Group Approach to Building Life Skills.* Bloomington, IN: National Education Service.

Eggert, Leona L., Christine D. Seyl, and Liela J. Nicholas. 1990. "Effects of a School-Based Prevention Program for Potential High School Dropouts and Drug Abusers." *The International Journal of the Addictions* 25: 773–801.

Eisenberg, T. 1975. "Labor Management Relations and Psychological Stress." *Police Chief* 42: 54–58.

Eitzen, D. Stanley, and George H. Sage. 2003. *Sociology of North American Sport,* 7th ed. Boston: McGraw-Hill.

El-Bassel, Nabila, Louisa Gilbert, Elwin Wu, Hyun Go, and Jennifer Hill. 2005. "Relationship Between Drug Abuse and Intimate Partner Violence: A Longitudinal Study among Women Receiving Methadone." *American Journal of Public Health* 95 (3; March): 465–470.

Eldred, C. A., and M. M. Washington. 1976. "Interpersonal Relationships in Heroin Use by Men and Women and Their Role in Treatment Outcome." *International Journal of the Addictions* 11: 117–130.

Eliyahu, Uri, Shai Berlin, Eran Hadad, Yuval Heled, and Daniel S. Moran. 2007. "Psychostimulants and Military Operations." *Military Medicine* 172 (4): 383–387.

Ellickson, Phyllis L. 1995. "Schools." In Robert H. Coombs and Douglas M. Ziedonis (eds.), *Handbook on Drug Abuse Prevention: A Comprehensive Strategy* to *Prevent the Abuse of Alcohol and Other Drugs,* 93–120. Boston: Allyn and Bacon.

Ellickson, Phyllis L., Robert M. Bell, and Ellen R. Harrison. 1993. "Changing Adolescent Propensities to Use Drugs: Results from Project ALERT." *Health Education Quarterly* 20: 227–242.

Elliot, Delbert S. 2001. *NYS Family Study: Problem Alcohol Use and Problem Behavior.* NIH Grant Award #1 RO1 AA11949-01A2. Bethesda, MD: National Institute on Alcohol Abuse and Alcoholism.

Elliott, Delbert S., David Huizinga, and Scott Menard. 1989. *Multiple Problem Youth: Delinquency, Substance Use and Mental Health Problems.* New York: Springer-Verlag.

Elwood, W. N., and M. L. Williams. 1997. "Powerlessness and HIV Prevention among People Who Trade Sex for Drugs ('Strawberries')." *AIDS Care* 9 (3; June): 273–284.

Employment Division of Oregon v. Smith, 494 U.S. 872 (1990).

Engs, Ruth. 1982. "Drinking Patterns and Attitudes Toward Alcoholism of Australian Human-Service Students." *Journal of Studies on Alcohol* 43: 517–531.

Ennett, Susan T., Nancy S. Tobler, Christopher L. Ringwalt, and Robert L. Flewelling. 1994. "How Effective Is Drug Abuse Resistance Education? A Meta-Analysis of Project DARE Outcome Evaluations." *American Journal of Public Health* 84: 1394–1401.

Epstein, Edward Jay. 1977. *Agency of Fear: Opiates and Political Power in America.* New York: G.P. Putnam's Sons.

Epstein, Jennifer A., Gilbert J. Botvin, and Tracy Diaz. 2001. "Linguistic Acculturation Associated with Higher Marijuana and Polydrug Use among Hispanic Adolescents." *Substance Use & Misuse* 36 (4): 477–499.

Erickson, Carlton K. 2007. *The Science of Addiction: From Neurobiology to Treatment.* New York: W.W. Norton and Company.

Erikson, Patricia G., Jennifer Butters, Patti McGillicuddy, and Ase Hallgren. 2000. "Crack and Prostitution: Gender, Myths and Experiences." *Journal of Drug Issues* 30 (4): 767–788.

Erowid Experience Vaults. 2000. Raoul, "I Felt my Soul being Ripped from my Body." Available online: http://www.erowid.org/experiences/exp.php?ID=1877 (accessed May 20, 2008).

European Association for Palliative Care, Expert Working Group. 1996. "Morphine in Cancer Pain: Modes of Administration." *British Medical Journal* 312: 823–826.

Evans, Richard I., Richard M. Rozelle, Maurice Mittelmark, William B. Hansen, Alice L. Bane, and Janet Havis. 1978. "Deterring the Onset of Smoking in Children: Knowledge of Immediate Psychological Effects and Coping with Peer Pressure, Media Pressure, and Parent Modeling." *Journal of Applied Social Psychology* 8: 126–135.

Fagan, Jeffrey. 1990. "Intoxication and Aggression." In Michael Tonry and James Q. Wilson (eds.), *Drugs and Crime,* 241–320. Chicago: University of Chicago Press.

————. 1994. "Women and Drugs Revisited: Female Participation in the Cocaine Economy." *Journal of Drug Issues* 24 (Winter–Spring): 179–225.

Fagan, Jeffrey, Joseph G. Weis, Yu-the Cheng, and John K. Watters. 1987. *Drug and Alcohol Use, Violent Delinquency, and Social Bonding: Implications for theory and Intervention*. San Francisco: URSA Institute.

Faley, Robert H., Lawrence S. Kleiman, and Patricia S. Wall. 1988. "Drug Testing in the Public and Private-Sector Workplaces: Technical and Legal Issues." *Journal of Business and Psychology* 3: 154–186.

Faupel, Charles E. 1981. "Drug Treatment and Criminality: Methodological and Theoretical Considerations." In James A. Inciardi (ed.), *The Drugs-Crime Connection*, 183–206. Beverly Hills, CA: Sage Publications.

————. 1985. "A Theoretical Model for a Socially Oriented Drug Treatment Policy." *Journal of Drug Education* 15: 189–203.

————. 1986. "Heroin Use, Street Crime, and the 'Main Hustle': Implications for the Validity of Official Crime Data." *Deviant Behavior* 7: 31–45.

————. 1987a. "Heroin Use and Criminal Careers." *Qualitative Sociology* 10 (2; Summer): 115–131.

————. 1987b. "Drug Availability, Life Structure and Situational Ethics of Heroin Addicts." *Urban Life* 15 (3; January): 395–419.

————. 1991. *Shooting Dope: Career Patterns of Hard Core Heroin Users*. Gainesville, FL: University of Florida Press.

Faupel, Charles E., and Penelope J. Hanke. 1993. "A Comparative Analysis of Drug-Using Women with and without Treatment Histories in New York City." *The International Journal of the Addictions* 28: 233–248.

Fay, Calvina L. 1996. "The Economic Value of Drug Prevention in Companies." Paper read in Zurich, Switzerland, June 22. Available online: http://sarnia.com/groups/antidrug/wrldnews/Economic.html (accessed June 2, 2008).

Fay, John. 1991. *Drug Testing*. Boston: Butterworth-Heinemann.

FBI. *See* Federal Bureau of Investigation.

Federal Bureau of Investigation (FBI). 1995. *Crime in the United States*. Available Online: http://www.fbi.gov (accessed September 20, 2008).

————. 2005. *Crime in the United States*. Washington, DC: U.S. Government Printing Office. Available online: http://www.fbi.gov (accessed September 20, 2008).

————. 2007. *Crime in the United States*. Washington, DC: U.S. Government Printing Office. Available online: http://www.fbi.gov (accessed September 20, 2008).

Federation of State Medical Boards. 1998. *Model Guidelines for the Use of Controlled Substances for the Treatment of Pain*. Available Online: http://www.fda.gov/ohrms/dockets/ac/03/briefing/3978B1_07_C-FDA-Tab%206.pdf. (Accessed March 30, 2009).

Fell, James C. 1987. "Alcohol Involvement Rates in Fatal Crashes: A Focus on Young Drivers and Female Drivers." *Proceedings of the 31st Annual Conference of the American Association for Automotive Medicine*, 23–42. Washington, DC: Center for Statistics and Analysis.

Fell, James C., and Robert B. Voas. 2006. "The Effectiveness of Reducing Illegal Blood Alcohol Concentration (BAC) Limits for Driving: Evidence for Lowering the Limit to .05 BAC." *Journal of Safety Research* 37 (3; June): 233–243.

Fell, Ronald D., Wayne C. Richard, and William L. Wallace. 1980. "Psychological Job Stress and the Police Officer." *Journal of Police Science and Administration* 8: 139–144.

Fergusson, David M., and L. John Horwood. 2000. "Does Cannabis Use Encourage Other Forms of Illicit Drug Use?" *Addiction* 95: 505–520.

Ferraiolo, Kathleen. 2007. "From Killer Weed to Popular Medicine: The Evolution of American Drug Control Policy, 1937–2000." *The Journal of Policy History* 19 (2): 147–179.

Fiddle, Seymore. 1963. "The Addict Culture and Movement into and out of Hospitals." In U.S. Senate Judiciary Committee Hearings, 3154–3162. Washington, DC: U.S. Government Printing Office.

———. 1976. "Sequences in Addiction." *Addictive Diseases: An International Journal* 2 (4): 553–568.

Field, Gary. 1992. "Oregon Based Drug Treatment Programs." In Carl G. Leukefeld and Frank M. Tims (eds), *Drug Abuse Treatment in Prisons and Jails* 142–155. NIDA Research Monograph Series #118. Washington DC: U.S. Government Printing Office.

Fields, Allen and James M. Walters. 1985. "Hustling: Supporting a Heroin Habit." In Bill Hanson, George Beschner, James M. Walters, and Elliot Bovelle (eds.), *Life with Heroin: Voices from the Inner City*, 49-73. Lexington, MA: Lexington Books.

Finnegan, Loretta P., and Kevin O'Brien Fehr. 1980. "The Effects of Opiates, Sedative-Hypnotics, Amphetamines, Cannabis, and Other Psychoactive Drugs on the Fetus and Newborn." In Oriana Josseau Kalant (ed.), *Alcohol and Drug Problems in Women*, 653–723, Vol. 5 in the series *Research Advances in Alcohol and Drug Problems*. New York: Plenum Press.

Fishbein, Diana H. 2000. "Neuropsychological Function, Drug Abuse, and Violence: A Conceptual Frmaework." *Criminal Justice & Behavior* 27: 139–159.

Fishbein, Diana H., and Susan E. Pease. 1990. "Neurological Links Between Substance Abuse and Crime." In Lee Ellis and Harry Hoffman (eds.), *Crime in Social, Biological and Moral Contexts*, 218–243. New York: Praeger.

Fitzgerald, T., L. Lundgren, and D. Chassler. 2007. "Factors Associated with HIV/AIDS High-Risk Behaviors among Female Injection Drug Users." *AIDS Care* 19 (1): 67–74.

Fitzpatrick, Joseph P. 1990. "Drugs and Puerto Ricans in New York City." In Ronald Glick and Joan Moore (eds.), *Drugs in Hispanic Communities*, 103–126. New Brunswick, NJ: Rutgers University Press.

Flay, Brian R. 1987. "Mass Media and Smoking Cessation." *American Journal of Public Health* 77: 153–160.

Fluke, Betty J., and Lillian R. Donato. 1959. "Some Glues Are Dangerous: Heavy Inhalation Can Cause Anemia or Brain Damage." *Empire Magazine,* supplement to the *Denver Post,* August 2, 24.

Flynn, Stephen. 1997. "Worldwide Drug Scourge: The Expanding Trade in Illicit Drugs." In Larry K. Gaines and Peter B. Kraska (eds.), *Drugs, Crime and Justice: Contemporary Perspectives,* 147–157. Prospect Heights, IL: Waveland Press. (Originally "Worldwide Drug Scourge: The Expanding Trade in Illicit Drugs." *The Brookings Review* 11 (1): 6–11 (1993).

Ford, Jason. 2007a. "Alcohol Use among College Students: A Comparison of Athletes and Nonathletes." *Substance Use and Misuse* 42: 1367–1377.

———. 2007b. "Substance Use among College Athletes: A Comparison Based on Sport/Team Affiliation." *Journal of American College Health* 55 (6): 367–373.

Ford, Julie M., and Andrew A. Beveridge. 2006. "Neighborhood Crime Victimization, Drug Use and Drug Sales: Results from the 'Fighting Back' Evaluation." *Journal of Drug Issues* 36 (2; Spring): 393–416.

Fossier, A. E. 1931. "The Marijuana Menace." *New Orleans Medical Surgical Journal* 84: 247.

Freeland, Jeffrey B., and Richard S. Campbell. 1973. "The Social Context of First Marijuana Use." *The International Journal of the Addictions* 8: 317–324.

French, Michael T., M. Christopher Roebuck, and Pierre Kébreau Alexandre. 2004. "To Test or Not to Test: Do Workplace Drug Testing Programs Discourage Employee Drug Use?" *Social Science Research* 33: 45–63.

Freudenrich, Craig C. 2000. "How Breathalyzers Work." Available online: http://www.howstuffworks.com/breathalyzer.htm (accessed June 2, 2008.)

Friedman, Jennifer, and Marixsa Alicea. 2001. *Surviving Heroin: Interviews with Women in Methadone Clinics.* Gainesville, FL: University Presses of Florida.

Friedman, Milton. 1972. "Prohibition and Drugs." *Newsweek,* May 1.

Frieze, Irene Hanson, and Patricia Cooney Schafer. 1984. "Alchol Use and Marital Violence: Female and Male Differences in Reactions to Alcohol." In Sharon C. Wilsnack and Linda J. Beckman (eds.), *Alcohol Problems in Women: Antecedents, Consequences and Intervention,* 260–279. New York: Guilford Press.

Fromme, Kim, and Julie Wendel. 1995. "Beliefs about the Effects of Alcohol on Involvement in Coercive and Consenting Sexual Activity." *Journal of Applied Social Psychology* 25 (23): 2099–2117.

Fu, Alex Z., Gordon G. Liu, and Dale B. Christensen. 2004. "Inappropriate Medication Use and Health Outcomes in the Elderly." *Journal of the American Geriatric Society* 52: 1934–1939.

Fullilove, Mindy Thompson, and Anne Lown. 1992. "*Crack 'hos* and *Skeezers*: Traumatic Experiences of Women *Crack* Users." *Journal of Sex Research* 29: 275–287.

Fullilove, R. E., Mindy Thompson Fullilove, B. P. Bowser, and S. A. Gross. 1990. "Risk of Sexually Transmitted Diseases among Black Adolescent Crack Users in Oakland and San Francisco, California." *Journal of the American Medical Association* 263: 851–855.

Fuqua, Paul. 1978. *Drug Abuse: Investigation and Control.* New York: McGraw-Hill.

Gable, R. S. 1993. "Toward a Comprehensive Overview of Dependence Potential and Acute Toxicity of Psychoactive Substances Used Nonmedically." *American Journal of Drug and Alcohol Abuse* 19: 263–281.

Galliher, John F., David P. Keys, and Michael Elsner. 1998. "Lindesmith v. Anslinger: An Early Government Victory in the Failed War on Drugs." *Journal of Criminal Law and Criminology* 88 (2): 661–682.

Gamella, Juan F., and Maria Luisa Jiménez Rodrigo. 2004. "A Brief History of Cannabis Policies in Spain (1968–2003)." *Journal of Drug Issues* 34 (3; Summer): 623–659.

Gamble, John W. 2004. "In the Presence of the Divine: The Use of Hallucinogens in Religious Practice." In C. K. Robertson (ed.), *Religion and Alcohol: Sobering Thoughts,* 111–144. New York: Peter Lang.

Gandossy, Robert P., Jay R. Williams, Jo Cohen, and Henrick J. Harwood. 1980. *Drugs and Crime: A Survey and Analysis of the Literature.* Washington, DC: National Institute of Justice.

Gawin, Frank H. 1991. "Cocaine Addiction: Psychology and Neurophysiology." *Science* 251 (March 29): 1580–1586.

Gendreau, Paul, and L. P. Gendreau. 1970. "The Addiction-Prone Personality: A Study of Canadian Heroin Addicts." *Canadian Journal of Behavioral Science* 2: 18–25.

Gerber, Jonathan K., and George S. Yacoubian Jr. 2001. "Evaluation of Drug Testing in the Workplace: Study of the Construction Industry." *Journal of Construction Engineering and Management* (November–December): 438–444.

Gerstein, Dean R., and Lawrence W. Green. 1993. *Preventing Drug Abuse: What Do We Know?* Washington, DC: National Academy Press.

Gfroerer, Joseph C., Li-Tzy Wu, and Michael A. Penne. 2002. *Initiation of Marijuana Use: Trends, Patterns, and Implications.* Analytic Series: A-17, DHHS Publication No. SMA 02-3711. Rockville, MD: Substance Abuse and Mental Health Services Administration, Office of Applied Studies.

Giacomuzzi, S. M., Y. Riemer, M. Ertl, G. Kemmler, H. Rossler, H. Hinterhuber, and M. Kurz. 2005. "Gender Differences in Health-Related Quality of Life on Admission to a Maintenance Treatment Program." *European Addiction Research* 11: 69–75.

Giancola, Peter R. 2000. "Executive Functioning: A Conceptual Framework for Alcohol-Related Aggression." *Experimental and Clinical Psychopharmacology* 8: 576–597.

———. 2007. "Alcohol and Aggression: A Test of the Attention-Allocation Model." *Psychological Science* 18 (7): 649–655.

Gill, Andrew M., and Robert J. Michaels. 1992. "Does Drug Use Lower Wages?" *Industrial and Labor Relations Review* 45: 419–434.

Gillmore, M. R., R. F. Catalano, D. M. Morrison, E. A. Wells, B. Iritani, and J. D. Hawkins. 1990. "Racial Differences in Acceptability and Availability of Drugs and Early Initiation of Substance Use." *American Journal of Drug and Alcohol Abuse* 16: 185–206.

Gil-Rivas, Virginia, Robert Fiorentine, M. Douglas Anglin, and Ellise Taylor. 1997. "Sexual and Physical Abuse: Do They Compromise Drug Treatment Outcomes?" *Journal of Substance Abuse Treatment* 14: 351–358.

Glasser, Ira. 2000. "American Drug Laws: The New Jim Crow." *Albany Law Review* 63 (3): 703–724.

Gleason, Philip M., Jonathan R. Veum, and Michael R. Pergamit. 1991. "Drug and Alcohol Use at Work: A Survey of Young Workers." *Monthly Labor Review* (August): 3–7.

Glick, Ronald. 1990. "Survival Income and Status: Drug Dealing in the Chicago Puerto Rican Community." In Ronald Glick and Joan Moore (eds.), *Drugs in Hispanic Communities*, 77–101. New Brunswick, NJ: Rutgers University Press.

Goffman, Erving. 1959. "The Moral Career of the Mental Patient." *Psychiatry* 22: 123–142.

———. 1963. *Stigma: Notes on the Management of Spoiled Identity.* Englewood Cliffs, NJ: Prentice-Hall.

Goldberg, Margaret E. 1995. "Substance-Abusing Women: False Stereotypes and Real Needs." *Social Work* 40 (6; November): 789–798.

Goldfried, Marvin R., and Michael Merbaum. 1973. "A Perspective of Self Control." In M. Goldfried and M. Merbaum (eds.), *Behavior Change through Self Control*, 3–34. New York: Holt, Reinhart and Winston.

Goldkamp, John S., and Doris Weiland. 1993. *Assessing the Impact of Dade County's Felony Drug Court.* Washington, DC: U.S. Department of Justice, Office of Justice Programs, National Institute of Justice.

Goldman, Fred. 1981. "Drug Abuse, Crime and Economics: The Dismal Limits of Social Choice." In James A. Inciardi (ed.), *The Drugs-Crime Connection*, 155–182. Beverly Hills, CA: Sage Publications.

Goldstein, Avram, and Harold Kalant. 1990. "Drug Policy: Striking the Right Balance." *Science* 249 (September 28): 1513–1521.

Goldstein, Paul J. 1979. *Prostitution and Drugs.* Lexington, MA: Lexington Books.

———. 1981. "Getting Over: Economic Alternatives to Predatory Street Crime among Street Drug Users." In James A. Inciardi (ed.), *The Drugs-Crime Connection*, 67–84. Beverly Hills, CA: Sage Publications.

———. 1985. "The Drugs/Violence Nexus: A Tripartite Conceptual Framework." *Journal of Drug Issues* (Fall): 493–506.

———. 1990. "Anabolic Steroids: An Ethnographic Approach." In Geraline C. Lin and Lynda Erinoff (eds.), *Anabolic Steroid Abuse*, 74–96. NIDA Research Monograph Series #102. Rockville, MD: National Institute on Drug Abuse.

Goldstein, Paul J., Patricia A. Belluci, Barry J. Spunt, and Thomas Miller. 1991. "Volume of Cocaine Use and Violence: A Comparison Between Men and Women." *Journal of Drug Issues* 21 (2; Spring): 345–367.

Goldstein, Paul, Henry H. Brownstein, Patrick J. Ryan, and Patricia A. Bellucci. 1989. "Crack and Homicide in New York City, 1988: A Conceptually Based Event Analysis." *Contemporary Drug Problems* 16: 651–687.

Goldstein, Paul, Douglas S. Lipton, Edward Preble, Ira Sobel, Tom Miller, William Abbot, William Paige, and Franklin Soto. 1984. "The Marketing of Street Heroin in New York City." *Journal of Drug Issues* 3 (Summer): 553–566.

Golub, Andrew Lang, and Bruce D. Johnson. 1999. "Cohort Changes in Illegal Drug Use among Arrestees in Manhattan: From the Heroin Injection Generation to the Blunts Generation." *Substance Use & Misuse* 34: 1733–1763.

———. 2001. "The Rise of Marijuana as the Drug of Choice among Youthful Adult Arrestees." *National Institute of Justice, Research in Brief* (June). Washington, DC: National Institute of Justice.

Golub, Andrew, Bruce D. Johnson, and Eloise Dunlap. 2005a. "Subcultural Evolution and Illicit Drug Use." *Addiction Research and Theory* 13 (3): 217–229.

———. 2005b. "The Growth in Marijuana Use among American Youths During the 1990's and the Extent of Blunt Smoking." *Journal of Ethnicity in Substance Abuse* 4 (3–4): 1–21.

Golub, Andrew, Bruce D. Johnson, Eloise Dunlap, and Stephen Sifaneck. 2004. "Projecting and Monitoring the Life Course of the Marijuana/Blunts Generation." *Journal of Drug Issues* 34 (Spring): 361–388.

Gomberg, Edith S. Lisansky. 1982. "Historical and Political Perspective: Women and Drug Use." *Journal of Social Issues* 38: 9–23.

Gomberg, Edith S. Lisansky, and Ted D. Nirenberg. 1993. "Antecedents and Consequences." In Edith S. Lisansky Gomberg and Ted D. Nirenberg (eds.), *Women and Substance Abuse*, 118–141. Norwood, NJ: Ablex Publishing.

Gonzales v. O Centro Espirita Beneficiente Uniao do Vegetal, 546 U.S. 418 (2006).

Gonzales v. Raich, 545 U.S. 1 (2005) 352 F.3d 1222.

Goode, Erich. 1970. *The Marijuana Smokers*. New York: Basic Books.

———. 1972. "Excerpts from Marijuana Use and Crime." In National Commission of Marijuana and Drug Abuse, *Marijuana: A Signal of Misunderstanding*, Appendix, Vol. 1, 447–453. Washington, DC: U.S. Government Printing Office.

———. 1975. "Marijuana and the Politics of Reality." In Frank R. Scarpitti and Paul T. McFarlane, *Deviance: Action, Reaction, Interaction*, 170–181. Boston: Addison-Wesley.

———. 1990. "The American Drug Panic of the 1980's: Social Construction or Objective Threat?" *The International Journal of the Addictions*. 25 (9): 1083–1098.

———. 1999. *Drugs in American Society*, 5th ed. New York: McGraw-Hill.

———. 2008. *Drugs in American Society*, 7th ed. New York: McGraw-Hill.

Goodhart, Fern Walter, Linda C. Lederman, Lea P. Stewart, and Lisa Laitman. 2003. "*Binge* Drinking: Not the Word of Choice." *Journal of American College Health* 52 (1; July–August): 44–46.

Gordon, Milton C. 1947. "The Concept of the Sub-Culture and Its Application." *Social Forces* 26 (October): 40–42.

Gorman, D. M. 1998. "The Irrelevance of Evidence in the Development of School-Based Drug Prevention Policy, 1986-1996." *Evaluation Review* 22: 118–146.

Gossop, Michael, John Marsden, and Duncan Stewart. 2000. "The UK National Treatment Outcome Research Study and Its Implications." *Drug and Alcohol Review* 19: 5–7.

Gossop, Michael, John Marsden, Duncan Stewart, and Tara Kidd. 2003. "The National Treatment Outcome Research Study (NTORS): 4–5 Year Follow-Up Results." *Addiction* 98: 291–303.

Gottfredson, M. R., and T. Hirschi. 1990. *A General Theory of Crime*. Stanford, CA: Stanford University Press.

Gould, Leroy, Andrew L. Walker, Lansing E. Crane, and Charles W. Lidz. 1974. *Connections: Notes from the Heroin World*. New Haven, CT: Yale University Press.

Graff, Harold, and John C. Ball. 1976. "The Methadone Clinic: Function and Philosophy." *International Journal of Social Psychiatry* 22: 140–146.

Granfield, Robert, and William Cloud. 1996. "The Elephant that No One Sees: Natural Reocvery among Middle-Class Addicts." *Journal of Drug Issues* 26 (1): 45–61.

Grant, Bridget F., and Devorah A. Dawson. 1996. "Alcohol and Drug Use, Abuse, and Dependence among Welfare Recipients." *American Journal of Public Health* 86 (10; October): 1450–1454.

Grasmick, Harold G., Charles R. Tittle, Robert J. Bursick Jr., and Bruce J. Arneklev. 1993. "Testing the Core Empirical Implications of Gottfredson and Hirschi's General Theory of Crime." *Journal of Research in Crime and Delinquency* 30: 5–29.

Green, Lesley L., Mindy Thomson Fullilove, and Robert E. Fullilove. 1995. "Stories of Spiritual Awakening: The Nature of Spirituality in Recovery." *Journal of Substance Abuse Treatment* 15: 325–331.

Greenberg, Stephanie, and Freda Adler. 1974. "Crime and Addiction: An Empirical Analysis of the Literature, 1920–1973." *Contemporary Drug Problems* 3: 221–270.

Grinspoon, Lester. 1971. *Marijuana Reconsidered*. Cambridge, MA: Harvard University Press.

———. 2000. "Wither Medical Marijuana?" *Contemporary Drug Problems* 27 (Spring): 3–15.

Grinspoon, Lester, and James B. Bakalar. 1976. *Cocaine: A Drug and Its Social Evolution*. New York: Basic Books.

———. 1979. *Psychedelic Drugs Reconsidered*. New York: Basic Books.

Grinspoon, Lester, and James B. Bakalar. 1993. *Marijuana: The Forbidden Medicine.* New Haven, CT: Yale University Press.

———. 1995. "Marihuana as Medicine: A Plea for Reconsideration." *Journal of the American Medical Association* 273 (23): 1875–1876.

———. 1997. *Marijuana: The Forbidden Medicine,* rev. ed. New Haven, CT: Yale University Press.

Grinspoon, Lester, and Peter Hedblom. 1975. *The Speed Culture: Amphetamine Use and Abuse in America.* Cambridge, MA: Harvard University Press.

Grossbard, Joel, Irene Markman Geisner, Clayton Neighbors, Jason R. Kilmer, and Mary E. Larimer. 2007. "Are Drinking Games Sports? College Athlete Participation in Drinking Games and Alcohol-Related Problems." *Journal of Studies on Alcohol and Drugs* 68: 97–105.

Gusfield, Joseph R. 1963. *Symbolic Crusade: Status Politics and the American Temperance Movement.* Urbana, IL: University of Illinois Press.

———. 1967. "Moral Passage: The Symbolic Process in Public Designations of Deviance." *Social Problems* 175: 175–188.

Guterman, Lila. 2000. "The Dope on Medical Marijuana." *Chronical of Higher Education* 46 (39; June 2): A21.

Haarr, Robin N., and Merry Morash. 1999. "Gender, Race, and Strategies of Coping with Occupational Stress in Policing." *Justice Quarterly* 16 (2): 303–336.

Haddock, C. Keith, L. Carrie Parker, Jennifer E. Taylor, Walker S. C. Poston, Harry Lando, and G. Wayne Talcott. 2005. "An Analysis of Messages about Tobacco in Military Installation Newspapers." *American Journal of Public Health* 95 (8): 1458–1463.

Haggerty, Kevin, Rick Kosterman, Richard F. Catalano, and J. David Hawkins. 1999. "Preparing for the Drug Free Years." *Juvenile Justice Bulletin* (July): 1–11 Washington, DC: Office of Juvenile Justice and Delinquency Prevention.

Halifors, Denise, Hyunsan Cho, Victoria Sanchez, Shereen Khatapoush, Hyung Min Kim, and Daniel Bauer. 2006. "Efficacy vs. Effectivness Trial Results of an Indicated 'Model' Substance Abuse Program: Implications for Public Health." *American Journal of Public Health* 96 (12; December): 2254–2259.

Hall, Wayne. 1997. "Evidence-Based Treatment for Drug Misuse: Bridging the Gap Between Aspiration and Achievement." *Addiction* 92 (4): 373–374.

Halpern, John H. 2004. "Hallucinogens and Dissociative Agents Naturally Growing in the United States." *Pharmacology and Therapeutics* 102: 131–138.

Halpern, John H., and R. Andrew Sewell. 2005. "Hallucinogenic Botanicals of America: A Growing Need for Focused Drug Education and Research." *Life Sciences* 78: 519–526.

Hammersley, Richard, and Valerie Morrison. 1987. "Effects of Polydrug Use on the Criminal Activities of Heroin Users." *British Journal of Addiction* 82: 899–906.

Hanke, Penelope J., and Charles E. Faupel. 1993. "Women Opiate Users' Perceptions of Treatment Services in New York City." *Journal of Substance Abuse Treatment* 10: 513–522.

Hanlon, Joseph T., Gerda G. Fillenbaum, Christine M. Ruby, Shelly Gray, and Arline Bohannon. 2001. "Epidemiology of Over-the-Counter Drug Use in Community Dwelling Elderly: United States Perspective." *Drugs and Aging* 18 (2): 123–131.

Hanlon, Thomas E., David N. Nurco, Timothy W. Kinlock, and Karen R. Duszynski. 1990. "Trends in Criminal Activity and Drug Use Over an Addiction Career." *Journal of Drug Issues* 16: 223–238.

Hansen, William B., C. Anderson Johnson, Brian R. Flay, John W. Graham, and Judith Sobel. 1988. "Affective and Social Influences Approaches to the Prevention of Multiple Substance Abuse among Seventh Grade Students: Results from Project SMART." *Preventive Medicine* 17: 135–154.

Hanson, Bill, George Beschner, James W. Walters, and Elliot Bovelle. 1985. *Life with Heroin: Voices From the Inner City*. Lexington, MA: Lexington Books.

Hanson, Meredith. 1993. "Overview on Drug and Alcohol Testing in the Workplace." *Bulletin on Narcotics* 2: 3–44.

Harachi, Tracy W., Richard F. Catalano, Sunah Kim, and Yoonsun Choi. 2001. "Etiology and Prevention of Substance Use among Asian American Youth." *Prevention Science* 2 (1): 57–65.

Hardesty, Monica, and Timothy Black. 1999. "Mothering Through Addiction: A Survival Strategy among Puerto Rican Addicts." *Qualitative Health Research* 9: 602–619.

Hargrove, Barbara. 1989. *The Sociology of Religion: Classical and Contemporary Approaches*, 2nd ed. Arlington Heights, IL: Harlan Davidson.

Harris, David A. 1998. "Car Wars: The Fourth Amendment's Death on the Highway." *The George Washington Law Review* 66: 556–591.

Harris, Mervyn. 1973. *The Dilly Boys*. Rockville, MD: New Perspectives.

Harris, Michael M., and Laura L. Heft. 1992. "Alcohol and Drug Use in the Workplace: Issues, Controversies, and Directions for Future Research." *Journal of Management* 18: 239–266.

Harrison, Lana D. 2001. "Understanding the Differences in Youth Drug Prevalence Rates Produced by the MTF, NHSDA and YRBS Studies." *Journal of Drug Issues* 31 (3): 665–694.

Harrison, Lana D., Patricia G. Erickson, Edward Adlaf, and Charles Freeman. 2001. "The Drugs-Violence Nexus among American and Canadian Youth." *Substance Use & Misuse* 36 (14): 2065–2086.

Hartjen, Clayton A., S. M. Mitchell, and N. F. Washburne. 1981. "Sentencing to Therapy: Some Legal, Ethical and Practical Issues. *Journal of Offender Counseling, Services and Rehabilitation* 6: 21–39.

Hartwell, Tyler D., Paul D. Steele, Michael T. French, and Nathaniel F. Rodman. 1996. "Prevalence of Drug Testing in the Workplace." *Monthly Labor Review* 119 (11; November): 35–42.

Harwood, Henrick, Douglas Fountain, and Gina Livermore. 1998. *The Economic Costs of Alcohol and Drug Abuse in the United States—1992*. Washington, DC: National Institute on Drug Abuse.

Hathaway, Andrew D. 2004. "Cannabis Careers Reconsidered: Transitions and Trajectories of Committed Long-Term Users." *Contemporary Drug Problems* 31 (Fall): 401–423.

Hawkins, J. David. 1979. "Reintegrating Street Drug Abusers: Community Roles in Continuing Care." In Barry S;. Brown (ed.), *Addicts and Aftercare*, 25–79. Beverly Hills, CA: Sage.

Hayano, David M. 1982. *Poker Faces: The Life and Work of Professional Card Players*. Berkeley, CA: University of California Press.

Hayghe, Howard V., 1991. "Anti-Drug Programs in the Workplace: Are They Here to Stay?" *Monthly Labor Review* 114 (April): 26–29.

Healey, David. 2000. "Emergence of Antidepressant Induced Suicidality." *Primary Care Psychiatry* 6: 23–28.

Hegarty, James D. 1995. "Suicide and Violence Associated with Fluexotine (Prozac)." Available Online: http://suicideandmentalhealthassociationinternational.org/suiporzac.html (accessed April 6, 2009).

Heien, Dale M. and David J. Pittman. 1989. "The Economic Costs of Alcohol Abuse: An Assessment of Current Methods and Estimates." *Journal of Studies on Alcohol* 50: 567–579.

Hellinger, Fred J. 1992. "Forecasts of the Costs of Medical Care for Persons with HIV: 1992–1995." *Inquiry* 29: 356.

Hellinger, Fred J., and John A. Fleishman. 2000. "The National Cost of Treating HIV Disease." *Journal of Aquired Immune Deficiency Syndromes* 24: 182–188.

Hendrickson, James C., and Dean R. Gerstein. 2005. "Criminal Involvement among Young Male Ecstasy Users." *Substance Use & Misuse* 40: 1557–1575.

Hepner, Randal L. 1998. "Chanting Down Babylon in the Belly of the Beast: The Rastafarian Movement in the Metropolitan United States." In N. S. Murrell, W. D. Spencer, and A. A. McFarlane (eds.), *Chanting Down Babylon: The Rastafari Reader*, 99–216. Philadelphia: Temple University Press.

Herd, Denise. 1987. "Rethinking Black Drinking." *British Journal of Addiction* 82: 219–223.

Hesselbrock, Michie N., and Victor M. Hesselbrock. 1993. "Depression and Antisocial Personality in Alcoholism: Gender Comparison." In Edith S. Lisansky Gomberg and Ted D. Nirenberg (eds.), *Women and Substance Abuse*, 142–161. Norwood, NJ: Ablex Publishing.

Hesselbrock, Michie N., Victor M. Hesselbrock, and Elizabeth E. Epstein. 1999. "Theories of Etiology of Alcohol and Other Drug Use Disorders." In Barbara S. McCrady and Elizabeth E. Epstein (eds.), *Addictions: A Comprehensive Guidebook*, 50–72. New York: Oxford University Press.

Hindmarch, Ian, and Rüdiger Brinkmann. 1999. "Trends in the Use of Alcohol and Other Drugs in Cases of Sexual Assault." *Human Psychopharmacology* 14: 225–231.

Hingson, Ralph, Timothy Heeren, Michael Winter, and Henry Wechsler. 2005. "Magnitude of Alcohol-Related Mortality and Morbity among U.S. College

Students Ages 18–24: Changes from 1998–2001." *Annual Review of Public Health* 26: 259–279.

Hirschi, Travis. 1969. *Causes of Delinquency.* Berkeley, CA: University of California Press.

———. 2004. "Self-Control and Crime." In Roy F. Baumeister and Kathleen D. Vohs (eds.), *Handbook of Self-Regulation: Research, Theory and Applications,* 537–552. New York: Guilford Press.

Hitz, D. 1973. "Drunken Sailors and Others: Drinking Problems in Specific Occupations." *Quarterly Journal of Studies on Alcohol* 34: 496–505.

Hoaken, Peter N. S., and Sherry H. Stewart. 2003. "Drugs of Abuse and the Elicitation of Human Aggressive Behavior." *Addictive Behaviors* 28: 1533–1554.

Hobbs, Thomas R. 1998. "Managing Alcoholism as a Disease." *Physicians News Digest* (February). Available online: http://www.physiciansnews.com/commentary/298wp.html (accessed June 2, 2008).

Hodgson, Thomas A., and Mark R. Meiners. 1982. "Cost-of-Illness Methodology: A Guide to Current Practices and Procedures." *Milbank Memorial Fund Quarterly* 60: 429–462.

Hoffman, John P., Angela Brittingham, and Cindy Larison. 1996. *Drug Use among U.S. Workers: Prevalence and Trends by Occupation and Industry Categories.* Rockville, MD: Substance Abuse and Mental Health Services Administration.

Hoffman, John P., Felicia Gray Cerbone, and S. Susan Su. 2000. "A Growth Curve Analysis of Stress and Adolescent Drug Use." *Substance Use and Misuse* 35 (5): 687–716.

Hoffman, John P., and S. Susan Su. 1997. "The Conditional Effects of Stress on Delinquency and Drug Use: A Strain Theory Assessment of Sex Differences." *Journal of Research in Crime and Delinquency* 34 (1): 46–79.

Holden, Constance. 1990. "Hairy Problems for New Drug Testing Method." *Science* 249 (September 7): 1099–2000.

Hollinger, Richard C. 1988. "Working Under the Influence (WUI): Correlates of Employees' Use of Alcohol and Other Drugs." *Journal of Applied Behavioral Science* 24: 439–454.

Holtman, Matthew C. 2007. "Disciplinary Careers of Drug-Impaired Physicians." *Social Science and Medicine* 64: 543–553.

Horowitz, Alan. 2000. "Narcotics Anonymous." In Clifton D. Bryant (ed.), *Encyclopedia of Criminology and Deviant Behavior*, Vol. 4, 438–442. Philadelphia: Taylor and Francis.

Horvath, Miranda, and Jennifer Brown. 2007. "Alcohol as Drug of Choice: Is Drug-Assisted Rape a Misnomer?" *Psychology, Crime and Law* 13 (5; October): 417–429.

Howard, Andrea A., Julia H. Arnsten, and Marc N. Gourevitch. 2004. "Effect of Alcohol Consumption on Diabetes Mellitus." *Annals of Internal Medicine* 140: 211–219.

Hrywna, Mary, Christine D. Delnevo, Eric S. Pevzner, and Kiane J. Abatemarco. 2004. "Correlates of Bide Use among Youth." *American Journal of Health Behavior* 28 (2): 173–179.

Hser, Yih-Ing, M. Douglas Anglin, and Chih-Ping Chou. 1988. "Evaluation of Drug Abuse Treatment: A Repeated Measures Design Assessing Methadone Maintenance." *Evaluation Review* 12: 547–570.

Hser, Yih-Ing, M. Douglas Anglin, and William McGlothlin. 1987. "Sex Differences in Addict Careers 1: Initiation of Use." *American Journal of Drug and Alcohol Abuse* 13: 33–57.

Hubbard, Robert L., Gail Craddock, and Jill Anderson. 2003. "Overview of 5-Year Followup Outcomes in the Drug Abuse Treatment Outcome Studies (DATOS)." *Journal of Substance Abuse Treatment* 25: 125–134.

Hubbard, Robert L., Mary Ellen Marsden, J. Valley Rachal, Henrick J. Harwood, Elizabeth R. Cavanaugh, and Harold M. Ginzburg. 1989. *Drug Abuse Treatment: A National Study of Effectiveness*. Chapel Hill, NC: The University of North Carolina Press.

Hughes, Carmel M. 2004. "Medication Non-Adherence in the Elderly: How Big is the Problem?" *Drugs Aging* 21 (12): 793–811.

Hughes, Everett C. 1958. *Men and their Work*. Glencoe, IL: Free Press.

Hughes, Patrick H., DeWitt C. Baldwin Jr., David V. Sheehan, Scott Conard, and Carla Storr. 1992. "Resident Physician Substance Use, by Specialty." *American Journal of Psychiatry* 149: 1348–1354.

Hughes, Patrick H., Nancy Brandenburg, DeWitt C. Baldwin Jr., Carla L. Storr, Dristine M. Williams, James C. Anthony, and David V. Sheehan. 1992. "Prevalence of Substance Use among U.S. Physicians." *Journal of the American Medical Association* 267: 2333–2339.

Huizinga, David, and Cynthia Jakob-Chien. 1998. "The Contemporaneous Co-Occurrence of Serious and Violent Juvenile Offending and Other Problem Behaviors." In R. Loeber and D. Farrington (eds.), *Serious and Violent Juvenile Offenders: Risk Factors and Successful Interventions*, 47–67. Thousand Oaks, CA: Sage.

Hunt, Dana. 1990. "Drugs and Consensual Crimes: Drug Dealing and Prostitution." Pp. 159–202 iIn Michael Tonry and James Q. Wilson (eds.), *Drugs and Crime*, 159–202. Chicago: University of Chicago Press.

Hunt, Geoffrey, and Kristin Evans. 2003. "Dancing and Drugs: A Cross-National Perspective." *Contemporary Drug Problems* 30 (Winter): 779–814.

Hutton, Fiona. 2005. "Risky Business: Gender, Drug Dealing and Risk." *Addiction Research and Theory* 13 (6): 545–554.

Hurd, Peter D., C. Anderson Johnson, Terry Pechacek, L. Peter Bast, David R. Jacobs, and Russell V. Luepker. 1980. "Prevention of Cigarette Smoking in Seventh Grade Children." *Journal of Behavioral Medicine* 3: 15–28.

Hyde, Gordon L., and James Wolf. 1995. "Alcohol and Drug Use by Surgery Residents." *Journal of the American College of Surgeons* 181: 1–5.

Iglehart, Austin S. 1985. "Brickin' it and Going to the Pan: Vernacular in the Black Inner-City Heroin Lifestyle." In Bill Hanson, George Beschner, James W. Walters and Elliot Bovelle (eds.) *Life With Heroin: Voices From the Inner City*, 111–133. Lexington, MA: Lexington Books.

Ihde, Aaron J. 1982. "Food Controls Under the 1906 Act." In James Harvey Young (ed.), *The Early Years of Federal Food and Drug Control*, 40–50. Madison, WI: American Institute of the History of Pharmacy.

Inciardi, James A. 1975. *Careers in Crime*. Chicago: Rand-McNally Publishing Co.

———. 1977. "The Changing Life of Mickey Finn: Some Notes on Chloral Hydrate Down Through the Ages." *Journal of Popular Culture* 11 (3): 591–596.

———. 1979. "Heroin Use and Street Crime." *Crime and Delinquency* (July): 335–346.

———. 1981a. "Introduction." In James A. Inciardi (ed.), *The Drugs-Crime Connection*, 7–16. Beverly Hills, CA: Sage Publications.

———. 1981b. "Marijuana Decriminalization Research: A Perspective and Commentary." *Criminology* 19: 145–159.

———. 1988. "Compulsory Treatment in New York: A Brief Narrative History of Misjudgment, Mismanagement, and Misrepresentation." *Journal of Drug Issues* 18: 547–560.

———. 1992. *The War on Drugs II*. Mountain View, CA: Mayfield Publishing Co.

———. 2002. *The War on Drugs III*. Boston: Allyn & Bacon.

———. 2004. "Proposition 36: What Did You Really Expect?" *Criminology and Public Policy* 3 (4; November): 593–598.

Inciardi, James A., Dorothy Lockwood, and Anne E. Pottieger. 1993. *Women and Crack-Cocaine*. New York: MacMillan Publishing Co.

Inciardi, James A., and Duane C. McBride. 1989. "Legalization: A High Risk Alternative in the War on Drugs." *American Behavioral Scientist* 32: 259–289.

Inciardi, James A. and Karen McElrath. 1998. *The American Drug Scene*, 2nd ed. Los Angeles: Roxbury.

Inciardi, James A., J. Ryan Page, Duane C. McBride, Dale D. Chitwood, Clyde B. McCoy, and H. Virginia McCoy. 1995. "The Risk of Exposure to HIV-Contaminated Needles and Syringes in Shooting Galleries." In James A. Inciardi and Karen McElrath (eds.), *The American Drug Scene: An Anthology*, 277–283. Los Angeles, CA: Roxbury Publishing Co.

Inciardi, James A., and Anne E. Pottieger. 1994. "Crack-Cocaine Use and Street Crime." *Journal of Drug Issues* 24: 273–292.

———. 1998. "Drug Use and Street Crime in Miami: Ann (Almost) Twenty-Year Retrospective." *Substance Use & Misuse* 33 (July): 1839–1870.

Inciardi, James A., and Robert A. Rothman. 1990. *Sociology: Principles and Applications*. New York: Harcourt, Brace, Jovanovich.

Inciardi, James A., and Christine A. Saum. 1996. "Legalization Madness." *The Public Interest* 123: 72–82.

Inciardi, James A., Hilary L. Suratt, Dale D. Chitwood, and Clyde B. McCoy. 1996. "The Origins of Crack." In Dale D. Chitwood, James E. Rivers, and James A. Inciardi (eds.), *The American Pipe Dream: Crack Cocaine and the Inner City*, 1–14. Fort Worth, TX: Harcourt Brace.

Institute for Substance Abuse Research. 1990. *Drugs of Abuse Digest: A Prevention Guide for the Family, School and Workplace*, 6th ed. Vero Beach FL: ISAR.

International Olympic Committee. 2000. *Olympic Movement Anti-Doping Code, Appendix A: Prohibited Classes of Substances and Prohibited Methods, 1st April, 2000.* Available online: http://www.nodoping.org/pos_anti_dop_code_e.html (accessed 27 June 2000).

Internet Mental Health. n.d. "Disulfiram." Available online: http://www.mentalhealth.com/drug/p30-a02.html (accessed June 2, 2008).

Ioannou, C. 1992. "Media Coverage versus Fluoxetine as the Cause of Suicidal Ideation." *American Journal of Psychiatry* 149: 572.

Irwin, John. 1980. *Prisons in Turmoil.* Boston: Little, Brown and Company.

Jackson, Rodney, Robert Scragg, and Robert Beaglehole. 1991. "Alcohol Consumption and Risk of Coronary Heart Diseease." *British Medical Journal* 303 (July 27): 211–216.

Jacobs, Barry. 1987. "How Hallucinogenic Drugs Work." *American Scientist* 75 (4): 386–392.

Jacobs, Bruce A. 1999. *Dealing Crack: The Social World of Streetcorner Selling.* Boston: Northeastern University Press.

Jacobs, James. 1989. *Drunk Driving: An American Dilemma.* Chicago: University of Chicago Press.

———. 1990. "Imagining Drug Legalization." *The Public Interest* 101: 28–42.

Jacobson, Mireille. 2003. "Drug Testing in the Trucking Industry: The Effect on Highway Safety." *Journal of Law and Economics* 46 (1; April): 131–157.

Jaffe, Jerome. 1979. The Swinging Pendulum: The Treatment of Drug Abusers in America. In: Dupont RI, Goldstein A, O'Donnell J eds. *Handbook on Drug Abus,* 3-16. Washington, DC: U.S. Government Printing Office.

James, Jennifer, Cathleen T. Gosho, and Robin Watson. 1976. "The Relationship Between Female Criminality and Drug Use." In Research Triangle Institute (ed.), *Drug Use and Crime: Report of the Panel on Drug Use and Criminal Behavior,* 441–455. National Technical Information Service Publication No. PB-259-167. Springfield, VA: U.S. Department of Commerce.

Janofsky, Michael. 2000. "Antidrug Program's End Stirs Up Salt Lake City," *New York Times,* September 15: B1.

Jellinek, Elvin M. 1960. *The Disease Concept of Alcoholism.* Highland Park, NJ: Hillhouse.

Jenkins, Philip. 2001. "The 'Ice Age': Social Construction of a Drug Panic." In James A. Inciardi and Karen McElrath (eds.), *The American Drug Scene,* 3rd ed, 231–247. Los Angeles: Roxbury.

Jessor, Richard. 1979. "Marihuana: A Review of Recent Psychosocial Research. In R. L. Dupont, A. Goldstein, & J.O'Donnell (Eds.), *Handbook on Drug Abuse,* 337–355. Washington, DC: U.S. Government Printing Office.

Jessor, Richard, and Shirley Jessor. 1977. *Problem Behavior and Psychosocial Development—A Longitudinal Study of Youth.* New York: Academic Press.

Jick, Susan S., Alan D. Dean, and Hershel Jick. 1995. "Antidepressants and Suicide." *British Medical Journal* 310: 215–218.

Jin Fuey Moy v. United States, 254 U.S. 189 (1920).

Johnson, Bruce D. 1973. *Marijuana Users and Drug Subcultures*. New York: Wiley.

———. 1980. "Toward a Theory of Drug Subcultures." In Dan J. Lettieri, Molly Sayers, and Helen Wallenstein Pearson (eds.), *Theories on Drug Abuse: Selected Contemporary Perspectives*, 110–119. Rockville, MD: National Institute on Drug Abuse.

Johnson, Bruce D., Flutura Bardhi, Stephen J. Sifaneck, and Eloise Dunlap. 2006. "Marijuana Argot as Subculture Threads: Social Constructions by Users in New York City." *British Journal of Criminology* 46: 46–77.

Johnson, Bruce D., Paul J. Goldstein, Edward Preble, James Schmeidler, Douglas S. Liptom, Barry Spunt, and Thomas Miller. 1985. *Taking Care of Business: The Economics of Crime by Heroin Abusers*. Lexington, MA: Lexington Books.

Johnson, Bruce D., Mangai Natarajan, Eloise Dunlap, and Elsayed Elmoghazy. 1994. "Crack Abusers and Noncrack Abusers: Profiles of Drug Use, Drug Sales and Nondrug Criminality." *Journal of Drug Issues* 24: 117–141.

Johnson, Chris W. 2007. "The Systemic Effects of Fatigue on Military Operations." *System Safety 2007: 2nd Institution of Engineering and Technology International Conference*, October 22–24, 2007. Available online: http://ieeexplore.ieee.org/stamp/stamp.jsp?arnumber=4399900&isnumber=4399889 (accessed November 6, 2008).

Johnson, Sandra H. 2003. "Providing Relief to Those in Pain: A Retrospective on the Scholarship and Impact of the Mayday Project." *Journal of Law, Medicine and Ethics* 31: 15–20.

———. 2004. "Relieving the Pain: Making Marked Changes to the Way Pain is Treated Through Research, Education and Policy Changes." *Saint Louis School of Law Magazine* (Spring): 10–12.

Johnson-Hill, Jack A. 1995. *I-Sight: The World of Rastafari: An Interpretive Sociological Account of Rastafarian Ethics*. Metuchen, NJ: Scarecrow Press.

Johnston, Lloyd D. 1973. *Drugs and American Youth*. Ann Arbor, MI: Institute for Survey Research. Rockville, MD: National Institute on Drug Abuse.

Johnston, Lloyd D., Patrick M. O'Malley, and Jerald G. Bachman. 2000. *Monitoring the Future National Results on Adolescent Drug Use: Overview of Key Findings, 1999*. Rockville, MD: National Institute on Drug Abuse.

———. 2003. *Teen smoking continues to decline in 2003, but declines are slowing* (December 19). Ann Arbor, MI: University of Michigan News and Information Services. Available online: www.monitoringthefuture (accessed May 30, 2008).

———. 2007. "Trends in 30-Day Prevalence of Use of Various Drugs for 8th, 10th, 12th Graders, 1991–2006." Available online: www.monitoringthefuture.org; (accessed October 22, 2007).

Johnston, Lloyd D., Patrick M. O'Malley, Jerald G. Bachman, and John E. Schulenberg. 2006. *Monitoring the Future National Survey Results on Drug Use, 1975–2005*. Vol. I, *Secondary School Students* (NIH Publication No. 06-5883). Bethesda, MD: National Institute on Drug Abuse.

Johnston, Lloyd D., Patrick M. O'Malley, Jerald G. Bachman, and John E. Schulenberg. 2007a. *National Survey Results on Drug Use from the Monitoring the Future Study, 1975-2006.* Vol. I, *Secondary School Students* (NIH Publication No. 07-6205). Rockville, MD: National Institute on Drug Abuse.

———. 2007b. "Overall, Illicit Drug Use by American Teens Continues Gradual Decline in 2007." Ann Arbor, MI: University of Michigan News and Information Services. Available online: http://www.monitoringthefuture.org (accessed 3/7/2008).

———. 2008. *Monitoring the Future National Results on Adolescent Drug Use: Overview of Key Findings, 2007* (NIH Publication No. 08-6418). Bethesda, MD: National Institute on Drug Abuse. Available online: http://www.monitoringthefuture.org (accessed February 28, 2009).

Joint Committee on New York Drug Law Evaluation. 1978. *The Nation's Toughest Drug Law: Evaluating the New York Experience.* Washington, DC: United States Department of Justice.

Jones, Ernest. 1953. *The Life and Work of Sigmund Freud.* Vol. 1, *The Formative Years and the Great Discoveries, 1856–1900.* New York: Basic Books.

Jones, Hendrée E. 2004. "Practical Considerations for the Clinical Use of Buprenorphine." *Science and Practice Perspectives* 2 (2; August): 4–19.

Joranson, David E., Karen M. Ryan, Aaron M. Gilson, and June L. Dahl. 2000. "Trends in Medical Use and Abuse of Opioid Analgesics." *The Journal of the American Medical Association* 283 (13; April 5): 1710–1714.

Jorquez, Jaime S. 1984. "Heroin Use in the Barrio: Solving the Problem of Relapse or Keeping the Tecato Gusano Asleep." *American Journal of Drug and Alcohol Abuse* 10: 63–75.

Joy, Janet E., Stanley J. Watson Jr., and John A. Benson Jr. 1999. *Marijuana and Medicine: Assessing the Science Base.* Washington, DC: National Academy Press.

Julien, Robert M. 2001. *A Primer of Drug Action: A Concise Nontechnical Guide to the Actions, Uses, and Side Effects of Psychoactive Drugs,* rev. ed. New York: W.H. Freeman and Company.

Kaestner, Robert. 1991. "The Effects of Illicit Drug Use on the Wages of Young Adults." *Journal of Labor Economics* 8: 318–412.

———. 1994a. "New Estimates of the Effect of Marijuana and Cocaine Use on Wages." *Industrial and Labor Relations Review* 47: 454–470.

———. 1994b. "The Effect of Illicit Drug Use on the Labor Supply of Young Adults." *Journal of Human Resources* 29 (1; Winter): 126–155.

Kandel, Denise. 1973. "Adolescent Marijuana Use: Role of Parents and Peers." *Science* 181 (September 14): 1067–1070.

———. 1975. "Stages in Adolescent Involvement in Drug Use." *Science* 190: 912–914.

Kandel, Denise, Kevin Chen, and Andrew Gill. 1995. "The Impact of Drug Use on Earnings: A Life-Span Perspective." *Social Forces* 74 (1): 243–270.

Kandel, Denise B., and Mark Davies. 1990. "Labor Force Experiences of a National Sample of Young Adult Men: The Role of Drug Involvement." *Youth and Society* 21: 411–445.

Kandel, Denise B., and Mark Davies. 1991. "Friendship Networks, Intimacy, and Illicit Drug use in Young Adulthood: A Comparison of Two Competing Theories." *Criminology* 29 (August): 441–469.

Kandel, Denise B., and Kazuo Yamaguchi. 1993. "From Beer to Crack: Developmental Patterns of Drug Involvement." *American Journal of Public Health* 83: 851–855.

Kandel, Denise B., Kazuo Yamaguchi, and Kevin Chen. 1992. "Stages of Progression in Drug Involvement from Adolescence to Adulthood: Further Evidence for the Gateway Theory." *Journal of Studies on Alcohol* 53: 447–457.

Kaplan, John. 1983. *The Hardest Drug: Heroin and Public Policy.* Chicago: University of Chicago Press.

Karan, Lori D. 1989. "AIDS Prevention and Chemical Dependence Treatment Needs of Women and Their Children." *Journal of Psychoactive Drugs* 21: 395–399.

Karmen, Andrew. 2007. *Crime Victims: An Introduction to Victimology.* Belmont, CA: Thomson Publishing.

Kaufman, Marc J., Jonathan M. Levin, Marjorie H. Ross, Nicholas Lange, Stephanie L. Rose, Thellea J. Kukes, Jack H. Mendelson, Scott E. Lukas, Bruce M. Cohen, and Perry F. Renshaw. 1998. "Cocaine-Induced Cerebral Vasoconstriction Detected in Humans with Magnetic Resonance Angiography." *Journal of the American Medical Association* 279 (5; February 4): 376–380.

Kaukinen, Catherine, and Alfred DeMaris. 2005. "Age at First Sexual Qassault and Current Substance Use and Depression." *Journal of Interpersonal Violence* 20 (10; October): 1244–1270.

Keh, Douglas I. 1991. "Friendship Networks, Intimacy, and Illicit Drug use in Young Adulthood: A Comparison of Two Competing Theories." *Criminology* 29 (August): 441–469.

———. 1996. *Drug Money in a Changing World: Economic Reform And Criminal Finance.* UNDCP Technical Series #4. Vienna, Austria: UN Office for Drug Control and Crime Prevention.

Kelly, Brian C. 2005. "Bongs and Blunts: Notes from a Suburban Marijuana Subculture." *Journal of Ethnicity in Substance Abuse* 4 (3–4): 81–97.

Kemp, Kathleen, Barry Savitz, William Thompson, and David A. Zanis. 2004. "Developing Employment Services for Criminal Justice Clients Enrolled in Drug User Treatment Programs." *Substance Use & Misuse* 39 (13–14): 2491–2511.

Kennet, Joel, and Joseph Gfroerer (eds.). 2005. *Evaluating and Improving Methods Used in the National Survey on Drug Use and Health.* DHHS Publication No. SMA 05-4044, Methodology Series, 5. Rockville, MD: Substance Abuse and Mental Health Services Administration, Office of Applied Studies.

Khantzian, E. J., and John E. Mack. 1994. "How AA Works and Why It's Important for Clinicians to Understand." *Journal of Substance Abuse Treatment* 11: 77–92.

King, Rufus. 1972. *The Drug Hang Up: America's Fifty-Year Folly*. Springfield, IL: Charles C. Thomas Publishers.

King, Ryan S. 2008. *Disparity by Geography: The War on Drugs in America's Cities*. Washington, DC: The Sentencing Project. Available online: http://www.sentencingproject.org/Admin/Documents/publications/dp_drugarrestreport.pdf (accessed October 15, 2008).

Kinlock, Timothy W., Kevin E. O'Grady, and Thomas E. Hanlon. 2003. "Prediction of the Criminal Activity of Incarcerated Drug-Abusing Offenders." *Journal of Drug Issues* 33 (4; Fall): 897–920.

Kirby, Michael, Aisling Denihan, Irene Bruce, Alicia Radic, Davis Coakley, and Brian A. Lawlor. 1999. "Benzodiazepine Use among the Elderly in the Community." *International Journal of Geriatric Psychiatry* 14: 280–284.

Kitzinger, Sheila. 1969. "Protest and Mysticism: The Rastafari Cult of Jamaica." *Journal for the Scientific Study of Religion* 8: 240–262.

Kiyaani, Mike, and Thomas J. Csordas. 1997. "On the Peyote Road: Worlds of the Shaman." *Natural History* 106 (2): 48–50.

Klatsky, Arthur L. 1999. "Moderate Drinking and Reduced Risk of Heart Disease." *Alcohol Health and Research World* 23 (1): 15–22.

Kleber, Herbert D. 1994. "Our Current Approach to Drug Abuse: Progress, Problems, Proposals." *New England Journal of Medicine* 330 (5): 361–365.

Kleber, Herbert D., and Frank Slobetz. 1979. "Outpatient Drug-Free Treatment." In Robert DuPont, Avram Goldstein, and John O'Donnel (eds.), *Handbook on Drug Abuse*, 31–38. Rockville, MD: National Institute on Drug Abuse.

Kleiman, Mark A. R. 1985. "Drug Enforcement and Organized Crime." In Herbert E. Alexander and Gerald E. Caiden (eds.), *The Politics and Economics of Organized Crime*, 67–87. Lexington, MA: D.C. Heath.

Kleiman, Mark A. R., and Kerry D. Smith. 1990. "State and Local Drug Enforcement: In Search of a Strategy." In Michael Tonry and James Q. Wilson (eds.), *Drugs and Crime*, 69–108. Chicago: University of Chicago Press.

Koch Crime Institute. 1999. "Manufacturing of Methamphetamine." Available online: http://www.kci.org/meth_info/making_meth.htm (accessed June 3, 2008).

Kolb, Lawrence. 1925. "Drug Addiction and its Relation to Crime." *Mental Hygiene* 9: 74–89.

Koob, George F., and Michel Le Moal. 2008. "Addiction and the Brain Antireward System." *Annual Review of Psychology* 59: 29–53.

Kopstein, Andrea N., and Joseph C. Gfroerer. 1991. "Drug Use Patterns and Demographics of Employed Drug Users: Data from the 1988 National Household Survey on Drug Abuse." In Steven W. Gust et al. (eds.), *Drugs in the Workplace: Research and Evaluation Data*, 11–24. NIDA Drug Abuse Reesearch Monograph Series, No. 100. Rockville, MD: National Institute on Drug Abuse.

Körner, Harald Hans. 2004. "From Blind Repression to a Thoughtful Differentiated, 'Four-Column' Strategy." *Journal of Drug Issues* 34 (3; Summer): 577–585.

Krahn, Dean D. 1993. "The Relationship of Eating Disorders and Substance Abuse." In Edith S. Lisansky Gomberg and Ted D. Nirenberg (eds.), *Women and Substance Abuse*, 286–313. Norwood, NJ: Ablex Publishing.

Kramer, Mark S. 1983. "Pharmacotherapy for Violent Behavior." In E. Gottheil, K. A. Druley, T. E. Skoloda, and H. M. Waxman (eds.), *Alcohol, Drug Abuse and Aggression*, xx–xx. Springfield, IL: Charles C. Thomas.

Kranzler, Henry R., and Raymond F. Anton. 1994. "Implications of Recent Neuropsychopharmacologic Research for Understanding the Etiology and Development of Alcoholism." *Journal of Consulting and Clinical Psychology* 62: 1116–1126.

Krauthamer, Gordon. 1998. "The Effectiveness of Preemployment Drug Testing." Paper prepared for the class Drugs and American Society, University of Maryland, College Park, Fall.

Krebs, Christopher P., and Kanielle M. Steffey. 2005. "Club Drug Use among Delinquent Youth." *Substance Use & Misuse* 40: 1363–1379.

Kroes, William H. 1976. *Society's Victims—The Police: An Analysis of Job Stress in Policing*. Springfield, IL: Charles C. Thomas.

Kroes, William H., B. L. Margolis, and J. J. Hurrell. 1974. "Job Stress in Policemen." *Journal of Police Science and Administration* 2: 145–155.

Ksir, Charles, Carl L. Hart, and Oakley Ray. 2008. *Drugs, Society and Human Behavior*, 12th ed. Boston: McGraw-Hill.

Kubrin, Charis, and Eric A. Stewart. 2006. "Predicting Who Reoffends: The Neglected Role of Neighborhood Context in Recidivism Studies." *Criminology* 44 (1; February): 165–197.

Laign, Jeffrey. 1987. "How Far Have We Really Come, Baby? Women's Addiction Treatment in 1987." *Focus* 10 (5): 14–15, 29–31.

Lane, Sandra D. 1993. "Needle Exchange: A Brief History." *The Aegis Law Library*. Available online: http://www.aegis.com/law/journals/1993/HKFNE009.html (accessed March 13, 2008).

Lange, W. Robert, B. Rodrigo Cabanilla, Gerri Moler, Kiane L. Frankenfield, and Paul J. Fudala. 1994. "Preemployment Drug Screening at The Johns Hopkins Hospital, 1989 and 1991." *American Journal of Drug and Alcohol Abuse* 20: 35–46.

Langevin, R., J. Bain, G. Wortzman, S. Hucker, R. Dickey, and P. Wright. 1988. "Sexual Sadism: Brain, Blood and Behavior." *Annals of the New York Academy of Sciences* 528: L163–171.

Lanternari, Vittorio. 1965. *The Religions of the Oppressed*. New York: Mentor Books.

Larson, Sharon L., Joe Eyerman, Misty S. Foster, and Joseph C. Gfroerer. 2007. *Worker Substance Use and Workplace Policies and Programs*. DHHS Publication No. SMA 07-4273, Analytic Series A-29. Rockville, MD: Substance Abuse and Mental Health Services Administration, Office of Applied Studies.

Laties, Victor G., and Bernard Weiss. 1981. "The Amphetamine Margin in Sports." *Federation Proceedings* 40: 2689–2692.

Laundergan, J. Clark. 1982. *Easy Does It: Alcoholism Treatment Outcomes, Hazelden and the Minnesota Model.* Center City, MN: Hazelden Foundation.

Lawrence, Jeffrey T. 1990. "The War on Drugs and Denominational Preferences: Farewell to Strict Scrutiny Analysis." *Brigham Young University Law Journal* (3): 1083–1105.

Leape, Lucian L., and John A. Fromson. 2006. "Problem Doctors: Is There a System-Level Solution?" *Annals of Internal Medicine* 144 (2): 107–116.

Le Dain Commission. 1972. *A Report of the Commission of Inquiry into the Non-Medical Use of Drugs.* Ottowa, Ontario: Information Canada.

Legal Action Center. 1989. "The Drug-Free Workplace Act: Background Materials." New York: Legal Action Center.

Lehrer, Evelyn L., Kathleen Crittenden, and Kathleen F. Norr. 2002. "Illicit Drug Use and Reliance on Welfare." *Journal of Drug Issues* 32 (1; Winter): 179–208.

Lemert, Edwin. 1951. *Social Pathology.* New York: McGraw-Hill.

Lender, Mark Edward, and James Kirby Martin. 1987. *Drinking in America: A History,* rev. ed. New York: The Free Press.

Leonard, Wilbert Marcellus, II. 1998. *A Sociological Perspective of Sport.* Boston: Allyn and Bacon.

LeRoy, Michael H. 1991. "Discriminating Characteristics of Union Members' Attitudes Toward Drug Testing in the Workplace." *Journal of Labor Research* 12: 453–466.

Leshner, Alan I. 1999. "Science-Based Views of Drug Addiction and Its Treatment," *The Journal of the American Medical Association* (October 13): 1320–1321.

———. 2003. "Accessing Opiate Dependence Treatment Medications: Buprenorphine Products in an Office Setting." *Drug and Alcohol Dependence* 70 (2; Supplement): S103–S104.

Lessem, Jeffrey M., Christian J. Hopfer, Brett C. Haberstick, David Timberlake, Marissa A. Ehringer, Andrew Smolen, and John K. Hewitt. 2006. "Relationship Between Adolescent Marijuana Use and Young Adult Illicit Drug Use." *Behavior Genetics* 36 (4; July): 498–506.

Leukenfeld, Carl G., and Frank M. Tims. 1990. "Compulsory Treatment for Drug Abuse." *The International Journal of the Addictions* 25: 621–640.

Levine, Samuel M. 1973. *Narcotics and Drug Abuse.* Cincinnati: Anderson Publishing Company.

Levy, Judith A., and Tammy Anderson. 2005. "The Drug Career of the Older Addict." *Addiction Research and Theory* 13 (3; June): 245–258.

Levy, Sharon, Sion K. Harris, Lon Sherritt, Michelle Angulo, and John R. Knight. 2006. "Drug Testing of Adolescents in General Medical Clinics, in School and at Home: Physician Attitudes and Practices." *Journal of Adolescent Health* 38: 336–342.

Lewis, Linden. 1989. "Living in the Heart of Babylon: Rastafari in the USA." *Bulletin of Eastern Caribbean Affairs* 15 (1): 20–30.

Lewis, Rupert. 1998. "Marcus Garvey and the Early Rastafarians: Continuity and Discontinuity." In N. S. Murrell, W. D. Spencer, and A. A. McFarlane (eds.), *Chanting Down Babylon: The Rastafari Reader*, 145–158. Philadelphia: Temple University Press.

Lewis, William F. 1993. *Soul Rebels: The Rastafari*. Prospect Heights, IL: Waveland Press.

Lex, Barbara W. 1993. "Women and Illicit Drugs: Marijuana, Heroin and Cocaine." In Edith S. Lisansky Gomberg and Ted D. Nirenberg (eds.), *Women and Substance Abuse*, 162–190. Norwood, NJ: Ablex Publishing.

Lichtenstein, Bronwen. 1997. "Women and Crack-Cocaine Use: A Study of Social Networks and HIV Risk in an Alabama Jail Sample." *Addiction Research* 5 (4): 279–296.

Lieberson, Alan D. 1999. *Treatment of Pain and Suffering in the Terminally Ill*. Available online: http://www.preciouslegacy.com (accessed June 3, 2008).

Light, Arthur B., and Edward G. Torrance. n.d. (1929 or 1930). *Opium Addiction*. Chicago: American Medical Association.

Lightwood, James, David Collins, Helen Lapsley, and Thomas E. Novotny. 2000. "Estimating the Costs of Tobacco Use." In Jha Prabhat and Frank Chaloupka (eds.), *Tobacco Control in Developing Countries*, 63–103. Oxford, U.K.: Oxford University Press.

Lightwood, James M., Ciaran S. Phibbs, and Stanton A. Glantz. 1999. "Short-Term Health and Economic Benefits of Smoking Cessation: Low Birth Weight." *Pediatrics* 104: 1312–1320.

Linder v. United States, 268 U.S. 5 (1925).

Lindesmith, Alfred R. 1938. "A Sociological Theory of Drug Addiction," *The American Journal of Sociology* 43: 593–613.

———. 1940. "'Dope-Fiend' Mythology." *Journal of Criminal Law and Criminology* 31: 199–208.

———. 1965. *The Addict and the Law*. Bloomington, IN: Indiana University Press.

Lindesmith, Alfred R., and John H. Gagnon. 1964. "Anomie and Drug Addiction." In Marshall B. Clinard (ed.), *Anomie and Deviant Behavior*, 158–188. New York: The Free Press.

Lindsay, Vicki. 2008. "Police Officers and Their Alcohol Consumption: Should We Be Concerned?" *Police Quarterly* 11 (1): 74–87.

Lingeman, Richard R. 1974. *Drugs from A to Z: A Dictionary*. New York: McGraw-Hill.

Lipp, Martin R., and Samuel G. Benson. 1972. "Physician Use of Marijuana, Alcohol and Tobacco." *American Journal of Psychiatry* 129: 612–616.

Lipton, Douglas S., and Michael J. Maranda. 1983. "Detoxification from Heroin Dependency: An Overview of Method and Effectiveness." *Advances in Alcohol and Substance Abuse* 2: 31–55.

Liska., Ken 1990. *Drugs and the Human Body*, 3rd ed. New York: Collier-MacMillan Publishers.

Liska, Ken. 2004. *Drugs and the Human Body*, 7th ed. New York: MacMillan Publishing Co.

Little, Ruth E., and Judith K. Wendt. 1993. "The Effects of Maternal Drinking in the Reproductive Period: An Epidemiologic Review." In Edith S. Lisansky Gomberg and Ted D. Nirenberg (eds.), *Women and Substance Abuse*, 191–213. Norwood, NJ: Ablex Publishing.

Logue, A. W. 1986. *The Psychology of Eating and Drinking*. New York: W.H. Freeman and Company.

Lofland, John. 1969. *Deviance and Identity*. Englewood Cliffs, NJ: Prentice-Hall.

Luck, Philip A., Kirk W. Elifson, and Claire E. Sterk. 2004. "Female Drug Users and the Welfare System: A Qualitative Exploration." *Drugs: Education, Prevention and Policy* 11 (2; April): 113–128.

Luckenbill, David F., and Joel Best. 1981. "Careers in Deviance and Respectability: The Analogy's Limitations." *Social Problems* 29 (2; December): 197–206.

Lum, Paula J., Clare Sears, and Joseph Guydish. 2005. "Injection Risk Behavior among Women Syringe Exchangers in San Francisco." *Substance Use & Misuse* 40: 1681–1696.

Lund, Adrian K., David F. Preusser, Richard D. Blomberg, and Allan F. Williams. 1989. "Drug Use by Tractor-Trailer Drivers." In Steven W. Gust and J. Michael Walsh (eds.), *Drugs in the Workplace: Research and Evaluation Data*, 47–67. NIDA Research Monograph 91. Rockville, MD: National Institute on Drug Abuse.

Lundberg, George D. 1972. "Urine Drug Screening: Chemical McCarthyism." *The New England Journal of Medicine* 287 (14): 723–724.

Lurie, P., A. Reingold, and D. Bowser. 1994. *The Public Health Impact of Needle Exchange and Bleach Distribution Programs in the United States and Abroad*. Washington, DC: National Academy Press.

Lynam, Donald R., Richard Millich, Rick Zimmerman, Scott P. Novak, T. K. Logan, Catherine Martin, Carl Leukefeld, and Richard Clayton. 1999. "Project DARE: No Effects at 10-Year Follow-Up." *Journal of Consulting and Clinical Psychology* 67: 590–593.

Maccoby, E. E., and J. N. Jacklin. 1974. *The Psychology of Sex Differences*. Palo Alto, CA: Stanford University Press.

MacCoun, Robert J., James P. Kahan, James Gillespie, and Jeeyang Rhee. 1993. "A Content Analysis of the Drug Legalization Debate." *Journal of Drug Issues* 23 (4; Fall): 615–630.

MacCoun, Robert, Beau Kilmer, and Peter Reuter. 2003. "Research on Drugs-Crime Linkages: The Next Generation" In *Toward a Drugs and Crime Research Agenda for the 21st Century*, 65–95. National Institute of Justice Special Report. Washington DC: National Institute of Justice.

MacGregor, Scott N., Louis G. Keith, Ira J. Chasnoff, Marvin A. Rosner, Gay M. Chisum, Patricia Shaw, and John P. Minogue. 1987. "Cocaine Use During Pregnancy: Adverse Perinatal Outcome." *American Journal of Obstetrics and Bynecology* 157: 686–690.

Maddux, James F. 1988. "Clinical Experience with Civil Commitment." In Carl G. Leukefeld and Frank M. Tims (eds.), *Compulsory Treatment of Drug Abuse: Research and Clinical Practice*, 35–56. National Institute on Drug Abuse Research Monograph Series #86. Washington, DC: U.S. Government Printing Office.

Maddux, James F., Sue K. Hoppe, and Raymond M. Costello. 1986. "Psychoactive Substance Use among Medical Students." *American Journal of Psychiatry* 143: 187–191.

Magura, Stephen. 2007. "Drug Prohibition and the Treatment System: Perfect Together." *Substance Use & Misuse* 42 (2–3): 495–501.

Maher, Lisa. 1990. "Criminalizing Pregnancy: The Downside of a Kinder, Gentler Nation?" *Social Justice* 17 (3): 111–135.

———. 1992. "Punishment and Welfare: Crack Cocaine and the Regulation of Mothering." *Women and Criminal Justice* 3 (2): 35–70.

———. 1997. *Sexed Work: Gender, Race and Resistance in a Brooklyn Drug Market*. Oxford: Clarendon Press.

Maher, Lisa, and Kathleen Daly. 1996. "Women in the Street-Level Drug Economy: Continuity or Change?" *Criminology* 34 (4): 465–490.

Malcolm, Barris P., Michie N. Hesselbrock, and Bernard Segal. 2006. "Multiple Substance Dependence and Coruse of Alcoholism among Alaska Native Men and Women." *Substance Use & Misuse* 41: 729–741.

Malson, Jennifer L., Eun M. Lee, Ram Murty, Eric T. Moolchan, and Wallace B. Pickworth. 2003. "Clove Cigarette Smoking: Biochemical, Physiological and Subjective Effects." *Pharmacology, Biochemistry and Behavior* 74 (3; February): 739–745.

Maltby, Lewis L. 1999. *Drug Testing: A Bad Investment*. New York: American Civil Liberties Union.

Marcoplos, Lucas. 2006. "Drafting Away from It All." *Southern Cultures* 12 (1): 33–41.

Marcus, Brend. 2004. "Self-Control in the General Theory of Crime: Theoretical Implications of a Measurement Problem." *Theoretical Criminology* 8 (1): 33–55.

Marijuana Policy Project. 2006. *State-by-State Medical Marijuana Laws: How to Remove the Threat of Arrest*. Washington, DC: Marijuana Policy Project.

Marijuana Policy Project. 2008. State-by-State Medical Marijuana Laws: How to Remove the Threat of Arrest. Washington D.C.: Marijuana Policy Project. Available Online: http://www.mpp.org/assets/pdfs/download-materials/SBSR_NOV2008.pdf (accessed April 8, 2009)

Marks, Robert E. 1992. "The Costs of Australian Drug Policy." *Journal of Drug Issues* 22: 535–547.

Marsh, Howard R. 1937. "Untold Tales of the Secret Service." *Liberty* (January 16).

Marsh, Jeanne C. 1982. "Public Issues and Private Problems: Women and Drug Use." *Journal of Social Issues* 38: 153–165.

Marshall, Shelly. 2001. "Rapid Detox No Magic Pill: Program Has Its Shortcomings and Dangers." Available online: http://alcoholism.about.com/library/weekly/aa010115a.htm (accessed June 18, 2008).

Marsiglia, Flavio Francisco, Stephen Kulis, and Michael L. Hecht. 2001. "Ethnic Labels and Ethnic Identity as Predictors of Drug Use among Middle School Students in the Southwest." *Journal of Research on Adolescence* 11 (1): 21–48.

Marsiglia, Flavio Francisco, Stephen Kulis, Michael L. Hecht, and Stephen Sills. 2004. "Ethnicity and Ethnic Identity as Predictors of Drug Norms and Drug Use among Preadolescents in the US Southwest." *Substance Use & Misuse* 39 (7): 1061–1094.

Martin, Daniel. 1999. "Power Play and Party Politics: the Significance of Raving." *Journal of Popular Culture* 32 (4; Spring): 77–99.

Martin, Jack K., and Paul M. Roman. 1996a. "Job Stress, Drinking Networks, and Social Support at Work: A Comprehensive Model of Employees' Problem Drinking Behaviors." *Sociological Quarterly* 37: 579–599.

———. 1996b. "Job Satisfaction, Job Reward Characteristics, and Employees' Problem Drinking Behaviors." *Work and Occupations* 23: 4–25.

Martin, Sandra L., Jennifer L. Beaumont, and Lawrence L. Kupper. 2003. "Substance Use Before and During Pregnancy: Links to Intimate Partner Violence." *American Journal of Drug and Alcohol Abuse* 29 (3; August): 599–617.

Mason, W. Alex, Rick Kosterman, J. David Hawkins, Kevin P. Haggerty, Richard L. Spoth, and Cleve Redmond. 2007. "Influence of a Family-Focused Substance Use Preventive Intervention on Growth in Adolescent Depressive Symptoms." *Journal of Research on Adolescence* 17 (3): 541–564.

Massing, Michael. 1999. "Beyond Legalization: New Ideas for Ending the War on Drugs—It's Time for Realism." *The Nation*, September 20, 11–15.

Matchan, Don C. 1977. *We Mind If You Smoke*. New York: Pyramid Books.

Mathers, Megan, J.W. Toumbourou, R.F. Catalano, J. Williams and G.C. Patton. 2006. "Consequences of Youth Tobacco Use: A Review of Prospective Behavioural Studies." *Addictions* 101 (7; July): 948–958.

Mathews, Ronnie E., Jr., Brendan M. McGuire, and Carlos Estrada. 2006. "Outpatient Management of Cirrhosis: A Narrative Review." *Southern Medical Journal* 99 (6; June): 600–606.

Mathias, Robert. 1996. "Marijuana Impairs Driving Related Skills and Workplace Performance." *NIDA Notes* 11 (1; January–February).

———. 1999. "'Ecstasy' Damages the Brain and Impairs Memory in Humans." *NIDA Notes* 14 (4). Rockville, MD: National Institute on Drug Abuse.

Maxwell, Jane Carlisle. 2005. "Party Drugs: Properties, Prevalence, Patterns and Problems." *Substance Use & Misuse* 40: 1203–1240.

———. 2006. *Diversion and Abuse of Buprenorphine: A Brief Assessment of Emerging Indicators*. Final Report submitted to the Substance Abuse and Mental Health Services Administration. Washington, DC: U.S. Government Printing Office.

Mayfield, Demmie. 1983. "Substance Abuse and Aggression: A Psychopharmacological Perspective." In E. Gottheil, K. A. Druley, T. E. Skoloda, and H. M. Waxman (eds.), *Alcohol, Drug Abuse and Aggression*, 139–149. Springfield, IL: Charles C. Thomas.

Mazerolle, Paul, Velmer S. Burton Jr., Francis T. Cullen, T. David Evans, and Gary L. Payne. 2000. "Strain, Anger, and Delinquent Adaptations: Specifying General Strain Theory." *Journal of Criminal Justice* 28: 89–101.

McAlister, Alfred L., Cheryl Perry, and Nathan Maccoby. 1979. "Adolescent Smoking: Onset and Prevention." *Pediatrics* 63: 650–658.

McAuliffe, William E. 1975. "A Second Look at First Effects: The Subjective Effects of Opiates on Nonaddicts." *Journal of Drug Issues* 5 (Fall): 369–399.

———. 1984. "Nontherapeutic Opiate Addiction in Health Professionals: A New Form of Impairment." *American Journal of Drug and Alcohol Abuse* 10: 1–22.

McAuliffe, William E., and Robert A. Gordon. 1974. "A Test of Lindesmith's Theory of Addiction: The Frequency of Euphoria among Long-Term Addicts," *The American Journal of Sociology* 79: 795–840.

McAuliffe, William E., Mary Rohman, Paul Fishman, Rob Friedman, Henry Wechsler, Stephen H. Soboroff, and David Toth. 1984. "Psychoactive Drug Use by Young and Future Physicians." *Journal of Health and Social Behavior* 25: 34–54.

McAuliffe, William E., Mary Rohman, Susan Santangelo, Barry Feldman, Elizabeth Magnuson, Arthur Sobol, and Loel Weissman. 1986. "Psychoactive Drug Use among Practicing Physicians and Medical Students." *The New England Journal of Medicine* 315: 805–810.

McBride, Robert. 1983. "Business as Usual: Heroin Distribution in the United States." *Journal of Drug Issues* 13: 147–166.

———. 1998. "Illegal Drugs: A Common Threat to the Global Community." Available online: http://www.whitehousedrugpolicy.gov/news/commentary/unchron.html (accessed July 27, 2000).

McCann, U. D., M. Mertl, V. Eligulashvili, and G. A. Ricaurte. 1999. "Cognitive Performance in (+/−) 3,4methylenedioxymethamphetamine (MDMA, 'ecstasy') Users: A Controlled Study." *Psychopharmacology* 143: 417–425.

McCaughan, Jill A., Robert G. Carlson, Russel S. Falck, and Harvey A. Siegal. 2005. "From 'Candy Kids' to 'Chemi-Kids': A Typology of Young Adults Who Attend Raves in the Midwestern United States." *Substance Use & Misuse* 40: 1503–1523.

McCoy, H. Virginia, James A. Inciardi, Lisa R. Metsch, Anne E Pottieger, and Christine A. Saum. 1995. "Women, Crack, and Crime: Gender Comparisons of Criminal Activity among Crack Cocaine Users." *Contemporary Drug Problems* 22: 435–451.

McCoy, H. Virginia, Christine Miles, and James A. Inciardi. 1995. "Survival Sex: Inner-City Women and Crack-Cocaine." In James A. Inciardi and Karen McElrath (eds.), *The American Drug Scene: An Anthology*, 172–177. Los Angeles, CA: Roxbury Publishing Co.

McCrady, B., and S. Delaney. 1995. "Self-Help Groups." In R. Hester and W. Miller (eds.), *Handbook of Alcoholism Treatment Approaches*, 173-175. Boston: Allyn and Bacon.

McDowell, David M., and Henry I. Spitz. 1999. *Substance Abuse: From Principles to Practice*. Philadelphia: Taylor and Francis.

McElrath, Karen. 1998. "Alcoholics Anonymous." In James A. Inciardi and Karen McElrath (eds.), *The American Drug Scene: An Anthology*, 2nd ed., 266–270. Los Angeles: Roxbury Publishing Co.

McElrath, Karen, Dale D. Chitwood, and Mary Comerford. 1997. "Crime Victimization among Injection Drug Users." *Journal of Drug Issues* 27 (4; Fall): 771–783.

McGlothlin, William H., and David O. Arnold. 1971. "LSD Revisited—A Ten-Year Follow-Up of Medical LSD Use." *Archives of General Psychiatry* 24: 35–49.

McGuire, William. 1964. "Inducing Resistance to Persuasion." In Leonard Berkowitz (ed.), *Advances in Experimental Social Psychology*, 191–229. New York: Academic Press.

McKeganey, Neil. 2006. "Safe Injecting Rooms and Evidence Based Drug Policy." *Drugs: Education, Prevention and Policy* 13 (1; February): 1–3.

McLean, Philip. 2003. "Economy of Columbia (sic)." Testimony before the Senate Foreign Relations Committee, October 29. Washington, DC: Center for Strategic and International Studies. Available online: http://www.csis.org/media/csis/congress/ts031029mclean.pdf (accessed November 12, 2008).

Mechanick, Philip, James Mintz, John Gallagher, Gary Lapid, Richard Rubin, and John Good. 1973. "Nonmedical Drug Use among Medical Students." *Archives of General Psychiatry* 29: 48–50.

Mehay, Stephen L., and Rosalie Loccardo Pacula. 1999. *The Effectiveness of Workplace Drug Prevention Policies: Does "Zero Tolerance" Work?* NBER Working Paper No. W7383. Boston, MA: National Bureau of Economic Research.

Mendelson, Jack H., and Nancy K. Mello. 1974. "Alcohol, Aggression and Androgens." In S. H. Frazier (ed.), *Aggression*, 225–247. Baltimore: Williams & Wilkins.

Mensch, Barbara S., and Denise B. Kandel. 1988. "Do Job Conditions Influence the Use of Drugs?" *Journal of Health and Social Behavior* 29: 169–184.

Merlin, Mark David. 1984. *On the Trail of the Opium Poppy*. Rutherford, NJ: Fairleigh Dickinson University Press.

Merton, Robert K. 1938. "Social Structure and Anomie." *American Sociological Review* 3: 672–682.

Messenger, Daniel S., Charles R. Bauer, Abhik Das, Ron Seifer, Barry M. Lester, Linda L. Lagasse, Linda L. Wright, Seetha Shankaran, Henrietta S. Bada, Vincent L. Smeriglio, John C. Langer, Marjorie Beeghly, and W. Kenneth Poole. 2004. "The Maternal Lifestyle Study: Cognitive, Motor, and Behavioral Outcomes of Cocaine-Exposed and Opiate-Exposed Infants through Three Years of Age." *Pediatrics* 113 (6; June): 1677–1685.

Messner, Steven F., and Richard Rosenfeld. 2007. *Crime and the American Dream*, 4th ed. Belmont, CA: Thomson.

Metsch, Lisa R., H. Virginia McCoy, and Norman L. Weatherby. 1996. "Women and Crack." In Dale Chitwood, James E. Rivers, and James A. Inciardi (eds.), *The American Pipe Dream: Crack Cocaine and the Inner City*, 71–88. Fort Worth, TX: Harcourt Brace.

Meyer, H. 1954. *Old English Coffee Houses*. Emmaus, PA: The Rodale Press.

Michalak, Laurence, Karen Trocki, and Jason Bond. 2007. "Religion and Alcohol in the U.S. National Alcohol Survey: How Important is Religion for Abstention and Drinking?" *Drug and Alcohol Dependence* 87: 268–280.

Mieczkowski, Tom, and Kim Lersch. 1997. "Drug Testing in Criminal Justice: Evolving Issues, Emerging Technologies." *National Institute of Justice Journal* 234 (December): 9–15.

Mill, John Stuart. 1975/1859. *Three Essays.* New York: Oxford University Press.

Miller, Norman S., and Norman G. Hoffman. 1995. "Addictions Treatment Outcomes." *Alcoholism Treatment Quarterly* 12 (2): 41–55.

Miller, Sara B. 2005. "Steps Toward More Drug Testing in Schools." *The Christian Science Monitor*, May 20.

Miller, Toby, and Marie Claire Leger. 2003. "A Very Childish Moral Panic: Ritalin." *Journal of Medical Humanities* 24 (1–2): 9–33.

Miller, William R. 1998. "Researching the Spiritual Dimensions of Alcohol and Other Drug Problems." *Addiction* 93 (7): 979–990.

Mills, James. 1987. *The Underground Empire: Where Crime and Governments Embrace.* New York: Dell.

Miron, Jeffrey A. 2001. "The Economics of Drug Prohibition and Drug Legalization." *Social Research* 68 (3; Fall): 835–855.

Moak, Darlene H., and Raymond F. Anton. 1999. "Alcohol." In Barbara S. McCrady and Esizabeth E. Epstein (eds.), *Addictions: A Comprehensive Guidebook,* 75–94. New York: Oxford University Press.

Modlin, H. C., and A. Montes. 1964. "Narcotics Addiction in Physicians." *American Journal of Psychiatry* 121: 358–363.

Moffitt, Terrie E. 1993. "Adolescence-Limited and Life-Course-Persistent Antisocial Behavior: A Developmental Taxonomy." *Psychological Review* 100 (4): 674–701.

———. 1997. "Adolescence-Limited and Life-Course-Persistent Offending: A Pair of Complementary Theories." In T. P. Thornberry (ed.), *Developmental Theories of Crime and Delinquency,* 11–54. New Brunswick, NJ: Transaction Press.

Mohler-Kuo, Meichun, Jae Eun Lee, and Henry Wechsler. 2003. "Trends in Marijuana and Other Illicit Drug Use among College Students: Results From 4 Harvard School of Public Health College Alcohol Study Surveys: 1993–2001." *Journal of American College Health* 52 (1): 17–24.

Moise, Rebecca, Beth G. Reed, and Virginia Ryan. 1982. "Issues in the Treatment of Heroin-Addicted Women: A Comparison of Men and Women Entering Two Types of Drug Abuse Programs." *International Journal of the Addictions* 17: (109–139).

Mokdad, Ali H., James S. Marks, Donna F. Stroup, and Julie L. Gerberding. 2004. "Actual Causes of Death in the United States, 2000." *JAMA* 291 (10): 1238–1246.

Monitoring the Future. 1999. *Purpose and Design.* Ann Arbor, MI: University of Michigan. Available online: http://monitoringthefuture.org/purpose.html (accessed June 3, 2008).

Montagne, Michael, Carol B. Pugh, and Joseph L. Fink III. 1988a. "Testing for Drug Use, Part 1: Analytical Methods." *American Journal of Hospital Pharmacy* 45: 1297–1305.

———. 1988b. "Testing for Drug Use, Part 2: Legal, Social and Ethical Concerns." *American Journal of Hospital Pharmacy* 45: 1509–1522.

Moore, Alan R., and Shaun T. O'Keefe. 1999. "Drug-Induced Cognitive Impairment in the Elderly." *Drugs and Aging* 15 (1; July): 15–28.

Moore, Joan. 1978. *Homeboys: Gangs, Drugs and Prison in the Barrios of Los Angeles.* Philadelphia: Temple University Press.

———. 1990. "Mexican American Women Addicts: The Influence of Family Background." In Ronald Glick and Joan Moore (eds.), *Drugs in Hispanic Communities*, 127–153. New Brunswick, NJ: Rutgers University Press.

———. 1991. *Going Down to the Barrio: Homeboys and Homegirls in Change.* Philadelphia: Temple University Press.

Moore, Roland S., Genevieve, M. Ames, and Carol B. Cunradi. 2007. "Physical and Social Availability of Alcohol for Young Enlisted Naval Personnel in and around Home Port." *Substance Abuse Treatment, Prevention, and Policy* 2: 17–38.

Morgan, H. Wayne. 1981. *Drugs in America: A Social History 1800–1980.* Syracuse, NY: Syracuse University Press.

Morgenstern, Jon, and Jeremy Leeds. 1993. "Contemporary Psychoanalytic Theories of Substance Abuse: A Disorder in Search of a Paradigm." *Psychotherapy* 30 (2): 194–206.

Mort, Jane R., and Rajender R. Aparasu. 2002. "Prescribing of Psychotropics in the Elderly: Why Is It So Often Inappropriate?" *CNS Drugs* 16 (2): 99–109.

Mosher, Clayton J., and Scott Akins. 2007. *Drugs and Drug Policy: The Control of Consciousness Alteration.* Thousand Oaks, CA: Sage Publications.

Mosher, Clayton, Thomas Rotolo, Dretha Phillips, Antoinette Krupski, and Kenneth D. Stark. 2004. "Minority Adolescents and Substance use Risk/Protective Factors: A Focus on Inhalant Use." *Adolescence* 39 (Fall): 489–502.

Moyer, Kenneth E. 1976. *The Psychobiology of Aggression.* New York: Harper and Row.

Mullahy, John, and Jody Sindelar. 1989. "Life-Cycle Effects of Alcoholism on Education, Earnings, and Occupation." *Inquiry* 26: 272–282.

———. 1991. "Gender Differences in Labor Market Effects of Alcoholism." *American Economic Review* 81: 161–165.

———. 1993. "Alcoholism, Work, and Income." *Journal of Labor Economics* 11: 494–520.

Mumola, Christopher J., and Jennifer C. Karberg. 2006. *Drug Use and Dependence, State and Federal Prisoners, 2004.* Washington, DC: Bureau of Justice Statistics.

Muntwyler, Jorg, Charles H. Henekens, Julle E. Buring, and J. Michael Gaziano. 1998. "Mortality and Lithe to Moderate Alcohol Consumption after Myocardial Infarction." *The Lancet* 352 (December 12): 1882.

Murphy, Sheigla, and Dan Waldorf. 1991. "Kickin' Down to the Street Doc: Shooting Galleries in the San Francisco Bay Area." *Contemporary Drug Problems* 18: 9–29.

Murray, David M., C.Anderson Johnson, Russell V. Luepker, and Maurice B. Mittelmark. 1984. "The Prevention of Cigarette Smoking in Children: A Comparison of Four Strategies." *Journal of Applied Social Psychology* 14: 274–289.

Murrell, Nathaniel Samuel. 1998. "Introduction: The Rastafari Phenomenon." In N. S. Murrell, W. D. Spencer, and A. A. McFarlane (eds.), *Chanting Down Babylon: The Rastafari Reader*, 1–19. Philadelphia: Temple University Press.

Murrell, Nathaniel Samuel, and Burchell K. Taylor. 1998. "Rastafari's Messianic Ideology and Caribbean Theology of Liberation." In N. S. Murrell, W. D. Spencer, and A. A. McFarlane (eds.), *Chanting Down Babylon: The Rastafari Reader*, 390–411. Philadelphia: Temple University Press.

Musto, David. 1973. *The American Disease: Origins of Narcotics Control*. New Haven: Yale University Press.

———. 1999. *The American Disease: Origins of Narcotics Control*, 3rd ed. New Haven: Yale University Press.

———. 2001. "They Inhaled." *New York Times Book Review*, August 12, 16.

Nadelmann, Ethan. 1988. "The Case for Legalization." *The Public Interest* 92: 3–31.

———. 1989. "Drug Prohibition in the United States: Costs, Consequences, and Alternatives." *Science* 245 (September 1): 939–947.

———. 1995. "Switzerland's Heroin Experiment." *National Review*, July 10, 46–47.

———. 1997. "Reefer Madness 1997: The New Bag of Scare Tactics." *Rolling Stone*, February 20, 51–53, 77.

———. 1998. "Commonsense Drug Policy." *Foreign Affairs* 77: 111–126.

———. 2002. Personal communication, March 12.

———. 2004. "Criminologists and Punitive Drug Prohibition: To Serve or to Challenge?" *Criminology & Public Policy* 3 (3; July): 441–450.

Nadelmann, Ethan, Jennifer McNeely, and Ernest Drucker. 1997. "International Perspectives." In Joyce H. Lowinson, Pedro Ruiz, Robert B. Millman, and John G. Langrod (eds.), *Substance Abuse: A Comprehensive Textbook*, 3rd ed., 22–39. Baltimore, MD: Williams & Wilkins.

Nakken, Craig. 1988. *The Addictive Personality: Understanding Compulsion in Our Lives*. San Francisco: Harper and Row.

National Association of Drug Court Professionals. 1997. *Defining Drug Courts: The Key Components*. Washington, DC: U.S. Department of Justice.

———. 2006. *The Commercial Value of Underage and Pathological Drinking to the Alcohol Industry*. New York: Columbia University.

National Center for Health Statistics. 2001. "Fastats on Alcohol Use." Available online: http://www.cdc.gov/nchs/fastats/alcohol.htm (accessed November 10, 2008).

National Center for Mental Health Promotion and Youth Violence Prevention. n.d "The New Drug Abuse Resistance Education (D.A.R.E.) Program" Available Online: http://www.promoteprevent.org/publications/EBI-factsheets/New%20 DARE.pdf (accessed April 4, 2009).

National Clearinghouse for Smoking and Health. 1969. *Use of Tobacco*. Washington, DC: U.S. Department of Health, Education and Welfare.

National Commission on Marijuana and Drug Abuse. 1972. *Marihuana: A Signal of Misunderstanding*. Washington, DC: U.S. Government Printing Office.

National Drug Intelligence Center (NDIC). 2001a. *Information Bulletin: OxyContin Diversion and Abuse*. Document No. 2001-L0424-001 (July). Washington, DC: U.S. Government Printing Office.

———. 2001b. *Raves*. USDOJ Information Bulletin. Washington, DC: U.S. Department of Justice.

———. 2005. *National Drug Threat Assessment 2005: Threat Matrix*. Product 2005-Q0317-006. Available online: http://www.usdoj.gov/ndic/pubs11/13817/13817p. pdf (accessed November 12, 2008).

———. 2007a. *Domestic Cannabis Cultivation Assessment 2007*. Available online: http://www.usdoj.gov/ndic/pubs22/22486/ (accessed November 13, 2008).

———. 2007b. *National Drug Threat Assessment 2008*. Product 2007-Q0317-003. Washington, DC: U.S. Department of Justice.

National Institute on Alcohol Abuse and Alcoholism. 2004. *NIAAA Newsletter* (Winter, no. 3). Bethesda, MD: U.S. Department of Health, Education and Welfare.

National Institute on Drug Abuse (NIDA). 1989. *Model Plan for a Comprehensive Drug-Free Workplace Program*. Rockville, MD: National Institute on Drug Abuse.

———. 1996. "Facts about Methamphetamine." *NIDA Notes* 11 (5): Rockville, MD: National Institute on Drug Abuse.

———. 1999. "Cocaine Abuse and Addiction." NIDA Research Report Series, NCADI # PHD813. Rockville, MD: National Institute on Drug Abuse.

———. 2000a. "Club Drugs: What are They?" *NIDA Notes* 14 (6). Bethesda, MD: National Institute of Health.

———. 2000b. "Gender Differences in Drug Abuse Risks and Treatment." *NIDA Notes* 15 (4). Bethesda, MD: National Institute of Health.

———. 2004. *Cocaine Abuse and Addiction*. NIDA Research Report Series, NIH Publication # 99-4342 (originally published May 1999). Rockville, MD: National Institute on Drug Abuse.

———. 2006a. *Methamphetamine Abuse and Addiction*. NIDA Research Report Series, NIH Publication # 06-4210 (originally published April 1998). Rockville, MD: National Institute on Drug Abuse.

———. 2006b. *Tobacco Addiction*. NIDA Research Report Series, NIH Publication # 06-4342 (originally published July 1998). Rockville, MD: National Institute on Drug Abuse.

———. 2006c. "Crack and Cocaine." From NIDA Infofax #13546. Rockville, MD: National Institute on Drug Abuse. Available online: http://www.nida.nih.gov/Infofax/cocaine.html (accessed November 7, 2007).

———. 2006d. "MDMA (Ecstasy) Abuse." Research Report Series, NIH Publication Number 06-4728 (March). Rockville, MD: National Institute on Drug Abuse.

National Organization for the Reform of Marijuana Laws (NORML). n.d.a. "Active State Medical Marijuana Programs." Available online: www.norml.org (accessed November 10, 2007).

———. n.d.b. *Arrests of the Rich and Famous*. Available online: http://www.norml.org/index.cfm?Group_ID=4439 (accessed May 31, 2008).

———. 2004. "States that Have Decriminalized". Available online: http://norml.org/index.cfm?Group_ID=6331 (accessed April 1, 2009).

National Treasury Employees Union v. Von Raab, 489 U.S. 656 (1989).

NDIC. *See* National Drug Intelligence Center.

Neal, Dan J., and Kim Fromme. 2007. "Hook 'em Horns and Heavy Drinking: Alcohol Use and Collegiate Sports." *Addictive Behaviors* 32: 2681–2693.

Nellis, Muriel. 1980. *The Female Fix*. New York: Penguin Books.

Nelson, David E., Paul Mowery, Scott Tomar, Stephen Marcus, Gary Giovino, and Luhua Zhao. 2006. "Trends in Smokeless Tobacco Use among Adults and Adolescents in the United States." *American Journal of Public Health* 96 (5; May): 897–905.

Nelson, Toben F., and Henry Wechsler. 2003. "School Spirits: Alcohol and Collegiate Sports Fans." *Addictive Behaviors* 28: 1–11.

Neuspiel, D. R., S. C. Hamel, E. Hochberg, J. Greene, and D. Campbell. 1991. "Maternal Cocaine Use and Infant Behavior." *Neurotoxicology and Teratology* 13: 229–233.

Newman, David M. 2008. *Sociology: Exploring the Structure of Everyday Life*, 7th ed. Thousand Oaks CA: Pine Forge.

New York City Transit v. Beazer, 440 U.S., 468 (1979).

Nichter, Mark, Gilbert Quintero, Mimi Nichter, Jeremiah Mock, and Sohalia Shakib. 2004. "Qualitative Research: Contributions to the Study of Drug Use, Drug Abuse, and Drug Use(r)-Related Interventions." *Substance use & Misuse* 39 (10–12): 1907–1969.

NIDA. *See* National Institute on Drug Abuse.

Normand, Jacques, Stephen D. Salyards, and John J. Mahoney. 1990. "An Evaluation of Preemployment Drug Testing." *Journal of Applied Psychology* 75: 629–639.

NORML. *See* National Organization for the Reform of Marijuana Laws.

Nurco, David N., Ira H. Cisin, and Mitchell B. Balter. 1981. "Addict Careers. II. The First Ten Years." *The International Journal of the Addictions* 16: 1327–1356.

Nurco, David N., Thomas E. Hanlon, Timothy W. Kinlock, and Karen R. Duszynski. 1988. "Differential Criminal Patterns of Narcotic Addicts Over an Addiction Career." *Criminology* 26 (3; August): 407–423.

O'Donnell, John A. 1967. "The Rise and Decline of a Subculture." *Social Problems* 15 (1; Summer): 73–84.

Oetting, E. R. 1993. "Orthogonal Cultural Identification: Theoretical Links Between Cultural Identification and Substance Use." In Mario R. De La Rosa and Juan-Luis Recio Adrados (eds.), *Drug Abuse among Minority Youth: Advances in Research and Methodology*, 32–56. NIDA Research Monograph 130. Rockville, MD: National Institute on Drug Abuse.

Office of Applied Studies. 2005. *Drug Abuse Warning Network, 2003: Area Profiles of Drug-Related Mortality*. DAWN Series D-27, DHHS Publication No. (SMA) 05-4023. Rockville, MD: Substance Abuse and Mental Health Services Administration, U.S. Department of Health and Human Services.

———. 2007. *Drug Abuse Warning Network, 2005: National Estimates of Drug-Related Emergency Department Visits*. DAWN Series D-29, DHHS Publication No. (SMA) 07-4256. Rockville, MD: Substance Abuse and Mental Health Services Administration, U.S. Department of Health and Human Services.

Office of National Drug Control Policy (ONDCP). n.d. *National Youth Anti-Drug Media Campaign*. Available Online: http://www.mediacampaign.org/ (accessed April 4, 2009).

———. 1998. *Pulse Check: National Trends in Drug Abuse, Summer 1998*. Washington, DC: U.S. Government Printing Office.

———. 2001a. *National Drug Control Strategy: 2001 Annual Report*. Washington, DC: Executive Office of the President.

———. 2001b. "Demonstrating the Effectiveness of Drug Treatment." Fact Sheet. Washington, DC: U.S. Government Printing Office.

———. 2002a. *National Drug Control Strategy: 2002 Annual Report*. Washington, DC: U.S. Government Printing Office.

———. 2002b. "What You Need to Know about Drug Testing in Schools." Available Online: http://staging.whitehousedrugpolicy.gov/pdf/drug_testing.pdf (accessed April 4, 2009).

———. 2004a. *The Economic Costs of Drug Abuse in the United States 1992–2002*. Washington, DC: Executive Office of the President.

———. 2004b. *Pulse Check: Drug Markets and Chronic Users in 25 of America's Largest Cities* (January). Washington, DC: U.S. Government Printing Office.

———. 2008. *National Drug Control Strategy: FY 2009 Budget Summary* Washington, DC: U.S. Government Printing Office.

Olsen v. DEA, 878 F.2d 1458, 1986.

ONDCP. *See* Office of National Drug Control Policy.

Orwin, Robert, Diane Cadell, Adam Chu, Graham Kalton, David Maklan, Carol Morin, Andrea Piesse, Saneev Sridharan, Diane Steele, Kristie Taylor, and Elena Tracy. 2006. *Evaluation of the National Youth Anti-Drug Media Campaign: 2004 Report of Findings*. Washington, DC: National Institute on Drug Abuse.

Osborne, Carl E., and Jacque J. Sokolov. 1989. "Drug Use Trends in a Nuclear Power Company: Cumulative Data from an Ongoing Testing Program." In Steven W.

Gust and J. Michael Walsh (eds.), *Drugs in the Workplace: Research and Evaluation Data*, 69–80. NIDA Research Monograph 91. Rockville, MD: National Institute on Drug Abuse.

Osgood, D.Wayne., Lloyd D. Johnston, Patrick M. O'Malley, and Jerald G. Bachman. 1988. "The Generality of Deviance in Late Adolescence and Early Adulthood." *American Sociological Review* 53: 81–93.

Oyez Project. 1995. *Vernonia School District v. Acton*, 515 U.S. 646 (1995). Available online: http://www.oyez.org/cases/1990-1999/1994/1994_94_590/ (accessed May 10, 2008).

———. 2002. *Board of Education of Independent School District No. 92 of Pottawatomie County v. Earls*, 536 U.S. 822 (2002). Available online: http://www.oyez.org/cases/2000-2009/2001/2001_01_332/ (accessed April 4, 2009).

Page, J. Bryan. 1990. "Streetside Drug Use among Cuban Drug Users in Miami." In Ronald Glick and Joan Moore (eds.), *Drugs in Hispanic Communities*, 167–191. New Brunswick, NJ: Rutgers University Press.

Palm, Jessica. 2007. "Women and Men—Same Problems, Different Treatment." *International Journal of Social Welfare* 16 (1; January): 18–31.

Pandina, Robert, and Robert Hendren. 1999. "Other Drugs of Abuse: Inhalants, Designer Drugs, and Steroids." In Barbara S. McCrady and Elizabeth E. Epstein (eds.), *Addictions: A Comprehensive Guidebook*, 171–184. New York: Oxford University Press.

Pantilat, Steven Z. 1999. "Just Say Yes: The Use of Opioids for Managing Pain at the End of Life." *The Western Journal of Medicine* 171 (4): 257–259.

Park, Jisuk, Rick Kosterman, J. David Hawkins, Kevin P. Haggerty, Terry E. Duncan, Susan C. Duncan, and Richard Spoth. 2000. "Effects of the 'Preparing for the Drug Free Years' Curriculum on Growth in Alcohol Use and Risk for Alcohol Use in Early Adolescence." *Prevention Science* 1: 125–138.

Parker, Keith D., Greg Weaver, and Thomas Calhoun. 1995. "Predictors of Alcohol and Drug Use: A Multi-Ethnic Comparison." *The Journal of Social Psychology* 135 (5): 581–590.

Parker, Robert Nash. 1995. *Alcohol and Homicide: A Deadly Combination of Two American Traditions*. Albany, NY: State University of New York Press.

Parks, Kathleen A., and Cheryl L. Kennedy. 2004. "Club Drugs: Reasons For and Consequences of Use." *Journal of Psychoactive Drugs* 36 (3; September): 295–302.

Paternoster and Mazerolle. 1994. "General Strain Theory and Delinquency: A Replication and Extension." *Journal of Research in Crime and Delinquency* 31 (3): 253–263.

Payne, Jennifer. 2007. "Women Drug Users in North Cumbria: What Influences Initiation into Heroin in this Non-Urban Setting?" *Sociology of Health & Illness* 29 (5; July): 633–655.

Pearlin, Leonard I., and Clarice W. Radabaugh. 1976. "Economic Strains and the Coping Function of Alcohol." *American Journal of Sociology* 82: 652–663.

Pellegrino, Edmund D. 1998. "Emerging Ethical Issues in Palliative Care." *The Journal of the American Medical Association* 279 (19; May 20): 1521–1522.

Peregoy, Robert M., Walter R. Echo-Hawk, and James Botsford. 1995. "Congress Overturns Supreme Court's Peyote Ruling." *NARF Legal Review* 20 (1): 1, 6–25.

Pernanen, K. 1976. "Alcohol and Crimes of Violence." In B. Kissin and H. Begleiter (eds.), *The Biology of Alcoholism: Social Aspects of Alcoholism*, Vol. 4, 351-444. New York: Plenum.

———. 1981. "Theoretical Aspects of the Relationship between Alcohol Use and Crime." In James J. Collins Jr. (ed.), *Drinking and Crime: Perspectives on the Relationship between Alcohol Consumption and Criminal Behavior*, 1–69. New York: Guilford.

Perry, Cheryl L., Kelli A. Komro, Sara Veblen-Mortenson, Linda M. Bosma, Kian Farbakhsh, Karen A. Munson, Melissa H. Stigler, and Leslie A. Lytle. 2003. "A Randomized Controlled Trial of the Middle and Junior High School D.A.R.E. and D.A.R.E. Plus Programs." *Archives of Pediatrics and Adolescent Medicine* 157: 178–184.

Perry, Cheryl L., Kelli A. Komro, Sara Veblen-dMortenson, Linda Bosma, Karen Munson, Melissa Stigler, Leslie A. Lytle, Jean L. Forster, and Seth L. Welles. 2000. "The Minnesota DARE PLUS Project: Creating Community Partnerships to Prevent Drug Use and Violence." *Journal of School Health* 70 (3; March): 84–88.

Pescor, Michael J. 1942. "Physician Drug Addicts." *Diseases of the Nervous System* 3: 2–3.

Peterson, Russell W. 2000. "A Cure Worse Than Crime" (op-ed). *Wilmington (DE) News Journal*, June 18.

Peterson, Ruth D. 1985. "Discriminatory Decision Making at the Legislative Level: An Analysis of the Comprehensive Drug Abuse Prevention and Control Act of 1970." *Law and Human Behavior* 9: 243–269.

Petry, Nancy M. 2000. "Effects of Increasing Income on Polydrug Use: A Comparison of Heroin, Cocaine and Alcohol Abusers." *Addiction* 95 (5): 705–717.

Pettiway, Leon E. 1997. *Workin' It: Women Living Through Drugs and Crime.* Philadelphia: Temple University Press.

Pisani, Roger G. 1995. "Advertising Industry." In Robert H. Coombs and Douglas M. Ziedonis (eds.), *Handbook on Drug Abuse Prevention: A Comprehensive Strategy to Prevent the Abuse of Alcohol and Other Drugs*, 217–248. Boston: Allyn and Bacon.

Platt, Jerome J. 1975. "'Addiction-Proneness' and Personality in Heroin Addicts." *Journal of Abnormal Psychology* 84 (3): 303–306.

Platt, Jerome J., G. Buhringer, C. D. Kaplan, Barry S. Brown, and D. O. Taube. 1988. "The Prospects and Limitations of Compulsory Treatment for Drug Addiction. Special Issue: A Social Policy Analysis of Compulsory Treatment for Opiate Dependence." *Journal of Drug Issues* 18: 505–525.

Platt, Jerome J., and Christina Labate. 1976. *Heroin Addiction: Theory, Research and Treatment.* New York: John Wiley and Sons.

Pletscher, A. 1991. "The Discovery of Antidepressants: A Winding Path." *Experientia* 47: 4–8.

Pope, Harrison G., Jr., and David L. Katz. 1994. "Psychiatric and Medical Effects of Anabolic-Androgenic Steroid Use: A Controlled Study of 160 Athletes." *Archives of General Psychiatry* 51 (5; May): 375–382.

Potter, Beverly A., and J. Sebastian Orfali. 1990. *Drug Testing at Work: A Guide for Employers and Employees.* Berkeley, CA: Ronin Publishing.

Powell, Arthur James. 2004. "Only in Paradise: Alcohol and Islam." In C. K. Robertson (ed.), *Religion and Alcohol: Sobering Thoughts*, 95–110. New York: Peter Lang.

Powell, Lisa M., Jenny Williams, and Henry Wechsler. 2004. "Study Habits and the Level of Alcohol Use among College Students." *Education Economics* 12 (2; August): 135–149.

Powis, Beverly, Michael Gossop, Catherine Bury, Katherine Payne, and Paul Griffiths. 2000. "Drug-Using Mothers: Social, Psychological and Substance use Problems of Women Opiate Users with Children." *Drug and Alcohol Review* 19: 171–180.

Preble, Edward, and John H. Casey Jr. 1969. "Taking Care of Business—The Heroin User's Life on the Street." *International Journal of the Addictions* 4 (1): 1–24.

Preble, Edward A., and Babriel V. Laury. 1967. "Plastic Cement: The Ten Cent Hallucinogen." *International Journal of the Addictions* 2 (2; Fall): 271–281.

Pringle, Kristine E., Frank M. Ahern, Debra A. Heller, Carol H. Gold, and Theresa V. Brown. 2005. "Potential for Alcohol and Prescription Drug Interactions in Older People." *Journal of the American Geriatric Society* 53: 1930–1936.

Putnam, Douglas T. 1999. *Controversies of the Sports World.* Westport, CT: Greenwood Press.

Putnam, Peter L., and Everett H. Ellinwood Jr. 1966. "Narcotic Addiction among Physicians: A Ten-Year Follow-Up." *American Journal of Psychiatry* 122: 745–748.

Quill, Timothy E. 1995. "You Promised Me I Wouldn't Die Like This! A Bad Death as a Medical Emergency." *Archives of Internal Medicine,* 155 (12; June 26), 1250–1254.

Quill, Timothy E., Rebecca Dresser and Dan W. Brock. 1997. "The Rule of Double Effect--A Critique of Its Role in End-of-Life Decision Making." *The New England Journal of Medicine* 337 (24 ; December 11), 1768–1771.

Rallason, Victoria, and Nicole Vogt. 2003. "Reduction of Polypharmacy in the Elderly: A Systematic Review of the Role of the Pharmacist." *Drugs Aging* 20 (11): 817–832.

Ramisetty-Mikler, Suhasini, Deborah Goebert, Stephanie Nishimura, and Raul Caetano. 2006. "Dating Violence Victimization: Associated Drinking and Sexual Risk Behaviors of Asian, Native Hawaiian, and Caucasian High School Students in Hawaii." *Journal of School Health* 76 (8; October): 423–429.

Ramos-Lira, Luciana, Catalina Gonzalez-Forteza, and Fernando A. Wagner. 2006. "Violent Victimization and Drug Involvement among Mexican Middle School Students." *Addiction* 101: 850–856.

Rankin, James G. 1994. "Biological Mechanisms at Moderate Levels of Alcohol Consumption That May Affect Coronary Heart Disease." *Contemporary Drug Problems* 21, 45–57.

Raskin, H. A., T. A. Petty, and M. Warren. 1957. "A Suggested Approach to the Problem of Narcotic Addiction." *American Journal of Psychiatry* 113: 1089–1094.

Ray, Marsh B. 1961. "Cycles of Abstinence and Relapse among Heroin Addicts." *Social Problems* 9 (2; Fall): 132–140.

Ray, Oakley. 1978. *Drugs, Society and Human Behavior*, 2nd ed. St. Louis: Mosby.

Ray, Oakley, and Charles Ksir. 1999. *Drugs, Society and Human Behavior* (8th ed.). New York: McGraw-Hill

Reed, Beth Glover. 1987. "Developing Women-Sensitive Drug Dependence Treatment Services: Why So Difficult?" *Journal of Psychoactive Drugs* 19: 151–164.

Register, Charles A., and Donald R. Williams. 1992. "Labor Market Effects of Marijuana and Cocaine Use among Young Men." *Industrial and Labor Relations Review* 45: 435–448.

Reid, Gary, Campbell Aitken, Lorraine Beyer, and Nick Crofts. 2001. "Ethnic Communities' Vulnerability to Involvement with Illicit Drugs." *Drugs: Education, Prevention and Policy* 8 (4): 359–374.

Reid, Jeanne. 1996. *Substance Abuse and the American Woman*. New York: The National Center on Addiction and Substance Abuse, Columbia University.

———. 1998. *Under the Rug: Substance Abuse and the Mature Woman*. New York: Center on Addiction and Substance Abuse, Columbia University.

Reiman, Jeffrey. 2007. *The Rich Get Poorer and the Poor Get Prison*, 8th ed. Boston: Pearson.

Reinarman, Craig. 2000. "The Social Construction of Drug Scares." In Patricia A. Adler and Peter Adler (eds.), *Constructions of Deviance: Social Power, Context, and Interaction*, 3rd ed., 147–158. Belmont, CA: Wadsworth/Thomson.

Reinarman, Craig, and B. C. Critchlow-Leigh. 1987. "Culture, Cognition and Disinhibition: Notes on Sexuality and Alcohol in the Age of AIDS." *Contemporary Drug Problems* 14: 435–460.

Reinarman, Craig, and Harry G. Levine. 1997. *Crack in America: Demon Drugs and Social Justice*. Berkeley, CA: University of California Press.

Renz, Loren. 1990. Private Foundations And The Crisis Of Alcohol And Drug Abuse. *Health Affairs: The Policy Journal of the Health Sphere* 9 (2): 193–201.

Renz, Loren and Steven Lawrence. 1998. "Health policy grant making by foundations in the 1990s." *Health Affairs: The Policy Journal of the Health Sphere* 17 (5): 216–229.

Research Triangle Institute. 1976. *Drug Use and Crime: Report of the Panel on Drug Use and Criminal Behavior*. Research Triangle Park, NC: Research Triangle Institute.

Rettig, Richard P., Manual J. Torres, and Gerald R. Garrett. 1977. *Manny: A Criminal-Addict's Story*. Boston: Houghton Mifflin Company.

Reuter, Peter. 1999. "Drug Use Measures: What are They Really Telling Us?" *National Institute of Justice Journal* (April): 12–19.

———. 2006. "What Drug Policies Cost. Estimating Government Drug Policy Expenditures." *Addiction* 101 (3; March): 315–322.

Rhodes, Tim. 1996. "Culture, Drugs and Unsafe Sex: Confusion about Causation." *Addiction* 91: 753–758.

Rhodes, William, Mary Lane, Patrick Johnston, and Lynne Hozik. 2000. *What America's Users Spend on Illegal Drugs, 1988–1998.* Office of National Drug Control Policy. Cambridge, MA: ABT Associates.

Ribeaud, Denis. 2004. "Long-Term Impacts of the Swiss Heroin Prescription Trials on Crime of Treated Heroin Users." *Journal of Drug Issues* 34 (1; Winter): 163–194.

Richardson, Gale A., and Nancy L. Day. 1994. "Detrimental Effects of Prenatal Cocaine Exposure: Illusion or Reality?" *Journal of the American Academy of Child and Adolescent Psychiatry* 33: 28–34.

Richardson, Gale A., Nancy L. Day, and Peggy J. McGauhey. 1993. "The Impact of Prenatal Marijuana and Cocaine Use on the Infant and Child." *Clinical Obstretrics and Gynecology* 36: 302–318.

Richmond, Robyn L., Linda Kehoe, Susan Hailstone, Alex Wodak, and Merryl Uebel-Yan. 1999. "Quantitative and Qualitative Evaluations of Brief Interventions to Change Excessive Drinking, Smoking, and Stress in the Police Force." *Addiction* 94 (10): 1509–1521.

Rickert, William S., Jack Robinson, and Byron Rogers. 1982. "A Comparison of Tar, Carbon Monoxide and pH Levels in Smoke from Marihuana and Tobacco Cigarettes." *Canadian Journal of Public Health* 73: 386–391.

Riley, Diane. 1993. *The Harm Reduction Model: Pragmatic Approaches to Drug Use from the Area Between Intolerance and Neglect.* Ottowa, Ontario: Canadian Centre on Substance Abuse. Available online: http://www.ccsa.ca/pdf/ccsa-004011-1993.pdf (accessed June 2, 2008).

Riley, Kevin J. 1996. *Snow Job? The War Against International Cocaine Trafficking.* New Brunswick, NJ: Transaction Books.

Rimm, Eric B., Edward L. Giovannucci, Walter C. Willett, Graham A. Colditz, Alberto Ascherio, Bernard Rosner, and Meir J. Stampfer. 1991. "Prospective Study of Alcohol Consumption and Risk of Coronary Disease in Men." *The Lancet* 338 (August 24): 464–468.

Rimm, Eric B., Paige Williams, Kerry Fosher, Michael Criqui, and Meir J. Stampfer. 1999. "Moderate Alcohol Intake and Lower Risk of Coronary Heart Disease: Meta-Analysis of Effects on Lipids and Haemostatic Factors." *British Medical Journal* 319 (December 11): 1523–1528.

Ritz, Mary C., and Michael J. Kuhar. 1993. "Psychostimulant Drugs and a Dopamine Hypothesis Regarding Addiction: Update on Recent Research." In S. Wonnacott and G. G. Lunt (eds.), *Neurochemistry of Drug Dependence,* 52. London: Portland Press.

Robertson, C.K. 2004. *Religion and Alcohol: Sobering Thoughts.* New York: Peter. Lang.

Robins, Lee N. 1974. *The Vietnam Drug User Returns.* Special Action Office for Drug Abuse Prevention Monograph, Series A, Number 2. Washington, DC: U.S. Government Printing Office.

Robinson v. California, 370 U.S. 660 (1962).

Rochford, Joseph, Igor Grant, and Gregory LaVigne. 1977. "Medical Students and Drugs: Further Neuropsychological and Use Pattern Considerations." *The International Journal of the Addictions* 12: 1057–1065.

Roman, Paul M. 1978. "Possible Effects of Using Alcohol to Control Distress: A Reanalysis of Pearlin and Radabaugh's Data." *American Journal of Sociology* 83: 987–991.

Room, Robin. 2005. "Stigma, Social Inequality and Alcohol and Drug Use." *Drug and Alcohol Review* 24 (March): 143–155.

Room, Robin, and Thomas Greenfield. 1993. "Alcoholics Anonymous, Other 12-Step Movements and Psychotherapy in the U.S. Population, 1990." *Addiction* 88 (4): 555–562.

Rosenbaum, Dennis. 2007a. "Just Say No to D.A.R.E." *Criminology and Public Policy* 6 (4): 815–824.

Rosenbaum, Marsha. 1981a. *Women on Heroin.* New Brunswick, NJ: Rutgers University Press.

———. 1981b. "Sex Roles among Deviants: The Woman Addict." *The International Journal of the Addictions* 16: 859–877.

———. 1981c. "Women Addicts' Experience of the Heroin World: Risk, Chaos, and Inundation." *Urban Life* 10: 65–91.

———. 1996. *Kids, Drugs and Drug Education: A Harm Reduction Approach.* San Francisco, CA: National Council on Crime and Delinquency.

———. 1999. *Safety First: A Reality-Based Approach to Teens, Drugs, and Drug Education.* San Francisco, CA: The Lindesmith Center.

———. 2004. "Random Drug Testing is No Panacea." *Alcoholism and Drug Abuse Weekly* 16 (15; April 12): 5–6.

———. 2007b. *Safety First: A Reality-Based Approach to Teens, and Drugs.* San Francisco, CA: The Lindesmith Center.

Rosenbaum, Marsha, and Sheigla Murphy. 1981. "Getting the Treatment: Recycling Women Addicts." *Journal of Psychoactive Drugs* 13: 1–13.

Rosenberg, Chaim M., and Joseph Liftik. 1976. "Use of Coercion in the Outpatient Treatment of Alcoholism." *Journal of Studies on Alcohol* 17: 58–65.

Rosenthal, Michael P. 1988. "The Constitutionality of Involuntary Civil Commitment of Opiate Addicts." *Journal of Drug Issues* 18: 641–661.

Rosett, Henry L. 1980. "The Effects of Alcohol on the Fetus and Offspring." In Oriana Josseau Kalant (ed.), *Alcohol and Drug Problems in Women,* 595–652, Vol. 5 in the series *Research Advances in Alcohol and Drug Problems.* New York: Plenum Press.

Rosin, Hanna. 1997. "The Return of Pot." *The New Republic* 216 (7): 18–24.

Rubington, Earl. 1967. "Drug Addiction as a Deviant Career." *International Journal of the Addictions* 2 (1; Spring): 3–20.

Ruitenberg, Annemeike, John C. van Swieten, Jacqueline C. M. Witteman, Kala M. Mehta, Cornelia M. van Duijn, Albert Hofman, and Monique M. B. Breteler. 2002. "Alcohol Consumption and Risk of Dementia: The Rotterdam Study." *The Lancet* 359 (January 26): 281–286.

Russell, M. A. Hamilton. 1971. "Cigarette Smoking: Natural History of a Dependence Disorder." *British Journal of Medical Psychology* 44: 1–16.

Sacco, R. L., M. Elkind, B. Boden-Albala, I. F. Lin, D. E. Kargman, W. A. Hauser, S. Shea, and M. C. Paik. 1999. "The Protective Effect of Moderate Alcohol Consumption on Ischemic Stroke." *Journal of the American Medical Association* 281 (January 6): 53–60.

Sack, Kevin, and Brent McDonald. 2008. "Popularity of a Hallucinogen May Thwart Its Medical Uses," *New York Times*, September 9, A1, A24.

Sackman, Bertram, M. Maxine Sackman, and G. G. DeAngelis. 1978. "Heroin Addiction as an Occupation: Traditional Addicts and Heroin Addicted Poly-Drug Users." *International Journal of the Addictions* 13: 427–441.

Sager, Ryan H. 1999. "Grass Roots." *National Review* 51 (21; November 8), 30–31.

Sales, Paloma, and Sheigla Murphy. 2000. "Surviving Violence: Pregnancy and Drug Use." *Journal of Drug Issues* 30 (4): 695–724.

SAMHSA. *See* Substance Abuse and Mental Health Services Administration.

Santayana, George. 1905. *Life of Reason, Reason in Common Sense.* New York: Scribner's.

Savisinsky, Neil J. 1998. "African Dimensions of the Jamaican Rastafarian Movement."In N. S. Murrell, W. D. Spencer, and A. A. McFarlane (eds.), *Chanting Down Babylon: The Rastafari Reader*, 125–145. Philadelphia: Temple University Press.

Scanlon, Walter F. 1991. *Alcoholism and Drug Abuse in the Workplace: Managing Care and Costs Through Employee Assistance Programs*, 2nd ed. New York: Praeger Publishing.

Schneider, Joseph. 1978. "Deviant Drinking as Disease: Alcoholism as a Social Accomplishment." *Social Problems* 25: 361–372.

Schuckit, Marc. 1983. "The Genetics of Alcoholism." In Boris Tabakoff, Patricia B. Sutker, and Carrie L. Randall (eds.), *Medical and Social Aspects of Alcohol Abuse*, 31–46. New York: Plenum Press.

———. 1985. "Genetics and the Risk for Alcoholism." *Journal of the American Medical Association* 254 (18; November 8): 2614–2617.

———. 1986. "Genetic and Clinical Implications of Alcoholism and Affective Disorder." *American Journal of Psychiatry* 143: 140–147.

———. 1988. "Weight Lifter's Folly: The Abuse of Anabolic Steroids." *Drug Abuse and Alcoholism Newsletter* 17: 8.

Schuckit, Mark A., and Maristela G. Monteiro. 1988. "Alcoholism, Anxiety and Depression." *British Journal of Addiction* 83: 1373–1380.

Schur, Edwin M. 1965. *Crimes Without Victims: Deviant Behavior and Public Policy.* Englewood Cliffs, NJ: Prentice-Hall.

———. 1971. *Labeling Deviant Behavior: Its Sociological Implications.* New York: Harper and Row.

Schwartz, Richard H., and Michael J. Sheridan. 1997. "Marijuana to Prevent Nausea and Vomiting in Cancer Patients: A Survey of Clinical Oncologists." *Southern Medical Journal* 90 (2; February): 167–172.

Schwarz, Judith Kennedy. 2004. "The Rule of Double Effect and Its Role in Facilitating Good End-of-Life Palliative Care: A Help or a Hindrance?" *Journal of Hospice and Palliative Nursing* 6 (2; April–June): 125–135.

Schwenck, Thomas L. 1997. "Psychoactive Drugs and Athletic Performance." *The Physician and Sportsmedicine* 25: 32–46.

Scitovsky, Anne A., and Dorothy P. Rice. 1987. "Estimates of the Direct and Indirect Costs of Acquired Immunodeficiency Syndrome in the United States, 1985, 1986, 1991." *Public Health Reports* 102 (1): 5.

Seeman, Melvin, and Carolyn S. Anderson. 1983. "Alienation and Alcohol: The Role of Work, Mastery, and Community in Drinking Behavior." *American Sociological Review* 48: 60–77.

Seeman, Melvin, Alice Z. Seeman, and Art Budros. 1988. "Powerlessness, Work, and Community: A Longitudinal Study of Alienation and Alcohol Use." *Journal of Health and Social Behavior* 29: 185–198.

Sells, S. B. 1979. "Treatment Effectiveness." In Robert DuPont, Avram Goldstein, and John O'Donnel (eds.), *Handbook on Drug Abuse*, 105–118. Rockville, MD: National Institute on Drug Abuse.

Senior, Kathryn. 1999. "Moderate Drinking Reduces Coronary Heart Disease Risk in Diabetes." *The Lancet* 354 (July 24): 311.

Shaw, Clifford, and Henry McKay. 1972. *Juvenile Delinquency and Urban Areas,* rev. ed. Chicago: University of Chicago Press.

Shaw, Elton. 1909. *The Curse of Drink; or Stories of Hell's Commerce.* City: [the author].Available Online: http://www.cimmay.us/e.shaw.html (accessed April 6, 2009).

Sheldon, Tony. 1997. "Dutch and Swiss Support Heroin on Prescription." *British Medical Journal* 315 (October 4): 835.

Shepard, Edward M., and Paul R. Blackley. 2005. "Drug Enforcement and Crime: Recent Evidence from New York State." *Social Science Quarterly* 86 (2; June): 323–342.

Shepard, Edward, and Thomas Clifton. 1998. "Drug Testing and Labor Productivity: Estimates Applying a Production Function Model." Research Paper #18, LeMoyne College of Industrial Relations. Syracuse, NY: LeMoyne College.

Sher, Kenneth J. 1991. *Children of Alcoholics.* Chicago: University of Chicago Press.

Sherman, Susan G. 2006. "Critical Condition Facing Needle Exchange Programs: The Politics of Science." *Substance Use & Misuse* 41: 827–829.

Shulgin, Alexander T. 1992. *Controlled Substances: A Chemical and Legal Guide to Federal Drug Laws*. Berkeley, CA: Ronin Publishing.

Sifaneck, Stephen J., Bruce D. Johnson, and Eloise Dunlap. 2005. "Cigars-for-Blunts: Choice of Tobacco Products by Blunt Smokers." *Journal of Ethnicity in Substance Abuse* 4 (3–4): 23–42.

Sifaneck, Stephen J., Charles D. Kaplan, Eloise Dunlap, and Bruce D. Johnson. 2003. "Blunts and Blowtjes: Cannabis Use Practices in Two Cultural Settings and Their Implications for Secondary Prevention." *Free Inquiry in Creative Sociology* 31 (1; May): 3–13.

Silver, G., and M. Aldrich. 1979. *The Dope Chronicles: 1850–1950*. New York: Harper and Row.

Simpson, D. Dwayne, and H. Jed Friend. 1988. "Legal Status and Long-Term Outcomes for Addicts in the DARP Followup Project." In Carl G. Leukefeld and Frank M. Tims (eds.), *Compulsory Treatment of Drug Abuse: Research and Clinical Practice*, 81–98. National Institute on Drug Abuse Research Monograph Series #86. Washington, DC: U.S. Government Printing Office.

Simpson, D. Dwayne, G. W. Joe, and S. A. Bracy. 1982. "Six-Year Follow-Up of Opioid Addicts after Admission to Treatment." *Archives of General Psychiatry* 39: 1318–1323.

Simpson, D. Dwayne, and S. B. Sells (eds.). 1990. *Opioid Addiction and Treatment: A 12-Year Follow-Up*. Malabar, FL: Krieger Publishing Co.

Singer, Merrill, Ray Irizarry, and Jean Schensul. 1991. "Needle Access as an AIDS-Prevention Strategy for IV Drug Users: A Research Perspective." *Human Organization* 50: 142–153.

Singer, Merrill, Freddie Valentin, Hans Baer, and Zhongke Jia. 1992. "Why Does Juan Barcia Have a Drinking Problem? The Perspective of Critical Medical Anthropology." *Medical Anthropology* 14: 77–108.

Skinner v. Railway Labor Executives' Association, 489 U.S. 602 (1989).

Skretting, Astrid. 2006. "The Nordic Countries and Public Drug-Injection Facilities." *Drugs: Education, Prevention and Policy* 13 (1; February): 5–16.

Slade, John. 1999. "Nicotene." In Barbara S. McCrady and Esizabeth E. Epstein (eds.), *Addictions: A Comprehensive Guidebook*, 162–170. New York: Oxford University Press.

Smeja, Carol M., and Dean G. Rojek. 1986. "Youthful Drug Use and Drug Subcultures." *The International Journal of the Addictions* 21 (9–10): 1031–1050.

Smith, Derek. 2007. "Alcohol and Tobacco Consumption among Australian Police Officers: 1989–2005." *International Journal of Police Science and Management* 9 (3): 274–286.

Smith, R. B., and Richard C. Stephens. 1976. "Drug Use and 'Hustling': A Study of Their Interrelationships." *Criminology* 14 (2; August): 155–176.

Smith, Stanley N., and Paul H. Blachly. 1966. "Amphetamine Usage by Medical Students." *Journal of Medical Education* 41: 167–170.

Soldz, Stephen, Dana Joy Huyser, and Elizabeth Dorsey. 2003a. "Characteristics of Users of Cigars, Bidis, and Kreteks and the Relationship to Cigarette Use." *Preventive Medicine* 37 (3; September): 250–258.

Soldz, Stephen, Dana Joy Huyser, and Elizabeth Dorsey. 2003b. "The Cigar as a Delivery Device: Youth Use of Blunts." *Addiction* 98: 1379–1386.

Sommers, Ira B. 2001. "Criminal Careers." In Clifton D. Bryant (ed.), *Encyclopedia of Criminology and Deviant Behavior*, Vol. 2, 155–158. Philadelphia: Taylor and Francis.

Sommers, Ira B., Deborah Baskin, and Jeffrey Fagan. 1994. "Getting Out of the Life: Crime Desistance by Female Street Offenders." *Deviant Behavior* 15: 125–150.

———. 1996. "The Structural Relationship between Drug Use, Drug Dealing and Other Income Support Activities among Women Drug Sellers." *Journal of Drug Issues* 26 (4; Fall): 975–1006.

Sommers, Andrew R. and Ramya Sundararaman. 2008. *Alcohol Use Among Youth.* Congressional Research Service Report RL34344. Washington DC: U.S., Gov't Printing Office. Available Online: https://secure.freedomsbell.org/leak/crs/RL34344.pdf (accessed April 6, 2009).

Speckart, George, and M. Douglas Anglin. 1986a. "Narcotics Use and Crime: A Causal Modeling Approach." *Journal of Quantitative Criminology* 2: 3–28.

———. 1986b. "Narcotics Use and Crime: An Overview of Recent Research Advances." *Contemporary Drug Problems* 13: 741–769.

Spell, Chester S., and Terry C. Blum. 2005. "Adoption of Workplace Substance Abuse Prevention Programs: Strategic Choice and Institutional Perspectives." *Academy of Management Journal* 48 (6): 1125–1142.

Spencer, William David. 1998. "Chanting Change around the World through Rasta Ridim and Art." In N. S. Murrell, W. D. Spencer, and A. A. McFarlane (eds.), *Chanting Down Babylon: The Rastafari Reader*, 266–283. Philadelphia: Temple University Press

Spencer, T., J. Biederman, T. Wilens, M. Harding, D. O'Donnell, and S. Griffin. 1996. "Pharmacotherapy of Attention-Deficit Hyperactivity Disorder Across the Life Cycle." *Journal of the American Academy of Child and Adolescent Psychiatry* 35: 409–432.

Spillane, Joseph F. 2000. *Cocaine: From Medical Marvel of Modern Menace in the United States, 1884–1920.* Baltimore, MD: The Johns Hopkins University Press.

Spoth, Richard, Max Guyll, and Susan X. Day. 2002. "Universal Family-Focused Interventions in Alcohol-Use Disorder Prevention: Cost-Effectiveness and Cost-Benefit Analyses of Two Interventions." *Journal of Studies on Alcohol* 63 (March): 219–228.

Spoth, Richard, Melissa Lopez Reyes, Cleve Redmond, and Chungyeol Shin. 1999. "Assessing a Public Health Approach to Delay Onset and Progression of Adolescent Substance Use: Latent Transition and Log-Linear Analyses of

Longitudinal Family Preventive Intervention Outcomes." *Journal of Consulting and Clinical Psychology* 67: 619–630.

Stampfer, Meir J., Graham A. Colditz, Walter C. Willett, Frank E. Speizer, and Charles H. Hennekens. 1988. "A Prospective Study of Moderate Alcohol Consumption and the Risk of Coronary Disease and Stroke in Women." *The New England Journal of Medicine* 319 (August 4): 267–273.

Standridge, John B., Robert G. Zylstra, and Stephen M. Adams. 2004. "Alcohol Consumption: An Overview of Benefits and Risks." *Southern Medical Journal* 97 (7; July): 664–672.

Staton, Michele, and Carl Leukefeld. 2002. "Heroin Maintenance and the United States." *Substance Use & Misuse* 37 (4): 549–554.

Stead, Martine, Bob Stradling, Anne Marie MacKintosh, Morag MacNeil, Sarah Minty, and Douglas Eadie. 2007. *Delivery of the Blueprint Programme: Report.* Stirling, UK: Institute for Social Marketing.

Steffy, Brian D., and D. R. Laker. 1991. "Workplace and Personal Stresses Antecedent to Employees' Alcohol Use." *Journal of Social Behavior and Personality* 6: 115–126.

Stephens, Robert S. 1999. "Cannabis and Hallucinogens." In Barbara S. McCrady and Esizabeth E. Epstein (eds.), *Addictions: A Comprehensive Guidebook*, 121–140. New York: Oxford University Press.

Sterk, Claire E. 1999. *Fast Lives: Women Who Use Crack Cocaine.* Philadelphia: Temple University Press.

Sterk-Elifson, Claire. 1996. "Just for Fun?: Cocaine Use among Middle-Class Women." *Journal of Drug Issues* 26 (1; Winter): 63–76.

Sterling, Eric. 1990. "Is the Bill of Rights a Casualty of the War on Drugs?" Remarks delivered to the Colorado Bar Association, 92nd Annual Convention, Aspen, September 14.

Stewart, Bob, and Aaron C. T. Smith. 2008. "Drug Use in Sport: Implications for Public Policy." *Journal of Sport and Social Issues* 32 (3): 278–298.

Stine, Susan M., and Thomas R. Kosten. 1999. "Opioids." In Barbara S. McCrady and Esizabeth E. Epstein (eds.), *Addictions: A Comprehensive Guidebook*, 141–161. New York: Oxford University Press.

Stoll, W. A. 1947. "Lysergsäure-diäthylamide, ein phantastikum aus der mutterkorn-gruppe." *Swiss Archives of Neurology and Psychiatry* 60: 1–2.

Stout-Weigand, Nancy, and Roger B. Trent. 1981. "Physician Drug Use: Availability or Occupational Stress?" *The International Journal of the Addictions* 16: 317–330.

Streel, Emmanuel, and Paul Verbanck. 2003. "Ultra-Rapid Opiate Detoxification: From Clinical Applications to Basic Science." *Addiction Biology* 8 (June): 141–146.

Strickland, T. L., I. Mena, J. Villanueva-Meyer, B. L. Miller, J. Cummings, C. M. Mehringer, P. Satz, and H. Myers. 1993. "Cerebral Perfusion and Neuropsychological Consequences of Chronic Cocaine Use." *Journal of Neuropsychiatry and Clinical Neurosciences* 5: 419–427.

Strike, Carol J., Ted Myers, and Margaret Millson. 2004. "Finding a Place for Needle Exchange Programs." *Critical Public Health* 14 (3; September): 261–275.

Substance Abuse and Mental Health Services Administration (SAMHSA). 1991. *How Drug Abuse Takes Profit Out of Business. How Drug Treatment Helps Put It Back.* U.S. Department of Health and Human Services (PHD574).

———. 1999c. *Summary of Findings from the 1998 National Household Survey on Drug Abuse.* Washington, DC: Substance Abuse and Mental Health Services Administration.

———. 1999d. *An Analysis of Worker Drug Use and Workplace Policies and Programs, 1997.* U.S. Department of Health and Human Services (PHD627).

———. 1999e. *Annual Survey of Federal Agency Drug Free Workplace, 1997.* Rockville, MD.: U.S. Department of Health and Human Services.

———. 2000a. National Survey of Substance Abuse Treatment Services, October, 2000. Available online: http://wwwdasis.samhsa.gov/00nssats/Append_A_nssats_2000.htm (accessed June 26, 2008).

———. 2000b. *Preliminary Results from the 1999 National Household Survey on Drug Abuse.* Rockville, MD: Substance Abuse and Mental Health Services Administration.

———. 2001. *Drug Abuse and Workforce Demographics.* Rockville, MD: U.S. Department of Health and Human Services.

———. 2003a. *Emergency Department Trends from the Drug Abuse Warning Network, Final Estimates, 1995–2002.* DAWN Series D-24, DHHS Publication No. SMA) 03-3780, Rockville, MD: Substance Abuse and Mental Health Services Administration, Office of Applied Statistics.

———. 2003b. "The National Survey of Substance Abuse Treatment Services (N-SSATS)." Drug and Alcohol Services Information System. The DASIS Report (December 12). Available Online: http://www.oas.samhsa.gov/2k3/NSSATS/NSSATS.pdf (accessed April 6, 2009).

———. 2004. *Results from the 2003 National Survey on Drug Use and Health: National Findings.* NSDUH Series H-25, DHHS Publication No. SMA 04-3964 Rockville, MD: Substance Abuse and Mental Health Services Administration, Office of Applied Studies.

———. 2005. *National Survey on Drug Use and Health.* Rockville, MD: Substance Abuse and Mental Health Services Administration.

———. 2006a. *Results from the2005 National Survey on Drug Use and Health: National Findings.* NSDUH Series H-30, DHHS Publication No. SMA 06-4194. Rockville, MD: Substance Abuse and Mental Health Services Administration, Office of Applied Studies.

———. 2006b. "Facilities Operating Opioid Treatment Programs: 2005." *The DASIS Report*, 36. Rockville, MD: Substance Abuse and Mental Health Services Administration.

———. 2007a. *Treatment Episode Data Set (TEDS): 1995–2005. National Admissions to Substance Abuse Treatment Services.* DASIS Series S-37, DHHS Publicatoin

No. (SMA) 07-4234. Rockville, MD: Substance Abuse and Mental Health Services Administration, Office of Applied Studies.

———. 2007b. *Results from the 2006 National Survey on Drug Use and Health: National Findings.* NSDUH Series H-32, DHHS Publication No. SMA 07-4293. Rockville, MD: Substance Abuse and Mental Health Services Administration, Office of Applied Studies.

———. 2008. *Results from the 2007 National Survey on Drug Use and Health: National Findings.* NSDUH Series H-34, DHHS Publication No. SMA 08-4343. Rockville, MD: Substance Abuse and Mental Health Services Administration, Office of Applied Studies. Available online: http://www.oas.samhsa.gov/nsduh. htm (accessed September 22, 2008) and http://www.oas.samhsa.gov/2k8/ hallucinogens/hallucinogens.cfm (accessed March 20, 2009).

Sue, David. 1987. "Use and Abuse of Alcohol by Asian Americans." *Journal of Psychoactive Drugs* 19 (1; January–March): 57–66.

Sunderwirth, Stanley G. 1985. "Biological Mechanisms: Neurotransmission and Addiction." In Harvey B. Milkman and Howard J. Shaffer (eds.), *The Addictions: Multidisciplinary Perspectives and Treatments,* 11–19. Lexington, MA: D.C. Heath.

Sutherland, Edwin H. 1939. *Principles of Criminology,* 3rd ed. Philadelphia: Lippincott.

Sutherland, Edwin H., Donald R. Cressey, and David F. Luckenbill. 1992. *Principles of Criminology,* 11th ed. Dix Hills, NY: General Hill.

Sutter, Alan G. 1969. "Worlds of Drug Use on the Street Scene." In Donald R. Cressey and David A. Ward (eds.), *Delinquency, Crime and Social Process,* 802–829. New York: Harper and Row.

Swena, Dennis D., and Will Gaines Jr. 1999. "Effect of Random Drug Screening on Fatal Commercial Truck Accident Rates." *International Journal of Drug Testing* 1. Available online: http://www.criminology.fsu.edu/journal/drugscreen.htm (accessed June 2, 2008).

Sykes, Gresham M., and David Matza. 1957. "Techniques of Neutralization: A Theory of Delinquency." *American Sociological Review* 22: 664–670.

Szalavitz, Maia. 2007. "Is There a College Substance Abuse Crisis?" Statistical Assessment Service (STATS) March 21. Available online: http://stats.org/ stories/2007/is_there_college_crisis_mar21_07.htm (accessed May 26, 2008).

Taggart, Robert W. 1989. "Results of the Drug Testing Program at Southern Pacific Railroad." In Steven W. Gust and J. Michael Walsh (eds.), *Drugs in the Workplace: Research and Evaluation Data,* 97–108. NIDA Research Monograph 91. Rockville, MD: National Institute on Drug Abuse.

Tammi, Tuukka. 2004. "The Harm Reduction School of Thought: Three Fractions." *Contemporary Drug Problems* 31 (Fall): 381–399.

Task Force Eleven. 1976. *Report on Alcohol and Drug Abuse: Final Report to the American Indian Policy Review Commission.* Washington, DC: U.S. Government Printing Office.

Taylor, Stuart P. 1983. "Alcohol and Human Physical Aggression." In E. Gottheil, K. A. Druley, T. E. Skoloda, and H. M. Waxman (eds.), *Alcohol, Drug Abuse and Aggression*, 280–291. Springfield, IL: Charles C. Thomas.

Taylor, Timothy B. 1984. "Soul Rebels: The Rastafarians and the Free Exercise Clause." *Georgetown Law Journal* 72: 1605–1635.

Teicher, Martin H., Carol Glod, and Jonathan O. Cole. 1990. "Emergence of Intense Suicidal Preoccupation During Fluoxetine Treatment." *American Journal of Psychiatry* 147: 207–210.

Terenius, Lars. 1993. "Opiate Receptors—The Historical Breakthrough in Drug Research." In S. Wonnacott and G. G. Lunt (eds.), *Neurochemistry of Drug Dependence*, 13–25. London: Portland Press.

Territo, Leonard, and Harold J. Vetter. 1981. "Stress and Police Personnel." *Journal of Police Science and Administration* 9: 195–208.

Terry, Charles E., and Mildred Pellens. 1928. *The Opium Problem*. New York: Committee on Drug Addictions, Bureau of Social Hygiene, Inc.

Theall, Katherine P., Claire E. Sterk, and Kirk W. Elifson. 2004. "Past and New Victimization among African American Female Drug Users Who Participated in an HIV Risk-Reduction Intervention." *The Journal of Sex Research* 41 (4; November): 400–407.

Theidon, Kimberly. 1995. "Taking a Hit: Pregnant Drug Users and Violence." *Contemporary Drug Problems* 22 (4; Winter): 663–686.

Thies, Clifford F., and Charles A. Register. 1993. "Decriminalization of Marijuana and the Demand for Alcohol, Marijuana and Cocaine." *The Social Science Journal* 30: 385–399.

Thomas, R. Buckland, Shula Avni Luber, and Jackson A. Smith. 1977. "A Survey of Alcohol and Drug Use in Medical Students." *Diseases of the Nervous System* 38: 41–43.

Thompson, Kevin M., and Richard W. Wilsnack. 1984. "Drinking and Drinking Problems among Female Adolescents: Patterns and Influences." In Sharon C. Wilsnack and Linda J. Beckman (eds.), *Alcohol Problems in Women: Antecedents, Consequences and Intervention*, 37–65. New York: Guilford Press.

Thorns, Andrew, and Nigel Sykes. 2000. "Opioid Use in Last Week of Life and Implications for End-of-Life Decision-Making." *The Lancet* 356: 398–399.

Thornton, Mark. 1991. *Alcohol Prohibition Was a Failure*. Policy Analysis No. 157 (July 17). Washington, DC: The Cato Institute.

Thornton, Sarah. 1995. *Club Cultures*. Cambridge, U.K.: Polity Press.

Thun, Michael J., Richard Peto, Alan D. Lopez, Jane H. Monaco, S. Jane Henley, Clark W. Heath, and Richard Doll. 1997. "Alcohol Consumption and Mortality among Middle-Aged and Elderly U.S. Adults." *The New England Journal of Medicine* 337 (December 11): 1705–1714.

Tobler, Nancy S. 1986. "Meta-Analysis of 143 Adolescent Drug Prevention Programs: Quantitative Outcome Results of Program Participants Compared to a Control or Comparison Group." *Journal of Drug Issues* 16: 537–567.

————. 1992. "Drug Prevention Programs Can Work: Research Findings." *Journal of Addictive Diseases* 11: 1–28.

Tobler, Nancy S., and Howard H.Stratton. 1997. "Effectiveness of School-Based Drug Prevention Programs: A Meta-Analysis of the Research." *The Journal of Primary Prevention* 18: 71–128.

Tomar, Scott L., and Gary A. Giovino. 1998. "Incidence and Predictors of Smokeless Tobacco Use among U.S. Youth." *American Journal of Public Health* 88 (1; January): 20–26.

Tondo, Leonardo, John Hennen, and Ross J. Baldessarini. 2001. "Lower Suicide Risk with Long-Term Lithium Treatment in Major Affective Illness: A Meta-Analysis." *Acta Psychiatrica Scandinavica* 104: 163–172.

Tonry, Michael, and James Q. Wilson. 1990. *Drugs and Crime*. Chicago: University of Chicago Press.

Trebach, Arnold. 1987. *The Great Drug War*. New York: MacMillan.

Trimble, Joseph E., Amado M. Padilla, and Catherine S. Bell. 1987. *Drug Abuse among Ethnic Minorities*. Rockville, MD: National Institute on Drug Abuse.

Uhl, George R., Tomas Drgon, Catherine Johnson, Oluwatosin O. Fatusin, Qing-Rong Liu, Carlo Contoreggi, Chuan-Yun Li, Kari Buck, and John Crabbe. 2008. " 'Higher Order' Addiction Molecular Genetics: Convergent Data from Genome-Wide Association in Humans and Mice." *Biochemical Pharmacology* 75: 98–111.

United Nations. 1997. *World Drug Report*. New York: United Nations Office on Drugs and Crime.

————. 1998. *Economic and Social Consequences of Drug Abuse and Illicit Trafficking*. United Nations Office on Drugs and Crime, Report, Number 6. Available online: http://www.unodc.org/pdf/technical_series_1998-01-01_1.pdf (accessed November 13, 2008).

————. 2001. *Alternative Development in the Andean Area: The UNDCP Experience*, rev. ed. New York: Office for Drug Control and Crime Prevention.

————. 2004. *World Drug Report*. New York: United Nations Office on Drugs and Crime.

————. 2006. "Coca Producing States Need Aid for Crop Substitution to Fight Illegal Drugs." U.N. News Service. Available Online: http://www.un.org/apps/news/story.asp?NewsID=18926&Cr=drugs&Cr1= (accessed March 14, 2008).

————. 2008a. *The Threat of Narco-Trafficking in the Americas*. New York: United Nations Office on Drugs and Crime.

————. 2008b. *World Drug Report*. New York: United Nations Office on Drugs and Crime.

United States Census Bureau n.d. Annual Estimates of the Resident Population for the United States, Regions, States, and Puerto Rico: April 1, 2000 to July 1, 2008 (NST-EST2008-01) Available Online: http://www.census.gov/popest/states/NST-ann-est.html (Accessed March 27, 2009).

United States Census Bureau. 2000. Historical National Population Estimates: July 1, 1900 to July 1, 1999. Available Online: http://www.census.gov/popest/archives/1990s/popclockest.txt (Accessed March 27, 2009).

United States Coast Guard. 2007. "Coast Guard Drug Seizure Statistics (In Pounds)." Available online: http://www.uscg.mil/hq/g-o/g-opl/Drugs/Statswww.htm (accessed February 18, 2008).

United States Congress. 1914. Public Law No. 223, 63rd Congress, December 17.

United States Courts Administrative Office. 2006. "206 Wiretap Report." Available online: http://www.uscourts.gov/wiretap06/Table32006.pdf (accessed February 26, 2008).

United States Customs. 2007. "Performance and Accountability Report, 2007". Available online: http://www.cbp.gov/linkhandler/cgov/toolbox/publications/admin/fiscal_2007_pub.ctt/fiscal_2007.pdf (accessed February 18, 2008).

United States Department of Agriculture. 2006. "Table 1—Cigarettes: U.S. output, removals, and consumption, 1950–2006." Available online: http://usda.mannlib.cornell.edu/usda/ers/92015/Tab01.xls (accessed December 14, 2007).

United States Department of State. 2008. International Narcotics Control Strategy Report, Vol. II. Money Laundering and Financial Crimes. Available online: http://www.state.gov/documents/organization/102588.pdf (accessed November 12, 2008).

United States Department of Transportation. n.d. Traffic Safety Facts 2004. Washington, DC: National Center for Statistics and Analysis.

United States House of Representatives. 1999. "Pain Relief Promotion Act." HR-2260/S-1272. Washington, DC: U.S. Government Printing Office.

———. 1988. Fact Sheet: The Human Costs of Drug Trafficking and Abuse. Select Committee on Narcotics Abuse and Control (August). Washington, DC: U.S. Government Printing Office.

United States House of Representatives, Ways and Means Committee. 1910. "Importation and Use of Opium", 12–13. Transcript of testimony. Washington, DC: U.S. Government Printing Office.

United States Senate. 1984. Impact of Drugs on Crime, 1984. Hearing before the Subcommittee on Alcoholism and Drug Abuse of the Committee on Labor and Human Resources, May 10. Washington, DC: U.S. Government Printing Office.

United States v. Behrman, 258 U.S. 280 (1922).

United States v. Jin Fuey Moy, 241 U.S. 394 (1916).

United States v. Oakland Cannabis Buyers Cooperative et al., 532 U.S. 483 (2001).

United States Surgeon General. 1964. Smoking and Health: Report of the Advisory Committee to the Surgeon General of the Public Health Service. Washington, DC: U.S. Government Printing Offfice.

U.S. See under United States.

Valliant, George E., J. R. Brighton, and C. McArthur. 1970. "Physicians Use of Mood Altering Drugs: A 20-Year Follow-Up Report." New England Journal of Medicine 272 (7): 365–370.

Van Raalte, R. C. 1979. "Alcohol as a Problem among Officers." *The Police Chief* 44: 38–40.

Vargas, Ricardo. 2005. "Strategies for Controlling the Drug Supply: Policy Recommendations to Deal with Illicit Crops and Alternative Development Programs." *Journal of Drug Issues* 35 (1; Winter): 131–150.

Vega, William Armando, Ethel Alderete, Bohdan Kolody, and Sergio Aguilar-Gaxiola. 1998. "Illicit Drug Use among Mexicans and Mexican Americans in California: The Effects of Gender and Acculturation." *Addiction* 93 (12): 1839–1850.

Venkatesh, Sudhir. 2008. *Gang Leader for a Day: A Rogue Sociologist Takes to the Streets.* New York: The Penguin Press.

Ventura, Lois A., and Eric G. Lambert. 2004. "Recidivism 12 Months after TASC." *Journal of Offender Rehabilitation* 39 (1): 63–82.

Vermeiren, Robert, Mary Schwab-Stone, Dirk Deboutte, Peter E. Leckman, and Vladislav Ruchkin. 2003. "Violence Exposure and Substance Use in Adolescents: Findings from Three Countries." *Pediatrics* 111 (3; March): 535–540.

Vernonia School District v. Acton, 515 U.S. 646 (1995). Available online: http://www.oyez.org/cases/1990-1999/1994/1994_94_590/ (accessed May 10, 2008).

Vesell, E. S. 1975. "Ethanol Metabolism: Regulation by Genetic Factors in Normal Volunteers Under a Controlled Environment and the Effect of Chronic Ethanol Administration." *Annals of the New York Academy of Sciences* 197: 79–88.

Violante, John M.. 2004. "Predictors of Police Suicide Ideation." *Suicide and Life Threatening Behavior* 34 (3; Fall): 277–283.

Violante, John M., James R. Marshall, and Barbara Howe. 1985. "Stress, Coping and Alcohol Use: The Police Connection." *Journal of Police Science and Administration* 13: 106–110.

Vold, George B., Thomas J. Bernard, and Jeffrey B. Snipes. 2002. *Theoretical Criminology*, 5th ed. New York: Oxford University Press.

Volkow, Nora D. 2006. "Testimony before the Subcommittee on Criminal Justice, Drug Policy, and Human Resources." Washington, DC: Committee on Government Reform, U.S. House of Representatives (July 26). Available online: http://www.hhs.gov/asl/testify/t060726a.html (accessed May 20, 2008).

Volkow, Nora D., Gene-Jack Wang, Joanna S. Fowler, Samuel J. Gatley, Jean Logan, Yu-Shin Ding, Robert Hitzemann, and Naomi Pappas. 1998. "Dopamine Transporter Occupancies in the Human Brain Induced by Therapeutic Doses of Oral Methylphenidate." *The American Journal of Psychiatry* 155: 1325–1331.

Voss, Harwin L. and Richard R. Clayton. 1984. "Turning on Other Persons to Drugs." *The International Journal of the Addictions* 19: 633–652.

Voy, Robert, with Kirk D. Deeter. 1991. *Drugs, Sport and Politics.* Champaign, IL: Leisure Press.

Wagner, Jon C. 1987. "Substance-Abuse Policies and Guidelines in Amateur and Professional Athletics." *American Journal of Hospital Pharmacy* 44: 305–310.

Wagner, Marcia, and Richard J. Brzeczek. 1983. "Alcoholism and Suicide: A Fatal Connection." *FBI Law Enforcement Bulletin* 52 (8): 8–15.

Waldorf, Dan. 1971. "Life without Heroin: Some Social Adjustments during Long-Term Periods of Voluntary Abstention." *Social Problems* 18: 228–243.

———. 1973. *Careers in Dope.* Englewood Cliffs, NJ: Prentice-Hall.

———. 1983. "Natural Recovery from Opiate Addiction: Some Social-Psychological Processes of Untreated Recovery." *Journal of Drug Issues* 13 (Spring): 237–280.

Waldorf, Dan, and Patrick Biernacki. 1981. "The Natural Recovery from Opiate Addiction: Some Preliminary Findings." *Journal of Drug Issues* 11 (Winter): 61–74.

Waldorf, Dan, Craig Reinarman, and Sheigla Murphy. 1991. *Cocaine Changes: The Experience of Using and Quitting.* Philadelphia: Temple University Press.

Wallace, Samuel. 1965. *Skid Row as a Way of Life.* Totowa, NJ: Bedminster Press.

Wallot, Hubert, and Jean Lambert. 1984. "Characteristics of Physician Addicts." *American Journal of Drug and Alcohol Abuse* 10: 53–62.

Walsh, J. Michael, and Jeanne G. Trumble. 1991. "The Politics of Drug Testing." In Robert H. Coombs and Louis Jolyon West (eds.), *Drug Testing: Issues and Options,* 22–49. New York: Oxford University Press.

Walters, James M. 1985. " 'Taking Care of Business' Updated: A Fresh Look at the Daily Routine of the Heroin User." In Bill Hanson, George Beschner, James M. Walters, and Elliot Bovelle (eds.), *Life with Heroin: Voices from the Inner City,* 31–48. Lexington, MA: Lexington Books.

Wambaugh, Joseph. 1975. *The Choirboys.* New York: Delacorte Press.

Warburton, Clark. 1932. *The Economic Result of Prohibition.* New York: Columbia University Press.

Watkins, Charles. 1970. "Use of Amphetamine by Medical Students." *Southern Medical Journal* 63: 923–929.

Watters, John K., Michelle J. Estilo, George L. Clark, and Jennifer Lorvick. 1994. "Syringe and Needle Exchange as HIV/AIDS Prevention for Injection Drug Users." *Journal of the American Medical Association* 271 (January 12): 115–120.

Waxman, Henry A., and Barbara Lee. 2008. Letter to John P. Walters, Director of the Office of National Drug Control Policy, dated February 15, 2008. Available online: http://oversight.house.gov/documents/20080219093736.pdf (accessed March 13, 2008).

Weaver, Michael F., and Sidney H. Schnoll. 1999. "Stimulants: Amphetamines and Cocaine." In Barbara S. McCrady and Esizabeth E. Epstein (eds.), *Addictions: A Comprehensive Guidebook,* 105–120. New York: Oxford University Press.

Webb et al. v. United States, 249 U.S. 96 (1919).

Wechsberg, W. M., W. K. Luseno, and W. K. Lam. 2005. "Violence Against Substance-Abusing South African Sex Workers: Intersection with Culture and HIV Risk." *AIDS Care* 17 (Supplement 1; June): S55–S64.

Wechsler, Henry, and S. Bryn Austin. 1998. "Binge Drinking: The Five/Four Measure." 1998. *Journal of Studies on Alcohol* 59: 122–124.

Wechsler, Henry, Andrea E. Davenport, George W. Dowdall, Barbara Moeykens, and Sonia Castillo. 1994. "Health and Behavioral Consequences of Binge

Drinking in College: A National Survey of Students at 140 Campuses." *Journal of the American Medical Association* 272: 1672–1677.

Wechsler, Henry, Jae Eun Lee, Meichun Kuo, Mark Seibring, Toben F. Nelson, and Hang Lee. 2002. "Trends in College Binge Drinking during a Period of Increased Prevention Efforts: Findings from 4 Harvard School of Public Health College Alcohol Study Surveys: 1993–2001." *Journal of American College Health* 50 (5; March): 203–217.

Weil, Andrew T.1975. "Letters from Andrew Weil: Mushroom Hunting in Oregon 1: One Hundred Pounds of Chanterelles" *Journal of Psychedelic Drugs* 7 (1): 89–102.

———. 1986. *The Natural Mind: A New Way of Looking at Drugs and the Higher Consciousness.* Boston: Houghton-Mifflin.

Weil, Andrew, and Winifred Rosen. 1983. *Chocolate to Morphine: Understanding Mind-Altering Drugs.* Boston: Houghton-Mifflin Co.

Weinberg, Martin S. 1966. "Becoming a Nudist." *Psychiatry: Journal for the Study of Interpersonal Processes* 29 (1; February): 15–24.

Weiner, Michelle D., Steve Sussman, Ping Sun, and Clyde Dent. 2005. "Explaining the Link Between Violence Perpetration, Victimization and Drug Use." *Addictive Behaviors* 30 (6): 1261–1266.

Weir, Erica. 2000. "Raves: A Review of the Culture, the Drugs, and the Prevention of Harm." *Canadian Medical Association Journal* 67 (2): 1843–1848.

Weisburd, David, Laura A. Wyckoff, Justin Ready, John E. Eck, Joshua C. Hinkle, and Frank Gajewski. 2006. "Does Crime Just Move around the Corner? A Controlled Study of Spatial Displacement and Diffusion of Crime Control Benefits." *Criminology* 44 (3; August): 549–592.

Weiss, Jeffrey G., Michael G. Shlipak, and Warren S. Browner. 2000. "The Alcohol Hangover." *Annals of Internal Medicine* 132 (11; June 6): 897–902.

Welborn, Angie A. 2006. *Religious Freedom Restoration Act: An Overview of Gonzales v. O Centro Espirita Beneficiente Uniao do Vegetal.* Congressional Research Service Report RS22392.

Weppner, Robert S. 1973. "An Anthropological View of the Street Addict's World." *Human Organization* 32 (2; Summer): 111–121.

Westermeyer, Robert W. n.d. "Reducing Harm: A Very Good Idea." Available online: http://www.habitsmart.com/harm.html (accessed March 8, 2008).

Wexler, Harry K. 2003. "The Promise of Prison-Based Treatment for Dually Diagnosed Inmates." *Journal of Substance Abuse Treatment* 25 (3; October): 223–231.

Wexler, Harry K., Gregory P. Falkin, Douglis S. Lipton and Andrew B. Rosenblum. 1992. "Outcome Evaluation of a Prison Therapeutic Community for Substance Abuse Treatment" In Carl G. Leukefeld and Frank M. Tims (eds), *Drug Abuse Treatment in Prisons and Jails* 156–175. NIDA Research Monograph Series #118. Washington DC: U.S. Government Printing Office.

White, David, and Marian Pitts. 1998. "Educating Young People about Drugs: A Systematic Review." *Addiction* 93: 1475–1487.

White, Helene Raskin, and D. M. Gorman. 2000. "Dynamics of the Drug-Crime Relationship." In Gary LaFree (ed.), *The Nature of Crime: Continuity and Change*, 151–218. *Criminal Justice 2000*, Volume 1. NCJ 182408. Washington, DC: U.S. Department of Justice.

White, Helene Raskin, Rolf Loeber, Magda Stouthamer-Loeber, and David P. Farrington. 1999." Developmental Associations between Substance Use and Violence." *Development and Psychopathology* 11: 785–803.

White, Helene Raskin, Robert J. Pandina, and Randy L. LaGrange. 1987. "Longitudinal Predictors of Serious Substance Use and Delinquency." *Criminology* 25 (3; August): 715–740.

White, William. 1979. "Themes in Chemical Prohibition." In William E. Link et al., (eds.), *Drugs in Perspective*, 117–182. Rockville, MD: National Institute on Drug Abuse.

White House. 2004. *National Drug Control Strategy Update* (March). Washington, DC: U.S. Government Printing Office.

Wiese, Jeffrey G., Michael G. Shlipak, and Warren S. Browner. 2000. "The Alcohol Hangover." *Annals of Internal Medicine* 132 (11): 897–902.

Wikler, Abe. 1952. "Mechanisms of Action of Drugs that Modify Personality Function." *American Journal of Psychiatry* 108: 590–599.

Wikler, Abraham. 1981. "Dynamics of Drug Dependence: Implications of a Conditioning Theory for Research and Treatment." In Howard Shaffer and Milton Earl Burglass (eds.), *Classic Contributions in the Addictions*, 352–366. New York: Brunner/Mazel.

Willcox, Sharon M., David U. Himmelstein, and Steffie Woolhandler. 1994. "Inappropriate Drug Prescribing for the Community-Dwelling Elderly." *Journal of the American Medical Association* 272: 292–296.

Williams College Neuroscience. 1998. "Synaptic Transmission: A Four-Step Process." Available online: http://www.williams.edu/imput/synapse/index.html (accessed May 20, 2008).

Williams, Jenny, Rosalie Liccardo Pacula, Frank J. Chaloupka, and Henry Wechsler. 2006. "College Students' Use of Cocaine." *Substance Use & Misuse* 41: 489–509.

Williams, Terry M. 1992. *Crackhosue: Notes From the End of the Line*. New York: Penguin Books.

Willson, Pam, Judith McFarlane, Ann Malecha, Kathy Watson, Dorothy Lemmey, Pamela Schultz, Julia Gist, and Nina Fredland. 2000. "Severity of Violence Against Women by Intimate Partners and Associated Use of Alcohol and/or Illicit Drugs by the Perpetrator." *Journal of Interpersonal Violence* 15 (9; September): 996–1008.

Wilsnack, Richard W., Albert D. Klassen, and Sharon C. Wilsnack. 1986. "Retrospective Analysis of Lifetime Changes in Women's Drinking Behavior." *Advances in Alcohol and Substance Abuse* 5: 9–28.

Wilsnack, Sharon C. 1984. "Drinking, Sexuality and Sexual Dysfunctions in Women." In Sharon C. Wislnack and Linda J. Beckman, *Alcohol Problems in*

Women: Antecedents, Consequences, and Intervention, 189–227. New York: Guilford Press.

Winger, Gail, Frederick G. Hofmann, and James H. Woods. 1992. *A Handbook on Drug and Alcohol Abuse: the Biomedical Aspects,* 3rd ed. New York: Oxford University Press.

Winick, Charles. 1961. "Physician Narcotic Addicts." *Social Problems* 9: 174–186.

———. 1962. "Maturing Out of Narcotic Addiction." *Bulletin on Narcotics,* 14 (January–March): 1–7.

———. 1974a. "A Sociological Theory of the Genesis of Drug Dependence." In Charles Winick (ed.), *Sociological Aspects of Drug Dependence,* 3–13. Cleveland, OH: CRC Press.

———. 1974b. "Drug Dependence among Nurses." In Charles Winick (ed.), *Sociological Aspects of Drug Dependence,* 155–165. Cleveland, OH: CRC Press.

Wish, Eric D., and Bernard A. Gropper. 1990. "Drug Testing by the Criminal Justice System: Methods, Research, and Applications." In Michael Tonry and James Q. Wilson (eds.), *Drugs and Crime,* 321–391. Chicago: University of Chicago Press.

Wisotsky, Steven. 1986. *Breaking the Impasse in the War on Drugs.* New York: Greenwood Press.

Wolfe, Ellen, Joseph Guydish, and Jenna Termondt. 2002. "A Drug Court Outcome Evaluation Comparing Arrests in a Two-Year Follow-Up Period." *Journal of Drug Issues* 32 (4; Fall): 1155–1172.

Wolfgang, Marvin E. 1958. *Patterns in Criminal Homicide.* Philadelphia: University of Pennsylvania Press.

Woods, S. C., and J. G. Mansfield. 1983. "Ethanol and Disinhibition: Physiological and Behavioral Links." In R. Room and G. Collins (eds.), *Alcohol and Disinhibition: The Nature and Meaning of the Link,* 4–23. Research Monograph #12, National Institute on Alcohol Abuse and Alcoholism. Washington, DC: Department of Health and Human Services, U.S. Public Health Service.

World Health Organization. n.d. "WHO's Pain Ladder". Available Online: http://www.who.int/cancer/palliative/painladder/en/. (Accessed March 30, 2009)

———. 1981. "Psychoanalytic Considerations of the Etiology of Compulsive Drug Use." In Howard Shaffer and Milton Earl Burglass (eds.), *Classic Contributions in the Addictions,* 133–153. New York: Brunner/Mazel.

Yablonsky, Lewis. 1965. *Synanon: The Tunnel Back.* New York: Penguin.

Yacoubian, George S., Julia K. Deutsch, and Elizabeth J. Schumacher. 2004. "Estimating the Prevalence of Ecstasy Use among Club Rave Attendees." *Contemporary Drug Problems* 31 (1; Spring): 163–177.

Yacoubian, George S. and Blake J. Urbach. 2002. "A Comparison of Drug Use Between Welfare-Receiving Arrestees and Non-Welfare-Receiving Arrestees." *Health and Social Work* 27 (3; August): 230–233.

Yesalis, Charles E., William A. Anderson, William E. Buckley, and James E. Wright. 1990. "Incidence of the Nonmedical Use of Anabolic-Androgenic Steroids." In Geraline C. Lin and Lynda Erinoff (eds.), *Anabolic Steroid Abuse,* 97–112. NIDA

Research Monograph Series #102. Rockville, MD: National Institute on Drug Abuse.

Yesalis, Charles E., R. T. Herrick, William E. Buckley, K. E. Friedl, D. Brannon, and James E. Wright. 1988. "Self-Reported Use of Anabolic-Angrogenic Steroids by Elite Power Lifters." *Physiological Sports Medicine* 16: 91–100.

Young, Amy, Carol Boyd, and Amy Hubbell. 2000. "Prostitution, Drug Use, and Coping with Psychological Distress." *Journal of Drug Issues* 30 (4): 789–800.

Young, James Harvey. 1961. *The Toadstool Millionaires: A Social History of Patent Medicines in America Before Federal Regulation.* Princeton, NJ: Princeton University Press.

Yuan, Jian-Min, and Ronald K. Ross. 1997. "FollowUp Study of Moderate Alcohol Intake and Mortality among Middle Aged Men in Shanghai, China." *British Medical Journal,* 314 (January 4): 18–23.

Zador, Deborah, Sandra Sunjic, and Shane Darke. 1996. "Heroin-Related Deaths in New South Wales, 1992: Toxicological Findings and Circumstances." *Medical Journal of Australia* 164 (February 19): 204–207.

Zane, Nolan, and Jeannie Huh Kim. 1994. "Substance Use and Abuse." In Nolan W. S. Zane, David T. Takeuchi, and Kathleen N. J. Young (eds.), *Confronting Critical Health Issues of Asian and Pacific Islander Americans,* 316–343. Thousand Oaks, CA: Sage Publications.

Zellner, William W. 2001. *Extraordinary Groups: An Examination of Unconventional Lifestyles.* New York: Worth Publishers.

Zemper, Eric D. 1991. "Drug Testing in Athletics." In Robert H. Coombs and Louis Jolyon West (eds.), *Drug Testing: Issues and Options,* 113–139. New York: Oxford University Press.

Zernike, Kate. 2001. "Antidrug Program Says It Will Adopt a New Strategy," *New York Times,* February 15, A1.

Zhang, Lening, William F. Wieczorek, and John W. Welte. 1997. "The Nexus Between Alcohol and Violent Crime." *Alcoholism: Clinical and Experimental Reesearch* 21: 1264–1271.

Zhang, Zhiwei. n.d. *Drug and Alcohol Use and Related Matters among Arrestees, 2003.* Washington, DC: Office of Justice Programs, National Institute of Justice.

Zhang, Zhiwei, Lynn X. Huang, and Angela M. Brittingham. 1999. *Worker Drug Use and Workplace Policies and Programs: Results from the 1994 and 1997 National Household Survey on Drug Abuse.* Substance Abuse and Mental Health Services Administration, Analytic Series A-11. Rockville, MD: Substance Abuse and Mental Health Services Administration.

Zilberman, Monica L., Hermano Tavares, Sheila B. Blume, and Nady el-Guebaly. 2003. "Substance Use Disorders: Sex Differences and Psychiatric Comorbidities." *Canadian Journal of Psychiatry* 48 (1; February): 5–13.

Zinberg, Norman E. 1984. *Drug Set and Setting: The Basis for Controlled Intoxicant Use.* New Haven, CT: Yale University Press.

Zlotnick, Cheryl, Marjorie J. Robertson, and Tammy Tam. 2002. "Substance Use and Labor Force Participation among Homeless Adults." *American Journal of Drug and Alcohol Abuse* 28 (1): 37–53.

Zuckoff, Mitchell. 2000. "Prozac Data was Kept from Trial, Suit Says." *Boston Globe*, June 8, A01.

Zwerling, Craig, James Ryan, and Endel John Orav. 1990. "The Efficacy of Preemployment Drug Screeing for Marijuana and Cocaine in Predicting Employment Outcome." *Journal of the American Medical Association* 264 (20; November 28): 2639–2643.

——. 1992. "Costs and Benefits of Preemployment Drug Screening." *Journal of the American Medical Association* 267 (1; January 1): 91–93.

INDEX

AA. *See* Alcoholics Anonymous (AA)

Action on Smoking and Health (ASH), 62

ADAM. *See* Arrestee Drug Abuse Monitoring Program (ADAM)

Additive drugs
  categories of
    anabolics, 230–231
    beta-blockers, 231–232
    diuretics, 232
    stimulants, 230

Adolescent Learning Experiences in Resistance Training (ALERT), 456

Agency of Fear, 339

Alcohol
  benefits from moderate drinking of, 267–269
  chronic or cumulative effects of, 18
  complications in pregnancy due to consumption of, 242
  consumption among Native American, 191
  and death caused by motor vehicle accident, 242
  as depressant, 75–76
  effect on motor skills performance, 9
  factors contributing use by police
    occupational subculture, 221
    stress, 219–221
  intoxication, 12, 76
  lethal dose for, 17
  sexual dysfunction caused by, 242
  subcultural drinking of, 221
  treatment for addiction of, 412–413
  use in nineteenth century America, 37–39

Alcohol dependence syndrome, 413

Alcoholic hepatitis, 241

Alcoholics Anonymous (AA), 412–413, 423, 485

Alcoholism, disease model of, 413

Alcohol Misuse Prevention Study (AMAS), 456

ALERT. *See* Adolescent Learning Experiences in Resistance Training (ALERT)

AMAS. *See* Alcohol Misuse Prevention Study (AMAS)

American Civil Liberties Union (ACLU), 478

American Indian Policy Review Commission, 190

American Medical Association (AMA), 45

American Pharmaceutical Association (APhA), 45

American society
  drug use in, 5
  forms of treatment and rehabilitative services in, 282
  patterns of alcohol and tobacco use and abuse in, 4

American Temperance Society, 51

Amotivational syndrome, 97, 338

Amphetamines, 42, 230

Anabolic steroids, 16, 102–103, 341
  consequences of chronic use of, 231
  use in sports, 230–231

Anaesthetic inhalants, 80–81

Angel dust, 395

Angina pectoris, 241

Anorexia nervosa, 179

Antabuse, 419

Antagonistic effect, 72, 73

Anticocaine legislation, 6

Anti-Drug Abuse Act, 61–62, 295

Anti-drug legislation
  Anti-Drug Abuse Act, 61–62
  Harrison Narcotics Act, 45–53
  Marihuana Tax Act, 53–55
  Pure Food and Drug Act, 44–45
  Renewed Drug Experimentation and the Controlled Substances Act, 55–60

Anti-opium ordinances, 45

Antisocial personality disorders, 151

Argot, 309

"Army disease," 35

Arrestee Drug Abuse Monitoring (ADAM) Program
  correctional statistics, 117
  for drug testing, 463
  evaluation of, 116–117
  prevalence of drug use revealed by, 114–116

Arrestee Drug Abuse Monitoring Program (ADAM), 350

ASH. *See* Action on Smoking and Health (ASH)